M E M O   5 - 1 9 5 0

Also by George F. Kennan

American Diplomacy, 1900–1950

Realities of American Foreign Policy

Soviet-American Relations, 1917–1920
Vol. I: Russia Leaves the War
Vol. II: The Decision to Intervene

Russia, the Atom, and the West

Soviet Foreign Policy, 1917–1941

Russia and the West Under Lenin and Stalin

On Dealing with the Communist World

The Fateful Alliance: France, Russia, and the Coming
of the First World War

Sketches from a Life

From Prague After Munich: Diplomatic Papers 1938–1940

Democracy and the Student Left

The Marquis de Custine and His "Russia in 1839"

Memoirs 1950–1963

The Cloud of Danger: Current Realities of American
Foreign Policy

Decline of Bismarck's European Order

The Nuclear Delusion

GEORGE F. KENNAN

MEMOIRS 1925-1950

PANTHEON BOOKS
NEW YORK

Library of Congress Cataloging in Publication Data

Kennan, George Frost, 1904–
Memoirs.

Reprint. Originally published: 1st ed. Boston:
Little, Brown, 1967–1972.
Includes indexes.
Contents: [1] 1925–1950—[2] 1950–1963.
1. Kennan, George Frost, 1904–   . 2. United
States—Foreign relations—Soviet Union. 3. Soviet Union
—Foreign relations—United States. 4. Ambassadors—
United States—Biography. 5. Historians—United States
—Biography. I. Title.
[E748.K374A3   1983]   327.2'092'4 [B]   83–4200
ISBN 0–394–71624–8 (v. 1)
ISBN 0–394–71626–4 (v. 2)

This book is dedicated to my four children
Grace
Joan Elisabeth
Christopher James and
Wendy Antonia
in the hope that, whatever other uses it may serve,
it will help them to understand something
of the strivings, bewilderments, failures,
and achievements in which their
father has been involved

Contents

MEMOIRS 1925-1950

1

A Personal Note

THERE are, of course, great variations in people's capacity to remember consciously their early youth. My own, I fear, falls at the weaker end of the spectrum. Beyond this, I wonder whether, in this rapidly moving age, every older man does not stand at a greater distance from his own childhood and adolescence than was the case when the pace of change was less precipitate — whether the immediacy of remembered experience is not impaired by the ruthless destruction of setting which the explosions of population and technological change have so often worked. I, in any case, see only dimly and uncertainly — too uncertainly to permit of confident judgments — the thin, tense, introverted Princeton student whose physical frame and reflexes I know myself to have inherited. More dimly do I perceive, behind him, the grubby military school cadet. Wholly untrustworthy and inadequate are the glimpses of the grade school boy, clad in the knickerbockers of the period, traveling back and forth between school and home on the new "pay-as-you-enter" streetcars of the Milwaukee street railways system (which thrilled him inordinately), retiring into sullen rages and sit-down strikes when required to attend Bournique's dancing school on Saturday afternoons, dreaming daydreams so intense and satisfying that hours could pass in oblivion of immediate surroundings. And when one moves still further into the past and arrives at the small child, the resources of memory fail altogether. I have found myself tempted to relate that this child was deeply affected, and in a certain sense scarred for life, by the loss of his mother shortly after his birth. This is, perhaps, a rational deduction, supported by a certain amount of circumstantial evidence from later years. But it is not really anything drawn from memory. The fact is that one moves through life like someone moving with a lantern in a dark woods. A bit of the path ahead is illuminated, and a bit of the path behind. But the darkness follows hard on one's footsteps, and envelopes our trail as one proceeds. Were one to be able, as one never is, to retrace the steps by daylight, one would find that the terrain traversed bears, in reality, little relationship to what imagination and memory had pictured. We are, toward the end of our lives, such different people, so far removed from the childhood figures with whom our identity links us, that the bond to those figures, like that of nations to their obscure prehistoric origins, is almost irrelevant.

There is another difficulty that confronts me when I try to describe the early self. In my own youthful consciousness, more, perhaps, than in the case of many others, the borderline between external and internal reality was unfirm. I lived, particularly in childhood but with lessening intensity right on to middle age, in a world that was peculiarly and intimately my own, scarcely to be shared with others or even made plausible to them. I habitually read special meanings into things, scenes, and places — qualities of wonder, beauty, promise, or horror — for which there was no external evidence visible, or plausible, to others. My world was peopled with mysteries, seductive hints, vague menaces, "intimations of immortality." For example, at the foot of the street we lived on in Milwaukee there was a particular entryway in a particular brick building — a dark, cavernous aperture, lurking behind a heavy romanesque archway of grimy brick, flush with the street — that held for me a sinister significance all its own. Behind it, I never doubted, lay a house of horror — horror unnamed, unmentionable, not to be imagined. It was plain, on the other hand, that the trunks of the trees in Juneau Park were populated by fairies. My cousin Catherine had told my oldest sister Frances that this was the case, and long, respectful contemplation of the park on my part convinced me that the hypothesis was probably correct.

How, then, if I am to consider my youth today in terms that could have meaning to other people, am I to weave my way effectively between what others could accept as reality and what they could not? How do I know what was real and what was not? To the extent that memory can carry me back at all into those dim recesses, it can do no more than to confront me with these uncertainties. Perhaps the house at the end of our street had indeed been the scene of some horrible unmentionable tragedy; perhaps it was affected by this, as houses sometimes are; and perhaps the fine antennae of the child picked up something of the ensuing desolation. Can I even be sure, for that matter, that there were not really fairies in Juneau Park? Things scarcely less strange have been known to happen. That it would be difficult to find the fairies there today I have no doubt. The automobiles have probably done them in, as they have done in so many other things in that now blighted region of central Milwaukee. But who can be sure what was there in 1910? Things are as we see them. It took two of us — the park and myself — to make possible a given view, a given apprehension, if you will, of the place. Fairies were a part of this view. To what extent they had their existence in the park and to what extent in me we shall never know. Perhaps a long and intensive self-analysis, along Freudian lines, would clarify such things. Were I a great artist, a great criminal, the subject of some highly complex and unusual experience, or one of exceptional personal failings and virtues, there might be reason for it. I am none of these things.

There are one or two aspects of family background that might bear mentioning. On my father's side there was nothing, since the removal of the family to this country from the north of Ireland in the early eighteenth century, but a straight line of pioneer farmers, digressing occasionally into the other free professions. Two of these forefathers were full-time farmers. One was a Presbyterian minister. One, after achieving a colonel's rank in the Revolutionary

War, ran a sawmill and tavern in Waterbury, Vermont, and represented that district in the first Vermont legislature. There was none that did not farm at least part time. Later generations moved on, first to upper New York State, then to Wisconsin. Their wives, too, were all of pioneer farming stock, though English, not Scottish.

These obviously were rugged and angular, not always attractive, people. The women, as a rule, brought more to the family in the way of education and the social graces than did the men. My father was the first of the latter to have a college education. The outstanding characteristic of all of them was an obdurate, tight-lipped independence, a reluctance to become involved with other people (unless in a church community), a fighting clear of every form of association that might limit one's freedom of individual choice.

Certain qualities of such a family were ones that had an effect on the mind of a descendant born at the outset of this century. Its members were neither rich nor poor. They never owned an appreciable amount of capital. There was not one who did not work long and hard with his hands. They were, on the other hand, as devoid of self-consciousness with regard to their poverty as they were of social bitterness over the fact that it existed. It never occurred to them to view it as a mark of inferiority, as an occasion for envy in the personal sense, or as a source of reproach to public authority. They accepted the logic of their passion for independence. They asked of government only that it leave them alone to struggle in their own way. When times were hard, as they often were, groans and lamentations went up to God, but never to Washington. Whoever emerged from such a family in the twentieth century emerged from it devoid of either pride or shame of station, without social grievance, oppressed neither by feelings of superiority nor of inferiority, prepared to relate himself on terms of equality to any other human being, with a total disregard for race, color, or nationality.

This detachment was particularly marked in its relation to the classic assumptions of Marxism. Not one of these American ancestors had ever been in significant degree an employer of labor; not one had ever sold his own labor to an entrepreneur, to be used for commercial gain. No family could have been more remote from that classic social predicament to which Marx, outstandingly, had drawn attention and to which his followers tended to ascribe so overwhelming a significance. This was a circumstance that would make itself felt — happily, as it seems to me — when, later in life, I would have to occupy myself long and intensively with the effects of Marxism's first great political triumph, the Russian Revolution. I could never concede to the classic Marxist predicament — to this dichotomy of the blood-sucking, corrupted capitalist versus the downtrodden, exploited, but socially pure worker — quite the sweeping ubiquity and reality that the Marxists claimed for it; but to the extent that it had currency and reality (and it obviously had *some*), it was something to which I could not relate myself personally either by my own experience or by that of the family. I could identify myself neither with the exploiter nor with the exploited. Insofar, then, as this sort of exploitation and injustice was a real phenomenon and not just a projection of the Marxist wish-image onto the society of the time, I retained the privilege of viewing it as the product of a tragic "misunderstanding" (to use Chekhov's charitable term) in the early development of modern industrial society, not as a dramatic encounter between demons and angels.

The fact is that in pioneer farming families such as ours the eighteenth century lasted a half-century longer than its name suggests — down to the 1860s — just as it did in the American South, and in Russia. The eighteenth-century culture that lingered on in these families was not that of the *ancien régime* in France, not that of London and the English establishment. It was the Puritan culture of Scotland and the northeast of England. Its remoteness from the affairs of the world protected it from the effects of the Napoleonic wars, its addiction to subsistence farming from the effects of the Industrial Revolution. My grandfather, to be sure, entering into his prime at the time of the Civil War, assumed the mannerisms and affectations of the Victorian age, and reveled in them. My father had them, too; but they sat poorly upon him. He was himself aware, increasingly as the years went by, of their tawdriness, their artificiality, their inadequacy as a guide to life. Yet the outlines of the new century that was dawning were disturbing, forbidding, partly incomprehensible in his eyes. He tended, therefore, to take refuge in the eighteenth century of his youth (he was born in 1851) and something of this atmosphere rubbed off on the household in which we children grew up.

It is, I suppose, to this shallowness of grounding in the nineteenth century, and this inherited partiality for the eighteenth, that I must attribute the discomfort I experience in my own status as a contemporary of the twentieth. The only advantage I can claim from this discomfort is the relative detachment it implies. None of us has all the qualities to be a good observer of his age; I am conscious of being lacking in a number of them; but it helps in this respect, however lonely and unsettling it may be in others, to be the guest of one's time and not a member of its household.

The other aspect of family background I should like to mention is that there was another George Kennan, a very well-known one, whose birth preceded that of my father by some six years. Many people have assumed I was his son; some still do. The error is not unnatural. There is, in fact, greater justification for this assumption than the true nature of the relationship would suggest. (He was actually a cousin of my grandfather.) The life of this elder Kennan and my own have shown similarities that give, to me at least, the feeling that we are connected in some curious way by bonds deeper than just our rather distant kinship. Aside from having the same name, we were, as it happened, born on the same day of the year. Both of us devoted large portions of our adult life to Russia and her problems. We were both expelled from Russia by the Russian governments of our day, at comparable periods of our careers. Both of us founded organizations to assist refugees from Russian despotism. Both wrote and lectured profusely. Both played the guitar. Both owned and loved particular sailboats of similar construction. Both eventually became members of the National Institute of Arts and Letters. Both had occasion to plead at one time or another for greater understanding in America for Japan and her geopolitical problems vis-à-vis the Asian mainland.

This elder George Kennan had no children of his own. In all devotion to the memory of my own father, whose son I recognize myself very much to be — in the sense that I inherited most of his weaknesses if not his virtues — I feel that I was in some strange way destined to carry forward as best I could the work of my distinguished and respected namesake. What I have tried to do in life is, I suspect, just the stort of thing the latter would have liked a son of his to try to do, had he had one. Whether he would have approved of the manner in which I have done it, I cannot judge.*

If the picture of an intellectual career in the Foreign Service is to be intelligible, it ought, I suppose, to include some reference to the higher educational experience that preceded it.

I came to Princeton directly from St. John's Military Academy. The progression was not a usual one. I owed it partly to the excitement and sense of revelation derived from reading Scott Fitzgerald's *This Side of Paradise* in my senior year at school, and partly to the help and encouragement of the St. John's dean, the late Henry Holt, a modest, shrewd, and dedicated pedagogue.

I arrived in Princeton on a hot evening in September 1921. The taxi carried me up University Place and down Nassau Street — along two sides of the campus; and as I discerned, through its windows, the shapes of the Gothic structures around Holder Hall, my penchant for the creation of imaginative wonders reached some sort of a crescendo. Mystery and promise, glamour and romance seemed to glow, like plasma, from these dim architectural shapes.

The reality was of course different. I was the last student admitted. I knew not a soul in college or town. I was given the last furnished room in the most remote of those gloomy rooming houses far off campus to which, at that time, late-coming freshmen were relegated. I was a year younger than most members of my class, and even more immature in manner than this tender age would suggest. I was hopelessly and crudely Midwestern. I had no idea how to

* For those who are curious about the extraordinary career of the elder George Kennan, I might say that an abridged edition of his celebrated work *Siberia and the Exile System* was published in 1958 by the University of Chicago Press. I wrote for this edition a brief introduction dealing with his career and his literary achievements.

approach boys from the East. I could never find the casual tone. My behavior knew only two moods: awkward aloofness and bubbling enthusiasm. I was afflicted from the start, furthermore, by a quality that has pursued me all my life: namely, of being the slowest and last to learn the ropes in any complicated organizational structure. Too shy to ask, I never found out. I went through Princeton as an innocent, always at the end of every line, always uninitiated, knowing few, known by few. Personal failings — pride, oversensitivity, a sullen refusal to be comforted, an insistence on knowing and experiencing the worst in order to be the more deserving of sympathy, at least in my own eyes — added to the discomfort.

Perhaps a bit of ill-fortune also played a part. Come Christmas of my freshman year, lacking the money to go home and fearing to burden my father if I asked him for it, I went to nearby Trenton and got a temporary job with the post office as a mail carrier. Bright and early on the first day of these labors I was given the usual leather sack, brimming with bundles of letters, and dispatched southward by trolley car to the slums of the city. The letters in the bundles, my supervisors assured me, were in perfect order; I had only to find the beginning street and the letters themselves would then guide me along my route.

Wet snow was falling this dark December day; an inch or two of it had already accumulated on the streets. Fumbling with the first of my bundles, I hopped off the car at the appointed stop. As I did so the bundle opened and broke; the letters spilled out partly on the rear platform of the car, partly onto the snow-covered street. Amid honking cars and clanging trolleys, I frantically gathered them up again and set forth on my rounds. But now they were in wild disorder; not even the streets, much less house numbers, followed in sequence. All day, I trudged desperately back and forth around those dreary, slush-covered thoroughfares, retracing my steps a dozen times, plaguing innumerable passersby with requests for directions, recoiling from the sights and smells that assailed me when people answered the doorbells. It was late evening before I disposed of my load; and I finished the day by eating my one meal — for fifty cents — in a squalid little restaurant somewhere along my beat.

So went the days before Christmas, not all as unhappy as this, but not dissimilar. By the afternoon of Christmas Day, the twenty-eight dollars then required for a day-coach passage to Milwaukee had been earned; and I went proudly home in this humble fashion. But somewhere along the line, whether in Trenton's slums or on the day coach, I had contracted scarlet fever.

The illness overtook me at home, suddenly and with violence, one ghastly afternoon around New Year's. There was great commotion in the family. This was long before the time of penicillin. The worst, not unreasonably, was feared. My sisters, sure that they had seen the last of me, were prematurely packed off, the same evening, to their respective colleges. I was relegated to the third floor of the house where, attended by a trained nurse, I remained in quarantine until Easter. When I returned to college, spring was upon us; the academic year was drawing to a close; coteries and friendships had already coagulated. To these tight and secure little communities there were now few paths of access, particularly to one who was younger than most of the others, behind in his studies, forbidden participation in sport, and too poor to share in the most common avocations.

I remained, therefore, an oddball on campus, not eccentric, not ridiculed or disliked, just imperfectly visible to the naked eye. In my sophomore year, during the celebrated Bicker Week when the club elections took place, in a veritable transport of false pride, self-pity, and thirst for martyrdom, I absented myself every afternoon from the campus, lest someone ask me to join a club. When, toward the end of the week, I was caught in my room one evening by a well-meaning acquaintance and urged to join one of the few clubs whose quotas were not yet filled, I was so unnerved by this sudden and unexpected attention that I promptly, almost in tears, said yes. But later I had pangs of conscience about the decision, resigned from the club, and ate for some months thereafter among the non-club pariahs, in a place called upper-class commons.

To eat in this gloomy refectory was a cruel experience, for in those days social distinctions cut deep. There were few of these social "rejects" (they numbered at that time perhaps one-third of the upperclassmen) who were not affected in some way — usually rendered either defensive or defiant — by the realization that they had been held to judgment by their fellow students and found wanting. So deep was the bitterness that one seldom spoke to a stranger at table; everyone feared that to open a conversation would lead the others to suppose that he couldn't take it. Yet cruel as it was there was something useful in the experience. It finally dawned on me, pondering this unhappy situation, that to be fair to oneself one had to make one's own standards, one could not just accept those of other people; there was always the possibility that those others, in the very rejection of us, had been wrong.

Friendships, of course, there ultimately were; but they were few, and tended to be formed with just such misplaced Midwesterners as myself. In Bernard Gufler, a Catholic intellectual from Kansas with a fine, wide-ranging mind, limitless curiosity, and great natural kindliness, I found a friend with whom I could pass long, and for me profitable, evenings in philosophic discussion; and the friendship, fed in later years by a common association in the Foreign Service, was to be a lifelong one. Again, there was my cousin, Charlie James, from Milwaukee, whom I knew like a brother. He was two classes below me, but we shared diggings in my last two years. With his entourage of Milwaukeean and Midwestern classmates, I felt personally at home; but my life was set off from theirs by my superior status as an upperclassman.

Finally, for a single academic year, there was a boy by the imposing name of Constantine Nicholas Michaelas Messolonghitis. Even poorer than myself, he had bummed rides to Princeton from Ohio and was trying to work his way through the upper-class years. (A born newspaperman, he later found his appointed place in life as a copy editor on the *New York Herald Tribune*.) His wide-eyed innocence about the East was even more staggering than my own; his uninhibited Greek hedonism was a good foil to my tense Presbyterian anxieties; in the easy glow of his provincial garrulousness (he was a character, in reality, from Thomas Wolfe) I softened and felt at home. Together, in the summer after junior year, we paid a poor man's visit to Europe. It was an adventure I look back upon now with a distinct absence of pride. We saw little, learned nothing, and must, as I now realize, have been awful nuisances to a long series of people — both those who were moved by kindness to help us, such as the understanding waitress in the London Lyons who would let us eat huge meals and then, with a wink, punch the check for a shilling; or those who had no choice but to occupy themselves with us, such as the unfortunate vice consul in Genoa into whose reluctant lap we tried insistently to lay the problems occasioned by our indigence. (Little did I dream, incidentally, that three years hence I would be in a similar position and would share this young man's revulsion toward any and all ragged students who looked to the government to save them from the predictable consequences of their own improvidence.) The dockside restaurants of Genoa, I may add, did no better by me than those of the slums of Trenton: I came away from the place with a raging amoebic dysentery, the aftereffects of which would haunt me for decades into the future.

In these circumstances, Princeton was for me not exactly the sort of experience reflected in *This Side of Paradise.* The portrayal in the hauntingly beautiful epilogue to *The Great Gatsby* of the Midwesterner's reaction to the fashionable East held, to be sure, such familiarity for me that when I first read it, while still in college, I went away and wept unmanly tears. Otherwise my college career bore little resemblance to Fitzgerald's. It is perhaps a mark of the difference between that day and this that it never occurred to me to hold the university to blame for my personal difficulties. On the contrary, I felt that I was fairly treated at its hands; I respected it intellectually; I took pride in it as an institution.

I knew none of my teachers well and cannot recall that I ever met any outside the official framework of the classroom or the faculty advisor's office. None, that I can recall, left any particular ideological imprint on me. But there were some I greatly respected for their intellectual power and integrity. The images of these have remained firmly in memory and have found their place, as such im-

ages often do, in the subtle web of admiration and attempted emula-
tion out of which personality is formed.

One of these was Raymond Sontag, later to be professor of European history at the University of California and editor of the
Documents on German Foreign Policy. I cannot remember what
was the exact subject matter of the course in diplomatic history in
which he instructed us; but the impression of his approach to the
subject: skeptical, questioning, disillusioned without being discouraged, was indelible.

Another such a one was Professor Joseph C. Green. He directed
and taught a massive freshman course popularly called Historical
Introduction, designed to give students an idea of the effect of such
things as climate, geography and resources on the character of human
civilizations. Ahead of its time in concept, this course was taught
with a vigor and severity that regularly left a considerable percentage of the freshman class by the wayside. For this reason it was
reputed to cause some measure of uneasiness in the dean's office. So
remorseless was the discipline of this course that some of the subject
matter has even stuck in my mind to the present day — something
that cannot be said, forty-five years later, of most college courses.
But more important, again, was the image of the man that directed
it: that of a stern, vigorous, and relentlessly conscientious scholar,
placing no demands on us that he did not meet to the fullest degree
himself. He later moved to Washington, entered the State Department, and came to direct, over the course of many years, the system
of examinations governing entrance to the Foreign Service. This he
did with the same implacable integrity that had inspired his teaching; and I wondered, sometimes, whether his unwillingness to make
the slightest concession — ever — to the political or social pressures
that were occasionally brought to bear, in that worldly capital, on
behalf of the admission of this or that individual candidate did not
arouse in his political superiors something of the same anxieties that
assailed the dean's office during his years at Princeton. He was re-
warded for these labors, in the end, by being not only eased out
of the position but left ostentatiously unconsulted, despite his years
of experience, when the whole examination system was revised in

1953, in connection with the report of the Wriston Committee. He deserves a recognition he has never fully received for having administered the Foreign Service examination system, over the span of several years, with a firm impartiality that could serve as a model for any nonpolitical career service.

One more teacher — anonymous, alas, because memory has obliterated his name — deserves a grateful mention. On account of the scarlet fever I was obliged to repeat, in my sophomore year, the usual freshman English course, a course devoted partly to composition but mostly to the analysis of some of the great classics of English literature. For some reason I rebelled intellectually against this course, misbehaved, and even failed, initially, to attend classes. What bothered me, if I remember correctly, was a feeling that English should not be taught that way: it was idle to go through the plays of Shakespeare trying to identify plots and climaxes — you either felt these plays as aesthetic and intellectual experiences or you did not. If you did not, nothing could help you; but if you did, what you should talk about was their content, their innermost spiritual and philosophic content, not their form. In any event, the young instructor who had me in his class finally summoned me to his presence and asked me, bluntly but not unkindly, what the hell was the matter with me. Softened by this personal attention, I professed repentance and agreed to make an honest effort. With all the perverseness of a person of that age, I then repaid his kindness by writing a theme for him on the subject of what was wrong with the teaching of English in American colleges. When the theme came back with the highest possible grade, I was taught an unforgettable lesson in generosity and restraint. Out of just such bricks of pedagogy, laid by modest masons of whom in later years not even the names are recalled, are built the educational edifices that really count.

I left college as obscurely as I had entered it. I absented myself heroically and self-consciously from all final ceremonies except the presentation of diplomas and hurried off.

It is not easy for me to picture myself as I was at that time. I prefer, in fact, not to try to do so; but I suppose there are occasions when one must. I see myself, emotionally and personally, as a rather ordinary youth, assailed by very ordinary weaknesses and passions. I was a dreamer, feeble of will, and something of a sissy in personal relations. I had inherited a detestation of scenes which I can only put down as a congenital weakness of the family. Many people plow more manfully through the inevitable brutalities of life. My greatest assets were a reasonably lucid and open intellect, lazy and passive when left to itself but capable of vigorous reaction when challenged; a high sensitivity to atmosphere and to other people's worlds of thought; and an almost total absence of intellectual preconception. With this intellect Princeton had done as well as it could, considering the educational conventions of the day. Literature I loved, and the understanding persistence of my teachers had given me a fair background in the English classics. For music I had a natural inclination, and I had picked up a bit about it on the side. Modern history and politics I had studied with increasing enjoyment and success as the college years progressed. But the whole great area of visual experience and appreciation had been grievously neglected. It had had no place in a Puritan home, where, as in so many Puritan families of an earlier day, the only real aesthetic awareness was literary. It had had no obligatory place even in the Princeton curriculum; and to the extent that it had existed there I had never come into contact with it. No one, to the day of my graduation, had ever taught me to look understandingly at a painting, or a tree, or the facade of a building.

I was, as I left Princeton, in some ways well schooled, but not really awakened. Princeton had prepared the mind for further growth. It had not stimulated in that mind any great latitude of curiosity. Nor had Princeton written upon it anything very much in the way of settled opinions, conclusions, or certainties in the field of public affairs. I can recall experiencing, as a fresh college graduate, the promptings of a vague Wilsonian liberalism; a regret that the Senate had rejected American membership in the League of Nations; a belief in laissez-faire economics and the values of competition; and a corresponding aversion to high tariffs. Beyond that, there was only a sensitive and impressionable *tabula rasa*. Some might make of this a reproach to the university. I chalk it up to its credit. It is the task of the university to prepare men for the formation of *their* prejudices, not to impregnate them with its own.

What I had most keenly missed to that point was the stimulus, and steadying effect, of association with older and wiser men. My father, now in his seventies, was too modest and honest, too conscious of his remoteness from the modern age and his inadequacy as a guide to it, to press himself upon me as a teacher. He contented himself with an occasional wistful admonition that I should not cease entirely, now that I was away from home, to go to church. Recognizing in him a shy, lonely, and not very happy person, I loved him, felt for him, wanted to protect him, and experienced little of the normal filial need for rebellion. But I was obliged to pick up my understanding of his mental world and reactions largely by bashful sidelong glances and had no free intellectual exchange with him.

I decided, on leaving Princeton, to try for the Foreign Service. This service was fairly new, having been established (by the Rogers Act) only in 1924. There had previously been a career Diplomatic Service and a similar Consular Service. Now the two were combined in a single professional organization, to stand entirely outside politics and to be run exclusively on the career principle. My decision to try for entry was dictated mainly, if my memory is correct, by the feeling that I did not know what else to do. During my upper-class years at college I had enjoyed the study of international politics and had prospered in it. Milwaukee held no charms for me. I feared falling into some sort of occupational rut and I thought that I would be best protected in the Foreign Service from doing so. The calculation, miraculously, proved to be correct. Some guardian angel must have stood over me at that point. It was the first and last sensible decision I was ever deliberately to make about my occupation.

Entrance into the Foreign Service generally involved, in those days, some months of special tutoring or other study and then the taking of written and oral examinations. The examinations were given once a year, in the spring.

I spent the summer of 1925, immediately after leaving college, working as a seaman on a coastal vessel that plied regularly between Boston and Savannah, Georgia. We received forty-eight cents an hour, worked up to sixteen hours straight on the days we came into port, and were quite happy.

In September I went on to Washington, took up residence in a boarding house (literally right out of the comic strip) on Church Street, and began as a pupil in the private tutoring school operated by a doughty Scottish pedagogue who made it his business to prepare young men for this purpose. When sober enough to teach, which was usually the case, he was an excellent teacher and, in addition to giving us adequate preparation for the examinations, imparted to us masses of intriguing general information.

The oral examining panel, headed by Under Secretary of State Joseph C. Grew, utterly terrified me. I was the first candidate to come before it and was so petrified by the experience that in my first words — to the effect that I was born in Milwaukee, Wisconsin — my voice broke into a falsetto on the second syllable of Wisconsin and set the board roaring with laughter. To my own surprise, I was accepted, along with seventeen other candidates (out of several hundred who had originally taken the written examinations) and was told to report for duty the following September.

A summer remained to be wasted; and I decided to waste it in Germany. I went first to Heidelberg, where I attended a few lectures, took lovely excursions up the Neckar, and squired a girl with an oval Renaissance face and black pigtails — very sweet and attractive, actually. We sat evening after evening on a bench on the hill, like thousands of couples before us, watching the sunset and enjoying the reflections of the round arches of the old bridge against the quiet waters of the river. Once my German uncle (an uncle by marriage, a lovely, civilized man from the old Frankfurt, with a goatee and pince-nez) came to see me, joined me in a walk along the hills, and made a lasting impression on me by remarking enviously in French, as we inspected the ruin of Heidelberg Castle (destroyed by the French in the late seventeenth century): *"Ce ne sont que les français qui puissent faire une si belle ruine."*

Heidelberg was followed by two or three weeks in a pension in Berlin, and then a fortnight or so at the seaside resort of Bansin, on the coast of the Baltic Sea. To this latter place I took Goethe's *Faust* and Spengler's *Untergang des Abendlandes*, wading persistently through them with the help of a dictionary. I spoke no English at all during those weeks. Many years before, in 1912, I had been taken to Germany as a boy of eight. For six months I had lived with my stepmother and my youngest sister in a pension in Kassel and had attended school there. Kassel had been chosen because my father, who knew German well, thought the purest German was spoken in that part of Germany. The city, being then the summer residence of the Kaiser, was considered, I am sure, elegant, refined, and residentially attractive. By the 1920s, my memories of Kassel had faded. They related mainly to the parks, the swans, the statue of Hercules leaning on his club at the head of the cascades that descended from Wilhelmshöhe, the tight smart uniforms of the guard regiments, the smell of the fish and cheese market, and the musical horn on the Kaiser's automobile. But the language, which I had acquired with the usual child's fluency in Kassel, now came back to me naturally and with ease. By the end of the summer I felt reasonably at home in it.

The first seven months of official service, beginning in the early autumn of 1926, were spent in what was then called the Foreign Service School. The institution occupied one large room on the eastern side of the first floor of the old State, War, and Navy Building, overlooking the White House grounds. There, while the lecturers droned on about passports, visas, and notarials, our inattentive eyes would sometimes be diverted by the spectacle of Calvin Coolidge, emerging from his offices to the White House lawn to be photographed with various groups of people — once, I seem to recall, with Indian feathers on his head. One bit of our training, however, seemed to me interesting and highly useful. We were asked, one day, to imagine that we were Ambassador Walter Hines Page, and that we were leaving our post at the Court of St. James's after long and distinguished service there. We were then to draft a letter to the British foreign minister apprising him of our intention to leave, asking for an audience with the king for the purpose of saying good-bye, and asking that Mrs. Page be similarly received by the queen. Anyone who subjects himself to such a task will understand, as we were then made to do, that diplomatic drafting is not a negligible skill; and he will appreciate the fact that the appropriate and graceful use of language is one of the prime requirements of the diplomatic profession.

On completion of the Foreign Service School, I was sent — on temporary assignment — to the consulate general at Geneva.

For anyone so callow, so unformed, so restless, so lacking in knowledge of himself and the world, there could have been no professional framework better than that of the Foreign Service. Its protective paternalism and sober training (more rigorous than now in the discipline of official style and deportment) served to steady down a young man by no means ready as yet for complete personal independence. The frequent changes of scene, the abundant intellectual stimuli, and the multitudinous glimpses the service afforded into the lives of other peoples and the workings of governments, all helped to broaden the horizons of one who was too timid to push or to ask many questions.

Most helpful of all was the new sense of responsibility. Within weeks after entry onto my first tour of duty abroad, I discovered that in this new role as representative (however lowly) of a government rather than of just myself, the more painful personal idiosyncracies and neuroses tended to leave me, at least in the office. I welcomed with surprised relief the opportunity to assume a new personality behind which the old introverted one could retire, be relieved of some of its helplessness, and even get some measure of perspective on itself. The moment of discovery, if I remember correctly, was an official American reception — a Fourth of July reception, I suppose it must have been — at the Hotel Beau Rivage in Geneva. As a new vice consul, attired in the resplendent cutaway that was *de rigueur* in those days, I was obliged to share with the other officers of the consulate general the duties of host. There on that summer day, with the orchestra playing on the terrace and the great lake shimmering beyond, with new guests constantly appearing and requiring to be greeted and welcomed, I suddenly became aware that I had a reputable and appointed place in the proceedings: I was now responsible for the well-being of others. For this reason I was something more than my usual self. I no longer had to relate myself to others as a species of naked intruder on the human scene. I had a role to play, a useful, necessary, legitimate role, helpful to others, requiring no justification or apology. If I played it creditably, I acquitted myself; there could be no need for further questions. Under this welcome mask I felt a hitherto unknown strength, a strength that was never entirely to fail me through a long Foreign Service career, at least not so long as I was in the office or appearing somewhere in the official role. From that time on, only in the odd moments of purely personal life, in the home or on vacation, would the silly student reappear — pouting, resisting, posing, refusing to be comforted, protesting that nothing was ever enough — reappear and require himself to be endured, not just by himself alone, now, but by all those who came, one after the other, to bear the burdens of a family intimacy. Like the actor on the stage, I have been able, all my life, to be of greater usefulness to others by what, seen from a certain emotional distance, I seemed to be than by what, seen closely, I really was.

The tour of duty at Geneva lasted only through the spring and summer of 1927. I gained little from it except some broad experience in consular work, the privilege of living with an old Genevan family, and daily practice in French. With the end of the summer I moved on to my first permanent post, at Hamburg.

Here, too, I did not stay long, but for quite different reasons. Hamburg, then the greatest port on the European continent, was a Social Democratic city, a great experiment, in fact, in the realization of a humane socialism. Here, as nowhere else except perhaps in Berlin, the immense moral and intellectual agony of the Weimar Republic was enacted daily, like a drama, before one's eyes, and I found it utterly fascinating. For the first time in my life I became preoccupied with the contemplation of events outside myself. I attended lectures at the excellent evening courses for adults run by the municipality. I rose early in the morning to do the assigned outside reading, before starting for the office. The sea having been at all times the greatest of my nonpersonal passions, I fell in love with Hamburg's most spectacular harbor. My work as a vice consul was concerned with American ships and seamen. I had a little office of my own, in the basement of the office building of the Hamburg-America Line, where I dealt with the captains and the stranded sailors. (A bullet hole in the desk commemorated, as I recall, the discontent one of the seamen had experienced with my predecessor; the latter, unharmed, had escaped by the window.) I missed no opportunity to get down into the harbor, and even once spent a blissful day, morning to night, on the bridge of one of the tugboats, as it pursued its appointed tasks.

The memories of those six months are all vivid, indelible ones; and although they were never reduced to any system of conclusions, I am aware that they had a deep effect on the image I formed of the post-World War I Europe. A diary entry tells, for example, of a rainy Sunday morning when I stood on the square before the Dammtor railway station watching, for the first time in my life, a Communist demonstration — ranks of shabby people with tense, troubled faces, marching defiantly and yet self-consciously under rain-soaked placards and red banners — and was suddenly moved to tears by the realization of their great earnestness, of the humble silence they were obviously obliged to endure on *other* days, of the fact that this, as they saw it, was *their* day, and that they were resolved to have their word, if only in the form of their banners and their numbers. The notes tell, again, of a lecture at the night school where the professor, a dumpy bearded little man with eyes full of suffering, read to us some of Franz Werfel's bitter poems of the recent war, and the whole tragic pathos of the postwar Germany was suddenly made real to me in the combination of his face and his words. I understood, in a flash of insight, as I wrote at the time, that "this man, whose entire personal and intellectual and religious life was obviously shattered to bits in the catastrophe of the war, and who has plodded through the chaos with a magnificent, unpretentious tenacity . . . has reconstructed out of the wreckage of his public and private ideals a new and higher philosophy for himself and for Germany," and that there were many others like him.

It was impressions such as these that bore in upon me how disgracefully incurious I had been to that point in life, how much I had missed, how spotty and unsatisfactory had been my education. A few months of such experiences served to convince me that before doing anything else I ought to continue formal education, to go on to some form of postgraduate study. I therefore announced my intention of resigning, signing myself as supercargo on a small American tanker, enjoyed a stormy four-week passage to Norfolk in the winter of 1928, and reported to the Department of State to complete the formalities of resignation. On arrival at the department, I was fortunate to encounter, first, my former chief and teacher at the Foreign Service School, Mr. William Dawson. Like a protecting angel, he intervened to save me from my foolishness. Himself a magnificent linguist, he reminded me that there was no need to resign: that if I was prepared to undergo training as a specialist for one of the rarer languages — Chinese, Japanese, Arabic, or Russian — I could have three years of graduate study at a European university without leaving the Foreign Service at all.

This intervention was decisive. I have always been grateful to Mr. Dawson for it. I selected Russian, partly because we then had no relations with the Soviet Union. It was logical to suppose that there would some day be favorable opportunities of service there for people knowing the language. But I also had a mind to the family tradition established by the elder George Kennan.

My application for special training in the Russian field was accepted. I was then sent out, in the summer of 1928, to begin the regime of practical service "in the field," followed by academic study, which the program of that day envisaged.

2

Training for Russia

FIVE and a half years elapsed from the time I was chosen to be trained as a Russian specialist to the time of my first service in Moscow. These years were all spent either in Berlin or in the Baltic capitals of Tallinn and Riga. I find them hard years to write about. I was obscure. My friends were obscure. Personal life was, for the purposes of this sort of a narrative, unexceptional. I read a great deal. I also wrote quite a bit — but mostly travelogues — the impressions of lonely expeditions to this place or that. To judge by the notebooks of those days, you would have thought that my usual companions were landscapes rather than people, as indeed they often were. The expeditions, almost exclusively to places in the various countries of the Baltic littoral, were deeply, unforgettably educational. The descriptions I wrote of them might have done as settings for events in novels. Without fictional accompaniment, they make monotonous and slightly melancholy reading. The reader will, with one exception, be spared them.

The arrangements for special Russian-language training envisaged, at that time, an initial period of regular Foreign Service work (not yet language study) in the respective field, to last twelve to eighteen months, followed by three years of postgraduate study at a European university. Since we then had no relations with the Soviet Union, the "field" consisted of the three Baltic cities of Tallinn, Riga, and Kovno, the capitals, respectively, of Estonia, Latvia, and Lithuania, in each of which the United States government had consular and diplomatic representation. All three of these countries had only recently been a part of the Russian Empire. All were soon to be part of Russia again. In all of them, at that time, a certain amount of Russian continued to be spoken, and a certain amount of Russian cultural life was to be pursued.

For some reason which now escapes me (probably because they had to fill some temporary vacancy in Berlin at just that time) I did not proceed directly to the Baltic but was detailed first, temporarily, to the Berlin consulate general. The detail lasted only a few weeks. I remember little about it. The city was always impressive to me, in its vast strong way, and at that time of year not unbeautiful. I inhabited a furnished room overlooking the square before the Schöneberger Rathaus — now the city hall of West Berlin. I patronized a small Anglo-American eating club, for bankers and diplomats, a club run, fortunately, by the English (who know how to do that sort of thing) and not by the Americans. I enjoyed as well as I could the amenities of the city. I interested myself, as I might have been expected to at that age and in these circumstances, in members of the other sex. I managed, in my spare time, to learn the Russian alphabet. At the end of this detail — in the beginning of July 1928 — I proceeded to Stettin and took ship, in company with a group of dreadfully seasick German boy scouts, for the Baltic.

The first assignment of my regular preliminary Russian training was as vice consul in Tallinn. Tallinn was then, and I hope still is, a lovely old Hanseatic town — a northern replica of the German Lübeck — surrounded, incongruously but not unattractively, by purely Russian suburbs. It lies on a bay of the Gulf of Finland, some sixty miles across the gulf from Helsinki. Two hundred and fifty miles away, at the head of the gulf, stands Leningrad.

In the little combined consular and diplomatic office that the United States government then maintained at Tallinn, there were only two Americans: the consul, who also held the diplomatic title of secretary of legation and was thus diplomatically accredited to the Estonian government, and myself, who had only the consular status. (The minister at Riga was accredited as chief of mission to all three Baltic countries; but his residence was in Riga, and he came only occasionally, as a visitor, to Estonia and Lithuania.) The consul was a timid, anxious man in middle age, who went through life with the worried air of one who earnestly tries to do things correctly but meets with constant frustration. Having little confidence in himself, he leaned heavily on the advice of a local Estonian clerk. The clerk combined a rather fuzzy intelligence with that outward claim to omniscience and infallibility which is, it has always seemed to me, the mark of a high percentage of the male population of the countries east of the Vistula and the Danube. The consul believed, however, in the authenticity of the posture, and would brook no challenge to it. I found myself, by consequence, barred from any usefulness in the diplomatic or political aspects of the work, and assigned to the more routine functions of the little office: the invoices, notarials, visas, accounts, and protection cases. This I did not mind too much. The work was at least varied (that is the advantage of a small office) and often amusing.

I recall being obliged, for example, to occupy myself at length with the manifold complications that ensued when an imaginative Estonian-American sharpster, accustomed to operating very close to the law of both countries, founded an enterprise the purpose of which was to salvage sunken ships of World War I vintage in Estonian waters. He raised capital for this venture from numbers of gullible Estonians, purchased or chartered a salvage tug in the United States, and brought it to Estonia with an American crew. The first object of its attentions was a venerable wreck, the stern of which still protruded from the water over a reef out at sea. To this, the tug was made fast, and operations were begun. But at this point a storm arose, as a consequence of which the tug sank, to add further enrichment to the underwater treasures of the Estonian coast, while the American crew took refuge on the protruding poop of the wreck. From this ignominious position they were happily salvaged by someone else — happily from their standpoint, and, to the extent that this was preferable to their being drowned, happily even from ours. But it was not *greatly* preferable, I must confess; because we now had the Estonian creditors of the wholly bankrupt enterprise about our ears, as well as the task of maintaining and repatriating the resentful crew. What happened to the entrepreneur I cannot recall; I have a faint idea that he absconded with the proceeds of the tug's insurance. Such, I may say, are the ennuis, but also the delights, of consular work. I rather loved it.

My recollection is that Estonia harbored, at that time, a total of nine native-born Americans, five of whom — the consul and his wife, a YMCA couple, and myself — lived in Tallinn. The consul once had me down for a weekend at his dacha at Hapsal, on the west coast. There, for some reason, I reverted to the worst reactions of my neurotic student youth, behaved with an atrocious lack of sociability, and merited the general ostracism I received thenceforth in the little diplomatic-consular community. I never saw the inside of an Estonian home, either. This last I found neither unfitting nor surprising; I was, after all, not primarily interested in Estonia and made no effort to learn the Estonian language. But the result of this combination of circumstances was that I lived mostly in solitude, except for the agreeable company of a cocker spaniel.

If this detachment had its strains, it also had its uses. I read a good deal — mostly contemporary German literature. (I thought and wrote, at that time, almost as much in German as in English.) I took, in company with the dog, a series of weekend expeditions: to Helsinki; to Narva; to the old university town of Tartu (Dorpat); to Pernau, on the southern coast; to the Russian-speaking province at the southeastern extremity of the country; to remote islands off the coast, with their simple communities of Swedish farmer-fishermen. I enjoyed this travel intensely, gathered impressions, recorded and treasured them with avidity. But above all, I began seriously in my spare time the study of Russian.

My teacher was an impoverished Ukrainian. He knew nothing about teaching languages, but he had the virtue of speaking, aside from his native Ukrainian, no word of anything but the language he was purporting to teach. He brought me, as teaching aids, the first-grade readers used in the schools in the Russian-speaking province just referred to. I admired and cherished these slender volumes, with their beautiful unreformed Cyrillic script,* their little vignettes and passages from Russian folklore and the classics, their naïve drawings of barnyards and animals and peasant children sledding. I learned by heart some of the poems and jingles they included. And I conceived then and there a love for this great Russian language — rich, pithy, musical, sometimes tender, sometimes earthy and brutal, sometimes classically severe — that was not only never to leave me but was to constitute in some curious way an unfailing source of strength and reassurance in the drearier and more trying reaches of later life.† Russian seemed to me, from the start, a natural language, in which words sounded the way they ought to sound, and might be expected to sound, as though one had once known it in some dead past and as though the learning of it was some sort of rediscovery. I turned to it with such real enjoyment and excitement that by the end of the year I could get around a bit in it. I even spent Christmas as a seeker of retreat in the Pskovo-Pecherski Monastery, near the Soviet border: a bit of old Russia, seventeenth-century Russia in fact, unspoiled in a way that would have been hard to duplicate anywhere in Russia proper. No one there spoke anything but Russian. When I left, I felt I was really getting on.

At the beginning of 1929 I was transferred to the legation at Riga. Riga was a much bigger city than Tallinn, though not entirely the great thriving center that it had been before the Russian Revolution. Here there was a large Western colony: some transient, like the diplomats; some resident, particularly the remnants of the former British commercial colony of Tsarist times. In Riga, one was at once embraced in an intensive foreign colony social life.

I am shocked to realize that I cannot recall what I did in those months at the legation chancery. Having not yet formally begun my Russian training, I was not a member of its vigorous and impor-

---

* Containing, that is, the letters that the Bolsheviki, in their reform of the orthography, had dropped from the alphabet.

† In making this statement, I am conscious of plagiarizing a passage from Turgenyev's *Verses in Prose* which was cited, for exemplary purposes, in a Russian grammar I once used. It reads, in my translation, as follows: "In the days of doubt, in the days of oppressive broodings over the fate of my native land, thou alone art my sustenance and my support, oh great, powerful, just and free Russian language. Were it not for thee, how could one keep from falling into despair . . . ?"

tant Russian section. I have vague recollections of fooling around with codes and couriers, translating articles about Latvian politics from the local Russian paper, and clearing shipments of embassy supplies through the customs.

Riga had the advantage of a variegated and highly cosmopolitan cultural life: newspapers and theaters in the Lettish, German, Russian, and Yiddish tongues, and vigorous Lutheran, Roman Catholic, Russian Orthodox, and Jewish religious communities. Throughout that region religion was still the common hallmark of nationality, so that if you asked a person what he was, he was apt to reply by telling you his religion rather than naming an affinity to any particular country. The politically dominant Letts, becoming increasingly chauvinistic as the years of their independence transpired, were concerned to put an end as soon as possible to all this cosmopolitanism and eventually did succeed, by 1939, in depriving the city of much of its charm. Their efforts in this direction were of course completed in 1940, in a manner they had neither foreseen nor desired, when the country was occupied by the Russians and incorporated into the Soviet Union. With this development the genial mingling of tongues and faiths that had once given Riga the proud title of "Paris of the Baltic" gave way all at once to the gray, dead shabbiness of isolation behind the impenetrable walls of Stalin's Russia; and national chauvinism was punished in a degree beyond its greatest deserts.

In addition to its more serious cultural amenities, Riga had a vigorous night life, much in the Petersburg tradition: vodka, champagne, gypsies, sleighs or drozhki with hugely bundled coachmen waiting at the door, a certain amount of gaiety, but even more of a nostalgic, despairing, shoot-the-works sentimentality — a mood, I may say, which had a tendency to prove highly irrelevant and unhelpful the next day. The nightclubs were, in fact, not the only relics of Tsardom in the sights and habits of the local scene. Riga was in many respects a minor edition of Petersburg. The old Petersburg was of course now dead, or largely dead — in any case inaccessible to people from the West. But Riga was still alive. It was one of those cases where the copy had survived the original. To live in

Riga was thus in many respects to live in Tsarist Russia — it was, in fact, almost the only place where one could still live in Tsarist Russia. Our legation there was partially manned by people from the staff of the old embassy at Petersburg; and I drew many years later on these impressions for the picture of the Petersburg embassy of 1917-1918 which I endeavored to recreate in *Russia Leaves the War*.

While in Riga I shared with other unmarried colleagues a spacious bachelor apartment on the top floor of a huge German-style apartment building called, for some reason, the Vorburg. My companions were intelligent, critical, and strongly argumentative people. The adjacent Soviet Russia, the scene now of Trotsky's expulsion, or Stalin's struggle with the Right opopsition, and of the beginnings of collectivization and the first Five Year Plan, overshadowed our Baltic world and dominated our thoughts and discussions. The apartment looked down on the so-called export harbor — a free-port area set aside for Soviet transit trade. The weather, for nine months of the year, was apt to be on the dreary side. (We were, after all, within thirty miles of Courland; and the weather of that historic duchy — *Kurländisches Wetter*, as the Germans called it — was proverbial for its foulness.) Over the long rainy weekends, arguments about Russia, Marxism, capitalism, the peasant problem, etc., droned endlessly on, rising and falling with the hours. Participants arrived, added their words and departed again, like casual players at a roulette game. And all the while, below us in the rain-drenched harbor could be heard the hooting of switch engines and the clanking of the strings of battered broad-gauged freight cars, as they finished their month-long treks to dockside from God knew where in the vast interior of Russia.

Here, too, there were expeditions — to Kovno, to Vilna, to the port of Memel. But above all there was, as a relief from Riga in summer, that magnificent, seemingly endless stretch of seashore known as the Riga Strand. Here the Russian-type dachas — summer bungalows — were strung out for miles and miles along the dunes, among the great glistening Scotch pines. I even got one of these cottages for myself: a tiny, single-room affair. I spent weekends there in June and July, bathing in the sea by day, bathing then later, in the nocturnal hours, in the magic and, to me, commandingly erotic twilight of the northern world in the weeks of the summer solstice — the twilight that has given the name to the "white nights" of Petersburg. It was a marvelous, diffuse half-light, marking the unbroken transition of the glow in the northern sky from sunset to sunrise — a condition of nature under the spell of which all human emotions and situations seemed to take on a heightened poignancy, mystery, and promise.

In the late summer of 1929 I went back to Berlin to begin the appointed term of intensive academic study in the Russian field. I matriculated as a student at the University of Berlin and enrolled, as an aspirant for its diploma, at the so-called Oriental Seminary (Seminar für Orientalische Sprachen) which formed a part of the university. This institution, originally established by Bismarck for the training of young German diplomats destined for service in the Orient, had endured as a general center for what would today be called "area studies" — but only for cultures other than Western. In the field of Russian studies its principal function seemed to be to grant, after appropriate examination, a diploma which entitled you to be a translator and interpreter before the German courts. It also offered a two-year course; but it was admitted that the course would not alone prepare you for the examination; you were expected to work on the side as well, or to take more than the two years. The examination was not only in the language but also in the history, particularly the constitutional and legal history, and the economic geography of Russia.

Profiting from the fact that I had learned a certain amount of Russian before coming to Berlin, I took the examination at the end of my first academic year, barely skimming through. There were only a handful of candidates—three, I think, of whom one had been born and brought up in Russia. The translation we were asked to do from Russian into German was a document out of the remote past — a decision of the supreme judicial tribunal of the former Russian Empire (the Governing Senate, as it was called), dished up to us in the original, with all the archaisms, legalisms, and abbreviations of the court record. The one from German into Russian I have forgotten. We were then given two hours to write an essay in Russian, without reference books, on the state of Russian agriculture on the eve of the Russian Revolution. I recently found among my papers the original of this essay, which they evidently returned. I think, in looking it over now, that they were very kind to me. I hope the translations were better, and venture to think it likely that they were.

The following academic year was spent in the study of Russian history at the university proper, and of Russian language and literature with private tutors. I participated in the seminars, respectively, of the two outstanding professors in Russian history, Otto Hoetsch* and Karl Stählin.†

Hoetsch, in addition to his academic commitments, was a prominent political figure and a Reichstag deputy on the conservative side. He was fearfully overburdened (in a way that I was to experience in my own person some three decades later) by the simultaneous claims of history and contemporary affairs. His field was more Eastern European than purely Russian history. His students struck me, for the most part, as forbiddingly advanced. Being poorly prepared, and coming in late, I got little from his seminar in the substantive sense, but found attendance worthwhile as a source of insight into both academic methods and personalities.

Stählin, then at work on what is to my mind one of the finest of modern histories of Russia, was a pure and dedicated scholar. He used his seminar students, after the German fashion, as aids to him in his work, sending them as researchers and investigators into this or that body of source material. I prepared a paper for him on the memoirs of the man who had been Kremlin librarian at the time of Napoleon's occupation of the city — memoirs that had heretofore remained without proper historical evaluation. Whether this was as useful to him as it was to me, I cannot tell; but to me as a student

* Otto Hoetsch, 1876-1946; professor of Eastern European History and International Relations at the University of Berlin, 1920-1935; at various times deputy in the Prussian Landtag and the German Reichstag; editor of *Osteuropa* and *Osteuropäische Forschungen.*

† Karl Stählin, 1865-1939; for many years professor in Russian History at the University of Berlin; author of *Geschichte Russlands.*

the experience of participating responsibly, if only in a very small way, in the preparation of a major work of history was a new one, and it had a value far beyond any study oriented just to the passing of exams.

My private tutors were for the most part simply highly cultured Russian emigrés, not systematic teachers. I conversed with them, and read aloud to them for long hours from the Russian classics or from Klyuchevski's famous lectures on Russian history — as a means, primarily, of mastering the mysteries of Russian syllable accentuation.

The father of this new system of language and area training, insofar as the Russian field was concerned, was the chief of the Division of Russian and Eastern European Affairs, Mr. Robert F. Kelley.* I shall have more to say about him at a later point. His concept of the purpose of the program, as I understood it, was to provide those of us who went through it with a background in Russian language and culture not dissimilar to that which would normally have been assumed on the part of a well-educated Russian of the old, prerevolutionary school. For this reason, stress was laid on basic linguistic, literary, and historical studies, not on Sovietology. Once, at the outset of my study in Berlin, I wrote to Kelley, pointing out to him that the Berlin University, almost alone among the universities of the West at that time, had excellent courses and lecture series on strictly Soviet subjects: Soviet finance, Soviet political structure, etc. I asked whether he did not want me to take some of these. The answer was negative. The sense of what he said was: stick to your knitting; get the essentials of a good Russian cultural background; the rest can come later. It was wise direction, for which I have always been grateful.

By the end of this second year in Berlin I had a pretty fair grounding in Russian history and literature and a workable command of the language. This last was to be further refined in subsequent years (nine, all told) in Russian-speaking environments; but

* Robert Francis Kelley, scholar, State Department official, and diplomat; for several years, beginning 1926, chief of the Division of Eastern European Affairs of the Department of State.

it sufficed at that time for every purpose of Foreign Service life and work. I was at this stage weary of study and wanted to get back to practical service. Kelley saw no objection to this, so it was decided that I should skip the normal third year of study. I was reassigned, instead, to Riga — but for work, this time, in the Russian section of the legation there. The establishment of diplomatic relations between the Soviet Union and the United States was still two years off, and this was the nearest thing to a Russian assignment that one could get.

Of personal life, during this period of study in Berlin, there is not much to be said. I was at a stage of my life when, to use the words that John Evelyn used to describe a similar stage in his own, I "now thought of nothing but the pursuit of vanity, and the confused imaginations of young men." I lived gracelessly, in stuffy, over-furnished Germanic rooms, where fussy landladies looked in twice a month to make sure that I had not soiled their lace curtains and Mecklenburgian housemaids cooked the main meal, brought me their little smudged shopping books for inspection, and complained about the price of vegetables at the market. Once I succeeded, with intense pride and excitement, in publishing an article in a liberal German magazine. I had friends: some German, some Anglo-American, some Russian. Of the latter, there was one family — mother, son, and daughter — who lived a penniless and precarious existence in a cellar in Spandau. None had regular employment; the son was trying to write; the daughter studied the piano; all were wildly impractical and helpless. I did what I could to alleviate their plight; but they lived from crisis to crisis, surviving only by a series of those miraculous last-minute rescues that God reserves for the truly innocent and utterly improvident. I was embarrassed by the reckless spontaneity of their devotion: enthusiastic visits at unexpected hours, elaborate gifts they couldn't possibly afford, etc. But I was grateful and reciprocated the affection in my way. I was pleased that they accepted me as a Russian, as one of them, not as a foreigner. Sharing their woes and crises, I felt like a Russian myself.

Perhaps the atmosphere of Berlin in those days, and the settings

of my own life, will best be illustrated by the following observations about the places in which I had lived, or was living, in this
great, pre-Hitlerian city. I find it in my diary notes, under date of
February 7, 1931. It serves as a reminder that the city was for me,
at that time, the nearest thing I had known to an adult home.

It has grown cold, at last. The dry snow, falling on the Kaiserallee
in the early twilight, swirls under the dirty wheels of the taxis.

There is frost on the windows of the trolley cars, and the wooden
floors are wet from the melted snow off people's feet. Above the frosted
windows there are singularly inappropriate advertisements of the streetcar company: "Into the great outdoors on the streetcars" — "*Mit der
Strassenbahn ins Freie.*" There are the names of all the places to which
the streetcar will take you: Tegelsee, Muggelsee, Wilhelmshorst, etc.,
and under each name there is a picture of a lake, with bullrushes and
sunshine and sailboats.

It makes little difference where you live in Berlin: you belong not to
the neighborhood but to the city.

In the Luisenstrasse . . . but that was long ago; the city has changed
and I have changed myself.

The windows of the room in the Mühlenstrasse looked out over the
square before the Schöneberger Rathaus. On the cool spring nights I
used to lean out the window and watch the square. One saw not only
the square, but also a corner of the Stadtpark. The thin young poplars
along the park looked very helpless and discouraged before the cold
mass of the Rathaus and the surrounding buildings. The corner of the
park was the end-stop for the 14 omnibus, and there would always be
two or three of them waiting there, before starting their return trip
back to the east. There would be a clanging of streetcars, and a rumbling of the motors of the waiting buses. A lone prostitute walked
round and round the block, like a nocturnal bird of prey, and I always
wondered what booty she found, down there in that unerotic part of
town. Sometimes there would be the remains of a market on the square,
old women packing things into rickety horse-drawn wagons or push-
carts, men sweeping the pavement. Other times there would be political
demonstrations, and young people with banners and drums and gym-
nasium suits and defiant faces.

The windows of the apartment in the Giesebrechtstrasse looked back

into the pitlike courtyard, called the garden. There were a few trees
there, and a bit of grass; also the garbage cans and an incredible number
of tawny, dirty cats. On summer nights one heard the cats and occasionally the faint roar of the elevated trains on the Stadtbahn. On warm
Sunday mornings, people would sit out on their high, iron balconies,
with coffee and the Sunday papers, and there would be a virulent
chorus of radios, playing church music and Wagnerian operas mixed
with strident gramophone jazz.

But the Giesebrechtstrasse may be said to have had a neighborhood,
inasmuch as it was near to the Kurfürstendamm. Not that one had
much personal contact with the boulevard. There was a bum café on
the corner, where the upholstery stank and nothing tasted good, but
where one could use the telephone without buying anything, which
was very helpful when one had locked one's self out of the apartment.
Once, when even that didn't work, I had to sleep (on credit) in the
new ultramodern hotel, a few doors farther up, and to breakfast the
next morning in the main dining room still attired in a dinner jacket,
to the astonishment of the waiters and the other guests. But the boulevard itself had life and lights. There was traffic on it at all times of the
day and night. It was always good to walk along the unused bridle
path in the center, late at night, and let one's self be hypnotized into
feeling that it all proved something.

In the Hitzigstrasse, the great old private mansions lowered back in
the shades behind high iron fences and cavernous front yards. Here,
too, traffic swept by night and day — high-hat, hurried traffic of taxis
and limousines — on its way between the west and the center of town,
reminding one constantly, in its steady rush, that this was no neighborhood at all, but only an unimportant stretch of the road between the
real centers of existence.

In den Zelten was like living in the country. There didn't even seem
to be a store near the place. Jammed in between the park and the quiet
canal-river, it was an eddy in the city's whirlpool, disturbed only on
summer nights by strains from the bands in the Kroll garden and the
beer gardens of the hoi polloi at the other end of the street.

Even here, now, in the suburbs, one is neighborless. The impersonal
villas stand blankly and mutely, side by side, all different and all dreadfully alike, along streets that are endless. In the quietness and flatness
of the terrain, there is still something that lets one feel the sandy pine

forest that was so recently here. One is rarely home in the daytime. At night there is welcome silence, broken only at infrequent intervals by the footsteps of some somber home-comer, or by the droning of a lonely trolley car, whining hopelessly, sleepily, through the night, from an unknown origin to an unknown destination.

* * *

In the summer of 1931, as my period of study in Berlin was nearing its close, I met a Norwegian girl — Annelise Soerensen. She was living in Berlin, with English cousins. We became engaged. She returned to Norway, in July, to break the news to startled and troubled parents. I followed shortly, to spend a month as a visitor at her home, before the wedding. The journey was, for obvious reasons, a memorable one for me. I journeyed, so far as I could, in the elegant Nash roadster I had acquired the year before and in which — automobiles being what they were in those days — I took great pride and satisfaction. Again, I shall let the account of the journey flow from the diary, for it, too, gives a sense of the time.

A bad road to Stettin. Harvesting going on in the fields.

It is Saturday, August 8. Banners are stretched across the village streets. "*Geh zum Volksentscheid*" is the appeal, and one can hear voices all over the far Pomeranian countryside: "*Kein Mensch hat Geld. Die Franzosen haben uns alles weggenommen. Erfüllungspolitik. . . .*"

In Stettin, I drive direct to the dock. Two drunken stevedores are having a fight by the corner of the warehouse. The thud of fists and the scuffling of shoes on the cobblestones echo across the quiet water of the slip.

While waiting for the ship to sail, Volodya and Shura, who have come along to bid me good-bye, disappear. After a while, they come back, laden with armfuls of flowers. With their last few marks, they have bought out an entire flower shop. They take it very seriously, this departure. Instinct, rather than any logical process of thought, tells them that while we may meet again soon, this day and this departure mark the termination of my residence in Berlin and that this is the real good-bye.

As the ship is moving away from the quay, a taxicab comes driving up with much honking. A stout lady descends, clutching a dozen parcels and waving an umbrella at the boat. We maneuver back to the dock. While the stout lady is bundled over the rail, we have a chance to shake hands again. Volodya hands me their new address on a crumpled slip of paper. Now we are off again. The engine pounds determinedly as we move down the slip. I stand in the stern and wave my handkerchief like the Germanest German, until the tiny waving spots of white on the dock have finally faded from view.

It is after six o'clock as we steam down the river. This trip has lost its romance since I made it three years ago on my way to the Baltic for the first time. Which only means that I have other eyes. Or perhaps I am just tired.

In the twilight, we churn down the long avenue of lighthouses that leads across the Stettiner Haff. Three years ago a storm was blowing here, and mean, choppy seas, like those on the Great Lakes, were tossing a motorboat moored to some of these pilings. Now all is quiet, and much less interesting.

It is already pitch dark when we reach the sea at Swinemünde. When we get a mile or two off shore, the lights from the resorts gleam brightly in a long, irregular string. I cannot bring myself to realize that there is life behind them, cafés and dancehalls and promenades. It seems to me that they only mask a desolate, deserted shore. Is it the depression, which deprives us of our illusions, this summer?

I stayed three days in Copenhagen, fussing with the car and trying to rest up. Instead of resting up, I contracted a wretched summer cold. I drove on up to Frederikshavn, near the northeastern tip of Denmark, and there boarded the old steamer which in those days made the wearisome daytime journey across the Skagerrak to Kristiansand, on the southern coast of Norway, my fiancée's home. All that day the fever gained on me as the vessel slithered and pounded in the characteristic Skagerrak sea. I arrived in the evening, to be introduced at once into a cozy, old-fashioned Norwegian family gathering, which proceeded long into the night, with coffee, brandy, cigars, and unhurried family talk. It was impossible to escape it or to plead illness. The evening was lived through and enjoyed as best it could be. I shudder still, though, to think what impression must have been made on this solid Norwegian family by the thin, slightly uncouth, very nervous, and rather unwell apparition of an American that they escorted from the boat. The parents surely went to bed with even more anxious feelings than those with which they had awaited the arrival of the vessel — and those, I understand, had not been exactly ones of confidence or elation.

All this did not prevent my being received into the family from that moment on like a son and brother, and treated thenceforth, over some thirty-five years, with an openhearted warmth and kindliness that ignored or accepted my failings and made the most of what was left. This was only the first of many visits to Norway; and I cannot leave it without recording a debt of gratitude to the memory of my wife's parents: to her mother — a warm, openhearted person, capable at times of childlike gaiety, but always against the background of a great maternal dignity and purity, a woman from whose lips I never heard an ungenerous or spiteful word; and her father: gaunt, gnarled, and taciturn, an oak root of a man, destined later to endure and survive mistreatment and concentration camp punishment at the hands of the Nazis — a stubborn and difficult person, but one from whom, again, over thirty years I never suffered a discourtesy or unkindness. No one who knew it could fail to love Norway for its nature; but even had the landscape been of the dreariest, one could not have failed to love it for such people. They gave to me in their undemonstrative way not only a second home but also, over the years, a second country.

We were married in mid-September. From the wedding dinner we went right to the night steamer for Frederikshavn and drove down to Central Europe through Denmark, casting the wedding corsage into the Kiel canal as we passed. For our honeymoon we went to Vienna, where neither of us had ever been. Vienna was shabby and rainy, but comfortable and inviting in an old-fashioned way. It seemed, as a city, to be resigned to the loss of its former imperial glamour, but quite sorry for itself. My wife's passport being still Norwegian, I labored long and in vain to persuade the hotel porter that we were really married, only to have him look paternally at me over his spectacles and to assure me stubbornly that "we understand." We saw the sights, fought over who was to hold the single guidebook, and finally, in the first serious adjustment to the married state, bought one for each. The papers, as I recall it, were full of the collapse of the Austrian Kreditbank. It was the beginning of the real agony of the economic crisis.

The wedding journey accomplished, we proceeded to Riga to establish our first home. Riga — enmired in the autumn rains and seen through the dusty windows of the Hotel Petersburg — looked empty and dreary. The illusion of glamour that had hung over the life of the place when seen through the eyes of an unattached bachelor to whom anything — after all — could happen fell suddenly away as one set about to introduce a young wife into its midst. Colleagues, formerly colorful and amusing, seemed guarded, remote, and undependable; and one realized at a stroke how pathetically thin and barren of meaning were those habits of casual good fellowship that normally lubricated the official and social encounters of the day. Alone, neither of us, I think, had felt isolated. Now, as a couple, we felt intensely, anxiously alone.

We found for a home the top two floors of a former factory owner's house, in the industrial suburb of Tornakalns. Factory owners in the Russian Empire had had a habit of living in or near the compounds of their plants (I always suspected this had something to do with the appeal of Marxism to Russian workers); and the house was a relic of those days. It stood across the street from a park. During the winter, except for the droning of the trolley cars just outside the wooden street fence, all was peaceful. But in early May, to our utter horror, a bandstand was erected in the park, on the other side of the street; a five-piece brass ensemble, most appallingly out of tune, began its labors every Saturday noon and continued until after one in the morning, and then again on Sunday, while young Latvian apaches danced on a wooden platform below them. They had only five tunes, one of which — as I shall never forget — was "Fiesta," and these were repeated endlessly, in unvarying order, over the weekends of the summer. You could retire to the innermost clothes closet of the house and bury your head in the clothes, it made no difference — the sound reached you. We tried to break the year's lease, but it was no good. It was autumn before it expired.

The ordeal was made worse by the fact that my wife was pregnant from the start, with the baby due in early summer. She announced this state of affairs by fainting, gracefully and elegantly, at a formal dinner at the residence of the dean of the diplomatic corps, Baron de Selys-Fanson, of Belgium, thus obliging me to carry her out before the eyes of the astonished guests, as though I were abducting her. But social life was not inordinate. Most of the winter and spring evenings were whiled away (until the band got started) with readings aloud from Conrad and dutiful obstetrical walks through the quiet gray streets of Tornakalns. The baby — daughter Grace — arrived without incident, one night in June. The nights were again white, and the river, I can recall, lay bathed in the golden reflections of the early sunrise as I drove back from the clinic.

By this time the economic crisis was upon us. I had had a bit of money, inherited from my mother. This now went the way of a great deal of other money in just those years, leaving me penniless. I am inclined, today, to think this was a blessing for me because from that time on I at least knew what I had earned and what I had not. But at the same time Congress reacted to the crisis by depriving us entirely of our rental and other allowances, and cutting our salaries through the shabby device of obliging us to take one month's leave without pay. The total cut in our official remuneration was, as I recall it, about 60 percent — and this abruptly, without warning. Caught with the year's lease on the house, there was nothing we could do about it until autumn. Then we moved in with the bachelors, in the Vorburg flat, for the winter. Later, we pinched pennies even further by renting a little dacha, at one hundred twenty dollars for the season, out at the Strand.

By the late summer of 1933, after some two years of this assignment, I was due for home leave. We parked the baby with the family in Norway, went to Copenhagen, and boarded a Moore-McCormack freighter for New York. This, though I did not know it at that time, was the end of my service in Riga.

I have said that the reader would be spared, with one exception, the records of travels around the Baltic area with which my own notebooks of that period are replete. But because these references to Riga and the Baltic in the years of the great depression have necessarily been cursory and devoid of vividness, I include, as a small example of landscape and atmosphere, the following account of a weekend visit paid, in company with my college friend Bernard Gufler (now stationed in Riga, and another inhabitant of the bachelor apartment) to the Courland port of Libau (Liepāja, in the Latvian). The time was late autumn 1932.

Libau is situated in southwestern Latvia, on the Baltic Sea. It had been, before World War I, a flourishing port, naval base, and manufacturing center. I described it, in a foreword to my account, as follows:

The most favorably situated of the few ice-free ports in northern Russia, terminus of the Libau-Romney Railway which penetrated into the heart of the Ukraine, natural base for the Russian navy, the city was well on the way, in 1913, to becoming one of the greatest ports of Northern Europe. The geographical settlements after the war, together with subsequent developments, have been such as to cut off almost entirely the trade and industry at this point, to paralyze a great deal of its economic life, and to leave the city a mere husk of its former self.

(There follows the account of our visit.)

We leave Riga by car in midafternoon. The short November daylight is already waning and a murky darkness is reclaiming the northern world.

The fall ice flow is in progress. They have taken out the pontoon bridge on this account and we have to go over the high iron bridge upstream. Below us, in the shadows, the black forms of the river tugs stand out against the white cakes of ice which they are breaking up.

In the eddy below the island, a dredge surrounded by barges is already frozen in.

The oiled road to Mitau, once a sector of the great military highway from Petersburg to the German border, is covered with the slimy mud of autumn which never dries up. The world about us is concealed in mist and darkness. The faint shades of peasant carts and high wagons loom up in the blur of the headlights. Some of the peasants have ridden days through icy fog and darkness to sell a load of produce in Riga for a dollar or two. They all sleep on the road, and their horses have a philosophical indifference to auto horns.

We get a train at Mitau and share a second-class compartment with two sleepy officers and a couple of German businessmen. These spacious cars, with their flat benches and smooth, imitation-leather upholstery, contrast favorably with the cramped coaches of the Western European roads, full of bad air and smelly upholstery. The officers soon burrow their faces into sooty palms and return to their slumbers. The Germans go out into the corridor to smoke long Russian cigarettes with hollow tips. The wheels set up their monotonous rumbling, and only the raindrops, streaking out of the blackness across the dirty window panes, remind one of the still Courland countryside which is flowing past outside — the swamps and forests, the muddy wagon roads, the lonely peasant farmsteads and rare villages, all drenched with the rains of autumn and shrouded in mist and darkness.

It is evening when we reach Libau. A horse droshki takes us from the station through the quiet provincial streets. Wet cobblestones and a lonely streetcar track gleam under the dim streetlights. Rain drips from the driver's fat back onto the leather cover over our laps. Hoofbeats resound against the walls of the low houses. We come to a square with one or two lighted shop windows, and stop before a building where a faint lamp shines out over the entranceway, behind flurries of rain. A boy scuttles out for the bags and we are led into a cold hotel, with a cavernous entrance hall, redolent of past grandeur.

We pass the evening in the town's one evening café. The two German train-companions, who incidentally have put up at the same hotel, have already installed themselves. There are two or three other miscellaneous guests and one table of Jews. The girls from the kitchen poke their heads through the kitchen door, to see the strangers. The Jews talk in tense low tones about the possibilities of getting past the American immigration laws by going to Cuba and being smuggled in from there. A little orchestra plays the last year's *"Schlagers"* from Berlin. So the night life wears on until shortly before midnight, when the Jews pay their bill, the orchestra packs its instruments, and the waitresses ostentatiously begin stacking the tables.

We take a walk before going to bed. A thin rain is falling. The streets are the narrow small-town streets of Northern Europe. They are dark and deserted at this time of night. The faint roar of the sea can be heard even in the center of the city, and we set off toward the west to find it.

The narrow streets soon widen out, and instead of the flat-fronted town houses, crammed up close against the sidewalk, we come to large low summer houses in the Russian style, set back behind spacious gardens. They lie in the shadows behind the trees, abandoned and boarded up for the winter. The roar of the sea is louder here. The street ends, and there is an imposing Renaissance building at the edge of a park. In summer this must be the main *"Kurhaus,"* without which no European resort can exist. Not a soul is in sight. A solitary streetlight shows the rain, sifting down through the naked branches of the linden trees. We pick our way through paths of the park, barely visible in the darkness, toward the sea. The park is not wide and we soon reach the other side. Here further progress is impossible; there are ditches and sand dunes ahead of us, and the darkness is complete. But the wind and the gusts of rain sweep over the dunes, redolent of the fresh night sea, and there is something young and untiring in the roar of the breakers.

Morning. The dawn comes late and faintheartedly, through gray skies and gusts of rain.

The local paper is on the breakfast table. Three and a half pages of outside news, from Riga, from Berlin, from Königsberg. One little column of local gossip announces that the Russian theater is soon coming from Riga, and that a guest singer is arriving from Königsberg to sing in the opera. Yes, there is still an opera. The prices for seats range from three and a half to fifteen American cents. The house brings in perhaps twenty to thirty dollars, on a good evening. From that, together with a little subsidy, the cast must be paid, and the orchestra, and the stage personnel, and the scenery, and the fuel, etc. Yet the opera goes on.

We set forth after breakfast on a tour of inspection, on foot. There is a large marketplace with all the features of an Eastern European provincial market; the fish wives, parked behind their barrels under huge umbrellas; the strings of little Russian doughnuts, yellow and polished and hard as rock; the stalls full of homemade wooden shoes, particularly favored by the vendors themselves, who have to stand all morning in the puddles between the cobblestones; the live pigs squealing in the burlap sacks, and a hundred other testimonials to the peculiarities of human needs and human enterprises. Leaving the marketplace, we come to a district of churches, and even go into one imposing Catholic church, an eighteenth-century structure in the red brick Gothic of northern Poland and East Prussia. A Polish school is not far away, and the stranger is reminded that the real hinterland of this port, cut off at present by Lithuania, is partly Polish.

Libau is no old town. Originally a fishing village, its development into a city was the result of the last partition of Poland and the inclusion of the Baltic provinces into the Russian Empire. Like the nearby ports of Königsberg and Memel, its natural hinterland, lying at the junction of German Lutheranism, Polish Catholicy, and Russian Orthodoxy, has been torn this way and that by repeated adjustments of national boundaries. Unlike Memel, it has not even an important river behind it, to serve as a natural thoroughfare of trade, and its real development as a port began with the construction of the railway, in the 1870s — the famous Libau-Romney Railway, which reached far back into the heart of the Russian breadbasket and gave the Ukraine an outlet on the shores of the Baltic. These quiet streets, with their two-story wooden buildings, their cobbled pavements, their young trees, are the product of the nineteenth century — the product of the tremendous economic expansion of nineteenth-century Russia. But the accuracy with which cultural influences are reflected in the faces of European cities is astounding, and one cannot fail to sense the proximity of the two great neighbors, Poland and Germany: Poland through the brick church and the cemetery with the Polish names and the unmistakably Catholic tombstones; Germany through the modern villas along the park by the sea and even through the very lay of the park and the linden trees.

We cross the dunes and come out on the broad beach. The southwest breeze is no longer strong, but a high surf is running and the sand has been washed white by the breakers. In the summer days before the war, this beach teemed with the society of imperial Petersburg and Moscow. As a summer seashore resort Libau shared with the hot cliffs of the Crimea, the pine-covered dunes of the Riga Strand, and the quiet beach at Hungerburg on the Gulf of Finland the favor of Russian society. The uniforms of officers and midshipmen (for this was the great naval port), ladies with long dresses and bustles, and with huge, many-colored beach parasols, children playing in the sand under the supervision of French and English governesses, flags, bunting, yachts, military bands — all these lent to this plain landscape, already tinged with the melancholy of the north, some of the glow and pomp of the capitals. But this is the year 1932 and the month of November. Only at the end of the beach, under the very shadow of the breakwater, a few peasants are raking up the seaweed that has been carried up on the sand, and are stowing it into carts.

From the top of the breakwater, one can survey the quiet expanse of the harbor. The long moles, several of them altogether, describe a semicircle far into the sea, around the mouth of the canal. Inside them the waters are smooth, troubled neither by the wind nor by the keels of ships. It is a weekday but the atmosphere is that of the quietest of Sundays. Not a human being is in sight. A lone ray of sunshine breaks through the jagged clouds and catches the shuttered windows of the abandoned customs house, across the water. Beyond it, on a narrow neck of land, one can see the huge bulk of the old emigrant house, which used to handle thousands of Russian emigrants a year, bound for another emigrant house in the waters of New York Bay. In the winter harbor, a single Latvian freighter lies high in the water, tied up for the winter, or perhaps for the duration of the crisis. Tufts of grass have sprung up between the cobblestones of the docks, but the big granite bits, so firmly implanted by the long arm of the Russian Empire, look as though they could wait many years more for the hawsers of ships before yielding to the corrosion of the elements.

We walk through the extended factory district which adjoins the harbor. It is a rare smokestack which can show a wisp of smoke these days. Occasionally the red brick walls which border the long streets are broken by pretentious houses, the residences of the owners. Now the windows are dark and the doors bolted. Only the porters' lodges seem to be inhabited, and there is something symbolic in this simple fact. It is as though all the remaining population of this town were living in the porters' lodges and the servants' quarters. With the astounding adaptability of human nature, remnants of life and activity have managed to settle themselves in the corners of the buildings which the mighty have abandoned.

> *They say the Lion and the Lizard keep*
> *The Courts where Jamshyd gloried and drank deep . . .*

Here it has not come to the lion and the lizard, and probably never will, but it is a reflection on our age that people should be settling down to a relatively primitive mode of life among the ruins of buildings erected for a far more highly organized and pretentious civilization. Is this only the war and the crisis? Will these docks again fill up with ships? these endless warehouses with goods? these factory chimneys with smoke? and these houses and hotels with people powerful enough to turn over the wheels of all this economic machinery? Or are these buildings already museum pieces, to be wondered at by future generations like the crooked medieval streets of Western European cities, and to be inhabited, like many a building in Russia, by people for whom their dignity and pretention are only a nuisance, and their original function a matter of indifference?

A little narrow-gauge tram car pounds back to the city between the deserted factories and the vacant lots. And in the late afternoon, when the train starts back to Riga, the same two Germans are already installed in the corridor of the second-class carriage, smoking their Russian cigarettes and staring patiently into the dark blankness of the rainstreaked windows.

* * *

The Russian Section of the American legation at Riga, in which I worked during these two years from the autumn of 1931 to the autumn of 1933, was a small research unit where, since there was no American representation in Russia itself, we received the major Soviet periodical and other publications, studied them, and reported as best we could to the United States government on conditions — primarily economic conditions — in the Soviet Union.

The suspicious Soviet mind at once stamped this little research bureau as a sinister espionage center. The mores of that part of the world no doubt afforded ample justification for such an assumption. It was, however, wholly erroneous. The United States government had not yet advanced to that level of sophistication. Incredible as this must have appeared to people schooled in the habits of the locale, we who worked in the Russian Section were exactly what we purported to be. We had no secret agents, and wanted none. Experience had convinced us that far more could be learned by careful, scholarly analysis of information legitimately available concerning any great nation than by the fanciest arrangements of clandestine intelligence. That the latter, if skillfully conducted, could on occasion usefully supplement the former, we would have been prepared to concede; but that they could replace it, or even rival it in importance, we would have firmly denied. We, in any case, had nothing to do with clandestine intelligence; and nothing gave us greater pleasure than to puncture, on the basis of demonstrable fact, the absurdities of the lurid reports about conditions in Russia received by various Western governments from secret intelligence sources and sent to us for comment.

My own particular job in Riga was economic reporting. I found it interesting, pursued it with a passion which I suspect drew smiles from blasé colleagues in the Department of State, and felt that I advanced gradually to a respectable knowledge of the Soviet economy and of Russian economic geography. By 1933, in fact, there were only three places in the non-Soviet world from which we in our little Russian Section felt that we had anything to learn in the study of the Soviet economy, and in some respects we considered ourselves the equal of any of them. One was the Birmingham Bureau of Research on Russian Economic Conditions, of the University of Birmingham; a second was the Wirtschaftsinstitut für Russland und die Oststaaten, in Königsberg,* which published the excellent *Osteuropamarkt;* the third was the institute for the study of the Russian economy at Prague, the so-called Economic Cabinet, founded and directed by the well-known emigré-Russian economist Serge Prokopovich. Supported by the work of these institu-

---

* Institute for the Economy of Russia and the Eastern European Countries.

tions, whose publications we received and studied, we felt we were building up a solid basis of reference material and statistical data which would serve to counterbalance with reasonable adequacy the efforts of the Soviet authorities to distort or suppress even the most elementary data on the progress of the Soviet economy.

Economic research, however, was lonely work, and life outside the office, especially in those days of economic crisis, pay cuts, and all manner of uncertainty, was something less than exciting. This had, as I see it in retrospect, advantages as well as disadvantages. I took to whiling away the long evenings and weekends in collecting material for what I conceived of as a biography of Anton Chekhov. The biography was never written — not, at least, by me.* Other things intervened. But the work of preparation led me through all thirty volumes of Chekhov's works, plus six fat volumes of his inimitable letters, not to mention a good deal of peripheral memoir material. There could, as it happened, have been no finer grounding in the atmosphere of prerevolutionary Russia than this great body of Chekhoviana, unparalleled as it was in perceptiveness, vividness, objectivity, and artistic feeling. And the fact that it was read precisely in the atmosphere of the Baltic States, where more of the prerevolutionary Russia was still present than in Russia proper, gave it a special immediacy.

In general, this period of service in Riga was simply a continuation of study. It involved no operational duties, no active responsibility. No one, in particular, could have been further than I was from the making of policy. But toward the end of my stay in Riga I had my first brief personal brush with the American policy-making process. Realizing that the whole question of "recognition" of the Soviet government was soon to be reexamined by the new administration, I spent several weeks on a study of the commercial treaties the Soviet government had concluded with other governments over the course of the years, examining particularly the extent to which

---

* In 1962 there appeared the fine biography of Chekhov by Ernest Simmons, which accomplished nine-tenths of what I had hoped to accomplish, and a good deal besides. (*Chekhov: A Biography*. Boston: Atlantic–Little, Brown and Company.)

these treaties had or had not afforded real protection to the interests of other governments. I wrapped up the findings in a long interpretative report which went forward to Washington in April 1933. Here I drew attention in particular to two examples of treaty language to which at different times the Soviet authorities had set their signature, but which had been proved by actual experience to be wholly inadequate for the protection of the foreign interests involved.

One of these passages consisted of the provisions of the German-Soviet Treaty of October 12, 1925, dealing with the arrest and detention of German nationals in the Soviet Union. This treaty was the most important of its kind the Soviet government had yet signed. It contained clauses (Article 11) providing that in case of arrest of a German citizen in Russia, notification of such arrest should be made to the German authorities within a week, at the latest, and that the arrested man might be then visited without delay by a German consular representative. These clauses represented the furthest the Soviet authorities had ever been willing to go in promising to foreign nationals in Russia some protection against arbitrary persecution or intimidation at the hands of the Soviet secret police. Nevertheless, as I was obliged to point out to Washington, the language of these provisions was quite inadequate to assure protection of German citizens in Russia. It failed, in particular, to include the vitally important provision that the visiting consul should be entitled to insist on interviewing the prisoner alone, without the presence of any Soviet officials and in conditions that satisfied him of the complete privacy of the interview. On the contrary, it was specifically provided that "officials of the courts or prisons" might *not* be required to withdraw during such an interview. It was clear that in these circumstances the prisoner could easily be intimidated into saying to the consul only what his jailors wished him to say; and indeed, in the subsequent German experience this repeatedly occurred. Particularly in the celebrated case of the so-called Shakhty Trial, in 1928, where German engineers employed in the Donets coal mines were charged with sabotage and other improper activities, it became clear that the language of the 1925 treaty failed to provide a legal basis that would have permitted German representatives to intervene effectively on behalf of the accused.

The other example of unsatisfactory language to which I drew attention at this time was a statement made by the Soviet delegation in the course of talks conducted with the Germans in 1928, after the Shakhty Trial. These talks were designed to clarify certain misunderstandings that had arisen concerning the interpretation of the 1925 treaty. Asked to explain what, in the Soviet view, constituted economic espionage, the Soviet delegation issued the following "advisory opinion," intended evidently as an assurance supplementary to the existing commercial treaty:

The widespread opinion that the dissemination of economic information from the Union of Soviet Socialist Republics is allowed only insofar as this information has been published in newspapers or magazines is erroneous. The right to obtain economic information is limited in the Union of Soviet Socialist Republics, as in other countries, only in the case of business and production secrets and in the case of the employment of forbidden methods (bribery, theft, fraud, etc.) to obtain such information. The category of business and production secrets naturally includes the official economic plans, insofar as they have not been made public, but not individual reports concerning the production conditions and the general conditions of individual enterprises.

The Union of Soviet Socialist Republics has also no reason to complicate or hinder the critical examination of its economic organization. It naturally follows from this that everyone has the right to talk about economic matters or to receive information about such matters in the Union, insofar as the information for which he has asked or which has been imparted to him is not such as may not, on the basis of special regulations issued by responsible officials or by the appropriate state enterprises, be made known to outsiders. (This principle applies primarily to information concerning economic trends and tendencies.) *

In bringing this statement for the first time to the attention of official Washington, I was at pains to point out its total inadequacy

* *Foreign Relations of the United States. The Soviet Union, 1933-1939,* pp. 34-35. Washington, D.C.: US Government Printing Office, 1952.

as a protection to foreigners against arrest and prosecution on charges of economic espionage. A careful examination of the language revealed, I wrote,

that actually the possibility of obtaining economic information in Russia is, for outsiders, extremely limited. The official economic plans, unpublished information about which is included among the type of information which cannot be sought by outsiders, embrace nearly the whole of Russian economic life. Furthermore, experience has shown that it is often the most elementary and important economic facts which, on the basis of "special regulations issued by responsible officials or by appropriate state enterprises," cannot be made known to outsiders. . . . Limited acquaintance with the Soviet economic press is sufficient to show that certain of the most important and elementary statistics, such as the size of the grain crop, the issuance of currency, the production of gold, etc., are included in this category. Consequently, not only the asking for information on these subjects but also the mere acceptance of such information is classified as economic espionage. According to the "advisory opinion" of the Russian delegation, a foreigner who even happened to be told the size of the total grain crop in Russia could be convicted of economic espionage by a Russian court.*

These two passages, in short, were brought to Washington's attention precisely as examples of language on which one ought not to rely, if one was concerned to assure the personal safety of one's nationals in Russia.

Imagine, then, my surprise when I picked up the newspaper, after conclusion of the negotiations with Litvinov in Washington, in November 1933, and saw that among the assurances Litvinov had been persuaded to sign, as conditions precedent to the extension of American recognition, both these questionable passages appeared, quite unchanged. The implication was unmistakable. Made aware by the State Department that the Soviet government had already set its signature to such language on other occasions, and

---

* Memorandum enclosed with Despatch of April 5, 1933, from American minister Robert Peet Skinner at Riga. National Archives, Department of State Files, 661.0031/30, pp. 48-49.

noting that the language itself looked technical and impressive, President Roosevelt, one had to assume, had simply seized on these passages and required Litvinov to sign them all over again, as undertakings toward us. I never learned whether, in doing this, he was unaware of the fact that the passages had been brought to Washington's attention precisely as examples of weak verbiage that had failed to be effective in protecting the interests of other countries dealing with the Soviet Union, or whether he knew this and did not care, considering merely that to an uncritical public, and particularly to a congressional public, the passages would look good. They did, in any case, convey successfully the impression that the American negotiators had been vigilant and professional: on to all the Soviet tricks, determined to let Litvinov get away with nothing.

This episode has remained in my mind as the first of many lessons I was destined to receive, in the course of a diplomatic career, on one of the most consistent and incurable traits of American statesmanship — namely, its neurotic self-consciousness and introversion, the tendency to make statements and take actions with regard not to their effect on the international scene to which they are ostensibly addressed but rather to their effect on those echelons of American opinion, congressional opinion first and foremost, to which the respective statesmen are anxious to appeal. The question, in these circumstances, became not: how effective is what I am doing in terms of the impact it makes on our world environment? but rather: how do I look, in the mirror of domestic American opinion, as I do it? Do I look shrewd, determined, defiantly patriotic, imbued with the necessary vigilance before the wiles of foreign governments? If so, this is what I do, even though it may prove meaningless, or even counterproductive, when applied to the realities of the external situation.

A long series of American statesmen have behaved this way in various situations and at various times. John Hay did so when he served up to the powers, in the Open Door incident, a note which he had not drafted and which he could scarcely have understood but which created the general impression that we Americans, highminded and imbued with virtue, had caught the main European powers in acts of wickedness and were sternly calling them to account. FDR did so on many occasions. Harry Truman, as we shall see later, did so when he gave to the "Truman Doctrine" message a universalistic and pretentious note, appealing to the patriotic self-idealization which so often sets the tone of discussion about foreign policy in our public life, but which is actually unrealistic and pernicious in its effect on the soundness of public understanding of our international situation. John Foster Dulles did so when he spoke of that "liberation" and that "massive retaliation" which, in reality, he had no intention of inflicting on anybody.

This list of examples could be continued indefinitely. I do not say that they are all reprehensible. Each statesman has to be the judge of the compromises he must make, in the form of a certain amount of showmanship and prestidigitation, in order to retain the privilege of conducting foreign policy at all. No one understood this better than FDR.

But I do say that this tendency has often placed on American statesmanship the stamp of a certain histrionic futility, causing it to be ineffective in the pursuit of real objectives in the national interest, allowing it to degenerate into a mere striking of attitudes before the mirror of domestic political opinion. Until the American press and public learn to detect and repudiate such behavior, the country will not have a mature and effective foreign policy, worthy of a great power.

Returning to the substance of the Litvinov assurances, it was fortunate for us that the political interests of the Soviet leaders, as they developed over the course of the ensuing years, did not suggest extensive political reprisals against American citizens in Russia. Those native-born Americans who came to Russia in particular for legitimate nonideological purposes, such as tourism or work under technical-assistance contracts, were seldom, if ever, molested. The Soviet police confined their more unpleasant attentions to persons born in Russia and claiming dual citizenship, persons with close family ties in the Soviet Union, and persons who had in some way involved themselves politically with the Communist movement. An American Communist visiting Russia in connection with the conspiratorial affairs of the party was, throughout the years of the purges, in much greater jeopardy than was the average bourgeois foreigner who had never professed or experienced any sympathy for the Soviet regime.

But had the political interests of that regime made it desirable that even the innocent American tourist or technician should become the victim of arrest, prosecution, and police pressures of one sort or another, the assurances Litvinov extended to us in 1933 would not have stood in the way, nor would they have provided our government with any adequate legal platform for intervention on behalf of the American, once he had been arrested. Repeatedly, in fact, over the course of the years, the Soviet police simply ignored that feature of the treaty language that concerned access to the prisoner on the part of official American representatives, holding Americans, or people claiming American citizenship, for weeks and months in detention while declining to permit American representatives to visit them, and usually failing even to apprise the American authorities that the arrest had been made.

In general, in matters concerning the residence and travel of foreigners in Russia, it was obviously the policy of the Soviet authorities to obligate themselves by treaty to do only those things that they would have done anyway, by unilateral decision dictated solely by their own interests, had no treaty existed. But beyond that it became amply evident in the course of time that the GPU, as the Soviet secret police authority was then called, was a law unto itself, and that in all matters concerning the treatment of foreigners in Russia the Soviet Foreign Office was powerless, regardless of treaty provisions, to exert any restraining influence over its actions. Extensive damage has been done to the fabric of Soviet foreign relations over the years by this vicious system, which confronts the representative in Moscow with two separate governments, one with power, the other powerless; or permits him to talk only with the powerless one, giving him no direct access to the other; and leaves him thus effectively without recourse, except for the highest sort of political intervention, when it comes to the protection of his nationals in the Soviet Union.

This feature of the Litvinov assurances — the one that dealt with the protection of American nationals in Russia — made a particular impression on me in view of my own involvement in unearthing the language that was used; but I viewed the assurances as a whole, I must say, with little enthusiasm. The outstanding issues over which recognition of the Soviet government had been withheld by the three preceding Republican administrations were of course, first, the insistence of the Soviet leaders, in their party if not their governmental capacity, on instigating and encouraging revolutionary activity in other countries, including the United States (an activity usually, and inadequately, described in our public discussions at that time as "propaganda"); and, second, their unwillingness either to honor the financial obligations of previous Russian governments or to make restitution to American firms and individuals for property in Russia nationalized in the course of the Revolution. Shortly before Litvinov's visit to Washington, the American minister in Riga, Mr. Robert Peet Skinner,* had invited from each of us in the Russian Section of the legation an individual opinion on the question of recognition. In replying, I had given it as my conviction that the Russians would not be willing to make any significant concessions on principle on either of these points. They would not do it in order to obtain American recognition; and they would not do it as a gesture of appreciation for recognition once obtained. Most of my colleagues had, I believe, expressed similar views. What happened subsequently confirmed their correctness.

I have no reason to suppose that these opinions (though they *were* forwarded to Washington) ever came to FDR's attention or that he would have paid any attention to them if they had. They offered no solution to his problem. He attached little importance to these particular issues for their own sakes (and with respect to the

---

* Robert Peet Skinner, 1866-1960; career diplomatist, well known for his effective service as consul general in London during World War I.

debts and claims, at any rate, I think he was right not to do so).*
He was concerned with them insofar as they meant things to influential sectors of American opinion; but here his concern was primarily to reassure, to allay apprehension, to give the impression that
things were being taken care of — not really to solve the issues. He
obviously considered the resumption of relations with Russia to be
desirable for the sobering influence it might exercise on the German Nazis and on the Japanese militarists; and if this effect could be
achieved only by throwing a certain amount of sand in the eyes of
the American Congress, press, and public, he was not averse to doing this.

Whether these calculations were correct — whether the establishment of United States–Soviet relations really had some effect as
a temporary restraint on the designs of these two aggressive powers
— I do not know. The Soviet leaders, in some ways very realistic
men but endowed with rather feverish political imaginations, certainly shared the expectation that it would have. I myself, at the
time, was skeptical. Never — neither then nor at any later date —
did I consider the Soviet Union a fit ally or associate, actual or
potential, for this country. The idea of trying to enlist Soviet
strength in a cause for which we were unwilling to develop and
mobilize our own semed to me particularly dangerous.

* The reasons for this view on my part are set forth in my *Russia and the West
under Lenin and Stalin* (Boston: Atlantic–Little, Brown and Company, 1960),
pp. 200-203.

3

Moscow and Washington in the 1930s

THE years immediately following the establishment of relations between the United States and the Soviet Union I spent mostly in Russia. They continued to constitute, like those spent in Riga and Berlin, primarily an educational experience.

I happened to be on leave, in Washington, when the negotiations with Litvinov took place and recognition of the Soviet Union was announced. Aside from lending a very minor hand in the preparation of the briefing papers for the American negotiators, I had nothing to do with the whole procedure. But one or two days after conclusion of the negotiations a friend introduced me to Mr. William C. Bullitt, who had been up to that point the new President's leading advisor on relations with Russia and had now been designated as our first ambassador to the Soviet Union. Bullitt plied me with questions. He soon discovered that I spoke Russian. I also happened to have the answers to certain questions he had on his mind about the Soviet economy. The result was that when he set out a few days later for Moscow, to present his credentials and to select buildings for a future embassy, he took me along as aide and interpreter. Together with one other American Foreign Service officer (Mr. Joseph Flack), I assisted him on the historic occasion of his presentation of credentials to Kalinin. And when, after a few days in Moscow, he himself started back to the United States to assemble an embassy staff, he left me behind as a sort of unofficial provisional representative, to maintain liaison with the Soviet authorities and to see to the preparation of the buildings. I was thus the first American official to reside regularly in Moscow in a representative capacity since the unhappy departure of Mr. DeWitt Poole* some fifteen years earlier — an event which I later had occasion to describe in the final chapter of my *Decision to Intervene*.†

I lived that winter in the National Hotel next door to what was to be, when completed, for many years our embassy chancery. My wife came and joined me. We had a male stenographer who lived across the hall. In addition to this, I met one day in the hotel bar a young American with ruffled hair, a strong Philadelphia-society drawl, and, as conversation soon revealed, a highly developed sense of humor. This was Mr. Charles W. Thayer, later to be a Foreign Service officer and, later still, an author and the humorous chronicler of this same period in the life of the American embassy at Moscow. He had come to Moscow as a tourist of sorts, hoping to get material for literary effort. Finding myself urgently in need of a man Friday, and he being rather bored with his National Hotel existence, I put him on the government payroll as a messenger at forty dollars a month and found for him, somehow, a battered Harley-Davidson motorcycle. On this vehicle he tore around town on my official business, the ear tabs of his Russian fur cap flapping wildly in the wind as he rode.

The four of us constituted the entire staff of the American embassy in Moscow at that time. We had no codes, no safes, no couriers, no security officers. Communications with our government went through the regular telegraph office and lay on the table for the Soviet government to see. Nevertheless, I felt that we, with our absence of bureaucracy, accomplished more in a few weeks than did the full embassy staff, when it arrived, over the first year of its existence.

It was, in truth, a wonderful and exciting time. The extreme cold of the Moscow winter was healthy and exhilarating. One

* DeWitt Clinton Poole, 1885-1952; career diplomat and academic administrator; entered diplomatic service, 1910; resigned, 1930; acting American consul general at Moscow, and later American chargé d'affaires in Russia, 1918.
† *The Decision to Intervene*, pp. 466-468. Princton: Princeton University Press, 1958.

could exist on four or five hours of sleep. Outside our door was the center of what was still in many respects the old Moscow. The great block of buildings between the hotel and the Kremlin had not yet been torn out. The three-car trains of trolley cars, bursting with their human load, jangled their way through the narrow street. Construction was just beginning on the Moscow subway. The streets around the hotel were full of youthful volunteers working on the subway — girls and boys in ther muddy, padded overalls. It was still a teeming but colorful and cozy town in which life — for us at least, but obviously for many others as well — was a pleasure. Even the political atmosphere was relatively favorable. The American journalists — a colorful company that included such figures as Walter Duranty, Bill Stoneman, William Henry Chamberlin, Ralph Barnes, and Linton Wells — invited us to their uproariously informal parties, and there we met Russians as well as Americans. I bear that pleasant winter in memory as an example of what Soviet-American relations *might*, in other circumstances, have been.

On arrival of the embassy staff in March 1934 I was appointed a regular diplomatic secretary in the new mission and continued, with the exception of some months spent in Vienna in 1935 for reasons of ill health, to serve in Moscow until the summer of 1937.

Words would fail me if I were to try to convey in this context the excitement, the enjoyment, the fascination, and the frustrations of this initial service in Moscow. We were fortunate in having within our mission, in addition to Charlie Thayer, a number of good friends with whom we shared not only a passionate preoccupation with the local scene but a common appreciation for its absurdities — and our own. We had a number of similar friends in other missions, particularly the German, French, and Italian. Most of us look back on those days, I suppose, as the high point of life — the high point, at least, in comradeship, in gaiety, in intensity of experience.

I ought, at this point, to say a special word about those friends of Moscow days, all of whom were to remain friends for life. If their names do not appear more frequently in this account, it is because what I am writing is conceived primarily as an intellectual autobiography, and I do not wish to saddle them — even by implication — with responsibility for any of my own thoughts or views. I would be giving a very inadequate account of my own development, however, if I failed to acknowledge their contribution to it.

The protracted habitual discussions that enlivened the long rainy weekends in Riga were, if anything, intensified by the move to Moscow. Never, I think, can there have been an American diplomatic mission where there was more off-duty discussion of the country to which it was accredited and the problems with which it was faced. The impressions that crowded in on us from every aspect of our Soviet environment were ones that challenged our own values unceasingly and in the most provocative way. In reacting to them, we felt an unlimited need for discussion among ourselves. These discussions were friendly but serious and sometimes passionate. What the others gained from them, they can say for themselves; but I feel that no experience in life did more to sharpen my mind and to refine my judgments on the whole problem of Russian communism than these daily arguments and explorations. The friends to whom I feel indebted in this way are too numerous to be all mentioned individually; but there are two whose influence must be particularly noted.

One of these was Loy Henderson,* my former colleague of Riga days. Despite his lack of special training in the Russian field, Henderson was a man of so active an intelligence, such deep seriousness and impressive sincerity, and such unbending conscientiousness not only in the performance of his duties but in his entire effort to cope with the problems presented to us by Soviet communism, that he left his impression on everyone who was associated with him. He was for considerable periods in charge of the mission in the absence of the ambassador; and the example he set of dedication and moral courage in the conduct of its work was one that affected it profoundly.

* Loy W. Henderson, born in 1892; entered the Foreign Service, 1922; secretary of embassy at Moscow, 1934 to 1938; later chief of the Division of Eastern European Affairs and, later still, of the Near Eastern Division, and ambassador to Iraq and India.

The other friend to whom special recognition must be given was Charles (Chip) Bohlen.* He and I were among the first to be trained as Russian specialists; and of all those early trainees, we were the ones to remain for the longest time and most intimately associated with Russian affairs. Nikolai Bukharin once observed (at his final purge trial, I believe) that intellectual friendship was the strongest of the bonds between men. Whether this is true of all men, I would not know. It was certainly true of Bukharin; and there was something in the intellectual challenge of Communist Russia that made it true for those of us who were obliged to receive that challenge and to react to it at first hand. My association with Bohlen at the embassy in Moscow in the 1930s was the beginning of a lifelong intellectual intimacy which, for me at least, was unique in its scope and intensity. A man of exceptional native brilliance, for whom Russian communism was to constitute a central interest throughout a long and distinguished professional career, a man interested (if the reader can grasp the logic of this contradiction) both passionately and dispassionately in everything that concerned the Russian scene, a man who never ceased to throw off thoughts and ideas like sparks from a sparkler, he was an incomparable critic for anyone else whose central interest was in Russian affairs. For the soundness of my own views, in particular, he always showed a special fraternal solicitude — a solicitude which I soon learned to recognize as a mark of respect and affection rather than derogation. That others should err was to him, I always suspected, regrettable but human. That I should err was intolerable. In numberless verbal encounters, then and over ensuing decades, our agreements and differences would be sternly and ruthlessly talked out, sometimes with a heat so white that casual bystanders would conclude we had broken for life. That he knocked numbers of unsound ideas out of my head I would be the first to admit. That he knocked enough — he would be the first to deny. What I owe him for this relentless

---

* Charles E. Bohlen, born in 1904; well known both in his capacity as advisor and interpreter to President Roosevelt during the war and later as ambassador to the Soviet Union and to France, had come up the same ladder of Russian specialization as I had, but had, like all the other Russian specialists, done his studying in Paris rather than Berlin.

discipline I cannot measure, but it takes a leading place in the formative influences of a lifelong effort to understand the shape of our relations with Russian communism. Life made us intellectual and professional brothers; and no friendship has ever meant more to me than his.

Among the forty-odd people — all men — whom Bullitt brought with him for his embassy staff when he returned to Moscow in early March 1934, there was one conspicuous omission, and that was a person available, qualified, and inclined to assume administrative responsibility. For this reason the first months witnessed a confusion in our official and personal lives for which one would probably have to reach back to the voyage of the Ford Peace Ship, during World War I, to find a parallel. We were housed, for those first months, in the top two floors of a hostelry called, euphemistically, the Hotel Savoy. It was at, or near, the head of the Kuznetski Most. Such offices as we had were in the partially furnished and still barnlike Spaso House, the ambassador's residence, two and a half miles away. Having no transport of our own, we tried to operate (at fantastic cost, incidentally) a shuttle service between the two buildings, with Lincoln touring cars (normally open, but with side curtains you buttoned on if it rained), supplied by the Intourist organization and driven by Soviet chauffeurs. But the latter were unused to the arrangement; there were no proper dispatchers or any workable communications. The system broke down constantly, leaving little groups of people helplessly stranded at one end or the other. Spaso House, furthermore, had no telephone switchboard, only one little phone upstairs and one down, both directly connected with the city. These tinkled halfheartedly and indiscriminately, day and night; and when one answered them there was often no reaction at the other end, only labored breathing and a baffling verbal silence.* At the Hotel Savoy, the telephone facili-

* Among the reasons (though not the most common) for this phenomenon was something of which we were informally advised, in a rather embarrassed confidence, from the Soviet side. Among the former Soviet inhabitants of Spaso House was the famous diplomatist, the second People's Commissar for Foreign Affairs, Georgi V. Chicherin. Now in disfavor and retirement, ill and half mad, Chicherin led a hermit's existence in a nearby flat. The only person he would admit to the premise, for the purpose of an occasional cleaning-up, was the Spaso House fur-

ties were even worse; and the restaurant service, ponderous and leisurely, seemed geared to the needs of the country squire of an
earlier day, in town to pass the time and to eat himself sick, not to
the staff of a modern embassy, interested in snatching a quick
luncheon snack.

These were only a small part of the complexities involved in the
effort to establish, in Moscow in 1934, the kind of embassy that our
government envisaged. The struggle continued through most of
that year and left little time for anything else. It was, however, a
struggle full of hilarity and good spirits; and it proceeded in a political atmosphere which, while not in all respects what one could
have hoped, was far more friendly, pleasant, and relaxed than anything Russia was to know for another two decades.

All this changed at the outset of the winter of 1934-1935. By this
time we had moved into our permanent premises, on the Mokhovaya, in the center of town, next to the National Hotel. For us the
Sturm und Drang period of initial establishment was at an end. We
were now in process of settling down to our regular diplomatic
work, insofar as work in Moscow could be said to have any regularity at all. But just at this time the circumstances in which this work
had to proceed were drastically altered by an event which marked
one of the most fateful turning points in modern Russian history:
the murder of Kirov, in Leningrad, on December 1.

Sergei Kirov, the head of the Communist Party organization in
Leningrad, was a powerful member of the leading group and indeed the one most commonly spoken of as a possible eventual successor to Stalin. We have, today, strong if not conclusive evidence
that by the autumn of 1934 a serious crisis had arisen in the leading ranks of the party over Stalin's growing tendency to brutal-

---

naceman, Seryozha; but since he was reluctant to speak directly over the phone
with anyone else at Spaso House, his method of signaling that the time had come
for Seryozha to pay a visit was to phone to the building and then, when the phone
was answered, to maintain a defiant, charged silence. I have never known whether
the reason for this arrangement was really a personal attachment to Seryozha on
Chicherin's part or whether Seryozha, in the light of other connections and
responsibilities he must be assumed as the Spaso furnaceman to have had, was the
only person authorized by the authorities to visit Chicherin. Perhaps the answer,
as was so often the case in Russia, was both.

ity, and particularly over his insistence that criminal proceedings, involving application of the death penalty, be instituted against those leading Communists who had had the temerity to oppose his own march to power in earlier years. It has been alleged, and I think it probably true, that Kirov, while of course too discreet to take any public stand on this issue, was known in authoritative party circles to be opposed to Stalin's course, and that he therefore appeared as the great hope of all those who feared and deplored the use of terror in the handling of intraparty differences. His murder appears, furthermore, to have occurred on the eve of a transfer from Leningrad to Moscow, long but unsuccessfully opposed by Stalin, which would have placed him in a position to make his influence much more strongly felt in the central bodies of the party. That the headquarters of the secret police in Leningrad had something to do with the murder, or at least with the murderer, is quite apparent; and the many allegations (encouraged by hints put out by Khrushchev in his "secret speech") that Stalin himself was not without complicity in the affair have never been specifically rebutted by the Soviet leadership.

Whatever may have been the circumstances of Kirov's assassination, it clearly became the point of departure for the great purges of the 1930s. With this event, the terrible cloud of suspicion and violence, of sinister, unidentifiable terror and *sauve qui peut* denunciations, began to gather over Russia, only to unleash upon it some months later the full horror of the purges, and to continue to darken it, in one degree or another, until Stalin's death in 1953. With this event the atmosphere for the conduct of any sort of diplomatic work in Moscow, by anyone, deteriorated drastically; and the honeymoon of Soviet-American relations, such as it was, came definitely to an end.

Three days after Kirov was murdered, I myself fell ill — so seriously that after some eight weeks in bed in Moscow I was shipped out to Vienna (January 1935) by a State Department generally as kind in such personal crises as it was obtuse in the great political ones. I remained in Vienna until November of that year. After an initial two months in hospital, I was well enough to return to work.

I was then put to political reporting in the Vienna legation, under the command of the redoubtable minister in that city, Mr. George Messersmith.*

I had already served under George Messersmith in Berlin and knew him well. He had a great reputation as a martinet and disciplinarian, but I personally never experienced anything but kindness and consideration at his hands. Tough he was, and strong-willed indeed. I had already learned in Berlin to admire the unflinching courage with which he invariably moved in on unpleasant situations. When I asked him, on one occasion, whence he had acquired this quality, he told me of an experience he had had in his early life as principal of a public high school. Political pressure had been brought to bear upon him to desist from the expulsion of a student who was a troublemaker and had defied his authority. Two of the political bigwigs of the state had descended on him in person and showered him with threats of the loss of his own position, and reprisals against the school, if he stuck to his guns. He stuck to his guns, but the strain was so great that when they left, he put his head down on his desk and wept. Nevertheless, his battle had been won, and since that moment he had never again let himself be influenced by fear of a scene or of personal unpleasantness. Now, in Berlin and subsequently in Vienna, this combative stoutness was being taken out on the Nazis, whom he detested and opposed with every fiber of his being.

Looking back on it today, I am aware that this dry, drawling, peppery man, his eyes always glinting with the readiness to accept combat, capable of being wrong like the rest of us but stern and incorruptible in his fight for what he considered right and decent, was one of those chiefs who left an indelible mark on my own concept of what American diplomacy could and should be.

On return from Vienna in 1935, there followed nearly two years of further service in Moscow. The work was mostly political re-

---

* George S. Messersmith, 1883-1960, a Foreign Service officer who had made much of his reputation as American consul general in Berlin, was minister at Vienna in 1934-1936. He later became Assistant Secretary of State for Administration, and then, successively, ambassador to Cuba, Argentina, and Mexico.

porting, and its benefits, once again, were primarily educational — there was little training in operational responsibility. The purges were now proceeding in high gear. It fell to me to follow their progress in detail, as well as one could do so from the Soviet press and the welter of unhappy rumors with which the Moscow atmosphere was then replete. We know more now than we did then about their background; but the view we then formed of their scope and significance was not inaccurate. To be forced to follow their course, day by day, and to write analytical dispatches about the entire process, was unavoidably a sort of liberal education in the horrors of Stalinism.

Of no smaller importance for me, personally, than this study of the political scene was the opportunity, now for the first time extensively available, to drink in impressions of Russia itself: of its life, its culture, its aspect, its smell. For the understanding of these things, I had by this time had six full years of preparation. As an object of curiosity, the country never palled for an instant; and as I look back on those years, I see their value primarily in this growing experience of the place itself.

It could well be asked how one could gain impressions at all, as a foreign diplomat in the Russia of the purges, in view of the fantastic measures taken by the regime to isolate all foreigners, and particularly diplomats, from the population at large. Actually, these measures were effective only to a degree. Some contacts and friendships with Soviet citizens continued to be cultivated, simply out of mutual liking and interest, though they naturally required ingenuity and discretion. Then there were the theater, sporting events, and public occasions of every sort where one could rub elbows with ordinary Russians and where, particularly if one knew Russian, one could absorb a great deal of what was in the air. Finally, there was travel. There were trips to Leningrad, to the south, to the Caucasus, trips on Moscow river steamers. Still interested in Chekhov, I made pilgrimages to places where he was known to have lived. I made similar expeditions into the countryside to find out what had become of some of the beautiful medieval churches described, and sometimes depicted, in Grabar's great history of Russian art. Many had fallen into decay, and few in Moscow then knew or cared about their existence.

These expeditions were made in good faith and without ulterior motive. My interest in both subjects was sincere. I would have undertaken the expeditions even had they yielded no side impressions. But side impressions they did yield, unfailingly and abundantly.

When I look back on those years in Moscow in the mid-Thirties, I believe that what I most gained from them was a feeling for the country — for the new Russia, as it had emerged from the ordeals of collectivization and the first Five Year Plan and as it was then entering the new ordeal of the purges. My greatest deficiency, as I see it now, was in knowledge of the history of the Russian revolutionary movement. This was hardly avoidable. The fine works of E. H. Carr, of Leonard Shapiro, of Isaac Deutscher, and of Franco Venturi were not yet available. None of us had the leisure to pursue the researches those great scholars were later to pursue. But even without this support, one could not live in Russia and occupy one's self with political reporting without getting a fair grounding in the nature of Stalinism.

My own case was perhaps unusual in that there were no pro-Soviet sympathies to be overcome. Distaste for the Stalin regime did not come by way of disillusionment of an earlier enthusiasm. Unlike many others who became professional observers of the development of Soviet power, I had never gone through a "Marxist period." Sometimes I suspect that it might have been better if I had. Many admirable students of Soviet affairs came by this road. In any case I had not.

The reason, I suppose, lay partly in the fact that it was in the Baltic states that I grew to a mature interest in Russian affairs. The brief and bloody periods of rule which the Russian and local Communists had enjoyed in Riga and Tallinn in 1919 had left no pleasant traces. But beyond that there was from the start a sheer intellectual distaste on my part for Russian Marxism. I was never able to accept or to condone the stony-hearted fanaticism that was prepared to condemn to the loss of all civil rights, to ignominy, persecution, and "liquidation as a class" entire great bodies of people — the "bourgeoisie" and large portions of the peasantry, the majority, in fact, of the Russian population — for no other reason than that their members had been born into certain stations in life. These savage class distinctions seemed to me only a mirror image of the feudal institutions Russia had so recently rejected. Like these, they penalized people solely on the criterion of birth, regardless of individual guilt. I could not see that it was better to tell a man that he and his family were condemned to persecution, frustration, and tragedy simply because he had been born a "bourgeois" than to tell him something similar because he had been born a serf or a Jew. I did not believe that being born to the possession of property or acquiring it by honest effort necessarily made men bad and deserving of chastisement any more than being born into a worker's family automatically assured their purity, their high-mindedness, and their worthiness of a privileged status. Nor could I pass over the fact that so many of those who placed themselves at the head of all this intolerance, and who were so ready to throw millions of other people onto what Trotsky called the "garbage heap of history" just because they were born on what was now the wrong side of the Russian tracks, were themselves anything else than proletarian in origin. Had the criterion of virtue really been the extent to which one had known the sweat of honest physical toil, most of these lily-handed Russian Communist intellectuals would have been in logic bound to join the bourgeoisie in their march to destruction. There were many facets of Soviet life that I respected and admired; but I could find little patience for the ideology itself. I saw it as a pseudo-science, replete with artificial heroes and villains; and much as I admired the Soviet leaders for their courage, their determination, and their political seriousness, I could experience only disgust for other features of their political personality: their professed hatred and rejection of large portions of humanity, their abundant cruelties, their claims to infallibility, their opportunism and unscrupulousness of method, their disregard for the truth, their conspiratorial secretiveness, and especially the love of power that so often and so obviously lurked behind the pretense of high-minded ideological conviction.

Holding these views, I came without false hopes or illusions, in the mid-1930s, to a more intimate acquaintance with the phenomenon of Stalinism at the apogee of its horror. But no one, of course, could have been fully prepared for the reality. If in earlier stages of the development of Soviet power there had been vestiges of belief that society would be genuinely benefited by all the cruelty and suffering, here, in the Russia of the purges, was cynicism, shamelessness, contempt for humanity — all triumphantly enthroned. Here was a great nation helpless in the toils of an unbelievably cunning, in many ways great, but monstrously ruthless and cynical man. So insistently were the evidences of Russia's degradation borne in upon me during the years of my residence in Moscow — so prolonged and incessant were the hammer-blow impressions, each more outrageous and heartrending than the other — that the effect was never to leave me. Its imprint on my political judgment was one that would place me at odds with official thinking in Washington for at least a decade thereafter.

* * *

I would like to let the views I held at given times reveal themselves now, so far as possible, in documents of the time, not from the promptings of hindsight. In what has survived of personal papers from those years in Moscow, 1933 to 1937, I find only two that seem of interest. The first was written evidently sometime in 1936 or 1937. For what purpose it was written, and what was done with it, I have not the faintest recollection. It does not appear to have been a governmental paper. I am quite sure it was never published. But there it is in my files, entitled "The War Problem of the Soviet Union."

The paper began with a description of the defiant and provocative attitude taken at all times by the Soviet regime toward non-Communist governments: regarding them by definition as enemies, willing to view peaceful relations with them only as some sort of a provisional abnormality — an armistice or a "breathing space" between conflicts. I described the stupendous program of militarization in which the Soviet government was then engaged — a program of which even collectivization and the various Five Year Plans were only constituent parts. I pointed to the spirit of chauvinism, of xenophobia, of suspicion and hatred for everything foreign in which this effort was being conducted. I recognized the interest manifested by the Soviet government in postponing hostilities to a day when its own military preparations might be further advanced. I recognized Stalin's willingness, with this in mind, to enter into pacts of nonaggression and mutual assistance with various powers and to accept the obligations of membership in the League of Nations. But I viewed this disposition as the reflection of a desire not so much to avoid the outbreak of another world war altogether as to assure that this war would be fought by others and among others — to embroil others, that is, against each other, and above all to prevent any sort of peaceful settlement among the Western European powers.

I recognized in full the seriousness of the Japanese threat to the Soviet Far East, although I also noted that Soviet policies in Asia had contributed to the rise of this threat. I was more skeptical about the reality of the Nazi menace to Soviet interests. That the Nazis were a menace to others I would not have denied. But Hitler's policy appeared to me as "outstandingly one of pan-Germanism," implying the extension of the power of the Reich "only to territories now or previously controlled or inhabited by Germans." This might, I observed, be interpreted to include certain states bordering on Russia; it could scarcely be interpreted to include Russia in her 1936-1937 borders, though there was always the possibility that the Ukraine might be offered by Hitler to Poland as compensation for territories lost in the west. These dangers, I thought, were in any case far off. Russian fears about them were "continually expressed with a histrionic vehemence which throws doubt on their sincerity, and are accompanied by a diplomatic activity better designed to aggravate than to allay the conditions to which they are attributed." There was, I believed, little reason to suppose that a Russian government determined to tend strictly to its own business would find itself "subjected to any immediate danger of aggression in the west." But the Soviet government did not answer to that description.

All in all, then, it seemed, I saw little prospect that the future of the Soviet Union would be a peaceful one. "Social fanaticism, militarism, chauvinism, and a cynical policy of driving the wedge between one's neighbors: these may be the means for postponing a war. They are not the means for avoiding it." It was possible to believe that Russia might keep out of a European war at the beginning. "In view of the frank cynicism with which she views treaty obligations, it may be questioned whether she would even comply with her undertakings regarding military assistance, unless this happened to coincide with her interests at the given moment." But this afforded small reason to hope that she would not eventually be drawn in to any major hostilities. Later, when other participants had weakened themselves, she would hardly resist the temptation to come in, "if only in the capacity of a vulture."

So much for the summary of the paper.

One sees today of course the weakness of such an analysis. The Nazi threat to Russia was certainly underrated, although one must not forget to what extent Hitler's final decision to attack Russia was influenced by the stubborn greediness of Soviet diplomacy, especially with regard to Finland and Bulgaria, as revealed in the talks with Molotov in November 1940, and by the very numerical enormity of the armed forces that Stalin was then maintaining along Russia's western frontier. Hitler dared not leave so imposing a force intact on his flank at a time when his inability to invade the British Isles was compelling him to widen his strategy into an attack against Britain's Mediterranean lifeline.

It was also not foreseen in my paper that the Soviet Union would itself, in the end, be directly attacked. But the belief that Stalin would endeavor to profit by hostilities among others was amply substantiated by his action against Finland in 1939-1940 as well as by his last-minute entry into hostilities against Japan and Bulgaria, just before the collapse of those powers. One can imagine how much more of this sort of thing there would have been had the Soviet armed forces remained unchallenged throughout the war, as Stalin had hoped they would, by those of any other great power, and thus virtually intact.

All in all, then, this was a sharply critical view of Stalin's diplomacy, but not, on balance, an inaccurate one. In particular it anticipated with reasonable clarity the Soviet policies that led to the Nazi-Soviet Nonaggression Pact. It was, however, a far cry from the trends of liberal opinion then prevailing in the West; and the growing divergence with certain of the basic tendencies of Roosevelt's Russian policy is evident.

My hopes for the long-term future of Soviet-American relations were marked at that time by no greater enthusiasm than my views on Soviet policy generally. In the spring of 1936 I prepared a study on this subject in which I attempted to look beyond the Stalin era and to make an estimate of just what, over the long term, one could expect in the development of bilateral relations between Russia and the United States. I do not have the text of it; I have only a summary, prepared by myself at some time in 1938. From this I shall quote briefly:

In the economic sphere I had to take into account the geographic similarity of the two countries, the probability that in many respects they would always be rivals rather than complementary factors in the economic world, and the jealous uncertainty which seemed to make Russian rulers so suspicious, so bureaucratic, and so Oriental in their business dealings. Culturally, I had to reckon not only with the natural understanding and sympathy of the peoples of the two countries, with their similar background in modern history,* and with their unquestionable potential value to each other, but also with the intense fear of most Russian governments of the possible effects of foreign influence on the popular mind: of that tendency which makes most Russian rulers prefer

* I had in mind here the similarity of the expansion of both nations toward the shores of the Pacific in the nineteenth century; their common experience of expanding frontiers into undeveloped territory; the simultaneity in the abolition of slavery/serfdom; the similarities in their modern industrial development; and the fact that in both instances the literary tradition was primarily one of the nineteenth century, influenced by Europe but not surrendering to it.

to keep their people in darkness rather than risk illumination by contact with foreign culture and foreign ideas. Politically, I had to go back into Russian history and to probe the origins of the traditional suspicion and diffidence on the part of the Russian rulers. I had to weigh the effects of climate on character, the results of century-long contact with Asiatic hordes, the influence of medieval Byzantium, the national origins of the people, and the geographic characteristics of the country — characteristics so little favorable to normal administrative control, to national unity, and to self-confidence.

The results of these investigations made me skeptical of any momentous future for Russian-American relations within our time. I did not despair of the possibility of a limited and unsensational measure of profitable cooperation between the two countries. But I was convinced that even this could be effectively realized only if our part in it was borne by persons who had the understanding and the qualifications necessary for the task: a gift for self-effacement, a decent educational background, an intellectual humility before the complexities of the Russian world, and, above all, an exceptional capacity for patience. Barring the enlistment of such persons on our part, I could see little future for Russian-American relations other than a long series of misunderstandings, disappointments, and recriminations on both sides.

Today, thirty years later, this estimate does not appear too pessimistic. But once again it was, as we shall see presently, a far cry from the outlook of FDR himself, and particularly of those whom he was soon to choose as advisors on policy toward the Soviet Union.

* * *

Through all of this growing involvement with major political problems, personal life — family, children, budgets, and salaries — continued to be lived and to preempt its usual share of time, worry, and emotional dedication. It is not primarily the subject of these reminiscences, but it cannot all be ignored.

By winter of 1936, another child was on the way. Pursuant to some quirk of American legislation (the well-known human proclivity for the repression of unpleasant memory has happily erased the details of it from my mind), a child born abroad to parents of whom one was not an American citizen was at that time in some sort of jeopardy from the standpoint of its future citizenship. It was decided, therefore, that Annelise would have to return to the United States to have the baby. I would follow, shortly after the baby's arrival, enjoy the home leave to which, by this time, I was entitled (although in those days you had to pay for it yourself), and eventually bring them all back again.

The baby was born in April at my sister's home in Highland Park, Illinois. I followed in May. I am appalled to realize how fleeting and inadequate are the memories of that summer. Of the journey home I recall only that it included for some reason a stop in London; that I went to the theater there; and that I was impressed, and in a sense reassured, by the greater subtlety and sophistication of the London stage after the strenuous heroics and muscle-flexing of the Stalinist Moscow theater.

For the journey from London to Illinois, memory is a blank. There is a faint impression of the new child, Joan Elisabeth, lying in her crib, placid and dignified, betraying as yet nothing of what growth and maturity were to make of her. There then followed a vacation at my sister's cottage on one of the southern Wisconsin lakes, in the part of the country where both the summers of boyhood and the years of military school had been spent. It was nearly a decade, now, since I had lived in America. I was overwhelmed by that complex of feelings that has found its classic description in the novels of Thomas Wolfe: nostalgia, the yearning for roots, a sense of the mystery of time, yet also — alienation and the realization that you can never go back. In an effort to rediscover the soil from which I had grown, I rented a bicycle and pedaled through the central portion of the state, even spending a night at the farm my grandfather had owned in the years just following the Civil War. The experience only emphasized the degree of my estrangement. The rural Wisconsin I remembered was largely the Wisconsin of the pre-automobile age. The intervening years had seen the general completion of the revolution in transportation that followed World War I. Those beautiful highways of central Wisconsin were now, as I noted in my journal, the most deserted places I had ever encountered. In the course of a one-hundred-mile journey I was destined to encounter on the open road no single fellow-cyclist, no single pedestrian, no single horse-drawn vehicle. . . . The occupants of the occasional machines that went whirring by . . . obviously had no connection in the social sense with the highway over which they were driving. . . . They were lost spirits, hovering for brief periods on another plane, where space existed only in time. To those of us who inhabited the highway — the birds and insects and snakes and turtles and chipmunks and the lone cyclist — the cars were only an abstract danger, a natural menace like lightning, earthquake, or flood, which had to be reckoned with and coped with (here the turtles, whose corpses strewed the pavement for miles, seemed to be at the greatest disadvantage) but to which we had no human relationship and which only accentuated . . . our loneliness.

I thought, by way of contrast, of the sociable English highway of Chaucer's day, sometimes full of human danger but full, also, of life and companionship. It seemed to me that we had impoverished ourselves by the change; and I could not, after the years in Europe, accustom myself to it. The sense of loss accompanied me even in the modest tourist homes of the little towns where I spent the evenings.

No one was at home, and I sat for a time alone on the porch in the darkness. The tree-lined street stretched away down the hill under the arc lights. The sidewalks were deserted, but a stream of sleek dark cars flowed between them. . . . Each car had its couple or its foursome inside, bent on pleasure — usually vicarious pleasure in the form of a movie or . . . a petting party. Woe to the young man or young woman who could not arrange to be included in one of these private, mathematically correct companies of nocturnal motorists. All the life of the evening flowed along in this fashion, segregated into quiet groups of twos or fours. There was no provision for anyone else. There was no place where strangers would come freely together, as in a Bavarian beer hall or a Russian amusement park. . . . Even the saloons were nearly empty.

I came away from the summer's visit aware that I was no longer a part of what I had once been a part of — no longer, in fact, a part of anything at all. It was not just that I had left the world of my boyhood, although this too was true; it was also that this world had left me. It had left everyone else, for that matter; but its departure had been sufficiently gradual so that those who remained had been less aware of its passage, and had adjusted in varying degrees to the change. I, like all other expatriates, simply had been left behind.

These feelings were only the first strong reminders of a reality which affects the situation of almost every professional diplomatist. Increasingly, now, I would not be a part of my country, although what it had once been would remain a part of me. I, not being a part of it, would nevertheless understand it. It, being still to some extent a part of me, would nevertheless not understand me. I would continue to pay it my loyalty. This was a matter of self-respect and of a deeper faith in the values of our civilization. What else, after all, could I be loyal to? But it would be a loyalty *despite*, not a loyalty *because*, a loyalty of principle, not of identification. And whatever reciprocation it evoked could never be one based on a complete understanding.

In the middle of the worst heat wave the country had known for sixty-one years, we made our way back, with the small child and the new baby and nineteen articles of luggage, to dockside at New York. The ship was carrying the American Olympic team to Germany for the games that were to take place there that summer. For a week we dodged the motions of gum-chewing supermen with crew cuts, and a variety of hefty amazons, as they practiced their particular skills on deck. The ship, completing its journey, came slowly up the Elbe on a lovely, still European summer evening; and the athletes, oblivious of linguistic differences, hurled wisecracks and frivolities at the bewildered Germans along the riverbank. From Hamburg the journey went by rail and boat to the south coast of Norway. There was no sleeping car available through Denmark. We had no Danish money; we sat up in the coaches all night; and I seem to recall that somewhere along the line we lost the baby's collapsible bathtub. On the long, rough journey by steamer across the Skagerrak my wife was prostrated with seasickness. I sat hour after hour on the top deck with the four-year-old, answering queries about why the ocean was deep. Once I was summoned down to the cabin to change diapers, a task which I performed expeditiously, to the helpless contempt of my wife, by throwing the soiled ones hastily out the porthole.

After two weeks in Norway, we wangled passage to Leningrad on the old *Bergensfjord,* which was going on a Baltic cruise. This was highly irregular, but connections did the trick. We were given one of the spacious old immigrant cabins, with about ten empty bunks, in the bow. The huge metal foremast went right through it. The only washing facilities were little tin basins, like serving bowls; and I recall my wife using one of these to bathe the baby: first turning it upside down and washing its head, then righting it and delicately polishing its little behind. In Copenhagen, to the horror of the Norwegian ambassador to Russia who was also on board, we tied the baby buggy to a pipe on the top deck and all went ashore to see the sights.

We made the approach to Leningrad in early morning one day at the end of August. The bleak Baltic autumn had already arrived. The sky was dark and troubled. A cold wind blew out of the north and stirred up a choppy sea. The flat coasts gradually emerged both to the north and the south: dim, melancholy and forbidding. We passed the great old island naval base of Kronstadt, with its barrack-like buildings and its grisly memories of naval mutinies, civil war, and the 1921 uprising. Then there were the embankments of the ship canal, jutting far out to sea among the shoals of the delta, and the miles of lumberyards and docks at the entrance of the Neva.

In Leningrad there was the usual confusion. There was a ghastly moment in the evening at the old Nikolayevski station when family, luggage, and I were all separated in the midst of vast pushing crowds of people, and nobody knew where our compartments were. But things worked out at the last moment, as they generally did in Russia. We arrived in Moscow the next morning in a downpour. The train was so long that our car stopped way out in the yards; no one could find us, and we got drenched making our way in to the platform. When we finally arrived at the familiar building on the Mokhovaya — the only place in the world where, at that moment, we fully belonged — and were welcomed by our friends, we realized that we were at last, in a deeper sense than in Wisconsin, in a deeper sense even than in Norway, at home. Such is the life of the Foreign Service.

The late William C. Bullitt was, in my opinion, a fine ambassador. I believe I reflect the views of others beside myself among those then stationed in Moscow when I say that we took pride in him and never had occasion to be ashamed of him. One should bear in mind, as I say this, that there is no scrutiny more critical than that to which an ambassador at a foreign post is subjected at the hands of his reserved and outwardly respectful career associates.

Bullitt, as we knew him at that time in Moscow, was charming, brilliant, well-educated, imaginative, a man of the world capable of holding his own intellectually with anyone, including such great intellects of the Communist movement as Radek and Bukharin, both of whom were then still around and had no objection to coming to the embassy to talk with him. He had an excellent knowledge of both French and German, which went far to compensate for his lack of knowledge of Russian. His was outstandingly a buoyant disposition. He resolutely refused to permit the life around him to degenerate into dullness and dreariness. All of us who lived in his entourage were the beneficiaries of this blitheness of spirit, this insistence that life be at all times animated and interesting and moving ahead.

His greatest weakness as a diplomatist (and it was the natural counterpart of his virtues) was impatience. He came to Russia with high hopes, and he wanted to see them realized at once. These hopes were not the result of any ideological sympathy for the Soviet regime; they reflected, rather, if my own impression is correct, a certain overoptimism concerning the impressionableness of the Soviet leaders. Here Bullitt was no doubt betrayed by his earlier experience with Lenin. He had gone to Russia in February 1919, during the Paris Peace Conference, with the blessing of Colonel House and at least the tacit consent of President Wilson and Prime Minister Lloyd George. He had dealt there with Lenin and other

Soviet leaders of that day. He had returned with Soviet proposals which were not ideal but which did offer the most favorable opportunity yet extended, or ever to be extended, to the Western powers for extracting themselves with some measure of good grace from the profitless involvements of the military intervention in Russia and for the creation of an acceptable relationship to the Soviet regime. He had been shabbily treated — disowned, in fact — on his return, by Wilson and Lloyd George. Both had ignored his proposals and had publicly denied, explicitly or implicitly, all responsibility for his journey. House, too, had washed his hands of him, and had turned — most unfortunately — to Herbert Hoover for further advice on the handling of the Russian problem at the peace conference. Bullitt had then resigned in protest from the American delegation to the conference.

All this had occurred at a time when the attitude of the Soviet regime toward the United States had not yet congealed — when there was still considerable vacillation among the Soviet leadership — when that leadership still included a number of people not disinclined to view the United States as something less than an entirely imperialistic and negative force in world affairs. Such pro-American tendencies in Moscow naturally received a severe rebuff in the treatment accorded to Bullitt by the Western leaders. Bullitt had never forgotten this. On returning to Russia as ambassador in 1933 he had hoped, I suspect, that the approach to the Roosevelt administration, free of the prejudices of 1919, free of the rigidities of the Republican regimes that had intervened over the preceding twelve years, and prepared to correct insofar as it could the errors of that earlier day, would evoke a favorable response on the Soviet side.

These hopes were quickly disappointed. This was, after all, the day of Stalin, not of Lenin. Bullitt soon became embittered over the behavior of the Soviet government in a whole series of questions. Increasingly, as the years 1934 and 1935 ran their course, he made himself the advocate of a hard line toward Moscow, a line which most of us in the embassy wholeheartedly supported but which FDR, caring little about the specific issues involved, had no intention whatsoever of adopting. Not only did he have no intention of adopting it, but since the mere recommendation of it reflected an outlook on Soviet-American relations that did not fit with the general orientation of his policy, he soon sidetracked Bullitt altogether as an advisor on Russian matters, no doubt blaming the deterioration of Soviet-American relations primarily on Bullitt's personal pique and impatience.

Bullitt spent, as I recall it, little time in Moscow after the early months of 1935. In the summer of 1936, he resigned as ambassador to the USSR and was soon given the Paris post in its place. Throughout much of the latter part of 1935 and 1936 the Moscow embassy carried on under the experienced and competent direction of Loy Henderson as chargé d'affaires *ad interim*. By the end of 1936 it was developing, we felt, into one of the best-informed and most highly respected diplomatic missions in Moscow, rivaled only by the German, which was at all times excellent. We were in many respects a pioneer enterprise — a wholly new type of American diplomatic mission — the model and precursor of a great many missions of a later day. We were the first to cope seriously, for example, with the problems of security — of protection of codes and files and the privacy of intra-office discussion — in a hostile environment. For this purpose, Bullitt brought in a detachment of Marine sergeants, in civilian clothes. But we were also the first to take a primarily intellectual and scholarly attitude to our work. We endeavored to carry forward into our reporting work the same scholarly approach and standards that had previously been adopted in Riga. We were profoundly imbued with a sense of the importance, present and future, of Soviet-American relations. We thought it of the utmost importance that the nature of the Soviet regime be correctly analyzed and that sound approaches be worked out for dealing with it. Our work in Moscow proceeded under formidable technical and physical difficulties, occasioned largely by the various minor harassments we never ceased to suffer at the hands of the Soviet authorities; but this only made us the prouder of our achievement. We regarded ourselves as a lonely and exposed bastion of American governmental life, surrounded by a veritable ocean of official Soviet ill will; and we took pride in our accomplishments precisely because of all this adversity.

I stress this situation because only against this background can one understand the degree of dismay, bewilderment, and discouragement with which, at the turn of the year 1936 to 1937, we learned of the appointment, as successor to Bullitt in the Moscow ambassadorship, of Mr. Joseph E. Davies,* and absorbed, upon his arrival, the first impressions of his person and his entourage. It is possible that we did Mr. Davies some injustice. Others will have to judge that in the light of history. Suffice it to say that he drew from the first instant our distrust and dislike, not so much personally (that was not of importance) but from the standpoint of his fitness for the office and of his motivation in accepting it. We doubted his seriousness. We doubted that he shared our own sense of the importance of the Soviet-American relationship. We saw every evidence that his motives in accepting the post were personal and political and ulterior to any sense of the solemnity of the task itself. We suspected him (and there could have been no more grievous failing in our eyes) of a readiness to bend both the mission and its function to the purposes of personal publicity at home. What mortified us most of all was the impression we received that the President himself knew nothing about, or cared nothing for, what we had accomplished in building up the embassy at Moscow; that the post, with all that it stood for, and all that depended on it, was for him only another political plum, to be handed out in return for campaign contributions.

All this struck deep. At the end of Mr. Davies's first day in Moscow, a number of us assembled in Henderson's rooms and solemnly considered whether we should resign in a body from the service. We properly decided against it. Mr. Davies, we decided, must be given a chance. We took a firm resolve (to which we stoutly adhered throughout the period of his service there) to keep our unhappiness to ourselves and to be loyal to him outwardly vis-à-vis the Russians and the other diplomats. But what then ensued did

---

* Joseph E. Davies, 1876-1958; lawyer, Democratic politician, and politically appointed diplomat; American ambassador to the USSR, 1936-1938.

little to reassure us. Had the President wished to slap us down and to mock us for our efforts in the development of Soviet-American relations, he could not have done better than with this appointment.

Mr. Davies's constituents in Moscow — those who received his confidence, before whom he aired his views, and whose opinions he consulted — were not the members of his official staff, they were the American journalists stationed there. This was borne in on us on countless occasions. I have, by way of example, vivid memories of the sessions of the second of the three great purge trials (the Radek-Pyatakov-Krestinski trial), in 1937. I attended as Mr. Davies's interpreter, hissing into his ear the best I could produce in the way of a simultaneous translation of Vyshinski's thundering brutalities, of the cringing confessions of some of the accused, and of the delicate innuendoes in the statements of some of the others. During the intermissions I was sent, regularly, to fetch the ambassador his sandwiches, while he exchanged sententious judgments with the gentlemen of the press concerning the guilt of the victims. I cannot recall, therefore, that I ever discussed the matter with him. His own reports make it evident that he placed considerable credence in the fantastic charges leveled at these unfortunate men.

It was part of Mr. Davies's concern for his newspaper image at home that American-Soviet relations should have the outward appearance of being cordial, no matter what gnashing of teeth might go on under the surface. This required many changes. It required turning the other cheek in the face of various Soviet harassments which, thus far, we had resisted on principle. It required a different tone in reporting, a different analysis of Soviet motives and intentions. To all of this not only were we career officers in Moscow an impediment, but so was the Division of Eastern European Affairs (commonly known as the Russian Division) in the Department of State.

This division had existed since 1924. It had been headed almost from the start, and with great distinction, by Mr. Robert F. Kelley, who was mentioned above in connection with my studies in Berlin. Kelley, a taciturn and infinitely discreet bachelor, was a graduate of Harvard and the Sorbonne. He had studied Russian much as others of us were later to study it under his general supervision. He was a scholar by instinct and dedication. He had built his division up on scholarly principles to a point where I am sure there was no geographic division in the Department of State that had a better knowledge of the area with which it dealt. He had assembled the best library on Soviet affairs in the United States. He had elaborate and voluminous files of materials collected from every possible source on every aspect of Soviet life. Litvinov, during the negotiations over recognition, paid him the bitter compliment of saying that the Division of Eastern European Affairs in the State Department had better records on the history of Soviet diplomacy than did the Soviet Foreign Office itself. But the division, well-informed as it was, took, as did we, a sharply critical view of Soviet policies and methods, and believed in standing up firmly to the Kremlin on the many issues in dispute, even if it had to be at the cost of a certain amount of open disagreement and unpleasantness.

It was not entirely surprising, then, that some five months after Mr. Davies's entry upon his duties as ambassador, Kelley was summoned one fine morning to the office of the Under Secretary of State and informed that the Division of Eastern European Affairs was abolished forthwith. The entire shop, he was told, was to be liquidated at once and its functions transferred to the Division of Western European Affairs — henceforth to be known as the Division of European Affairs. The beautiful library was to be turned over to the Library of Congress, to be dispersed there by file numbers among its other vast holdings and thus to cease to exist as a library. The special files were to be destroyed. The division was to be reduced to two desks in the new European division, one for Russian affairs and one for the Baltic and Poland.

I never learned the real background for this curious purge. It was rumored that the Western European Division considered that we in the Russian Division "took Russia too seriously" — that we gave it attention, that is, out of proportion to that given by other divisions to other countries. I have no doubt there was something in this; but it was surely not the whole story. There is strong evidence that pressure was brought to bear from the White House. I was surprised, in later years, that the McCarthyites and the other right-wingers of the early Fifties never got hold of the incident and made capital of it; for here, if ever, was a point at which there was indeed the smell of Soviet influence, or strongly pro-Soviet influence, somewhere in the higher reaches of the government.

The Russian Division, in any case, was abolished — with a suddenness more characteristic of Soviet politics than of American administrative procedure. Kelley was packed off to the embassy at Ankara, and retired from the service some years later. My friend Bohlen, serving in Washington at the time of the change, wrapped up in brown paper several hundred of the most valuable reference books from the former library and hid them in the attic of the State Department, thus saving them from anonymity in the Library of Congress. I, just at that point, was brought back to Washington to occupy the new Russian desk as its first permanent incumbent, Bohlen being ordered to Moscow in my place. Together, before his departure, he and I rescued the hidden books and restored them to bookcases in the half of a room that was now to be my province.

I served only one year on the so-called Russian desk. Things could not have been more quiet. I shared the room with my former college friend, classmate, and roommate of the Riga bachelor quarters, Bernard Gufler. He occupied himself with the Polish and Baltic affairs. We whiled away the official doldrums with the continuation of the philosophic and political discussions we had inaugurated as college sophomores, twelve years earlier, and had continued in Riga. Three times, during the course of the year, if my memory is correct, I was summoned to the august presence of the chief of the Western European Division. On one memorable occasion I was even called to the chambers of the Secretary of State, Mr. Cordell Hull, whom I had never met and was never to see again. The problem, on that occasion, concerned some American Communists who had disappeared in Russia. I recall only being signally unsuccessful in trying to explain to the bewildered Secretary why it was that Russian Communists, at the height of the purges, arrested their own American followers. At the end of the brief interview he thought, I suspected, that I was as unbalanced as the Russians whose behavior

I had tried to make intelligible. These four interviews constituted the only occasions on which senior officials of the Department of State concerned themselves sufficiently intensively with Russian affairs, during the course of that year, to cause them to want to consult with the "expert" on the Russian desk. They could thus be taken as the measure of the official attention which Russia received in Washington in those idyllic times. The Western European Division, obviously, was serious in its determination "not to take Russia too seriously."

My departure from the Russian desk at the end of one year was ostensibly the response to my plea that it was hard to support a wife and two children in Washington on five thousand dollars a year with no rent allowance. I am still grateful for the understanding shown. I have always suspected, however, that the decision was made easier for the Western European Division by the recognition that my views on policy toward Russia were badly out of accord with those of the new ambassador in Moscow and indeed with those of the administration itself. In any case, when the time came to leave, it was not to Russia but to Prague that the orders read. Six years would pass before I would again be active in the Russian field.

4

Prague, 1938–1939

THE journey to Prague was not uneventful. The ship left
Sandy Hook at 2 P.M. on the afternoon of the New England
hurricane (taking her pilot with her because it was too rough to let
him off) and steamed directly into the eye of that great storm. As
the remaining days of the voyage slipped past, the Munich crisis
drew to its climax. Europe was again on the verge of war. The ship,
originally bound for Hamburg, received instructions to terminate
its passage and discharge its passengers at Le Havre. On arrival
there, a bewildered company of travelers, only a fraction of whom
had been bound for France, were hustled off into a special train and
dumped, late that evening, in Paris. It was clear that no dependents
should proceed to Prague — the ones already there were being
evacuated. So at five o'clock the following morning, on the day of
the Munich Conference, I kissed my sleeping family good-bye in
the hotel room and hurried to the airport to get what turned out to
be the last regular airplane ever to go from Paris to the 1918-1938
Czechoslovakia. As we took off, at Le Bourget, a special plane was
warming up on the runway, preparing to take Daladier to Munich.

Prague was blacked out and in a state of military emergency.
The results of the Munich Conference became known, as I recall it,
on the morning after my arrival. I was present on the Vaclavsky
Namesti as they were being announced over the loudspeakers; and
one of my first impressions of the post-Munich Prague was thus the
sight of crowds of people weeping, unabashedly, in the streets at

this death knell of the independence their country had enjoyed for a brief twenty years. Within a matter of hours, the German forces were occupying the border regions — closing in around the heart of Bohemia and Moravia. The atmosphere was already that of war; and it was thus at this moment that for me personally the war — my war, so to speak — began. It was destined to last for nearly eight years.

In view of the blackout and the evacuation of dependents, I found all the male staff residing in the residence quarters of the legation. Both chancery and residence were at that time installed in the Schoenborn Palace. This fine old building, situated in the marvelously picturesque part of Prague known as the Mala Strana, contained some eighty rooms, many of them huge. In the basement, I recall, one could still see the great stables with marble mangers for twenty-four horses. The legation chancery and the residence quarters for the minister occupied only a small portion of the building, the remainder being left in a state of desuetude. The residential quarters alone contained, in addition to several bedrooms, at least three, and I think four, huge salons. Immediately back of the building the lovely garden rose in terraces up the hill, culminating in a fruit orchard and a structure known as the Glorietta. From there one had a magnificent view over the roofs of the Mala Strana to the river, with the lovely old Charles bridge, and across the little valley to the ancient fortress hill, the Hradčany, center and shrine of the Czech nation.

At the time of my arrival, the United States government was in the process of completing the construction, under one of the terraces of this garden, of a concrete air raid shelter. It was, as I recall it, the only shelter of this sort to be completed for any of our diplomatic missions in Europe before the outbreak of war. It is an eloquent commentary on the difficulty of foresight in international affairs that not only was this the first of our diplomatic premises to be abandoned — abandoned, in fact, before the war had really begun and long before any bombs began to fall — but that Prague itself was almost the only European capital to escape any serious measure of aerial destruction.

The American minister in Prague at that time was a man whose name was not only familiar but legendary in the consciousness of every member of the American Foreign Service: Mr. Wilbur J. Carr. This was Mr. Carr's first diplomatic post. For forty years prior to this appointment he had served as an administrative official in the Department of State. He had been, in that capacity, the real architect of the State Department's career services — at first only of the old Consular Service; then, after 1924, of the new, combined Foreign Service. For decades it had been he who, year after year, armed with an imperturbable patience, a studied softness of speech, and a transparent integrity, had been obliged to confront the congressional committees on whose good graces the budget of the Department of State depended and to defend and justify the department's requests. He had often been criticized by members of the department and the Foreign Service for the modesty of the demands he put to the Congress; but I personally always suspected that it was this modesty of demand, coupled with that limpid honesty which no member of Congress ever dared to doubt, which made it possible for him to get as much as he did.

Now, in 1938, this long and quiet bureaucratic career had come to an end. The appointment as minister to Czechoslovakia was conceived by his superiors, we suspected, as a well-deserved tribute to a long life of unassuming service, and as a suitable way of rounding it off. Mr. Carr was no longer young, and one might well have wondered how effective forty years of labor in the vineyard of governmental bureaucracy would prove to be as preparation for a diplomatic assignment. It proved in this instance to be admirable. Quiet, dignified, affable; thoroughly schooled in all the intricacies of governmental and diplomatic procedure; accustomed to the frustrations of governmental routine and skilled in the arts of patience and of quiet persuasion by which alone that routine could be successfully assailed; kindly, understanding, and yet astute in his treatment of junior personnel — Wilbur Carr was a first-rate chief of mission. It was only to be regretted that he had come so late to a function for which he was obviously excellently fitted.

As in the case of many another able diplomatic representative,

there was little or nothing Mr. Carr could do to alter an unhappy
— in this case disastrous — course of events in the country to
which he was accredited. We all felt small and helpless in the face
of what was happening around us. But one of the first prerequisites
of usefulness in the diplomatic profession is the ability to recognize
the limits of one's possibilities, and this Mr. Carr did. I recall in this
connection an evening during that period of my stay at the residence when I waited long and vainly, in my bedroom, for the usual
call to dinner from the butler. Finally, wondering what had happened, I ventured into the great salons. There, in the brightly
lighted room, I came upon the minister peacefully sleeping in an
armchair. The servants stood respectfully behind the curtains of
the dining room, not daring to wake him. The sight of the old gentleman, thus peacefully at rest in the solitary splendor of his heavily
curtained salons while outside in the growing darkness a Europe
seething with fear and hatred and excitement danced its death
dance all around us, struck me as a symbolic enactment of the helplessness of all forces of order and decency, at that moment, in the
face of the demonic powers that history had now unleashed.

Two incidents from those first days in Prague stand out in my
mind, both as useful lessons in personal humility. The old diplomatic service was often charged with complacency and arrogance.
We who belonged to it tended to put these charges down to popular ignorance and jealousy. We considered ourselves innocent and
misunderstood. But were we, always, I wonder?

One morning, only three or four days after my arrival, there
burst into our office an attractive young lady wearing a collegiate
American fur coat and tossing, in her indignation, a most magnificent head of golden hair. Without further ado, she proceeded to
burn us all up for our sleepy inactivity. The advance of the Germans into the Sudeten area was causing the Czech inhabitants of
that region, she said, to flee by the hundreds of thousands. Within a
day or two these hordes would be descending on Prague. No one
was making any provision to feed them, to house them, to care for

them. It was time for us to bestir ourselves. "Why," she demanded to know, "don't you *do* something about it?"

The other secretary of the legation and I responded with a weary and polite disdain. What in the world could we "do" about it? These were the days before Food for Peace and foreign aid. Our little legation chancery, with its total staff of some six or eight persons, did not have at its disposal stocks of food or clothing or housing; we had trouble enough getting the Congress to provide the pay for four local clerks. Besides, we suspected that her fears were exaggerated, as indeed they turned out to be. We relegated her, therefore, to the category of ignorant, impractical do-gooders, and were relieved to get her out of the office.

All this would have been unexceptional, were it not that the lady, Martha Gellhorn, was one I would know in later decades as a valued and respected friend, and would admire precisely for these qualities of courage and generosity she was then indulging. I realize today that we both, on that harrowing morning in Prague, had lessons we could have taught each other.

The second incident was even more striking. In those days, as the German forces advanced like encroaching waves over all the borders of Bohemia, no trains were running, no planes were flying, no frontier stations existed. Yet in the midst of this confusion we received a telegram from the embassy in London, the sense of which was that our ambassador there, Mr. Joseph Kennedy, had chosen this time to send one of his young sons on a fact-finding tour around Europe, and it was up to us to find means of getting him across the border and through the German lines so that he could include in his itinerary a visit to Prague.

We were furious. Joe Kennedy was not exactly known as a friend of the career service, and many of us, from what we had heard about him, cordially reciprocated this lack of enthusiasm. His son had no official status and was, in our eyes, obviously an upstart and an ignoramus. The idea that there was anything he could learn or report about conditions in Europe which we did not already know and had not already reported seemed (and not without reason) wholly absurd. That busy people should have their time taken up arranging his tour struck us as outrageous. With that polite but weary punctiliousness that characterizes diplomatic officials required to busy themselves with pesky compatriots who insist on visiting places where they have no business to be, I arranged to get him through the German lines, had him escorted to Prague, saw to it that he was shown what he wanted to see, expedited his departure, then, with a feeling of "that's that," washed my hands of him — as I thought.

Had anyone said to me then that the young man in question would some day be the President of the United States and that I, in the capacity of chief of a diplomatic mission, would be his humble and admiring servant, I would have thought that either my informant or I had taken leave of our senses. It was one of the great lessons of life when memory of the episode returned to me, as I sat one day in my Belgrade office, many years later, and the truth suddenly and horribly dawned. By just such blows, usually much too late in life, is the ego gradually cut down to size.

I remained in Prague one year — until the outbreak of the World War. Midway through the year, in March 1939, the Germans completed the extinction of the Czechoslovak state by marching into Prague and extending their occupation to all of Bohemia and Moravia. Our legation was of course at that point formally abolished; but I remained, alone, under orders of the Department, looking after the palace, keeping the little chancery going with a skeleton staff, and continuing my work as a political observer. When the war broke out in 1939 I was transferred to the embassy at Berlin, in whose bailiwick the occupied Czechoslovakia now fell — as indeed most of the rest of Europe was soon to do.

My position during that year in Prague, and particularly during the months that followed the entry of the German forces into the city and the total suppression of the Czechoslovak state, was a unique one. The great corps of foreign pressmen who had gathered there for the Munich crisis soon departed for more agitated shores. In the end I was left as practically the only Western political observer regularly residing in what remained of Czechoslovakia. The fate of a small nation already occupied and suppressed by the Germans was not of great interest to the metropolitan dailies of the Western countries. Czechoslovakia had gone down the drain, and that was that. But it was not uninteresting to me. Horrified but fascinated by what was taking place before my eyes, I poured forth a stream of letters and reports to the government.* Not more than five people, I suppose, ever read them in Washington. My reward for the effort would be to be left for nearly three years thereafter to do administrative work at the Berlin embassy. But I was not downhearted. I wrote with pleasure and enthusiasm, aware that I was gradually mastering the complexities of the situation and was writing better than I had ever written before. More than a decade of experience in writing reports for the Department of State had now begun to teach me the art of writing without an audience, or at least without a reacting one; and I was learning to enjoy it.

Almost everything that I had previously experienced was useful to me in observing and in trying to understand the drama of the disintegration of the initial Czechoslovakia that was now taking place before my eyes. With a knowledge of Russian, it was not too difficult to learn enough of the Czech, Slovak, and Ruthenian tongues to read the papers and to carry on conversations of sorts with people who spoke nothing else. Long years of residence in Germany and Austria meant that the Germans, who were now the other leading parties to this drama, were no mystery to me. Service in Vienna, in particular, had given me some idea of the old Central Europe out of which the state of Czechoslovakia had emerged. My status as an observer, wholly unencumbered with administrative duties, left me free to do a good deal of traveling outside Prague. Impressions were therefore vivid, revealing, and absorbing.

I came to Prague devoid of any sympathy for the Nazis and deeply moved by the plight of the Czechs as the most recent victims of Hitler's imperialism, yet far from sharing that sentimental enthu-

---

* This body of *reportage*, emanating from the residence and service in Prague, is too voluminous and specialized in content to warrant inclusion in this volume. It is in process of publication, as a special volume, by Princeton University Press.

siasm for the Beneš regime and the post–World War I order of Central Europe which had inspired so many English and American liberals. I had no sympathy for the fragmentation of sovereign power in the Danube basin to which the outcome of the First World War had led. I deplored the breakup of the Austro-Hungarian Empire. I had unpleasant recollections of the narrow linguistic nationalism of the Czechs, as I had experienced it on the occasion of a brief visit to Prague some years before. The Little Entente, on which the Czechs, with French encouragement, had tried to base their security, had seemed to me an artificial, unwise arrangement, founded in the quicksands of the vengeful, emotional, and unrealistic spirit that dominated French policy in the years just after World War I. My sympathies went out to the Austrians, for whom so few had then a good word to say and whom the Czechs in particular had treated, during the period of their own independence, with such unbending hostility and rejection. I felt that the Czechs owed much, not only of what their capital city was but also of what they themselves were, to the positive sides of their long association with Vienna; they might, I thought, have been at greater pains to acknowledge it.

And finally, my interpretation of the Munich crisis, which had now reached its climax, was different from that of most Western liberals. I did not believe in the good faith of the Soviet professions of willingness to leap to the aid of Czechoslovakia — always provided the French did likewise. The Soviet leaders, I believed, knew very well that neither military geography nor the well-founded anxieties of the Polish and Rumanian governments would permit, in actuality, any major Russian military move to assist the Czechs. They were therefore safe in undertaking to go to war if France and England would do likewise. The burden of the military struggle was bound to fall on others.

If, then, I deplored the failure of the French and British to stand up to Hitler in the crisis, even at the risk of a war, I did so for reasons different from those which were common to most of Western liberal opinion.

Some, if not all, of these preconceptions were reflected in what I wrote during the early stages of my service in Prague. Only a few days after my arrival — a few days after Munich, that is — I recorded as follows, for what purpose I cannot today recall, my initial reactions to the Czechoslovak scene of the post-Munich period, reactions that were not devoid of hope that recent developments, for all their tragedy, would have at least *some* positive consequences. I described in detail the tragedy of the Czechs, for whom I had the keenest sympathy. But one did not, I thought, need to share their despair in order to understand it.

In this crowded heart of Europe, where neighborly jealousies run so high, there can never be any solution of the ills of the day which will satisfy both Jack and Tom alike. It is comforting to reflect that if no good wind can fail to blow ill, no ill wind can fail to blow good. Change will always involve suffering, but one can at least hope that such changes as occur will lead in the direction of greater economic security and greater racial tolerance for people sadly in need of both. And while recent events, to be sure, have done no immediate service to either of these goals, there is hope that their ultimate results may lead in this direction.

Czechoslovakia is, after all, a Central European state. Its fortunes must in the long run lie with — and not against — the dominant forces in this area. It is generally agreed that the breakup of the limited degree of unity which the Hapsburg Empire represented was unfortunate for all concerned. Other forces are now at work which are struggling to create a new form of unity where individualism and sectionalism have held sway for two decades. To these forces, Czechoslovakia has been tragically slow in adjusting herself. It is idle at this late date to attempt to apportion the blame for this fact between the country's own statesmen and its foreign advisors. The adjustment — and this is the main thing — has now come. It has come in a painful and deplorable form. But it has relieved the Czechoslovak state of liabilities as well as assets. It has left the heart of the country physically intact. Finally, and perhaps most important of all, it has preserved for the exacting tasks of the future a magnificent younger generation — disciplined, industrious, and physically fit — which would undoubtedly have been sacrificed if the solution had been the romantic one of hopeless resistance rather than the humiliating but truly heroic one of realism.

Unfortunately, it proved impossible to maintain for long the temperate optimism of this initial reaction. It became evident, as the autumn wore on and deepened into winter, that the Germans were themselves undecided as to the future of the rump Czechoslovakia left by the Munich settlement, and were as yet unprepared to find for it a stable place in the new order of Europe. Repeatedly, I found myself obliged to point out in my reports not only the hesitating and contradictory quality of German policies toward Bohemia and Moravia but also the dilemma that had been created for the Germans by the effects the Munich settlement had had on Slovakia and Ruthenia. In the winter months, just prior to the final German takeover of Prague, I paid visits to Slovakia and Ruthenia and wrote long reports on conditions in those provinces. These reports reflected the conviction that the situation then prevailing there could not long endure. Prague, itself hard pressed by a thousand trials and difficulties, was being asked to finance, support, and defend these highly deficit provinces while being faced with nothing but defiance and subordination on the part of the irresponsible pseudo-Nazi elements the Germans had assisted to power there. In addition to this it was clear that the borders of the rump Czechoslovakia, particularly in the Slovak and Ruthenian region, were so absurdly and unfortunately drawn that they would not even serve German purposes from the standpoint of East-West communications, in the event of war between Germany and any power further to the east. I could see no stability, therefore, in the existing state of affairs. "Slovakia's brief achievement of autonomy," I was obliged to write in Jaunary 1939, "was only an incidental and temporary outcropping of the slow shift of power in the Central European area from Vienna and Budapest northward to Berlin. Its loss of autonomy, when it comes, will have to be regarded as an inevitable reversion to the natural state of affairs." Similarly, I was obliged to conclude my report on Ruthenia, written in early March 1939, by confessing to the impression "that somehow or other, and in the not too distant future, the unwieldy remnant of what was once Ruthenia will find its way back to the economic and political unit in which it most naturally belongs, which is Hungary. (Actually, this happened before the report reached Washington.) And finally, in the case of the so-called Historic Provinces — Bohemia and Moravia — which formed the heart of the former Czechoslovakia, a dispatch written in late January 1939 for Minister Carr's signature summed up the situation as follows:

. . . the situation in Bohemia is still precarious. The Germans would evidently like to see the territory remain nominally independent for the immediate future, but only on conditions which make it extremely difficult for any Czech government to operate. There is a limit to what any Czech regime can do for Germany, and sooner or later the Germans will have to choose between continuing to tolerate in their midst an independent Czech state which can never identify itself entirely with the National Socialist ideology, or proceeding to an occupation of Bohemia and endeavoring to cope with all the new problems which this step would bring in its train.

Six weeks later, as everyone knows, Hitler chose the second of these alternatives and proceeded to occupy the remainder of Bohemia and Moravia, including the city of Prague, permitting Slovakia to become nominally independent, and tossing Ruthenia to the Hungarians. In this way he demolished, for the time being, the Czechoslovak state as established in 1919. The action must stand, historically, as one of his greatest mistakes. It destroyed the Munich settlement and with it the last grain of confidence in his word on the part of the governments and public opinion of the Western countries. It discredited Neville Chamberlain and placed the British in a position where they had no choice but to extend a guarantee to Poland and to react with force to any further Nazi encroachments to the east. It left Hitler himself no choice, now, but to desist from irredentist claims against Poland that had been part of German policy even before he came to power, or accept a strong risk of war with the Western powers.

The entry of the German forces into Prague on March 15 was, for all of us Americans who witnessed it and who experienced the stresses and excitements of that day, a harrowing experience. For some days, the clouds had been gathering, and we had known that something ominous was cooking. But it was not until the early morning of the fifteenth that we could be certain of what the Germans had in mind. I have in my diary notes the account of the remainder of that day; and this will suffice, perhaps, to recall the atmosphere of the time. I was wakened by a phone call at four-thirty in the morning.

The shaky voice of a terrified acquaintance told me that the German troops would begin the occupation of Bohemia and Moravia at six o'clock. I phoned the military attaché and asked him to get a confirmation from the military authorities. Then I called the Czechoslovak Press Bureau where a depressed female voice told me that the report was true. Determined that the German army should not have the satisfaction of giving the American legation a harried appearance, I shaved meticulously before going to the office. The wind was howling and the snow was falling in the dark streets as I made my way to the legation. A light was on the Italian legation. The cop on duty outside looked at me strangely, and I wondered if he knew what was up.

The minister was already at his desk in the chancery. The staff gradually assembled, and we got off a cable. It began to get light. Two disheveled men, ashy-pale with fear, came up to ask for asylum. They had been Czech spies in Germany, they said, and they were known to the local Gestapo. Their faces were twitching and their lips trembling when I sent them away. They were followed by two German Social Democrats, fugitives from the Reich. They seemed almost dazed with terror. They seemed to accept my statement that I could do nothing for them, but they wouldn't leave. They refused to believe that they had to leave that building, where they still could not be touched, and to go out into the streets where they were no more than hunted animals. A Jewish acquaintance came. We told him that he was welcome to stay around there until he could calm his nerves. He paced wretchedly up and down in the anteroom, through the long morning hours. In the afternoon, he decided to face the music and went home.

About seven o'clock, I took a ride around town. A full blizzard was blowing, by this time, and the snow was staying on the streets. The downtown section was crowded, partly by the normal early-morning traffic of people going to work but partly by people running about and making last-minute preparations of all sorts. The news was widely spread by this time, and many of the women were weeping into their handkerchiefs as they walked.

Back to the office after breakfast. A stream of desperate persons was by this time arriving at the legation, and we had to post a man down at the gate to turn those away whom we did not know well. But even the others were only too numerous.

About ten o'clock, word came that the German troops had already reached the palace. Parry and I set out in my car to verify this, for the palace was only a short distance away. Driving up the hill on the Nerudova, just before my own apartment, we met a German armored car stopped in the middle of the narrow street. The driver was evidently trying to find the German legation and had stopped there, by the Italian legation, to ask the way. A crowd of embittered but curious Czechs looked on in silence. The soldier in the turret sat huddled up against the driving snow, nervously fingering the trigger of his machine gun as he faced the crowd. It seemed to me that the two famous eagles on the baroque portico of the Italian legation had a distinctly startled air as they witnessed this scene, like one who was prepared to say something very important and has had the wind unexpectedly taken out of his sails.

For the rest of the day, the motorized units pounded and roared over the cobblestone streets; hundreds and hundreds of vehicles plastered with snow, the faces of their occupants red with what some thought was shame but what I fear was in most cases merely the cold.

By evening the occupation was complete, and the people were chased off the streets by an eight o'clock curfew. We drove through the town around midnight. It was strange to see these Prague streets, usually so animated, now completely empty and deserted. Tomorrow, to be sure, they would fill with life again, but it would not be the same life that had filled them before; and we were all acutely conscious that in this case the curfew had indeed tolled the knell of a long and distinctly tragic day.

It was after the German occupation of Prague and the consequent withdrawal of our legation that the most intensive period of my work as a reporting officer ensued. I now had nothing to do, and there was nothing that the Department of State wanted me to do, other than political reporting. The legation was now closed. I was effectively my own boss. For form's sake I submitted my reports through, and over the signature of, the consul general, Mr. Irving Linnell, who was the ranking officer at the post. But my independence in the writing of them was complete.

It is clearer to me today than it was then that the treatment of the Czechs, now that they were entirely under German control, was for Hitler not just a question that could be judged on its own merits as a matter of relations between the German and Czech peoples, but primarily something that had to be fitted in with, and subordinated to, his general policy of the moment toward Eastern Europe and the Soviet Union. Determined now not only to regain Danzig and to wipe out the Polish Corridor but also to gain dominant political influence and access to raw materials much further to the east, he was faced with three alternative routes of approach to this objective. First, he could attempt to play on the national feeling of the Ukrainians and to stimulate a demand for an independent Ukrainian state under Nazi influence, along the lines of what the Germans had attempted to do during the occupation of the Ukraine in 1918. This could be done only at the expense of relations with both Poland and the Soviet Union, and at the risk of a simultaneous war against both, into which the Western powers would almost certainly be drawn. Second, he could pursue the possibility of a deal with Poland at the expense of the Soviet Union — a deal whereby the Poles would satisfy German aspirations with respect to Danzig and Poland's western border and would be recompensed at the expense of the Soviet Union. But this, of course, meant making war in alliance with Poland against the Soviet Union; and for this the Poles were scarcely to be had. The third alternative was a deal with the Soviet Union at Poland's expense, with at least the possibility that the Western powers, who had now put up with so much, would remain passive for a further period.

Like a lot of other people, I quite failed to see this latter alternative in advance of the event; nor did I consider myself well enough acquainted with what was happening in the higher reaches of European diplomacy (I knew, after all, only what was in press and radio) to relate the experiences of the Czechs to these questions of high policy in any adequate way. I did, to be sure, point out in my dispatches, immediately after the occupation of Prague, that the sacrifice of Ruthenia meant the abandonment by the Germans of the dream of a puppet Ukraine and that therefore if the Germans were going to expand further to the east, such expansion would "have to be carried out on a less subtle and more frankly militaristic basis." After that, my task consisted largely of pointing to the continued evidences of German indecision and vacillation in policy toward Central Europe, to the numerous contradictions and dilemmas into which the Germans had propelled themselves by their brutal and reckless destruction of the status quo in that area, and to the growing evidence that they had no serious intention of giving real meaning, permanence, or stability to the new form of government — namely, the Protectorate of Bohemia and Moravia, which they had established, on paper at least, in what was left of the Historic Provinces. By consequence of this last situation, it also fell to me to describe to official Washington the utter failure of the Germans to win any sympathy among the Czech population; the growing bitterness and cynicism of those Czechs whom the Germans left, almost contemptuously, as helpless figureheads in the Protectorate government; the shameless financial corruption and economic plundering of the province by the new German masters; and finally, the establishment in the minds of the Czechs of the possibility of a world war as the only hope for liberation and a better future. "Just as the Czechs waited for the [First] World War to wrest their freedom from the Austrian Empire," I wrote in mid-April 1939,

so now they place their hopes again on war as the development which will bring the restoration of their political freedom. There is probably no country in Europe where war — and war at the earliest possible date — is so universally desired as in the Protectorate of Bohemia and Moravia. One hears this sentiment expressed daily on every hand. In the event of an unsuccessful war at any time during the next few years, the Germans will probably find that the Czech spirit of independence, despite the subjection of the people to all the propaganda methods of the modern totalitarian state, has shown surprising powers of endurance.

Time and again I was forced to emphasize this psychological failure of the Germans, and its significance not just for the future of this particular area but for the prospects of a successful Nazi hegemony in Europe generally. "One can predict," I wrote in mid-May 1939,

no successful future for the German attempt to rule the Historic Provinces. Inflation, impoverishment, economic disruption, bitterness, lack of confidence, and the moral disintegration of public administration can reap no good harvest either for victors or vanquished. . . . Until the German people develop greater spiritual power and greater political maturity they will stand little chance of success as heirs to the responsibilities which were borne for many centuries — and at times not uncreditably — by the Catholic Church and the Hapsburg Empire.

I thought it likely, I wrote a week later,

that the Germans will find themselves forced in the end to sweep away the last figments of Czech autonomy, to place their reliance solely on their bayonets and to attempt to crush by sheer force the powerful Czech nationalism which they have hitherto tried to exploit. In this case, it is outright war: an undeclared war in which imprisonments, shootings, deportations, intimidation, and bribery on the one side would be pitted against passive resistance, sabotage, espionage, and conspiracy on the other. If it comes to this, the Germans will probably hold the upper hand without undue difficulty as long as the broad basis of National Socialist power remains intact. But they will have no happy time of it, and if the tide ever turns, Czech retaliation will be fearful to contemplate.

By midsummer relations between the Germans and the Czechs had come to an obviously unstable and unsatisfactory deadlock, a deadlock in which the Germans held, of course, all the physical and military cards, while honorable and wholly un-Nazi Czechs were permitted to carry on without hindrance as ostensible heads of the

Protectorate government. But in the very fact that the Germans were doing nothing to resolve this deadlock, people began to suspect that things more important than just German-Czech relations were in the wind. In late August, only four days before Ribbentrop flew to Moscow to conclude the famous German-Soviet Nonaggression Pact and thus to unleash the second world war of this century, I wrote a long analysis of the Prague scene which began with the following paragraph:

Another summer is now drawing to an end — the unhappiest which this area has known since the days of the World War. It has been a strange summer, characterized by frequent and destructive electrical storms which damaged crops to the extent of hundreds of millions of crowns and seemed grimly symbolic of the rapidly alternating hopes and fears in the minds of the people. Work has gone on as usual. Even now the peasants are struggling — encouraged by the Germans and deterred by the frequent showers — to get in the harvest before the newest crisis reaches its culminating point. And the industries are busy enough trying to still the insatiable appetite of the Reich for their products. But all other manifestations of human activity seem afflicted by a strange lethargy, almost a paralysis. Everything is in suspense. No one takes initiative; no one plans for the future. Cultural life and amusements continue in a halfhearted, mechanical spirit. Theaters and public amusements attract only scanty and indifferent crowds. People prefer to sit through the summer evenings in the beer gardens or the little parks along the rivers, to bandy the innumerable rumors in which they themselves scarcely believe, and to wait with involuntary patience for the approach of something which none of them could quite describe but which they are all convinced must come and must affect all their lives profoundly. The near future should show whether this waiting attitude is the result of a sound instinct or whether it merely expresses the natural reluctance of a people which has just awakened from a twenty-year dream of independence to accept again the status of a nation of servants.

In the concluding passages of this dispatch, the last of its kind that I was to write in Prague, I speculated on the effects of the events of the last year on the future of the Czech people:

Whether there is war or not, the Bohemia and Moravia of the future will never be quite the same as those which were left by President Beneš and his advisors last autumn. Time does not stand still and the turbulent events of the last year have not been without their modifying effect on Czech character. It is true that if the pendulum ever starts to swing in the other direction, there may be terrible anti-German excesses. It is likewise true that German clumsiness has given to Beneš's name a superficial boulevard popularity which his personality on its own merits was never able to command. But that the Czechs will ever restore in full their past institutions and their past leaders is doubtful. Misfortune has left many marks; and among them is a deep sense of the necessity for unity and discipline in a small people so unhappily situated as themselves. Few will wish for the return of the many squabbling political parties, the petty bourgeois timidity, and the shallow materialism which seems to have characterized at least the lower organs of public administration under the former regime. Czech nationalism will flourish indeed, but with it there will be a demand for greater personal responsibility and greater spiritual authority among those who pretend to lead.

This was in general an unhappy time, full of darkening clouds, vague fears and disturbing premonitions. One was kept going, to some extent, by unreal hopes. Had I been able to foresee, at that point, what specific meaning history would give in the postwar period to these dim and groping appreciations, premonition would have given way, I think, to a total despair.

5

Wartime Service in Germany

IT was the intention of the Department of State, in transferring
me from Prague to Berlin at the outbreak of war in 1939, that I
should continue, but now from Berlin, the reporting role on which
I had been engaged while in Czechoslovakia. But the Berlin embassy, as I soon discovered, was faced at that moment with formidable administrative problems for which the department had made no
adequate provision. The state of war was already adding, as it always does, innumerable burdens and complications to the work of a
neutral diplomatic mission. Among other things, we were taking
over the interests of France and Great Britain: the protection of
their nationals, their diplomatic property, their prisoners of war,
and the tasks connected with the exchange of their official personnel. And in addition to this, there were many new problems
affecting American interests themselves. Out of sheer sympathy for
Alexander Kirk,* the chargé d'affaires, I offered my services as
administrative officer, and continued to carry this burden during
much of the time I served there. To this arrangement the Department of State tacitly acquiesced, having no better solution and
being increasingly uninterested, it seemed, in political reporting
from within the area commanded by the German government.

This administrative burden of the Berlin embassy, incidentally,
grew steadily as the war progressed. In the summer of 1940 the ten

* Alexander Kirk, born in 1888; long-time American career diplomat; later
American ambassador in Egypt and in Italy.

major consular offices which our government had maintained in various German cities were closed on the insistence of the German government, and all their work, insofar as it could not be liquidated entirely, was transferred to the Berlin embassy. The increasingly desperate situation of the German Jews, and Jews from the German-occupied areas, and the heavy attendant pressures brought to bear upon us to effect their release and removal to the United States, added to the burden. These pressures tended often to be generated in powerful congressional circles at home and to be passed on, unmitigated, to us by a Department of State anxious to get itself out of the firing line and too timid to point out to the Congressmen what could and could not (sometimes in the light of the laws they themselves had created) be done to aid such people.

As the Nazi conquest proceeded, new countries were added to the list of those whose interests we were protecting. By the time of Pearl Harbor there were, I believe, about eleven of them. And we had the responsibility for representing the interests of these countries not just in Germany alone, but also throughout the wider and steadily expanding sphere of German-occupied Europe, so that in the end we stood as the sole representatives for most of Europe of the interests of the United States and a good part of the remainder of the Western world.

All of this burden was absorbed and carried forward with an American staff which, even at the end, numbered together with its dependents only some ninety-nine persons, aided by an equally modest figure of German personnel. Compared with the official missions the United States maintains today in the larger European capitals, where literally hundreds and hundreds of Americans are employed for responsibilities scarcely comparable in scope with those we then carried, this is, of course, a ridiculously small number. It will not be hard to imagine what strain was involved for the embassy personnel.

This strain was increased by the usual wartime hardships and inconveniences of personal life — hardships and inconveniences which I, incidentally, having occasion to live in both capitals at one time or another during the war, found to be considerably greater in Berlin than in London. Particularly the first war winter — 1939-1940 — was a difficult one. Canals were frozen. Fuel was short. Whole blocks of huge apartment houses could not be heated at all and had to be evacuated in zero weather. Both rationing and black-out rules were severe. Private automobiling was banned entirely. Air raid precautions, too, were stricter than in London. No one was allowed on the streets during the period of an alarm. People caught out at evening parties by the sounding of the air raid sirens were often obliged to enjoy their host's hospitality until the all-clear sounded shortly before dawn. Under these conditions the problems faced in getting night-duty personnel back and forth between their homes and the embassy and in meeting couriers and other travelers who arrived at night at remote suburban stations (the long-distance trains were no longer routed into the center of the city after the bombings) can easily be imagined. They were heightened by the fact that when the war began the embassy possessed not a single official vehicle, nor would the government buy it one. Kirk contemptuously purchased out of his own pocket a small Renault, with a trailer for luggage, and successfully solicited the department's gracious consent that it should be placed on the inventory of official property.

I find it impossible to convey in this sort of account the atmosphere of the great city of Berlin in wartime. It is symbolized for me, in memory, by the recollection I have of my homeward progress as I left my work in the embassy on winter evenings: the groping in pitch blackness from column to column of the Brandenburg gate, feeling my way by hand after this fashion to the bus stop; the waiting for the dim blue lights of the bus to come sweeping out of the obscurity; then the long journey out five and a half miles of the "east-west axis"; the dim, hushed interior of the bus, lightened only by the sweeps of the conductor's flashlight; the wonder as to how the driver ever found his way over the vast expanse of unmarked, often snow-covered asphalt which that wide and endless street presented; the eerie walk home at the other end, again with much grop-

ing and feeling for curbstones; the subdued voices of other pedestrians heard but not seen; and finally the confrontation with the
facade of what appeared, from outside its blackout curtains, to be a
dark and deserted home; and the ultimate pleasant discovery, always with a tinge of surprise, on opening the door that behind the
curtains was light, at least a minimal measure of warmth, at times
(when she was not taking the children somewhere) a wife, and a
coziness all the more pronounced for the vast darkness and uncertainty of the war that lay outside.

Insofar as one could feel at home amid such abnormalities and
discomforts, I felt fairly at home in Berlin. I had lived there before.
Setting and language were familiar. Except for occasional visits to
the Foreign Office on official business, I had nothing to do with the
regime, nor did most of the people I knew. The Berliners themselves — the simple people, that is — were, of all the major urban
or regional elements among the German population, the least Nazi-
fied in their outlook. They could never be induced to give the Nazi
salute. They continued to the end to greet each other with the usual
"Guten Morgen" in place of the obligatory *"Heil Hitler."* Nor did
they evidence any particular enthusiasm for the war. I can testify
(because I stood among crowds of them on the Pariserplatz, outside
our embassy, on that particular day) that they witnessed with a
reserved, sullen silence the victory parade of the troops returning
from the successful completion of the Polish campaign. Not even
the most frantic efforts of professional Nazi agitators could pro-
voke them to demonstrations of elation or approval. The news of
the fall of Paris was received with the same inscrutable silence and
reserve. I rode miles, that afternoon, on the enclosed upper deck of
a bus, where practically everyone's conversation was audible. I
heard no one as much as mention the event; the talk was all of food
cards and the price of stockings.

Indeed, what struck one most about wartime Berlin was the undemonstrative but unmistakable inner detachment of the people
from the pretentious purposes of the regime, and the way in which
ordinary life went on, as best it could, under the growing difficul-

ties of wartime discipline. The war dominated the public prints; but it was, so far as concerned the Berliners and to a large extent common people in other great cities as well, the regime's war, not theirs.

My diary notes from that time contain many items to illustrate this disparity between the regime's undertakings and the preoccupations of common people. Perhaps the following, written sometime in late 1939, will serve to make the point.

It was about midnight on a Saturday night when I left a bar in the Binnenalster district of Hamburg and started to grope my way homeward through the darkened streets.

The war had been on about a month. The blackout had become routine. The weather, on this particular evening, was clear. A wan moon threw down just enough light to reveal the curbstones, lampposts, and other obstructions. Except for an occasional ghostly bus, rumbling along behind its dimmed lights, there was no traffic. The quiet streets stretched away, empty and desolate, into the moonlight. Only the shadowy rustling forms of pedestrians, looming up and fading again in the gloom, indicated that there was still life in the city. People talked, if at all, in semiwhispers; and their quietness redoubled the mystery which — to an outsider — hung over their identity, their nocturnal movements, their reactions to this darkness — to this war.

On a streetcorner a woman emerged, walking toward me. She paused and said: "Shan't we go somewhere?" She spoke cheerfully and graciously, with none of the usual false intimations of tenderness. I suggested we go and have a drink. Oh no, she could not afford to waste time that way. Was I not interested in anything else? I confessed that I was not. But a few moments dickering resulted in a compromise whereby I agreed to pay the fee for the usual service and she to honor me with her company in a public "*Lokal*." So she led me to her favorite bar and there we settled down, I over a bad highball, she over a "half-and-half" and a new box of cigarettes.

In the lighted barroom I could see her clearly for the first time. She was still a young woman with a good figure and a fresh, firm face. Her clothes were in such good taste that one might almost have been deceived about her profession. She had been on the street, she told me, for several years — off and on. Just now she was only out for an hour or two each night, because she had a job during the daytime. She

packed parcels in a factory, for nineteen marks a week. It was hard;
it ruined your fingernails; but it was better than being in the labor
camp, and if she hadn't been wise and gotten a job in advance, that was
what would have happened to her.

The labor camp?

Yes, didn't I know? Some months ago they had rounded up all the
street girls and all the bar hostesses under thirty (the old ones could
stay) and had taken them away to a labor camp in the country. "There
were seventy-five of us on my corner alone, at one time, and we all
lived well. Now I'm the only one. We used to support this whole
section of town. The hairdressers and the tradespeople are desperate.
We were the best part of their trade, and the only ones who tipped
well. It's foolish to try to stop this sort of thing. It existed before the
war. It existed in the Stone Age. It always will exist."

"But the girls you work with in the daytime," I asked, "don't they
have any normal social life that you could share?"

"Those girls!" she snorted with contempt. "I have nothing in common with them. They are uneducated little beasts from Altona. They
live in a different world. I couldn't live the way they do. I have to
have money and culture. I never talk to them. They wonder where
I get my clothes. One week I even forgot to draw my pay."

"But you continue to run a risk in going on the street. Won't it end
up in the labor camp anyway?"

"Yes, there's a risk, all right. The other night I watched a cop haul
in two others. They were crossing the Jungfernstieg. He saw me too
and told me to stop. I ran all the way to the Café Vaterland and when
I got there I was still shaking so that I couldn't light a match. But I
won't have to keep it up much longer. You see, I'm engaged. My fiancé
is with the army. He's a flyer now. He's in Poland. When he comes
back, he'll marry me — perhaps. He says he will."

"Does he know what you do?"

"Good God, no! He'd be furious."

"Why do you keep on taking this risk, then?"

"Well, you see, when I first met him, I told him I had two thousand
marks. I didn't really, of course. Now I have to earn them before he
comes back."

"Don't be silly. Go to him and tell him about it. He'll pass it up."

"Oh, you don't know that man. He's terrible. He's a complete egoist.

He's used to having everything he wants. I don't dare peep. He never thinks of me. Sometimes I cook eggs for us in the morning: two for him and two for me. He eats them all. He never thinks about whether there's one left for me. He never asks me how I feel. He only loves me physically."

"Why do you stay with him? Do you love him?"

"Not the way he does me. He disgusts me. I lie there beside him and I hate him and I think to myself: 'The damn fool. He thinks he's beautiful, and yet he's just like any other man.' "

"But?"

"But I can't help it. He has me where he wants me. When he speaks to me, I am as little as that finger. I am as nothing. I sit at work and make up my mind to be firm with him, but when the phone rings and I hear his voice, I just say '*Ja*.'

"Once I tried to be firm with him. He left me money and told me to buy an umbrella. I told him: 'You go buy that umbrella yourself.' He got white in the face and stalked out. I took the money and went out and drank it all up. Next day he came back. 'Where's that umbrella?' 'There isn't any umbrella.' 'Where's the money?' 'It's here' [pointing to her stomach]. He went away again and he didn't come back. After two days I went right to the nightclub where he worked. He was as nice as sugar to me and he took me home. I said to him: 'You've been with another woman.' He said: 'No.' 'Your word of honor?' 'No.'

"I found the other woman. I told her he was married and not to dare ever set eyes on him again. And she didn't. But it makes no difference. There are plenty of others. And whenever I make him mad, he doesn't fight; he just goes with another woman. What can you do?

"We were so happy at first. You have no idea. We had an apartment. I bought the furniture for it. We had so much fun. We used to play that I was the bar hostess and he the guest, and I would serve him drinks and he would say: '*Gnädiges Fräulein*, may I seduce you?' And I took good care of him. No one could have taken better care of him than I did. I did everything for him. Women like me — we really *are* decent. Believe me, we are. We don't do any of the nasty things respectable women do. We don't blackmail men. We don't hound them. I know a woman who calls herself respectable. She has seven men. She spends every night with a different one, and swears to every one that she loves him. I couldn't do that. And all the women who don't take money but take flowers and candy and clothes and attention and flattery. They're the whores, not we. We're honest."

The curfew hour was approaching. I paid the bill and gave her her fee from the change. She pocketed it with silent dignity. We were good friends by this time.

Before we left, I said to her: "I'm afraid it's the labor camp for you after all, in the end."

She gave a sad little laugh, and said: "I know it." I saw her through the darkness to her apartment house, not far away. She unlocked the street door and turned on the dim blue light in the outer hall. We shook hands in farewell, and then she modestly turned one powdered cheek to me.

"You may kiss me, now," she said.

While I walked home, four great pencils of light from the searchlights to the north lazily followed a target plane across a black sky.

It was only after I got home it occurred to me that neither of us had mentioned the war.

It will be easily understood that in the face of such experiences it was hard for me, in the ensuing years, to go along with the devil-image American opinion invariably ascribes to its particular political opponent of the moment. It was hard to associate oneself with much of the American press and of Washington officialdom in picturing the German people as a mass of inhuman monsters, solidly behind Hitler and consumed with a demonic enthusiasm for the ruin and enslavement of the rest of Europe.

* * *

I must here record a small debt of gratitude and admiration to Alexander Kirk. A confirmed bachelor, profoundly saddened by the recent death of an adored mother who, while she was alive, had preempted much of both his companionship and his emotional life, Kirk drowned the inner emptiness in the performance of his arduous official duties. Such were the demands of wartime service that he spent sixteen to eighteen hours daily in his office, catching brief intervals of sleep in a little adjoining alcove. He was a carry-over from an older day when to be rich entitled you to be eccentric, and he made the most of the privilege. He kept, in the swank Grunewald district, an enormous mansion (selected, he always maintained, because it was the only house he could find in Berlin with *only one* red room), where he maintained a staff of Italian servants and in which he gave a large buffet luncheon every Sunday noon, as a means of revenging himself for such hospitality as his position required him to accept. But for himself food meant nothing; he saw no reason why you could not live exclusively on vitamin pills and concentrates, like an Arctic explorer, and nearly ruined his health trying to do so. He took a box at the opera for the season; and his only recreation, so far as we could observe, was to leave his office at some point during the evening, drive to the opera, slink into the back of the box for a portion of the performance, and leave again, unseen by the audience, before it was ended.

Deliberately, I think, as a gesture of defiance and self-protection, and in the indulgence of a fine sense of the theatrical, Kirk worked at giving himself the aspect of exactly that sort of American career diplomat of which the American philistine has always been most suspicious: elegant, overrefined, haughty, and remote. It was a manner of enlivening life by playing the buffoon. He was anything but an intellectual. He never wrote anything if he could help it. He was even suspicious of many of our efforts at interpretative reporting, discouraged them, and preferred that we make our points obliquely by a shrewdly selective coverage of the Nazi press. His understanding was intuitive rather than analytical. His conversation consisted largely of weary, allusive quips. His posing sometimes went so far as to raise doubts whether he was serious.

But behind this facade of urbane and even exaggerated sophistication there lay great intuitive shrewdness and a devastatingly critical sense of humor, directed to himself as well as others. No one impressed him. He treated the most pretentious women like sluts, and they glowed in response. He was seen, on one occasion, to greet an ebullient American butter-and-egg man by unctuously sticking out one fin and saying (who of my age could forget the "Kirk's soap" of the advertisements of our boyhood?): "My line's soap; what's yours?" He despised the Nazis and held them at arm's length with a barbed irony. Even at the height of their military successes, he declined to entertain for a second the possibility that they might win the war. "They have undertaken," he would insist, "something they cannot finish. They will find no stopping point. That is the cardinal sin: to start something you cannot finish."

I have realized, in subsequent years, that I learned much from Kirk — more, perhaps, than from any other chief. Unintellectual as he was, his instincts were very sound; and when one learned enough to see through the poses and to look for the deeper meaning of the quips, he was a good teacher. I am particularly indebted to him for the impressive lesson he gave me, by example even more than by precept, of the importance of the means as compared with the ends. The only thing worth living for, he once told me, was good form. He himself had little to live for; there were moments when he would have liked to leave this life; but suicide would be an abrupt act, and abruptness was the height of bad form. "Never, never, do anything abrupt," he advised me. "It never pays." He disclaimed all further interest in the Foreign Service, since his mother's death. He had entered it, he solemnly maintained, only to spare her having her bags inspected at frontiers. But he could not just resign, especially in wartime; that would have been abrupt. "When the war is over," he said, "I shall leave it so gradually and quietly that no one will know I am gone."

He did. After service as ambassador in Egypt and Italy, he sidled, quietly and unobserved, out of all of our lives. For many years, I had no word from him. It was rumored that he lived in solitude on a ranch somewhere in the Southwest. Someone even once gave it to me as his understanding that Kirk kept a table set in his dining room at all times as though for a smart diplomatic dinner; and that if you appeared there, as a self-invited guest, he would personally cook and serve you a meal, to the accompaniment of the usual la-de-da chatter, after which he would tell you how infinitely he regretted that the villa had no guest bedroom. This was no doubt apocryphal, but it was symptomatic of the somewhat exotic reputation he had.

Be that as it may, when he left Berlin, it may have been Kirk who was in my debt when it came to administration of the embassy, but it was I who was in his debt when it came to personal, and even political, philosophy.

* * *

In late February 1940 I was sent off to Italy to meet the Under Secretary of State, Mr. Sumner Welles, and his party on their arrival at Naples and to accompany them on their journey to Berlin. Mr. Welles had been dispatched by President Roosevelt to the four European capitals of Rome, Berlin, Paris, and London to ascertain the views of the leading European statesmen on the possibilities for the negotiation of an end to the hostilities and the establishment of a just and permanent European peace. Up to that time, it will be recalled, the western front had been inactive. It was clear that unless the war could be in some way terminated before the advent of spring, hostilities would begin in the west on a serious scale, and the struggle would assuredly develop into another great and tragic one, from which it would be unlikely that the United States could remain aloof. If there were the slightest possibility of averting this catastrophe, the President wanted to know about it before it was too late.

Since Mr. Welles's itinerary did not include the Soviet Union, it occurred to someone in Washington that it might be useful to him to have attached to his party on at least a portion of his trip one person versed in Soviet affairs, who could be present to answer any questions that might arise concerning the probable attitude and reactions of the Soviet government.

I thought at the time that there was a certain naïveté in the belief that anything was to be learned by such a visit, particularly from the Nazi leaders, which could not have been better ascertained through consultation of our regular diplomatic representatives on the spot. I doubt today that anything was developed in Mr. Welles's conversations with the leading statesmen (certainly nothing was in Berlin) that was not already well known to the embassies concerned. But this was FDR's way of doing business, and he was entitled to the indulgence, in this respect, of his own preferences.

Nothing, actually, came of my own assignment. Mr. Welles seemed unaware of my presence and evinced no interest in my views on Russia. So little did I enter into the ken of the party that on leaving Rome for Berlin they forgot me entirely. I learned of their departure only when I happened to see the cavalcade of official cars pass me on the street, late one evening, on its way to the station. I tore back to the hotel, packed, took off for the station, and arrived, breathless, just as the red carpet was being rolled up, only to find that there was no berth for me on the special car which housed the party.

I was not, in the circumstances, of much use to Mr. Welles. I doubt that this was any great loss to him or to the government. I had no answers — no hopeful answers, at any rate — to his questions, any more than anyone else did. I tried, while nursing a ghastly wartime cold in my hotel room in Rome, to set down on paper some views on the broader questions that interested him. I presented the paper to Pierrepont Moffat, chief of the Division of European Affairs, who accompanied him on his journey. I doubt that Moffat even read it himself, but he sent it back to me after a decent interval, and I have it today, a small though not greatly gratifying reminder of my outlook as of that moment.

I began by warning against putting too great a reliance on the differences between Hitler and the German people when it came to judging the prospects for war and peace. Some of the German people, I wrote, might have lost the edge of their enthusiasm under the pressure of wartime privation, others might have been shocked and estranged by the character of Hitler's regime. The fact remained that

the man is acting in the best traditions of German nationalism, and his conception of his own mission is perhaps clearer than that of his predecessors because it is uncomplicated by any sense of responsibility to European culture as a whole. The colossus is genuine; and it now stands defiant before the French and the British, unified and disciplined, armed with a destructive power never before seen in history, determined to dominate Europe or to carry the entire continent to a common destruction.

I then went on to examine the courses open to the British and the French:

They can, if they like, arrive at an armistice with Hitler. He would probably be glad enough to make such an arrangement at this time. He needs the breathing space in order to consolidate past gains. He needs time to develop the new sources of raw materials now open to him in Poland, in Slovakia, in Rumania, and in Russia. He needs time to extricate his Russian admirers from their ghastly folly in Finland. He needs time to rebuild his submarine fleet and to complete the hundreds of other armament tasks held before him in the Four Year Plan. Finally, he needs time to let the martial spirit die down in the Allied countries, to watch the effect of anticlimax on morale, to measure the cooling-off of the outlying parts of the empire, to see the demobilization of bewildered and frustrated troops on the other side, to let the impression sink in on the rest of Europe that the French and British were afraid to fight him.

He would probably be willing to pay for such an armistice by concessions with respect to the form of government in parts of Poland, in Bohemia and Moravia — possibly even in Austria. These concessions would have as little practical value as if he were to pay in the depreciated currencies of those three countries. To talk of a granting of "self-government" or of "political independence" for any of these territories is, so long as Germany is not thoroughly shattered, the purest nonsense. In Austria, the Nazi Party and the German army would continue to underlie the framework of whatever bogus government might be established. For Bohemia, bereft of its strategic frontiers, stripped of all war materials, and with vast quantities of its substance — of lands, industries, and financial resources — already passed into German ownership, any "independence" would be a mockery. Poland, humiliated, discouraged, and profoundly demoralized, would be quite incapable of reorganizing its national life at this moment on a reduced territory and in the face of two powerful, ruthless neighbors, and would have to be controlled and supported by one of them. The Nazi machine is a cog machine, and the cogs work only in one direction.

What sort of peace would Hitler hope to gain from such concessions? It would, I am afraid, be a state of peace very little different, as far as he is concerned, from the present state of war. The ultimate goal, the defeat of France and England, would not be lost sight of for an instant. There would be — and would need to be — no demobilization. Soldiers might be furloughed; they would not be demobilized. The Nazi system is built on the assumption that war, not peace, represents the normal condition of mankind.

I then proceeded to warn against the siren songs of the German conservatives (I had in mind Schacht and Papen) who held out the hope of overthrowing Hitler and setting up a government of "reasonable men," with whom one could "do business," if only the Allies would give them, in advance, assurances of good treatment that could be dangled before the German people to wean them from existing loyalties. I warned similarly against building hopes for peace around the known differences between Hitler and the army leaders: these differences, I thought, were tactical rather than strategic. I warned against the assumption that Hitler could be moved to restraint, and to the acceptance of peace, simply by economic pressures — by attempts to cut off Germany's raw materials. I argued, finally, against basing hopes for peace on the prospects for internal disintegration of the Nazi regime. The German state of the moment, I argued, was not an anachronism which tomorrow would sweep away.

If Germany had indeed set the clock back, as Edgar Mowrer claims, we could be happier, for there is hardly a stone on the continent of Europe which does not speak of the superiority of the past. But what has happened has been no setting back of the clock. Germany has simply been unified and thoroughly so. What Bonaparte and Napoleon III left undone in this direction, Versailles completed, and Hitler is now stamping out the last vestiges of particularism and class differences. That he is doing this by reducing everything to the lowest and most ugly common denominator is neither here nor there. German unity is a fact. Hitler may go but the unity will remain, and with it, barring outside interference, will remain — must remain — the jealousy, the uncertainty, the feeling of inferiority, the consequent lust to dominate Europe which are all that most Germans really have in common.

I saw, therefore, no virtue in a mere cessation of hostilities for its own sake. The further prosecution of the war would indeed be terrible; but if it resulted "in the reestablishment of Europe, however weakened, on a relatively sound political basis, no amount of sacrifice could be too great." If, on the other hand, it ended merely with a repetition of the mistakes of Versailles, then its further prosecution would be "not worth even those few lives that have already been lost." And I ended with a plea for a policy aimed at the eventual partition of Germany, at repair of the damage done by the rise of national states in Germany and Italy, at a return to the particularism of the eighteenth century — a return to the small kingdoms, the chocolate soldiers, the picturesque localisms of an earlier day.

I read this paper today with astonishment. Leaving aside the puerility of the nostalgic conclusion, it stands, for me, as a reminder of the subtle ways in which one's views gradually and imperceptibly change. I was to become, in later years, a strong partisan of the view that the Allies had missed a chance precisely by failing to deal with the German conservatives and the army leaders. And I came away from Germany, some two and a half years later, with quite different feelings about the German people — feelings that took more thoughtfully into account the true complexity of their historical experience and recognized the existence within them of elements whose positive qualities, including courage and humanity, defied all efforts at negative generalization.

My views on just these subjects were affected by something that occurred not long after the Welles visit. Kirk, when he left Germany in October 1940, turned over and entrusted personally to me the most delicate and valuable of his clandestine "contacts" among the German oppositionists. This was Count Helmuth von Moltke. A great-grandnephew of the famous nineteenth-century military leader, Moltke was then serving as a civilian legal aide to the German general staff.

It had been Kirk's custom to meet discreetly, from time to time, with Moltke for discussions of the general political situation. It was, in fact, largely from Moltke that he had derived his conviction that the war, all early German military triumphs notwithstanding, would end badly for Germany. Moltke, despite — or perhaps because of — his intimacy with the centers of military decision-taking on the German side, held strongly to this same view.

The meetings between the two men were not in themselves of any great impropriety. They involved no specific political deals or arrangements. Moltke, after all, had no popular following; he could speak for scarcely anyone besides himself. And nothing, God knows, could have been further from the thoughts of FDR or Cordell Hull than to authorize Kirk to have political dealings with the conservative German opposition. But meetings in wartime between anyone occupying so sensitive a position as that of Moltke, on the one hand, and the American chargé d'affaires, on the other, would scarcely have commended themselves to Moltke's military superiors, and much less to the Gestapo, unless Moltke had consented to serve as a decoy and informer — and nothing could have been more foreign to his nature. Hence the conspiratorial character of the meetings.

After Kirk's departure, I met several times, secretly and alone, with Moltke. I sought him out first, by prearrangement, in the blackout — in a little study-apartment which he kept over a garage in the center of the old residential district near the Tiergarten. Later, when the Russian campaign was on, he became for some reason bolder. He cheerfully came to lunch, one time, with my wife and myself. He once filled me with astonishment and consternation by walking into the American embassy in broad daylight and asking to see me. I received him immediately, took him out onto the balcony of the office, where traffic noises were likely to drown out the effectiveness of microphones, and asked him how he had dared to do this. Oh, he replied, the Gestapo would never believe that anyone coming this openly could be coming for anything other than a legitimate purpose.

A tall, handsome, sophisticated aristocrat, in every sense a man of the world, Moltke was also, at the same time, everything that by the logic of his official environment he might have been expected not to be: a man of profound religious faith and outstanding moral courage, an idealist, and a firm believer in democratic ideals. I found him, on that first occasion, immersed in a study of the *Federalist Papers* — to get ideas for the constitution of a future democratic Germany; and the picture of this scion of a famous Prussian military family, himself employed by the German general staff in the midst of a great world war, hiding himself away and turning, in all humility, to the works of some of the founding fathers of our own democracy for ideas as to how Germany might be led out of its existing corruption and bewilderment has never left me. I consider him, in fact, to have been the greatest person, morally, and the largest and most enlightened in his concepts, that I met on either side of the battle lines in the Second World War. Even at that time — in 1940 and 1941 — he had looked beyond the whole sordid arrogance and the apparent triumphs of the Hitler regime; he had seen through to the ultimate catastrophe and had put himself to the anguish of accepting it and accommodating himself to it inwardly, preparing himself — as he would eventually have liked to help prepare his people — for the necessity of starting all over again, albeit in defeat and humiliation, to erect a new national edifice on a new and better moral foundation.

I was particularly impressed by the extent to which Moltke had risen, in his agony, above the pettiness and primitivism of latter-day nationalism. "My own homeland of Silesia [where he had his estates] will go," he once told me, "to the Czechs or the Poles." (It did.) This was sad for him, he admitted, but it was not important. "For us," he was to write shortly thereafter to a friend in England, "Europe after the war is less a problem of frontiers and soldiers, of top-heavy organizations or grand plans. . . . Europe after the war is a question of how the picture of man can be reestablished in the breast of our fellow citizens." *

Moltke was not destined to survive the war. It was scarcely to be expected that he should. His opposition to the Nazi regime, never exactly a secret, became more flagrant and more irritating to the authorities as the war ran its course. Himself a Protestant, he defied

---

* *A German of the Resistance: The Last Letters of Count Helmuth James von Moltke,* p. 28. London: Oxford University Press, 1948.

the regime, for example, by giving refuge in his own home in Silesia to the local Catholic school and permitting it to carry on there after its own premises had been closed by the Gestapo. He was arrested and imprisoned, on relatively minor charges, before the abortive putsch of July 20, 1944. He was thus not formally involved in that disaster, being already in confinement when it occurred; but certain of those arrested in the July 20 affair were brought, under torture, as I understand it, to reveal more about him than the Gestapo had previously known. He was then tried by a Volksgericht and hung, at the Ploetzensee prison, in early 1945. With his death, to which he went bravely and movingly, the future Germany lost a great moral force.

I record all this because the image of this lonely, struggling man, one of the few genuine Protestant-Christian martyrs of our time, has remained for me over the intervening years a pillar of moral conscience and an unfailing source of political and intellectual inspiration.

Another man who opposed Hitler as best he could during the war and who, incidentally, befriended me at some risk to himself was Gottfried Bismarck, grandson of the great Chancellor, and governor at that time of the province of Brandenburg. In 1940 he and his wife invited me for a weekend to their country estate in West Prussia. I realized, on arrival there, that the invitation itself had been a source of considerable tension between him and the local Gestapo. It was clear that my presence as a guest at his home caused much indignation in local Nazi circles. Nevertheless, he invited me once again a year later — this time to spend the Christmas of 1941 with him and his family. I accepted. Pearl Harbor and the declaration of war intervened, and nothing came of it; but the invitation itself was a brave and defiant gesture. He and his wife Melanie were both arrested during the war, after my departure. He was condemned to death, but the execution was delayed, and the regime fell before it could be carried out. His wife, I was told, had the bones of her face broken in Gestapo beatings, but also survived. I visited them again after the war, at the old Chancellor's former estate, near Hamburg; but shortly after that the hazards of the highway completed what the Gestapo had failed to complete, and both were killed in a motor accident.

In the face of such experiences, I was shocked to realize, in talking with President Franklin Roosevelt later in the war, that he was one of the many people who could not easily distinguish World War II from World War I and still pictured the Prussian *Junkertum* as a mainstay of Hitler's power just as it had been, or had been reputed to be, the mainstay of the power of the Kaiser. Actually, Hitler found his main support in the lower middle class and to some extent in the nouveau riche. The older Prussian aristocracy was divided; but from its ranks came some of the most enlightened and courageous of all the internal opposition Hitler was ever to face.

The spring of 1940 brought, as everyone had expected, the activization of the war in the west. The greatest surprise was that it should have begun with the German attack on Denmark and Norway. We know today that the British themselves, toying as they did with the idea of an expeditionary force across northern Norway to Finland, and finally deciding to encroach on Norwegian neutrality themselves by mining the leads along the Norwegian coast, had a heavy responsibility for Hitler's decision to put the move on Scandinavia ahead of the campaign against the Low Countries and France. At the time, of course, all this was obscure. We in the Berlin embassy did, however, have a few days' warning of the attack against Norway. My wife and two small daughters were at that time with the family at Kristiansand. I was able to get them away and back to Germany just two days before the German warships shelled that town. This they did in the first hours of the surprise attack, the inhabitants being obliged to flee up into the snow-covered hills until the shelling was over. We kept the children in Berlin over the summer; but in early autumn, just before the inauguration of the British night bombing attacks on the city, I took Annelise and the children to Italy, and saw them all off, late one night, from a deserted dock in Genoa — the tear-stained faces peering wretchedly out at me from the thick glass of the portholes, at dock level. Wondering whether I would ever see them again, I made my way back through the false paradise of Switzerland to Berlin for the last year of duty there before our own entry into the war.

These spring campaigns widened greatly, of course, the area of German occupation in Europe. It fell to me, in the course of service in Berlin, to visit at one time or another practically all the occupied regions. I had already lived in occupied Bohemia. I had been to Danzig just after the German attack. I was dispatched to the Low Countries and France, on the heels of the invading German forces, to establish communication with such of our official personnel as had not been evacuated prior to the entry of the German troops. I saw the bombed-out area of Rotterdam while it was still smoking. I saw the eerily deserted Paris of June 1940 after the panicky flight of almost its entire population, surely one of the strangest and most unreal spectacles of modern times. Later that year, to my own surprise, the German government permitted me to pay a Christmas visit to my wife's family in Kristiansand, a journey which took me to occupied Denmark as well as to Oslo and the south of Norway.

These journeys were depressing experiences. In the face of the visible evidences of sweeping Nazi successes, there being no reason as yet to reckon with the likelihood of an armed conflict between Germany and Russia, and with our own Congress still strongly committed to a policy of neutrality, it was difficult to foresee anything else than a complete German military victory on the European continent. How hard it was, in these circumstances, to retain hope for any brighter future will perhaps be most clearly shown by the diary notes of one of these journeys to German-occupied Europe — in this case a visit paid to Holland very shortly after the German seizure of that country:

> The Hague, Friday,
> June 15, 1940

Rain — a misty English rain, smelling of spongy meadows and of the nearby sea — sifted down through the great lime trees onto the cobblestone streets of The Hague.

In the afternoon . . . I walked out to Scheveningen, getting thoroughly drenched in the process. A half a gale was blowing from the northwest and the great breakers were fighting their way in onto the sands in a melee of foam. The rainswept boardwalk was deserted; and out at sea, in those mine-infested waters, no vessels moved.

The electric railway station was dark and deserted. I was not sure at first that the trains were running. In the guardroom, a few German soldiers sat drinking beer, and an ugly waitress chucked one of them under the chin. On the train back to The Hague my only fellow passengers were four little schoolchildren who chattered cheerfully, impervious to the gray day, the rain-streaked windows, the deserted places, and all the ruin.

The train deposited us at a big station somewhere in the eastern part of the city. It took me nearly an hour to find my way back to the legation. The search led through miles of sober streets, across bridges, along quiet canals, through shady little squares. I watched the sturdy, impassive, stubborn people trundling their bicycles and pushing their barges. Their fidelity to habit and tradition was so strong that it seemed as though nothing could ever change them. But try as I might, I could see little but ruin and decline ahead for most of them. What could Germany give this country economically to replace her lost position as the center for a colonial empire, as a transit point for overseas trade? These provinces, like Norway and Denmark, lived largely off their overseas connections. They were Europe's windows to the outside world. But would a Europe dominated by Germany, confined to a continental, autarkic economic policy, deprived — at least in its northern sections — of all its colonial empires, a Europe which had killed the great economic vortex of England off its own coast — would such a Europe need much in the way of windows to the outside world? Rotterdam would remain as a transit harbor, yes. But that alone, together with the growing of some flowers and vegetables, would scarcely suffice to maintain the dense population and the high standard of living of these water-bound provinces.

One could only expect that to the spiritual misery attendant upon the destruction of a great culture and a great tradition there would be added the misery of foreign exploitation and economic decline, and that someday large parts of these Dutch cities, sinking back into the swamps from which they had been so proudly and so competently erected, would become merely a curiosity for the edification of future generations of German tourists and would perhaps help to give the latter a sense of appreciation — tardy and helpless appreciation — for the values their forefathers had so lightheartedly destroyed.

The Hague, Saturday,
June 16, 1940

I took another long walk this morning, only to hear a German military band playing on a square to a sizable audience of placid, politely applauding Dutchmen, and to see a place, only a block or two from the legation, where bombs had wiped out most of the inside of a city block.

In the afternoon, Elting* drove me around in his car. First we went over to a small nearby town, to see our consul at Rotterdam, who had his office and home destroyed in the bombing and had taken temporary quarters there. We found him at home, and had drinks with him. The room opened completely on one side, toward the garden. There the rain drizzled onto rich grass and a little weed-covered canal, and everything was very Dutch and very sad and peaceful. Across the canal, a stream of people passed on bicycles, and a beautiful copper beech shimmered in the rain.

From there we drove to Rotterdam. We came into town along a normal city street, with shops open, trams running, crowds of busy people on the sidewalks. Suddenly, with as little transition as though someone had performed the operation with a gigantic knife, the houses stopped and there began a wide open field of tumbled bricks and rubbish. Here and there a wall or even the gutted framework of a house remained, but in most places there was only a gray plain of devastation. The main streets leading through this great ruined area were left untouched. Trams and motor cars ran on them as usual, and the unfathomable Dutch wheeled along on their bicycles as though nothing unusual had occurred. At one of the main corners of the city, traffic was still fairly thick, but not a building was left standing anywhere near, and the impression gained was that it was a crossing out somewhere in the country, between fields that had been used as dumping grounds for debris and refuse.

Most striking of all, apart from the ghastly scope of the destruction (the number of houses destroyed must have run into thousands) was

---

* Howard Elting, Jr., career Foreign Service officer, then serving as secretary of legation at The Hague.

the utter absence of transitions. Where bombs had not fallen, everything seemed in perfect order. Where they had fallen, there was simply
nothing left at all. I saw a shop doing business and people living in a
house on one side of which there was a perfectly normal city scene
and on the other side of which, beginning right at the side of the house,
there stretched nothing but a desert of bleached, smoking debris, as far
as the eye could see. . . .

We drove back along the broad highway from Rotterdam to The
Hague, the highway on which the German transport planes had landed
on that first morning of the invasion. The hedges were damaged in
some spots, where the big machines had swung off the road to check
their momentum. At the entrance to the airport near The Hague a
crowd of Dutch people were leaning on their bicycles and staring
through the fence at some smoldering debris beside the gutted administration building. We too stopped to look, but an infuriated German air
force lieutenant screamed at the sentry to make the Americans move
on, and we obediently took our departure.

Sunday, June 17, 1940

Got up early in the morning to take a six o'clock train back to Berlin.
The five-hour trip across occupied Holland, in the dead hours of Sunday morning, was very dull indeed. It was still raining; the towns were
empty; one had a feeling of the world's being forsaken by everyone
but the cows. I read the German paper, pondered gloomily on the
propaganda patter about the "senseless resistance," and reflected that
if there were anything in this war that had made any sense to me at all,
it was the resistance that had produced the ruins of Rotterdam.

Under the stimulus of these experiences, the study of German
occupational policies, and of the efforts of the Germans to play the
role of a *Herrenvolk* throughout the remainder of Europe, became
something of a hobby for me, and a diversion from my administrative duties. Nobody else was studying it. The months spent in
Prague under German occupation had given me both an interest
and a basis for comparisons. I wrote, therefore, a number of volun-
tary reports on individual regions, and topped these off in the
spring of 1941 (at a time when we still scarcely dared to base hopes
on the maturing of a German-Soviet conflict) with a long report

analyzing the German occupational policies and experiences in general. (Long afterward, when I returned to Washington, I asked the man on the German desk in the State Department whether they had received this and whether it had been of any interest. The answer was: yes, they had received it, but it had been of no use because the discussion was not broken down by individual countries and therefore it could not be cut up and distributed to the "country desks" in the various Washington agencies. So no one had read it.)

I was driven, by this effort, to what was for me a surprising but significant conclusion. It was that even in the event of a complete military victory the Nazis would still face an essentially insoluble problem in the political organization and control of the other peoples of the continent. The main basis for this conclusion was the reflection that the Nazi ideology, based on nothing other than a glorification of the supposed virtues of the German people themselves, had no conceivable appeal to people, and especially young people, outside Germany itself; that it was bound, in fact, to be inadequate as a political basis even for puppet regimes set up under German encouragement and composed of people fully prepared, subjectively, to accept German guidance.

This realization first came to me as I listened, on the train going to Holland in June 1940, to a discussion between a German Nazi, a businessman, and a Dutch Nazi sympathizer — the latter, incidentally, an intelligent person. The Dutchman, I find recorded in my notes,

told the German of Dutch tradition and of the bourgeois conservatism of the Netherlands and pointed out regretfully how hard it would be to train Dutch youth, who had only a small country to fall back on and no great conquests to look forward to, to be National Socialists. As the train pulled into The Hague, I could not help remarking to him that he would indeed have a hard time creating a Dutch National Socialist movement: for either it would be truly Dutch, in which case it would be only an unsuccessful competition for the German movement, or it would be pan-Germanic, in which case all the values of Dutch nationalism would be sacrificed and the adherents, instead of being superior Dutchmen, would only become inferior Germans.

By the time my inquiries into German occupational policies were completed, I was persuaded that there was, from the German standpoint, no hopeful answer to the problem. The Germans were faced with a dilemma, either to try to remain permanently in military occupation of most of the remainder of Europe, something which was physically almost impossible and which would inevitably lead to the disaffection of large elements in their own military forces; or to accommodate themselves in some way to regimes differently inspired than their own — regimes which would pursue aims by no means identical, and at times even in conflict, with those of German national socialism. Had I known what difficulties were being created for Hitler, even at that time, by his Spanish, Italian, and Vichy-French associates, my conviction of the insolubleness of this dilemma would have been even stronger.

I stress this conclusion now because I realize that it had a marked effect later on my assessment of the prospects for political success of the Soviet leadership in its effort to play the part of an imperial power, dominating and guiding the behavior of other states, particularly in Eastern Europe. This problem could sometimes be solved, it seemed to me, when the subject nation was very much smaller than the master, or where it was geographically so placed as to render quixotic the very thought of any real and total independence. But when one was dealing with larger peoples, situated at some distance from the would-be metropolitan power, the same realities would eventually come into play as those that affected Hitler's effort to consolidate his power over German-occupied Europe. True, the Soviet leaders, in contrast to the Nazis, had an ideology that was universal in its pretensions and had therefore at least a theoretical chance of commending itself to other peoples. For this reason the full applicability of these realities to the Soviet case was less visible to me in the immediate postwar years than later, when it was clear that nationalism, rather than communism, was becoming the dominant political force throughout the Communist world. But more and more, beginning with this scrutiny of the German occupational problems in 1939-1941, I was brought to recognize the continued and undiminished relevance in the modern world of Gibbon's assertion that "there is nothing more contrary to nature than the attempt to hold in obedience distant provinces." Out of this grew my feeling that one must not be too frightened of those who aspire to world domination. No one people is great enough to establish a world hegemony. There are built-in impediments to the permanent exertion by any power of dominant influence in areas which it is unable to garrison and police, or at least to overshadow from positions of close proximity, by its own troops.

The summer of 1940 passed without the expected and dreaded invasion of Britain. By October 17 I was able to write to a friend in the department that while rumors were still current of some new military initiative even in the interval before winter, time was now short, and I could give them little credence:

Reports from many sources indicate a greater reserve in influential German circles with respect to the duration of the war, and it is surely not without significance that the *DAZ* [*Deutsche Allgemeine Zeitung*] felt called upon to reassure its readers last Sunday in a long editorial entitled "Winter" that Germany will have no difficulty in surviving another "long and indecisive war winter." *

In the American embassy at Berlin we were, as I see it now, slow to recognize that in Hitler's logic the inability to invade Britain would inevitably spell the necessity of invading Russia. I came close to the reasons for this in another passage of the same letter, but failed to draw the necessary conclusions:

It is difficult not to take notice of the varying degrees of enthusiasm with which German-Russian cooperation is discussed on the respective sides of the *Interessengrenze*. All the glowing references to this subject seem to come from Berlin; whereas the Russian expressions of opinion,

---

* It was about this time that the wit of the Berliners, fastening on the German war song "*Wir fahren, wir fahren, wir fahren gegen Engeland*" (We are marching, marching, marching against England) revised it in such a way as to make it read: "*Wir fahren, wir fahren, wir fahren schon seit Jahren, mit langen weissen Haaren, gegen Engeland*" (We are marching, marching, marching; we have for years been marching; with hair whitened by the passage of time we go on marching, against England).

as far as I see them, are marked by a very obvious dryness, and are interspersed with occasional sharp cracks of the Russian ruler over the German knuckles. It is quite evident that in at least one highly important field, namely Rumania, there has been no close collaboration and no marked confidence between the two governments. Questions of quality aside, the Rumanian frontier is one on which the Russians should be able to mass very formidable quantities of men and equipment and any [German] drive toward Greece and Turkey will have to take into account the disposition of these forces on its flank.

Had I only thought things through to the realization that the inability to crack the nut of Britain at the center would force Hitler to try to solve the problem by attacking Britain's Mediterranean lifeline through the Balkans, then I would have seen how precisely the consideration noted above would have impelled him to try to eliminate Soviet military strength in order to free his eastern flank for a concerted Mediterranean operation. But to complete the picture, I would also have had to know what I had then no means of knowing, namely with what blind stubbornness Molotov would insist, during his forthcoming visit to Berlin, on a complete Soviet military control of Bulgaria and on other desiderata only slightly less acceptable than this to German interests. We were aware that things did not go well in Molotov's talks with the German leaders; but none of us suspected that Stalin would so seriously overrate his own bargaining power as to make upon the Germans, as a price for Russia's collaboration in the wider war against Britain's world position, demands so greedy and extreme that they would convince Hitler he had no choice but to attempt to eliminate Russia as a factor in the world situation in order to get on with his principal job.

The situation was further obscured by the attack on Yugoslavia in the spring of 1941, a venture which was indeed of questionable strategic soundness and may, insofar as it delayed preparations for the attack on Russia, have cost Hitler the success of the Russian operation and, by the same token, the war itself. Small wonder, in these circumstances, that we failed to recognize the move against Yugoslavia as the prelude to an attack on Russia. As the spring wore on, however, other evidences began to accumulate of German preparations for action on a major scale in the east. We passed all these evidences on to Washington, which — as is now well known — tried in vain to warn Stalin. So when the news of the attack broke, on June 22, we were not taken entirely by surprise. It was clear to me, nevertheless, that the German attack represented a fundamental change in the situation with which our government was faced and called for new policy decisions of the most momentous and fateful nature. These decisions would involve nothing less than the formulation of a new policy toward Eastern and Central Europe — a policy more actively responsible and more far-reaching in its implications than any we had as yet found it necessary to formulate. At the end of the First World War we had, to be sure, incurred a certain responsibility by the part we took in setting up an independent Polish state and in sanctioning the breakup of the Austro-Hungarian Empire; but both of these things had been done in deference to the abstract and poorly thought through principle of self-determination, without regard to specific realities of power. We would now have to make up our minds as to whom, specifically, we would like to see exercise the dominant political influence in the eastern part of Europe in the aftermath of the war. To envisage as an aim of policy a continued Nazi control was unthinkable. But the spectacle of the Soviet Union as the latest victim of Nazi aggression would be bound to arouse uncritical sympathy and enthusiasm in American opinion. The first radio broadcasts from England and America in the hours following the German attack confirmed this. Would this sympathy not cause us to forget that, while Russia's immediate task would now be defensive, her long-term aims, in the event of victory, might not be exactly that? And would there not be a danger that we would end up, in this way, sponsoring Soviet policies toward Eastern Europe which we would someday come to regret?

With such thoughts in mind I sat down on June 24, two days after the launching of the German attack, and wrote a personal note to my friend Loy Henderson, then a deputy chief of the Division of European Affairs in the Department of State with particu-

lar responsibility for our relations with Russia and Eastern Europe.
(I kept no copy of it, but Loy was kind enough to send me back
the original some years later.) "I feel strongly," I wrote in this
letter,

that we should do nothing at home to make it appear that we are following the course Churchill seems to have entered upon in extending
moral support to the Russian cause in the present Russian-German
conflict.

It seems to me that to welcome Russia as an associate in the defense
of democracy would invite misunderstanding of our own position and
would lend to the German war effort a gratuitous and sorely needed
aura of morality. In following such a course I do not see how we could
help but identify ourselves with the Russian destruction of the Baltic
states, with the attack against Finnish independence, with the partitioning of Poland and Rumania, with the crushing of religion throughout
Eastern Europe, and with the domestic policy of a regime which is
widely feared and detested throughout this part of the world and the
methods of which are far from democratic. It is, I believe, no exaggera-
tion to say that in every border country concerned, from Scandinavia
— including Norway and Sweden — to the Black Sea, Russia is generally more feared than Germany. . . .

It is obvious that the Russian involvement in this struggle is not the
result of any concern for the principles underlying the Allied cause
and that Russia, despite its present involvement, has little desire to see
England emerge a real victor. Russia has tried unsuccessfully to purchase security by compromising with Germany and by encouraging
the direction of the German war effort toward the west. Throughout
the war the Moscow government has been most vehement in insisting
that its own policy was based on sheer self-interest and in expressing
its determination to do nothing to aid any warring power. It has thus
no claim on Western sympathies; and there is no reason apparent to me
why its present plight should not be viewed realistically at home as that
of one who has played a lone hand in a dangerous game and must now
alone take the moral consequences. Such a view would not preclude
the extension of material aid wherever called for by our own self-
interest. It would, however, preclude anything which might identify
us politically or ideologically with the Russian war effort. In short, it

seems to me that Soviet Russia could more soundly be regarded as a "fellow traveler" in the accepted Moscow sense, rather than as a political associate.

In this reaction, put forward nearly half a year before the United States entered the Second World War, there was embodied the essence of the disagreement that was to hold me in opposition to our governmental policy for some five years to come; hold me in opposition until the movement of the pendulum of official thinking from left to right would bring it close to my own outlook in the years 1946 to 1948, only to carry it away once more in the other direction, with the oversimplified and highly militarized view of the Russian problem that came to prevail after 1949.

The remaining months of 1941, down to Pearl Harbor, swim in my memory. I remember only a feeling that things were now out of control — not only out of *our* control (we, after all, in our poor overworked embassy, had never at any time had any influence on the course of events) but out of everyone's control. Day by day I followed, on a large map of Russia that hung on the wall of my office, the advance of Hitler's army across the great regions of forest and swamp to the west of Moscow, comparing it at every turn with the similar advance of Napoleon's army in the year 1812. (The similarities in timing and geography were often striking.)

As the German penetration into Russia proceeded, our own relations with the German government, never better than frigid at any time since the beginning of the war, continued to deteriorate. No one knew how the end would come. But many of us sensed it to be near.

The news of Pearl Harbor reached us, on that memorable December Sunday evening, in the faint signals of the shortwave radio news broadcasts from the United States. Happening to hear it myself, I aroused the chargé d'affaires (Mr. Leland Morris) and as many as I could of the other officers by telephone. We met in the embassy, late that night, to consider our course now that the end seemed near. Our country was now at war with Japan; and it was clear that this situation might at any moment develop into war with Germany.

For four days we lived in excruciating uncertainty as the Germans deliberated whether or not to support their Japanese associates by declaring war on the United States. One by one, during those four days, our channels of communication with the outside world ceased to function. Telegrams, even to our government, were no longer accepted at the telegraph office. By late Tuesday, our telephones mysteriously ceased to function. It became impossible to communicate with Washington or with anyone else. We were now on our own.

Realizing that we would look like fools if the declaration of war did not come, but also realizing that we would appear as worse than fools if it did come and we had failed to take this step, we burned our codes and our classified correspondence during the night from Tuesday to Wednesday. Finally, on Thursday, the announcement was made that Hitler was to speak in the Reichstag. As the hour for his speech approached, the square in front of the embassy filled up with sound trucks and mobs of people — to what purpose we were not sure. We closed the metal blinds on the windows on the ground floor and waited for the storm; but it failed to come. Instead, while Hitler was fulminating against us in the Reichstag, the telephone suddenly and mysteriously came to life — to admit a phone call from the Foreign Office saying that a car and an officer of the protocol section would arrive in a few moments to escort the chargé d'affaires to the presence of the foreign minister. The officer appeared almost instantaneously. I was obliged to receive and entertain him while we waited for the chargé to make his preparations; and a stiffer conversation has never transpired. Poor Morris was then hauled off to the Wilhelmstrasse — to be kept standing while Ribbentrop, striking ferocious attitudes, read out loud the declaration of war and then, after screaming at him: *"Ihr Präsident hat diesen Krieg gewollt; jetzt hat er ihn"* (Your President has wanted this war; now he has it), turned on his heel and stamped away.

Uncertain what to do with us, now that we were officially enemies, the Foreign Office decided to consult the Führer. He had evidently left, just after his speech, for field headquarters; and it took two days to get a reply. This, when it finally came on Saturday morning, was laconic, and packed with Hitlerian fury: "By the end of the week the Americans must be out of Berlin." I was accordingly summoned to the Foreign Office on Saturday afternoon and was told that all American embassy personnel would be required to liquidate their residential establishments forthwith and to report to the chancery, with not more than two pieces of hand luggage, at eight o'clock the following morning. This, over the course of a hectic and sleepless night, was in some way accomplished. At eight o'clock on Sunday, December 14, we assembled at the embassy, only to find the building, inside and out, already guarded by members of the Gestapo, and ourselves their prisoners.

Before that Sunday morning was over, we were taken in buses to the station, packed into two special trains, and sent away for five months of confinement, incommunicado, under armed guard and Gestapo supervision, in a building on the outskirts of Bad Nauheim, near Frankfurt. A few other American officials and journalists, picked up in other parts of Europe, were added to our company. The number eventually reached one hundred and thirty. Not until the end of April 1942 did the United States government bother to communicate with us, which it could easily have done through the Swiss. For knowledge of what plans, if any, were being made for our exchange and removal, we remained dependent over the winter on such crumbs of gossip or information as we could eke out of the Germans or the Swiss representatives who occasionally visited us.

During these five and a half months, I bore personally the immediate responsibility for disciplinary control of this motley group of hungry, cold, and worried prisoners, as well as for every aspect of their liaison with their German captors. Their cares, their quarrels, their jealousies, their complaints filled every moment of my waking day. The details of this ordeal would alone make a book. I shall not go into them here. The experience taught me something about the behavior of human beings in adversity: the untrustworthiness and failure of a minority at one end of the human spectrum; the rather passive response to leadership on the part of a majority in the middle; the extraordinary faithfulness, courage, and general excellence of a few. I came away with a new admiration for one portion of mankind, but a portion which, as I now recognized, would never be more than a minority. For the majority at the center, I felt a mixture of sympathy and solicitude. For the remainder, there was only horror and repulsion.

Particularly disillusioning were the endless complaints about food which I was compelled to receive, and of which I was often obliged, somewhat against my will, to make myself the spokesman in dealings with the Germans. It is true that we received only the German civilian rations, far less than those to which regular prisoners of war were entitled; also that we had none of the Red Cross parcels that the war prisoners normally received. We were, by consequence, appreciably less well fed than the prisoners were, and most of us were emaciated when we emerged from the experience. But we were not the only people in Europe who were hungry at that time, and more important things were at stake than the filling of our bellies.

We were sent out through Spain and Portugal, in mid-May, to be exchanged in Lisbon against a similar party of Germans. We accomplished the rail journey from Frankfurt to Lisbon in two special trains. In Spain, which we traversed at night, we found it necessary to lock the doors of the trains to keep the more exuberant members of our party (primarily the journalists) from disappearing into the crowded, chaotic stations in search of liquor and then getting left behind. I was myself in charge of the first of the trains, and was up all night trying to keep my unruly flock together. We reached the Portuguese frontier — our first breath of peace and normalcy — in the early morning, at a little mountain station. Ted Rousseau, then assistant naval attaché in Lisbon, now curator of the Department of Paintings at the Metropolitan Museum of Art, was there to meet us. Leaving my charges imprisoned in the train, I went out to greet him. After the usual politenesses, I inquired whether by any chance one could breakfast in the station. The an-

swer was affirmative. Thereupon I, who had been for five months
on the receiving end of the food complaints, took final revenge
upon my fellow internees by repairing to the station buffet and eating a breakfast of several eggs, leaving the rest of them to nurse their
empty bellies over the remaining six or seven hours of rail journey
before making themselves sick, as all of us did, on the rich fare of
Lisbon. As for myself, I whiled away those remaining hours in the
train by trying to compose a set of farewell verses to my companions of the last five months. I find among my papers the results of
this poetic effort; and I offer them here, as reminders of the atmosphere of the moment, explaining only that the structure in which
we had been housed at Bad Nauheim had been known, before its
wartime conversion to the status of a military hospital, as Jeschke's
Grand Hotel; and the little stream that flanks its walls was called,
most appropriately, the Usa. Here are the verses:

> *From you, embattled comrades in abstention,*
> *Compatriots to this or that degree,*
> *Who've shared with me the hardships of detention*
> *In Jeschke's Grand and guarded hostelry —*
>
> *From you, my doughty champions of the larder,*
> *Who've fought with such persistency and skill,*
> *Such mighty hearts, such overwhelming ardor,*
> *The uninspiring battle of the swill —*
>
> *From you, my friends, from your aggrieved digestions,*
> *From all the pangs of which you love to tell,*
> *Your dwindling flesh and your enraged intestines:*
> *Permit me now to take a fond farewell.*
>
> *For five long months you've slept and nursed your bellies,*
> *Or strolled along the Usa's quiet shores,*
> *Eaten your rolls and failed to eat your jellies,*
> *While others toiled and tramped and fought the wars.*
>
> *The world might choke in food-restricting measures;*
> *Chinese might starve; and Poles might waste away;*
> *But God forbid that you — my tender treasures —*
> *Should face the horrors of a meatless day.*

This, fortunately or otherwise, was as far as I got. The exercise was interrupted by arrival in Lisbon and by the experiencing, on my part, of an urgent need to go out and find a good restaurant.

Although the experience of this internment had not been pleasant, although it had in fact been considerably less pleasant than the bare facts recited above would suggest, the Department of State took little notice of it. When the department did finally take cognizance of our plight and consent to communicate with us by telegram for the first time, which was shortly before our departure and exchange, it did so only for the purpose of informing us that by decision of the comptroller general (which, we were allowed to infer, it was disinclined to challenge) none of us were to be paid for the months we had been in confinement: we had not, you see, been working. A second telegram (the only other word we ever received from Washington during our confinement) was to inform us that, contrary to the original intention to remove us all, half of us were to be left behind, in German custody, in order to free space on the exchange vessel for Jewish refugees. Why? Because individual Congressmen, anxious to please individual constituents, were interested in bringing these refugees to the United States, and this — although the refugees were not citizens — was more important than what happened to us. The department was obviously more concerned to relieve itself of congressional pressures than to worry about a group of its own employees, many with long and creditable records, whose fidelity to duty, and to duty in peculiarly difficult circumstances, had caused them to fall into enemy hands. Although Mr. Morris and I succeeded in warding off both of these particular blows, it will be understood that these were not exactly the greetings we had hoped for upon liberation from five months of imprisonment. The unpleasantness of the resulting impression was reinforced when, upon arrival at Lisbon, we found awaiting us telegrams curtly assigning some of our most valuable people to service on the Iberian peninsula, and telling them to go to work the following day. The department obviously had not the faintest idea of the condition, nervous and physical, in which these people found themselves, and had not bothered to use its imagination. Neither those particular orders nor the reception the rest of us received upon arrival in the United States were accompanied, so far as I can recall, with any expression of appreciation on the government's part either for the services we had performed in wartime Germany or for the rigors of confinement to which this service had led.

This was not the last time I was to have occasion, in the course of a wartime experience, to reflect on the obvious injustice of the approach of the government and large parts of our public to the men of the Foreign Service in time of war. In their relation to the draft, in particular, these men were placed in a position no one ought ever to have been asked to endure. They were specifically advised by their superiors in the State Department that they were more needed in the Foreign Service, where their experience and qualifications lay, than in the armed services, and that it was therefore desirable that they should apply for deferment from the draft call. The department itself, however, was unwilling to approach their draft boards and to request such deferment (to do this might, after all, have led to congressional criticism); therefore, it was suggested that the officers should do it themselves. Most of them did, and most were deferred. In many instances the work which they then proceeded to perform, so long as the war was on, was no less integrally a part of the war effort than was the service of men in uniform. Not only this, but in not a few cases the dangers and hardships of work in the Foreign Service in wartime proved little if any smaller than those to which a great many men in the armed services were subjected. All this did not save them, however, from constant reminders, and in many instances reproaches, about their civilian status. They were denied, in Allied countries, even those modest privileges and amenities that were available to the lowest ranks of armed forces personnel.* The American press repeatedly carried articles charging them, sometimes individually and by name, with being

---

* On service in London, later in the war, I had a male clerical assistant who had seen combat as a regular soldier in France during the First World War. He was denied access to the great military mess in Grosvenor House, only two blocks from our office, and had to seek his lunches alone in the greasy spoons along Oxford Street, on account of his present civilian status.

draft dodgers. On one occasion, later in the war, when I asked a chief of mission to grant leaves of absence for several obviously overworked and tired officers, the refusal was accompanied by the observation that they ought all to be in uniform, anyway. This observation cut to the heart, and I never forgot it. It did not apply to me personally. I was already too old to be subject to the draft, or indeed even to volunteer for service in the ranks. But looking over the complement of Foreign Service officers, at that post, it seemed to me that their wartime service compared not unfavorably with that of many men in uniform.

6

Portugal and the Azores

THE exchange vessel arrived in New York about the beginning of June 1942. I was fortunate enough to be given a long vacation over the midsummer. It was used for the happy adventure of seeking and finding the first home we ever owned — a large but neglected farmhouse in southern Pennsylvania — and installing ourselves in it.

In August I returned to the department for temporary duty. I was assigned to a desk in the Personnel Section. Here there was presented to me, for appropriate disposal, a heap of old files, odds and ends of one sort or another, which the others in the section did not know what to do with.

Earlier in the summer, before going on leave, I had handed to the assistant secretary for administration, Mr. Howland Shaw, two papers I had written during the internment, one on the project of a Foreign Service Academy, the other on the need for an immediate and drastic expansion of the corps of Foreign Service officers to meet the rapidly growing requirements of the wartime situation and the further needs that the postwar period was bound to bring. These two papers I now found, to my dismay, among the odds and ends that had been tossed at me to dispose of. I realized from the absence of markings on them that I was the only person in the Department of State destined to read them and to act responsibly on them. Sadly, I marked them both for the files; but I could not resist adding weakly, for the benefit of the files, the notation: "I find this a good idea."*

On the Friday before Labor Day weekend came orders to proceed at once — over the weekend, in fact — to Portugal to assume the duties of counselor of legation. This was to be my formal position and I was to have all the normal duties and responsibilities that went with it. But in addition to this I was asked, privately and informally, to take the lead in trying to straighten out the dreadful confusions which our various intelligence people had created, among themselves and with the British, in their efforts to insert themselves into the already seething cauldron of espionage and counterespionage that wartime Lisbon constituted. This last task I was, I believe, eventually able to accomplish to general satisfaction. The effort was not without the usual lurid byplay — sometimes (and usually) laughable, sometimes fantastic, sometimes hair-raising. But all this, too, belongs in a different sort of book, if in any at all; and I shall restrict myself here to another aspect of the year and a half's experience in Lisbon, namely, my own part in the effort of the United States government to obtain from the Portuguese government facilities in the archipelago of the Azores which would permit us to fly great numbers of land-based aircraft to Europe, via the Azores, for participation in the Normandy invasion.

The American minister at Lisbon in 1942 was a political appointee from Florida, Mr. Bert Fish,† a friend, reputedly, of Senator Claude Pepper. A small, rotund man with a head as bald then as my own was eventually to become, Mr. Fish seldom left his official residence in Lisbon. His appearances at the legation chancery were few and far between. He spent most of his days ensconced in an armchair in his bedroom, his feet on a pillow, listening to the broadcasts of the BBC and such other English-language channels as he

---

* The result of the failure to expand the Foreign Service at that time was that vast competing services had to be built up to meet the needs of the war and postwar periods. These were necessarily recruited and selected on wholly different and less rigorous standards. Later, of course, it became necessary to blanket their personnel into the Foreign Service, often at higher ranks, thus violating the entire principle of fair competition in entry and advancement.

† Bert Fish, 1875-1943; American minister at Lisbon, 1941-1943.

could pick up. I visited him every morning, brought him the day's batch of official papers and got his reactions and orders. I found him to be, despite his physical inactivity and apparent isolation, a shrewd and thoughtful observer of events, who kept up amazingly well both with happenings and personalities on the Lisbon scene. I was, as I soon learned, by no means the only person from whom he received visits and gathered the local gossip. And I must say that on the rare occasions when he entertained, he did so with much Southern charm and dignity, seldom forgetting a face or a name, taking a keen interest in every one of his guests.

All this was to the good; but I became increasingly concerned, as I got into the new job, over our obvious lack of political contact with the Portuguese government. So far as I could learn from the official files and from the memories of persons on the legation staff, at no time since the entry of the United States into the war had there taken place anything resembling a political discussion between the American minister and the Portuguese Prime Minister. At no time had we discussed with the Portuguese at a responsible level such things as the compatibility of our interests generally, in the face of the wartime situation, or the prospects for our postwar relationship. This struck me as not only unsatisfactory, but in some respects dangerous. The war and its consequences were bound, at some point, to require a clarification and a new definition of the Portuguese-American relationship. Portugal was still officially neutral, but clearly any drastic change in the fortunes of war (and such changes had to be expected one way or another, at a relatively early date) would immediately introduce problems for the solution of which some reasonable intimacy of understanding between ourselves and the Portuguese would be essential. In early 1943 I wrote a long dispatch to the department, recounting the history of the Anglo-Portuguese Alliance and showing why the scope of that most ancient and honorable of international engagements had now to be widened in such a way as to allow for the sharing, by the United States, in both the benefits and the responsibilities of the British side. I hoped in this way to stir Washington to an interest in the whole problem of relations with Portugal. But there was no reaction. I also pressed Mr. Fish to seek an interview — perhaps several of them — with Salazar on his own accord, even without instructions, and to see whether the two men could not arrive at some sort of a personal meeting of the minds which could provide a background for the inevitable future encounter between the interests of the two countries. But Mr. Fish could not be moved in this direction. He viewed Salazar with a wary respect. "Ah ain't goin' down there and get mah backsides kicked around," he told me on one occasion. "He's too smaht for me." And there the matter rested.

In June of 1943 I paid a brief visit to Washington, primarily to fetch back to Portugal with me a small daughter who had been left in school in Washington. During my absence Mr. Fish was suddenly taken ill and died. This meant that on return to Lisbon I immediately became chargé d'affaires, fully responsible — for the first time — for the conduct of what was now, by virtue of wartime circumstances, a major diplomatic mission.

My friend, Princeton classmate, and fellow Foreign Service officer W. W. Butterworth* was at that time conducting with great distinction, in the capacity of director general of the United States Commercial Corporation, the important economic warfare activities of our government on the Iberian peninsula. From him I learned, on returning to Lisbon, that negotiations had been undertaken in utmost secrecy between the British and the Portuguese for the acquisition by the British of military facilities in the Azores. The negotiations were just then being inaugurated by a British team which had come secretly to the Portuguese capital for this purpose. The use of the Azores, it appeared, was practically essential to the movement of land-based aircraft from North America to Britain in sufficient quantity to support a future landing on the continent.†

* W. Walton Butterworth, born 1903, Foreign Service officer and career ambassador; Assistant Secretary of State for Far Eastern Affairs, 1949-1950; ambassador in Sweden, 1950-1953; ambassador to European Coal and Steel Community, 1956-1962; ambassador to European Communities, 1958-1962; since 1962 ambassador in Canada.

† The American Joint Chiefs of Staff estimated at the time, as I later learned, that the movement to Europe via the Azores of the planes needed for the forth-

This secret British approach to the Portuguese was based, of course, on the provisions of the Anglo-Portuguese Alliance, and amounted in effect to its invocation by the British side. It was the second time that this had occurred in a century. In the First World War, just as in the Second, the Portuguese made it clear that while they themselves preferred to remain neutral and proposed to do so if the decision were left to them, they would not fail to come into the war if asked by the British to do so in the name of the alliance. For several hundred years Portuguese security had rested on the British interest in Portugal's independence and integrity which this venerable international contract brought to expression, and the Portuguese did not take it casually. Asked to honor it, in the First World War, they had done so unquestioningly. It was clear that they would do so again in the Second World War if the request were made to them in that way. But they were determined not to take the step *unless* the request were made to them in this way. And if they were to make military facilities available to Britain, then they wanted first to have detailed discussions of what the step might mean to Portugal and how she was to be protected from the various adverse consequences it might be expected to have. All this was under discussion in the secret talks with the Portuguese on which the British had then embarked.

As the summer went on the British in Lisbon loyally kept Butterworth and myself confidentially informed of the progress of their initiative. The negotiations were brought to a successful conclusion on August 17; and it was agreed that the entry of British forces onto certain of the islands of the archipelago, for the purpose of preparing the military bases, would begin on October 8.

The delicacy of this undertaking, and the need for utmost secrecy with regard to it in all preliminary stages of negotiation and initial landing of forces, was obvious. Had the Germans gotten

---

coming Normandy landings would effect a saving of approximately 51.5 million gallons of high octane aviation fuel, as well as releasing sizable numbers of transport aircraft and ground personnel that would otherwise have been tied up in the effort to move the planes by the less direct and more costly northern route. (*Foreign Relations of the United States, 1943, Europe*, Vol. II, pp. 547-548. Washington, D.C.: US Government Printing Office, 1964.)

wind of the negotiations they would, at the least, have come storming in with protests and threats against the Portuguese, who were after all still officially a neutral power; and at the worst they would have moved at once against Portugal in some way, probably with attacks against Portuguese shipping on the high seas, without even awaiting the results of their protests. In addition to this, the absence of suitable harbors at the places involved meant that the vessels of the initial British expeditionary force would have to lie, during certain of the unloading operations, in deep water offshore, where they would be sitting ducks for any German submarines to whose commanders their presence there might be known. For this reason the arrangement could be publicly revealed only four days *after* landing of the forces began. Meanwhile, it was of vital importance that there be no leaks of any sort.

Butterworth and I, concerned to do our part in assuring security, kept Washington informed only through top secret letters addressed to the Secretary of State in person. It was my hope that these letters would elicit something in the way of a reaction on Washington's part, if only to tell us that our government was aware of what the British were doing and to give us some guidance as to the attitude we should take toward the whole procedure. Obviously, the change in Portugal's relationship to the war which these preparations portended was one of greatest importance to American as well as British interests. It had a host of implications for the work of the official establishments which Butterworth and I headed. It was bound to have important effects, in particular, on our economic warfare policy toward Portugal — an area of policy in which our government, and Butterworth's corporation especially, was intimately involved. But not a word was received in reply or even in acknowledgment of our communications; and as the day for implementation of the British arrangement approached, I could only hope and assume that what the British were doing was the result (as indeed anything of this gravity should have been) of the most careful consultation and agreement between their government and ours.

Friday, October 8, was, I reiterate, the day on which the British

landings were to begin. Three days earlier, on Tuesday of that
week, I received a telegram from the Department of State, bearing
the highest security designation (as would indeed all further communications on this matter), and instructing me, if asked, *but only
if asked*, to give assurances to the Portuguese Prime Minister that
the United States was prepared to respect Portuguese sovereignty
in all Portuguese possessions. It was obvious that these assurances
stood in connection with the British landings.

What to make of this? "If asked," the message read. Well, I had
as yet received no such query. I therefore put the message in the
safe and waited.

Two days passed, bringing us to the crucial Friday on which the
British were to begin their landings. On arrival at the office Friday
morning, I found a message instructing me to go ahead and present
the assurances at once, without awaiting any query from the Portuguese. Very well. Off I went to the Foreign Office, to arrange an
interview with Dr. Salazar.

The chief of the American Section, Mr. Leitao, was suspicious
and reluctant to help. Salazar, he said, was out of town. He was not
expected back for some days. (Actually, he was at the Spanish
frontier, two hundred and fifty miles away, informing General
Franco of what was now taking place.) He could be asked to return only if some serious reason could be offered. Could I tell him,
Leitao, what I wished to see Dr. Salazar about? I could not. But I
gave him a hint. I recalled in my own mind that some months previously, on the occasion of the entry of our forces into North Africa,
Mr. Fish and I had been obliged to arouse the elderly Portuguese
President, General Antonio Oscar de Fragoso Carmona, in the wee
hours of the night in order to present to him similar assurances of
the intention of our government, in connection with the North African operation beginning in just those moments, to leave Portugal
strictly alone and to show every respect for her sovereignty. On
that occasion, too, the Foreign Office had been reluctant, at first, to
make the appointment. Then, too, they had wanted to be told what
it was all about, and we had been obliged to disappoint them. I now

reminded my Portuguese friend of that earlier occasion, and told him that the present request was not dissimilar.

This satisfied him. The telegraph wires were put to work at once. A few hours later I was notified that Salazar would return to Lisbon expressly to see me and would receive me at his private residence at 10 o'clock on Sunday morning.

About 9:30 Sunday morning, on my way to this appointment, I stopped at the legation chancery to pick up the necessary papers and to see if any further messages had come in. A top-priority message was indeed just arriving, and was in process of being decoded. The decoding was completed only a few minutes before ten. A glance at the message filled me with consternation. I was, it said, under no circumstances to present the assurances; nothing was to be done pending further instructions. No explanations were offered for this sudden decision.

What *was* I to do? I had persuaded the Prime Minister, the political leader of the country, to make a journey of two hundred and fifty miles, on a weekend, to see me. The appointment was now only five minutes off. I could not possibly cancel it at this late moment. Yet what could I say?

In black despair I made the short journey to the modest palace which Salazar used as a residence. Admitted to his presence, I confessed to him, miserably, that I had received instructions which made it unnecessary and difficult for me to take up with him the matter I had originally been instructed to see him about. But then, feeling that I simply had to do something to save the situation, I took a deep breath, pointed out to him that I was aware that no one on our side had at any time discussed with him the elements of Portuguese-American relationship in the light of the wartime situation, and proposed that we take advantage of the occasion to have just such a discussion. He, though visibly puzzled, asked me to go on. I sallied bravely forth with some views of my own on the common interest we had in the security of the Atlantic region. Soon we were embarked on a cautious but not unfruitful discussion of some of the more long-term aspects of our mutual relations. He was, when I left, mollified and not wholly displeased, but still very puzzled.

I returned to the legation and reported to Washington what I had done and why. But even this report failed to break Washington's baffling reticence. I was left to wonder why the assurances had been withheld. Was there, I wondered, a sudden disposition somewhere in Washington *not* to respect Portuguese sovereignty at this delicate moment, a disposition, perhaps, to seize something ourselves without even asking Portuguese permission? I did not like to think so, but could I be sure? I recalled that earlier in the war we in the legation had been obliged to intervene vigorously in Washington to prevent various eager beavers in General Donovan's OSS from developing plans for a revolt against Portuguese authority on the part of the inhabitants of the Azores, plans based — apparently — on the theory that Salazar was a dangerous Fascist and in league with the enemy.

All this was Sunday, October 10. Monday passed without incident, but also without further enlightenment. On Tuesday, the initial debarkation of British forces having been successfully accomplished, the news of the extension of military facilities in the islands to the British was made public. The excuse of the Portuguese for this departure from neutrality, vis-à-vis the Germans, was of course the Anglo-Portuguese Alliance. Nevertheless, the Germans naturally responded with a menacing diplomatic note, and for the remainder of the week the Portuguese trembled lest the Germans take some sort of military action against the Portuguese mainland or begin the sinking of Portuguese ships at sea.

The following Sunday morning, October 17, I again paid my Sunday morning visit to the office to check on the telegraphic correspondence. Once again, a top-priority message was coming in but it was a long one, this time, and took long to decode. With horror and stupefaction I read the sheets as they emerged from the code room. "The following instructions," the message began,

are given you by direction of the President, to be executed on October 18 or as soon thereafter as possible, if at such time no military action has been taken by Germany against Portugal.

You are aware [I was not, incidentally] that we have held in suspense certain negotiations in order to avoid interference with the negotiations leading up to the Anglo-Portuguese Agreement of August 17. Our negotiations were designed to make available for us certain facilities in the Azores for our Army and Navy. You are now directed to seek an interview with Dr. Salazar and to request the following facilities: . . .*

There then followed a list of facilities several times more pretentious than all that the British, even invoking their ancient alliance, had ever dreamed of requesting: a naval base, a seaplane base, bases for landbased aircraft on three different islands, cable and communications systems, observation posts, radar, facilities for accommodation of American naval vessels in each of the Azores ports with "unrestricted port facilities and shore accommodations for necessary personnel," etc. It was perfectly clear that facilities of these dimensions would simply sink the economy and administration of the islands under their own weight. The Portuguese share in what went on in the islands would, in the face of such an establishment, necessarily be reduced to secondary dimensions. The primitive economy of the islands would be debauched by the amount of outside money brought in and expended. The islanders themselves, heretofore self-respecting people, would inevitably be moved to abandon their humble farms and other pursuits and to embrace, for the superior remuneration involved, the status of servicing personnel for the bases. It was idle to pretend that this represented anything other than a virtual takeover of the islands by our armed forces for the duration of the war and the ruination of the culture and traditional mode of life of the inhabitants.

Salazar, I knew, was utterly unprepared for anything of this nature. The British had perhaps warned him (even this was not certain) that we would probably wish, at some point, to make use of the facilities they were obtaining; but they had, so far as I then knew or now know, never intimated that demands of this nature might be in the offing. He, in fact, considered that what he had conceded so reluctantly to the British represented the payment of the entire debt demanded on the strength of the Anglo-Portuguese

* *Ibid.*, pp. 554-556.

Alliance; and he was congratulating himself, no doubt, on having survived the greatest crisis of Portugal's relationship to the war without exposing his country to invasion or blockade. To permit the Americans now to seize in effect the entire archipelago of the Azores and to turn it into one great naval and air base would be to reopen the whole question of Portugal's wartime relations with Germany, and to do so over an issue far less defensible, from the Portuguese standpoint, than the deal with the British. This time Salazar would have no Anglo-Portuguese Alliance, far predating the issues of this particular war, to use as an excuse. To accept such demands would unquestionably involve the complete abandonment of Portugal's nominal neutrality, which Salazar had worked so hard to preserve and which, as he understood it, the Allies desired him to preserve. The effect on Spain, with whose leader he had just been talking, would also be incalculable. It might, who could tell, tip the Spaniards into the war on the German side and jeopardize Portugal's independent position on the Iberian peninsula.

In addition to this, there was the matter of our guarantee of Portuguese sovereignty. Salazar was surely now aware (the British must have told him) that this was being withheld. This would mean, in his eyes, that he was being asked to deal under the threat: "Either give us these facilities at once or we shall seize them."

And suppose, I had to ask myself, we did force his hand. What would he then do? Obviously he would turn to the British — turn to them in the name of precisely that same alliance which Portugal had just honored, honored at British request for the second time in one century, and honored at considerable risk to herself. He would turn to the British and say: "We have just honored this alliance. Are you prepared to do so? Is your honor and your fidelity to the oldest of your engagements less than ours? If not, you will now please protect us from the Americans." To Churchill, with his strong sense of history and tradition, this would have been of powerful appeal.

I took the message over to the British ambassador, Sir Ronald Hugh Campbell, an experienced colleague with whom I had been able at all times to collaborate effectively and happily. He, too, paled when he read it. It was obvious to us both that we were in the face of a major and dangerous misunderstanding between our two governments.

What, again, was I to do? The instruction had come to me "by direction of the President." The President's orders were not normally to be trifled with, particularly not orders on military matters in wartime. Yet to execute it could and probably would, only too obviously, open Pandora's box.

I slept on the problem. The next day I wired Washington. I was, I said, reluctant to enter into a discussion with the department, or to ask the department to do so with the President, over an order given me by the President. Yet there were in my opinion compelling reasons why we should not take this course. Would the department, instead of requiring me to proceed at once with the execution of the instruction, not permit me "to return immediately to Washington and to explain, if necessary, personally to the President the reasons for my views." I had asked the British, I added, to make no comment of their own to Washington before I had opportunity to present my views, because I had "no desire to evade the direct responsibility which I bear for the execution of these orders."* But I did wish to remonstrate.

For two days it was now my turn to tremble. Then the reply came. The President saw no reason for my return to Washington; he wished me to cable my views.

I sat down and drew up a long message, reciting the various reasons why such an approach to the Portuguese could have no good effect and why it might have a number of bad ones. I pointed out in particular that I had no *quid pro quo* to offer the Portuguese for the abandonment of their neutrality; the British had already bargained away, in order to obtain their facilities in the Azores, all the trump cards of the Allied side relating to economic warfare measures and problems of supply, shipping, etc. These cards were no longer in our hands. Then, realizing that it would be unwise to confront Washington simply with negative views, I outlined the man-

---

* These citations from the official correspondence, and the ones that follow, are from *ibid.*, pp. 556-562.

ner in which I thought we could obtain Portuguese consent to our use of the facilities already granted to the British.

The answer, which came promptly, filled me with joy and relief. The President desired, it was said, to leave to my "judgment and discretion the manner of approach to these negotiations and the extent to which our desiderata should be presented to Dr. Salazar." I should just bear in mind that the need for the facilities was imperative and urgent. The department, however, did take issue with the argument I had advanced to the effect that I had no *quid pro quo* to offer to the Portuguese for such concessions. I had, the department considered, a number of such *quid pro quo*'s. "First among these in importance is the assurance to respect the sovereignty of Portugal and its entire colonial empire, assurances that have thus far been withheld."

This last disturbed me. Did it mean that the assurances would not be granted until the Portuguese came across with satisfactory concessions? I doubted that Dr. Salazar would even consent to discuss the matter with such a threat hanging over his head. I asked Butterworth, who had had rich experience in dealing with the Portuguese, what he thought Salazar would do if asked to negotiate under these conditions. "In my opinion," Butterworth replied, "Salazar would say, 'If I have brought my country to such a pass that we can conduct our foreign relations only under blackmail, then I am not a fit person to guide the destinies of this country'; and he would then pick up his hat and leave the position of the premiership."

This made a great deal of sense; but I had, this time, no choice. Once more I got into touch with the Foreign Office and asked for an appointment with the Prime Minister. Now, however, the reaction was somewhat different. There came a phone call asking me to call on the ranking permanent official of the Foreign Office, the venerable and experienced secretary general, Dr. Luis Teixeira de Sampayo. Sampayo received me kindly but went right to the point. He reminded me of what had occurred the preceding Sunday, when I had had the first appointment. He knew, he said, that I had originally intended to talk to Dr. Salazar about something in the nature of a guarantee of Portuguese sovereignty, but I had then, pursuant to instructions from my government, refrained from speaking about this. Now, I was asking for an appointment again. The Portuguese were puzzled. They would like to know where matters stood with this question of the guarantee. The inference was clear: no assurances, no appointment with Dr. Salazar.

Once again the agony was acute. I was under specific instructions not to give the assurances at this time. Yet it was clear that without giving them, I would not even gain access to the Prime Minister. And the need for the facilities, I had been told, was "imperative and urgent." There was no time for deliberation. I knew that if I even showed signs of hesitation or uncertainty, real damage could be done. I decided to take the risk. "Oh, that," I said. Yes, it was quite true: we *had* been on the point of extending such assurances. But then it had occurred to us that it might be embarrassing to the Portuguese if assurances of this nature were forthcoming from *us*, a third party, just at the moment when the Portuguese government was trying to stress publicly that its departure from a strict neutrality had been undertaken only in deference to the alliance with the British. If, I went on, there was no such feeling, and if I would not be embarrassing the Portuguese government by doing so, I would be glad to return to my legation, to have the assurances written up, and to present them before the day was out. Dr. Sampayo, looking much relieved, said he wished I would do just that.

I returned to the legation chancery. It was late Saturday afternoon. My secretary had left for the day. I sat down and typed out myself, in direct violation of the written orders I had in my safe, a communication assuring the Portuguese government that "in connection with the agreement recently concluded between Portugal and Great Britain the United States of America undertakes to respect Portuguese sovereignty in all Portuguese colonies." Having dispatched this communication to the Foreign Office, I sent off a wire to Washington explaining in detail what I had done, and why.

The following day, Sunday, October 24, I was informed that Salazar would receive me on the forthcoming Wednesday. I immediately began to prepare for the interview. But it was not to be — at least not then. Before the interview could take place, another telegram arrived from Washington. It contained no word of comment on what I had reported about the guarantee. It instructed me, simply and ominously, to take the next plane for the United States.

The air journey from Portugal to the east coast of the United States was performed in those days by what was left (some of them had been turned over to the British for the duration of the war) of Pan American's fleet of great Boeing seaplanes — the original "Pan American Clippers." These few planes (I believe there were at one time only nine of them) constituted the only civilian air link between North America and Europe. With heroic efficiency Pan American Airways kept them moving constantly around the shores of the North Atlantic on a circuit of some fourteen thousand miles. The planes were not normally capable of flying the Atlantic westbound, so the voyage from Lisbon to New York went via Africa, the east coast of South America, the Caribbean, and Bermuda. The trip took five days and nights. The crew was changed three times, but the same little group of passengers sat there day and night, getting off every few hours at refueling stops. The temperature at these stops varied wildly — in winter as much as one hundred degrees between certain of the African and South American stops and New York. I made the journey twice; and I felt each time, at the end of it, as I imagine one might feel after some sort of five-day debauch: unnerved, overtired, jittery, not myself.

I spent the wearing hours and days of this particular journey trying to comfort myself over what seemed a probable personal catastrophe. I had, after all, simply done my best. As a civilian I could probably not, I reflected, be court-martialed.*

On arrival in New York I took a train for Washington. Getting in there late in the day, I at once phoned to the chief of the European Division, Mr. Harrison Freeman (Doc) Matthews.† He gave

---

* There were, I was told some years later, those in military circles who seriously insisted that I ought to be hanged.

† Harrison Freeman Matthews, career Foreign Service officer; chief of the European Division of the Department of State from August 1943; later ambassador to the Netherlands, to Sweden, and to Austria.

me no explanations but told me to be in his office the next morning at eight-fifteen.

I showed up the following morning, still jittery from the long, sleepless journey. Nothing yet was said to me to explain my recall; indeed, there were no explanations of any sort. We simply got into a car and were driven to the Pentagon. There we were joined by the Under Secretary of State, Mr. Edward R. Stettinius, Jr. He had just assumed — three days earlier, if my memory is correct — the functions of Acting Secretary of State, in the absence of Mr. Cordell Hull. Even the position of Under Secretary was one which he, being without previous diplomatic experience, had clothed for only about one month. In these circumstances it was not surprising that his familiarity with this complicated matter was something less than complete.

After a delay of a few minutes, during which we spoke only trivialities, the three of us were ushered into a large room which, I soon realized, could only be the office of the Secretary of War, Mr. Henry Stimson. The Secretary himself, easily recognizable from his photographs, occupied the main desk. There were many other people in the room, mostly people in uniform. I was able to recognize the Secretary of the Navy, Mr. Frank Knox, and General George Marshall. The Joint Chiefs of Staff, I believe, were there in full; and it was clear from the insignia that a number of others were officers of very high rank. This was, in other words, as impressive a gathering of the top military command of the country as could conceivably have been assembled at that moment. I was, however, introduced to no one, not even to the Secretary of War; and I had no official knowledge of who any of them were.

The three of us civilians took seats side by side, like prisoners in a dock, along a side wall of the room. There then followed a morning I shall always remember for its sheer horror. It may be recalled that through this entire affair, from the day the British first spoke to us about their intention to undertake negotiations with the Portuguese over the Azores to the moment of my arrival in this room, I had not been given the slightest word of guidance from my own government, with the single exception of the department's brief comment about the *quid pro quo*. I had been told nothing about our calculations or intentions. Nothing had been said to me to explain the fantastic list of facilities in the Azores we wished to acquire. Not one word of background had been offered about our government's dealings with the British on this subject, although it was obvious that extensive exchanges must have taken place. I had not been told why I had been called home or to what purpose I had been summoned into this illustrious company.

Considerable time was taken up while maps were procured for the Secretary of War and various features on them were pointed out to him by people at his elbow. Then followed prolonged palaver among the military about various messages and communications. These last were referred to by number and by the complicated groups of initials to which the military are addicted, and the discussion meant nothing to me. Only after that did there ensue a general discussion, and even then a good part of it, in view of my total lack of background, went over my head. Finally the point was reached where the question was put to me: why had I thought it unwise to go ahead with our demands? Assuming they were familiar with the message in which I had explained all this, I merely recapitulated the headings of the main arguments. (I was later told that, owing to a mix-up in communications, they had never seen that message; but no one explained this at the time.) I then gave it once more as my view that it would probably be possible for us to obtain permission to make use of the airfield the British were already putting into shape. "What field was that?" came the challenge. "The Lagens field, on Terceira Island," I replied. "Hell," bellowed a gentleman whom I thought I recognized as the chief of the Air Force — General Henry H. (Hap) Arnold — "that's nothing but a goddam swamp." There was such finality in this declaration that I cannot recall even arguing the point, though my impression was a wholly different one.* (Actually regular use of the field by Amer-

* See account of President's meeting with the Joint Chiefs of Staff November 18, 1943, on the USS *Iowa* en route to the Cairo and Tehran Conferences (*Foreign Relations of the United States. The Conferences at Cairo and Tehran, 1943*, p. 260. Washington, D.C.: US Government Printing Office, 1961). Fleet Admiral Ernest J. King, then naval member of the Joint Chiefs of Staff, is recorded as ob-

ican transport aircraft began exactly three weeks after this discussion.)

The discussion was by this time becoming acrid. It was as confusing, I suspect, for the Secretary of War as it was for me. He, in any case, finally turned to Mr. Stettinius and, giving a nod in my direction, asked: "Who is this young man?" Stettinius turned to Matthews for help, and after a moment of whispered prompting, vouchsafed that it was our chargé d'affaires in Lisbon, Mr. Kennan. "Our what?" inquired Mr. Stimson. It was explained that the minister had died and I had been left in charge. "Well," said the Secretary of War, with the air of one who finally sees a ray of light at the end of a dark tunnel, "I think it's high time that we had a full-fledged ambassador who could give proper attention to our affairs at this important post. Will you see to that, Mr. Secretary?" Mr. Stettinius told Matthews to make a note of it, and then, turning to me, he said, "I think you may go, now."

Miserably, I slunk away, allowed myself to be escorted once more through the endless corridors of the building, and was soon released into the fresh air and the normality of the great spaces around the Pentagon. I taxied, out of force of habit, back to the region of the old State Department. There, having no official home within the building and knowing no one else to talk to, I walked around for a time and then lunched in one of the little restaurants along 17th Street. As I sat there over my lunch, indignation mounted. It was not only the unfairness involved in asking anyone, chargé or ambassador or what you will, to handle a delicate, complicated, and vital matter of this sort without a single word of guidance or briefing. What stung still more was the realization that these various people, for all their lofty rank and enormous power, were unquestionably wrong. I knew more about Portugal, and about the ins and outs of this situation, than any of them did. I could only assume, from the nature of the questioning and from the manner of my dismissal, that they had in some way succeeded in dissuading the President from his intention to let me play this

serving on this occasion that "the airfields in the Azores were much better than had been expected."

my own way, and that they were proposing to go ahead and place upon the Portuguese, through a newly appointed ambassador, the demands against which I had already remonstrated. I knew that this was not only unnecessary but was fraught with danger of serious complications both as between the British and ourselves and in its effect on the relationship of the Iberian peninsula as a whole to the war. I resolved then that if I was to go down, I would go down fighting. So I went back to the Department of State and sought out Matthews, now returned from the Pentagon. I could not, I said, just leave it at that. Where could I turn? He suggested Admiral William D. Leahy, the President's chief of staff. I readily assented. He called up the admiral and arranged for me to be received at once.

Admiral Leahy listened patiently, and I believe with some astonishment, to what I had to say. He told me that the man I should see was Harry Hopkins, and arranged for me to be taken at once to Hopkins's office. Hopkins lost no time on politenesses or pleasantries. For the better part of an hour he paced up and down and cross-questioned me as though I were a suspected criminal. The questions were sharp, skeptical, and menacing in tone. I realized that if I failed to pass this test, things would not go well with me. When he had asked his fill of questions, he pondered a brief moment and then asked: "Where are you staying?" I told him. "You go back there," he said, "and don't let yourself get out of reach of the telephone." Shortly after I arrived at the home where I was a guest, the telephone rang. It was Hopkins, instructing me to return at once to the White House. This time I was taken through a different set of corridors, asked to pass through a different door, and found myself, to my consternation but also to my relief, alone in a room with the President of the United States.

FDR waved me jovially to a seat at the other side of his great desk. There was no need for me to repeat my story to him. Hopkins had already briefed him. He asked me no questions but set out at once to give me his own thoughts. He failed to understand, he said, how Salazar could possibly suspect that he, Franklin Roosevelt, would not see to it that we evacuated and returned to the Portuguese in good shape, when the war was over, any facilities we might be permitted temporarily to use in the islands. Why, had he not, as Under Secretary of the Navy during the First World War, personally supervised the dismantling of the naval bases we had had on two of the Azores islands at that time? His face lit up. "I'll tell you what I'll do," he said. "You come back here tomorrow morning and I'll give you a personal letter which you can take back to Portugal and present to Dr. Salazar; and then you just go ahead and do the best you can."

I replied that I could think of nothing better; but I wondered whether there wasn't some misunderstanding here. I had the impression, from the morning I spent in the Pentagon, that people there were proposing to follow an entirely different course.

"Oh, don't worry," said the President with a debonair wave of his cigarette holder, "about all those *people* over there" (having in mind, of course, no less than the Secretaries of War and Navy and the Joint Chiefs of Staff — in short, the entire high command of the American armed forces in wartime).

No injunction could have been more pleasing to my ears. As puzzled as ever, but feeling that my position was now impregnable, I happily picked up his letter the following morning and made my return to Portugal. I at once sought and obtained an interview with Salazar. Even with the President's letter to support me, it was not easy to overcome his reservations and suspicions. He was — and still is, I am sure — a man of principle, and he wanted to get things straight. He began the interview by saying that he had been called a fascist by the American press, and wanted to know what was our definition of a fascist. But these questions were talked out; and I was soon able to report that he was not only prepared to permit us to make liberal use of the facilities granted to the British in the Azores, if appearances were kept up in certain respects, but that he was even not disinclined to permit Pan American Airways to construct — albeit for the account of the Portuguese government — a second airport there, which we could eventually use on favorable terms.

The back of the problem had now been broken, and from this

time on the entire project went forward successfully — but not for long with *my* participation. The wheels of the Washington bureaucracy had continued to revolve in their relentless way, President or no President. Just as I was having the first of the interviews with Salazar about the bases, there arrived on the Lisbon scene the new chief of mission whom Mr. Stimson had asked Mr. Stettinius to have appointed — in the person of a career diplomat: Mr. Henry Norweb. I liked and respected Mr. Norweb. I would, in normal circumstances, have enjoyed serving under him. But by this time the whole subject of the facilities on the Azores was so much "my baby" that it was obvious to us all — to him, to the department, and to myself — that it would be easier for him to take over and to carry forward the responsibility for this matter if I were not around. I was therefore summoned home and reassigned before the negotiations over the Azores were fully completed.

Much of the documentation relating to this episode has now been published in the *Foreign Relations* series.[*] In many instances the respective documents came to my attention in this way for the first time. For anyone familiar with the details of my own experience, they go fairly far to explain the background. No one reading just these documents, however, would ever suspect how the whole episode appeared at the time to the American chargé d'affaires in Lisbon whose name occasionally appears in their pages. This is one of my reasons for telling this tale.

I have subsequently learned (it does not even appear in the documents) that my sudden recall to Washington had nothing to do with the guarantee. The suggestion came from someone in the Pentagon who had received my first message, in which I objected to placing on the Portuguese the demands in question and offered to come home and face the President, but had not seen the subsequent one in which I stated my reasons for opposing the demands; nor, apparently, had he seen the President's reply, authorizing me to go ahead and negotiate after my own fashion. And the Department of

[*] *Foreign Relations of the United States, 1943, Europe,* Vol. II, pp. 527-576. Washington, D.C.: US Government Printing Office, 1964.

State, regarding its role at that time as nothing more than that of a messenger boy for the Pentagon and accustomed to sneezing whenever the Pentagon caught cold, had faithfully implemented the suggestion for my recall, not bothering to inquire into the misunderstanding and apparently indifferent to the fact that yanking me home in this way and at this time seriously interfered with the whole course of the negotiations. As for the guarantee, the suggestion of withholding it had come, it seems, from Ambassador John Winant in London, who thought the withholding of it could be a means of putting pressure on the Portuguese; the department, again unwilling to take any independent initiative or responsibility, had simply passed it along, heedless of the effect. There was apparently no objection in Washington to my extending the assurances at my discretion; but no one had bothered to tell me this.

There was a brief epilogue to this incident which must also be recorded. On the day when I picked up the President's letter, I took occasion, before leaving Washington, to call on Matthews at his office in the State Department to say good-bye. He was out of the room when I arrived, and I was asked by his secretary to make myself at home and wait. I seated myself back in the shadows, at the rear of the room, on one of the black leather sofas which were standard equipment in the old State, War, and Navy Building. Just as Matthews was reentering the room, the Acting Secretary of State, Mr. Stettinius, who had been accompanying him down along the hall, also put his head in the door for a moment, and, not seeing me, said substantially the following: "By the way, Doc, the Portuguese ambassador was just in to see me. He thanked me for some damn guarantee, and said that he always knew we would want facilities in the Azores. Now what in the name of hell did he mean by that?"

7

The European Advisory Commission

THE assignment that followed on this tour of duty in Portugal was to the embassy at London. There I was to serve, with the rank of counselor of embassy, as political advisor to Ambassador John G. Winant in his capacity as American delegate to the newly established European Advisory Commission.

The decision to set up the European Advisory Commission had been taken at the meeting of the three foreign ministers — British, Russian, and American — which took place in Moscow in October 1943. The suggestion came from the British, who originally envisaged the body, in the words of Lord Strang, as "an advisory organ which would serve as a clearinghouse for any European problems of common interest connected with the war (other than those relating to military operations). . . ." * This concept, however, was considerably too wide for American tastes. It conflicted, in particular, with FDR's aversion to anything that might commit him in advance, or restrict his freedom of action, with respect to the postwar settlement in Europe — a matter which he recognized as having domestic-political as well as foreign-political implications for this country. The President would obviously have preferred, in fact, that there be no such commission at all; but the very reasonable desire of the State Department to get on with *some* sort of preparations for a joint Allied approach to the problems of the German surrender and the immediate post-surrender treatment of Germany,

* Lord Strang, *Home and Abroad*, p. 202. London: Andre Deutsch, Ltd., 1956.

problems which were taking on a new urgency as the time for the invasion of the continent drew nearer, evidently had sufficient force to compel his very reluctant assent to the establishment of the commission. Secretary of State Cordell Hull did insist, however, in deference to the President's feelings, and probably his own as well, on a considerable narrowing of the body's charter over that which the British had envisaged; refusing to permit it to occupy itself with anything at all beyond the problems of surrender terms, zones of occupation, and machinery for the enforcement of the surrender terms. Even this modest measure of activity on the commission's part met, as we shall presently see, with a resistance violent almost to the point of insubordination at the hands of the Civil Affairs Division at the United States War Department.

The commission was set up in London at the turn of the years 1943 and 1944. The United States government, instead of appointing a special representative who could have concentrated on this work, named as its delegate Mr. Winant, who, as ambassador in London, had a host of other duties, and in whose harried official life the commission could figure only as a secondary and not always welcome diversion. The Soviet government followed suit, similarly naming its ambassador in London as its delegate. The British, on the other hand, appointed one of the ablest of their officials, Sir William Strang, Under Secretary of State in the Foreign Office, as their delegate, and gave him ample time and staff for this work. They alone were adequately represented.

The British, in proposing establishment of this commission, envisaged that its members would function as an independent group of advisors, examining the problems at hand, taking counsel with one another, and sending joint recommendations to the respective governments. But both the American and Soviet governments insisted on holding their representatives on such short leash that they could in no way join Strang in functioning in this manner. The American representative could come up with no thoughts and make no suggestion to his colleagues which had not already come to him as instructions from Washington; and since Washington appeared to have a total absence of thoughts, and only the tardiest and most grudging of suggestions, this obviously limited drastically what the American representative could do. Each of the governments concerned insisted, furthermore, that no "recommendation" should be put forward by this "Advisory Commission" which had not been cleared with itself in advance. Little remained, therefore, of the body's advisory function. What did remain was actually a place, rather than a body — a place at which official positions could be filed and registered, it being left to the respective governments to reconcile these positions or not to reconcile them, as the spirit moved them. Obviously, a man (in this case Ambassador Winant) whose own opinions were neither wanted nor invited, and who could lay before his colleagues on the commission only that which his government had already approved, had no latitude of operation himself, and small need of a political advisor to help him.

I returned to Washington from Lisbon in the last days of 1943 to receive such instructions as the department had to offer before taking up my new duties. So far as I could learn from my superiors in the department, their attitude toward the commission was dominated primarily by a lively concern lest the new body should at some point and by some mischance actually do something, and particularly lest the American delegation, through overeagerness or inadvertence, contribute to so unfortunate an occurrence. Uneasiness centered particularly on my own person as a result of my recent adventures in the matter of the Azores bases — adventures which, despite their generally favorable outcome, many in the department still viewed with a disapproval bordering on sheer horror. It was for this reason, I suppose, that I was especially admonished by Assistant Secretary of State James Clement Dunn, as I left for my new post in London, to bear constantly in mind that in wartime the Department of State had only an advisory role with respect to matters of policy, and that it gave advice only when asked.

I arrived in London in time for the first working session of the European Advisory Commission on January 14, 1944. What followed is in essence so similar to what had recently occurred in Portugal (though less dramatic) that I shall describe it only in the most general terms.

The British, who were well prepared, at once laid on the table a draft surrender instrument and detailed proposals for future zones of occupation in Germany. (The zonal boundaries described in this British proposal are, with very minor exceptions, the ones that were later adopted; and the western boundary proposed for the Soviet zone is the one still in force today.) We Americans, of course, had no instructions on either subject — or, for that matter, on any other. We forwarded the British proposals to Washington and waited for a reaction.

Several weeks went by. No word from Washington. Repeated telegraphic appeals for instructions went unanswered. Our British colleagues became restive, we ourselves acutely embarrassed.

On February 18 the Soviet delegate put forward his government's reaction to the British initiative. The Russians submitted their own alternative draft of the surrender terms. The British proposals on zones of occupation, on the other hand, they accepted practically *in toto*. We Americans still had no instructions and could only inform Washington what the Russians had done.

We were, however, puzzled by the Russian action. We were not officially informed as to what had taken place at the Tehran Conference (neither was the Department of State, for that matter). We now suspected that some sort of prior agreement on zones of occupation must have been reached between the Russians and the British at Tehran. There was, actually, no justification for this particular suspicion. The British proposals, as I was to learn many years later, had been drawn up some months before within the British government and had been made known to our military authorities at the time of the President's departure for Cairo in mid-November 1943. They had been discussed between the President and the American Joint Chiefs of Staff on the way to Cairo. They had been discussed again at Cairo in the Combined (Anglo-American) Chiefs of Staff.* Of all this, no one in the White House or in the military establishment gave to us, or apparently even to the State Department, at any time the slightest inkling of official information, despite

* William M. Franklin, "Zonal Boundaries and Access to Berlin," *World Politics,* Vol. XVI, No. 1 (October 1963).

the fact that we were now supposed to negotiate with the British and Soviet governments on precisely this subject.

We in the American delegation in London continued, therefore, during the remainder of February to stumble along in total darkness. In early March Washington finally broke its silence. We received, first, a draft surrender instrument. It was quite different from the other two that had been proposed, and was not accompanied, as I recall it, by any explanation, guidance, or commentary. All we could do was to place it on the table before the other delegates and shrug our shoulders. Then on March 8 came a most curious communication on the subject of zones of occupation. It was worded not as a proposal to be put forward in negotiation among governments, but as a military directive from the American Joint Chiefs of Staff (who were mentioned as the authority for it) to some unspecified subordinate echelon. It consisted, to my present recollection, of a single sentence purporting to describe in rough geographic terms the zone the United States proposed to occupy in northern Germany. The eastern border of this zone, so far as we could reconstruct it from the cryptic description given, was one that made no sense at all. It cut, apparently without rhyme or reason, across geographic and administrative boundaries. Since it failed to extend as far as the Czechoslovak frontier, there was left an entire area the intended disposition of which was unclear.

This curious one-sentence directive was accompanied by no word of explanation or background information; nor did the message contain anything at all in the way of comment on the zonal boundaries the Russians and British had already proposed. Insofar as it indicated anything, our directive suggested a boundary for the Russian zone considerably east of the present one. The proposed American zone was to include, it could be calculated, 51 percent of the population and 46 percent of the territory of Germany. It was clear that very strong and well-founded arguments, probably coupled with some tangible means of pressure, would be required to persuade the Russians, who had already agreed with the British on a line further west, to accept one considerably less advantageous to themselves.* But we had not even been given any arguments to offer, not to mention any means of pressure. We had no idea what the line proposed by the Joint Chiefs of Staff represented, what its rationale was supposed to be, why we wanted just this line and no other.

My suspicion of this strange document was heightened when I was told privately by one of the military officers who had accompanied the President to the recent Cairo Conference that he suspected the description to represent an attempt to reduce to words something President Roosevelt had once casually drawn on a chance scrap of paper while en route to Cairo. Someone in the military establishment, he thought, must have picked this up, treasured it away, and now, basing himself on the presidential authorship, persuaded the Joint Chiefs of Staff to put it forward as an American proposal. But if this was true, then it was clear that this had been conceived by the President before the European Advisory Commission had been established, in a discussion which had no specific relation to the work of the commission, and at a time when the President could not have had any knowledge of the recent British and Soviet proposals. Would he really still wish to insist on this casual sketch as a negotiating position, in the light of what the British and Russians were proposing? Had he, in fact, been again, and recently, consulted at all? This seemed highly unlikely.

I objected strenuously to our putting this curious instruction on the table as an American negotiating position. I simply could not agree that it constituted proper and adequate instruction for a diplomatic representative embarking on an important and delicate phase of international negotiation. My colleague, Mr. Winant's military advisor, General Cornelius W. Wickersham, a distinguished

---

* It must be remembered that the present boundary of the Soviet zone, when proposed by the British in 1944, looked considerably more favorable to the Western powers than it does today. Few people then anticipated that the Western forces would advance far enough to meet the Soviet forces on this line when the German collapse came. The Soviet agreement to occupy the present eastern zone was greeted with relief in particular by people who had previously feared that the Russians might not be willing to enter Germany at all, but would leave the entire burden of the final defeat of Hitler to the forces of the West. (Strang, *op. cit.*, p. 213.) Little did these people understand Soviet political ambitions.

lawyer in civilian life, and a very reasonable man with whom I was able to collaborate at all times amicably and happily, understandably felt obliged to take the opposite position. "The Joint Chiefs have passed this," he said. "We have to fight for it, my boy; we have to fight for it." "How does one fight," I objected, "for something which makes no sense and which one does not understand oneself?"

The immediate problem was resolved by an agreement that General Wickersham and myself should return to Washington and see what could be done to straighten out the confusion. This we did — traveling in a military transport plane. The heating system of the plane gave out in the depths of night somewhere over the wintry ocean between Iceland and Newfoundland, reducing the temperature in the cabin to many degrees below zero and, incidentally, freezing the brakes. The vehicle, on hitting the snow-covered landing strip at Gander in the winter dawn, skated along like a toboggan and finally slithered to a stop, with its load of half-frozen passengers, some ten feet before the open sea at the end of the runway. An hour or two later, however, we were off again for what was — in the planes of that day — the long remaining trek to Washington.

Once again, then, I arrived in Washington rather dazed and unnerved by the vicissitudes of wartime intercontinental travel. Once again the Department of State had no suggestions for me, and would offer no help. Once again I saw no choice but to go to the President and try to explain to him why an instruction emanating from our military authorities could not be carried out.

I should perhaps make clear at this point that I personally had no desire to see the boundary between the Soviet and the Western zones drawn any further west than was absolutely necessary. Had my opinion been inquired, I should certainly have favored one that at least afforded to the Western zones a direct territorial access to Berlin. But my opinion had never been asked. It had in fact been made clear to me that the Department of State did not even wish it to be volunteered. There was nothing I could do in the circumstances but to try to assure that the positions we took were at least coherent and defensible — a description to which the one we had been told to take did not answer.

Once again the President received me graciously. But I had difficulty, this time, in getting through to him what it was I had come to see him about. He was now already locked into his celebrated conflict with the British over which of us should have the northern, and which the southern, of the contemplated two Western zones This was what was on his mind, and this was what he wanted to talk about. When I finally managed to convey to him that it was a confusion relating primarily to the boundary of the *Soviet* zone that I had on my mind, he was quite surprised. When I explained to him the nature of the confusion and showed him the instruction we had received in London, he laughed gaily and said, just as I had expected him to say: "Why that's just something I once drew on the back of an envelope." I asked him whether he would himself see to the removal of the confusion, or whether there was something more I should do about it. He said I could relax — he would see to it that the mixup was straightened out. (On May 1, instructions went out to Ambassador Winant to approve the boundaries of the Eastern zone as already proposed by the British and the Russians.)

This was the end of my brief service as Mr. Winant's counselor for the work of the European Advisory Commission. I was at this point physically exhausted; a rest had become necessary. The Department of State, its worst fears confirmed by this last example of my deplorable insistence on straightening out the confusions of wartime diplomacy, received the news of my physical difficulty with what I suspect to have been some relief, urged me to make the vacation a good long one, and assured me that I had no need to worry further about the affairs of the EAC — another officer would be sent at once to take my place. I therefore went away to my farm for a blissful five weeks of planting trees, and did not return to Washington until the beginning of May.

The background of this entire episode: of the department's stubborn reticence and of the curious manner in which we were ultimately instructed, has been reconstructed from the historical record in the excellent articles published respectively by my friend Mr. Philip E. Mosely, who succeeded me as Mr. Winant's counselor on the EAC delegation, and Mr. William M. Franklin, now director of the Historical Office of the Department of State.* The main source of the trouble was, quite clearly, the Civil Affairs Division of the War Department, which refused initially even to take part in any interdepartmental discussion looking to the instruction of the American representative on the EAC, and which later, having grudgingly consented to take part, did so in a manner so lacking in both candor and enthusiasm as to give the impression of sabotage. So unhelpful, in fact, were the representatives of the Civil Affairs Division that, not content with declining to approve any instructions to Ambassador Winant over long periods of time, they even — according to Mr. Mosely — "vetoed draft messages informing him that he should not expect an early reply." Apparently in their view there was to be no communication with Mr. Winant at all. And when, as a result of pressure brought to bear on them through higher echelons of government, they finally came up with the cryptic proposals on surrender terms and zones of occupation to which I have referred, they refused to accompany them with any background or explanation.

As conduct on the part of people sharing responsibility for the instructing of an American envoy on major subjects of international negotiation, I find this irresponsible and seriously reprehensible. But the blame cannot be assigned exclusively to the War Department and its Civil Affairs Division. The Department of State must accept its share.

I think I understand the difficult position in which the Department of State found itself during the Second World War. The late Mr. Cordell Hull has described in his memoirs the manner in which policy questions were handled by the President during the war years. The arrangement that emerged in 1942, as described by Mr.

* Philip E. Mosely, "The Occupation of Germany," *Foreign Affairs*, Vol. XXVIII, No. 4 (July 1950), pp. 580-604; William M. Franklin, "Zonal Boundaries and Access to Berlin," *op. cit.*

Franklin in the article referred to above, was that "Roosevelt would work to win the war with Churchill, Chiang, Stalin and the Joint and Combined Chiefs of Staff, while the Department of State would take care of the more routine foreign relations and would formulate plans for the post-war settlement." In practice this meant, of course, that the Secretary of State found himself repeatedly uninformed and unconsulted on vitally important matters relating to America's foreign policies, only to have the responsibility for action and decision abruptly thrown at him from time to time by the President or by circumstances, in questions with which he was not even properly conversant.

The main responsibility for this regrettable and dangerous state of affairs was of course the President's. But I think it may well be asked whether responsible officials of the Department of State were justified in enduring this state of affairs and in collaborating, as they did, in the farcical and near-tragic confusions to which it repeatedly led. I find it difficult, for example, to understand how they could, in the Portuguese case, accept so passive a role — how they could to such an extent exclude themselves as active participants in a governmental process — as to yank an American representative abruptly home at the suggestion of the War Department when that representative was in the midst of important international negotiations; to do this at a time when the department could see clearly that the War Department's suggestion was the result of a confusion; and to do this, incidentally, without so much as a word of explanation to the representative himself. I fail to understand how a Department of State which had primary responsibility in the field of diplomatic representation could mechanically pass on to the President the suggestion of a Secretary of War for the appointment of a diplomatic representative when it could see clearly that the Secretary of War, in making this suggestion, was laboring under a serious misunderstanding. I fail, finally, to see how senior State Department officials could transmit to Ambassador Winant, with a shrug of the shoulder and without any sort of comment or explanation, a document emanating from the Joint Chiefs of Staff which made no substantive sense and was not even responsive to the known realities of the situation, and expect the ambassador to place it on the negotiating table as a serious American proposal.

Presumably, the standing instructions or understandings under which the Department of State was then operating gave it no formal right to intervene in such matters. But surely there are limits to such passivity and to such a formal disclaimer of responsibility. The President, as I myself demonstrated, was not unwilling to have such confusions brought to his attention nor was he unwilling to take steps to correct them when he was given knowledge of them. Why it should have been left to a junior officer such as myself to jeopardize his own career by going directly to the President on these two separate occasions — why the Department of State could not have taken upon itself this minimal responsibility — was a mystery to me at that time. It remains a mystery to the present day.

The work of the European Advisory Commission was of course addressed almost exclusively to the problems of Germany. Germany was a country in which, aside from living there as a child and again as a private student, I had served or studied more than five years in official capacity, and nearly three of these years during the war then in progress. I cannot recall, however, that I was ever consulted, during my service as political advisor to Mr. Winant or at any other time, on any problem of substance relating to the future treatment of Germany, or that I ever had opportunity to present to him or to the government any view of my own on this subject.

After my return to Washington, in 1943, my friend and colleague, the late Henry P. Leverich, with whom I had served in the Berlin embassy earlier in the war and who was now concerned with postwar planning for Germany in the State Department, took me as a visitor, on one occasion, to a meeting of the so-called Germany Committee in which such matters were studied. He showed me in this connection an official policy paper which was then under consideration, concerning utilization of German personnel by a future military government. This provoked from me a written memorandum addressed to the questions of principle involved in this sort of planning, questions that included, as I saw it, not just the employment practices of the future military government in the narrow sense, but indeed the wider problems of denazification and of our political approach generally to the post-hostilities Germany. I have no reason to suppose that this memorandum ever reached the eyes of those who took responsibility for our policy toward Germany in the immediate post-hostilities period. After 1947, to be sure, the outlook I expressed in this paper came to be generally accepted, it seems to me, as the basis for American policy. But for the first two or three years following the German surrender the policies adopted were in general those against which this paper inveighed.

Since to my mind a sensible policy toward Germany was the first requirement of a sound postwar policy with relation to the Soviet Union itself, the despair and in some instances horror (I have in mind the Nuremberg War Crimes Trial) with which I viewed our immediate postwar policies toward Germany did more to give me a sense of hopelessness and frustration in the immediate post-hostilities period than did such differences as I had with the administration over the handling of our bilateral relations with Moscow itself. It is for this reason that the following passages from the memorandum handed to Leverich, representing the only contribution I ever had occasion to make to our thinking about the post-hostilities treatment of Germany, may not be out of place in this record.

I began by summing up the basic view expressed in the working paper I had been shown. It was, as I understood it,

that, assuming it to be our duty to insure that Germans employed in administrative capacities are not enemies of democratic reconstruction, we should endeavor to eliminate from the administrative machinery of the German state all persons belonging to certain broad categories which comprise at least three million individuals.

I then stated my objections to this view:

(*1*) In the first place, it is impracticable. It presumes a degree of knowledge and of coordination in matters of personal intelligence which could never be achieved on a tripartite basis. There is no thornier or more thankless task in the field of foreign affairs than that of trying to probe into the political records and motives of masses of individuals in a foreign country. It is impossible to avoid injustices, errors, and resentment. It involves the maintenance of a huge, and necessarily unpopular, investigative apparatus. I should place the proposed program for Germany clearly beyond the capacity of our own intelligence agencies. To attempt to encompass it on a tripartite basis would merely give rise to inter-Allied differences. There is little likelihood that the Allies would agree, even outwardly, on the categories to be eliminated. Neither British nor Russians attach much importance to ideological distinctions in their approach to foreign peoples; and both are apt to be more concerned with the immediate usefulness of individuals to their own purposes than with the former views which these individuals may have professed.

If we attempt to carry out the program indicated, we will not succeed. People will either escape notice entirely; or they will prove their indispensability on technical grounds; or they will disappear and pop up elsewhere under other names; or they will see that records are destroyed; or they will ingratiate themselves with one of the Allies and play this favor off against the other two. We will eventually get caught up in a round of denunciation, confusion, and disunity from which none but the Germans would stand to profit.

(2) Second, the project, even if it could be successfully carried out, would not serve the purpose for which it is designed. We would not find any other class of people competent to assume the burdens of those we had eliminated. Whether we like it or not, nine-tenths of what is strong, able, and respected in Germany has been poured into those very categories which we have in mind.* To remove these categories would

---

* Twenty years later Mr. Robert Murphy, who was our first political representative in Germany after the war, had this to say in his memoirs about the actual experience of our military government there in the immediate post-hostilities period (the "JCS 1067" to which he refers was the basic directive prepared in the War Department, governing our occupational policies):

. . . JCS 1067 prohibited employment as executives or skilled workmen of any Germans who had been more than nominal members of the Nazi party. And we were promptly made aware that the great majority of executives and skilled workmen in Germany had undeniably been Nazis. . . . We had to dismiss thousands of efficient workers because their records placed them in categories which JCS 1067 marked for automatic exclusion. . . . It did not make us any happier when we learned that many of the workers whom we had been compelled to discharge found jobs immediately in the Russian, French and British zones.

From Robert Murphy, *Diplomat Among Warriors*, p. 284. New York: Doubleday and Company, 1964.

mean to saddle some alternative regime — presumably composed of our occupying forces and such liberal Germans as could be found and commonly accepted by the Allies — with a task far beyond its power, and simultaneously with an embittered, irresponsible opposition of unparalleled strength and prestige. The only result could be the final discrediting in Germany of all that the Western powers stand for, the assumption of the cloak of martyrdom by the nationalist elements, and the eventual triumphant return of the latter in the role of the liberators of Germany from a bungling, pseudodemocratic puppet regime. We must never forget that the forces of liberalism in Germany are pitifully thin and weak. To place upon them the strain of major responsibility before their shoulders are broad enough to bear it may easily lead to their final destruction.

(3) Finally, I should like to plead that the elimination of nationalist elements by action on our part is not only impracticable and inefficacious, but also unnecessary. The main purpose of our post-hostilities action on Germany is, as I take it, to assure that that country will not again become the seat of a program of military aggression which might threaten our security. For this, we all agree, it must be demonstrated to Germany that aggression does not pay. But I do not see that this involves the artificial removal of any given class in Germany from its position in public life. Let us rather assume — for there is ample justification for doing so — that nationalist Germany *is* Germany; and let us then set about not to relieve that nationalist Germany of the very responsibilities it might most justly be required to bear, but to hold it strictly to its tasks and to teach it the lessons we wish it to learn. The best treatment for the present ruling class in Germany is not an obliging removal from office at the very moment when the exercise of office has become an ugly burden, but a grim demonstration that Germany is not strong enough to threaten the interests of other great powers with impunity and that any unsuccessful attempt in this direction will inevitably lead to catastrophe. It is precisely the strong nationalistic ruling caste which must become convinced of this. Once they realize it, the realization will soon take the guts out of their own nationalism. It will probably eventually lead to their own political demise, for they have no program, in reality, but the greatness and power of Germany. But if they then go, it will be through the logic of history and through the organic development of German political life, not through the premature, and unavoidably inept, interference of foreign

powers. The political development of great peoples is conditioned and determined by their national experiences, but never by the manipulations of foreign powers in their internal affairs.

Let the impact of defeat, therefore, be as tremendous as possible. Let the immediate impressions of failure be so vivid and unforgettable that they become a part of the national consciousness of the German people for all time. But having done this, let us then abandon the concept of punishment in the treatment of Germany — for prolonged punishment can never be effective against an entire people. And let us not confuse for everyone the clear outlines of responsibility by trying to interfere with the natural consequences which total defeat must inevitably produce. It is our job to create the unforgettable impression. It is up to the Germans to react to it.

These passages clearly reveal one of the reasons for my lack of confidence, during the final phases of the war, in the plans that were being evolved for the postwar treatment of Germany; namely, the extent to which these plans were founded on hopes of collaboration with the Russians in the approach to this problem. It was not just that any attempt at such collaboration was bound, as I saw it, to be unsuccessful; more dangerous still was the possibility that in deference to this chimera we would refrain from going ahead with the development of constructive plans for the handling of affairs within the Western zones, and would thus miss the golden moment, psychologically, for setting German life on a new and more hopeful course. I laid great stress on the need for immediate constructive measures of rehabilitation of economic life and civilian morale, and felt it important to get on with the necessary plans rather than diverting ourselves with pipedreams of collaboration with the Russians. In arriving at these views, I was probably over-rating somewhat the seriousness of the negative results that were bound to flow from the determining conditions of the immediate post-hostilities period, as they could then be foreseen: the enormous influx of refugees, the economic dislocations, the breakdown of existing administration; and I was definitely taking too negative a view of the political climate in which the Allied military government would have to function.

On the other hand, it must be recognized that the hesitant and confused policies with which we entered upon our post-hostilities responsibilities in Germany proved within a year or two to be inadequate and unworkable; and if they had not been abandoned and replaced in 1947 by a different approach, many of the disastrous results I then feared might have become reality.

A particular reason for the unhappiness I felt over what we were planning to do in the post-hostilities treatment of Germany related to the question of punishment for war crimes. In a memorandum I once started to prepare for the eyes of Ambassador Winant while I was in London (it was not invited by him, and I cannot recall that I ever actually showed it to him), I find the following passage:

There can be few people connected with the conduct of our foreign affairs who have had more intimate knowledge than I of German atrocities, or more personal cause for indignation on this score. I have seen a good deal of German occupation, in a number of countries; and persons very close to me have been the victims of the most revolting forms of Gestapo brutality. In what I say on this subject, therefore, I am speaking neither in ignorance nor in sentimental condonation of the excesses which Germans have committed during this war.

But the day we accepted the Russians as our allies in the struggle against Germany we tacitly accepted as facts, even if we did not ourselves adopt, the customs of warfare which have prevailed generally in Eastern Europe and Asia for centuries in the past and which will presumably continue to prevail long into the future.

These customs, I stress, are general; they are not the peculiar property of the Germans.

History, in judging the individual cruelties of this struggle, will not distinguish between those of victor and vanquished. If our judgments are to stand the test of history, they must be made with this in mind.

If others wish, in the face of this situation, to pursue the illumination of those sinister recesses in which the brutalities of this war find their record, they may do so. The degree of relative guilt which such inquiries may bring to light is something of which I, as an American, prefer to remain ignorant.

All in all, then, it was with deep misgivings about our German policy that I returned, in the spring of 1944, from the brief encounter with it occasioned by the assignment in London. I regarded as unreal the hopes for collaboration with the Russians in the governing of Germany. Partly for this very reason, but partly for wider reasons as well, I was opposed to any elaborate program of denazification. I had no sympathy with the Nazi leaders; but I was most reluctant to see us associate ourselves with the Russians in judging and punishing their conduct. Subsequent experience shows these misgivings to have been somewhat overdrawn but not entirely without substance. They entered prominently, in any case, into the lively uneasiness over American policy toward Germany that was to dominate my attitude during the forthcoming two years of service in Moscow.

* * *

When I returned to Washington, following my vacation in the spring of 1944, the department, I think, had no clear idea as to what it wanted to do with me. Chip Bohlen, now serving as liaison officer between the department and the White House, heard that the minister-counselor of the Moscow embassy, Maxwell M. Hamilton, was about to be transferred, and that the ambassador there, Mr. Averell Harriman, was looking for a new minister-counselor. Bohlen introduced me to Harriman; the three of us dined together one evening at Harriman's suite at the Mayflower; and it was agreed that I should be given the assignment. The arrangement was made in full cognizance of the fact, which I took pains to emphasize, that my views on policy toward the Soviet Union were not exactly those of the administration.

The job of minister-counselor at Moscow was viewed by all of us at that time as primarily an administrative one. The embassy was divided into two sections, roughly equal, as I recall it, in size of personnel: the embassy proper, comprising the civilian component, which I was to head; and the military mission, headed by General John R. (Russ) Deane. Sharing, as it was proper for an ambassador to do, the President's view that the preferred source of advice on matters of high policy in wartime was the military establishment, Mr. Harriman had little intention at that moment (if I read his mind correctly in retrospect) of looking to the civilian side of his mission for advice on such matters. What was wanted, at that particular juncture, was someone who could direct the routine work of the embassy proper under the unusual wartime conditions. Previous experience and linguistic competence appeared to recommend me for the job.

I left Washington in early June 1944 and flew to Lisbon, where my family was staying. After making arrangements for the family to follow me shortly (this was allowed only as an exception; wives were not normally permitted to come to Moscow at that time, unless they were prepared to work regularly as employees of the embassy), I set off alone, via the Mediterranean and Iran, to my new post. The journey, which included a visit to the headquarters at Caserta, Italy, of the Supreme Commander of the Mediterranean, yielded a copious crop of travel notes. The reader may well be spared the bulk of these. I include, however, as a variation of the diet of pure politics, the description of and the reflections induced by stopovers in Cairo and in Baghdad.

Including these passages, I should perhaps observe that my entire diplomatic experience took place in rather high northern latitudes. Lisbon, situated on the same latitude as Washington, D.C., was the southernmost of my various posts. I recognize this to have been a regrettable limitation on both experience and intellectual horizon. The negative impressions produced by occasional brief encounters with places farther south in Africa and the Middle East (these two were not the only ones) were largely, I am sure, the result of these blind spots. As such, they were no doubt shallow and misleading. But they, too, affected — for better or for worse — future thoughts and outlooks on international affairs. So I include these two glimpses as symptomatic of the reservations I was to entertain, at a much later date, with regard to what another generation would know as "foreign aid to underdeveloped nations."

It was June 19 when I left Caserta by air in early morning for what I recorded then and there as the most unpleasant day of travel I could recall. I had stayed at Caserta as a guest of the Supreme Commander, and had been driven to the airport, pennants flying and sirens screaming, in his personal car. In Malta, however, the magic of this lofty patronage was no longer palpable; my lowly status as a civilian caught up with me once again; I was disdainfully denied a cup of tea in the officers' canteen — and in the enlisted men's, too, for that matter — on the grounds that I had no British military money. Hungry and thirsty, I pursued my weary way, on the bucket seats of slow but indefatigable DC-3s, toward Cairo. At Benghazi I encountered the worst heat I had ever experienced.

It was like the breath of a furnace. The atmosphere was blurred and vibrant with heat. Off across the desert there was a mirage of the sea. All afternoon the plane droned on across the Cyrenaica and the Western Desert. Hellfire Pass moved slowly beneath us, deserted and still in the afternoon glare — only a ridge of rock and sand — the signs of all the recent struggle and suffering already swallowed up in the unconquerable insistence of the desert, like the sea, on its own tremendous, boundless uniformity. At El Alamein, there were still the remains of trenches and gun emplacements, but another year or two will finish them as well.

It was already evening and getting dark when we reached the airport of our destination, thirty or forty miles outside of Cairo. Crowded into the back of a truck, we bounced along for another hour and a half in the darkness, the diffused glow of the desert sunset filling the sky behind us. At ten o'clock at night I found myself, more dead than alive, standing disconsolately in the lobby of Shepherd's Hotel. They had no room for me. They would change neither my dollars nor my pound checks. There was no one at the legation who seemed to be able to make sense on the telephone. The berobed porters who had carried my bags stood looking at me impatiently, waiting for the tip which I couldn't give them. Outside lay only the totally strange, blacked-out city. It was one of life's low moments. In the small hours of the morning, after agonized exertions, I finally found myself accommodation on a sofa in the apartment of a kind American YMCA secretary.

Tuesday, June 20, 1944
Wednesday, June 21

These two days were too alike to describe separately. Egypt, that triangle of irrigated desert around the delta of a polluted stream, was suffering from a heat wave. The hot breath of the Sahara enveloped miles and miles of brown plaster walls. The mud flats on the outskirts steamed and stank under the fiery African sky. In the streets of the foreign quarter the glare lay, white and burning, between the blank concrete walls of the villas. People barricaded themselves in their houses against the heat; and limousines were parked in shady basement garages, that they should not become too hot to sit in.

On the evening of the first day, when the sun had set and the sky had cooled, the heat could be felt rising back, like steam, from the baked earth. Elderly Britishers, groggy from their siesta, sauntered out for their game of golf. Itinerant Arabs, who had lain stretched out in the shade of a wall on the pavement through the heat of the day, arose, shook some of the dirt out of their robes, and began to beat their torpid donkeys into a resumption of the interminable trek from nowhere to nowhere. The jeeps and command cars, moving down the road from the pyramids, passed a string of dromedaries plodding slowly, patiently up the timeless hill to the timeless desert. In the Hotel Mena, the doors were thrown open to the terraces. The bar began to serve drinks outside. In the music room, surrounded by elaborate Moorish gratings, the pale-faced Polish refugee woman with the dog played Chopin on the piano; and a lone rat, sick and confused with the heat, ducked miserably around on the tiled floor, among the potted palms, searching for the exit to the darkness and freshness of the garden.

On the evening of the second day, the great heat ended in a sandstorm. The dry clouds rolled and turned as they swept across the city. The wind whistled in the shutters of the hotel as if in the rigging of a ship at sea; and there was a steady hissing as the sand hit the walls and windows of the building. The palm trees of the garden tossed and moaned, their long branches clattering wildly under the scourging of the wind. The guests sat in the lounge, with shutters closed and electric lights on, and listened, like people snowbound in a blizzard, to the howling of the wind outside.

During the night the wind died down. At dawn, when I got up to go to the airport, it had become cool; and a clear fresh air lay over the sleeping city. But the sun was rising, great and ominous, on the cloudless sky; and it would not be long, I knew, before the heat and corruption of the day would descend once more upon the fertile, sinister land.

Friday, Saturday, Sunday
June 23-25, 1944. Baghdad

All day we were barricaded in the legation (where the temperature never fell below 90°) by the much fiercer heat outside. We might look out the windows (as one looks out the windows in zero weather in the north) and see the burning dusty wind tearing at the eucalyptus trees and the flat, bleached country enveloped in the colorless sunshine of the desert; a sunshine with no nuances, no shades, no shadows — a sunshine which does not even brown the skin, but only strikes and penetrates and dissolves with its unbending hostile power. Into this inferno of heat only "mad dogs and Englishmen," as Noel Coward used to sing, could dream of venturing. At night, it cooled off considerably, and we slept in reasonable comfort on the roof. But by that time the real mad dogs and the jackals had come in from the desert, and it was not safe to walk in the outlying district where the legation was situated. The only tolerable time of day, when it would have been possible to break out of the prison walls, was the early morning.

The dryness of the heat was nerve-racking. One had to keep drinking water from morning to night; and even then the kidneys had a tendency to cease working entirely.

In general, it was possible to keep healthy only by a very strict and scientifically conceived discipline and routine of private life.

So much for the handicaps; what of the possibilities of service in Baghdad? A country in which man's selfishness and stupidity have ruined almost all natural productivity, where vegetation can survive only along the banks of the great rivers which traverse its deserts, where climate has become unfavorable to human health and vigor.

A population unhygienic in its habits, sorely weakened and debilitated by disease, inclined to all manner of religious bigotry and fanaticism, condemned by the tenets of the most widespread faith to keep a full half of the population — namely, the feminine half — confined and excluded from the productive efforts of society by a system of indefinite house arrest, deeply affected — and bound to be affected — by the psychological habits of pastoral life, which have ever been at variance with the agricultural and industrial civilization.

This people has now come just enough into contact with Western life so that its upper class has a thirst for many things which can be obtained only in the West. Suspicious and resentful of the British, they would be glad to obtain these things from us. They would be glad to use us as a foil for the British, as an escape from the restraints which the British place upon them.

If we give them these things, we can perhaps enjoy a momentary favor on the part of those interested in receiving them. But to the extent that we give them, we weaken British influence, and we acquire — whether we wish it or not — responsibility for the actions of the native politicians. If they then begin to do things which are not in our interests, which affect the world situation in ways unfavorable to our security, and if the British are unable to restrain them, we then have ourselves at least in part to blame and it is up to us to take the appropriate measures.

Are we willing to bear this responsibility? I know — and every realistic American knows — that we are not. Our government is technically incapable of conceiving and promulgating a long-term consistent policy toward areas remote from its own territory. Our actions in the field of foreign affairs are the convulsive reactions of politicians to an internal political life dominated by vocal minorities.

Those few Americans who remember something of the pioneer life of their own country will find it hard to view these deserts without a pang of interest and excitement at the possibilities for reclamation and economic development. If trees once grew here, could they not grow again? If rains once fell, could they not again be attracted from the inexhaustible resources of nature? Could not climate be altered, disease eradicated?

If they are seeking an escape from reality, such Americans may even pursue these dreams and enter upon the long and stony road which could lead to their fruition. But if they are willing to recall the sad state of soil conservation in their own country, the vast amount of social improvement to be accomplished at home, and the inevitable limitations on the efficacy of our type of democracy in the field of foreign affairs — then they will restrain their excitement at the silent, expectant possibilities in the Middle Eastern deserts, and will return, like disappointed but dutiful children, to the sad deficiencies and problems of their native land.

On June 28 I continued my journey to Tehran and was surprised to find myself already — in atmosphere at least — halfway back in Russia.

At the Tehran airport, I was met by an officer of the legation: a lugu-
brious gentleman who declared himself ill and answered all questions
about Persia either in tones of black despair or with a mysterious eva-
siveness which was evidently intended to have dire implications. He
was very kind, however, loaned me money and fixed me up with a
room in a hotel. The hotel was dirty and noisy. At night an orchestra
played in the garden, and the cars came and went with officers and
officials of at least four different nationalities.

I went for a walk in the evening. I was surprised to find myself in
a city that seemed, after all, very Russian. In the straight cobbled street,
the high fences, the Russian signs, the crowds strolling in the evening
darkness, and the cosmopolitan babble of tongues, I could even sense
the familiar breath of summer evenings years ago, in Reval [Tallinn].
It was impressive to think of those two capitals, so far apart and yet
so near, bound together by that vast fluid influence which is Russia.

On the following morning, our chargé d'affaires arranged for me to
live out at the American army camp, so I moved out there. They gave
me a cabin-apartment to myself. There, fortified with a number of
books, I settled down to lead a life of repose and solitude until the
Russians might be prepared to grant me a visa to enter Russia.

Saturday, July 1, 1944

Journey from Tehran to Moscow

We arrived at the Russian airport at 5 A.M. There we waited nearly
an hour before taking off. A horse, saddled but halterless, with an
officer's sword tossing and clattering by the saddle, had gotten loose
on the airfield, and was capering about among the big parked planes.
After the horse had been corralled by twenty or thirty of the airport
officials, to the accompaniment of great shouting and laughter, a Russian
lieutenant, scheduled to leave with our plane, was missing. He was apparently some sort of a courier. A jeep was finally sent for him; and he
arrived, pale with fright over his dereliction, stammering in confusion
that it was "the first time."

The first leg of our journey took us over the mountains and the sea,
to Baku. Then we flew direct to Stalingrad: over the Caspian, again,
as far as Makhachkala, then overland. That leg of the trip was a rather
desolate one, especially the one or two hundred miles of country north
of Makhachkala, which evidently consisted chiefly of salt marshes.

At Stalingrad, everything except the airport building (which they were still working on) appeared to have been destroyed. Near the airfield there were dumping grounds of wrecked planes and tanks. There was an air of busy reconstruction about the airport building. Lunch was served in a little *"stolovaya"* where they had only one glass, and chairs were scarce; but everyone was good-natured and helpful about it. How deeply one sympathizes with the Russians when one encounters the realities of the lives of the people and not the propagandistic pretensions of their government.

8

Moscow Again—and Poland

THE first weeks in Moscow were a strange and unsettling experience. In many respects I had the feeling of one returned from the dead: privileged to witness the progress of life on earth some years after his own death but barred, by delicacy rather than injunction, from reminding others of his previous life and resultant memories. Neither in the embassy nor in the diplomatic corps was there a single soul who had been there during the years of my previous assignments in Moscow. I was then already, at the age of forty, the senior member of the diplomatic corps in length of service in Russia.* My colleagues represented a new generation, with new interests. Particularly was this true in our own embassy. There, thoughts and memories of early years of the embassy's existence had been obliterated by the war, by the many changes of personnel, and by the fresh impressions of the recent move to Kuibyshev, where the foreign diplomatic missions had been obliged to take refuge while the Germans were at the gates of Moscow.

During the first four weeks after my arrival, my predecessor being still there and in occupancy of the minister-counselor's apartment, Mr. Harriman kindly permitted me to live in Spaso House — the ambassador's residence. Here, in deference to the exigencies of

---

* Had I remained longer than I did in Moscow, on this assignment, I would no longer have enjoyed this status. In the person of the new Swedish ambassador, Mr. Rol Solman, the corps was shortly to be augmented by an experienced and talented diplomatist whose initial service in Russia, as a junior official, had far predated my own.

wartime service, the usual amenities of an ambassadorial residence had been generally dispensed with. The building housed, in addition to the personal entourage of the ambassador, a number of junior military and civilian personnel, and a species of wartime mess was being operated under the supervision of the ambassador's daughter Kathleen, who served, with casual graciousness, as mistress of the house.

For me, Spaso House was of course full of memories. I had assisted Bullitt, in 1933, in the selection of the building. Shortly after that I had been obliged to press for the removal of the Soviet officials (including the diplomat Karakhan, famous for his previous service in China and soon to be executed in the purges), who were still residing in it at the time it was offered to us. I had supervised the alteration and refurbishing of the building in preparation for Bullitt's arrival, in 1934. Together with Charlie Thayer, I had personally unpacked and carried into the place the first items of the ghastly official furniture that was sent out from Washington to equip the chancery. Later, in the days of Joe Davies, but during one of his frequent absences from the post, Thayer and I had played detective in the empty building, he spending an uncomfortable night concealed in the great sand-floored attic and I the same in the former billiard room, to see whether we could catch the individuals who, only too obviously, were installing primitive listening devices in preparation for the ambassador's return.

These were just some of the recollections of Spaso House on the personal side. They were fortified by a host of others, relating to official and social events that had taken place at one time or another in the great building. I had, in short, a certain proprietary feeling about the place. Now, on returning to Moscow, I found it inhabited by a race of people to whom all this past history meant little or nothing. They listened with no more than a bored incredulity when one attempted to speak about these memories, and I soon learned that it was better not to do so.

Outside the little oasis of the diplomatic colony there stretched still, fascinating and inviting, the great land and life of Russia, more interesting to me than any other in the world. I could not enter into this life as a participant. The wartime association between Russia and the United States had changed nothing, I soon learned, in the isolation of American diplomats from the population. It was obvious that in the eyes of the secret police we, though nominally allies, were still dangerous enemies, to be viewed with suspicion and held at arm's length from Soviet citizens — lest we corrupt them, I suppose, with insidious tales of another life, or pry from them secrets on the preservation of which, even from ostensibly allied powers, Russia's security was somehow seen to depend. This did not, however, preclude strolling through the city and its environs or visiting the parks and the theaters; and I, consumed with curiosity and yearning for a new familiarity with the atmosphere of the country, threw myself upon this privilege like a thirsting man on a stream of clear water: roaming the boulevards and parks in the evenings, taking off on random weekend jaunts into the countryside, simply for the pleasure of mingling, anonymously, with ordinary people and feeling myself in a small way a part of them and their life. It was, of course, a rule of the game that I must never, if I could avoid it, confess my identity, for this might have frightened and embarrassed others; but so long as they did not know who I was, they could scarcely be blamed for talking with me.

To the Soviet authorities in Stalin's time particularly but not, unfortunately, then alone, any spontaneous curiosity on the part of a foreigner about life in Russia, beyond what the regime had itself deliberately chosen to reveal, was highly suspect. I have no doubt that to them my various jaunts and explorations represented nothing other than a sophisticated form of espionage. To what extent these suspicions were justified the reader may himself judge from the following account of a Sunday expedition, undertaken scarcely a week after my return to Moscow. It will serve, too, as an illustration of the atmosphere of wartime Moscow into which I was plunged.

July 9, 1944

It was a fine July morning: Moscow summer weather at its best. I started off bright and early to seek out and sketch one of the two remaining churches in the Moscow Oblast (beside the Cathedral of St. Basil on the Red Square) supposed to date from the time of Ivan the Terrible.

The sun rises early at this time of the year in Moscow. As I walked over to the subway, it was already flooding into the cobbled streets and bathing the peeling facades of the shabby old houses which were once the homes of Moscow's upper class and which today — despite all the crowding and deterioration — still retain the charm of most Russian architecture of the Empire period.

From the subway exit near the Bryansk Station crowds of people, many bearing primitive hoes and other strange implements, emerged onto the vast asphalted void before the station, blinked to adjust themselves to the glare of sunshine, made out in the distance, across the square, the suburban ticket windows, and broke into a competitive hundred yard dash toward this first objective. Frantic crowds were already milling and pushing around at the ticket windows, and the new arrivals threw themselves into the contest with militant enthusiasm.

The suburban train was waiting at the platform. Although the locomotive had not yet been attached, every seat was taken, every aisle was full, every outdoor platform was packed, every bumper had its occupant. Even the steps up to the platforms were covered with clusters of clinging humanity. Latecomers, myself included, scurried desperately up and down the platform, searching for a toehold somewhere on the long string of cars.

I finally found a step, a bottom step, which seemed to have room for one more single foot, and hopped onto it. A young girl, observing my success, immediately jumped up behind me and threw both arms around me to clutch the guard rails. Hanging widely out over the platform, she shouted exuberantly to an invisible companion down the platform: "Sonya, Sonya: I have found a seat!"

We waited. The locomotive was finally brought up and attached. The scrambling of the latecomers up and down the platform took on a frantic and tragic air. The locomotive whistled. A flock of ragged little boys, with burlap sacks slung over their shoulders in true hobo fashion, suddenly appeared over the cement walls of the railway yard and scuttled across the adjacent empty platform under the nose of the armed guard. Just as the train began to move they settled themselves, with contemptuous professional ease, on the brake beams. We were off.

Slowly, almost silently, the long heavy train pulled up the grades on the further side of the Moscow River. The skirt of the girl behind me flicked each of the switches and signal towers, as we went past; but she failed to notice it, and continued to wave triumphantly to the invisible Sonya, who had apparently found a similar "seat" farther down the line. Beyond the right-of-way, there were endless victory gardens, chiefly of potatoes. All over the countryside, you could see the backs of the women working in the fields, hilling the potatoes with their great square hoes. At one spot, we passed tanktraps and trenches. Here, the Russians had evidently planned to defend the railroad against the advancing Germans in 1941. The sky was an incredibly deep blue and was lined in the distance with the rich white clouds of the Russian plain. Here and there, a poplar stood up among the fields, leaves trembling in the breeze; and off on the horizon there was always the cold dark line of the pine forests.

On the crowded platform of our car conversation was buzzing. I could hear only snatches of it. Someone had read in the morning paper the new decree about marriage and divorce, and the idea of premiums for large families was giving rise to a series of hilarious comments among the women. Just above me, a peasant girl was relating her own sufferings and those of her native village at the hands of the Germans. The tale began with the hiding of a barrel of honey and ended with the demise of her husband and her relatives. I could hear the conclusion, flung out to the sympathetic audience with all the throaty eloquence of the Russian tongue: "Who has need of me now? To whom am I now necessary?"

I tried repeatedly to turn around and climb up a step, in the hopes of hearing more of these discussions, but in doing so, I jostled the old peasant woman above me. She descended upon me with virulence: "What's the matter with you, anyway, comrade?" she shouted. "Such vulgarity. After all. That's the tenth time you've jostled me. And you with the outward appearance of a cultured man." There did not seem to be any suitable answer to this, so I stayed on my step until my station was reached.

The tower of the church that had attracted my interest could be seen from the station. I made my way to it without difficulty. The old structure stood in a little patch of woods, surrounded by suburban bungalows. Paths ran crisscross, here and there, through the woods, sustaining a steady stream of Sunday strollers. A service was going on in the church. The drone of the choir floated out onto the sunny outdoors and mingled there with the hum of insects, the conversational voices on the paths, the sound of the breeze in the treetops. It was not the best church singing, but it was correct and forthright. I wondered who, in the motley population of this suburban district, had taken the trouble to learn the long variations — some beautiful, some tedious — of the Gregorian chants.

I sat down on a knoll and spent an hour or two sketching. Except for the trees, which forced me to sketch at an exact 45-degree angle, the church would have been a good subject. I have a feeling that the date of its origin was a little later than John the Terrible, but it was a venerable and worthy old-timer, whatever its date.

The service was a long one. It was over just as I finished sketching. The congregation, mostly old women, emerged, babbling, and dispersed. An old beggarwoman and two women with children remained on the stone porch. Then the priest, in high boots and what looked to be a new blue robe, came out the side door, locked it after him, walked around the church, chased the women off the porch, and stamped jerkily away, shaking his wispy gray beard in ill temper, complaining in a low mutter that he had nothing to eat.

I went back to the station, to get information about trains and to find something to drink. The place was crowded. A train was apparently almost due, going back to town. There was a little hut where they were selling mineral water and *kvass;* but you had to have your own receptacle to take it away, so I gave up.

People were already collecting on the platform for the expected train. At the end of the platform, on the cinder path, a blind woman was sitting, an old blind beggarwoman. She sat patiently, intoning an endless song about the origins and trials of her affliction, singing the words like a priest in her high feeble voice. When someone put a ruble in her hand, she would start up, fumble for her little bag, put the ruble in, and then insert into her song a few words of appreciation, repeated several times for good measure: "Thank you, my nice one, my own one; thank you, my good provider. May the Lord grant you a great health." Then she would return to the complaints and reminiscences.

I decided that it was too early to go back to town and walked away. As I crossed the tracks, I could still hear the droning, cackling little voice: "I do not see the great white light; I do not see the light of God."

Near the church, there was a little brick house, in old Russian style. It had a brick wall around it, and corner towers on the wall, as though in imitation of an old Kremlin. It was all very run down. The tiny yard enclosed by the fence was high in weeds.

A soldier with only one leg was standing at the door, on crutches. I asked him what the house was. A woman in a white dress, carrying a shopping net in one hand, came up at that moment and interrupted. "He wouldn't know," she said. "It's old, the house. It's from the time of John the Terrible. It used to belong to some boyar. We live in it. Would you like to see the inside?"

I followed her up the dark, winding staircase into an upstairs room. A man was sitting there at a table doing nothing. She introduced him as her husband. He, too, was lame, and had the undefinable look of a veteran, bored and bewildered with the humdrum of civilian life after all the adventure and comradeship of the front. The room was divided in the middle by a big cupboard. I had the impression that behind the cupboard was somebody else's apartment. The part of the room we sat in, being bedroom, living room, dining room, and bathroom combined, was crowded with objects, and had the air of a storehouse. The profusion was such that all thought of attractive arrangement had been abandoned. The walls were thick. The window arches had a curious naïve shape. I began to believe that they might really be old, although I still suspected the little Kremlin wall outside as being a product of the well-known passion of our grandfathers' generation for miniature.

How did she like living in a boyar's house, I asked. It was damp, my hostess said, pointing to big blotches of moisture on the ceiling. Besides, the stove didn't work. It was a calamity, that stove.

I looked with respect at the little tile and brick structure in the corner. Its antiquity seemed unchallengeable, its inadequacy scarcely to be doubted.

Did she know anything more about the house?

No, not much. It had once belonged to the church. Both buildings had originally been part of the boyar's estate. There had been a big manor house "right over there," built at a later date; and before the First World War ("in the peaceful time") it had housed a historical museum. But it had burned down, and now no one remembered much about it. Was I an artist? She had seen me sketching the church.

No, I was not an artist. I showed them my sketchbook by way of proof and took my leave.

I set off to the north: along a lane, through a woods, down into a ravine, across a stream, and up the other side. Somewhere in the woods a woman was singing, in a clear strong voice, a voice you would never hear anywhere but in Russia. On the other side of the ravine two women were working in a small potato field, and a man was lying on his back in the grass and watching them. The women had broad faces, brown muscular arms, and the powerful maternal thighs of the female Slav. They laughed and joked as they worked; and it was clear that they enjoyed the feeling of the sun on their bodies and the dark earth, cool and sandy, under their bare feet. I asked them the way to the Minsk railway. After they had told me, they turned again and bent to their work with all the easy, unhurried strength of their people.

I must say that never, except possibly during my later experience as ambassador in Moscow, did the insistence of the Soviet authorities on isolation of the diplomatic corps weigh more heavily on me, or more deeply affect my thinking, than in these first weeks following the return to Russia in the final months of the war. It accorded poorly not only with the outward facade of wartime cordiality and collaboration among allies which the Western powers, at any rate, were endeavoring to maintain, but also with the intimate feelings of many of us then serving there. We were sincerely moved by the sufferings of the Russian people as well as by the heroism and patience they were showing in the face of wartime adversity. We wished them nothing but well. It was doubly hard, in these circumstances, to find ourselves treated as though we were the bearers of some species of the plague.

I find in my notes an account, from late July 1944, of a talk with a Soviet acquaintance. We had first spoken of their ideology as opposed to ours, and I had voiced my distaste for the thought of living under a dictatorship. The conversation then continued as follows:

"Here," my friend said, "we have to have a dictatorship. Left to themselves, our people would know no measure. They have no restraints. They would get out of hand."

"I have no comments to make," I replied, "on your system. That's your business. The rights and wrongs of it are determined by your history and traditions, by the habits of thought and behavior of your people. These are things I don't attempt to judge. I only wish you didn't find it necessary to hold your friends perpetually at arm's length. I come back here after all these years of absence, and I find the same absurd system of isolation of foreigners as existed ten years ago. Here we are supposed to be allies, and you continue to treat us individually as spies."

"We must teach our people to assume that every foreigner is a spy. It is only in this way that we can train them to exercise the self-control which they should exercise as citizens of a great power."

"Look here," I said, "this espionage business is a disease with you. You are more afraid of espionage than any country in the world. One would think you were some weak little country, the life of which depended on the extent to which it could keep out foreign influence. Haven't your victories given you any self-confidence? Where is the logic of it? If we were hostilely inclined to you, do you think that we would support your war effort, that we would place at your disposal billions of dollars worth of the products of the labor of our people, year after year? Do you seriously believe that our government would give you this tremendous support and then instruct its diplomats to engage in all sorts of dirty little intrigues against you?"

"Our people," my friend replied, "must not be allowed to forget that they live in a capitalist environment, that a friend may be a friend today and an enemy tomorrow. We cannot permit you to associate closely with them. You will tell them all sorts of things about your countries, about your higher standard of living, about what you consider to be your happier life. You will confuse them. You will weaken their loyalty to their own system."

"Very well," I said. "You can continue to do this. You can continue to act on the theory that the world is your enemy. You can continue to send out one generation after another of embittered and insulted diplomats from your little college of diplomacy. But you must be prepared to accept the results of this policy, to accept the repercussions of the resentment and sense of grievance it inevitably spreads."

My friend laughed. "We are not afraid of that," he said. "We are satisfied with the arrangement."

He paused for a moment. I got up to leave. He stopped me at the door.

"We are being very successful these days," he said. "The more successful we are, the less we care about foreign opinion. This is something you should bear in mind about the Russian. The better things go for him, the more arrogant he is. That applies to all of us, in the government and out of it. It is only when we are having hard sledding that we are meek and mild and conciliatory. When we are successful, keep out of our way."

*   *   *

On another Sunday morning in that same summer of 1944 I had the unpleasant experience of standing at the curb on one of the great boulevards near Spaso House and watching the passage of some fifty thousand German prisoners in process of being marched several miles across town from one railway station to another. The object of the operation was plainly to make a spectacle of the men before the population of the city.

It was a hot day. The rays of the sun were already dancing over the vast expanse of asphalt which the boulevard presented.* The men, presumably just out of freight cars, were obviously exhausted and — I have no doubt — hungry. They were marched, purposely, at a fast clip. Now and then, mounted Soviet guards — members, apparently, of the border and internal guard units of the police establishment — rode their horses brutally into the rear ranks of the densely arranged units, forcing the men to stumble about and to run on the double quick. Occasionally, one or another of them fainted and was hauled off to the gutter, to be picked up afterward.

It was not a very great brutality, as brutalities of war go. The Germans, God knows, had done many times worse, and on a scale far greater, with the Russian prisoners taken in the first summer of the war, permitting hundreds of thousands if not millions to die of hunger and exposure in the stockades, and then mistreating the sur-

---

* Once proper boulevards with parks in the middle, these thoroughfares had, allegedly on Stalin's orders, been cleared of their verdant center strips. They now presented very wide stretches of sheer asphalt, dangerous to both pedestrian and motorist.

vivors in a thousand different ways. Even compared to the fate that awaited these same German prisoners when they arrived at their unknown destinations, for hard labor or confinement, the ordeal they were now undergoing on the boulevard was, I suspect, a minor one.

Still, I came away from the sight shaken, saddened, and unsatisfied. These prisoners were young men — many of them no older, surely, than our college students. Five years ago, when the war began, they had been mere boys. Each had a home and a mother somewhere; and not even the strongest revulsion to the Nazi system could let one forget that many of these homes must have been decent ones, marked by affection, tenderness, and a genuine political helplessness, if not innocence. How these young men would have behaved had they grown older and achieved personal power and responsibility, no one could tell. But surely they had never been consulted about the great issues of this war, still less about the abominations of the Nazi system. Their presence at the front was not their doing. As front line fighting men, it was not to be assumed that they had been prominently involved in the beastliness perpetrated by the Gestapo, the SS, and the punitive police detachments in the rear of the German lines. Was it right, then, I asked myself, to punish them all for the acts of a government to whose power their fathers had consigned them already as children and whose policies they had never had the faintest opportunity to oppose? Was brutality ever sanctioned, or sanctionable, as a measure of revenge? If one fought against an enemy ostensibly *because* of his methods, and permitted oneself to be impelled by the heat of the struggle to adopt those same methods, who, then, could be said to have won? Who was it, in this situation, who had imposed his methods on the other? Whose outlook could be said to have triumphed?

I recognized, at that moment, that I stood temperamentally outside the passions of war — and always would. I had my moments of indignation, many of them; the days, in fact, were seldom without them. Wherever I lived — in Berlin, in Moscow, in Washington — the evidences in the daily prints of hypocrisy, of deliberate falsehood, of vindictiveness and pettiness of spirit, had never failed, and never would fail in the future, to send me into elaborate physical heavings, and mutterings of outraged sentiment. The family came to know these unfailing symptoms. But it was primarily against people's methods rather than against their objectives that indignation mounted in such moments. Objectives were normally vainglorious, unreal, extravagant, even pathetic — little likely to be realized, scarcely to be taken seriously. People had to have them, or to believe they had them. It was part of their weakness as human beings. But methods were another matter. These were real. It was out of their immediate effects that the quality of life was really molded. In war as in peace I found myself concerned less with what people thought they were striving for than with the manner in which they strove for it. Whatever such an outlook implied — whether weakness of character or qualities less reprehensible (and on this question there will never, I am sure, be wide agreement) — I was never a man for causes.

* * *

Despite all our good resolutions, it proved unfeasible from the ambassador's standpoint as well as from my own for me to remain entirely detached from political problems. Of these, the first to assail us in the weeks following my return to Moscow was the one that was to encumber Soviet-American relations more than any other over the ensuing year: the problem of Poland.

A word or two of recapitulation may not be out of order at this point, for the problem was a complex one, and not all readers will have the details clearly in memory. During the period of the German-Soviet Nonaggression Pact the Soviet government, having in effect agreed with the Nazis on the destruction of the Polish state and the partitioning of its territory between Russia and Germany, naturally refused to recognize the Polish government-in-exile, established in London, which for obvious reasons could not accept the legitimacy of the partition. At the same time the Soviet police authorities proceeded to deport from the Soviet-occupied portion of Poland to the interior regions of Russia and Siberia, under conditions of extreme brutality and cruelty, people in the number of several hundred thousand — probably over one million.* These people were, in the overwhelming majority of cases, guilty of no specific offenses whatsoever against the Soviet occupational authorities. They were removed because they belonged, or were thought to belong, to categories of persons (and by no means all of them reactionary categories) whose continued presence might complicate the consolidation of a Communist regime in that region. So appalling were the circumstances of their deportation and their subsequent treatment in the Soviet Union that a large proportion of them, as much as 50 percent it is sometimes claimed, have never been heard from since. In addition to this, the Soviet authorities had taken into detention nearly 200,000 members of the Polish armed forces — men whose sole offense had consisted, so far as one can see, in the effort to defend their country when it was attacked in 1939. And of these, nearly ten thousand officers — many of them reserve officers: doctors, lawyers, the cream in some measure of the Polish intelligentsia — had been individually executed in the Katyn forest, in the spring of 1940, by Soviet police detachments detailed for this purpose, the executions being carried out at the edges of mass graves into which, after receiving their shot in the neck, the bodies were pushed. This was done, I reiterate, despite the fact that the Polish army was guilty of no attack on the Soviet Union; indeed, it had scarcely offered any military resistance to the Soviet occupation. Nor was any effort made, in the destruction of the officers, to establish any distinctions whatsoever of individual guilt. They were simply destroyed "as a class."

This last stupendous crime did not become definitely known until the Germans stumbled on the graves in the winter and spring of 1943. Of the deportations, much was of course known at an earlier date; but Western opinion was never fully aware, during the war years, of the full monstrosity of what had been done by the Soviet police authorities during the Nonaggression Pact period,

* The authorities of the government-in-exile have placed the figure at 1,600,000, including some 180,000 war prisoners. Vyshinski, in October 1944, admitted to a figure of 387,932 Poles originally "in confinement" in Russia, but this evidently failed to include Jews, "Ukrainians," etc., as well as those not "in confinement." My own impression is that the number of civilian deportees must have reached at least the neighborhood of 1 million, and perhaps as much as 1.2 million.

both to the civilian population of eastern Poland and to the officer prisoners of war.

In the summer of 1941, following the German attack, the Stalin regime, then in a dangerous and desperate military situation, yielded to the importunities of the Western Allies and agreed to recognize the Polish government-in-exile, to grant an amnesty to Poles incarcerated or detained in one way or another in the USSR, and to permit the formation on Soviet territory, under command of Lieutenant General W. Anders, of a Polish army, to be recruited from the Polish war prisoners and other Poles in the Soviet Union. One is obliged to wonder whether Stalin, in making these concessions, was really aware of what his own police had done in the case of the nearly ten thousand officers; for the effort to establish a Polish armed force of this nature was bound to direct attention to the absence of these men and to lead to demands that they be produced and permitted to join the new force. However that may be, considerable concessions were made, at that time, to Allied pressures for a decent treatment of the Polish exiled government. There was one point, however, where these concessions stopped short. While willing to admit that the agreement with the Nazis no longer had validity, Stalin proved unwilling, even in the moments of his greatest military extremity, to agree to restore to Poland after the war the areas into which Soviet forces had entered by agreement with the Nazis in 1939. And the British, then the ones most prominently involved on the Western side in defense of the interests of the government-in-exile, seeing in the resistance of the Russian armies the only chance of defeating Hitler, refrained from pressing the point.

By the end of 1941, only a few weeks after making these concessions to the Poles, Stalin appears to have begun (probably in view of the improvement of Russia's military situation) to repent of them. He set about, in any case, to deprive them, where he could, of real meaning. This it was not difficult for him to do. One by one, measures were put in hand, at that time and during the ensuing fifteen months, to reduce and eventually to negate the value of the concessions. The Soviet authorities first refused to recognize the

Polish citizenship of those deportees from the former Soviet-occupied area of Poland who could not prove that they were of Polish ethnic origin, thus simply appropriating to Soviet citizenship, without the slightest consultation of their own wishes, all those who were classifiable as Jews, Ukrainians, Byelorussians, or other non-Polish ethnic groups. This obviously greatly narrowed the body of persons to whom the representatives in Russia of the government-in-exile could have access. All sorts of difficulties were placed in the path of the recruitment and formation of the Polish armed force in Russia; and such units as could be assembled were finally removed, by common agreement, from the Soviet Union. A committee of Polish Communists, wholly disinclined to recognize the authority of the government-in-exile, was permitted, and no doubt encouraged, to establish itself on Soviet territory, where it was obviously to be held in reserve as a possible alternative to the exiled government. The efforts of the government-in-exile to maintain an official establishment on Soviet territory and carry out a relief action for the survivors of the deportations were gradually and progressively harassed to a point where they lost practically all meaning. In January 1943 the Soviet government finally put a complete end to the usefulness of that establishment by announcing that all Poles remaining on Soviet soil were henceforth to be considered as Soviet citizens. This meant that the representatives of the London Polish government could no longer even inquire of the fate of these people, much less bring them any assistance. Finally, when — in April 1943 — the discovery of the bodies at Katyn was announced by the Germans, and the Polish government-in-exile asked for an investigation by the International Red Cross (and it is hard to see how it could have done less), the Soviet government responded by breaking off relations with the government-in-exile promptly and entirely.

Just before returning to Moscow, in 1944, I spent ean evening with the counselor of the Polish embassy in Washington, the late Jan Wszelaki. Together we went over this whole sorry story in an effort to reconstruct the motives and purposes of the Soviet government. I came away from this discussion with the strong feeling that while Stalin's hostile actions toward the government-in-exile were no doubt partly attributable simply to Russia's improved military and political position, they were not fully explicable except in terms of an acute embarrassment, on the Soviet side, over excesses perpetrated by the Soviet police authorities against the Poles in 1939 and 1940, and a resulting determination that there should be in Poland in the postwar period no government that would have either the inclination or the ability to probe uncomfortably into the past and to make a public issue of these actions of the Soviet authorities. This meant, if my calculations were correct, that things stood much worse with the Polish government-in-exile than the Western governments were at that time prepared to believe: that we were confronted here with a situation far uglier and more recalcitrant than was generally recognized. What was bothering Stalin was not, as many of our people tended to assume, just the desire to have a "friendly government" on the other side of the Polish frontier. What was bothering him was the need for the collaboration of any future Polish political authority in repressing evidences and memories of actions by Soviet police authorities in the period 1939-1941, for which no adequate and respectable excuse could ever be found. It was clear that a Polish authority which could be depended on to give such collaboration could never be other than a Communist one, under close Soviet control.

While in Tehran, on my return journey to Russia, I entered in my diary some thoughts about the Polish situation which reflected these impressions. Realizing that I was about to travel through Soviet territory all the way from the Persian border to Moscow and that I could not be sure that my papers would not be gone through at some point by curious members of the Soviet secret police, I phrased my thoughts here in a manner calculated to stand Soviet scrutiny if they had to; but I found that I had to temper them very little to make them adequate to this purpose. Here, the diary passage:

I had occasion, during the period I was in Iraq, to reflect on the Polish-Russian question. I could scarcely do otherwise; for I have no doubt that this question will arise repeatedly, during the period of my stay in Moscow, to plague the relations between the United States and the Soviet Union. It is all very well for Comrade Borisov to write to the editors of *War and the Working Class* that this question can be settled between the Soviet Union and Poland directly, and needs no interference from without. The fact remains that for millions of people in our country this question has become the test of the willingness of Russia to pursue a decent, humane, and cooperative policy in Europe. If Russia is prepared to pursue such a policy, then the tremendous latent possibilities of American-Russian relations have before them an open road to fruition. If not, then there remains for the Anglo-Saxon powers only the division of Western Europe into spheres of influence and the establishment of a relationship to Russia which can serve the interests of neither party. For many people in our country, the attitude of Russia in the Polish problem will be the touchstone of Russia's relations with the West.

I think that I understand as well as anyone the complications of the Russian position. It is of course not the territorial question which causes the real difficulty, but the question of the Polish government. Here the Soviet government is making things unnecessarily hard for itself; and it is clear that those responsible for Soviet policy are either incorrectly informed by persons within their own sphere of authority or have arrived at an incorrect appraisal of the situation.

Reasonable people everywhere will understand that the current policies of the Soviet government, with all their tremendous importance for the future of Europe, cannot and must not be compromised by disputes over past errors in judgment of individual groups or individuals within the Soviet government. I am sure that the Polish government, whatever tactical mistakes it may have made in the past, would understand this as well as anybody else, at the present moment. The demand in Russia for the complete suppression and liquidation of the Polish government, with all its records and archives and memories, may serve the interests of certain groups within the Soviet government who know themselves to be responsible for past mistakes. It will not serve the interests of the Soviet government or of the Soviet people as a whole. For if the present Polish government is ruined and driven to despair, it will merely become the core of a Polish emigration which for years will continue to make propaganda over the alleged excesses of Russian authorities toward Polish forces and civilians during the period of the Russo-German Nonaggression Pact. Whereas if any reasonable arrangement can be made with that government (and such an arrangement would not necessarily preclude either extensive territorial arrangements or the reconstitution of the Polish government to include people such as Witos and others) there can be no doubt that the Polish leaders would be willing enough to let bygones be bygones; and the Russian government would always have, in its own tremendous strength, the guarantee of that undertaking. If the present course is continued, it means that the entire international future of Russia is to be jeopardized for the internal political security of a few individuals in Russia who once made unsound decisions.

By the end of June 1944, when I reentered Russia, the whole Polish problem was coming to a head as the result of the entry of Soviet forces, for the first time, onto territory the status of which as Polish not even the Soviet government was inclined to dispute. Instead of permitting the government-in-exile to send its own officials to this territory and to take over, or at least have a hand in, the administration of civil affairs there, the Soviet government gave every evidence of an intention to permit the Polish-Communist Committee, now blossoming out into a "Committee of National Liberation," to establish itself politically on the liberated territory, at Lublin.

The government-in-exile was naturally frantic with anxiety over this turn of events. The Western governments, too, having tried for three years to temporize with the problem, now found themselves obliged to face up to it. The Premier of the London Polish government, Mr. Stanislaw Mikolajczyk, visiting President Roosevelt in June, was pressed by the President, and by Churchill as well, to travel to Moscow and to make his appeal directly to Stalin. Stalin, though obviously reluctant, was finally persuaded to receive him. On July 27 Mikolajczyk left London for Moscow. That same day the Soviet newspapers announced, obviously in anticipation of this visit, the conclusion of an agreement between the Soviet government and the Polish-Communist Committee of National Liberation, permitting the latter to assume "full direction of all the affairs of civil administration" in all areas of Poland as soon as these areas ceased to be included in the zone of direct military operations. This was as clear an indication as one could want that Stalin had no intention of permitting the government-in-exile to reestablish its authority on any portions of Poland overrun, as indeed all of Poland was eventually sure to be, by the Red army.*

On July 26, the day before the announcement of the agreement just mentioned, Ambassador Harriman told me in confidence of Mikolajczyk's impending visit, and asked me for my opinion as to what, if anything, we should wire to Washington in the way of advance comment on the event. We agreed that we would both sleep on the problem. The following morning, with the news of the agreement with the Lublin Poles (as the members of the Committee of National Liberation were now being called) now before me in the morning papers, I wrote out my views. I gave it to the ambassador as my belief that it was most unlikely that this visit would produce any reconciliation of the government-in-exile with the Lublin group. To support this opinion, I offered the following considerations:

1. The Russians have recently had — and still are having — unparalleled success on the field of battle. They are elated and proud almost to the point of hysteria. They will be confident that they can arrange the affairs of Eastern Europe to their own liking without great difficulty, and they will not be inclined to go far out of their way either for the Poles or for us.

2. Mikolajczyk has had no recent invitation to come to Moscow. The visit was arranged at the insistence of the British and not the Russians. The most he has to go on is a grudging admission by Stalin that he will not refuse to see him if he comes — together with a warning that it would be better for him to see the Moscow-controlled Poles. This indicates that Stalin has no real interest in the visit and no plans for gaining anything from it.

3. It was made clear in Moscow that a reorganization of the [Lon-

---

* On the last day of 1944, the Soviet government finally announced its recognition of the National Committee, at Lublin, as the legitimate government of Poland, and it thus became the origin of the present Polish-Communist regime.

don] Polish government is a prerequisite for the straightening out of Polish-Russian relations. This reorganization has not taken place.

4. The new Polish Committee of Liberation has already taken a stand violently opposed to the government-in-exile. Considerations of prestige will inhibit a change in this stand.

I added that I thought the best Mikolajczyk could expect to get would be a post in a Polish government composed largely of the present members of the Committee of Liberation, together with certain pro-Soviet Poles from abroad, like Lange, and this — only if he were prepared not only to disavow but also to join in the denunciation of many of his present associates among the Poles in exile, including the President and Sosnkowski.

On the boundary question, finally, I stated that the boundary would, of course, be determined in the final instance according to political and strategic considerations, as Moscow saw them, and that the final result would be masked over by the ethnologic formula embodied in the Polish manifesto — than which nothing could be more flexible.

I thought it best not to mention in this memo my own dismal suspicions as to the deeper reasons for the unwillingness of the Soviet government to deal with the Polish government-in-exile. There was a general reluctance in Allied circles at that time to dwell on, or make issues of, past actions of the Soviet government, particularly those taken in the Nonaggression Pact period. In addition to this, when it came to the murdered officers, I had no proof — nothing more than a general intuitive idea, in fact, based on experience and on the limited evidence then available — as to what was likely and what unlikely to have been the case. I was particularly loath to bring up these matters at that moment because it was just about this time, if my memory is correct, that the ambassador sent one or two of his personal aides to Katyn in company with a group of foreign journalists whom the Soviet authorities, anxious to persuade them of German guilt for the murder of the officers, had invited to view the graves. I had not been consulted in connection with any of this. I was not familiar with any of the documentation beyond what the Soviet government had itself seen fit to publish in the press. I could not take upon myself the burden of trying to prove, from my modest vantage point, charges of the most grievous nature against the Soviet government, and particularly ones which my own government did not wish to have raised or discussed. I therefore fell in, at least when it came to official correspondence, with the tacit rule of silence which was being applied at that time to the unpleasant subject in question.

In the light of my conviction that their cause was already a lost one, I experienced only with the most intense discomfort such social contacts as we had with the members of the Mikolajczyk party during their stay in Moscow. They were, in my eyes, the doomed representatives of a doomed regime, but no one could be so brutal as to say this to them; nor would it have increased my usefulness in Moscow if it had come to the attention of the Soviet authorities, as it probably would have, that I was saying things of this sort. On August 1, three days after the party's arrival, I recorded in my personal notes my reactions to the visit. I prefaced the entry by the following excerpts, taken from Bernard Pares's history of Russia, dealing with the attitude of the Russian government toward the Poles in the wake of the Napoleonic wars.

Gentlemen, yet a little patience, and you will be more than satisfied with me.

— Speech of Alexander I to the Poles, at Vilna, July 1814

Alexander loyally performed his promise to give a constitution to Poland.

— Pares writing of the year 1815

Russians . . . felt the contradiction of the grant to Poland of rights which were not yet given in Russia.

— Pares writing of the year 1830

The Polish Constitution was replaced by an Organic Statute which abolished the Polish Diet and army and practically repealed the constitutional loyalties. . . . Poland fell entirely under Russian bureaucratic government. . . . It was as if Russia could only hold Poland by uncivilizing it.

— Pares writing of the year 1832

I then went on with the following observations:

Had dinner last night at the British embassy with the Polish Prime Minister, Mikolajczyk, and the members of his entourage. They had now been here two days. The Prime Minister had seen Molotov. He had not yet seen Stalin. He himself was apparently encouraged by his talk with Molotov. The members of his entourage were depressed.

The British ambassador proposed a toast to the success of their mission; and since Mikolajczyk had been encouraged to come here by our President and by the British Prime Minister, we clearly had to maintain a general attitude of confidence and good cheer.

I found the evening a hard one. I was probably the only non-Pole present who had enough experience of Eastern Europe to be thoroughly aware of the factors involved. I knew that an agreement between the Poles and the Russians would be possible. I knew that such an agreement could even contain strong assurances of the independence of Poland. I knew that there could be solemn engagements on the part of the Russians not to interfere in Polish internal affairs. I knew that the Red army itself, during its period of occupation, would be entirely dignified and decent in its attitude toward the Poles.

But I also knew that entirely regardless of present intentions the force of circumstances would eventually transform such an agreement from a charter into a harness for the Poles; that Russians, in the long run, would be no more inclined at present than they were a hundred years ago to accept "the contradiction of the grant to Poland of rights which were not yet given in Russia"; that Russian conceptions of tolerance would not go far beyond those things with which Russians were themselves familiar; that the Russian police system would inevitably seep into Polish life unless sharp measures were taken on the Polish side to counteract it, and that such countermeasures would inevitably be deemed provocative and anti-Russian in Moscow. I knew, in short, that there is no border zone of Russian power. The jealous and intolerant eye of the Kremlin can distinguish, in the end, only vassals and enemies; and the neighbors of Russia, if they do not wish to be the one, must reconcile themselves to being the other.

In the face of this knowledge, I could only feel that there was something frivolous about our whole action in this Polish question. I reflected on the lightheartedness with which great powers offer advice to smaller ones in matters affecting the vital interests of the latter. I was sorry to find myself, for the moment, a part of this. And I wished that instead of mumbling words of official optimism we had had the judgment and the good taste to bow our heads in silence before the tragedy of a people who have been our allies, whom we have helped to save from our enemies, and whom we cannot save from our friends.

Two days later I was put again to the ordeal of pursuing polite conversation with Mikolajczyk and the other visiting Poles — this time at a luncheon in our own embassy. Again, the notes speak for themselves:

One of the Poles asked me point-blank what I thought of their chances. I replied that I thought the Russians, all things considered, wanted an agreement, but that I could not imagine that they would be inclined to go far out of their way to get it. I thought that the Poles could consider themselves well out of it if they could reach any satisfactory arrangement which would make it possible for Poles in exile to return to their native country and work there for its future. But I warned him that I usually leaned to the pessimistic side, and advised him to take that into account.

Before Mikolajczyk left Moscow, there began the tragic and dramatic episode of the Warsaw uprising. This, more than anything that had occurred to that point, brought the Western governments face to face with what they were up against in Stalin's Polish policy. For if the inactivity of the Red army forces as they sat, passive, on the other side of the river and watched the slaughter by the Germans of the Polish heroes of the rebellion was not yet eloquent enough as an expression of the Soviet attitude, then the insolent denial by Stalin and Molotov to Ambassador Harriman of permission for use of the American shuttle base in the Ukraine to facilitate the dropping of arms and supplies to the beleaguered Poles, and the significant demand, expressed on the same occasion, that we withdraw the shuttle bases entirely, left no room for misunderstanding. I was personally not present at this fateful meeting with Stalin and Molotov; but I can recall the appearance of the ambassador and General Deane as they returned, in the wee hours of the night, shat-

tered by the experience. There was no doubt in any of our minds as
to the implications of the position the Soviet leaders had taken. This
was a gauntlet thrown down, in a spirit of malicious glee, before the
Western powers. What it was meant to imply was: "We intend to
have Poland, lock, stock, and barrel. We don't care a fig for those
Polish underground fighters who have not accepted Communist authority. To us, they are no better than the Germans; and if they
and the Germans slaughter each other off, so much the better. It is a
matter of indifference to us what you Americans think of all this.
You are going to have no part in determining the affairs of Poland
from here on out, and it is time you realized this."

It has been my opinion, ever since, that this was the moment
when, if ever, there should have been a full-fledged and realistic
political showdown with the Soviet leaders: when they should have
been confronted with the choice between changing their policy
completely and agreeing to collaborate in the establishment of truly
independent countries in Eastern Europe or forfeiting Western-
Allied support and sponsorship for the remaining phases of their
war effort. We no longer owed them anything, after all (if indeed
we ever had). The second front had been established. The Western
Allies were now on the European continent in force. Soviet territory had been entirely liberated. What was now at stake in Soviet
military operations was exclusively the future of non-Soviet territories previously overrun by the Germans. We in the West had a
perfect right to divest ourselves of responsibility for further Soviet
military operations conducted in the spirit of, and with the implications of, the Soviet denial of support for the Warsaw uprising.

All these things occurred in the summer of 1944: five months
before Yalta, eight or nine months before the crisis over Polish
affairs that occurred at the time of the death of President Roosevelt.
It will be understood that I, holding these views, followed only
with greatest skepticism and even despair the progress of our
further dealings with the Soviet leaders, in 1944 and 1945, over
Poland. The Yalta Declaration, with its references to the reorganization of the existing Polish-Communist regime "on a broader democratic basis" and to the holding "of free and unfettered elections

. . . on the basis of universal suffrage and secret ballot," struck me as the shabbiest sort of equivocation, certainly not calculated to pull the wool over the eyes of the Western public but bound to have this effect. With boredom and disgust I served, in the spring of 1945, as Ambassador Harriman's aide and interpreter through the many hours of unreal, repetitive wrangling with Molotov and Vyshinski as to who, among the non-Communist Poles, might be invited to participate in the discussions looking to the formation of a coalition Polish government.* I never doubted that it was all a lost cause.

My last responsible encounter with the Polish problem occurred when, shortly after Franklin Roosevelt's death, Harry Hopkins, himself with only a few weeks to live, visited Moscow to see what could be salvaged from the wreckage of FDR's policy with relation to Russia and Poland.

At some point during his visit, after at least the first — and I believe the second as well — of his interviews with Stalin, Hopkins summoned me to Spaso House to inquire my opinion. I was amazed at this. I did not know him well. I had not been kept informed about his dealings with Stalin; and I had not expected to be consulted on these matters. He described to me Stalin's terms for a settlement of the Polish problem, as developed in his talks at the Kremlin, and asked whether I thought we could do any better. I said I did not. Did I think, then, that we should accept these terms and come to an agreement on this basis? I did not; I thought we should accept no share of the responsibility for what the Russians proposed to do in Poland.

"Then you think it's just sin," he said, "and we should be agin it."

"That's just about right," I replied.

* The reference here is to the several sessions of the Commission, composed of Soviet Foreign Minister Molotov and the British and American ambassadors in Moscow, that had been established by the Yalta Conference to consult with the "present [Polish] government." My disgust would have been even greater had I known that while we talked, the Soviet authorities were quietly arresting, behind our backs, some of those very Polish political figures we were discussing for inclusion in the group to be consulted, and were putting pressure on them, unbeknownst to us, to become Soviet agents.

"I respect your opinion," he said, sadly. "But I am not at liberty to accept it."

There was one more aspect of the Polish problem that lay heavily on my mind during those first months in Moscow. This was the question of the western boundaries of the future Poland. On December 18, 1944, *Pravda* devoted nearly half of its entire foreign affairs page to an article by Dr. Stefan Jedrichowski, propaganda chief of the Lublin Committee and an important representative of that committee in Moscow, dealing with the question of the future German-Polish border. Jedrichowski recommended in this article that the future border of Poland should extend from Stettin south along the Oder and Lower Neisse rivers to about the most northerly point of the Czechoslovak border, near Görlitz. Stettin itself was to become a Polish port. The appearance of the article in *Pravda* meant, plainly, that the Soviet government sponsored the claim — that this was, in effect, the Soviet position as to where the future border should be.

I did not then know that this arrangement had already been substantially agreed to, specifically by Churchill and tacitly by Roosevelt, at the Tehran Conference a year earlier.* Not knowing this, I took the liberty, immediately upon reading Jedrichowski's article, of setting forth for the ambassador some thoughts of my own on the implications of such an arrangement. The Poles, I wrote, would obviously not have the manpower, technically or administratively, to make much of the newly acquired territory in the west, nor would they be able to defend it with their own resources. The result would be to increase their dependence on the Soviet Union. The Russians, I continued,

know this perfectly well. They know that the farther the western frontier of Poland is advanced into Germany, the greater will be the dependence of the Poles, economically and militarily, on the Soviet

---

* The understanding reached at Tehran was not specific with relation to the southern portion of the future German-Polish boundary. It left uncertain whether this was to be along the eastern or the western of the two Neisse rivers. (See Herbert Feis, *Churchill, Roosevelt, Stalin*, p. 287. Princeton: Princeton University Press, 1957.)

Union, and the less the significance of whatever frontier may be drawn in the east. They know that to fix the line of the Oder as the western-most limit of Germany must inevitably bring this dependence to a point where no Polish regime in the territory east of that line can be anything more, in effect, than a local authority, and where the Polish territory must become, by the unalterable logic of events, the military, economic, and political responsibility of the Soviet Union.

The appearance of this article [the Jedrichowski article] in this setting [i.e., in the prominent place given it by *Pravda*] must thus be taken to mean that the Russians have definitely decided that their strategic frontier, i.e., the line to which their immediate military, economic, and political responsibilities will run, will be the line from Stettin along the Oder and Lower Neisse rivers to the northernmost sector of the Czech frontier, and that they have found the moment opportune to announce this to the world public. . . .

This, in turn, has implications of the most far-reaching character. It makes unrealistic the idea of a free and independent Poland. It establishes a border in Central Europe which can be defended only by the permanent maintenance of strong armed forces along its entire extent. Despite Churchill's unconvincing optimism as to the ease with which new homes can be found in Germany for six million people (I believe the figure is too low) it renders the economic and social problems of the remainder of Germany — of those sections of Germany, in other words, which are of the most direct interest to the nations of the Atlantic community — highly difficult of solution, and reduces radically the possibilities for stability in that area. In this sense, it can operate only at the expense of ourselves and the British.

We may not be able to prevent the realization of this project. . . . But I think we are being unrealistic if we fail to recognize it for what it is and give it its proper place in our thinking about the future of Europe. Above all, I see no reason why we should have to share responsibility for the complications to which it is bound to lead.

This memorandum was written a full six weeks before the discussions over Poland that took place at the Yalta Conference. I cite it here because I think it brings out sharply the basic elements of the unrealism that prevailed in the entire approach of FDR to the problems of Eastern Europe in those final months of the war. It should have been clear more than a year earlier, at the time of the Tehran Conference, that in undertaking to move Poland some two hundred miles west at the expense of Germany, the Allies were agreeing to the establishment of a Polish state which could not be other than a military and political protectorate of the Soviet Union. A border so unnatural as the Oder-Neisse one could be maintained and defended, in the long run, only by armed force — and armed force on a scale greater than Poland itself could be expected to muster. Nor could the Poles be expected to place reliance, for the defense of such a border, on the Western powers. This had all been gone through once before, in 1938 and 1939. Even at that time, the Western powers had proved a weak reed. In the face of the Oder-Neisse border, a future Germany would obviously have irredentist claims far stronger and more reasonable than those that Hitler was able to put forward in 1939 (and even these, as the Western powers realized, had something to be said for them). A Poland carved out of a good portion of Germany would be simply obliged, in the interests of its own defense, to assure itself at all times of Russian support, and to accept it pretty much on Russia's terms. In these circumstances it made little sense to go on arguing with Stalin and Molotov about the composition of a future Polish government, as though there were a real chance of genuine Polish independence. This was simply an attempt, and an unpromising one at that, to lock the stable door after the horse was stolen.

9

Moscow and the Victory in Europe

ALL of the papers from which were taken the excerpts dealing with the Polish problem, reproduced in the last chapter, were either entirely private ones, shown to no one at all at the time, or memos written for the ambassador. He did not normally comment on opinions of this sort; and if any of these memos were ever forwarded to Washington, I, at any rate, have no recollection of it. With the exception of the brief talk with Harry Hopkins, I had no opportunity to discuss these matters with anyone in authority in our government or to get their reaction to my own views, at the time. Had I been able to do this, I suppose that the answer to what I have just said, with relation to the western borders of Poland and to many of the other questions I was raising in that summer and autumn of 1944, would have been that neither Poland nor any other of the Eastern European countries would be dependent, in the postwar period, on Russian protection because plans were going forward for the establishment of a new international organization designed to protect and ensure international peace, and it would be this organization that would bear the load of assuring the stability of the postwar frontiers.

I was of course aware of these plans for establishment of a United Nations Organization. The Department of State had made no secret of them. They represented, as it seemed, the escape of the Secretary of State from the frustrations occasioned by his exclusion from the province of policy-making while the war was on. If he was not permitted to influence our wartime diplomacy, he could at least divert himself, and lend some aura of significance to his activity, by encouraging and directing planning for the postwar order. In this area, accordingly, in contrast to all the areas of wartime policy itself, the department plunged ahead with boldness and enthusiasm. Just at the time of my return to Russia I found our government, and the British, busily engaged in pressing the wary and unenthusiastic Russians to join in talks looking to the formation of a future international organization for peace and security. I considered this effort of persuasion to be unwise and regrettable because it helped to feed the impression, already conveyed to the Soviet leaders in many other ways, that it was *we* who were anxious for their collaboration and friendship, *we* who wanted something from *them*, we who, for some reason, could not face the problems of the postwar era without dangling before our public opinion at least the facade of Big Three collaboration. All this, as I saw it, was bound to fortify their belief in the strength of their own position and to increase the severity and greediness of their asking price for the very collaboration we were anxious to have. But none of these reflections had merit, at that time, in the eyes of my superiors in Washington. The Russians were finally prevailed upon to join us in three-power discussions of the issues involved. And from August 21 to September 28 there took place, in consequence, the first phase of the Dumbarton Oaks Conference, devoted to the exploration of just these possibilities.

Aside from having misgivings about the tactical desirability of pressing this sort of planning upon the Russians at that time, I could take no comfort from the idea itself. It seemed to offer no promising avenue of escape from the dangers of the situation to which the progress of the war, supported by our own policies, was inexorably tending. Lacking anyone to say these things to, and with a view only to the clarification of my own thoughts, I set forth, on August 4, 1944, some initial reactions to the press reports of the Dumbarton Oaks discussions:

Underlying the whole conception of an organization for international security is the simple reasoning that if only the status quo could be rigidly preserved, there could be no further wars in Europe, and the European problem, as far as our country is concerned, would be solved. This reasoning, which mistakes the symptoms for the disease, is not new. It underlay the Holy Alliance, the League of Nations, and numerous other political structures set up by nations which were, for the moment, satisfied with the international setup and did not wish to see it changed. These structures have always served the purpose for which they were designed just so long as the interests of the great powers gave substance and reality to their existence. The moment this situation changed, the moment it became in the interests of one or the other of the great powers to alter the status quo, none of these treaty structures ever stood in the way of such alteration.

International political life is something organic, not something mechanical. Its essence is change; and the only systems for the regulation of international life which can be effective over long periods of time are ones sufficiently subtle, sufficiently pliable, to adjust themselves to constant change in the interests and power of the various countries involved.

An international organization for preservation of the peace and security cannot take the place of a well-conceived and realistic foreign policy. The more we ignore politics in our absorption with the erection of a legalistic system for the preservation of the status quo, the sooner and the more violently that system will be broken to pieces under the realities of international life.

Those provisions of our proposals that are designed to prevent a great nation from conquering and dominating a small nation reflect a thinking which is naïve and out of date. We ignore completely the time-honored conception of the puppet state which underlies all political thought in Asia and Russia, and occasionally appears in Eastern and Central Europe as well. This conception alone mocks any legalistic formulas for the regulation of international life. Try asking the head of the Outer Mongolian Republic whether Mongolia has any grievances against Russia. He will pale at the thought. He is personally in the power of the Russian police system, and his people live under the shadow of the Red army. . . .

The conception of law in international life should certainly receive every support and encouragement that our country can give it. But it cannot yet replace power as the vital force for a large part of the world. And the realities of power will soon seep into any legalistic structure which we erect to govern international life. They will permeate it. They will become the content of it; and the structure will remain only the form. International security will depend on *them:* on the realities of power — not on the structure in which they are clothed. We are being almost criminally negligent of the interests of our people if we allow our plans for an international organization to be an excuse for failing to occupy ourselves seriously and minutely with the sheer power relationships of the European peoples.

I was not, in 1944, strongly averse to the establishment of a new world organization, per se. It was not greatly needed, I thought; but if pursued realistically, with a clear recognition of its obvious limitations, it would do no harm. What worried me was the establishment of such an organization on the expectation that it could serve in any significant way to mitigate the consequences of the forthcoming communization of Eastern and parts of Central Europe — that it could serve, in effect, to contain and to correct the disbalances bound to flow from the foreseeable outcome of military operations. Woodrow Wilson in 1919 had expected something similar of the League of Nations, only to be grievously disappointed. This last point was met, of course, in the arguments of people in Washington, by reference to the fact that the United States had declined to accept membership in the League of Nations. Good enough, I thought to myself at the time; but even American participation could not in itself make up for the inherent weaknesses of such an organization, particularly not when American statesmen were themselves admitting that the whole concept depended on a friendly and intimate postwar collaboration among the great powers, which, as one saw it in Moscow, was certainly not to be. Stalin, after all, laid no value on a peaceful world per se. He was interested in a world where the interests of his own personal power would prosper. If "peace" would cause them to prosper better than "war," he would be for peace. But the deadly political struggle would continue; and if the day were to come when violence — particularly violence among others from which Russia could hope to remain aloof — would serve his purposes better than peace, no international organization would restrain him from a provocatory, inflammatory policy.

Insofar as Stalin attached importance to the concept of a future international organization, he obviously did so in the expectation that the organization would serve as the instrument for maintenance of a great power hegemony — a US–UK–Soviet hegemony, that is — in international affairs. This hegemony would be predicated, as he conceived it, on a far-reaching political harmony among the three powers; but this harmony would be based, in turn, on an acceptance by the other two of the sphere of influence in Eastern and Central Europe which, by the summer of 1944, the Soviet Union was already in process of establishing; and the world organization would then be expected to serve as a means of enlisting British and American support in the maintenance of this sphere of influence.

It is not surprising, all this being so, that when in the course of the Dumbarton Oaks discussions the United States government took the position that one of the permanent members of the future Security Council should not be permitted to vote in a dispute to which it was a party, Stalin sensed trickery. Attempts, as he foresaw, could easily be made to dislodge the Kremlin from its preeminent position in one or another of the countries within its sphere of influence. If the matter then developed into an international clash, and came before the world organization, the Soviet government would have no legal recourse. The Soviet negotiators were therefore instructed to oppose the American proposal, pointing out that if the political solidarity of the great powers were maintained, nothing of this sort would be necessary.

The matter became one of the two major points on which it proved impossible to reach agreement at Dumbarton Oaks. There was a flutter of alarm in Washington. Fears were entertained in the State Department that the entire project for an international organization would come under domestic political attack in the United

States if the great powers should be permitted to vote, and thus to enjoy the right of veto, in conflicts to which they were a party. An anxious telegram went forward from the President to Stalin, begging him to instruct his delegation to yield; but the reply, received in Washington on December 15, was negative. To yield on this point, Stalin said, would be to nullify the understanding reached at the Tehran Conference that plans for the postwar period had to be based on the principle of Allied unity. Besides, there was a lot of anti-Soviet prejudice abroad in the world; even the smaller countries, after all, had an obligation to weigh carefully the consequences to which any disruption of big-power unity could lead.

This reply occasioned much further perturbation in Washington, and much discussion as to whether a further appeal should not be made. The flurry found its reflection in Ambassador Harriman's upstairs study in Spaso House, where the officers of the embassy, too, discussed the deadlock and puzzled over what could and should be done. I cannot recall the specific tenor of the discussion, but there must, I think, have been a suggestion from some quarter (probably Washington) that we should, in effect, throw ourselves on Stalin's mercy, pointing out the domestic political embarrassment he was causing to the administration and asking him by implication to help us out in our domestic political difficulty.

I was violently opposed to this suggestion. I had always thought it unwise and improper for American statesmen to plead domestic political pressures, or the pressures of public opinion, as an argument to support their positions vis-à-vis other governments. It was our own business, I considered, not that of other governments, to resolve such divisions in American opinion. Others should not be invited to involve themselves in our domestic-political process. I had been shocked on being told, at an earlier time, that FDR had once sent a private request to Stalin to use his influence with the American Communist Party to prevent it from supporting him, FDR, in a presidential election, lest this support prove embarrassing to him. The same hackles now rose at the suggestion that we should ask Stalin's help in easing the position of our government vis-à-vis public or congressional opinion in the matter of the future international organization. I could conceive of giving the Russians a warning; I could not approve the idea of approaching them with another supplication. I therefore sat down the following morning (December 16, 1944) and addressed a memo to the ambassador which contained the following passages:

We should realize clearly what we are faced with. It is this — that as far as border states are concerned the Soviet government has never ceased to think in terms of spheres of interest. They expect us to support them in whatever action they wish to take in those regions, regardless of whether that action seems to us or to the rest of the world to be right or wrong. We are not expected to inquire as to whether those deeds are good ones or bad ones. I have no doubt that this position is honestly maintained on their part, and that they would be equally prepared to reserve moral judgment on any actions which we might wish to carry out, i.e., in the Caribbean area.

Our people, for reasons which we do not need to go into, have not been aware of this quality of Soviet thought, and have been allowed to hope that the Soviet government would be prepared to enter into an international security organization with truly universal power to prevent aggression. We are now faced with the prospect of having our people disabused of this illusion. This involves the danger that bitter things may be said at home, either sincerely or for purposes of domestic political advantage, which will offend Moscow's abnormal sensibilities and cause violent repercussions on our relations. Our task is to soften and ease this readjustment as much as possible.

It is absolutely essential that we maintain at this moment a cool head and a clear, dignified position. There is one thing we must not do: we must not admit to the Russians that their stand in this matter can have domestic political repercussions in our country, and thereby put ourselves in the position of supplicating them to take action which would affect a domestic political situation. The moment we do this, they will feel that they have us really on the run and will begin to crack the whip for fair. They might agree to retract slightly from their position about the voting in the Council of the proposed organization, or at least to try to sweeten the pill for our public by some disarming declaration. But they would demand a high price for this. They would probably try to devise their action in such a way that they could undo its effects at will. In this way, they would hold the whip hand over us constantly. And even then their action would be superficial. They would scarcely change their basic position, whatever apparent concessions they might make.

Instead of going as supplicants to the Russians, we should go to them as one bringing a friendly warning. Our position should be as follows: we would regret to have to make it plain to our public that Russia alone, of all the great powers, was unwilling to submit her future actions to the judgment of international society. We would regret this because it would only fortify and widen in our public opinion those very suspicions of Russia which we ourselves have been helping to eliminate. It would disillusion our people as to the possibilities of really effective international collaboration, and it would force them to abandon many of the splendid hopes that they have had for the future character of our relations. It would make it difficult for this or for any other American administration to do for the Russian people the things which all of us would like to be able to do. But the choice lies with Russia and with Russia alone. If this position is adhered to and if repercussions in American public opinion are unfavorable, Russia has only herself to blame.

The immediate crisis was surmounted by the simple expedient of an agreement to disagree at Dumbarton Oaks, and the issue itself was finally resolved, as is known, by the heads of state, at Yalta, through the now familiar distinction between procedural and political questions. I could, however, take little satisfaction from this accommodation or from the other evidences of progress made in the ensuing months in the preparations for a new international organization. The world of thought that had inspired Mr. Hull and his associates with such exalted enthusiasm as they addressed themselves, earlier in war, to these preparations was foreign to me, intellectually and personally. I followed with bitter skepticism what I happened to learn of the progress of the Yalta discussions and other exchanges on these subjects. I considered them only the further deepening of unresolved misunderstandings, and rather hoped, I must confess, that they would fail: not because I did not wish for

international amity, not because I was even against the principle of
a world organization per se, but because I felt that any agreements
on major matters arrived at with the Russians at that time, and in
the face of the prevailing misunderstandings, could have no other
than a tragic ending.

In the period just prior to my return to Russia in 1944 I had been
uncertain as to the validity of my own misgivings about our policy
toward Russia. It seemed to me, as I have said, that this policy was
based on grievous misunderstandings; but could I be sure? I had not
been in Russia for several years. In particular, I had not been there
during the war. Perhaps there had really been significant changes.
Perhaps my impressions and views were out of date. Perhaps the
great traumatic experiences of Russia in the war — the intimacy between people and regime and the association with foreign allies in a
common military undertaking — had brought to the Soviet leaders
what no other experience had succeeded in bringing to them: a realization of the extent to which men everywhere were involved in a
common predicament — a sense of the unreality of the antagonisms
conjured up by Marxian doctrine — a recognition that there could
be such things as confidence and collaboration even between countries that called themselves Communist and ones that did not — a
readiness to believe that differences in social systems might not,
after all, be the final determinants of relations between sovereign
states, that other and more hopeful factors might also be involved.

It did not, I repeat, seem to me *likely* that things should be this
way. I had seen no objective evidence that they were. But could I,
having been so long absent from Russia, be sure that the evidence I
had was adequate? Colleagues who *had* been in touch with the Russian problem had a more encouraging impression of the state of
affairs.

It was for these reasons that I was, at the time of my return,
prepared to reserve judgment until I could see for myself.

Several weeks of life and work in Moscow during that summer
of 1944 sufficed to dispel these uncertainties. What I saw during
that time was enough to convince me that not only our policy to-

ward Russia, but our plans and commitments generally for the shaping of the postwar world, were based on a dangerous misreading of the personality, the intentions, and the political situation of the Soviet leadership.

I had, of course, no obligation to exert myself to dispel this misunderstanding. It had been understood, when I took the post, that I was not to have political responsibility; and I had, God knows, in view of my experiences at other wartime posts, no reason to believe that my views would be interesting or welcome to people in official Washington. But it was hard to remain silent in the face of so tragic a recognition. Conscience forced me to attempt to reduce to words on paper the view I held of the nature of the Soviet leaders and of the situation in which they found themselves as they entered upon this final phase of the war, and to make this statement at least available to those who had responsibility for the formulation of American policy. It would be up to them, then, to draw the logical conclusions, if by chance they should be interested.

The result, completed in September 1944, was an essay of some thirty-five pages entitled *Russia — Seven Years Later*. The text, never previously published in full, is appended in the Annex to this narrative.* In it I poured forth, as in nothing else I ever wrote, the essence of what I knew about Russia generally, and Stalin's Russia in particular, as a phenomenon on the horizon of American policy makers. It was a better paper, broader, more balanced, and more specific than the so-called X–Article, written two and a half years later, which went in part over the same ground and in fact drew heavily on the earlier statement.† It laid out my interpretation of the evolution of Soviet foreign policy over the years of the Stalin era, assessed the situation in which the Soviet leaders found themselves at the time, and forecast in general terms the lines of their reaction and behavior in the immediate postwar period.

The paper began with an appraisal of the influence of the war on the relationship between the Soviet regime and the people. It con-

* A large portion of this paper has been published in *Foreign Relations of the United States, 1944, Europe,* Vol. IV, pp. 902-914. Washington, D.C.: US Government Printing Office, 1966.
† The nature and background of the X–Article will be discussed in Chapter 15.

tinued with an estimate of the extent of the demographic changes the war was bringing, and an appraisal of their effect, and that of the forthcoming expansion of the Russian sphere of interest in Eastern Europe, on the balance of forces between Russia and the West. These changes would not, I thought, be sufficient to support the thesis that old Europe was "finished" or that one had to expect "the early establishment of Russian domination throughout the continent." But they did mark a considerable displacement of the power balance in favor of the Russians.

Two hundred million people, united under the strong and purposeful leadership of Moscow and inhabiting one of the major industrial countries of the world, constitute a single force far greater than any other that will be left on the European continent when this war is over; and it would be folly to underestimate their potential — for good or for evil.

Turning to the prospects for Russian economic life in the postwar era, I pointed out that the regime would continue to be faced with the problem of distributing the proceeds of its various revenues among three main areas of expenditure: military expenditures, increase in fixed capital, and improvement of the living standards of the people. In facing this problem, it would be guided by its principal goal, which was "to increase the relative power and prestige of the Russian state in the world at large." And it would "see the way to the achievement of this goal in the increase of fixed capital" (i.e., in the forced development of heavy industry). As for foreign trade, the Soviet leaders would not, in the postwar period, be dependent on it, or inclined to give up for the sake of it, anything deemed vital or important to Russia's security or progress. They would gladly accept foreign governmental credits, but in doing so they would assume that the governments granting such credits would have acted "in their own interests and with their eyes open," and would do what they could to assure that such outside assistance should not "become the cause of widespread feelings of gratitude or sentimental enthusiasm among the Russian population." (This point was emphasized in view of the widespread anticipation in liberal American circles that the Soviet government would gratefully avail itself of American financial assistance in the postwar period, and that appreciation for the financial assistance would reinforce the expected political collaboration.)

After a discussion of cultural trends, I turned to the political questions, particularly those of foreign policy, that were central to the purpose of the paper. I began with an historical digression. Sketching the origins of the exaggerated fear of the outside world and preoccupation with security that had always dominated the psychology of Soviet officialdom, pointing to the waning of the original Soviet hopes that the security problems of the Soviet regime would be solved by the spreading of revolution to other countries, I went on to trace the reaction of Stalin to the accession of Hitler to power in Germany, and the development of a policy during the mid-1930s based on the hope of embroiling the Western powers with Hitler as the best means of assuring Russia's immunity to German attack, or at least of reducing the force of such an attack if it could not be avoided. I analyzed Stalin's reaction to the growing evidence, in the late 1930s, that the Western powers were not going to be caught on this hook and could not be expected to oppose further German expansion to the east; and I showed how this impelled him to embrace, even at that time, a program of territorial and political expansion, based largely on Tsarist examples, designed to provide Russia with a wider protective glacis against attack from the west. This program, as I saw it,

meant the reestablishment of Russian power in Finland and the Baltic states, in eastern Poland, in northern Bukovina, and in Bessarabia. It meant a protectorate over western Poland, and an access to the sea for the Russian Empire somewhere in East Prussia. It meant the establishment of dominant Russian influence over all the Slavs of Central Europe and the Balkans. . . . Finally, it meant Russian control of the Dardanelles through the establishment of Russian bases at that point.

This, I argued, was the program that had inspired the conclusion of the Nonaggression Pact with Hitler. It continued, now, to lie at the basis of Soviet hopes and plans for the immediate postwar era. If it could be realized by "collaboration" with the Western powers, so much the better; if not, it would be pursued by other means. The course of military operations gave good grounds to suppose that the Kremlin would have it within its power, at the conclusion of hostilities, to achieve most of these objectives whether the Western powers liked it or not. Soviet troops would, after all, be in occupation of nearly all these regions when the war came to an end. In these circumstances, Stalin stood little to lose by talking agreeably about "collaboration."

What dangers could collaboration bring to a country which already held in its hand the tangible guarantees of its own security? On the contrary, if it were properly exploited, participation in arrangements for world security might even be made into a form of reinsurance for the protection of Russia's interests. Considerations of prestige, furthermore, would demand that Russia not be missing from any of the councils of the world powers.

It was idle in these circumstances, I thought, to worry about whether or not the Soviet leaders intended to "communize" the countries their forces were overrunning. What they were interested in was power itself; the form this power might take was a secondary consideration and would be determined by considerations of expediency.

For the smaller countries of Eastern and Central Europe, the issue is not one of communism or capitalism. It is one of the independence of national life or of domination by a big power which has never shown itself adept at making any permanent compromises with rival power groups . . . It is not a question of boundaries or of constitutions or of formal independence. It is a question of real power relationships, more often than not carefully masked or concealed.

I then turned to an examination of the personalities of Stalin and the men around them. None of Stalin's leading advisors, I pointed out, was personally identified with the policy of collaboration with the Western powers. There was none who had not been in high position in the late 1930s and at the time of the conclusion of the Nonaggression Pact with the Germans. There was none who had not been associated with policies decidedly hostile to Britain and the United States. It was not easy to believe that they had really changed their views. They were men who knew little of the outside world from personal experience. "To them, the vast pattern of international life, political and economic, can provide no association, can hold no significance, except in what they conceive to be its bearing on the problems of Russian security and Russian internal life." Who knew what strange images and impressions were created in the minds of these men by what they heard of life beyond Russia's borders, or what conclusions they drew from those images? It would be strange if they were not to some extent the victims of their own propaganda.

So long as this situation endured the Western powers would be, I thought, in a precarious position in the conduct of their relations with Russia. Western statesmen could never know, in the face of the extreme secrecy with which the entire process of decision-taking in the Kremlin was surrounded, "when, unbeknownst to them, people of whom they have no knowledge, acting on motives utterly obscure, will go to Stalin with misleading information and with arguments to be used to their disadvantage — information which they cannot correct and arguments which they have no opportunity to rebut." In such circumstances, it was doubtful whether even the friendliest of relations could be considered dependable. Until the "Chinese Wall of the spirit" * with which the Kremlin had contrived to separate itself and its people from the outside world had been broken down, men of good will abroad could have no assurance that their efforts on behalf of better relations with Russia would not lead to tragedy, instead of to the results they were seeking.

I completed this dissertation with some reflections on the philosophic difficulty involved for Americans in the attempt to under-

---

* This was a play on words. The area of Moscow immediately adjacent to the Kremlin had originally been separated from the remainder of Moscow by a wall called the Chinese Wall.

stand the realities of Russian life and thought, and ended with this melancholy, but for myself personally most prophetic, passage:

Distance, necessity, self-interest, and common sense may enable us, thank God, to continue that precarious and troubled but peaceful coexistence which we have managed to lead with the Russians up to this time. But if so, it will not be due to any understanding on our part of the elements involved. Forces beyond our vision will be guiding our footsteps and shaping our relations with Russia. There will be much talk about the necessity for "understanding Russia"; but there will be no place for the American who is really willing to undertake this disturbing task. The apprehension of what is valid in the Russian world is unsettling and displeasing to the American mind. He who would undertake this apprehension will not find his satisfaction in the achievement of anything practical for his people, still less in any official or public appreciation for his efforts. The best he can look forward to is the lonely pleasure of one who stands at long last on a chilly and inhospitable mountaintop where few have been before, where few can follow, and where few will consent to believe that he has been.

So much for the content of *Russia — Seven Years Later*. It would have been improper for me to send this paper, with its far-reaching implications for American policy, directly to anyone in Washington. It was the prerogative and the responsibility of the ambassador to decide whether it should go to Washington at all. I presented it, accordingly, to him. Some days later he returned it — without comment. Whether he had read it in full, or in part, or not at all, is something I do not know to this day. Evidently, he did send it to Washington, for a portion of it was recently reproduced in one of the volumes of our diplomatic correspondence published by the Department of State. I must doubt that he himself would even now remember the episode. I was puzzled and moderately disappointed, at the time, over his failure to react. That he might wish not to comment on the political content of the document, I could understand. I did think he might have observed, if he thought so, that it was well written. I personally felt, as I finished it, that I was making progress, technically and stylistically, in the curious art of

writing for one's self alone. But I would have welcomed reassurance.

* * *

A word or two is perhaps due at this point about the remarkable
man who was my chief in Moscow, Averell Harriman. I was, as
mentioned above, his "number two" on the civilian side of his mission. In this capacity I was thrown closely together with him in my
work for a period of some two years. From the professional, if not
from the personal standpoint, few could have had the opportunity
to observe him more intimately.

Circumstances were by no means all conducive to an easy relationship. He had at that time, I think, little liking for, or confidence
in, the Foreign Service. In this he followed closely the example of
the President and Harry Hopkins. It was obvious that the military
establishment seemed to him to be more central to his wartime
functions and concerns than did the civilian; and he had a tendency,
initially at least, to turn to the military side for advice and companionship. For this, one could scarcely blame him. He had at his side,
in the person of General John Deane, a senior military aide of the
highest quality: modest, unassuming, scrupulously honest, fair-
minded and clear-sighted. And it was, after all, our military collaboration with the Red army that still stood highest on the list of our
official concerns at that time.

But beyond this the traditional niceties of our diplomatic training
left him cold. I am sure that he, like many other people, would have
considered most of them to be affectations, peculiarly out of place
in wartime. He had no interest in the social-representational side of
the diplomatic function — either his or ours. He had that curious
contempt for elegance that only the wealthy can normally afford;
and if style interested him at all, it was more in horsemanship and
painting than in language or in mode of life. Unique in his single-
mindedness of purpose, it was his nature to pursue only one interest at a time. When we were associated with each other in Moscow this interest was, properly and commendably, the prospering
of the American war effort and American diplomacy, as Presi-

dent Roosevelt viewed and understood it. To the accomplishment of his part in the furtherance of this objective he addressed himself with a dedication, a persistence, and an unflagging energy and attention that has no parallel in my experience. He recognized no interests outside his work. Personal life did not exist for him. His physical frame, spare and sometimes ailing, seemed at best an unwelcome irrelevance; I had the impression that it was with an angry impatience that he took cognizance of the occasional reminders of its existence, dragged it with him on his daily rounds of duty, and forced it to support him where continuation without its support was not possible. Like my former chief, Kirk, in Berlin, he worked eighteen to twenty hours a day. No detail was too small to escape his attention. He wanted to know everything about everything. There were times when, after we had interrupted our labors in the wee hours of the morning, supposedly out of deference to the demands of our protesting bodies, he would be on the phone again before — as it seemed to me — I had scarcely gotten to sleep, demanding to know what implementation I had given to the decisions of the night.

Of me, as his senior subordinate, he demanded a knowledge of the details of the area of my responsibility no less encyclopedic than his own. The normal leisurely pace of an embassy chancery, and the coordination of its work with the other normal demands, social and personal, of a diplomatic existence, was not for him. An order once given, in no matter how trivial an affair, he expected — not unreasonably, as I recognize from the distance of the years — it to be executed forthwith. It made no difference what else lay on the docket, what else had been planned. I often think: what a trial I must have been to him, running around with my head in the usual clouds of philosophic speculation, full of interests other than my work, inclined to delegate responsibility and to forget about it cheerfully so long as all went well, bombarding him with bundles of purple prose on matters which, as I am sure he thought, it was the business of the President to think about, not mine — and all this when there was detailed, immediate work to be done. Small wonder that he was often peremptory. He didn't shout you down, for he never shouted; but he had a way of riding roughshod over unsolicited suggestions. A hundred times I came away from our common labors asking myself, without finding an answer: "Why do I still like this man?"

The difficulty was increased by the fact that he, in contrast I suppose to myself, regarded himself more as an operator than as an observer. He had no great interest in the general run of Foreign Service reporting. Accustomed to doing things in a big way and endowed with a keen appreciation for great personal power, always enjoying, in fact, the mere proximity of the very great, he dealt only with people at the top. I have no doubt that he felt, and not without justification in a country where power was so highly personalized as in the Soviet Union of that day, that he could learn more that was important in one interview with Stalin than the rest of us could derive from months of pedestrian study of Soviet publications. He concentrated on what is indeed the central function of the diplomat: to serve as a sensitive, accurate, and intelligent channel of communication between one's own government and another one. And this, I must say, he did supremely well. No diplomatist ever executed more punctiliously the instructions he had for communication with the leaders of a foreign government. None ever kept more careful notes, or reported more fully or conscientiously on what had transpired in the respective interviews or exchanges. None — be it said to his eternal credit — was ever less inclined to distort the record, however imperceptibly, in order to show himself and his performance off to good advantage. Nothing was more foreign to his nature. His integrity in the performance of his duties was monumental and unchallengeable.

It is characteristic that the critical observations I have had to make about Averell Harriman have all been ones of detail. The appreciative ones are not, for they relate to his virtues; and his virtues, as I knew him in Moscow, were virtues in the grand manner. He was a towering figure on our Moscow scene, outwardly unassuming but nevertheless commanding in appearance, without petty van-

ity, intensely serious but never histrionic in his seriousness, imperious only when things or people impeded the performance of his
duty. The United States has never had a more faithful public servant. He never invited our affection, nor gave the impression that he
would have reciprocated it; but in a curious way I think he had it,
at least from those of us who were thrown constantly together with
him. He had, in any case, our appreciative respect, and that of everyone else who knew him. I once asked a Russian friend what the
Russians thought of him. "They look at him," she replied, "and
they say to themselves: there goes a man [*vot muzhchina*]!" In
this, I think, she spoke for us all.

I, in any case, can do no other than record my gratitude to him
— for his patience with me, for what he taught me, for the example
he set. If he received in silence the anxious needlings on political
matters with which I plagued him in the months following my return to Moscow in 1944, he had good reason to do so. It was not his
business, as the President's personal representative in another great
country in wartime, to discuss with a subordinate statements and
interpretations that challenged so intimately the outlooks and policies to which the President was committed. He soon showed, by his
own official acts, that he had not been obtuse to the same evidences
of misunderstanding that caused me such concern. This was, I am
sure, a better way for him to indicate such agreement as he may
have found with my reflections and arguments than by verbally
holding, so to speak, my intellectual hand.

*   *   *

The autumn and winter of 1944-1945 wore on, with military operations on the Russian front now moving rapidly to their victori-
ous conclusion. Our windows looked out to the Red Square, and
every few evenings, in celebration of a victory at some point along
the enormous battle line, the cannons boomed and fireworks burst
over the square, the flashes of light reflecting themselves weirdly
against the oversized golden stars that had replaced the Tsarist double eagles on the Kremlin towers.

For us in the embassy, the approach of victory brought new

problems. There took place successively, during those months, the conclusion in Moscow of armistice agreements with the Finns, the Rumanians, and the Bulgarians. In each of these I was, in some small way, involved. I fussed and fumed, and plagued Averell, over the fact that the Russians, on coming into possession of the American-owned oilfields in Rumania, impudently set about to haul away to the Caucasus, for their own uses, the movable American property which they had been specifically asked, in advance, to protect. Similar unhappiness was produced by the operation of the tripartite control commissions that were set up to govern, provisionally, the enemy countries in the Balkans overrun by the Soviet armies. Here the Soviet commanders, who were by governmental agreement *ex officio* chairmen of the respective commissions, at once began to ride roughshod over their British and American colleagues, withholding information from them, ignoring their views as well as the interests of their governments, while the NKVD and its local agents, over whom the local Soviet commanders seemed either unwilling or unable to exert control, set about to isolate the Allied officers from the population, as though they were not allies but dangerous enemies (which indeed in the Soviet view they were).

The Russian commanders were well within their rights in asserting their authority in the commissions in this manner, for the Western Allies had done much the same, conversely, in the Allied Control Commission for Italy. But I could see no reason why this obliged us to continue to be represented on the commissions; and I personally questioned the desirability of our doing so. I felt (as I pointed out in a memo of December 5, 1944, dealing with the plans for an armistice agreement with Hungary) that this would merely saddle us "with moral responsibility for an armistice regime, the operation of which we have no means of influencing." The argument made no impression, however, on the United States government. Our military representatives on the respective commissions found themselves obliged to struggle unhappily along over the ensuing months, their personal helplessness being demonstrated daily to the local populations, while the United States accepted a share of responsibility before the respective populations for the highly political operations, useful only to the Kremlin, on which the chairmen of the commissions and other Soviet officials were engaged.

February and March 1945 brought the repercussions of Yalta and the endless, frustrating rounds of argument with Molotov over the question as to who was and who was not to be invited to take part in discussions looking to the formation of a new Polish government. In April there came signs of a strong and growing anxiety on the President's part over Soviet reactions and practices; and then, close on the heels of the first really unpleasant exchanges between the two leaders, the shattering news of the President's sudden death. After that, things moved rapidly, and for us hectically, to the final collapse of German resistance in early May.

In mid-April 1945, there arrived in Moscow, for a brief stopover, the man who was at that time our ambassador in China: Major General Patrick J. Hurley. He had been in Washington, consulting with the State Department and the President. Now he was on his way back to his post at Chungking.

Ambassador Hurley had visited Moscow once before, in September 1944, when first proceeding to his post in China. He had been accompanied on that occasion by Mr. Donald Nelson, Chairman of the War Production Board. The two men had talked with Molotov; and General Hurley had carried away from the interview (if we are to judge by his own account) a most remarkably optimistic impression of Soviet intentions toward China. He summed up as follows, in a later message (February 4, 1945), what he understood Molotov's views to be:

(*1*) The so-called Chinese Communists are not in fact Communists at all.

(*2*) The Soviet Government is not supporting the Chinese Communists.

(*3*) The Soviets do not desire dissensions or civil war in China.

(*4*) The Soviets complain of Chinese treatment of Soviet citizens in China but frankly desire closer and more harmonious relations in China.*

* *United States Relations with China,* Department of State Publication 3573, p. 93. Washington, D.C.: US Government Printing Office, 1949.

Now, in April 1945, things had moved on. The Yalta Conference had come and gone. We had undertaken to reconcile the Chinese Nationalists to the territorial and other concessions to the Soviet Union envisaged at Yalta. The Russians, on the other hand, had agreed to conclude a pact of friendship and alliance with Nationalist China. The time had now come for direct Chinese-Soviet discussions. The Chinese, however, were understandably puzzled and skeptical over the earlier optimistic reports they had received from General Hurley concerning Soviet intentions. They wanted further information about this before sending their own envoy to Moscow. This, presumably, was the background of General Hurley's second visit.

Ambassador Harriman was in the United States at that time. General Hurley wanted to see Stalin, and did so on April 15. Although I was chargé d'affaires and would normally have been present at any such interview, I cannot recall that any suggestion along this line was forthcoming from the general; and I, being in some ways just as happy not to be involved in his affairs, did not press the matter. I could not fail, however, to see the report of the interview which he drew up immediately afterward, before resuming his journey to Chungking, because it was left for us to dispatch through our telegraphic channels, and I was obliged to approve its dispatch. Its content gave me much trouble, for it did not check at all with the view of the Soviet outlook on Chinese matters that some of us in the embassy had formed. It was, once again, much more optimistic than anything warranted by the situation as we knew it. I studied it together with Mr. John Paton Davies, the embassy secretary most familiar with Chinese affairs, and we both felt that if permitted just to go as it stood, it would give a serious misimpression. We even doubted that it accorded with Ambassador Harriman's views; and we thought it not right to permit a message to go forward without comment which might run counter to his own interpretation. We therefore sat down and drafted the following personal message from me to Mr. Harriman, designed to bring some corrective into General Hurley's sanguine picture:

I refer specifically to the statements which were attributed to Stalin to the effect (1) that he expressed unqualified agreement with our policy in China as Ambassador Hurley outlined it to him, (2) that this policy would be supported by the Soviet government, and (3) that we would have his complete support, in particular, for immediate action directed toward the unification of the armed forces of China with full recognition of the Chinese National government under the leadership of Generalissimo Chiang Kai-shek. . . .

There was, of course, nothing in Ambassador Hurley's account of what he told Stalin to which Stalin could not honestly subscribe, it being understood that to the Russians words mean different things than they do to us. Stalin is of course prepared to affirm the principle of unifying the armed forces of China. He knows that unification is feasible in a practical sense only on conditions which are acceptable to the Chinese Communist Party. . . .

Actually I am persuaded that in the future Soviet policy respecting China will continue what it has been in the recent past: a fluid resilient policy directed at the achievement of maximum power with minimum responsibility on portions of the Asiatic continent lying beyond the Soviet border. This will involve the exertion of pressure in various areas in direct proportion to their strategic importance and their proximity to the Soviet frontier. I am sure that within the framework of this policy Moscow will aim specifically at: (1) Reacquiring in substance, if not in form, all the diplomatic and territorial assets previously possessed on the mainland of Asia by Russia under the Czars. (2) Domination of the provinces of China in central Asia contiguous to the Soviet frontier. Such action is dictated by the strategic necessity of protecting in depth the industrial core of the USSR. (3) Acquiring sufficient control in all areas of North China now dominated by the Japanese to prevent other foreign powers from repeating the Japanese incursion. This means, to the Russian mind, the maximum possible exclusion of penetration in that area by outside powers including America and Britain. . . .

It would be tragic if our natural anxiety for the support of the Soviet Union at this juncture, coupled with Stalin's use of words which mean all things to all people and his cautious affability, were to lead us into an undue reliance on Soviet aid or even Soviet acquiescence in the achievement of our long-term objectives in China.*

* *Ibid.*, pp. 96-97.

This interpretation met, in general, as the China White Paper makes clear, with Ambassador Harriman's agreement.

I cite this episode here, because it provides a wonderful example of the element of irony that runs through so much of diplomatic history. Davies, with his brilliant, imaginative mind and his wide background of experience in China, was a rock of strength to us at that time in the Moscow embassy. I owe largely to him whatever insight I was able to muster in those years into the nature of Soviet policies toward the Far East. He was a man of broad, sophisticated, and skeptical political understanding, without an ounce of pro-Communist sympathies, and second to no one in his devotion to the interests of our government. To reflect that here, trying to bring some element of realism and sobriety into the view of General Hurley on the question of Soviet intentions, was a man who only shortly thereafter would have to suffer years of harassment and humiliation at the hands of congressional investigating committees and executive loyalty boards largely because of charges, inspired largely by this same General Hurley, to the effect that he was naïve or pro-Communist in his sympathies — to realize this is to recognize the nightmarish quality of that world of fancy into which official Washington, and much of our public opinion, can be carried in those times when fear, anger, and emotionalism take over from reason in the conduct of our public life.

* * *

I cannot recall that I felt any great elation over the end of the war in Europe. Like everyone else, I was glad that the bloodshed and destruction of the battlefields was coming to a close. I had never doubted the necessity of the total destruction of German Nazism. But I could derive little comfort from the circumstances in which the war was ending. It was clear to me, as already stated, that no tripartite collaboration for the governing of Germany would be workable. Yet we Americans were continuing to base our plans on dreams of such collaboration. We had made no realistic plans, and had come to no adequate agreement with the British, for the establishment in the Western zones of the constructive and hopeful sort of order by which alone, it seemed to me, one could hope to resist effectively the political pressures which the German Communists, with Soviet support, could be expected to bring to bear. Meanwhile, tales were reaching us in depressing abundance — in some instances from decent members of the Soviet armed forces, themselves disgusted with the behavior of their comrades — of the wild brutalities and atrocities being perpetrated by a portion of Soviet troops (rarely the fighting men themselves, more often the rear echelon people) as they made their way into Germany and other areas liberated from the German forces. Was this, I wondered, the sort of victory we had hoped for? Was the price not such as to make a large portion of the victory unreal?

It was May 9, one day after V–E Day in the west, before the Russians, still suspicious lest the Germans continue resistance in the east even after surrendering to the British and Americans, consented to accept the fact that the war in Europe was over and to let their people know it. The news got about in Moscow in the very early hours of the morning of the tenth; and by daybreak a holiday mood so exuberant as to defy all normal disciplinary restraints was gripping the city.

The American flag was of course hung out from our combined chancery and staff residence quarters in the center of town; and from the National Hotel, wall to wall with our building, there hung the national flags of those unfortunate Allied representatives who had been unable to find premises of their own in Moscow and who still conducted their official activities (as we had done for several months after arrival in 1934) from their hotel rooms.

About ten o'clock in the morning, contingents of young people, apparently students, marching with songs and banners along the street before these buildings, spied the Allied flags on the National Hotel and burst into cordial cheers. Then, as they moved beyond the hotel, they discovered the Stars and Stripes, reacted with what appeared to be in most instances a surprised delight, stopped their march, and settled down to demonstrate before the embassy building feelings that were obviously ones of almost delirious friendship. The square before the building was commodious — it could have held two hundred thousand people — and soon our initial well-wishers were augmented by thousands of others, who joined in the friendly cheering and waving and showed not the slightest desire to move on. We were naturally moved and pleased by this manifestation of public feeling, but were at a loss to know how to respond to it. If any of us ventured out into the street, he was immediately seized, tossed enthusiastically into the air, and passed on friendly hands over the heads of the crowd, to be lost, eventually, in a confused orgy of good feeling somewhere on its outer fringes. Few of us were anxious to court this experience, so we lined the balconies and waved back as bravely as we could.

As a gesture of reciprocation, I sent one of our people across the roof of the National Hotel and procured from the hotel a Soviet flag, which we hung out together with our own. This produced new roars of approval and enthusiasm. But it did not seem enough. Being at that time chargé d'affaires (the ambassador was away), I thought it incumbent on me to say at least a word or two in appreciation. The balconies were too high to permit one to be heard; so I went down to the first floor and climbed out onto the pedestal of one of the great columns that lined the front of the building. With me among others (for some cockeyed reason buried in the agreeable confusions of the day) came a sergeant of the military mission in uniform — a man who was, as I understood it, a preacher in real life. Our appearance produced new transports of approval on the part of the crowd. The police, who had been holding the people away from the walls of the building, and one party agitator who had obviously been sent to try to assume leadership of the people and get them to move on, were now good-naturedly shoved aside, and the crowd pushed over the little barrier that lined the sidewalk, and onto the grass plots at the foot of the building, so that they now surrounded the pedestal. I shouted to them in Russian: "Congratulations on the day of victory. All honor to the Soviet allies"—which seemed to me to be about all I could suitably say. At this, roaring with appreciation, they hoisted up a Soviet soldier on their hands to the point where he could reach the pedestal. He pulled himself up into our company, kissed and embraced the startled sergeant, and pulled him relentlessly down to the waiting arms of the crowd. There, bobbing helplessly over a sea of hands, he rapidly receded from our view (and did not come back until the next day, I was told). I myself successfully escaped back into the building.

All day long, and well into the evening, this great crowd remained, waving and cheering, before the building. The Soviet authorities were naturally not entirely pleased with this situation, particularly because this was, so far as we could learn, the only place in Moscow where any demonstration of anything resembling these dimensions took place. A single polite though slightly suspicious cheer on the part of the crowd, accompanied by evidences of determination to destroy the "remnants of fascism" (meaning any form of opposition to Soviet political purposes), might, one feels, have been considered in order, but certainly not this warmth, this friendliness, this enthusiasm, demonstrated before the representatives of a government of whose iniquities, as a bourgeois power, Soviet propagandists had spent more than two decades trying to persuade people. It is not hard to imagine what mortification this must have brought to both party and police. Without their solicitous prearrangement not even a sparrow had fallen in a Moscow street for twenty-seven years, and now, suddenly — this! Continued efforts were made to get the crowd to move on. A bandstand was even hastily erected and a brass band put into operation on the other side of the square. But it was all to no avail. The crowd stayed. We ourselves were even a little embarrassed; we had no desire to be the sources of such trouble on a day of common rejoicing. We had done nothing, God knows, to invite the demonstration, or to encourage its prolongation, once it had started. But we were even more helpless than the authorities.

The evening of this memorable day brought an episode which, taken in connection with the epilogue it was to have four years later, seems to me to provide a striking illustration of the Stalinist-propagandist mentality. Mrs. Winston Churchill was, as it happened, visiting Moscow just at this time. A reception in her honor, to which I was invited in my quality as chargé d'affaires, was scheduled for that evening in the premises of the Society for Cultural

Relations with Foreign Countries. Shortly before my wife and I were to leave for this reception, I received a phone call from an English journalist, Mr. Ralph Parker, formerly correspondent in Prague for the *New York Times*, asking whether he and his Soviet-Russian wife might come up to our flat in order to watch the demonstration from the balcony. I knew Parker fairly well. I had helped him and a Czech lady friend to escape from Prague on the entrance of the Germans into that city in 1939, they being in bad odor with the Nazis for certain left-wing activities in which they had involved themselves. In Moscow we had had pleasant, but not close, social relations. He was known to be far to the left in his sympathies. His Soviet wife was widely believed in the diplomatic corps, correctly or otherwise, to be not only a faithful Communist but also a police informer. However, Moscow being a Communist city, we were accustomed to social relations with people who were party members, and even with some who were police informers. And so far as Parker himself was concerned, the wartime political association had tended to blur the distinction between honest anti-fascism and Communist political sympathies. I therefore thought nothing of telling him that he and his lady were welcome to come up and use the balcony in our absence.

They arrived just as we were leaving for the reception. He went out on the balcony for a few moments, then came back into the room in order to take leave of us before we left the flat. "Isn't this wonderful?" he asked me. I replied that it was, but that it also made me sad. Asked to explain, I observed that those people out there in the crowd had been through so much, and they naturally now hoped for so much from victory; yet the world was still full of troubles; Russia faced major problems of reconstruction; things would not be put back together again all at once; peace could scarcely be what these people dreamed of it as being.

So much for the incident itself. Four years later a book was published in Moscow, over Parker's signature, entitled *Zagovor protiv Mira (The Conspiracy Against Peace)*. Parker had by this time given up his work for non-Communist Western newspapers, thrown in his lot completely with the Soviet government, and burned his bridges to the West. What his exact status was, whether a Soviet citizen, or a member of some Communist Party, I do not know. Obviously, he was entirely under Soviet control. I suspect that he was by this time in some way a blackmailed man. The book, in any case, was a vicious attack on the United States government and particularly on its embassy in Moscow — the most unscrupulous, mendacious, and nauseating sort of Stalinist propaganda. It is difficult to believe that he had written it himself. He was, after all, an intelligent man. But the authorship was ostensibly his.

In the foreword to this book, after first describing the scenes on Victory Day in the squares and streets immediately around our embassy, Parker went ahead to give the following account of his visit to our flat on the evening of Victory Day (passages in brackets are my own comments):

On Mokhovaya Street I made my way through the crowd of Muscovites that was pushing past [the reader will note the implication that there was no crowd assembled before the Embassy, only passersby] and entered the building of the American Embassy. At a closed window [the windows had been wide open all day long, with members of our staff coming and going to and from the balconies] stood the tall figure of George F. Kennan, the Counselor of the Embassy of the United States in Moscow. Standing in such a way that he could not be seen from below, he watched the crowd. [This language was evidently chosen to expunge from the record, as a "nonhappening," the fact that I had actually appeared before the crowd and had addressed it; the official version had to be exactly the opposite in each case: far from exposing myself to the crowd, I had tried to conceal myself from it; far from addressing it, I had preserved a sullen silence.] The noise on the street became slightly weaker, dying away to a dull, echoing roar.

I noticed on Kennan's face, as we watched this moving scene, a strangely unhappy and irritated expression. Then, casting a last glance at the crowd, he moved away from the window and said bitterly: "They rejoice. . . . They think the war has ended. But it is really only beginning."

Before leaving the Embassy I noted that in place of the portrait of Roosevelt — whose brilliantly smiling face had previously presided over the room — there hung on the wall a portrait of Truman. [This last was purest nonsense. Portraits of both Presidents hung in the office; there was no portrait of either in our flat. But the legend was now being built that Truman, sabotaging Roosevelt's policy of collaboration, had begun, from the day of victory, to launch and press the cold war.]

On that particular day I failed to give proper attention to Kennan's words. But now, four years later, I recall them just as clearly as everything else that I saw and heard on the day of victory: the streams of people pouring into Moscow from the suburbs, the meetings of those who had solemnly sworn to each other to meet again "when the war is over," the sincere and friendly yearning of the Soviet people for peaceful collaboration with their former military allies.

The things that have occurred since that solemn and bright day have shown me that the real meaning of the words spoken by this American diplomat on the Day of Victory consisted precisely in the denial of this policy of peaceful coexistence.

I cite this passage as an illustration of the process of dreamlike distortion to which most reality having political implications has always had to be subjected before it could be made to fit into the image which the Russian Communist Party has cultivated of itself and its experiences. In tens of thousands of instances, over the course of the years, real events had to be denied, false ones invented, or true facts distorted beyond recognition, in order to produce a version that was compatible with the party's neurotic vision of the environment in which it lived and of its own reaction to that environment. Like a vast, collective Walter Mitty, it pictured itself moving fearlessly and heroically through a host of dangers, frustrating and defeating an endless series of dragons in human form. The result was that for every situation or event having political meaning there were always two versions: the true one and the fabricated one. There was usually some recognizable connection between them, but it was often so faint as to be discernible only with difficulty. The fabricated version having once been created, it at once became the authoritative one, and was then treated with all the respect and seriousness which would have been owing to the actual truth. If it invited indignation against the outrages of wicked enemies, indignation was manifested; if it suggested admiration for the superlative wisdom, shrewdness, courage, and altruism of the lead-ers of the Russian Communist Party, admiration was duly paid. So-viet officials, and indeed most of the literate public, were often per-fectly well aware of the existence and nature of both versions, the real one and useful one; and they were capable of talking, if they so desired, in terms of the one or of the other, depending on circum-stances. But it was seldom considered safe to talk in terms of the real one, once the other had been manufactured and made known. In this way two images of reality accommodated themselves to each other in the same breast, one to be brought forward in the presence, or even the suspected or possible presence, of the party, the other to be hugged to the innermost recesses of the personality and to be revealed, if ever, only in the most intimate and unpolitical family circle.

In describing a set of circumstances which did not actually occur on V-E Day but which bore a faint, dreamlike resemblance to something that did occur and which nurtured the image that the party liked to cultivate of itself and its experiences, Parker was merely functioning as the party's chosen agent in defining the sec-ond, preferred, and from now on authoritative version. It has never ceased to be a source of wonder to me that a political regime com-posed of men obviously perfectly sane and robust in their personal psychic makeup could, as a collective political entity, exhibit in so extreme a degree the characteristic symptoms of an advanced psy-chosis.

The cessation of hostilities in Europe clearly marked an historic turning point in Soviet diplomacy. The international position of the Soviet Union had been fundamentally changed by the great widen-ing of the area of its effective power produced by the advance of the Soviet armies into the heart of Europe. Stalin's dream of the acquisition of a protective glacis along Russia's western border had now been realized — in a measure greater, I am sure, than he had ever dared to hope — greater, perhaps, than he even found com-fortable. Obviously, new considerations would now have to prevail in the inspiration of Soviet foreign policy; new responsibilities would have to be met. Things could never again be as they had been before the war.

Reflecting on what all this meant for Russia and for the West and for their mutual relations, I experienced again, in the days following the cessation of hostilities in Europe, a need to put thoughts to paper. The result was another fair-sized document, entitled — this time — *Russia's International Position at the Close of the War with Germany*. It, too, having never previously been published, is reproduced in full in the Annex to this volume. Whereas the earlier paper, *Russia — Seven Years Later*, was addressed mainly to internal conditions in the Soviet Union, this one was directed to the problem of what was soon to be called the "satellite" area. In it were set forth for the first time — indeed, the writing of it evoked for the first time — thoughts that were to be basic to my view of Russia and its problems in future years.

The first words of this paper echoed the apprehension I had voiced to Parker when he came away from my balcony on the evening of V–E Day. "Peace, like spring," I wrote,

has finally come to Russia; and the foreign resident, weary of both Russia's wars and Russia's winters, finds himself wanly wishing that the approaching political season might not be like the Russian summer: faint and fleeting, tinged with reminders of rigors that recently were and rigors that are soon to come.

The relative expansion of Russia's power had come to pass, I pointed out, not through any great increase in her own strength (her demographic and industrial potential had not been greatly changed in comparison with the prewar levels) but through "the disintegration of the power of neighboring peoples." When the Far Eastern war was over, Russia would find herself for the first time in her history "without a single great power rival on the Eurasian land mass" and in control of large areas of that land mass outside her own borders — some of them ones to which her power had never before extended. This great expansion of real power involved responsibilities and problems for Russia as well as advantages. Some of the non-Russian areas now overrun by the Soviet forces had once been part of the Tsarist Empire; but they had proved in the end to be sources of weakness for the empire rather than of strength. The prominence of representatives of the national minorities in the revolutionary movement that led to the breakdown of 1917 had demonstrated this. The Soviet state, deprived of these areas during the first two decades of its existence, had probably been stronger by virtue of this circumstance. But now it was shouldering once more the burden of their possession — and more.

As an imperialist power, confronting the smaller states of Eastern Europe, Russia had of course great elements of strength. She also had important weaknesses. There was the natural and congenital difficulty involved in the ruling of people of different tongue, tradition, and national feeling. It took men to staff a Communist-type government. If these men were Russians, they would either be insensitive to a foreign environment, and in that case inept; or, if sensitive, they would soon become de-Russianized and disaffected. If they were natives, there would be lack of intimacy; nationalistic feelings would eventually break through; there would be loss of control. In addition to this, there were the problems of political appeal and ideology. Land reform on the Communist pattern might have a momentary appeal to the peasantry in these Eastern European countries; but it was a card one could play only once, and its effect would not be lasting. Russian control, furthermore, would probably be detrimental to living standards. The Russians had never shown themselves to be good economic administrators. Such industrial progress as they had achieved at home had been purchased at a terribly high price. Would the ideological appeal suffice to overcome these handicaps? Soviet Marxism was a dated doctrine. Even in Russia, its fire, as a political-emotional force, had largely died away.

What remains is capable of inspiring patriotism and nationalist sentiment, both for defense and for imperialist aggrandizement. But it is incapable of commanding that ultimate fund of human idealism on which the revolution, like the churches of all ages, was once able to draw. The deepest confidence, the most intimate hopes, the finest ideals: these are no longer the Kremlin's to command. It has before its gates a submissive but no longer an inspired mass of followers.

If this was true even in Russia, how effective would the ideological approach be when applied to the Eastern European countries, where it would have the forces of nationalism and the natural prejudice against imported foreign doctrines to contend with? In view of all these weaknesses, I thought it would be difficult for Russia to maintain successfully its recently acquired power in Eastern Europe unless it could enlist in this cause the moral and material support of the West. Did it seem strange that one should expect and seek such support? Not to Soviet minds. The Soviet leaders knew that the American public, in particular, had been taught to believe that intimate collaboration with the Soviet Union was both possible and necessary; that without it further wars were inevitable; and that to obtain it one had only to establish the proper personal relationships of cordiality and confidence with the Russian leaders; if there were troubles, that could only mean that the Western statesmen had not tried hard enough. These propositions were of course not true. The Russians knew they were not true. In particular was it not true that peace depended on the sort of intimate collaboration with Russia that Americans had been taught to envisage and to hope for. All that was really required to assure stability among the great powers was "the preservation of a realistic balance of strength between them and a realistic understanding of the mutual zones of vital interest." This, too, the Russians understood. But these American prejudices naturally worked to Soviet advantage; and they were susceptible of further exploitation. This explained the hopes entertained by the Soviet leaders that the West, and America in particular, could be induced to lend moral and material support to the maintenance of a Soviet Empire in Eastern Europe that ill accorded with the brave professions of the Atlantic Charter. If the West should deny this support, then, of course,

Russia would probably not be able to maintain its hold successfully for any length of time over *all* the territory over which it has today staked out a claim . . . The lines would have to be withdrawn *somewhat.**

But in addition, the West in this case would be made to feel the full bite of Soviet displeasure. Moscow would, as Trotsky had once threatened, "slam the door so that all Europe would shake." But if people in the West kept their nerves and held to their line, Soviet displeasure would not be disastrous. There were limits to Soviet power.

Should the Western world stand firm . . . and should democracies prove able to take in their stride the worst efforts of the disciplined and unscrupulous minorities pledged to the service of the political interests of the Soviet Union, Moscow would have played its last real card. . . . Further military advances in the west could only increase responsibilities already beyond the Russian capacity to meet. Moscow has no naval or air forces capable of challenging the sea or air lanes of the world.

This, then, was my assessment of Russia's international position at the end of the war with Germany. There were three features of it to which I would invite special attention:

1. That the Russians, for reasons internal to their own structure of power, would probably not be able to maintain their hegemony successfully over the entire area they had taken under their control in Eastern Europe unless they had the blessing and the assistance of the West in doing so; lacking that support, there would have to be a certain retraction of their political positions.

2. That the sort of fulsome collaboration with Russia our people had been taught to expect was not really essential to the preservation of world peace — a reasonable balance of power and understanding on spheres of influence would do the trick; and

3. That Moscow would have no reason to contemplate a further military advance into Europe; the danger for the West was not Russian invasion — it was the Communist parties in the Western

---

* (Italics added 1967, GFK.) This withdrawal did of course occur in the ensuing years: in Yugoslavia, in northern Greece, in Trieste, in Austria, and in a sense in Finland.

countries themselves, plus the unreal hopes and fears the Western peoples had been taught to entertain.

The attentive student of the issues of the postwar period will not fail to discern in these three propositions the basic elements of the containment doctrine, as it was to be enunciated two years later in the X–Article. I emphasize them here to show that, right or wrong, my views about the problem faced by the West as it confronted Soviet power in the postwar years were ones arrived at not in the anxieties and disillusionments of 1947, when they first became publicly known, but rather in the impressions of wartime service in Moscow itself, and in the effort to look ahead from that vantage point, on the heels of the Allied victory, into the uncertain future of Russia's relationship to the West.

This paper, too, was handed to the ambassador. Again, so far as I can recall, it was returned to me without comment. I have no evidence that it was ever forwarded to Washington. A faint prompting of memory suggests to me that it may have been read by Harry Hopkins, when he visited Moscow in that same month of May 1945. But by the time he returned to the United States he was a very sick man and was no longer playing a major role in the formulation of American foreign policy.

10

From V–E Day to Potsdam

IN AN interpretive report from the Moscow embassy, dated May 19, 1945, and based on the Soviet press coverage for the last weeks before V–E Day, the following observations were made:

It can safely be said that no group of people anywhere are more conscious of the critical quality of the post-hostilities period, of its dangers and possibilities, than the leaders of the Soviet Union. Themselves the bearers of a regime forged in the chaotic aftermath of the last war, they are keenly aware that it is in this period of civil and social confusion following on the heels of general military conflict that the lines are drawn which congeal into permanency and determine the overall pattern of the future. They attach even greater importance to the decisions of the next few weeks than to the decisions of possible future peace conferences. For these later decisions, in the Soviet view, will be largely the products of the actual blows that will have been struck while the iron was hot.

I, being not uninvolved in the authorship of this message, was understandably anxious that we in our government should now analyze correctly the problem we faced in the post-hostilities Soviet Union and should devise policies designed to hold to a minimum the damage already done to the prospects for European stability by the military and political situation to which the final phases of the war on the Russian front had led. For this reason not only did I fill my private notes with the record of various anxieties, but I plagued whosoever might be prepared to listen, primarily the ambassador, with protests, urgings, and appeals of all sorts on matters of policy. The number of documents that poured forth from my pen during these months was, I blush to say, too great to permit their inclusion in any such volume as this. But since the thoughts they set forth were ones which would, at a later date, enter prominently into various statements of my views that received wide public attention, I would like to summarize them here. In doing this, I shall stick mainly to the problems of policy. The analysis of the Russian situation itself is clearly indicated in the two long papers to which I have already had occasion to refer.

I continued, throughout this immediate post-hostilities period, to be an advocate — the only such advocate, I suppose, in the higher echelons of our governmental service — of a prompt and clear recognition of the division of Europe into spheres of influence and of a policy based on the fact of such division.

The reasons for this were two. I remained convinced, in the first place, as I had been even prior to the German surrender, that it was idle for us to hope that we could have any influence on the course of events in the area to which Russian hegemony had already been effectively extended. I felt that we were only deceiving ourselves and the Western public by clinging to the hope that what the foreseeable future held in store for most of these countries could be anything less than complete Communist domination and complete isolation from the West, on the Soviet pattern. This being so, I saw no reason why we should go out of our way to make things easier for the Russians in this area either by aid programs of one sort or another or by sharing moral responsibility for what they were doing. I preferred that we should have nothing to do with what was now, only too obviously, going to occur.

When in February and March 1945 there began, for example, the difficulties over Rumania occasioned by Vyshinski's sudden visit to Bucharest and his brutal measures of reorganization of the Rumanian government, I opposed the tenor of the notes of protest with which we were assailing Molotov: notes in which expressions of plaintive surprise were mingled with empty pleadings to the Soviet authorities to do otherwise than they were doing. "I see nothing to be gained," I wrote, on March 8,

by continuing this fruitless polemic with Molotov. His tune has been set for him by whatever body determines Soviet policy; and he will not change it unless he becomes convinced, and can convince his associates, that there are tangible and overpowering reasons for doing so. No mere expression of opinion on our part would constitute such a reason. Unless we are prepared to take some concrete measure, such as a public disassociation of our government from the whole affair or a withdrawal of our representation from the Control Commission, it is not likely that the Russians will see any reason to pay attention to our views. It is by no means certain that they would alter their . . . policies in Rumania even if we were to take some action.

One month later the subject was Czechoslovakia. In contrast to the Balkan countries of Hungary, Rumania, and Bulgaria, Czechoslovakia had not been at war with the Soviet Union. Its status, officially, was that of a liberated ally. In some way or other which I have never fully understood — as a result, perhaps, of the great popularity Beneš enjoyed in the Western countries — the impression got about in the West that an independent government was being re-established in that country. It was an assumption for which I saw no evidence. Personal acquaintance with the Czechoslovak ambassador in Moscow, Mr. Zdenek Fierlinger, had given me the impression that we had to do in his person not with the representative of a free and independent Czechoslovakia but with one who was to all intents and purposes a Soviet agent; and I was extremely skeptical about the real independence of a political authority that would be represented by such a man in the Russian capital. What little we were able to learn, furthermore, about what was occurring in that part of Czechoslovak territory occupied by Soviet forces made it evident that every device of infiltration, intimidation, and intrigue was being brought into play with a view to laying the groundwork for establishment of a Communist monopoly of power in that country. This impression was confirmed when, around the time of the German collapse, our own government found itself prevented, by Soviet obstruction, from sending American representatives to the Czechoslovak regime now officially restored to its own territory. Washington, declaring it to be "highly desirable" that our representatives should arrive promptly at the seat of the Czechoslovak government, asked us to take this matter up with the Soviet government and to request that they be permitted at once to proceed to their posts. This, again, I opposed. The matter should be left, I felt, squarely with the Czechoslovak authorities. If they were unable to arrange it — if, that is, their position vis-à-vis the Russians was so ignominious that they were unable to receive foreign representatives except at the gracious pleasure of the Soviet government — that in itself was "so revealing of the character of their relations with the Russians that I think . . . it should be taken into account in determining the general desirability of our stationing representatives there at this time." The non-Communist members of the Czechoslovak government, I went on to say, were after all no more than honored prisoners of the Russians. American representatives with the Czechoslovak government would find themselves frustrated and powerless.

Their presence will merely be used to lend respectability to a stooge government and to discourage those people who still hope . . . for the restoration of democratic processes, for the Russians will exhibit them around the place as evidence that the Western world approves Russian policies and is associated with them.

Even in the case of Yugoslavia, I bristled at the concern shown in Washington over the question whether Marshal Tito's regime was "representative," and also at the suggestion that, if it turned out to be true that there was little opposition to his regime, we should at once take steps to ingratiate ourselves with it. I saw justification neither for the question nor for the conclusion.

We do not, after all, interest ourselves in the question of whether Stalin has or has not the majority of the population behind him in Russia and it would be illogical . . . for us to take a different stand with respect to a government so similar to that of Moscow. . . . Tito is a man of strict Marxist training. He will do for the capitalist world precisely that which he feels the interests of the Communist revolution demand. In this he will be influenced not by the personal cordiality of the Western representatives in Belgrade but by the strength and decisiveness of the governments they represent.*

The first reason for my inclination to favor a "sphere of interests" policy was, then, the conviction that we could not expect to have any significant influence on events in the area under Soviet control and that it would be undignified and even misleading to keep on acting as though we expected to do so. The second reason was the impression I had gained that in deference to this pipe dream of a general European collaboration, and out of a fear, in particular, lest the Russians be offended if we took any important action without them, we were neglecting positive undertakings for the reconstruction of a vigorous and hopeful state of affairs in the part of Europe which really was accessible to our influence. It seemed to me that if we waited too long to create creditable conditions there, the resulting situation would be one on which the Communist parties of the western portion of the continent, now greatly strengthened by their recent association with the resistance movements, could easily capitalize. We were thus in danger of losing, like the dog standing over the reflecting pool, the bone in our mouth without obtaining the one we saw in the water.

It is possible that I overrated the extent to which things were being thus held up in deference to the chimera of Soviet collaboration. I had in mind, among other things, the United Nations Relief and Reconstruction Agency (UNRRA) operations, and also the elaborate plans being entertained by our Treasury Department (they had been launched at the Bretton Woods International Monetary and Financial Conference in July 1944) for establishment of an International Monetary Fund and an International Bank for Reconstruction and Development. The motives for which the Russians might be expected to interest themselves in UNRRA would have little in common, it seemed to me, with the general altruistic

---

* Diary note, December 3, 1945.

interest in European reconstruction by which our people were motivated: the Soviet leaders would use their participation in this organization primarily for political purposes, and would do what they
could to see that relief was distributed in such a way as to benefit
their political cause. And it seemed wildly unrealistic to expect that
they, with their jealously closed and controlled economy, and with
a currency that had no status on the world markets, with a wholly
arbitrary and artificial price structure and a total monopoly of foreign trade, would be suitable partners for collaboration in the international monetary field, even if their purposes had been similar to
ours, which they were not.

But the point on which my anxieties focused in this respect was,
as always, Germany. Hostilities were now at an end. The test of
our attitudes and policies was now at hand. From all I could learn,
the behavior and outlooks of the American military authorities
were still deeply affected by what I had felt to be the disgraceful
anti-British and pro-Soviet prejudices that certain of our military
leaders had entertained during the war. Shades of the Azores crisis
and of the European Advisory Commission rose before me when,
on one memorable evening in the autumn of 1945, I had occasion to
sit alone with a very high-ranking military officer at Ambassador
Robert Murphy's house in Berlin and to endure reproaches leveled
at me, and at us "State Department people" generally, for our anti-
Soviet attitudes and our inability "to get along with the Russians"
— an inability which, I was permitted to understand, we could easily overcome if we would only take an example from the military
establishment. I continued, accordingly, in those immediate post-
hostilities months, to fidget lest we, in anticipation of a Soviet collaboration that was never to be, delay in getting on with the establishment of sound and creditable conditions in the Western zones of
Germany where we had the power to act. The Russians had, as
they saw it, little to gain from a real collaboration with us in the
reconstruction of Europe; but they had much to gain by dangling
before our eyes the prospect of such collaboration and inducing us
to defer constructive measures of our own until it could be realized.
The continuing distress in the West could only play into the hands

of the eager, waiting Communist parties of the Western countries.

In an undated draft, reposing among other personal papers and obviously written in the summer of 1945, I find the following passage:

The idea of a Germany run jointly with the Russians is a chimera. The idea of both the Russians and ourselves withdrawing politely at a given date and a healthy, peaceful, stable, and friendly Germany arising out of the resulting vacuum is also a chimera. We have no choice but to lead our section of Germany — the section of which we and the British have accepted responsibility — to a form of independence so prosperous, so secure, so superior, that the East cannot threaten it. This is a tremendous task for Americans. But it is an unavoidable one; and along these lines, not along the lines of fumbling unworkable schemes of joint military government, must lie our thinking.

Admittedly, this is dismemberment. But dismemberment is already a fact, by virtue of the Oder-Neisse line. Whether or not the remainder of the Soviet zone is rejoined to Germany is not now important. Better a dismembered Germany in which the West, at least, can act as a buffer to the forces of totalitarianism than a united Germany which again brings these forces to the North Sea.

. . . While we should carry out loyally the obligations we have already assumed with regard to the Control Commission, we should entertain no false illusions or hopes about the possibilities of tripartite control . . . We are basically in competition with the Russians in Germany. We should not compromise in the Control Commission on anything which is really of importance in the running of our zone.*

It will be understood, against the background of these convictions, that I viewed the labors of the Potsdam Conference with unmitigated skepticism and despair. I cannot recall any political document the reading of which filled me with a greater sense of depression than the communiqué to which President Truman set his name at the conclusion of these confused and unreal discussions. It was

---

* This passage sounds, I must confess, startlingly similar to the arguments destined to be used against me some twelve years later by my celebrated opponents in their attacks on the 1957 BBC Reith lectures. I shall try, at a later point in this account, to explain why, after twelve years, I found myself on the other side of this argument.

not just the knowledge that the principles of joint quadrupartite control, which were now supposed to form the basis for the administration of Germany, were unreal and unworkable. The use in an agreement with the Russians of general language — such words as "democratic," "peaceful," and "justice" — went directly counter to everything I had learned, in seventeen years of experience with Russian affairs, about the technique of dealing with the Soviet government. The assertion, for example, that we and the Russians were going to cooperate in reorganizing German education on the basis of "democratic ideas" carried inferences wholly unjustifiable in the light of everything we knew about the mental world of the Soviet leadership and about the state of education in Russia at that time.*
Even more shocking was the announced intention on our part to collaborate with the Soviet government in reorganizing the German judicial system "in accordance with the principles of democracy, of justice under law, and of equal rights for all citizens without distinction of race, nationality or religion." For the further statement that "democratic" political parties would be not only permitted but "encouraged" to function throughout Germany "with rights of assembly and of public discussion" it is difficult to find any ameliorating explanation whatsoever. Anyone in Moscow could have told our negotiators what it was that the Soviet leaders had in mind when they used the term "democratic parties." Not even the greatest naïveté could excuse the confusion worked on public understanding in Germany itself and the other Western countries by the use of this term in a document signed by Stalin as well as by Messrs. Truman and Attlee.

As for reparations, what was done at Potsdam under this heading seemed to me only the further extrapolation of a program of wholly unreal hopes and intentions that had been inaugurated at Tehran and that was bound eventually to end (as indeed it finally did with General Clay's decision of May 3, 1946, to halt all further

---

* The fact that I, at that moment, had one of my daughters in a regular Soviet school probably served to intensify my feelings on this subject. I am happy to state that she was treated at all times with utmost tact and consideration by her Russian teachers, who were dedicated pedagogues of the highest quality; but to say that the school was concerned to inculcate "democratic ideas" into its pupils, as we understand this term, would be grossly inaccurate.

deliveries of reparations from the American zone to the East) in complete breakdown. Some months earlier, I had had occasion to say, in a private letter, that it was silly to suppose that we could collaborate effectively with the Russians on such a program. Reparations would, I wrote, simply be a matter of "catch as catch can" in the respective zones. We would get precisely what we would be able and disposed to take in our own zone, no more. The Russians could be depended upon to do just as they pleased in the area under their occupation, and would not be inhibited in this respect by any agreements with us. I having entertained these views even in 1944, and the events of the intervening months having amply confirmed their correctness, it will be easily understood why I viewed without enthusiasm the continued temporizing with the whole reparations problem at Potsdam.*

There was, finally, the question of the trial of war criminals. This, too, was a matter on which tripartite discussions had been under way well before Potsdam; but the Potsdam communiqué, engaging once more the prestige of the three governmental leaders behind the program of an early joint trial of certain major figures, marked a point of no return. I have already mentioned my aversion to our proceeding jointly with the Russians in matters of this nature. I should not like to be misunderstood on this subject. The crimes of the Nazi leaders were immeasurable. These men had placed themselves in a position where a further personal existence on this earth could have had no positive meaning for them or for anyone else. I personally considered that it would have been best if the Allied commanders had had standing instructions that if any of these men fell into the hands of Allied forces they should, once their identity had been established beyond doubt, be executed forthwith.

---

* These views were, if my memory is correct, shared to a considerable extent by Ambassador Harriman. On April 6, 1945, he wired Washington that he had "no reason to doubt that the Russians are already busily removing from Germany without compunction anything (repeat anything) which they find it to their advantage to remove." Mr. Walter Millis, writing as editor of *The Forrestal Diaries* (New York: Viking Press, 1951, pp. 40-41), understood it to be the ambassador's view at that time that "it would be a long time before the achievement of any firm agreement with the Russians on reparations and restitutions."

But to hold these Nazi leaders for public trial was another matter. This procedure could not expiate or undo the crimes they had committed. It could have been justified only as a means for conveying to the world public the repudiation, by the conscience of those peoples and governments conducting the trial, of mass crimes of every sort. To admit to such a procedure a Soviet judge as the representative of a regime which had on its conscience not only the vast cruelties of the Russian Revolution, of collectivization, and of the Russian purges of the 1930s, as well as the manifold brutalities and atrocities perpetrated against the Poles and the peoples of the Baltic countries during the wartime period, was to make a mockery of the only purpose the trials could conceivably serve, and to assume, by association, a share of the responsibility for these Stalinist crimes themselves. The only implication this procedure could convey was, after all, that such crimes were justifiable and forgivable when committed by the leaders of one government, under one set of circumstances, but unjustifiable and unforgivable, and to be punishable by death, when committed by another set of governmental leaders, under another set of circumstances. It was difficult to arrive at any other interpretation. It was not possible to accept the proposition that our governmental leaders were excusably ignorant of what had been done in the name of the Soviet state by the Stalinist police authorities. The record was reasonably adequate. Even the most minimal study would have sufficed to establish the evidence. There were several of us who could have testified to it, had our knowledge and experience been consulted.

I know that these observations, and the earlier references to the deportations from eastern Poland and the shooting of the Polish officers, will be received indignantly in Moscow today. On the theory that "no real friend of Russia would tell the truth about us," the Soviet leaders, or their propagandists, will stamp what I have said as "vile slander" of the Soviet peoples and will interpret it as the expression of a vicious hostility to themselves and to everything Russian. I would like, for this reason, to add the following:

I doubt that there could be anyone in the Western world who has deeper feeling than do I for the qualities of the Russian people or greater respect for the paths of heroism and suffering by which this people has groped its way from the degradation of earlier despotisms toward the ideal of human dignity and social responsibility. I know of no people that is more sensitive, generally, to moral values, and none that has done more in modern times to clarify — through the treatment of moral issues in its great literature as well as through the tremendous earnestness of its political and philosophical debates — fundamental problems of social and political ethics. That great crimes should have been committed some years ago by persons acting in the name of the Soviet peoples is an ironic and tragic fact, which all of us would prefer to forget. But it is a fact of which not only the Soviet peoples but their present leaders will have to take account and with which they will eventually have to come to terms if they are to have any possibility of advancing further along the great historical path to which all that was valuable in recent and modern Russian intellectual and political life, beginning with the Decembrists, has been committed. There is no more reason to deny or to ignore the fact of these crimes than there was in the case of the injustices of Tsardom. On the contrary, no fully valid and useful approach to the problems of Russia's future will ever be evolved that does not take them into account and face up to their implications. I, in particular, have no more reason to pass them by in silence than did my relative, the elder George Kennan, have reason to conceal from the American public the mistakes committed by the Tsarist authorities in the establishment and maintenance of the Siberian exile system.

The overwhelming majority of people in the Soviet Union are not by nature cruel. They have no greater fondness for cruelty than people anywhere else in the world. They hold, on the contrary, extraordinary reserves of the capacity for kindness, for tenderness, and, at their best, for a sort of saintliness which, as reflected in their own literature, has entered into, and changed, the consciousness of great portions of mankind. If things have been done in their name that abuse and distort for the outside eye these magnificent qualities, that is a problem of historical interpretation and of reconciliation with the national conscience: a problem to which the Soviet peoples themselves must find the answer. The sooner they undertake the search for this answer, the better. The foreigner, meanwhile, who has occasion to retrace the events of the Thirties and early Forties, to record his reactions to them, and to note their bearing on later developments, will be doing no favor to the Russians themselves, or even to their rulers, by ignoring these unhappy circumstances.

Not the least depressing, to me, of the published results of the Potsdam Conference, was the sanctioning and further refinement of the earlier decisions relating to the severance of East Prussia from Germany, the partition of that province between Russia and Poland, and the cession to the Soviet Union, in particular, of the administrative center and port of Königsberg. Mr. Truman cannot, in all fairness, be blamed for the general tenor of these arrangements. They had found at an earlier date the approval in principle of FDR and of Winston Churchill. But the casualness and frivolity with which these decisions were made, the apparent indifference on the American side, then and ever since, to their real economic and other effects, and the misimpressions conveyed at the time to the American public have all seemed hard to excuse.

Let us take just the case of the city of Königsberg. Why, in the first place, it was found necessary to stress specifically in the Potsdam communiqué the cession of this city to the Soviet Union, when it had already been made clear, in the description given of the new border, that Königsberg fell within the boundaries of the Soviet Union, is not apparent. But beyond this, one wonders why it was necessary for the American negotiators to accept without question the inaccurate and even nonsensical statements with which Stalin supported his demand for the city, and to connive at relaying these absurdities to the American public.

According to the records of the conference, Stalin, repeating what had already been said at Tehran, "complained that all ports of the Baltic freeze. They froze for shorter or for longer periods but they froze. . . . It was necessary [for Russia, that is] to have at least one ice-free port at the expense of Germany." *

This statement, implying that Russia needed Königsberg as an ice-free port, made no sense whatsoever. Russia already possessed on the Baltic Sea (assuming that one was prepared to concede the legitimacy° of her possession of the Baltic countries, and no one, at Potsdam, seemed disposed seriously to challenge it) three perfectly good ports that were substantially ice-free: the former Windau (now Ventspils), Libau (now Liepāja), and Baltic Port (now Baltisky). Königsberg, on the other hand, lies forty-nine kilometers from the open sea, at the end of an artificial canal which is frozen several months of the year and has to be kept open, if it is to be kept open at all, by icebreakers. Königsberg is, furthermore, accessible only to moderate-sized vessels, with a draft not exceeding about twenty-five feet. In both of these respects its qualities are not materially different from those of the major port of Riga, which had already fallen to the Soviet Union through its conquest and annexation of the Baltic countries. Thus it was true neither that Russia lacked ice-free ports on the Baltic nor that Königsberg would have filled such a need had it existed. Yet Stalin's statements on this subject went unchallenged, so far as I can ascertain, at all the wartime conferences; and Mr. Truman made himself a party to the absurdity by solemnly informing the American public, in his personal report on the conference, that he had agreed to satisfy the age-old Russian yearning for an ice-free port.†

These territorial changes seemed to me to be doubly pernicious, and the casual American acquiescence in them all the less forgivable, because of the fact that they served, like other territorial con-

* *Foreign Relations of the United States. Diplomatic Papers. The Conference of Berlin, 1945,* Vol. II, p. 305. Washington, D.C.: US Government Printing Office, 1960.

† An interesting sidelight to this curious set of circumstances is the fact that the second, post–World War II edition of the large *Soviet Encyclopedia,* published in 1953, specifically described Königsberg as "ice-free," although the earlier edition of this encyclopedia, published before the war, made no such allegation. The grounds for this assertion can be no other than Stalin's statement. The conclusion to which the reader is impelled is that what creates geographic conditions, in any given instance, is the political convenience of the Soviet government. If anyone thought, after 1945, that he saw ice in the canal at Königsberg, he didn't. It was an illusion fed by anti-Soviet prejudice.

cessions to the Russians, simply to extract great productive areas from the economy of Europe and to permit the Russians, for reasons of their own military and political convenience, to deny these areas and their resources to the general purposes of European reconstruction. This observation concerns not just the moment of Potsdam but what became evident in the ensuing months and years: namely that this entire area was never to be developed in such a way that it could again contribute measurably in our time to the economic life of the continent. Although Stalin based his demand for Königsberg, for example, on the argument that Russia needed the place as a port, there is no evidence that it has ever subsequently been used in this way to anything like the extent it was used when it was part of Germany. And this is characteristic of the situation in the province of East Prussia as a whole. The disaster that befell this area with the entry of the Soviet forces has no parallel in modern European experience. There were considerable sections of it where, to judge by all existing evidence, scarcely a man, woman, or child of the indigenous population was left alive after the initial passage of Soviet forces; and one cannot believe that they all succeeded in fleeing to the West.* The economic life of the place was shattered beyond belief. I myself flew low, in an American plane, over the entire province shortly after Potsdam, and the sight was that of a totally ruined and deserted country: scarcely a sign of life from one end of it to the other.

It was idle for the Russians to pretend, or for others to believe, that they had prospects of redeveloping in any adequate manner this once highly developed area, and particularly their own portion of it (i.e., the portion that passed under Soviet sovereignty), from which they had swept the native population clean in a manner that had no parallel since the days of the Asiatic hordes. Yet whoever seizes a territory of this nature assumes, it seems to me, a certain responsibility to the world at large for its use as a productive entity.

* Stalin himself cheerfully affirmed, at Potsdam, that "no single German remained in the territory to be given Poland." (*Foreign Relations of the United States. Diplomatic Papers. The Conference of Berlin, 1945*, Vol. II, p. 211. Washington, D.C.: US Government Printing Office, 1960.) This was fortunately exaggerated. Over one hundred thousand Germans were still present at that time in the area in question. But they constituted only a fraction of the former population.

Particularly was this true when the territory in question was an important agricultural province, and when Europe faced an enormous and urgent problem of food relief. There were some, I suppose, to whom 2.5 million human inhabitants of East Prussia could be regarded as expendable; but what about the 500,00 horses, the 1.4 million head of cattle, the 1.85 million pigs that were once to be found in the place? And what about the near 4 million tons of wheat, 15 million tons of rye, and 40 million tons of potatoes it had once produced annually? It is obvious that nothing was further from the thoughts of Soviet generals, as their forces swept over this province, than a concern for its productive capacity, or a sense of responsibility to the rest of Europe for the preservation of that capacity. All that sort of thing was left to us Americans. We could, if we wished, make up the deficit.

I have never been able to understand the indifference of our statesmen, and of our public, to these circumstances. It is one thing for a great country to develop a territory for its own uses. It is another thing for it first to devastate and then to appropriate to itself, or to its sphere of influence, an area which it is incapable of restoring, or is disinclined to restore, even to the levels of productivity that prevailed at the outset of this century. It is another thing, in other words, to take fertile territory merely in order to turn it, because this suits one's military convenience, into a wilderness.

Another question which at that time lay on the minds of most of us in the American embassy at Moscow was the future of Soviet-American economic and financial relations.

The American administrations of that day, both FDR's and Mr. Truman's, have often been reproached over the intervening years for the abrupt cancellation of Lend-Lease to Russia in the summer of 1945, and the failure to offer to the Soviet Union the large-scale loan which, in the view of some, the Soviet leaders had been encouraged to believe they would receive. Connected with these problems, as we were obliged to view them at the time, was the whole question of future trade between the United States and the Soviet Union. Connected with them, also, was the question of the extent to which the USSR should be a beneficiary of the arrangements being established at that time for relief and reconstruction in Europe under the facilities of UNRRA.

I must confess that if the United States government deserves criticism for taking a hard line in any or all of these problems, I deserve greater criticism for taking a still harder one, for taking it earlier, and for inspiring and encouraging Washington in its stiffness.

Far from disapproving the cancellation of Lend-Lease after the termination of our military partnership with Russia in 1945, I considered, as already mentioned, that barring some satisfactory political understanding with the Soviet Union, we should have considered at least an extensive curtailment of this program at the time of the Warsaw uprising, in the summer of 1944. And as for the problems of future trade with Russia and a possible credit to the Soviet government, my views were made plain as early as December 3, 1944, in a memo to the ambassador which I signed, together with two other officers, commenting on plans then being bruited about in certain of the Washington planning committees for extension of a credit of 3.5 billion dollars to the Soviet Union in the immediate post-hostilities period.

The Russians had evidently at that time already indicated their interest in receiving such a credit and had expressed a desire for terms which would include interest at 2.5 percent, with amortization to begin only after the lapse of ten years. Assuming these to be the terms, and assuming Soviet exports to the United States to run at a maximum of 100 million dollars per annum in the postwar years (and we thought this was definitely on the optimistic side),* our conclusions as of December 3, 1945, were as follows:

We would regard one and a half to two billion dollars as the maximum that could safely be extended in the way of an immediate postwar credit — on the understanding that this would have to include obligations carried over from wartime transactions (i.e., Lend-Lease, etc.). . . .

We thus consider that credits in the amount of three and a half billion

* Actually, Soviet exports to the United States turned out to average, for the years 1947 to 1959, inclusive, only $15,740,000 per annum.

dollars, exclusive of protocol items . . . would be unsound. A large portion of them could probably not be met upon maturity, and would have to be prolonged. This would only have the effect of mortgaging prospective Soviet exports to the United States for a period of further decades in advance, thereby complicating the problem of payment for future exports from this country to Russia.

We then went ahead to make the following comments on the Soviet attitude toward foreign economic exchanges generally, and on the implications of this attitude for our government and its economic planning:

We do not consider the intentions of the Soviet government have yet been made sufficiently clear in deeds to warrant the assumption on our part that in furthering the military industrialization of the Soviet Union during the post-hostilities period we will not again, as in the cases of Germany and Japan, be creating military strength which might some day be used to our disadvantage. . . .

Actually, the Soviet government views foreign trade in general as a political-economic weapon designed to increase the power of the USSR relative to that of other countries. It will view imports from our country only as a necessary means of hastening the achievement of complete military-economic autarchy of the Soviet Union. Once such autarchy has been substantially achieved, it is not certain that the Soviet government will continue to be interested in large scale imports from the United States, except on terms quite incompatible with our interests. On the contrary if, by virtue of a lopsided forcing of machinery and machine tool exports to Russia, large sections of our private industrial plant become dependent on the orders of the Soviet trade monopoly for the maintenance of their production and employment, the Russians will eventually not hesitate, if it suits their book, to exploit this dependence, together with their influence over organized labor groups, to gain political and economic objectives which have nothing to do with the interests of our people.*

---

* This last gloomy prognostication was based on my memories of the unhappy position of dependence on Soviet orders in which the machine tool manufacturers of Germany, and particularly of Saxony, had found themselves during the economic crisis at the beginning of the 1930s. It is a danger that has not matured in our case, but which should never be lost sight of when it comes to trading with a foreign governmental trade monopoly.

I find these views reiterated, and made more explicit, in another undated draft memorandum, written to all appearances in the late summer of 1945. It will stand as a fair example of the views I was putting before the ambassador and the State Department at that time.

I know of no justification, either economic or political, for any further granting of Lend-Lease aid to Russia, for any agreement on our part that Russia, not being a contributor to UNRRA, should receive any substantial amount of UNRRA aid, or for any extension of U.S. government credit to Russia without equivalent political advantage to our people.

In taking this view I have in mind that:

1. The Russians have no great need for foreign aid unless they insist on straining their economy by maintaining a military strength far beyond the demands of their own security. Their resources and productive powers, agricultural and industrial, are sufficient to assure fairly rapid recovery without outside aid.

2. The present Soviet economic program is one of military industrialization, designed to serve political purposes antagonistic to our interests. Our government has no reason to further this program.

3. The only sound possibility of repayment of a credit is provided by Russian exports to the United States. Even if expanded to several times their prewar value, these exports would not be large enough to pay interest and amortization and large long-term credits and yet maintain a healthy level of current Soviet purchases in the US. . . .

4. Soviet trade is a state monopoly. Much as we talk about our objections to trusts, monopolies, and cartels in our country, we seem to make an exception on behalf of the greatest of all trusts, which is the Soviet government . . . I approve of trade with Russia. But it should be conducted in such a way as to avoid any dependence of a large section of the American business community on the Soviet foreign trade monopoly.

I should add that in these respects, as in many others, my views, after undergoing a useful critical refinement at the hands of Ambassador Harriman's judgment, received his prudent and effective support and found acceptance, in the main, in Washington. I find, in retrospect, nothing to regret about this, either on my own part or his, or on that of the government. A large credit to the Soviet government, in the circumstances of that day, would have been obviously unsound and would unquestionably have led to bitter disagreements and recriminations at a later date, both as between the two governments and in American domestic politics. As for Lend-Lease, a large proportion of the 11 billion dollars' worth that we sent, including shipments to the amount of 244 million dollars under the later Protocol of October 15, 1945 (for which no payment has yet been made), reached Russia after the termination of hostilities against Germany, and was used primarily for purposes which had nothing to do with the war against our common enemies. In addition to this, the Russians benefited by UNRRA aid to the tune of another 249 million dollars; and we turned over to them several million dollars more in the form of reparations from our zone of Germany (including finally, as I was infuriated to note at some point in 1947, a flock of karakul sheep which our military authorities declared to be German war booty on the basis of the character of their fur). All this being the case, it seems to me that we did not do badly by the Russians in that immediate post-hostilities period; and I find nothing to repent in the fact that I used my influence to prevent our largesse from going further than it did.

11

The Long Telegram

MY views on all that had to do with possible economic aid to Russia were influenced, I suspect, by the impressions of a journey that I had opportunity to make, within the Soviet Union, not long after the ending of hostilities in Europe.

On return to Russia in the previous summer, I had filed a request with the Soviet Foreign Office for permission to visit western Siberia — and particularly the metallurgical center at what was then called Stalinsk-Kuznetsk, some two hundred miles southeast of Novosibirsk and a similar distance northwest of what was then the border of Tannu-Tuva. The great steel mill there was one of the two major projects of this nature completed during the 1930s, the other being the better-known Magnitogorsk plant, in the Urals. Although many foreigners had visited Magnitogorsk, no Westerner, so far as I could ascertain, had been in Kuznetsk for several years. I had never seen any of the leading Soviet industrial plants and thought it would be interesting to see one that had been less commonly visited by foreigners. In addition to this there was, again, the example of my distinguished nineteenth-century namesake. I wanted, before leaving Russia again, to see at least a small portion of the vast Siberian territory where so many of his travels had taken place and with which his name was so widely associated.

For months following the submission of my request, there had been no response from the Foreign Office. I had concluded, by spring, that it was destined to join the long list of similar requests to

which the Soviet authorities had not wished to say yes but had also
not wished to say no and had therefore said nothing at all. I had, in
fact, almost forgotten about the matter when, in the spring of 1945,
I was suddenly called to the Foreign Office and told that I might
go.

The trip was made some time in the summer — I cannot remember just when. I wrote a copious literary account of the experience
— an account which the reader is now mercifully to be spared,
because no copy of it can be found. The journey to Novosibirsk
was made by rail: four days and nights in the end compartment of a
sleeping car, walled off from the other passengers by two NKVD
officers in uniform who "chanced" to be occupying the adjoining
compartment.

In Novosibirsk I spent some days seeing the various sights of this
burgeoning Siberian Chicago. On the afternoon of the last of these
days, the departure for Kuznetsk being scheduled for early the following morning, I was taken out of town to visit a state farm in the
neighborhood. A very impressive farm it was, too, with great herds
of fine cattle, and country that took your breath away with its
beauty, its fertility, and its sense of space and strength. The tour of
the farm finished, I suggested an immediate return to town, plead-
ing the need for early retirement in view of the next day's departure. But I was told that "tea" was being prepared in the orchard,
for my benefit, and was made to understand that this was *de rigueur*.

Tea turned out to be a long wooden table under the fruit trees,
literally groaning with every sort of food, a total of ten or twenty
people there to do the honors, and an insistence that the various
courses be washed down with tumblers, not liqueur glasses, of very
fine vodka. The repast lasted into the evening. Among my hosts
was a burly young party secretary from Novosibirsk, obviously a
person of considerable competence and power, informal to a degree
that would have made him feel perfectly at home in the great
American West (to which, indeed, Siberia has many similarities).
At the conclusion of the "tea," he and I were both in exceptional good humor. He suggested I ride back into town with him
in his jeep, which I did. By the time we reached town, the humor

was even better. We agreed that sleep was a dreary idea, and he undertook to show me the night life of Novosibirsk. This he did with enthusiasm, in a tour that lasted long into the night. Memories of this tour are not as clear as one could wish. My NKVD escort was curtly dismissed by my companion, early in the game. For one lovely evening I was, to all intents and purposes, a member of the Soviet governing elite. We visited several theaters, barging in through side doors, staring down anyone who questioned our arrival, and installing ourselves without ceremony in the government box. I have a faint recollection that we watched some Isadora Duncan dancers performing on a bandstand in a park, and they were terrible. We visited a circus, watched a lady put her head in the lion's mouth, and after having a good second look at the lady agreed — to our great mutual satisfaction — that we were lost in admiration for the courage of the lion. We ended up by routing out, in the early morning hours, a very mussed and sleepy stationmaster and obliging him to give us a conducted tour of what, my host assured me, was one of Russia's greatest railway stations, not to be omitted on any properly conducted tour of the city.

The days in Kuznetsk were similarly agreeable. I arrived there, after a train ride of some eighteen hours during which, still fortified by the state farm "tea," I deplored the very thought of food, only to find myself confronted, at three in the morning, with another groaning table of hors d'oeuvres, accompanied this time with Siberian liqueurs (made in Kuznetsk, and the pride of the city), and required to endure all over again that well-meant but sometimes trying refrain of Russian hospitality: "You don't eat anything. You don't like it, huh?"

The same buffet table, with the same hors d'oeuvres, replenished from time to time as circumstances required, remained before us during the entire period of my stay there; it was our sole source of sustenance, but a very luxurious one; and three times a day my delighted hosts, for whom in wartime these delicacies were scarcely a daily fare, applied themselves vigorously to its destruction and pressed me to do likewise. They, too, like my party friend in Novosibirsk, were genial and thoroughly friendly.

Most pleasant of all was the return trip, by air, to Moscow. It took three days and involved overnight stops in Chelyabinsk and Kazan. For some reason the NKVD seemed to have lost track of me at this point. The office at Novosibirsk was, I suppose, done with me, and the center at Moscow had not yet picked me up. The result was that I had, for once, the feeling of not being a stranger, of belonging to a company of ordinary Soviet people. My companions on the plane, in any case, did not seem to recognize me as anything out of the ordinary. At the airport in Omsk, sitting in the grass under the shade of the wing of the plane in the heat of the day, I read aloud to a group of them, at their request, from a volume of Aleksei Tolstoy's *Peter the Great* which I had with me. In the evenings I shared their company in the little airport dormitories as though I were a common citizen like the rest of them. I felt immensely at home among them, and never did the artificial barriers that separated people like myself from Soviet citizens in Moscow seem more absurd and more deplorable.

On the last day of this journey, sitting on a crate in the stern of a DC-3 and watching the great plain of the region just west of the Volga as it slowly receded beneath us, I fell to thinking, in connection with these friendly fellow passengers, of the problem of American aid to Russia. It was a problem which, what with Lend-Lease, Red Cross aid, UNRRA, and talk of a major loan to the Soviet government, had been much on our minds in the preceding months. The Russian people, as the experiences of this visit had just emphasized for me, were a great and appealing people. The sufferings they had recently undergone were enormous. These sufferings had been incurred partly in our own cause. One would have liked to help, but could one? When a people found itself under the control of a strongly authoritarian regime, and especially one hostilely inclined to the United States, there was very little that Americans could do to help them, it occurred to me, without helping the regime to which they were subject. If economic assistance were to be extended, say in the form of consumer goods, the regime would first impugn our motives; then it would turn to the people and say: "Who but we could have been clever enough to get this aid for you from the wicked imperialists?" And finally it would simply divert to its own purposes an equivalent volume of resources which it would otherwise have had to make available to the people, leaving the total allocation to the civilian sector exactly what it would otherwise have been. If, on the other hand, we tried to bring injury to the regime, by means of economic pressure of one sort or another, the regime would simply find means to pass this injury on to the civilian population, using it as proof both of foreign hostility to the people themselves and of the indispensability of its own protection and authority. People and regime, in other words, were bound together in a common dialectical relationship, so that you could not help people without helping regime, and you could not harm regime without harming people. In these circumstances it was better, surely, to try neither to help nor to harm, but rather to leave people alone. It was, after all, *their* predicament, not ours. We could not interfere in it, whether benevolently or malevolently, without producing effects we did not mean and did not desire to produce, and without sowing confusion as to our own motives.

In the postwar years, as the problems of foreign aid gradually advanced to the status of a major item in our national discussions about foreign policy, I was to have many an occasion to return to these reflections. They have lain, ever since those hours on the plane, at the basis of the hesitations and skepticism I have experienced with respect to the possibilities of foreign aid in general — with respect to the whole concept of wreaking, by intervention, even benevolent intervention, from without — great and useful changes in the lives of other peoples.

In the period following the end of hostilities with Japan, Ambassador Harriman was repeatedly called away from Moscow for temporary duties elsewhere. This altered somewhat my own situation, insofar as it now became necessary for me to present views directly, from time to time, to the Department of State, and to handle personally the American official visitors who were now in increasing numbers making their appearance in the Soviet capital.

In September, during one of the ambassador's absences, we re-

ceived the visit of a group of members of Congress. They wanted
to see Stalin. Although unenthusiastic, and not hopeful, I had no
choice but to ask for the appointment. I knew that such a request
would not normally be granted. The chances were particularly slim
in this instance because I had been obliged to request a similar interview, just at this time, for Senator Claude Pepper of Florida, a
member of the Senate Foreign Relations Committee, whose visit
happened to coincide with that of the Congressmen. To my amazement both interviews were granted — to take place, if my memory
is correct, within a day of each other. I escorted both parties to the
Kremlin and interpreted for them both in their interviews.

I cannot recall the tenor of the discussion between the Congressmen and Stalin (the Washington archives, I am sure, would show
it); but I have a vivid memory of our approach to this occasion.
The interview was scheduled, I believe, for 6 P.M., in Stalin's office
in the Kremlin. Just prior to it was scheduled a visit of the congressional party to the Moscow subway system. Having seen the Moscow subway on a great many occasions, I decided not to accompany them on that last venture, but arranged to pick them up, at
5:30 P.M., at the exit from the Mossovyet subway station, where
their tour was to end. I came there at the proper time and waited
until well after 5:30. To my growing concern no Congressmen appeared. Inquiry elicited the information that the party was being
entertained at "tea" somewhere in the bowels of the subway system. I never discovered the premises in which this repast was being
served, but frantic indirect messages finally brought my compatriots to the surface, at about ten minutes before six. To my horror
I discovered that the "tea" served to them by their genial hosts of
the Moscow subway had, like the tea of Novosibirsk, been not only
of the nonalcoholic variety: varying amounts of vodka, depending
on the stoutness of character and presence of mind of the individual
concerned, had been poured into my charges while they were on
the verge of their interview with the great Soviet leader.

We tore away, in two limousines, in the direction of the Kremlin,
I riding in the front seat of one of the cars. As we approached the
Kremlin gate, protected by what was probably the most vigilant

and elaborate system of guarding of any place in the world, I was horrified to hear, from the interior of the car behind me, a raucous voice saying: "Who the hell is this guy Stalin, anyway? I don't know that I want to go up and see him. I think I'll get out." Elaborate arrangements had been made, including even the submission of every passport to the Foreign Office, to assure admission of the party to the Kremlin, and I knew that if anyone were missing, things would be royally gummed up. So I said with great definiteness: "You'll do nothing of the sort. You will sit right there where you are and remain with the party." There ensued the formalities at the gate. Doors were opened, identities were established, seats were looked under. A car full of armed men was placed before us, and another one behind. Thus guarded, we drove off up the short incline to the heart of the Kremlin. At this point the same raucous voice became audible once more behind me: "What if I biff the old codger one in the nose?" My heart froze. I cannot recall what I said, but I am sure that never in my life did I speak with greater earnestness. I had, as I recollect it, the help of some of the more sober members of the party. In any case, our companion came meekly along. He sat in Stalin's office at the end of the long table, facing Stalin, and did nothing more disturbing than to leer and wink once or twice at the bewildered dictator, thus making it possible for the invisible gun muzzles, with which the room was no doubt studded, to remain sullenly silent.

The episode was a small one, but I must say that it was one of the impressions (and there were many of them in the course of a Foreign Service career) that gradually bred in me a deep skepticism about the absolute value of people-to-people contacts for the improvement of international relations. On the other hand, I must also say that our congressional visitors varied, in their capacity to derive profit for themselves and to cause the interests of our government to prosper by their visits, from the very worst to the very best. Their number contained some shrewd and serious men, who not only were able to give us valuable support when they returned to Washington, but whose reactions and advice, while they were in Moscow, were useful to us and much appreciated.

Actually, both of the interviews with Stalin passed off successfully, although that of Senator Pepper was also not without its
minor difficulties. I had naturally, and without second thought,
asked for his appointment with Stalin on the strength of his quality
as a member of the Senate Foreign Relations Committee — as a
statesman, in other words. It was granted on this understanding. To
my consternation the Senator, on the eve of the interview, confided
to me that he was combining his official interests on this journey
with a certain amount of journalistic activity — writing articles, in
fact, for publication by a syndicate of Florida newspapers. What
did I think? Would it be all right for him to write a story on his
interview with Stalin, and should he send it from Moscow or wait
until he had left the country?

Had I known, of course, that he was coming as a journalist, the
request for an appointment should have made this clear and should
have gone through other channels. I cannot remember how the
problem was finally solved. I recall only the sense of hopelessness I
experienced in trying to explain to the Russians why a distinguished
statesman, discussing serious problems of international affairs with a
foreign governmental leader, would be interested in exploiting for a
very minor private gain whatever value the interview might have in
the eyes of the commercial mass media. I knew that ten years of
patient explanations would not suffice to make them understand
why this could be regarded as a creditable procedure; and I would
have been the worst to undertake the explanation, for I fear my
sympathies, in this case, were on the Russian side.

* * *

I should perhaps say a word at this point about Stalin. The impression one gains of a public figure from seeing him at first hand is
of course a different thing, and far less important, than the impression one gains from long and careful study of his public career. I
have set forth in another context* my view of Stalin as a statesman.
Here a word or two about his person.

* *Russia and the West under Lenin and Stalin,* **Chapter** 17, Boston: Atlantic-
Little Brown and Company, 1960.

His was a low-slung, smallish figure, neither markedly stout nor thin, inclining, if anything, to the latter. The square-cut tunic seemed always a bit too large for him; one sensed an effort to compensate for the slightness of stature. Yet there was also a composed, collected strength, and a certain rough handsomeness, in his features. The teeth were discolored, the mustache scrawny, coarse, and streaked. This, together with the pocked face and yellow eyes, gave him the aspect of an old battle-scarred tiger. In manner — with us, at least — he was simple, quiet, unassuming. There was no striving for effect. His words were few. They generally sounded reasonable and sensible; indeed, they often were. An unforewarned visitor would never have guessed what depths of calculation, ambition, love of power, jealousy, cruelty, and sly vindictiveness lurked behind this unpretentious facade.

Stalin's greatness as a dissimulator was an integral part of his greatness as a statesman. So was his gift for simple, plausible, ostensibly innocuous utterance. Wholly unoriginal in every creative sense, he had always been the aptest of pupils. He possessed unbelievably acute powers of observation and, when it suited his purposes, imitation. (If he later destroyed his teachers, as he usually did, this was really the mark of his high respect for them.) By the same token he was, of course, a great, if terrible (in part: great *because* terrible), teacher of politics. Most impressive of all was his immense, diabolical skill as a tactician. The modern age has known no greater master of the tactical art. The unassuming, quiet facade, as innocently disarming as the first move of the grand master at chess, was only a part of this brilliant, terrifying tactical mastery.

Those of my colleagues who saw more of him than I did have told of being able to observe other aspects of his personality: of seeing the yellow eyes light up in a flash of menace and fury as he turned, momentarily, on some unfortunate subordinate; of witnessing the diabolical sadism with which, at the great diplomatic dinners of the war, he would humiliate his subordinates before the eyes of foreigners, with his barbed, mocking toasts, just to show his power over them. I myself did not see these things. But when I first encountered him personally, I had already lived long enough in Russia to know something about him; and I was never in doubt, when visiting him, that I was in the presence of one of the world's most remarkable men — a man great, if you will, primarily in his iniquity: ruthless, cynical, cunning, endlessly dangerous; but for all of this — one of the truly great men of the age.*

*　　*　　*

Immediately after this interview with Stalin, I had occasion to make a brief visit to Helsinki. As a small respite from this heavy diet of political problems, but also because it illustrates something important in the life of every Westerner who lives in Russia, I adduce at this point that portion of the diary notes from this journey that deals with the passage from Russia into Finland.

I should perhaps remind the reader that the territory of the Karelian Isthmus, over which the train begins to pass as soon as it leaves the suburbs of Leningrad, had been bitterly fought over, fought over twice, in fact, during the war. Occupied by Soviet forces and taken formally into Soviet possession with the collapse of Finnish resistance a year earlier, it had at the time I saw it simply been left, like great parts of East Prussia, untouched by human hands and permitted to become a wilderness. The onetime modern Finnish town of Vyborg, as I recorded in my diary, had been completely destroyed and was, so far as I could see, devoid of habitation. On my return journey I left the train in early morning when it stopped at the Vyborg station, and roamed about among the ruins of the place. While I was doing this it began to rain heavily. I took refuge from the rain in what had once been the doorway of a fine modern department store, now gutted and wrecked. Not having seen a living being on my entire walk, I was surprised, standing there in the doorway, to hear a noise behind me. Looking around, I discovered that I was sharing the shelter of the doorway with a goat. The two of us, it seemed, were for the moment the sole inhabitants of this once thriving modern city.

---

* The above was written before I read Svetlana's book about her family. This has widened, and changed somewhat, my view of Stalin; but since the present discussion relates to the experiences of 1945-1946, I let the description stand as written.

What the account of this trip may serve to illustrate is that curious feeling of relief and release which overcomes every sensitive Westerner as he leaves the charged political climate of Russia and returns to the more reassuring atmosphere of the West. It is the feeling which causes all Westerners, in fact, to use the terms "in" or "out" to distinguish their presence on Soviet territory from their presence elsewhere. It is something apparently unaffected by wars, devastations, and political upsets. I am sure that this contrast between Russia and non-Russia, never wholly absent from the mind of the Western resident in Russia, affects subconsciously, and perhaps not unjustly, his judgments about a great many political problems that do not normally concern his person at all. My diary goes on to note:

September 6, 1945

[The train for Helsinki left in late evening.] The only other Intourist guest who was going there was a somewhat gloomy Mexican in a beret, who spoke with a perfect Texas accent. Just as we went out the front door of the hotel, the bus which was to have taken us to the station started up and disappeared without us into the darkness — to the amazement and consternation of the Intourist girl who had been delegated to accompany us. For a long time I stood out on the square, looking at the stately outlines of St. Isaac's Cathedral that loomed out faintly in the darkness, while the Mexican described to me the course of his diarrhea. Another bus, not ours, stood empty and deserted by the curb. A drunken Soviet soldier came weaving along out of the darkness, hammered indignantly at the door of the empty bus, and then asked the white-bearded doorman when it left. "That's not your bus," replied the doorman. "Where do you want to go?" "I want to go west," the soldier replied, "as near as you can get to the Soviet border." The Intourist girl, who had arrived on the scene just in time to hear this last crack, quickly hustled us back into the lobby, where we waited until another bus could be made ready.

September 7, 1945

When I woke in the morning we were just pulling out of ruined and deserted Vyborg. It was overcast, and there was a strong cold wind. Rays of early morning sunshine, slipping through the clouds, slanted across the earth, caught the gutted shells of apartment buildings, and flooded them momentarily with a chill, pale gleam. Below us the port lay quiet and empty. An abandoned water-filled boat washed gently beside the remnants of a pier. But the light of morning was fresh on the harbor. The water rippled gaily in the breeze, as though it were not bounded on three sides by these mute testimonials to man's capacity for desolation. A gull, wheeling and circling over the inner basin, rejoiced in the new day, in the prospect of fish below, and in its own graceful strength.

After leaving Vyborg, we moved slowly through a devastated and deserted country. Weeds and scrub trees were growing on the abandoned farms. The houses, doorless and windowless, were obviously sinking gradually back into the new vegetation around them. When you occasionally got a glimpse into the interiors, you saw that the floors were full of rubbish and offal. And you knew that the rank new vegetation still concealed tens of thousands of live land mines.

After an hour we reached the new Finnish border and stopped at the first Finnish station. Here everything was suddenly neat and cheerful. A new station building had been erected: simple and of wood, but with a certain distinctive modern touch. The platform was in good repair and clean. There was a freshly painted kiosk where newspapers were on sale. But the station was almost deserted. Food was not in evidence. The sky was gray. Everything was a little sad.

Our Russian locomotive retired, leaving our sleeping car, together with two "soft" cars full of Russians bound for the new naval base at Porkkala Udd, to wait for the Finnish train. We had long to wait. I paced up and down the platform in the wind, a slave to the Anglo-Saxon habit of exercise. The Russians stared vacantly out the windows of their car, and on their faces was that same stoical emptiness with which Russians stare out of train windows all over their vast, melancholy Russian world.

The sidings were full of freight cars loaded with Finnish goods being shipped to Russia as reparations. Little cars, wheels and tracks for a narrow gauge logging railroad, bright with shiny metal and new paint, were carefully stored and lashed on big gondola cars. On others there were piles of clean sawn lumber, neatly cut and carefully stacked. All these contributions bore the mark of orderly, conscientious Finnish workmanship. I wondered at first whether such offerings did not sometimes rouse pangs of shame among the inhabitants of the great shoddy

Russian world into which they were moving. But on second thought I was inclined to doubt this very strongly.

The station platform was almost deserted. A lithe young Finn, with a knife in his belt, gave side glances of hatred and contempt at the Russian cars as he went about his work as a switchman. Wood smoke from the little switch engine was torn away by the wind and carried across the clearing, its odor reminiscent of the north woods at home. A Finnish railwayman in uniform rode sedately up to the station building, parked his bicycle, and went inside to transact his business. A peasant cart drove up with a family in the back. The family might well be hungry, but the horse was fat and sleek and trotted with a happy briskness which no Russian horse possesses. Over the entire scene there lay the efficiency, the trimness, the quietness, and the boredom of bourgeois civilization; and these qualities smote with triple effect on the senses of a traveler long removed from the impressions of bourgeois environment.

The Finnish locomotive finally appeared, picked us up and started off with us through the forests at a pace which seemed positively giddy after the leisurely lumbering of Russian trains. There was a dining car. There was not overly much to eat, but what there was was well prepared; the place was well run and inviting; the other passengers were friendly, unafraid, and unsuspicious. All day long we moved through a beautiful northern country, the forests broken with lakes, farms, meadows, and herds of cattle. The Russians continued to stare out the window with impassive and apparently unappreciative faces. By evening we were in Helsinki.

* * *

The Potsdam Conference, as will be recalled, established the Council of Foreign Ministers, on which were to be represented the five leading powers that had been involved in the wars against Germany and Japan, and had assigned to this council, as its first task, the drafting of peace treaties for Italy, Rumania, Bulgaria, Hungary, and Finland. The initial meeting of this council, at London in September 1945, broke down in wrangling over procedure, a breakdown which merely reflected, and was in fact the product of, deeper disagreements, primarily over the nature of the governments

that were being established under Russian pressure in the Eastern
European countries. To resolve this deadlock, the Americans, anxious to get on with the drafting of the treaties, proposed a meeting
of the foreign ministers of the Big Three to discuss not only the
problems of procedure that had arisen at London but a number of
other problems that were proving troublesome. The proposal was
accepted; and the three foreign ministers — Molotov, Ernest Bevin,
and James F. Byrnes — met in Moscow, in December 1945.

I am frank to say that I regarded this meeting, rightly or
wrongly, with the same feelings of detachment and skepticism with
which I had viewed the earlier meetings of the heads of state. I had
not been drawn in any way into the preliminary planning. The entire world of thought out of which these encounters arose was foreign and distasteful to me. I had never met Mr. Byrnes or had any
communication with him. For the effort to rescue something of the
wreckage of the Yalta Declaration on Liberated Europe, to preserve, that is, some fig leaves of democratic procedure to hide the
nakedness of Stalinist dictatorship in the respective Eastern European countries, I had nothing but contempt. I simply did not believe
in its reality. I found it absurd to suppose that anything essential
was going to be changed by the inclusion of one or two non-Communist ministers in the cabinets of countries which already had
a police system along the pattern of the Soviet NKVD, entirely
under Russian control. I saw little to be gained by our having anything at all to do with the new regimes in these countries. If peace
treaties were unavoidable, I saw no reason to preserve in this respect the facade of tripartite unity. I would have preferred that we
negotiate such treaties independently, and that the documents be as
brief and noncommittal as possible, consisting in fact of nothing
more than a mutual agreement to terminate the state of war. I deplored any and every effort to convey to the American public the
impression that our own government had any residue of influence
in the Soviet-dominated area, or that the countries in question faced
anything less than the full rigor of Stalinist totalitarianism.

It was, in these circumstances, with a weary sense of meaningless
duty that I went through such minor motions as were required of

me in connection with the visit of the Secretary of State to Moscow in that first postwar December, and my memories can add nothing to the record of the substance of the discussions that then took place. But such of my diary notes as concern this visit may be not wholly without interest, as evidences of the atmosphere and impressions of the time. The first of them related to the day of the arrival of the Secretary of State.

Friday, December 14, 1945

This was a lively day. We were expecting the Secretary and his party. A full blizzard was blowing. Calls to the Soviet weather people in the early morning brought forth the information that weather conditions were impossible and no planes would be coming in. About 12:00 we were told that the Secretary's plane had left Berlin at 11:00. This came from a minor official of the Foreign Office. The Red army and the airport people said they knew nothing about it. At 1:30, just as I was leaving for lunch, Brooks Atkinson came in and said he had just been told by the British embassy that they had heard that the plane had turned back to Berlin. Thinking this very likely, I went home and had a leisurely lunch; came back to find one of the attachés talking on the phone to a distressed Foreign Office official who claimed that the plane was just then coming in and might arrive at any time at the Central Military Airport. I asked where Ambassador Harriman was. They said he had gone to some airport 20 miles south of town because he had heard that the Secretary might arrive there. I grabbed Horace Smith and the little duty car and together we tore out to the Central Military Airport. A howling blizzard was blowing. The field was just one white blur, with no distinction between sky and snow. You couldn't see across it at all. However, a radio sound truck was driving out into the obscurity as we arrived, and there were a number of Russian cars about. We were taken up into a little building at the edge of the field. Two or three journalists came along and joined us. In a few minutes we heard the sound of motors and looked out to see a four-motored plane passing over the roof of the building. We rushed out onto the field. The snow flurry had passed, and visibility was now better. Dekanosov,*

---

* One of the Soviet deputy foreign ministers; a protégé of Beria, taken to diplomatic work directly from a career in the secret police; later executed (1953) in connection with Beria's demise.

with one Foreign Office assistant and a lot of NKVD, was out there. Somebody had put up two iron posts with the Soviet and American flags. The plane, which had managed to land somehow or other, appeared out of the soup, taxiing up the field, wheeled around and stopped in front of us. The gangplank was pushed out through the snow and we went through the official reception. The Secretary, in a light coat and no overshoes, standing in deep snow, said his hellos and gave his speech over the microphone, while the wind howled through the little company. I then took him to the first available car and drove him, together with Ben Cohen and his military aide, to Spaso House. There Kathy gave them drinks and soup and kept them busy until the ambassador arrived from his wasted journey. Then I went back to the office to clear up papers.

Thoroughly enraged by a telegram from the department asking us to invite the Soviet government to a conference to work out mutual tariff reductions next March, I spent the evening writing an eloquent telegram demonstrating why it shouldn't be done.

Wednesday, December 19, 1945

Was invited by ambassador to attend the conference this afternoon. Unfortunately, the session turned out to consist of two brief meetings of about five or ten minutes each.

Bevin looked highly disgusted with the whole procedure. It was easy to see by his face that he found himself in a position he did not like. He did not want to come to Moscow in the first place and was well aware that nothing good could come of the meeting. The Russians knew his position, and were squeezing the last drop of profit out of it. As for Byrnes, Bevin saw in him only another cocky and unreliable Irishman, similar to ones that he had known in his experience as a docker and labor leader. Byrnes, as the British saw it, had consistently shown himself negligent of British feelings and quite unconcerned for Anglo-American relations. He had conceived the whole idea of this meeting in his own head and had taken it up with the Russians before saying a word about it to the British or giving them any warning that this was to be done. He had further offended the British by giving a copy of the Ethridge report to the Russians but not to the British embassy, despite the fact the latter had opened its files to Ethridge

when he was here and that his visit was largely at British initiative.*
Finally, Byrnes had come to Moscow with a paper to present to the
Russians on atomic energy which had been cleared with neither of the
other powers [Britain and Canada] which shared in holding the secret
of the manufacture of atomic energy, and this within six weeks after
Attlee's visit to Washington and conferences with the President. When
Bevin had remonstrated against the presentation to the Russians of any
document on this subject which had not been cleared with British and
Canadian governments, Byrnes had given him two days, namely until
today, Wednesday, to submit this document to London and get the
approval of the British cabinet. Bevin thought he had the assurance of
Byrnes that meanwhile nothing would be submitted to the Russians;
and indeed no other understanding would have made any sense. Nevertheless, on Tuesday evening, with no word to the British, Byrnes had
sent the document to the Russians. Bevin could view this only as an
instance of direct bad faith and was furious.

Molotov, conducting the meeting, sat leaning forward over the table,
a Russian cigarette dangling from his mouth, his eyes flashing with
satisfaction and confidence as he glanced from one to the other of the
other foreign ministers, obviously keenly aware of their mutual differences and their common uncertainty in the face of the keen, ruthless,
and incisive Russian diplomacy. He had the look of a passionate poker
player who knows that he has a royal flush and is about to call the last
of his opponents. He was the only one who was clearly enjoying
every minute of the proceedings.

I sat just behind Byrnes and could not see him well. He plays his
negotiations by ear, going into them with no clear or fixed plan, with
no definite set objectives or limitations. He relies entirely on his own
agility and presence of mind and hopes to take advantage of tactical
openings. In the present conference his weakness in dealing with the
Russians is that his main purpose is to achieve some sort of an agreement, he doesn't much care what. The realities behind this agreement,
since they concern only such people as Koreans, Rumanians, and
Iranians, about whom he knows nothing, do not concern him. He wants

---

* Mr. Mark Ethridge, publisher of the *Louisville Courier-Journal*, had been sent
by Mr. Byrnes on a special mission to Rumania, Bulgaria, and Greece, to make an
independent assessment, for the United States government, of political conditions
in those countries.

an agreement for its political effect at home. The Russians know this. They will see that for this superficial success he pays a heavy price in the things that are real.

After the meeting I walked home with Matthews and he stayed for supper. Frank Roberts* and his wife joined us. By the end of the evening, Matthews looked so crestfallen at the things that he had heard from Roberts and myself that I felt sorry for him and had to try to cheer him up. In the introduction of newcomers to the realities of the Soviet Union there are always two processes; the first is to reveal what these realities are, the second is to help the newcomer adjust himself to the shock.

Friday, December 21, 1945

Talked with the Bulgarian minister this morning. He began by censuring the opposition for not taking part in the [Bulgarian]election, claiming that they had voluntarily cut themselves off from participation in Bulgarian political life. Being somewhat impatient, I told him that what bothered us was not really questions of parliamentary representation or procedure but the fact that we were faced there with a regime of police oppression which did not hesitate to proceed in the most ruthless manner against the lives and liberties of individual citizens. It was our belief that in this atmosphere of terror and intimidation no real democracy could live. He became quite excited at this, and spoke thereafter much more frankly, admitting that the Communists were only a minority but pointing to the desirability of concluding peace and getting Russian troops out of the country.

Lunch with Roberts and Cadogan and two or three other people from the British delegation. Chip was there and I think he and I rather shook Cadogan's composure with our observations on the technique of dealing with the Soviet government.

Saturday, December 22, 1945

Was just settling down this evening for a quiet weekend when Page came over and told me the ambassador wanted a memorandum for the Secretary to present on the economic situation in Hungary. I went down to the office and worked until 3 A.M. with Horace Smith getting the memorandum up.

---

* Sir Frank Roberts, at that time my opposite number in the British embassy in Moscow. He was later to serve as British ambassador in Moscow, as well as in

Sunday, December 23, 1945

Went down to the office in the morning and finished work on the memorandum. After that I went to Spaso to a stag luncheon for Molotov and Bevin. Sat next to Tsarapkin, who was relatively human. Bevin caused much amusement among the Americans and considerable bewilderment among the Russians by the dour informality of his asides during the luncheon. When a toast was proposed to the king, he added good-humoredly, "and all the other dockers." He told a story afterward to explain this remark. When Harriman raised his glass to the success of the conference, Bevin assented and added: "And let's hope we don't all get sacked when we get home." Molotov left the minute luncheon was over. Later in the afternoon they were all hard at work again and worked most of the night.

The memorandum on the Hungarian economic situation, incidentally, was never used.

This evening the Russians put on a special performance of *Zolushka* (Cinderella) at the Bolshoi, for the visiting foreign ministers. I did not learn about it until late in the afternoon, and, feeling that Annelise and I ought to be there, took two of the last tickets on the list of those allotted to the embassy. When we got there, the theater was already packed to the last seat, spotlights were trained on the empty imperial box where the appearance of the foreign ministers was expected, and Molotov and his aides were waiting nervously in the hall outside. As is always the case when the big curtain is down, the theater was stuffy and hot and people were fanning themselves with their programs. The orchestra were all in their places waiting to strike up the national anthems. I found myself in a box with the ambassador's aide and one of his private secretaries. After we had waited another fifteen minutes, I said laughingly to the private secretary that I supposed the Secretary of State had forgotten to come. "Oh, no," the secretary replied, "they are only sitting up in his room at the embassy telling stories and having drinks and no one dares go in and interrupt them." I immediately tore out of the box and downstairs to the administrator's office, to telephone. The phone was in use when I got there and I stood in the crowded office for a moment waiting for a chance to use it. Just as the phone became free and I was about to dial the embassy a man in the shiny

Paris and Bonn. I knew him not only as a diplomatist of outstanding experience and ability but as a loyal colleague and valued friend.

blue civilian clothes so characteristic of the secret police came into the office, walked up to me, and said with a slight smile on his face: "They have just left." I went back to the box and sure enough in five minutes Mr. Byrnes appeared, having kept several thousand people, including numerous members of the Soviet government, waiting for something like a half an hour.

The performance was absolutely first-rate; one of the best I have ever seen, but it fell very flat on the audience. I understand that Stalin was somewhere in the theater, though not in the imperial box. For this reason the audience, except for the diplomatic corps, was apparently composed mostly of secret police people, who were doubtless afraid that any excessive display on their part of enthusiasm for the performance might look as though they were being diverted from their duties.

* * *

It is axiomatic in the world of diplomacy that methodology and tactics assume an importance by no means inferior to concept and strategy. Over the eighteen months I had now spent on this assignment in Moscow, I had experienced unhappiness not only about the naïveté of our underlying ideas as to what it was we were hoping to achieve in our relations with the Soviet government but also about the methods and devices with which we went about achieving it. The two aspects of our diplomacy were, of course, closely related. Methodology was itself in large measure a reflection of the image we had formed of the Soviet leadership and of the manner in which it could be expected to react to various stimuli. But methodology was nevertheless a subject that deserved attention in its own right. Perhaps it was the visit of Secretary Byrnes to Moscow that caused the pot of my patience to boil over with relation to this area of our diplomacy, as it had boiled over with respect to so many others. My reaction to this boiling over was, in any case, the usual one of reaching for my pen; and at some time in the winter of 1946 I produced the first three sections of what was intended as another *magnum opus*, directed this time to the specific problem of Soviet-American relations. It was never finished. (Possibly it was overtaken, as a literary effort, by the major telegraphic essay of which I shall have occasion to speak presently.) Being unfinished, my recollection is that it was never used in any way. I include in the Annex to this volume an excerpt from it, on the subject of the technique of dealing with Russia (pages 560-565), which represents a crude attempt, but one of the first of its kind (the first in my recollection, at any rate), to draw up a useful set of rules for dealing with the Stalin regime.

I prefaced this set of rules with an analysis of the process of decision-taking in the Soviet Union, trying to bring out the fact that it was wrong and useless to attempt to appeal to subjective feelings on the part of Soviet statesmen or negotiators: they could be influenced only by their assessment of how a given proposal or desideratum advanced by a foreign government would affect the interests of their regime; it was idle, therefore, to appeal to alleged common purposes or to an assumed high-mindedness on their part; one had to demonstrate at every point what would be "in it for them" in the way of advantage if they accepted our views, or of disadvantage if they did not. There then followed the rules themselves, designed to constitute, in their aggregate, a guide to the technique of dealing with (I reiterate) the *Stalin* regime. (This was, after all, the only Russian regime with which I had then had personal experience.) I offer here only the main headings of these rules. The comment and elucidation of each will be found in the full text of the document, appended.

A. *Don't act chummy with them.*

B. *Don't assume a community of aims with them which does not really exist.*

C. *Don't make fatuous gestures of good will.*

D. *Make no requests of the Russians unless we are prepared to make them feel our displeasure in a practical way in case the request is not granted.*

E. *Take up matters on a normal level and insist that Russians take full responsibility for their actions on that level.*

F. *Do not encourage high-level exchanges of views with the Russians unless the initiative comes at least 50 percent from their side.*

G. *Do not be afraid to use heavy weapons for what seem to us to be minor matters.*

H. *Do not be afraid of unpleasantness and public airing of differences.*

I. *Coordinate, in accordance with our established policies, all activities of our government relating to Russia and all private American activities of this sort which the government can influence.*

J. *Strengthen and support our representation in Russia.*

The student of Soviet-American relations who reads these rules today will have, no doubt, two questions in his mind as he completes the reading of them. One is whether they have been observed in the subsequent years and continue to be observed today. The other is whether they are still applicable now that Stalin is dead and the world situation has changed in important ways. My answer to both these questions would be: only partly. But to explain this answer now would be to jump ahead of my story.

In mid-February 1946 I was taken with cold, fever, sinus, tooth trouble, and finally the aftereffects of the sulpha drugs administered for the relief of these other miseries. The ambassador was again absent; he was, in fact, now in process of leaving his post for good. I was therefore in charge. Bedridden by these various *douleurs*, I suffered the daily take of telegrams and other office business to be brought currently up to my bedroom, and coped as best I could with the responsibilities that flowed from it all.

Among the messages brought up on one of these unhappy days was one that reduced us all to a new level of despair — despair not with the Soviet government but with our own. It was a telegram informing us that the Russians were evidencing an unwillingness to adhere to the World Bank and International Monetary Fund. The message, it appeared, had been inspired by the Treasury Department. It should be remembered that nowhere in Washington had the hopes entertained for postwar collaboration with Russia been more elaborate, more naïve, or more tenaciously (one might almost say ferociously) pursued than in the Treasury Department. Now, at long last, with the incomprehensible unwillingness of Moscow to adhere to the Bank and the Fund, the dream seemed to be shattered, and the Department of State passed on to the embassy, in tones of bland innocence, the anguished cry of bewilderment that had floated over the roof of the White House from the Treasury Department on the other side. How did one explain such behavior on the part of the Soviet government? What lay behind it?

The more I thought about this message, the more it seemed to be obvious that this was "it." For eighteen long months I had done little else but pluck people's sleeves, trying to make them understand the nature of the phenomenon with which we in the Moscow embassy were daily confronted and which our government and people had to learn to understand if they were to have any chance of coping successfully with the problems of the postwar world. So far as official Washington was concerned, it had been to all intents and purposes like talking to a stone. The Russian desk in the State Department had understood; but it had generally been as helpless as we were, and beyond it all had been an unechoing silence. Now, suddenly, my opinion was being asked. The occasion, to be sure, was a trivial one, but the implications of the query were not. It was no good trying to brush the question off with a couple of routine sentences describing Soviet views on such things as world banks and international monetary funds. It would not do to give them just a fragment of the truth. Here was a case where nothing but the whole truth would do. They had asked for it. Now, by God, they would have it.

I reached, figuratively, for my pen (figuratively, for the pen was in this case my long suffering and able secretary, Miss Dorothy Hessman, who was destined to endure thereafter a further fifteen years studded with just such bouts of abuse) and composed a telegram of some eight thousand words — all neatly divided, like an eighteenth-century Protestant sermon, into five separate parts. (I thought that if it went in five sections, each could pass as a separate telegram and it would not look so outrageously long.) These sections dealt respectively with:

the basic features of the Soviet postwar outlook;

the background of that outlook;

its projection on the level of official policy;

its projection on the level of unofficial policy. i.e., policy implemented through "front" organizations and stooges of all sorts;

the implications of all this for American policy.

I justified this outrageous encumberment of the telegraphic process by saying the department's query involved "questions so intricate, so delicate, so strange to our form of thought, and so important to the analysis of our international environment that I cannot compress the answers into a single brief message without yielding to . . . a dangerous degree of oversimplification."

The text of this document is reproduced in the Annex. I shall not attempt to summarize it here. I read it over today with a horrified amusement. Much of it reads exactly like one of those primers put out by alarmed congressional committees or by the Daughters of the American Revolution, designed to arouse the citizenry to the dangers of the Communist conspiracy. The fact that this is so demands its explanation but — again — not at this point in the narrative.

The effect produced in Washington by this elaborate pedagogical effort was nothing less than sensational. It was one that changed my career and my life in very basic ways. If none of my previous literary efforts had seemed to evoke even the faintest tinkle from the bell at which they were aimed, this one, to my astonishment, struck it squarely and set it vibrating with a resonance that was not to die down for many months. It was one of those moments when official Washington, whose states of receptivity or the opposite are determined by subjective emotional currents as intricately imbedded in the subconscious as those of the most complicated of Sigmund Freud's erstwhile patients, was ready to receive a given message. Exactly what happened to the telegram, once it entered into the maw of the communications system of the capital, I do not know. To say the least, it went "the rounds." The President, I believe, read it. The Secretary of the Navy, Mr. James Forrestal, had it reproduced and evidently made it required reading for hundreds, if not thousands, of higher officers in the armed services. The Department of State, not at all disturbed by the reckless use of the telegraphic channel, responded with a message of commendation. With the receipt in Washington, on Washington's Birthday 1946, of this telegraphic dissertation from Moscow, my official loneliness came in fact to an end — at least for a period of two to three years. My reputation was made. My voice now carried.

Six months earlier this message would probably have been received in the Department of State with raised eyebrows and lips pursed in disapproval. Six months later, it would probably have sounded redundant, a sort of preaching to the convinced. This was true despite the fact that the realities which it described were ones that had existed, substantially unchanged, for about a decade, and would continue to exist for more than a half-decade longer. All this only goes to show that more important than the observable nature of external reality, when it comes to the determination of Washington's view of the world, is the subjective state of readiness on the part of Washington officialdom to recognize this or that feature of it. This is certainly natural; perhaps it is unavoidable. But it does raise the question — and it is a question which was to plague me increasingly over the course of the ensuing years — whether a government so constituted should deceive itself into believing that it is capable of conducting a mature, consistent, and discriminating foreign policy. Increasingly, with the years, my answer would tend to be in the negative.

There remains, to complete this record of service in Moscow during and just after the war, one ominous matter to be mentioned. It was a cloud that appeared on the horizon in the last months of my service there, a cloud decidedly larger than a man's hand in the literal sense but not appreciably larger as it then appeared to me.

The reader will note that in all this structure of thought concerning Stalin's Russia and the problem it presented for American statesmanship, the nuclear weapon played no part. Those of us who served in Moscow in the last months of 1945 and the spring of 1946 were of course aware of its existence and of the use that had been made of it in Japan. But I cannot recall that this awareness affected perceptibly my own view of our relations with the Soviet Union. I saw, then as later, no positive role for weapons of such power in the pattern of our relations with the Soviet Union.

I can find in my papers from that time only one document that dealt with this matter at all. Its tenor was strictly negative, the reflection only of an anxiety lest this matter be handled on the basis of the same effort to curry favor with the Stalin regime that seemed to me to have inspired our other policies up to that time. I reproduce it here in full, for this is a sensitive subject, on which there will be highly critical judgments, and I would like the record to be complete.

The document was a dispatch to Washington, dated September 30, 1945. What evoked it, I do not know. Probably I had picked up some reflections of the view, then entertained by at least some people in Washington, that we should place at Moscow's disposal, as a pledge of our good faith, complete information on the new weapon and the methods of its production. This, in any case, is what I wrote.

I have no hesitation in saying quite categorically, in the light of some eleven years' experience with Russian matters, that it would be highly dangerous to our security if the Russians were to develop the use of atomic energy, or any other radical and far-reaching means of destruction, along lines of which we were unaware and against which we might be defenseless if taken by surprise. There is nothing — I repeat nothing — in the history of the Soviet regime which could justify us in assuming that the men who are now in power in Russia, or even those who have chances of assuming power within the foreseeable future, would hesitate for a moment to apply this power against us if by doing so they thought that they would materially improve their own power position in the world. This holds true regardless of the process by which the Soviet government might obtain the knowledge of the use of such forces, i.e., whether by its own scientific and inventive efforts, by espionage, or by such knowledge being imparted to them as a gesture of good will and confidence. To assume that Soviet leaders would be restrained by scruples of gratitude or humanitarianism would be to fly in the face of overwhelming contrary evidence on a matter vital to the future of our country.

It is thus my profound conviction that to reveal to the Soviet government any knowledge which might be vital to the defense of the United States, without adequate guarantees for the control of its use in the Soviet Union, would constitute a frivolous neglect of the vital interests of our people. I hope the department will make this view a matter of record, and will see that it is given consideration — for whatever it is worth — in connection with any discussions of this subject which may take place in responsible circles of our government.

I realize, in reading this over, that it might seem to run contrary, though only partially and obliquely so, to the views of several very wise and farseeing people, in Washington and elsewhere. I am free to recognize that it is the product of only the tiniest smattering of knowledge and reflection. It represented nothing other than an honest and earnest reaction to available information. Had I then known what I now know, I would, obviously, have seen little point in writing it at all. Had I known, in particular, how profound and fearful was the problem I was thus casually biting into, in how much deeper a range of philosophic reflection than any I then conceived the answers would have to be sought, and how formidable a measure of unpreparedness lay between us all and the discovery of those answers, my heart would have been even heavier than the clumsy naïveté of our wartime responses to Stalinist power had already made it.

12

The National War College

THE success of the long telegram from Moscow changed my life. My name was now known in Washington. I became qualified, in people's minds, as a candidate for a different order of position than the ones I had previously occupied. In April 1946 I was transferred to Washington and assigned as the first "deputy for foreign affairs" at the newly established National War College. This institution, conceived as the senior of the various midcareer educational establishments of the armed services, was scheduled to open its door in the fall of that year to the first batch of officer-students. My status was to be in effect that of one of the three deputy commandants. My particular function would be to devise and direct the more strictly political portions of the combined military-political course of instruction.

We arrived in Washington in late May. Most of June and July was taken up with the working out of a curriculum for the college. In late July and early August, I undertook, at the request of the Department of State, a speaking tour to the Middle West and the West Coast — more specifically, to Chicago, Milwaukee, Seattle, Portland, the San Francisco area, and Los Angeles.

This was my first extensive experience with public speaking. (It was, alas, far from being the last.) I had lectured on Russian history to my fellow internees at Bad Nauheim. I had spoken once or twice, nervously and fumblingly, before private audiences at this or that foreign post. But never had I involved myself in anything of such dimensions. It was a mark of my inexperience that I prepared no written texts for these appearances, relying for the substance of my statements on a few scribbled notes, on the resources of memory, and on the inspiration of the moment. Having failed to preserve the notes, I have no clear idea of what I did say. Whatever it was, it must have been marked by more enthusiasm and spontaneity than coherence. But audiences, however much or little edified, seemed to be attentive and appreciative. Their reactions, in fact, sometimes startled me. On the second of these occasions — some sort of a League of Women Voters luncheon in my native city of Milwaukee — a clergyman at the speaker's table, who had sat staring at me with a disconcerting smile throughout my presentation, approached me afterwards, shook my hand, and said, enigmatically: "Boy, you missed your calling."

In their readiness or ability to understand what I was talking about, the audiences varied markedly. The best were the stag groups of businessmen: skeptical, critical, but hardheaded, thoughtful, schooled in the sort of dialectical approach that permitted you to oppose a competitor without finding it necessary, or even desirable, to destroy him, and therefore capable of understanding that the Soviet-American antagonism might be serious without having to be resolved by war. The most difficult, not in the sense that they were hostile but rather that they were unprepared for, and troubled by, what I had to say, were the academic ones. I discussed this in an account of the tour which I submitted, upon its completion, to one of the officials of the Department of State who had inspired it. There hung over these academic audiences, I wrote,

something of the intellectual snobbery and pretense, the jealousies and inhibitions, and the cautious herd-instinct which have a habit of creeping into college faculties, whether liberal or conservative. . . . But added to this were two other elements which made things difficult. One of these was a bias against the State Department as such. The other was a geographic inferiority complex, if I may call it that: a feeling that the East, including the State Department, was haughty and supercilious and neglectful of the wisdom and vision that flourished in centers of learning on the West Coast. . . . There was a certain neurosis there: a resentment of the fact that things are still centered in the East; a desire to see the Pacific area just as important — and recognized as being as important — as the Atlantic. This played a particularly noticeable role in the discussion of Russian questions, for I could see that many of my listeners viewed the development of "collaboration" with Russia as one of the things that were going to increase the activity and importance of their particular area. They had set high hopes on the development of relations across the Pacific between our West Coast . . . and Siberia. Their noses were out of joint over the failure of these hopes to materialize, and they were inclined to put the blame on the State Department.

I could not help but gain the impression, incidentally, that these West Coast academic audiences included a sizable number of people who, if not themselves Communist Party members, had been strongly influenced from that side. I suppose it was the recent residence in Moscow that made me sensitive to this situation; in any case, accustomed as I was to a concern for governmental security, I was disturbed by it. I had no doubt, I wrote to the State Department,

that every word I said was being dutifully reported to the Soviet consul before the day was out. There is no great harm in this; and I did not alter what I said for that reason; but if the department has people going out there to talk on subjects more confidential in character, it had better exercise some check on who is admitted to the meetings.

The atomic scientists included in the group at Berkeley had puzzled me particularly. "The exact nature of their views," I wrote,

is still nebulous to me; they seemed to combine a grudging approval of Mr. Baruch's proposals for an International Atomic Energy Authority with an unshakable faith that if they could only get some Soviet scientists by the buttonhole and enlighten them about the nature of atomic weapons, all would be well. I don't think it ever occurred to them that a realization of the tremendous destructive possibilities of atomic energy might be less inclined to scare the Russians into international collaboration than to whet their desire to find a way of using it without danger to themselves. Politically these people are as innocent as six-year-old maidens. In trying to explain things to them I felt like one who shatters the pure ideals of tender youth. Fortunately for them, they didn't believe much of what I said and left, I am sure, unshaken in the comfortable conviction that such evil as exists in the world has its seat in the State Department, which doesn't want to understand. . . .

On rereading these passages, I recognize that they might suggest I was headed for a job as staff consultant to the late Senator Joe McCarthy or to the House Un-American Affairs Committee. To offset this impression, and to make it clear that this was not my only reaction to the problem of communism in our own society, I ought perhaps to include the following remarks, of which I find record in the notes for a talk which I gave at the University of Virginia, some six months later:

In particular, I deplore the hysterical sort of anticommunism which, it seems to me, is gaining currency in our country: the failure to distinguish what is indeed progressive social doctrine from the rivalry of a foreign political machine which has appropriated and abused the slogans of socialism. I am far from being a Communist; but I recognize in the theory of Soviet communism (in the theory, mark you, not the practice) certain elements which I think are probably really the ideas of the future. I hate to see us reject the good with the bad — throw out the baby with the bath — and place ourselves in that way on the wrong side of history.

. . . So here, again, I return to the need for greater coolness, greater sophistication, greater maturity and self-confidence in our approach to this whole problem of Russia and communism.

* * *

I do not, as I say, have any written record of what it was that I was saying in the various speeches delivered around the country in the summer of 1946. But I do have a record of sorts — a stenographic record that somebody made — of what I said shortly after return from that journey, on the occasion of an appearance by myself and Llewellyn Thompson (also only recently returned from a period of service in Moscow) before a large meeting of members of the personnel of the Department of State. The date was September 17, 1946. Here, too, I spoke without a written text, but the stenographic record of what I said may be taken, I think, as a pretty good summary of what I had just been saying to audiences around the country.

I began by emphasizing the duality of the political personality that had confronted us in Moscow. There was one side of this personality with which we could sympathize and which we could to some extent admire; there was another of which this could not be said. One saw in the positive side "a great devotion to principle: a sort of Spartan-puritan strictness of thought, combined with a real eagerness to know about the West, to learn about us, to share with us thoughts and ideas." This was mixed, to be sure, with oversensitivity, with pride, with a shame for Russia's backwardness; but these were understandable things. The other side of the personality was so full of ill will that it was "hard to believe that it is sincere." One had to assume that it was inspired by some ulterior purpose. What was clear was only that we had to have a policy which took account of, and was addressed to, both of these personalities: a policy "devised in such a way as to encourage and not to antagonize the one, while discouraging and discrediting the other."

The tough side could only be confronted by superior military and political force.

I don't think that we can influence them [the Soviet leaders] by reasoning with them, by arguing with them, by going to them and saying: "Look here, this is the way things are." I don't believe that is possible. I have seen it tried by the hour. . . . I don't mean our policy should not be frankly . . . and adequately stated to them at every turn of the game. . . . I think we should go to them and put it right on the line, but not with the idea that they are going to turn around and say: "By George, I never thought of that before. We will go right back and change our policies." . . . They aren't that kind of people.

This did not mean, I was at pains to point out, that they did not hear or understand what one was trying to say. They were simply steeled against it.

If you talk to any fanatic, what is in the back of his mind is: "This fellow talks from premises that are profoundly wrong; he is trying to seduce me intellectually; my job is to try to hold out against him."

The behavior of the Soviet leaders could be changed, I thought, only

by the logic of a long-term set of circumstances which makes it evident that noncollaborative purposes on their part will not pay — will redound to Russia's disadvantage, whereas a more kindly policy toward us would win them advantages. If we can keep them maneuvered into a position where it is always hard and unprofitable for them to take action contrary to the principles of the United Nations and to our policies and where there is always an open door and an easy road to collaboration; if we can maintain that situation, keeping cool nerves, and maintaining it consistently, not in a provocative way but in a polite way, a calm way, preserving at all times our own strength and our firmness, but never blustering or threatening, always keeping the door open for them when they finally do decide to come in — I personally am quite convinced that they will not be able to withstand . . . that sooner or later the logic of it will penetrate their government and will force changes there.

I felt it necessary to warn my listeners that this measured optimism did not mean that I saw an early end to the iron curtain, any end to it, in fact, within the lifetime of those of us present. The iron curtain was suspended, I thought,

from the basic backwardness of Russia; from the differentness of Russia; from its close proximity to the Orient; from its love-hate complex with respect to the West; from its fear that the West will be superior and will put something over on it; and at the same time from its basic faith that they in Russia have something way down there, behind all the . . . poverty and misery, that they could teach us, too; and they don't want to lose it.

The curtain, then, was there to stay. But if we handled ourselves correctly, we could bring about a situation within a reasonable time, and by that I mean an historical time — five or ten years — where we can have much pleasanter relations with them than we have today in the sense of things being more normal, more quiet, and people not being all excited about our difficulties.

The Soviet leaders were, after all, not anxious to have a showdown with us at this point in history — of that I was sure. We still had with us the preponderance of world opinion. This represented a superior force. It gave us a decisive edge of advantage. And this edge

should enable us, if our policies are wise and nonprovocative, to contain them both militarily and politically for a long time to come.

It is for obvious reasons that I have underlined here the word "contain." The reader will wish to note that this use of it occurred months before I was called to any policy-making position in government, before General Marshall had even become Secretary of State, and before I had any intimacy with anyone in the policy-making echelons of official Washington.

The months at the War College were intensely enjoyable. We lived (as a result, I seem to recall, of the kindly intervention of General Eisenhower) in one of the row of generals' houses that line the western side of the point at Fort McNair, in southeast Washington. Their back doors looked out on the shining waters of the Washington channel and the Potomac. The benevolent paternalism of the army, which kept one's house up, supplied transportation, and rendered a thousand other useful personal services, was pleasing and reassuring. Beyond that, we were now for the first time living within striking distance of our Pennsylvania farm. Energies, at that stage of life, were great. Enthusiasm for agriculture and for the improvement of property was huge. We went to the farm practically every weekend, jogging happily on Friday afternoons across the lovely northern Maryland countryside, so similar to that of the southern Pennsylvania which it adjoins. It came to have a very special meaning to me, emotionally, that countryside: tidily farmed, prosperous, and lush in summer; quiet, brooding, patiently waiting in winter; spoiled only moderately, as yet, by that reckless semi-urbanization with which Americans love to desecrate the beauty and health of their continent. At the farm itself there were always thousands of things to be done (most of which, incidentally, never would be). Saturdays flew by in veritable orgies of labor on various "projects." The energies of guests were employed no less enthusiastically and no less inefficiently than our own. Then, on Sunday mornings, there would be the sad cleaning up and preparing of the house for another week of its customary solitude, followed by the long trek back amid Sunday-afternoon traffic; and finally — the sudden confrontation with the other world, the urban one, in the form of the fat stacks of the waiting Sunday paper and the insistent phone calls of people who had been trying to reach us ever since Friday noon.

This way of life has its disadvantages, as many other Americans have discovered; but it yielded pleasures and satisfactions untold. So long as I pursued it, during the years I spent in Washington, I remained healthy. When, for one reason or another, I omitted these weekend expeditions to the country, I fell ill. And in the contacts with our country neighbors, who never received us other than courteously and helpfully, I discovered not only an endless source of useful and friendly advice on practical matters, but the beneficent influence of a shrewd, reassuring common sense in the approach to life and its problems generally: a common sense that gave new, and sometimes healing, perspective to the trials, excitements, and disappointments of a hectic official existence.

I had as my associates on the command staff of the War College: Vice Admiral Harry W. Hill, USN, who was commandant; and the two deputy commandants: Major General Alfred M. Gruenther, of the army, and Brigadier General Truman H. Landon, of the air force. All three of these officers had distinguished careers behind them and even more distinguished ones ahead. Harry Hill would go on to be superintendent of the Naval Academy; Al Gruenther — to a whole series of illustrious positions, including that of Supreme Allied Commander of the NATO forces in Europe; Ted Landon — to the command of our air forces in Europe.

No one, I think, ever had finer associates than I did in these three men. I respected and admired them all, and never found anything but pleasure in our mutual association.

The college was intended as the senior establishment for in-service training in the problems of national policy, military and political. This being only the inauguration of its existence, the program for the first year was necessarily experimental. We were in a position to try out ideas of method and substance in teaching; and this was in itself exciting. But our possibilities were not limited to that. We could, through our activities, contribute in a way that no previous institution could do to the thinking about problems of national policy that was going on all over Washington in that winter of transition and uncertainty. Senior officials from both military and civilian echelons of the government, as well as people from the legislative branch, attended our lectures and occasionally lectured themselves. The Secretary of the Navy, James Forrestal, to whose vision and driving initiative the college largely owed its existence, took the keenest interest in what went on there, attended personally a number of the lectures (including some of my own), and gave us every support. Other officers of Cabinet rank, generals, and Senators sat at our feet as we lectured. The college came to provide a sort of academic seminar for the higher echelons of governmental Washington generally.

At my side, in the work of political instruction, were three civilian professors: Hardy Dillard of the University of Virginia, Sherman Kent and Bernard Brodie, both of Yale. All were stimulating thinkers and teachers as well as agreeable companions.

The students, an even hundred in number, were officers in the armed services, of the ranks between, and including, lieutenant colonel and brigadier general, or their equivalents, plus ten Foreign Service officers. Most of the officers from the armed services were men with recent distinguished war records, but they had by no means been chosen for this alone. Mature, thoughtful, keen, pleased to be there and anxious to make the most of it, they were a joy to teach. One learned from them as one taught.

Al Gruenther directed the administration of the college; and it was due largely to his relentless administrative energy, coupled with his infectious, teasing humor, that the program of that first experimental year moved forward as it did: smartly, smoothly, and with great élan. All in all, I have never known a more enjoyable professional experience.

The seven months of residence and work at the War College, from September 1946 to May 1947, were the occasion for a veritable outpouring of literary and forensic effort on my part. I look back today with a slightly horrified wonder on the energies this frenzy reflected. I was now in demand. I lectured not only at the National War College itself but in a number of other places as well: the Naval and Air War Colleges, the Naval Academy, the Carlisle Barracks (where I came directly from a weekend at my nearby farm and was so exhausted physically that I communicated it to others and put everyone to sleep); on the Yale, Virginia, Williams, and Princeton college campuses; before various private and semiprivate groups around the East. In the course of some thirty-five weeks, in addition to speaking many times extemporaneously or from notes, I wrote about seventeen formal lectures or articles, generally about five thousand words in length. Each was usually the product of at least three complete rewritings before reaching final form. Astonishment at my own energy is excelled only by admiration for that of my secretary, Dorothy Hessman, who had now followed me from Moscow to the War College, and who contrived to type uncomplainingly this endless torrent of prose, in addition to all the correspondence.

The War College course, particularly during the autumn term, was focused on the interrelationship of military and nonmilitary means in the promulgation of national policy. It was a course, in short, on strategic-political doctrine. This was the first time I had personally ever had occasion to address myself seriously, either as a student or as a teacher, to this subject. It was also the first time the United States government had ever prescribed this area of inquiry for study in an official academic institution embracing in its student body and teaching staff all three of the armed services, as well as the State Department. Not only were we all new to this subject, personally and institutionally, but we had, as we turned to it, virtually nothing in the way of an established or traditional American doctrine which we could take as a point of departure for our thinking and teaching. It was a mark of the weakness of all previous American thinking about international affairs that there was almost nothing in American political literature of the past one hundred years on the subject of the relationship of war to politics. American thinking about foreign policy had been primarily addressed to the problems of peace, and had taken place largely within the frameworks of international law and international economics. Thinking about war, confined for the most part to military staffs and institutions of military training, had been directed almost exclusively to the technical problems of military strategy and tactics — to the achievement, in short, of victory in purely military terms. There had, of course, been Mahan; and his importance was not negligible. But he had addressed himself almost exclusively to the problems of sea power; and the assumptions underlying his work had now been extensively undermined by changes in weaponry as well as in international political patterns. We found ourselves thrown back, perforce, on the European thinkers of other ages and generations: on Machiavelli, Clausewitz, Gallieni — even Lawrence of Arabia. We had the admirable compilation *Makers of Modern Strategy*, edited by E. M. Earle* to draw on; and in my own case, at least, this proved invaluable. But it was obvious that in no instance was the thinking of these earlier figures fully relevant or remotely adequate to the needs of a great American democracy in the atomic age. All of this, clearly, was going to have to be rethought. A strategic-political doctrine would have to be devised for this country which gave promise not simply of expanding the material and military power of a single nation but of making the strength of that nation a force for

* Princeton: Princeton University Press, 1943.

peace and stability in international affairs and helping, in particular, to avoid the catastrophe of atomic war. It was my hope, as we proceeded so buoyantly to the inauguration of this new governmental institution for strategic-political study, that it would come to serve as a home for the development of such a doctrine.

To what extent the college has served this purpose in subsequent years, I cannot say. I suspect that its possibilities in this direction have been somewhat limited by the established practice of frequent rotation of command among senior officers of the various armed services — a practice which inevitably hampers to a certain extent the continuity of concept and direction — as well as by lack of permanent research activities that could have given depth, refinement, and authority to the thinking that took place on the pedagogical level.

But for myself, personally, the confrontation with these problems, during the initial year, was enormously stimulating and interesting. I realize now that it was at that time — in the background reading, in the attendance at lectures by distinguished outsiders, in the agonizing over my own lectures — that some of the ideas were conceived that have been basic to my views on American policy ever since.

One of these related to the purpose of warfare. The precedents of our Civil War, of the war with Spain, and of our participation in the two world wars of this century, had created not only in the minds of our soldiers and sailors but in the minds of many of our people an unspoken assumption that the normal objective of warfare was the total destruction of the enemy's ability and will to resist and his unconditional capitulation. The rest, it was always assumed, was easy. This sort of victory placed you in a position to command total obedience on the part of the defeated adversary; it thus opened the way to the unhindered realization of your political objectives, whatever they might be.

The most significant of the appreciations to which I came during that year at the War College was that this approach to the cultivation and use by our country of armed forces would no longer work. I doubted that it had been a sound one even in the pre-atomic

age. It seemed to me that in each of the two world wars, the application of it, while successful in the immediate military sense, had
complicated — very gravely indeed — the problems of the peace.
But now that arsenals — our own at the moment, but others, presumably, before too long — included such things as atomic weapons and now that our outstanding adversary was so great a country
as Russia, it was clear that such concepts were unrealistic. The existence of atomic weapons meant that total war would either be
suicidal or, if the adversary lacked such weapons, indiscriminately
destructive to a degree impossible to contemplate and out of accord
with every principle of humanity in warfare. But beyond that,
there was the fact that Russia was simply not occupiable. To occupy it exceeded our physical possibilities, even on the most optimistic estimate. And it exceeded our political and moral possibilities
as well. We were not set up to govern, even temporarily, great
numbers of people in other parts of the world. The experience in
Germany, I felt, had shown that.

This meant, it seemed to me, a need for return to much earlier
concepts. The doctrine of total war had been a doctrine of the
nineteenth and twentieth centuries. We would now have to revert
to the concepts of limited warfare prevalent in the eighteenth century. The aims of warfare, accordingly, would have to become limited. If weapons were to be used at all, they would have to be employed to temper the ambitions of an adversary, or to make good
limited objectives against his will — not to destroy his power, or his
government, or to disarm him entirely. We would have to revert to
the view of Talleyrand: that "nations ought to do one another in
peace the most good, in war — the least possible evil." For this, we
would have to recognize the wisdom shown by Gibbon when he
listed among the elements of strength in the European civilization
of the eighteenth century the fact that the armies of the European
powers were "exercised in temperate and indecisive conflicts." Man
would have to recognize, in short, that the device of military coer-
cion could have, in the future, only a relative — never an absolute
— value in the pursuit of political objectives.

The second concept I carried away from that first year at the

War College was an idea nowhere specifically expressed. It was rather in the nature of an assumption, which I should no doubt have expressed on many occasions in the ensuing years but didn't. It was the assumption that we would never wish to use, or even contemplate the use of, atomic weapons otherwise than in retaliation for their use against us. I came close to expressing this assumption in a talk given on January 23, 1947, to the National Defense Committee of the United States Chamber of Commerce. I did not question, on that occasion, the necessity of our holding and cultivating atomic weapons. Until there was a workable international agreement on their removal from national arsenals, with safeguards against their production and use by others, we had, I thought, "the sad duty" of retaining our preeminence in this field. There could be no greater protection for our own people against atomic attack than "the deterrent effect of overwhelming retaliatory power in the hands of this country." But, I added, I was saying these things

with full confidence that the people of this country will never sanction the unprovoked and aggressive use of such weapons against the other peoples of the world.

From these two appreciations — the imperative need for acceptance of limited warfare, and the impossibility of contemplating the use of the atomic bomb as a forward weapon — I went ahead to develop a concept of the peacetime requirements of our armed force establishment which laid emphasis on the maintenance of small, compact, alert forces, capable of delivering at short notice effective blows on limited theaters of operation far from our own shores. This, was, of course, not all that was needed. We would have to maintain our capacity "to mobilize our strength rapidly if a clear threat of major war developed." But we would also need "small mobile forces," made up on a task-force basis out of units from all three of the services, and capable of commitment to combat on very short notice.

We must remember that the first line of American defense might be many thousands of miles from American shores. We already hold a number of outlying bases which it is essential for us to staff, and it might be necessary for us on very short notice to seize and hold other . . . outlying island bases or peninsular bases on other continents, if only for the purpose of denying the use of them to others during the period required for further military preparations. But here, again . . . the greatest value of our forces lies in their quality as a deterrent. If we do not maintain such forces, there will always be an incentive to unruly people elsewhere to seize isolated and limited objectives on the theory that we would be able to do nothing about it at the moment and that they could count on making the seizures with impunity and talking about it afterward. . . .

Translated into terms of the actual development of our armed forces this meant, of course, strengthening the Marine Corps, strengthening interservice collaboration, and maintaining task-force units in a state of high alertness. The time of this statement was a little more than three years before the Communist attack on the Korean peninsula. The inadequacy of what had been done, in the meantime, to prepare for just that sort of a contingency was a measure of the great distance that still remained, in 1947, between the War College, and particularly its foreign affairs deputy, and those congressional committees and Pentagon chiefs who controlled the actual shaping of our armed establishment.

13

The Truman Doctrine

I SEEM to recall that at some time during the first weeks of 1947, while I was still at the War College, Mr. Dean Acheson, then serving as Under Secretary of State, called me to his office and told me that General George Marshall, who had only recently assumed the office of Secretary of State, had in mind the establishment within the department of some sort of a planning unit — something to fill, at least in part, the place of the Divisions of Plans and Operations to which he was accustomed in the War Department. It was likely, Mr. Acheson indicated, that I would be asked to head this new unit when my tour of duty at the War College was completed. I gained no very clear understanding of what was involved; I am not sure that Mr. Acheson had gained a much clearer one from General Marshall. But that some such thing was in store for me, I understood.

I was, therefore, less surprised than I might otherwise have been when, on February 24, Mr. Acheson again summoned me to his office, told me of the crisis of policy that had arisen for us as a result of the decision of the British government to abandon its special support for Greece, and asked me to participate in the deliberations of a special committee that was being established to study the whole problem of assistance to Greece and Turkey.

The committee met that same evening (February 24), as I recall it, under the chairmanship of my old friend and colleague of Riga and Moscow days Loy Henderson, who was now chief of the Division of Near Eastern Affairs in the department. It was my own recollection that we had before us, on that occasion, the task of recommending whether to respond affirmatively at all to the problem posed for us by the British withdrawal, or whether to leave the Greeks and Turks to their own devices. Henderson's recollection (and in the divergence between the two you have a good example of the danger of relying on pure memory, unsupported by written evidence, as a source for diplomatic history) was that this question, so far as the Department of State was concerned, had already been decided in principle by the Acting Secretary of State and himself over the preceding weekend and that the task of the committee was to outline in more detail the course of action that should be recommended to the President and General Marshall (then in Moscow) and to make suggestions as to how it should be explained and justified to other governmental departments, to the Congress (whose action would obviously be necesary to give it effect), and to the public. However this may be (and I gladly yield to Henderson's recollection as more likely to be right than my own), I gave it as my opinion that we had no choice but to accept the challenge and to extend the requisite aid; this was the consensus of the group as a whole; an appropriate recommendation was drawn up; and I returned to my home late that evening with the stimulating impression of having participated prominently in a historic decision of American foreign policy. If, on this occasion, I somewhat overrated the effect of my own voice, it would not be the last time that egotism, and the attention my words seemed often to attract on the part of startled colleagues, would deceive me as to the measure of my real influence on the process of decision-taking.

Mr. Joseph Jones, in his excellent book *The Fifteen Weeks*,* has described in great and faithful detail the various discussions, consultations, clearances, and literary struggles that took place within the government in the ensuing days before the President was in a position to present to the Congress, two weeks later, his famous Truman Doctrine message. It was (I learn from Mr. Jones's book) on the day before the State Department's final draft of this message went to

* New York: Harcourt, Brace and Company, 1955.

the White House, presumably about March 6, that I came over to the department to have a look at the paper. What I saw made me extremely unhappy. The language to which I took particular exception was not the product of Henderson's pen or of any of his associates in the geographic divisions. It had been produced, at the initiative of the department's public relations office, in a subcommittee of the State-War-Navy Coordinating Committee (SWNCC), which evidently felt itself under the necessity of clothing the announced rationale for the President's decision in terms more grandiose and more sweeping than anything that I, at least, had ever envisaged. (More about that later.) I remonstrated, by my own recollection, to Henderson. Mr. Jones says I also remonstrated to Mr. Acheson; and I have no doubt that I did, although I do not specifically recall it. I produced, in any event, some alternative language, though I have no record of what it was. Whether these remonstrations met with much understanding in substance, I cannot remember. In any case, they came too late. No one wanted to repeat the agony of collective drafting that had been invested over the preceding days in the production of this historic piece of paper.

Faced, as any autobiographer is, with the danger of mistaking hindsight for recollection, I am fortunate in finding among my papers one that not only sets forth in detail the reasons, as I saw them at the time, why it was desirable that our government should respond to the challenge of the British move but also explains, by clear implication, the reasons for my unhappiness over the wording of the President's message. We in the faculty of the War College used the Greek crisis, just at that time, as the basis for a problem which we assigned to various committees of the students. We asked them, in effect, to supply some of the individual components of the President's decision on this question. Twice, on the heels of the President's presentation to Congress, I discussed this problem informally before the student body. On the first of these occasions, March 14, two days after presentation of the President's message, I commented on the terms of the War College problem itself. On March 28, after the student answers were in, I discussed the solutions to it and gave the reasons why I, personally, had felt that we had been right to accept the challenge of the British action. It is the stenographic records of these two statements that I find in my papers.

First, as to my understanding of the background of the decision: I accepted the conclusion, to which many others in the government had arrived, that (and I use the words of the War College presentation) "if nothing were done to stiffen the backs of the non-Communist elements in Greece at this juncture the Communist elements would soon succeed in seizing power and in establishing a totalitarian dictatorship along the lines already visible in other Balkan countries." I did not view the prospect of such a Communist takeover as "*in itself* any immediate and catastrophic setback to the Western world." I considered that the Russians and their Eastern European associates were poorly set up to take responsibility either for the governing of Greece or for the support of the Greek economy. Eventually, I thought, all this might boomerang on them in the form of serious economic difficulties and other problems, which the West might even ultimately exploit to good advantage. But Communist rule, I thought, "would probably be successfully consolidated in the long run and might some day have most unfortunate strategic consequences from the standpoint of any military adversary of the Soviet Union." And more important still were the probable repercussions which such a development would have on neighboring areas.

In this last connection, I took up first the question of Turkey. I pointed out that the situation of Turkey differed quite fundamentally from that of Greece. There was no serious Communist penetration in Turkey — no comparable guerrilla movement. The Turks had nothing to fear but fear. "If . . . the Turks do not lose their nerves, if they keep their internal political life relatively clean and orderly and refuse to become involved in negotiations with the Russians on a bilateral basis over complicated questions such as that of the Straits, they will probably continue to enjoy a temporary and precarious immunity to Russian pressure." But, I pointed out, should they be increasingly encircled by Communist-dominated entities, it would plainly be harder for them to maintain this stance.

Aid to Greece was therefore important as a support for stability in Turkey as well.

It should be noted that this view of the problem of Turkey afforded no rationale for the mounting of a special aid program for Turkey itself. The accent was put on internal morale and on firmness of diplomatic stance, not on military preparations. It was for this reason that I was not happy to find in the draft of the President's message to Congress a proposal for aid to Turkey as well as to Greece. I suspected that what was intended primarily was military aid, and that what had really happened was that the Pentagon had exploited a favorable set of circumstances in order to infiltrate a military aid program for Turkey into what was supposed to be primarily a political and economic program for Greece. Since it was important, in my view, that the Soviet threat be recognized for what it was — primarily a political one and not a threat of military attack — it seemed unfortunate that the picture of what was needed in Greece should be confused by association with something that was not needed — or, if needed, was needed for entirely different purposes — in Turkey.

To return to the exposé at the War College: From Turkey, I moved on to the subject of the Middle East. What would be the repercussions there of a Communist takeover in Greece? Here again my conclusions were somewhat different from those of other people. I did not underrate the seriousness of Russian-Communist penetration among the restless intelligentsia of the Moslem capitals. But I questioned the ultimate ability of the Russians to disaffect and dominate the entire Moslem world. Not only was their ideology in conflict with the Moslem faith, but they were just not that good. Even in northern Iran and among the Kurds their recent performance, as political intriguers, had not been impressive. If they were to expand still further in this area they would "soon encounter the far more vigorous political society of Arabia itself and contiguous areas, where the fire of Moslem ideology burns with a purer and fiercer flame, and where resistance to Communist political pressure would be of a far sterner quality than in the lands to the north and east." It was not, then, for the long term that I feared the fillip to Soviet penetration of the Middle East which a Communist coup in Greece would certainly provide. But I had to recognize that the immediate repercussions might be ones unsettling to such fragile stability as the region then enjoyed. And this in turn might have effects in relation to the situation in an area even more important from the standpoint of our security: Western Europe.

It was hard to overestimate, in those days of uncertainty and economic difficulty, the cumulative effects of sensational political events. People were influenced, as I pointed out on that occasion to the War College, not just by their desires as to what *should* happen but by their estimates of what *would* happen. People in Western Europe did not, by and large, want Communist control. But this did not mean that they would not trim their sails and even abet its coming if they gained the impression that it was inevitable. This was why the shock of a Communist success in Greece could not be risked.

In Western Europe, too, I added, it was not likely that Communist domination could last indefinitely. But while it lasted, it could do great damage.

Because floodwaters must — by the laws of nature — some day subside is no reason that one should welcome them on his place. . . . We have no cause to assume that Europe as we know it — and as we need it — would never recover from the blow which even a brief period of Russian control would deal to her already weakened traditions and institutions. . . . The waves of Communist authority might some day recede but we could have no reason to expect that American prestige and influence could easily reenter the territories thus liberated. . . .

I went on, then, to point out that if we were to leave Europe to the Communists, the resulting problem of security for the United States "might not be one of external security alone."

Remember that in abandoning Europe we would be abandoning not only the fountainheads of most of our own culture and tradition; we would also be abandoning almost all the other areas in the world where progressive representative government is a working proposition. We would be placing ourselves in the position of a lonely country, culturally and politically. To maintain confidence in our own traditions and institutions we would henceforth have to whistle loudly in the dark. I am not sure that whistling could be loud enough to do the trick.

I know that there are many people — and probably some among you — who will reply indignantly that I am selling short the strength and soundness of our institutions — who will maintain that American democracy has nothing to fear from Europe's diseases and nothing to learn from Europe's experiences.

I wish I could believe that that were true. I wish I could believe that the human impulses which give rise to the nightmares of totalitarianism were ones which Providence had allocated only to other peoples and to which the American people had been graciously left immune. Unfortunately, I know that that is not true. After all, most of us are only Europeans once or twice removed; and some of us are less removed than that. There are openly totalitarian forces already working in our society. Do you think that they could fail to derive new confidence and new supporters from such a series of developments? And it is not even with these small existing groups of extremists that the real danger lies. The fact of the matter is that there is a little bit of the totalitarian buried somewhere, way down deep, in each and every one of us. It is only the cheerful light of confidence and security which keeps this evil genius down at the usual helpless and invisible depth. If confidence and security were to disappear, don't think that he would not be waiting to take their place. Others may lull themselves to sleep with the pleasing assumption that the work of building freedom in this country was accomplished completely and for all time by our forefathers. I prefer to accept the word of a great European, the German poet, Goethe, that freedom is something that has to be reconquered every day. And in that never-ending process of reconquest, I would hate to see this country lose all its allies.

So much for the reasons for our limited intervention in Greece. Why, then, approving this action, did I take exception to the language of the President's message?

I took exception to it primarily because of the sweeping nature of the commitments which it implied. The heart of the message and the passage that has subsequently been most frequently quoted was this:

I believe it must be the policy of the United States to support free peoples who are resisting subjugation by armed minorities or by outside pressures.

I believe that we must assist free peoples to work out their own destinies in their own way.

This passage, and others as well, placed our aid to Greece in the framework of a universal policy rather than in that of a specific decision addressed to a specific set of circumstances. It implied that what we had decided to do in the case of Greece was something we would be prepared to do in the case of any other country, provided only that it was faced with the threat of "subjugation by armed minorities or by outside pressures."

It seemed to me highly uncertain that we would invariably find it in our interests or within our means to extend assistance to countries that found themselves in this extremity. The mere fact of their being in such a plight was only one of the criteria that had to be taken into account in determining our action. The establishment of the existence of such a threat was only the beginning, not the end, of the process of decision. I listed, in my presentation to the War College, three specific considerations that had supported our decision to extend assistance to Greece:

A. The problem at hand is one within our economic, technical, and financial capabilities.

B. If we did not take such action, the resulting situation might redound very decidedly to the advantage of our political adversaries.

C. If, on the other hand, we do take the action in question, there is good reason to hope that the favorable consequences will carry far beyond the limits of Greece itself.

These considerations, I pointed out, did not necessarily apply to all other regions. I doubted, for example, that any of them would fully apply in the case of China: the first most definitely would not.

But if this was the case, then why use language that suggested that all that was required was proof of the existence of a threat of "subjugation by armed minorities or by outside pressure" — that this was the sole criterion of our response?

Were I reacting today to the Truman Doctrine message, I would certainly have added to this list of specific requirements the willingness and ability of the threatened people to pick up and bear resolutely the overwhelming portion of the responsibility and effort in their own defense against both direct and indirect aggression — not just to sit back and hedge against the possibility that resistance might not be effective and leave the burden of the struggle to us. I would also take exception to the repeated suggestions, in the text of that message, that what we were concerned to defend in Greece was the democratic quality of the country's institutions. We would find it necessary to give aid, over the ensuing years, to a number of regimes which could hardly qualify for it on the basis of their democratic character. It was unwise to suggest that this, too, was an essential criterion. But these omissions, the recognition of which does indeed reflect the promptings of hindsight, only reinforce the validity of the objections to the language of the message that suggested themselves at the time.

I was not alone in my awareness of the danger that the sweeping language of the message might be subject to misinterpretation. Mr. Acheson was himself at pains to try to dispel among the members of the Congress the impression that what the President had said represented some sort of a blank check. The fact that we were prepared on principle to extend aid in such situations did not mean, he explained in his testimony before the Senate Committee on Foreign Relations on March 24, 1947, that our action in other instances would always be the same as in Greece. "Any requests of foreign countries for aid," he said in his opening statement,

will have to be considered according to the circumstances in each individual case. In another case we would have to study whether the country in question really needs assistance, whether its request is consistent with American foreign policy, whether the request for assistance is sincere, and whether assistance by the United States would be effective in meeting the problems of that country. It cannot be assumed, therefore, that this government would necessarily undertake measures in any other country identical or even closely similar to those proposed for Greece and Turkey.

Nevertheless, the misapprehension already conveyed was, as I see it, never entirely corrected. Throughout the ensuing two decades the conduct of our foreign policy would continue to be bedeviled by people in our own government as well as in other governments who could not free themselves from the belief that all another country had to do, in order to qualify for American aid, was to demonstrate the existence of a Communist threat. Since almost no country was without a Communist minority, this assumption carried very far. And as time went on, the firmness of understanding for these distinctions on the part of our own public and governmental establishment appeared to grow weaker rather than stronger. In the 1960s so absolute would be the value attached, even by people within the government, to the mere existence of a Communist threat, that such a threat would be viewed as calling, in the case of Southeast Asia, for an American response on a tremendous scale, without serious regard even to those main criteria that most of us in 1947 would have thought it natural and essential to apply.

On many occasions, both before and after this Greek-Turkish episode, I have been struck by the congenital aversion of Americans to taking specific decisions on specific problems, and by their persistent urge to seek universal formulae or doctrines in which to clothe and justify particular actions. We obviously dislike to discriminate. We like to find some general governing norm to which, in each instance, appeal can be taken, so that individual decisions may be made not on their particular merits but automatically, depending on whether the circumstances do or do not seem to fit the norm. We like, by the same token, to attribute a universal significance to decisions we have already found it necessary, for limited and parochial reasons, to take. It was not enough for us, when circumstances forced us into World War I, to hold in view the specific reasons for our entry: our war effort had to be clothed in the form of an effort to make the *world* (nothing less) "safe for democracy." It was not enough for us, in World War II, that the Japanese attacked us at Pearl Harbor and that both Japanese and German governments declared war on us: we did not feel comfortable until we had wrapped our military effort in the wholly universalistic — and largely meaningless — generalities of the Atlantic Charter. Something of this same compulsion became apparent in the postwar period in the tendency of many Americans to divide the world neatly into Communist and "free world" components, to avoid recognition of specific differences among countries on either side, and to search for general formulas to govern our relations with the one or the other. I think, in this connection, of the periodic wrangling in Congress, in connection with the annual aid bills, over the question whether most-favored-nation treatment should be extended, or various forms of aid be granted, to "Communist" countries or to countries "forming part of the Communist conspiracy" or whatever general language one chose to employ — the idea being always to define a category of states and to compel the executive to behave in a uniform way with relation to all of them. Seldom does it seem to have occurred to many congressional figures that the best thing to do would be to let the President, or the Secretary of State, use his head.

To this day I am uncertain as to the origins of this persistent American urge to the universalization or generalization of decision. I suspect it to be a reflection of the extent to which we are a people given to government by laws rather than by executive discretion. Laws, too, are general norms, and Congress, accustomed to limiting executive discretion through the establishment of such norms in the internal field, obviously feels more comfortable when its powers with relation to foreign policy can be exercised in a similar way. Unable to control executive decisions on a day-to-day basis, many Congressmen and Senators feel, I suspect, a need for general determinations defining the latitude within which those decisions may be taken.

14

The Marshall Plan

ON April 28, 1947, Secretary of State Marshall returned from Moscow, where he had been attending the latest meeting of the Council of Foreign Ministers. He returned shaken by the realization of the seriousness and urgency of the plight of Western Europe, where economic recovery had failed to proceed as expected and where something approaching total economic disintegration seemed now to be imminent. The result of the talks with the Russians had compelled him to recognize, however reluctantly, that the idea of approaching the solution to Europe's problems in collaboration with the Russians was a pipe dream. It was plain that the Soviet leaders had a political interest in seeing the economies of the Western European peoples fail under anything other than Communist leadership. The general realized that for us to delay action to shore up these economies, merely lest independent action disrupt great power "collaboration," was simply to play into Communist hands. We had already delayed too long. The hour was late. Time was running out. "The patient," as he put it in his radio address to the nation on the day of his return, "is sinking while the doctors deliberate."

The following day he summoned me to his office. It would not be possible for me, he said, to finish out the year at the War College as I had planned. I would have to come over to the State Department and set up the Policy Planning Staff without delay. Europe was in a mess. Something would have to be done. If he did not take the initiative, others would. Others, particularly people in Congress, would start coming up with ideas of their own about what ought to be done for Europe. He would then be forced on to the defensive. He was determined to avoid this if he possibly could. He wished me to assemble a staff and address myself to this problem without delay. I had a limited time (I cannot remember whether it was ten days or two weeks; I remember only that it was brief) in which to give him my recommendations as to what he ought to do. He then added characteristically (as several historians have already correctly recorded) that he had only one bit of advice for me: "Avoid trivia."

Once again, the background of the conception of the Marshall Plan has been so well and accurately set forth by Mr. Jones, in his book already referred to, that there could be no useful purpose served by going over the same ground here. I can do no more than relate in somewhat greater detail the circumstances of my own participation.

General Marshall's order placed me in some difficulty. The staff, as of that moment, did not exist. I myself had speaking engagements — four just for the next fortnight, and three of them outside of Washington — which it would be most awkward to cancel, and which in fact I kept. In addition to preparing and delivering these lectures, I now had to find and equip staff premises in the new State Department Building, into which the department was just in process of moving. I was supposed, on no notice at all, to scratch together something in the nature of a staff. Then, in company with these newly and hastily selected staff members, I was supposed to review the whole great problem of European recovery in all its complexity, to tap those various sources of outside advice which we would never be forgiven for not tapping, to draw up and present to the Secretary the recommendations he wanted, and be prepared to defend these recommendations against all governmental critics, including ones unavoidably more deeply versed in the details of the subject matter than myself, and ones who could be expected to show no charity or mercy toward a man who came as an invader of their hitherto private bureaucratic premises.

The staff was formally established on May 5, 1947. The departmental order setting it up defined as follows the major functions it was to fulfill:

1. Formulating and developing, for the consideration and approval of appropriate officials of the department, long-term programs for the achievement of U.S. foreign policy objectives.

2. Anticipating problems which the department may encounter in the discharge of its mission.

3. Undertaking studies and preparing reports on broad politico-military problems.

4. Examining problems and developments affecting U.S. foreign policy in order to evaluate the adequacy of current policy and making advisory recommendations on them.

5. Coordinating planning activities within the Department of State.

It was idle to suppose that one could assemble, on such short notice and against such pressure, a staff of distinguished outsiders, broadly representative in competence, whose names might have carried weight with the public. Nor was this what the Secretary wanted. The opinion of such a group (even if it could have arrived at any clear and concise opinion; few such groups could) would have carried too much weight — would merely have put both Secretary of State and President on the spot and would have left them little scope for their own judgment. It was clear, in the circumstances, that we would have to draw on people whose greatest qualifications, as in my own case, were simply that they were favorably known and available. I am sure that many other groups, no less qualified than the one I gathered around me, could have been culled at that time from the senior echelons of the department, if availability had not been a factor. To the extent that the fortunes of American policy may be said to have rested on us, at that particular moment, they rested in effect on the general level of competence of people of our rank and reputation in department and Foreign Service.

My associates, so hastily gathered together, fortunately turned out to be, without exception, able, honorable, and intellectually hard-headed people, sufficiently familiar with the department to draw at many points on the wisdom and expertise which the lower echelons of that institution always harbor (however little or poorly they are used), and sufficiently stout in argument to put me personally over the bumps, to drive whole series of clichés and oversimplifications out of my head, to spare me no complications, and to force me into an intellectual agony more intensive than anything I had ever previously experienced.* They included Joseph E. Johnson, who had previously taught at Williams College and would later become president of the Carnegie Endowment for International Peace; Colonel Charles Hatwell (Tick) Bonesteel III, a talented officer of the regular army (at present our commander in South Korea) who had been seconded to the Department of State as special assistant to the Under Secretary and who was to play a prominent part in later phases of development of the European recovery program; Jacques Reinstein, able and imaginative economist, who had only recently occupied himself extensively with the problems of the economy of occupied Germany; Ware Adams, a Foreign Service officer of experience and good sense, then on duty in Washington; and Carleton Savage, erstwhile personal assistant to Cordell Hull, whose long experience with Washington outside the department as well as within it, and whose fine instinctive feeling in particular for the reactions of American public opinion generally and of people in Congress in particular, were of great value to us.

Together, aware of the almost fortuitous quality of our association but aware, too, of the awesome responsibility that rested upon us, we sweated as best we could through the examination of Europe's problems and of our own country's possibilities for being helpful with relation to them. We had advice and assistance, of course, from many sides. We were far from being the only people, or even the first, in official Washington to sweat over these same

---

* So earnest and intense were the debates in our little body in those harried days and nights that I can recall one occasion, in late evening, when I, to recover my composure, left the room and walked, weeping, around the entire building.

problems. We had access to the valuable views and studies of people on the economic side of the department. (Will Clayton, then serving as Under Secretary of State for Economic Affairs, did not get back from Europe until mid-May, and the important memorandum he prepared on the subject of European recovery came too late to be of use to us in the preparation of our initial paper; but his views filtered through to us, I am sure, in other ways.) The appreciations and judgments that entered into Dean Acheson's speech of May 8 before the Delta Council in Cleveland, Mississippi, were both helpful and authoritative for us in the approach to our own task. We were able to examine (at a preliminary stage, as I recall it) the studies of the special committee of the State-War-Navy Coordinating Committee which had been set up some weeks earlier, by consequence of Mr. Acheson's foresight, to examine the possible needs of the various countries for assistance. We were able to draw personally into consultation a considerable number of qualified people around the department and in other branches of the government. We endeavored, in this way, to pull together all the elements of the intensive study of this problem, and the thinking about it, that were going on by this time in many parts of the government.

I do not have at hand, as I write these lines, any records of the staff discussions or consultations that preceded the final drafting of our report to Secretary Marshall. I do have, however, the text of a lecture dealing with the entire problem of European recovery which I delivered at the War College on May 6, the day after the staff's official establishment, just as we were entering upon our struggle with this problem. Since the picture of what was at stake, as portrayed in this lecture, differs somewhat from the picture of it that flows from other official representations of that period, some passages may be of interest.

I began by examining the reasons why the Russians had not thought it to their advantage to come to any agreement with us over Germany at the recent meeting of the Council of Foreign Ministers. They had been moved, I thought, by two considerations: one, the belief that we would soon suffer an economic crisis that would serve to reduce our interest and our weight in world affairs; but second, by the expectation that we would not alone be able to halt the economic deterioration now taking place in Western Europe and that this deterioration would soon begin to play politically into the hands of the Communist elements there. They thought it probable that we Americans, in particular, would not

be able to muster, as a nation, the leadership, the imagination, the political skill, the material resources, and above all the national self-discipline necessary to bring material stability, confidence, and hope for the future to those areas of Western Europe which have been brought low by the effects of the war. . . . The Russians consider that the economic problems of these countries cannot be solved without the aid of the resources of those areas of Eastern and Central Europe which they now control; and for this reason they feel that they have only to continue to deny those resources for a while longer in order to put themselves in a position where they will be able practically to name the political price on which they will make them available.

. . . They feel, in other words, that Europe is in reality theirs, although Europe may not know it; that they have already woven an invisible network of economic dependence around those proud nations of the continent which still fancy themselves to be free; and that they have only to await patiently the day when American failure to relieve the intolerable economic conditions of those areas will allow them to begin to draw tighter the cords of that invisible network and bring the west of Europe into the shadows which have already enveloped the east.

I then went on to discuss, in turn, the situations that prevailed in Italy, France, Austria, and Germany.

In Italy economic recovery had progressed, in many respects, not badly. There was lack of confidence, to be sure, and a flight of capital. There was need for a long-term foreign loan, and for stringent measures of financial and social discipline. The problem of finding money for a loan did not look too difficult. But when one came to the financial and social discipline, it was another matter.

The Communist Party . . . has over two million members and controls 19 percent of the seats in Parliament. . . . It has substantial control of the key positions in the labor movement. From these strong positions, it has the capacity to interfere seriously with any measures which might have the effect of stimulating confidence in a non-Communist future for Italy.

In France the pattern was not dissimilar. In one respect the situation there was even better.

France, alone . . . of the countries we are dealing with, has an over-all economic plan: a four-year plan known as the Monnet Plan, around which she is endeavoring to orient her economy . . . [a plan] designed to put her by the end of 1950 in a position where she will no longer require any special sort of assistance from the outside world.

The financing of this plan, insofar as it had to come from outside sources, did not present insuperable difficulties. It appeared to require only about one and a half billion dollars, of which a third was already available. But the successful completion of the plan demanded increased imports from other European countries, notably Italy and Germany, imports which would scarcely be forthcoming unless recovery took place there, too. The initial progress made in implementation of the Monnet Plan had not been encouraging. Again, much depended on the political support which the execution of the plan would now receive. If "all important factions in French political life" were determined to see it succeed, there would be no serious cause for concern.

But . . . the real question is the Communist Party. . . . With 28.5 percent of the votes and with control of the French labor movement, the French Communists, whether in the government or out of it, probably have a decisive capacity to influence the fulfillment of the Monnet Plan.

The French Communists, I pointed out, had to be careful how they handled themselves with relation to the problem of economic recovery. They

cannot afford to put themselves openly in the position of opposing economic rehabilitation of France. That is their weakness. . . .

What is the moral for us? I think it is the same as in the case of Italy. Any assistance extended to France by us, directly or indirectly, must be anchored in some sort of undertaking which will bind at least the French government, if not French labor as well, to see that there is no dirty work at the crossroads.

Turning to Austria, I pointed out that we had in effect waited for two years, in the hopes of reaching some sort of agreement with the Russians, before attempting to face the problem of Austria's rehabilitation. This line of procedure had not helped us much, and it had certainly not helped the Austrians. One could of course go on talking. Something might come of it. You never knew in international life — anything was possible.

But I think it may be fairly stated, as a working rule for dealing with the Russians, that only those people are able to get along *with* them who have proven their ability to get along *without* them. And I think it would not be misplaced effort if we were to do some planning right now for the rehabilitation of the three western zones [of Austria] alone, leaving out the Soviet zone. I cannot find that much thinking has been done along these lines in our government. It undoubtedly presents greater problems than the planning for Austria as a whole. But the problems do not appear . . . insuperable. The cost . . . ought to be well under the half-billion-dollar mark. . . . The day may come when the price of a firm position in Central Europe will run much higher.

That brought me to the question of Germany. I think it may properly be said that the emphasis placed on the correction of our previous occupational policies and on the prompt and vigorous rehabilitation of the German economy was the point at which my own view of the problem of European recovery differed most sharply from the views then being held in other quarters in Washington. For this reason, I shall quote in full the passages of the May 6 lecture dealing with this problem. I must say that as I spoke these words, I was conscious of the futile pleas for the use of the Germans in the postwar process of European recovery with which I had returned from Germany in 1942, of the bitter memories of the European Advisory Commission, and of the fatuous provisions of

the Potsdam Conference relating to four-power control and administration of Germany — provisions that had caused us to lose nearly
two years of valuable time.

Let us recapitulate the situation. We carried the war to completion and
accepted the unconditional surrender of Germany in accordance with
a set of arrangements which left us with the sole responsibility for a
section of Germany which had never been economically self-supporting in modern times and the capacity of which for self-support had
been catastrophically reduced by the circumstances of the war and the
German defeat. At the moment we accepted that responsibility, we had
no program for the rehabilitation of the economy of our zone, prefer-
ring to leave all that to later settlement by international agreement, and
we had no agreement with our Allies on any program of rehabilitation
of German economy on a national or even regional scale. We were
not even clear in our own minds whether we wanted German economy
rehabilitated. Sometimes we thought we did. Sometimes we thought
we didn't. Sometimes we just agreed to disagree among ourselves.

In these circumstances we let the economic situation slide for two
years, refraining from drawing up any real program for the rehabilitation of our zone (and by real progam, I mean one that had a visible,
definite goal connected with the interests of this country), and we gave
precedence in our occupational policy to a political program designed
to accomplish the denazification and democratization of German public
life. Since we were unwilling to let people starve entirely, we made up
from the pockets of our own taxpayers the very considerable costs of
keeping the Germans in our zone barely alive. But in the absence of
international agreement with the Russians, we made no serious effort
to restore German economy to a point where it could play any appreciable role in solving the general economic problem of Western Europe
and/or removing from our shoulders any important part of the burden
of keeping life going in those areas.

Today we find ourselves before the recognition that the economic
rehabilitation of Western Europe is of urgent and primary importance.
The restoration of German productivity, if only in a part of Germany,
is essential to that rehabilitation. We cannot wait for Russian agreement
to achieve that restoration. For this reason it might be supposed that
the decks were now cleared for an intensive program to restore a high
level of productivity as far as possible throughout the west of Germany.

For the first time now we have indications that even the French might go along with us on such a matter. We have indeed taken certain steps in that direction, chief of which has been to agree in principle with the British on the economic unification of our two zones and on their joint development under a program which should make them within some two or three years at least no longer the object of the charity from part of the Big Three.

But I have not seen convincing evidence that we have yet allotted to this program the priorities which it is going to have to receive if it is to have any chance of cutting through the obstacles which lie in its path. Many of these obstacles are to be found in the political concepts with which we have been working in Germany. I do not see that any of these have been substantially modified in deference to the needs of the economic program. . . .

Finally, I see that while we have agreement with the British in principle on the economic unification of our two zones, we appear to be deadlocked in disagreement with them at the moment over the channels whereby that program should be implemented.

I do not blame any of our people in Berlin for this failure to agree. I hope I will never be one of those who assume that whenever an American fails to agree with somebody else it is the American who is wrong. But in this case that which is at stake is an economic program of crucial urgency: a program on which tens of millions of people are waiting as a matter almost of life and death, a program which may prove decisive for the balance of power in Europe. The achievement of agreement with the British on this issue thus deserves the highest attention of our government; and if such agreement cannot be achieved promptly by the best good will and the broadest view on our part of the factors involved, then it is high time we drew some far-reaching and very unpleasant conclusions for the future of our whole occupation of Germany and of our policies in Western Europe.

In my opinion it is imperatively urgent today that the improvement of economic conditions and the revival of productive capacity in the west of Germany be made the primary object of our policy in that area and be given top priority in all our occupation policies; and that this principle be adopted as a general line of procedure of this government, binding on all of its departments and agencies. *

---

* Italics added by GFK.

If this is done, I think that here, again, the economic problem before us is not insoluble. Although it is harder than any other we have discussed, the figures still do not run into impossible dimensions. But unless it is done, we must inevitably continue to flounder and our chances of proving the Russians wrong in their calculations about Western Europe will be very much diminished.

It was, as the near future would show, the Marshall Plan which, in addition to the beneficent influence it exerted on our European allies, finally broke through the confusion of wartime pro-Sovietism, wishful thinking, anglophobia and self-righteous punitivism in which our occupational policies in Germany had thus far been enveloped, and placed us at long last on what was, and for six years remained, a constructive and sensible path.

So much for the intellectual background of the Planning Staff recommendations on the problem of a European recovery program. The paper embodying these recommendations was handed to General Marshall on May 23. The ideas by which it was inspired came from many sources; the drafting was largely my own. It has never, to my knowledge, been made public in its entirety. Extensive portions of it, including the most important ones, were quoted in Mr. Jones's above-mentioned book and in Harry Bayard Price, *The Marshall Plan and Its Meaning*.*

Being under the impression that it would take a long time, at best, before a comprehensive program of European recovery could be worked out and have any significant psychological effect, we began our paper by dividing the problem into its short-term and its long-term aspects. For the short term, we recommended a crash program for the immediate improvement of European coal production, designed to eliminate what appeared to us to be the most urgent and serious of bottlenecks in the economies of the Western European countries generally — namely, the supply of industrial fuel.

Turning then to the long-term problem, we described this as one resulting "in large part from the disruptive effect of the war on the economic, political, and social structure of Europe." The war had

---

* Ithaca, New York: Cornell University Press, 1955.

produced "a profound exhaustion of physical plant and vigor." The staff did not see Communist activities as the root of these difficulties. It recognized

that the Communists are exploiting the European crisis and that further Communist successes would create serious danger to American security. It [the Staff] considers, however, that American effort in aid to Europe should be directed not to the combatting of communism as such but to the restoration of the economic health and vigor of European society. It should aim, in other words, not to combat communism but the economic maladjustment which makes European society vulnerable to exploitation by any and all totalitarian movements and which Russian communism is now exploiting.

We then went on to stress the need for a sharp line of division, in point of responsibility as well as procedure, between our own role in the approach to this problem and that of the European countries immediately involved.

It is necessary to distinguish clearly between a program for the economic revitalization of Europe on the one hand, and a program of American support for such revitalization on the other.

In a passage which later found its way, almost verbatim, into General Marshall's Harvard speech, we went on to spell out, as we saw them, the implications of this division of responsibility:

It would be neither fitting nor efficacious for this government to undertake to draw up unilaterally and to promulgate formally on its own initiative a program designed to place Western Europe on its feet economically. This is the business of the Europeans. The formal initiative must come from Europe; and Europeans must bear the basic responsibility for it. The role of this country should consist of friendly aid in the drafting of a European program and of the later support of such a program, by financial and other means, at European request.

There followed a listing of requirements which seemed to us essential for the success of any such undertaking.

The first was that the European countries get together and agree on a coordinated program of recovery on a European scale.

The program which this country is asked to support must be a joint one, agreed to by several European nations. While it may be linked to individual national programs, such as the Monnet Plan in France, it must, for psychological and political, as well as economic, reasons, be an internationally agreed program. The request for our support must come as a joint request from a group of friendly nations, not as a series of isolated and individual appeals.

The reason for this last requirement is, I think, fairly obvious. Had it not been insisted upon, the United States would have been confronted with a whole series of competing national demands, all padded and exaggerated for competitive purposes, all reflecting attempts to solve economic problems within national frameworks rather than on an all-European basis. This would have forced us to make choices bound to be politically unpopular in many quarters, with the respective European governments in a position to shift onto our shoulders the blame for any features of the programs that were particularly disagreeable to sections of their electorate. But beyond this, we had serious doubts about the success of any movement toward European recovery that rested merely on a series of uncoordinated national programs; we considered that one of the long-term deficiencies of the European economy as a whole was its excessive fragmentation, the lack of competitive flexibility in commercial exchanges, the lack, in particular, of a large consumer's market. By insisting on a joint approach, we hoped to force the Europeans to begin to think like Europeans, and not like nationalists, in their approach to the economic problems of the continent.

The second requirement was really a warning light, raised in connection with the prospective reactions of our own Congress:

This European program must envisage bringing Western Europe to a point where it will be able to maintain a tolerable standard of living on a financially self-supporting basis. It must give promise of doing the whole job. The program must contain reasonable assurance that if we support it, this will be the last such program we shall be asked to support in the foreseeable future.

It was clear that we could not in good conscience recommend to the Congress another interim program which failed to get to the heart of the problem. Dean Acheson had listed, in his recent Delta speech, the impressive series of contributions we had already made, since termination of hostilities, to economic recovery in other parts of the world. We had, as he pointed out, contributed nearly three billion dollars in foreign relief. (Much of this, obviously, had gone to Europe.) We had made a direct loan of three and three-quarters billion dollars to Great Britain. We had taken the lead in organizing the International Bank for Reconstruction and Development and the International Monetary Fund, and had subscribed liberally to these two institutions. Yet obviously, all of this had not been sufficient. Congress, it was clear, would not now be prepared to give further support unless it could be convinced that this would do the trick and that there would not be further demands.

In addition to the above, we thought it essential that:

(*a*) there be maximum use of existing international facilities and resources;

(*b*) that there be safeguards to assure that the European governments exerted the full force of their authority in execution of the programs; and

(*c*) that wherever possible, other than at the expense of the success of the program, there be arrangements for reimbursement of this country.

The problem of the area to which a European recovery program might suitably be extended was treated, in the May 23 paper, only in connection with the relationship of the arrangements in question to the Economic Commission for Europe. This was a time when enthusiasm for the United Nations Organization, and hopes for its predominant role in world affairs, ran high. There were many in Washington who still felt that it would be wrong for us to encourage the preparation and promulgation of any European recovery program otherwise than through some body, connected with the United Nations, on which the Russians and the Eastern European Communist countries were represented. A suitable body of this sort seemed now to be in existence, in the form of the Economic Commission for Europe, which had only recently been established by the Economic and Social Council of the United Nations. The commission had been formed and was just then in session at Geneva. There were many of our consultants who feared, and not without some reason, that if, in stimulating the preparation of a recovery program of Europe, we bypassed this commission, into whose area of responsibility the economic recovery of Europe plainly fell, we would be damaging the usefulness not only of the commission but of the United Nations itself in the entire field of world trade and economics.

I addressed myself to this problem in the War College lecture of May 6. The ECE, I pointed out, was beginning to absorb several of the ad hoc organizations that had been set up to deal with various phases of Europe's economic problems. In some of these, the Russians participated; in others — not. If the Russians, I said on that occasion,

had similarly refrained from participating in the new overall European Commission, there might have been a relatively good chance of clearing through it a plan for general Western European collaboration. And perhaps it was for this very reason that the Russians surprised everyone by showing up unannounced at the last moment with a delegation of twenty-three members. . . . In any case, the Russians are there, and we have to reckon with them. Any proposals for the ordering of the economic life of Western Europe will have to undergo their minute and suspicious scrutiny. I do not think they can afford to blackball outright any effective and promising scheme if people understand that the future of Western Europe depends on that. But they may try to worm themselves into the administration of it, and then they will drag their feet so that the thing will never work at all unless it works to their benefit.

Despite these obvious dangers, I thought initially that the ECE would have to come into the picture at some point. The best procedure, it seemed to me, would be to let the Western European countries work out a tentative program and submit it to the commission. If it found acceptance there, the United Nations could accept sponsorship of it and submit it to this country for support, as a United Nations project. But what if the commission failed to accept it? What if — as I posed the question in the War College lecture —

the Russians spiked it by bringing in a plethora of extraneous questions or by trying to link it to Russian participation in the administration of the Ruhr or put themselves in other ways in a position where they could control the execution of the program and exploit it for their own political purposes? What do we do then?

The answer I then gave to my own question was one which was destined to constitute my own basic line on this question, and that of the staff, throughout the coming weeks:

In that case I think we can only say "no" to the whole business as pleasantly and firmly as we know how, and proceed to deal with the countries individually or severally outside the United Nations, laying down essentially the same requirements as we laid down in the European Commission.

If they were not willing to meet those requirements — if Communist influence within those countries was strong enough to cause them to hold back — if they were not willing, in other words, to guarantee that our money would be spent carefully and economically to achieve the purposes for which it was granted — then there would be no use in our giving it at all. If the peoples of Western Europe were to reject American aid on those terms, then that in itself would be equivalent to a final vote for Russian domination. And then there would be nothing more that we could do except to make crystal clear precisely where the responsibility lay for the hardships that lay ahead.

The question . . . is going to be fought out on political ground. Unless the Communists get key positions in the administration of such a program, they will fight it everywhere, tooth and nail. They will portray it as a sinister effort to fasten American hegemony onto the peoples of Western Europe. The only thing which can silence them and force them to acquiesce . . . will be public opinion . . . enlightened public opinion, a public opinion which understands that this is the only way Western Europe can be saved from disaster.

This view found its reflection in the Planning Staff paper of May 23. It would be best, the staff thought, to stimulate initiative in the first instance from ECE, but to do so in such a way that the Eastern European countries would "either exclude themselves by unwillingness to accept the proposed conditions or agree to abandon the exclusive orientation of their economies." *

The staff paper ended with a plea that an effort be made, in connection with the advancement of the idea of a European recovery program, to correct what seemed to us to be the two main misimpressions that had been created in connection with the Truman Doctrine. These were:

(*a*) That the United States approach to world problems is a defensive reaction to Communist pressure and that the effort to restore sound economic conditions in other countries is only the by-product of this reaction and not something we would be interested in doing if there were no Communist menace;

(*b*) That the Truman Doctrine is a blank check to give economic and military aid to any area in the world where the Communists show signs of being successful. It must be made clear that the extension of American aid is essentially a question of political economy in the literal sense of that term and that such aid will be considered only in cases where the prospective results bear a satisfactory relationship to the expenditure of American resources and effort.

We then went ahead to describe those specific qualities of the situation in Greece that had justified our limited intervention there — very much as I had defined them in my earlier presentation of

---

* Actually, our hopes for the possible use of ECE as a center for European recovery received a severe setback from the account Will Clayton gave us, on his return from Europe, of the behavior of the Soviet delegation at the first meeting of that body.

March 28 to the War College. It ought to be made clear, we thought, that "in other areas we should have to apply similar criteria."

This, then, was the Planning Staff's recommendation to General Marshall. Copies went, I believe, to Mr. Acheson, to Will Clayton, to Ben (Benjamin V.) Cohen as counselor of the department, and to Chip Bohlen, then serving as special assistant to the Secretary. The following morning, General Marshall had a meeting in his office, at which all of these latter gentlemen, in addition to a number of other senior officials of the department, were present. Here, the general went around the circle, asking for comments on the paper.

Several of the comments were critical. Doubt was expressed, in particular, that the Europeans would themselves be able to draw up an effective program. The extension of the offer to Europe as a whole was also questioned: what, it was asked, would we do if the Russians accepted?

When all the others had spoken, I was asked to answer the criticisms. This I did, along the lines already indicated. I thought the Europeans could get together on a satisfactory program; if they couldn't, there was nothing we could do for them anyway. As for the Russians: we would simply play it straight. If they responded favorably, we would test their good faith by insisting that they contribute constructively to the program as well as profiting from it. If they were unwilling to do this, we would simply let them exclude themselves. But we would not ourselves draw a line of division through Europe.

When my piece was spoken, General Marshall thanked us and dismissed us, keeping his own opinion to himself, as was his wont, until he had opportunity to reflect and to make his decision. I cannot recall that I was further consulted in the ensuing days. The general was an orderly man. He had asked us for a recommendation and he had received it. He had enlisted with relation to it the best critical advice he could get. It was now, as he — I am sure — saw it, his responsibility. I learned of his final decision when I saw the text of the Harvard speech, in which the substance of our paper found

— along with the thoughts and suggestions of several other people — almost total acceptance.

The authorship of the Marshall Plan has been variously claimed, and variously imputed. Obviously, a considerable number of people, of whom Messrs. Acheson, Clayton, and Bohlen were only the most senior and distinguished, had a prominent hand in its origins. The function of the Planning Staff was primarily to bring together the knowledge and views of all these people, to cull out of them a workable recommendation for the principles on which our approach to this problem might be based and for the procedure that might best be followed, and to accept formal responsibility before the Secretary of State for this recommendation. This we did. A number of the elements of the final recommendation, including particularly the insistence that the Europeans get together on a joint program, were by no means original with us. We were indebted to others for many insights, even though we, in the final analysis, had to make our own opinion of their value. Our principal contributions consisted:

(*a*) in establishing the principle that the Europeans should themselves take the initiative in drawing up a program and should assume central responsibility for its terms;

(*b*) in the insistence that the offer should be made to all of Europe — that if anyone was to divide the European continent, it should be the Russians, with their response, not we with our offer; and

(*c*) in the decisive emphasis placed on the rehabilitation of the German economy and the introduction of the concept of German recovery as a vital component of the recovery of Europe as a whole.

Any judgment of the role of the Planning Staff in the origins of the Marshall Plan will have to rest on the relative importance ascribed to these three features of it.

Historically viewed, the authorship of the Marshall Plan lies, of course, squarely with General Marshall and President Truman. It lies with General Marshall for his service in seeking what he considered the best advice he could get, in enlisting that advice in the manner most calculated to assure its orderly preparation and presentation, in exposing it to the most qualified criticism he could find, and then in accepting before President, Congress, American public opinion, and the world at large responsibility for what was a bold and far-reaching act of statesmanship, by no means without great risks. As a man who never shirked responsibility for his mistakes, regardless of whose recommendation they flowed from, he deserves unstinted credit for his successes. But President Truman deserves that credit, too, for his perception and political courage in selecting as Secretary of State one of the most experienced, most selfless, and most honorable of America's professional public servants, in giving to that man his confidence and a wide latitude of action, and then supporting him in an individual initiative which, had it misfired, could have brought embarrassment and misfortune to the administration.

In the circle of advisors to whom General Marshall experienced and expressed a sense of indebtedness in connection with the evolving of the concept of the European recovery program, the Planning Staff, I am glad to say, was not omitted. Two years later, in June 1949, the chiefs of mission of the countries participating in the Marshall Plan tendered a dinner to President Truman and General Marshall in Washington, to celebrate the second anniversary of the Harvard speech. The general, being then in retirement, asked my help in editing the speech he was to make in response to the toast that would obviously be drunk in his honor. I was myself (as a result, I suspect, of General Marshall's tactful suggestion) among the guests at the dinner. When he had finished his response to the toast, General Marshall turned to me and, with his own inimitable graciousness, raised his glass. Four days later I received from him the following note, written by hand at his home in Virginia:

Dear Kennan:

While I thanked you informally for your helpfulness in the doctoring of my speech for Sunday night I want to tell you more formally that I greatly appreciated the time and trouble you gave to the matter and the quality of advice you gave me. Incidentally, it was certainly very appropriate for you to participate in the drafting of the speech since you performed a similar service, to a more important degree, in the preparation of the initial speech two years ago.

Faithfully yours,

G. C. MARSHALL

* * *

This is, I think, as good a place as any to say a word about General Marshall. I knew him only late in his life — during his final tour of duty in a long life of service to the nation. I was not close to him personally (few people were, I gather), but during the year and eight months of our association in the Department of State, from May 1947 to the end of 1948, I had the only office adjoining his own, and enjoyed the privilege (which I tried never to abuse) of direct entry to him, through our common side-door. Officially, then, the association was a fairly close one, and I had many opportunities to observe him in his work as Secretary of State.

There could be no one whose memory has less need of a eulogy from me than George Marshall. Like everyone else, I admired him, and in a sense loved him, for the qualities I saw in him, some of them well known, some less so: for his unshakable integrity; his consistent courtesy and gentlemanliness of conduct; his ironclad sense of duty; his imperturbability — the imperturbability of a good conscience — in the face of harassments, pressures, and criticisms; his deliberateness and conscientiousness of decision; his serene readiness — once a decision had been made — to abide by its consequences, whatever they might be; his lack of petty vanity or ambition; his indifference to the whims and moods of public opinion, particularly as manifested in the mass media; and his impeccable fairness and avoidance of favoritism in the treatment of subordinates (there was no one in the Department of State whom he called by the first name; every one of us, from top to bottom, was recognized simply by his surname, with no handle to it). I did not always agree with his political judgment; nor did I feel that he had always been well advised, in earlier years, on Russian matters. There were times when I had to disagree with him, and to give him unwelcome advice. But he had never held himself out as a political pundit. His official concern with political matters was not the result of his own initiative or request. And these limitations did not affect his personal qualities.

I have a feeling that I puzzled him. He was not used to people like me. But he recognized that I gave him what I could in the way of loyalty and service; and he treated me with a certain amused forebearance and respect.

He was, properly and commendably, chary of praise. Aside from the letter mentioned above, with its laconic words of appreciation, the nearest thing to a word of commendation that I ever had from him was on an occasion when I joined him in acting as host to two or three guests for luncheon in his office. He asked me to pour the drinks, which I nervously did. He, observing my efforts, then delivered himself of the following pronouncement: "Kennan, they tell me you are a good head of a planning staff, and for all I know you are, but . . ." (with a touch of military crescendo) "who the hell ever taught you to put the ice in before the whiskey?"

I can recall one other episode that endeared him to me beyond all others. It was in the spring of 1948. The success of the Marshall Plan was now so sweeping that Bohlen and I both felt the time had come for some conciliatory gesture on the part of this government — some gesture making it clear that our purpose was not to humiliate the Soviet government or to press it against a closed door — that we were entirely willing to talk over our problems at any time. We recommended to General Marshall that a statement along these lines be made to the Soviet government. The recommendation was accepted; and Ambassador Walter Bedell Smith was instructed to make to Molotov, and did so make, a statement on behalf of the United States government containing the assurance that "the door is always wide open for full discussion and the composing of our difficulties."

This gambit bounced back upon us in the most painful way. Molotov, inspired no doubt by his crafty master in the Kremlin, exploited it against us by affecting to understand it as an invitation for a high-level "parley" and announcing Soviet acceptance of the proposal. This unleashed a storm of speculation and protest. Our Western European friends, taken by surprise, descended on us — even personally on the Secretary — in droves, angrily demanding explanations. Were we going to negotiate with the Russians behind their backs? The administration had to climb down and to make an embarrassing confession that this was not at all what it had intended. It fell then under a cross fire of criticism from the columnists and editorial writers: some charging it with ineptness for issuing an unintended invitation, others — for not going through with the parley once we had invited it. Herblock, in the *Washington Post*, showed Harry Truman at bat, with the ball whizzing by him untouched, and the umpire calling, "Strike one."

I was appalled at what I had done. For two evenings, I walked the streets of Foxhall Village, trying to think out the course of events and to discover where our error had lain. On the third day, I went in to the general to render my accounting. He was absorbed in a pile of papers.

"General," I said, "I know that a man should try to learn from his mistakes, and not weep over them. I have spent two days, now, trying to figure out what it was that we did wrong. For the life of me, I cannot see it. I think we were right, and that the critics are wrong. But where there is so much criticism, there must be some fault somewhere."

General Marshall put down his papers, turned ponderously in his chair, and fixed me penetratingly over the rims of his glasses. I trembled inwardly for what was coming.

"Kennan," he said, "when we went into North Africa, in 1942, and the landings were initially successful, for three days we were geniuses in the eyes of the press. Then that business with Darlan began and for another three weeks we were nothing but the greatest dopes.

"The decision you are talking about had my approval; it was discussed in the Cabinet; it was approved by the President.

"The only trouble with you is that you don't have the wisdom and the perspicacity of a columnist. Now get out of here!"

* * *

Despite what was now an extremely intensive preoccupation with the affairs of state, I tried to contribute where I could to the work of the War College throughout the remainder of the academic year. On June 18, I spoke again, and for the last time, to the students of the college, and endeavored to explain to them, on the basis of six weeks' experience, what the task of a governmental planner in the field of foreign affairs was like. For this I found it necessary to use a parallel:

I have a largish farm in Pennsylvania. The reason you never see me around here on weekends (or rather, the reason you would never see me around if *you* were here weekends) is that I am up there to look after that farm. The farm includes two hundred thirty-five acres, and a number of buildings. On every one of those acres, I have discovered, things are constantly happening. Weeds are growing. Gullies are forming. Fences are falling down. Paint is fading. Wood is rotting. Insects are burrowing. Nothing seems to be standing still. The days of the weekend, in theory days of rest, pass in a . . . succession of alarms and excursions. Here a bridge is collapsing. No sooner do you start to repair it than a neighbor comes to complain about a hedgerow which you haven't kept up — a half-mile away on the other side of the farm. At the very moment your daughter arrives to tell you that someone left the gate to the hog pasture open and the hogs are out. On the way to the hog pasture you discover that the beagle hound is happily liquidating one of the children's pet kittens. In burying the kitten you look up and notice that a whole section of the barn roof has been blown off, and needs instant repair. Somebody shouts pitifully from the bathroom window that the pump must have busted — there's no water in the house. At that moment a truck arrives with five tons of stone for the lane. And as you stand helplessly there, wondering which of these crises to attend to first, you notice the farmer's little boy standing silently before you with that maddening smile that is halfway a leer, and when you ask him what's up, he says triumphantly: "The bull's busted out and he's eating the strawberry bed."

That's the only way I know to tell you what policy planning is like. The world is a big world. It has at least two hundred thirty-five big acres on it. On each of these something is incessantly happening. A nimble and astute person, working furiously against time, may indeed succeed in getting himself to a point where he thinks that with respect to one of those two hundred thirty-five acres he is some three or four months ahead of events. . . . But by the time he has gotten his ideas down on paper, the three or four months have mysteriously shrunk to that many weeks. By the time he has gotten those ideas accepted by others, they have become days. And by the time others have translated those ideas into action, it develops that the thing you were planning for took place day before yesterday, and everyone wants to know why in hell you did not foresee it a long time ago.

But suppose, I went on, you decide that you must not be put off by the plethora of urgent demands — that you must take one particular part of this harried globe and concentrate on the exploration of it. We might assume, for example, that you were examining the plight of a friendly European country which had not been able to revive its economic life by its own resources in the wake of the war. You are confronted immediately with a babble of tongues and conflicting opinions:

You say: "This shouldn't be so difficult. Why don't we tell these people to draw up a plan for the reconstruction of their economic life and submit it to us and we'll see whether we can support it or not?"

That starts it off. Someone says: "That's no good. They are too tired to draw up a plan. We have to do it for them."

Someone else says: "Even if they do draw up a plan, they wouldn't have the internal economic discipline to carry it out. The Communists would spike it."

Someone else says: "Oh, it isn't the Communists who would spike it — it is the local business circles."

Then someone says: "Maybe what we need isn't a plan at all. Maybe we just haven't given them enough in the past. If we just give them more, things will work out all right."

Another then says: "That's probably true, but we've got to figure out how the money is going to be spent. Congress just won't pour money down any more ratholes."

Then somebody says: "That's right; we need a program. We've got to figure out just what's to be done with the money and make sure that it does the whole job this time."

To that someone else replies: "Ah, yes, but it would be a mistake for us to try to draw this program up all by ourselves. The Commies would just take potshots at it and the European government would shrug off the responsibility."

Then someone says: "That's absolutely right. The thing for us to do is to tell these Europeans to draw up a plan and submit it to us and we'll see whether we can support it or not."

And then you ask: "Didn't somebody say that before?" And we're off again.

These words describe, perhaps, better than more formal ones the sort of intragovernmental debates that preceded the formulation of the Marshall Plan.

That final lecture to the War College, from which these excerpts are taken, was not all facetious. This was less than a fortnight after the Harvard speech. The success of the approach General Marshall had outlined in that speech was by no means yet assured. The tremendous problems with which it was designed to deal were still before us. I tried, in the final passages of my talk, to describe the danger they presented. These passages are perhaps worth recalling, as a reminder of the gravity of the problems to which, in 1947, the so-called "doctrine of containment" was addressed:

There is no use blinking the seriousness of our position. We have won a war in Europe — on the battlefield. It has cost us far more than we realized. It has cost us not only the lives of our people, the labor of our people, the depletion of our national resources. It has also cost us the stability of our international environment, and above all the vigor and strength — temporarily — of some of our real and natural allies.

Worst of all, it was not a complete victory. We of the Anglo-American world were not strong enough — at least not when we needed to be — to put down all of the forces that threatened our existence. We were forced to ally ourselves with a part of them in order to defeat the other part. That alone would not have been too unfortunate. But we were unable to encompass that without deceiving ourselves and our peoples as to the nature of that alliance.

Great modern democracies are apparently incapable of dealing with the subtleties and contradictions of power relationships. You men have examined here the crucial decisions of the war. I should say that the greatest error of the war on our side was the failure to distinguish clearly the personality of our Russian allies and to recognize and to explain frankly to our peoples the real nature of our wartime association with them. This failure, this lack of preparation for the aftermath of war, has caused us to suffer since the termination of hostilities set-backs which come close to balancing out the gains of our military victory over Germany.

Today we Americans stand as a lonely, threatened power on the field of world history. Our friends have worn themselves out and have sacrificed their substance in the common cause. Beyond them — beyond the circle of those who share our tongue and our traditions — we face a world which is at the worst hostile and at best resentful. A part of that world is subjugated and bent to the service of a great political force intent on our destruction. The remainder is by nature merely jealous of our material abundance, ignorant or careless of the values of our national life, skeptical as to our mastery of our own fate and our ability to cope with the responsibilities of national greatness. Left to itself, that remainder would not threaten us, at least not at this stage; for its aims are basically national, parochial ones. It embraces no national unity endowed with such human and material resources as to permit it to dream of world domination. But the towers of the Kremlin cast a long shadow. On many of these countries, otherwise content to tolerate if not to welcome the existence of our country as a great power, these shadows have already fallen. And that, gentlemen, is a dangerous thing; for the more I see of the life of this international society the more I am convinced that it is the shadows rather than the substance of things that move the hearts, and sway the deeds, of statesmen.

This was the way the world looked to one of us, at least, on the eve of the great turning point produced by the European response to the Harvard speech. It had been primarily the shadow, rather than the substance, of danger which we, in contemplating a European recovery program, had been concerned to dispel. It may be well to recall this in connection with the arguments over interpretation of the so-called X–Article and the "Doctrine of containment" which were now soon to ensue.

The presentation of the paper of May 23, 1947, was not the end of the Planning Staff's preoccupation with the problem of European recovery. The paper had been hastily produced. There were a number of aspects of the problem to which we wished to give more detailed study. We worked steadily for another two months, refining the whole concept, and at the end of that time presented another and much longer paper, designed not as a recommendation to the Secretary of State but rather as guidance and background for people who would now be concerned with the implementation of the project on the operational level. This paper, entitled, "Certain Aspects of the European Recovery Program from the US Standpoint," was completed on July 23. In it, we examined in greater detail the source of the American interest in Europe's recovery, the elements which that recovery would have to embrace if it was to be successful, the general considerations that ought to govern America's relationship to the program, the demands of individual countries (notably Britain, Germany, and Austria), the possibilities for private American participation, etc. The paper is too long to be cited or summarized here. It is my hope that it may some day be published in full, because I think it gives the most succinct and yet comprehensive picture of the official rationale of what our government attempted to do in this connection.

There is, however, one aspect of it I would like to mention. This was the very sharp line that was drawn between the problem of European recovery and the problems of economic growth that existed elsewhere in the world. Europe's needs, it was stated in this paper, were

clear in outline, readily susceptible of short-term solution, and of urgent importance to the interests of this country and of world recovery in general. . . . They lent themselves to special treatment. There was no reason to believe that the approaches here applied to Europe will find any wide application elsewhere.

Except in Korea and Japan, the needs of people in other areas differed in fundamental respects from those of Europe. In Europe, it was a case of releasing capacities for self-help that were already present. This was a short-term problem. Elsewhere, it was a matter not of releasing existing energies but of creating new ones. This was a long-term problem. For this, new organizational machinery would be necessary. Here, the need would be for some sort of instrumentality, near government but not entirely of it, through which technical know-how could be drawn from American industry and made available to other peoples.

Seen historically, from the perspective of two decades, this distinction between Europe's needs and those of other areas seems too obvious to be challenged. This was, however, not the case at the time. Throughout the period of preparation of the legislation making possible American aid to Europe's recovery, and for years thereafter, those of us who had had to do with the original Marshall Plan concept would be plagued with demands from the congressional side that we draw up or inspire similar programs for China, for the Middle East, or for Latin America. Congressman Walter Judd, of Minnesota, was particularly insistent that something of the same nature be attempted for China, and blamed the later demise of the Nationalist government there — I have no doubt — partly on our unwillingness to pursue this suggestion. Nothing that we could point to in the way of differences between the problems and situations of the two areas — neither the primitiveness of the existing industrial base in China, nor the unpromising nature of the political background, nor any of the other gaps that existed in China's ability to absorb and to use effectively outside financial capital — could shake his belief, and that of many other people, that the principles invoked to govern our relationship to Europe ought to have universalized validity. The congenital American aversion to regional approaches, and the yearning for universal ones, were too strong to be entirely overcome even by the success of the Marshall Plan — on the contrary, they were only stimulated by it.

15

The X – Article

AMONG the many papers prepared in the winter of 1946-1947, there was one that was written not for delivery as a lecture and not for publication but merely for the private edification of Secretary of the Navy James Forrestal. Ever since the receipt in Washington of the long telegram of February 22, 1946, Mr. Forrestal had taken a lively personal interest in my work. It was, I suspect, due to his influence that I was assigned to the War College and later chosen by General Marshall to head the Planning Staff.

During the period of my service at the War College — in December 1946, to be exact — Mr. Forrestal sent me a paper on the subject of Marxism and Soviet power, prepared by a member of his immediate entourage, and asked me to comment on it. This I found hard to do. It was a good paper. With parts of it I could agree; other parts were simply not put the way I would have put them. The whole subject was one too close to my own experience and interests for me to discuss it in terms of someone else's language. I sent the paper back to him with the observation that rather than commenting I would prefer, if he agreed, to address myself to the same subject in my own words. This, he replied, he would like me to do.

The result was that on January 31, 1947, I sent to him, for his private and personal edification, a paper discussing the nature of Soviet power as a problem in policy for the United States. It was a literary extrapolation of the thoughts which had been maturing in my mind, and which I had been expressing in private communications and speeches, for at least two years into the past. Even the term "containment" which appeared in the course of the argument was, as we have just observed, not new.

Mr. Forrestal read the paper. He acknowledged it, on February 17, with the words: "It is extremely well-done and I am going to suggest to the Secretary* that he read it."

Now I had, as it happened, spoken informally, early in January, at the Council of Foreign Relations, in New York, on the same general subject. The editor of the council's magazine *Foreign Affairs*, Mr. Hamilton Fish Armstrong (a great editor and, incidentally, one with whom this association was to be the beginning of a long and close friendship), asked me whether I did not have something in writing, along the lines of what I had said to the council, that could be published in the magazine. I had no text of what I had said on that occasion, but I thought of the paper I had prepared for Mr. Forrestal. In early March, therefore, I sought and obtained Mr. Forrestal's assurance that he had no objection to its publication. I then submitted it (March 13) to the Committee on Unofficial Publication, of the Department of State, for the usual official clearance. In doing so, I explained that it was the intention that it should be published anonymously. The committee pondered it at leisure, found in it nothing particularly remarkable or dangerous from the government's standpoint, and issued, on April 8, permission for its publication in the manner indicated. I then crossed out my own name in the signature of the article, replaced it with an "X" to assure the anonymity, sent it on to Mr. Armstrong, and thought no more about it. I knew that it would be some weeks before it would appear. I did not know how my position would be changed in the course of those weeks, or how this would affect the interpretations that would be placed upon the article when it was published.

In late June, as I recall it, the article appeared in the July issue of *Foreign Affairs*, under the title: "The Sources of Soviet Conduct." Its appearance was followed shortly (July 8) by that of a

* Presumably, the Secretary of State.

piece in the *New York Times* from the pen of the well-known and
experienced Washington columnist Mr. Arthur Krock, hinting at
the official origin of the article and pointing to the importance that
attached to it by virtue of that fact. He, I later learned, had been
shown the article by Mr. Forrestal at a time when it was no more
than a private paper lying around in Mr. Forrestal's office. His keen
journalistic eye had at once recognized it when it appeared in print;
and he had put two and two together.

It was not long, after the appearance of Mr. Krock's piece, before the authorship of the article became common knowledge.
Others began to write about it, to connect it with the Truman Doctrine and Marshall Plan, to speculate on its significance. It soon
became the center of a veritable whirlpool of publicity. *Life* and
Reader's Digest reprinted long excerpts from it. The term "containment" was picked up and elevated, by common agreement of
the press, to the status of a "doctrine," which was then identified
with the foreign policy of the administration. In this way there was
established — before our eyes, so to speak — one of those inde-
structible myths that are the bane of the historian.

Feeling like one who has inadvertently loosened a large boulder
from the top of a cliff and now helplessly witnesses its path of destruction in the valley below, shuddering and wincing at each successive glimpse of disaster, I absorbed the bombardment of press
comment that now set in. I had not meant to do anything of this
sort. General Marshall, too, was shocked. It was a firm principle, for
him, that "planners don't talk." The last thing he had expected was
to see the name of the head of his new Planning Staff bandied about
in the press as the author of a programmatical article — or an article
hailed as programmatical — on the greatest of our problems of foreign policy. He called me in, drew my attention to this anomaly,
peered at me over his glasses with raised eyebrows (eyebrows before whose raising, I may say, better men than I had quailed), and
waited for an answer. I explained the origins of the article, and
pointed out that it had been duly cleared for publication by the
competent official committee. This satisfied him. He was, as I have
already observed, an orderly man, accustomed to require and to

respect a plain delineation of responsibility. If the article had been cleared in this manner, the responsibility was not mine. He never mentioned the matter again, nor did he hold it officially against me. But it was long, I suspect, before he recovered from his astonishment over the strange ways of the department he now headed.

Measured against the interpretations that were at once attached to it, and have continued to a considerable extent to surround it ever since, the article that appeared in *Foreign Affairs*, in June 1947, suffered, unquestionably, from serious deficiencies. Some of these I might have corrected at the time by more careful editing and greater forethought, had I had any idea of the way it was to be received. But I cannot lay these failures exclusively to the innocent and unsuspecting manner in which the article was written. Certain of the public reactions were ones I would not, in any event, have foreseen.

A serious deficiency of the article was the failure to mention the satellite area of Eastern Europe — the failure to discuss Soviet power, that is, *in terms of* its involvement in this area. Anyone reading the article would have thought — and would have had every reason to think — that I was talking only about Russia proper; that the weaknesses of the Soviet system to which I was drawing attention were ones that had their existence only within the national boundaries of the Soviet state; that the geographic extension that had been given to the power of the Soviet leaders, by virtue of the recent advances of Soviet armies into Eastern Europe and the political exploitation of those advances for Communist purposes, were irrelevant to the weaknesses of which I was speaking. Obviously, in mentioning the uncertainties of the Soviet situation — such things as the weariness and poor morale among the population, the fragility of the constitutional arrangements within the party, etc. — I would have had a far stronger case had I added the characteristic embarrassments of imperialism which the Soviet leaders had now taken upon themselves with their conquest of Eastern Europe, and the unlikelihood that Moscow would be permanently successful in holding this great area in subjection.

To this day, I am not sure of the reason for this omission. It had something to do, I suspect, with what I felt to be Mr. Forrestal's needs at the time when I prepared the original paper for him. I have a vague recollection of feeling that to go into the problems of the satellite area would be to open up a wholly new subject, confuse the thesis I was developing, and carry the paper beyond its intended scope. Whatever the reason, it was certainly not that I underrated the difficulties with which the Soviet leaders were faced in their attempt to exercise political dominion over Eastern Europe. It has been noted above, in Chapter 9, that even as early as V-E Day, two years before, I had expressed the view that the Russians were over-extended in this area. Without Western support, I had written at that time

Russia would probably not be able to maintain its hold successfully for any length of time over all the territory over which it has today staked out a claim . . . The lines would have to be withdrawn somewhat.

Similarly, in the long telegram I had sent to Washington from Moscow, in February 1946, I had pointed out that the Soviet internal system

will now be subjected, by virtue of recent territorial expansions, to a series of additional strains which once proved a severe tax on Tsardom.

Had I included these appreciations in the X-Article, and added to the description of the internal weaknesses of Soviet power a mention of the strains of Moscow's new external involvement in Eastern Europe, I would have had a far stronger case for challenging the permanency of the imposing and forbidding facade which Stalin's Russia presented to the outside world in those immediate postwar years.

A second serious deficiency of the X-Article — perhaps the most serious of all — was the failure to make clear that what I was talking about when I mentioned the containment of Soviet power was not the containment by military means of a military threat, but the political containment of a political threat. Certain of the language used — such as "a long-term, patient but firm and vigilant containment of Russian expansive tendencies" or "the adroit and vigilant application of counterforce at a series of constantly shifting geographical and political points" — was at best ambiguous, and lent itself to misinterpretation in this respect.

A third great deficiency, intimately connected with the one just mentioned, was the failure to distinguish between various geographic areas, and to make clear that the "containment" of which I was speaking was not something that I thought we could, necessarily, do everywhere successfully, or even needed to do everywhere successfully, in order to serve the purpose I had in mind. Actually, as noted in connection with the Truman Doctrine above, I distinguished clearly in my own mind between areas that I thought vital to our security and ones that did not seem to me to fall into this category. My objection to the Truman Doctrine message revolved largely around its failure to draw this distinction. Repeatedly, at that time and in ensuing years, I expressed in talks and lectures the view that there were only five regions of the world — the United States, the United Kingdom, the Rhine valley with adjacent industrial areas, the Soviet Union, and Japan — where the sinews of modern military strength could be produced in quantity; I pointed out that only one of these was under Communist control; and I defined the main task of containment, accordingly, as one of seeing to it that none of the remaining ones fell under such control. Why this was not made clear in the X-Article is, again, a mystery. I suppose I thought that such considerations were subsumed under the reference to the need for confronting the Russians with unalterable counterforce "*at every point where they show signs of encroaching upon the interests of a peaceful world.*"

So egregious were these errors that I must confess to responsibility for the greatest and most unfortunate of the misunderstandings to which they led. This was the one created in the mind of Mr. Walter Lippmann. It found its expression in the series of twelve pieces attacking the X-Article (later published in book form as *The Cold War, A Study in U.S. Foreign Policy*, New York: Harper and Brothers, 1947) which he published in his newspaper column in the late summer and autumn of 1947. As I read these articles over today (and they are well worth the effort), I find the misunderstanding almost tragic in its dimensions. Mr. Lippmann, in the first place, mistook me for the author of precisely those features of the Truman Doctrine which I had most vigorously opposed — an assumption to which, I must say, I had led squarely with my chin in the careless and indiscriminate language of the X-Article. He held up, as a deserved correction to these presumed aberrations on my part, precisely those features of General Marshall's approach, and those passages of the Harvard speech, for which I had a primary responsibility. He interpreted the concept of containment in just the military sense I had not meant to give it. And on the basis of these misimpressions he proceeded to set forth, as an alternative to what I had led him to think my views were, a concept of American policy so similar to that which I was to hold and to advance in coming years that one could only assume I was subconsciously inspired by that statement of it — as perhaps, in part, I was. He urged a concentration on the vital countries of Europe; he urged a policy directed toward a mutual withdrawal of Soviet and American (also British) forces from Europe; he pointed with farsighted penetration to the dangers involved in any attempt to make of a truncated Western Germany an ally in an anti-Soviet coalition. All these points would figure prominently in my own later writings. He saw them, for the most part, long before I did. I accept the blame for misleading him. My only consolation is that I succeeded in provoking from him so excellent and penetrating a treatise.

Nevertheless, the experience was a painful one. It was doubly painful by reason of the great respect I bore him. I can still recall the feeling of bewilderment and frustration with which — helpless now to reply publicly because of my official position — I read these columns as they appeared and found held against me so many views with which I profoundly agreed. A few months later (April 1948), lying under treatment for ulcers on the sixteenth floor of the Naval Hospital in Bethesda, very bleak in spirit from the attendant fasting and made bleaker still by the whistling of the cold spring wind in the windows of that lofty pinnacle, I wrote a long letter to Mr. Lippmann, protesting the misinterpretation of my thoughts which his articles, as it seemed to me, implied. I never sent it to him. It was probably best that I didn't. The letter had a plaintive and overdramatic tone, reflecting the discomfort of flesh and spirit in which it was written. I took a more cruel but less serious revenge a year or two later when I ran into him on a parlor car of the Pennsylvania Railroad, and wore him relentlessly down with a monologue on these same subjects that lasted most of the way from Washington to New York.

But the terms of the unsent letter still hold, as I see them, a certain interest as expressions of the way the Lippmann columns then affected me.

I began, of course, with a peal of anguish over the confusion about the Truman Doctrine and the Marshall Plan. To be held as the author of the former, and to have the latter held up to me as the mature correction of my youthful folly, hurt more than anything else.

I also naturally went to great lengths to disclaim the view, imputed to me by implication in Mr. Lippmann's columns, that containment was a matter of stationing military forces around the Soviet borders and preventing any outbreak of Soviet military aggressiveness. I protested, as I was to do on so many other occasions over the course of the ensuing eighteen years, against the implication that the Russians were aspiring to invade other areas and that the task of American policy was to prevent them from doing so. "The Russians don't want," I insisted,

to invade anyone. It is not in their tradition. They tried it once in Finland and got their fingers burned. They don't want war of any kind. Above all, they don't want the open responsibility that official invasion brings with it. They far prefer to do the job politically with stooge forces. Note well: when I say politically, that does not mean without violence. But it means that the violence is nominally *domestic*, not *international*, violence. It is, if you will, a police violence . . . not a military violence.

The policy of containment related to the effort to encourage other peoples to resist this type of violence and to defend the *internal* integrity of their countries.

I tried, then, to explain (I could have done it better) that the article was in reality a plea — addressed as much to our despairing liberals as to our hotheaded right-wingers — for acceptance of the belief that, ugly as was the problem of Soviet power, war was not inevitable, nor was it a suitable answer; that the absence of war did not mean that we would lose the struggle; that there was a middle ground of political resistance on which we could stand with reasonable prospect of success. We were, in fact, already standing on that ground quite successfully. And I went ahead to point proudly (and rather unfairly, for after all, Lippmann had approved and praised the rationale of the Marshall Plan in his articles) to what had already been accomplished. I cite this passage here, not as a correction to Mr. Lippmann, to whose arguments it was not really an answer, but as a sort of epilogue to the discussion of both Marshall Plan and X-Article.

Something over a year has now gone by since General Marshall took over his present job. I would ask you to think back on the state of the world, as he faced it last spring. At that time, it was almost impossible to see how Europe could be saved. We were still caught in the fateful confusion between the "one-world" and the "two-world" concepts. The economic plight of the continent was rapidly revealing itself as far worse than anyone had dreamed, and was steadily deteriorating. Congress was in an ugly frame of mind, convinced that all foreign aid was "operation rathole." The Communists were at the throat of France. A pall of fear, of bewilderment, of discouragement, hung over the continent and paralyzed all constructive activity. Molotov sat adamant at the Moscow council table, because he saw no reason to pay us a price for things which he thought were bound to drop into his lap, like ripe fruits, through the natural course of events.

Compare that with today? Europe is admittedly not over the hump. But no fruits have dropped [into Molotov's lap]. We know what is West and what is East. Moscow was itself compelled to make that unpleasant delineation. Recovery is progressing rapidly in the West. New hope exists. People see the possibility of a better future. The Communist position in France has been deeply shaken. The Western nations have found a common political language. They are learning to lean on each other, and to help each other. Those who fancied they were neutral are beginning to realize that they are on our side. A year ago only that which was Communist had firmness and structure. Today the non-Communist world is gaining daily in rigidity and in the power of resistance. Admittedly, the issue hangs on Italy; but it hangs, in reality, on Italy alone. A year ago it hung on all of Europe and on us.

You may say: this was not the doing of US policy makers; it was others who worked this miracle.

Certainly, we did not do it alone; and I have no intention of attempting to apportion merit. But you must leave us some pride in our own legerdemain. In international affairs, the proof of the pudding is always in the eating. If the development of the past year had been in the opposite direction — if there had been a deterioration of our position as great as the actual improvement — there is not one of you who would not have placed the blame squarely on the failure of American statesmanship. Must it always, then, be "heads you win; tails I lose" for the US Government?

* * *

In the years that have passed since that time, the myth of the "doctrine of containment" has never fully lost its spell. On innumerable occasions, I have been asked to explain it, to say whether I thought it had been a success, to explain how it applied to China, to state a view as to whether it was still relevant in later situations, etc. It has been interpreted by others in a variety of ways. Pro-Soviet writers have portrayed it as the cloak for aggressive designs on the Soviet Union. Right-wing critics have assailed it precisely for its lack of aggressiveness: for its passivity, for its failure to promise anything like "victory." Serious commentators have maintained that it was all very well in 1947 but that it lost its rationale with the Korean War, or with Stalin's death, or with the decline of bipolarity.

It is hard for me to respond to all these criticisms. What I said in the X-Article was not intended as a doctrine. I am afraid that when I think about foreign policy, I do not think in terms of doctrines. I think in terms of principles.

In writing the X-Article, I had in mind a long series of what seemed to me to be concessions that we had made, during the course of the war and just after it, to Russian expansionist tendencies — concessions made in the hope and belief that they would promote collaboration between our government and the Soviet government in the postwar period. I had also in mind the fact that many people, seeing that these concessions had been unsuccessful and that we had been unable to agree with the Soviet leaders on the postwar order of Europe and Asia, were falling into despair and jumping to the panicky conclusion that this spelled the inevitability of an eventual war between the Soviet Union and the United States.

It was this last conclusion that I was attempting, in the X-Article, to dispute. I thought I knew as much as anyone in the United States about the ugliness of the problem that Stalin's Russia presented to us. I had no need to accept instruction on this point from anybody. But I saw no necessity of a Soviet-American war, nor anything to be gained by one, then or at any time. There was, I thought, another way of handling this problem — a way that offered reasonable prospects of success, at least in the sense of avoiding a new world disaster and leaving the Western community of nations no worse off than it then was. This was simply to cease at that point making fatuous unilateral concessions to the Kremlin, to do what we could to inspire and support resistance elsewhere to its efforts to expand the area of its dominant political influence, and to wait for the internal weaknesses of Soviet power, combined with frustration in the external field, to moderate Soviet ambitions and behavior. The Soviet leaders, formidable as they were, were not supermen. Like all rulers of all great countries, they had their internal contradictions and dilemmas to deal with. Stand up to them, I urged, manfully but not aggressively, and give the hand of time a chance to work.

This is all that the X-Article was meant to convey. I did not suppose, in saying all this, that the situation flowing immediately from the manner in which hostilities ended in 1945 would endure forever. It was my assumption that if and when the Soviet leaders had been brought to a point where they would talk reasonably about some of the problems flowing from the outcome of the war, we would obviously wish to pursue this possibility and to see what could be done about restoring a more normal state of affairs. I shared to the full, in particular, Walter Lippmann's view of the importance of achieving, someday, the retirement of Soviet military power from Eastern Europe, although I did not then attach quite the same political importance to such a retirement as he did. (In this he was more right than I was.)

No one was more conscious than I was of the dangers of a permanent division of the European continent. The purpose of "containment" as then conceived was not to perpetuate the status quo to which the military operations and political arrangements of World War II had led; it was to tide us over a difficult time and bring us to a point where we could discuss effectively with the Russians the drawbacks and dangers this status quo involved, and to arrange with them for its peaceful replacement by a better and sounder one.

And if the policy of containment could be said in later years to have failed, it was not a failure in the sense that it proved impossible to prevent the Russians from making mortally dangerous encroachments "upon the interests of a peaceful world" (for it did prevent that); nor was it a failure in the sense that the mellowing of Soviet power, which Walter Lippmann took me so severely to task for predicting, failed to set in (it did set in). The failure consisted in the fact that our own government, finding it difficult to understand a political threat as such and to deal with it in other than military terms, and grievously misled, in particular, by its own faulty interpretations of the significance of the Korean War, failed to take advantage of the opportunities for useful political discussion when, in later years, such opportunities began to open up, and exerted itself, in its military preoccupations, to seal and to perpetuate the very division of Europe which it should have been concerned to remove. It was not "containment" that failed; it was the intended follow-up that never occurred.

When I used the term "Soviet power" in the X-Article, I had in view, of course, the system of power organized, dominated, and inspired by Joseph Stalin. This was a monolithic power structure, reaching through the network of highly disciplined Communist parties into practically every country in the world. In these circumstances, any success of a local Communist party, any advance of Communist power anywhere, had to be regarded as an extension in reality of the political orbit, or at least the dominant influence, of the Kremlin. Precisely because Stalin maintained so jealous, so humiliating a control over foreign Communists, all of the latter had, at that time, to be regarded as the vehicles of his will, not their own. His was the only center of authority in the Communist world; and it was a vigilant, exacting, and imperious headquarters, prepared to brook no opposition.

Tito's break with Moscow, in 1948, was the first overt breach in the monolithic unity of the Moscow-dominated Communist bloc. For long, it remained the only one. It did not affect immediately and importantly the situation elsewhere in the Communist world. But when, in the period between 1957 and 1962, the differences between the Chinese and Russian Communist parties, having lain latent in earlier years, broke to the surface and assumed the form of a major conflict between the two regimes, the situation in the world Communist movement became basically different. Other Communist parties, primarily those outside Eastern Europe but partly the Eastern European ones as well, had now two poles — three, if Belgrade was included — to choose among. This very freedom of choice not only made possible for them a large degree of independence; in many instances it forced that independence upon them. Neither of the two major centers of Communist power was now in a position to try to impose upon them a complete disciplinary control, for fear of pushing them into the arms of the other. They, on the other hand, reluctant for the most part to take the risks of total identification with one or the other, had little choice but to maneuver, to think and act for themselves, to accept, in short, the responsibilities of independence. If, at the end of the 1940s, no Communist party (except the Yugoslav one) could be considered anything else than an instrument of Soviet power, by the end of the 1950s none (unless it be the Bulgarian and the Czech) could be considered to be such an instrument at all.

This development changed basically the assumptions underlying the concept of containment, as expressed in the X-Article. Seen from the standpoint upon which that article rested, the Chinese-Soviet conflict was in itself the greatest single measure of containment that could be conceived. It not only invalidated the original concept of containment, it disposed in large measure of the very problem to which it was addressed.

Efforts to enlist the original concept of containment with relation to situations that postdate the Chinese-Soviet conflict, particularly when they are described in terms that refer to some vague "communism" in general and do not specify what particular communism is envisaged, are therefore wholly misconceived. There is today no such thing as "communism" in the sense that there was in 1947; there are only a number of national regimes which cloak themselves in the verbal trappings of radical Marxism and follow domestic policies influenced to one degree or another by Marxist concepts.

If, then, I was the author in 1947 of a "doctrine" of containment, it was a doctrine that lost much of its rationale with the death of Stalin and with the development of the Soviet-Chinese conflict. I emphatically deny the paternity of any efforts to invoke that doctrine today in situations to which it has, and can have, no proper relevance.

16

Japan and MacArthur

THE work performed by the Planning Staff in relation to the European recovery program was, as we have seen, of a highly urgent nature. It was addressed of necessity to the needs of a single geographic area. Its requirements were such that until we had completed it, we had no time or opportunity to examine anything else. It was late summer of 1947 before we could, so to speak, come up for air, look around us, and attempt to take stock of America's world position as a whole.

As this *tour d'horizon* proceeded it became increasingly clear to me that the theaters of our greatest dangers, our greatest responsibilities, and our greatest possibilities at that moment were the two occupied areas of Western Germany and Japan. These places were the centers, respectively, of the two greatest industrial complexes of East and West. Their recovery was essential to the restoration of stability in Europe and East Asia. It was essential, if any sort of a tolerable balance of power was to be established in the postwar world, that they be kept out of Communist hands and that their great resources be utilized to the full for constructive purposes.

In both places — in Japan, that is, where General Douglas MacArthur had the supreme command, and in our own zone of Western Germany — we, the United States government, had what might be called a totality of responsibility. We had invited this upon ourselves. We had demanded and received unconditional surrender. That was equivalent to demanding and receiving dictatorial power. We had purposely relieved our erstwhile opponents of every shred of responsibility for what was now to come. Together with our allies we were theoretically in a position to control both internal developments and external relationships of those areas. Here, in contrast to other areas of our international relations, we were not confronted with any local sovereign government which had to be pressed, wheedled, or persuaded before we could achieve what we wanted. It was our cake. We had only to cut it.

However, looked at from the standpoint of the State Department in 1947, there were certain disturbing factors that entered into the picture.

First, although it was clear that these areas represented, in the light of their importance and of our own powers of control, two of our most important pawns on the chessboard of world politics, they were pawns over which we in the State Department had virtually no power of disposal and even the President an imperfect one. The American commanders in these countries occupied, in reality, highly independent positions. They would not have admitted it, but they were virtually laws unto themselves. The virtual elimination of the State Department as a factor in policy-making during the war, in favor of the military, carried over into the postwar period insofar as the military still had forces and occupational responsibilities abroad. If the commanders looked to anyone at all in Washington for guidance, it was to the War Department, and most immediately, I suppose, to its Civil Affairs Division. But the latter, as we have already seen in connection with the European Advisory Commission, was scarcely the most collaborative of the other governmental agencies with which the State Department had to deal. And even here, as it seemed to us, the commanders asked for guidance primarily when they felt a need for the cover of higher authority in some awkward or disagreeable decision for which they did not want to accept exclusive responsibility. Otherwise they were, we suspected, not much easier to control from the War Department's standpoint than from ours.

The difficulty was compounded by the fact that the commanders had, as a rule, two hats: an American one and an international one.

In part, they executed American directives; in part, they were the executors of international agreements among the allies. Pressed in the field of competence associated with one of these hats, they promptly took refuge under the other. This flealike agility and flexibility gave them extraordinary powers of resistance to any Washington-generated pressures which went contrary to their own views and inclinations.

Not only was it difficult to tell these commanders what to do, but it was not always easy to find out what they were doing. In Germany this was less of a problem. The State Department had its own representative there in the person of Ambassador Robert Murphy, a career Foreign Service officer of great experience, judgment, and prestige; and he kept us reasonably well informed. But in Japan there were real difficulties. MacArthur would not even hear of State Department advice on the political problems of his occupational responsibility. Lines of communication, such as they were, had to run through the War Department. There was a State Department representative at MacArthur's headquarters in Tokyo; but his office constituted only a subordinate unit — a sort of diplomatic protocol section — within the hierarchy of the headquarters. Its access to information, its opportunities for regular liaison at higher levels in headquarters, and its facilities for private communication with the State Department were all inadequate. The deficiencies were counterbalanced as far as they could be by the personal qualities of the man who headed this office from 1947 to 1952 — Mr. William J. Sebald, an able and experienced officer with a deep background in Japanese affairs — but his usefulness had to be developed in spite of, rather than because of, the organizational framework in which it was imbedded.

The difficulty of controlling the commanders was further complicated by the direct appeal they enjoyed to the public and congressional opinion. They were in effect official hosts to all who visited their theaters of operation. Without their benevolent approval and support, press correspondents found it difficult to obtain the facilities for their work. Distinguished visitors became willy-nilly their guests, depended on them for all facilities of residence and travel, and left in most instances with a feeling of personal indebtedness for courtesies and acts of hospitality extended. The commanders enjoyed, in effect, the perquisites of the monarchs of an older day: a benevolent nod from them opened many doors, whereas without that nod it was difficult for any stranger, journalistic or congressional or official, to make useful firsthand observations and to form well-founded judgments on the practices and policies of the occupation.

In all of this the commanders found themselves supported and protected by that curious admiration that many Americans, but particularly American legislators, seem to feel toward any other American who, in the uniform of our armed services, exercises extensive power over people in another land. Americans who would have protested violently at the first sign of paternalism or arbitrariness in the behavior of the United States government at home with relation to other Americans found it not only entirely in order but wholly admirable and inspiring — a source of pride, in fact — that an American commander should exercise a wholly autocratic power, untrammeled by legislative controls, in a foreign country; and they tended to sympathize extensively with that commander whenever corrupt, distrusted Washington attempted to interfere in any way in the exercise of his power. In making this observation I am not criticizing the generals in question. They were not responsible for the position in which they found themselves. In all cases known to me from that postwar period they exercised their great power with a high degree of responsibility and humanity. They deserved the respect which must be paid in general to benevolent despotism wherever encountered. I am merely pointing out that these commanders enjoyed something of the same sympathies which I suppose were once addressed to Belisarius by itinerant Byzantines visiting the Italy that rested under his command, enjoying his hospitality, and listening to his complaints about the inept and ignorant interference he had to endure from the imperial court at Constantinople.

The truth of the matter is that any great military-occupational government at once takes on certain of the aspects of a sovereign

government and is in a position to require that it be treated accordingly, even by the government it purports to represent. Ceasing to
be primarily an instrument of policy, it becomes in large measure a
policy-making center in its own right. Whoever in Washington
takes responsibility for placing a major American armed establishment anywhere beyond our borders, particularly when it is given
extensive powers with relation to civil affairs in the area where it
is stationed, should remember that he is not thereby creating just
an instrument of American policy — he is committing himself seriously to the insights, interests, and decisions of a new bureaucratic
power structure situated far from our shores and endowed with its
own specific perspective on all problems of world policy; and to
this extent he is resigning his own power of control over the use to
be made of America's resources in the process of international life.

If, then, the first of the factors that gave rise to uneasiness, as you
looked at Germany and Japan in 1947 from the standpoint of one
concerned with the formulation of national policy, was the limited
degree of Washington's control over what went on there; the second was the nature of the directives, both international and national, by which the occupational establishments were ostensibly
governed and by which they were at any rate influenced. In large
part these directives had been evolved in the final phases of the war.
They reflected at many points the love for pretentious generality,
the evangelical liberalism, the self-righteous punitive enthusiasm,
the pro-Soviet illusions, and the unreal hopes for great-power collaboration in the postwar period which, as we have seen, had per-
vaded the wartime policies of the Allied powers. These distortions
were now in process of modification by the discipline of experience;
but in 1947 there had been no general revision of the directives
themselves; no systematic attempt had been made to bring them into
accord with a new situation not originally anticipated but now
widely recognized to exist. Occupational policy, as a result, was at
that time in a state of uncertain and unsatisfactory transition, reflecting at some points recent and more realistic appreciations, but
still bound in many ways to unrealistic and wholly inadequate directives. In part these directives were the reflections of interna-

tional agreement, and any attempt to alter them thus presented formidable problems. In other instances the power to change them lay theoretically with our government. But in these latter instances formal authority lay with the War Department. The State Department could only suggest and advocate; it had no power to act on its own.

In the case of Germany, conditions did not seem to call at that time for any reexamination or new initiative on the part of the Planning Staff. The failure of the recent Moscow talks of the foreign ministers had cured whatever illusions had previously endured about the possibilities for four-power administration of Germany. The implications of this situation had finally been recognized in the form of the agreement with the British on the economic merging of the British and American zones, an agreement which was by mid-1947 already in process of implementation. This, plus the discipline which participation in the European recovery program might be expected to exert on the occupational regime, afforded reason to hope that, for the immediate future at least, Western Germany would progress in the desirable direction: toward the recovery, that is, of its own productivity, the development of its ability to contribute to the recovery of the remainder of Europe, and the achievement of a reasonable measure of domestic-political stability.

But the situation in the Far East was another matter. China was now unmistakably slipping rapidly into Communist control. We saw nothing the United States could do about this. We were decidedly not convinced that this development, which we deplored no less than anyone else, was occurring for lack of anything that the United States could provide. Our government had, admittedly, made its mistakes there; but the basic reason for the deterioration of the situation lay in the political weaknesses of the Nationalist regime itself — weaknesses which, in our opinion, would be more apt to be indulged and encouraged than corrected by further infusions of American aid.

On the other hand, this deterioration of the situation in China did not strike us as fatal, in itself, to American interests. China was not a strong industrial power. She showed no promise of becoming one for a long time in the future. In particular, she could not become in any short space of time a strong military power anywhere beyond the mainland of Asia. She had no ability to develop amphibious power on any serious scale. While I, at any rate (I shall not speak here for my colleagues), doubted at that time, and very wrongly so, the ability of the Chinese Communists to establish and maintain their rule for long over *all* of China, I also recognized — and this played a certain part in the assessment of the dangers of a Communist takeover — that even if they should succeed — precisely, in fact, *in the event* that they should succeed — in doing so, it was unlikely that they would themselves remain for long under Russian control. "I think," I said in a lecture to the War College on May 6, 1947,

. . . there is a good chance that if you let the Russians alone in China they will come a cropper on that problem just as everybody else has for hundreds of years . . . As long as [the Chinese Communists] remain a little minority movement fighting for their lives . . . they have to keep on fairly good terms with Moscow. If they were to become a majority, if they were to come to control, let's say, a large portion of the territory of China, I am not sure their relations with Moscow would be much different from those of Chiang today, because they would be much more independent, much more in a position to take an independent line vis-à-vis Moscow.

If, then, the deterioration of the situation in China did not seem to constitute in itself any intolerable threat to our security, what it did do was to heighten greatly the importance of what might now happen in Japan. Japan, as we saw it, was more important than China as a potential factor in world-political developments. It was, as I have already observed, the sole great potential military-industrial arsenal of the Far East. Americans, laboring under that strange fascination that China has seemed to exert at all times on American opinion, tended to exaggerate China's real importance and to underrate that of Japan. I considered then, and hold to the opinion today, that if at any time in the postwar period the Soviet leaders had been confronted with a choice between control over China and control over Japan, they would unhesitatingly have chosen the latter. We Americans could feel fairly secure in the presence of a truly friendly Japan and a nominally hostile China — nothing very bad could happen to us from this combination; but the dangers to our security of a nominally friendly China and a truly hostile Japan had already been demonstrated in the Pacific war. Worse still would be a hostile China *and* a hostile Japan. Yet the triumph of communism in most of China would be bound to enhance Communist pressures on Japan; and should these pressures triumph, as Moscow obviously hoped they would, then the Japan we would have before us would obviously be a hostile one.

It was with such reflections in mind that we in the Planning Staff turned our attention at the end of the summer of 1947 to the situation in Japan and the state of occupational policies there. What we found appeared at first sight distinctly disturbing. The theory was, of course, that as soon as the objectives of the occupation — primarily demilitarization and collection of reparations — had been achieved, the occupation of the country would be terminated by the conclusion of a treaty of peace. General MacArthur had given it publicly as his view on March 17, 1947, that Japan was now ready for such a treaty. The State Department had followed suit. It had sent out invitations on July 11 to the eleven states members of the Far Eastern Commission (the inter-Allied body seated in Washington to which General MacArthur was theoretically responsible in implementing the terms of the Japanese surrender) suggesting an early preliminary conference to prepare a draft treaty. This initiative had run into stubborn opposition from the Russians and the Chinese Nationalists; and it was clear that for the moment nothing would come of it. But it had brought us very close at one point to a position in which, had the others agreed, we would have been obliged to go through with the conclusion of a treaty and then, presumably, to evacuate Japan and leave her to her own devices.

It was with amazement and concern that I personally took note of this state of affairs in the summer of 1947 and attempted to relate it to what I could learn of the situation in Japan. If one was to regard the protection of Japan against Communist pressures as a legitimate concern of the United States government, then it was simply madness to think of abandoning Japan to her own devices in the situation then prevailing. She had been totally disarmed and demilitarized. After cession to the Soviet Union of southern Sakhalin and the Kurile Islands, and with the Russians in occupation of North Korea, she was semisurrounded by the military positions of the Soviet Union. Yet no provision of any sort had been made by the occupational regime for her future defense; nor could we discover that anyone in our government or in any of the Allied governments had given any thought in their planning for a peace treaty to the question of how this need was to be met in the post-treaty period. In addition to this, Japan's central police establishment had been destroyed. She had no effective means of combatting the Communist penetration and political pressure that was already vigorously asserting itself under the occupation and could be depended upon to increase greatly if the occupation was removed and American forces withdrawn. In the face of this situation the nature of the occupational policies pursued up to that time by General MacArthur's headquarters seemed on cursory examination to be such that if they had been devised for the specific purpose of rendering Japanese society vulnerable to Communist political pressures and paving the way for a Communist takeover, they could scarcely have been other than what they were.

We could of course not be sure of these judgments. It was too difficult to obtain through the devious governmental channels then available precise and satisfactory information about what SCAP (as MacArthur's headquarters was bureaucratically termed) *had* actually done, and *was* doing. But this was the way things looked on available surface evidence; and in the face of such a situation it seemed to us that our people had wandered very close to serious danger in taking the initiative for the launching of peace treaty negotiations. In the refusal of the Russians and Chinese to go along, we had been luckier than we deserved. The resulting deadlock now gave us opportunity to review the situation and to have a new look at our thinking and our policies generally with relation to Japan. For this the Planning Staff seemed to be a suitable organ. We could not, in fact, avoid occupying ourselves with this problem if we were to evolve anything like a coherent view of American policy as a whole. But it was clear that for the accomplishment of any such study we would have to have better factual information than we were able to get through the indirect channels of the War Department. And it would hardly do to try to work out and advance ideas on this whole subject without some sort of discussion and consultation with General MacArthur personally.

These reflections underlay a preliminary paper that I presented to General Marshall on October 14, 1947, inviting his attention to the dangers of any early relinquishment of our control over Japan. I pointed out that the occupation, as things then stood, was running into a situation of diminishing returns. A continued effort just to implement existing concepts and directives was not likely to bring Japan to a point where the consequences of a treaty of peace could be safely contemplated. There was need, before going any further with moves toward a peace treaty, for thorough discussion of these matters with General MacArthur personally and for a careful study of the adequacy of SCAP's existing directives.

This matter was the subject of several oral discussions I had with the Secretary of State over the course of the ensuing weeks. The upshot of these talks was a decision that I myself should make a journey to Japan, as soon as this could be arranged, for the purpose of studying the whole problem on the spot and discussing in detail with General MacArthur the difficult and delicate problems of policy it presented.

* * *

In the weeks that elapsed before my departure for Japan at the end of February 1948, I wrote and presented to General Marshall two papers of a general interpretive nature relating to the world situation and the problems it presented for American policy. It is interesting to recall today the high spots of these reviews, for they illustrate well the way the world looked at that time to at least one of those responsibly concerned with the formulation of American policy.

The first of these papers, presented on November 6, 1947, dealt with the world situation. I began by giving it as my view that the containment of Communist expansionism had thus far proceeded successfully. The expansion of the area of Soviet political domination had been halted. If the European recovery program should be successfully carried forward, the Communists would probably not be able to resume their political advance in Europe. But the American part in the devising and supporting of this program had stretched American resources dangerously far. It would be unwise for us to continue to exert such an effort of containment alone or largely alone. There was need to restore a balance of power by strengthening local forces of independence and getting them to assume a greater part of the burden.

The halt in the Communist advance, I considered, had placed the Communists before the necessity of consolidating their power throughout Eastern Europe. For this reason they would soon find themselves obliged to clamp down entirely on Czechoslovakia. So long as Communist power had been advancing generally in Europe, it had been to Russian advantage to allow to the Czechs the outward appearances of freedom; but now that the advance had been halted, they could no longer afford this luxury. Czechoslovakia could too easily become a path of entry for truly democratic forces into Eastern Europe generally. We had to expect a "sweeping away of democratic institutions and a consolidation of Communist power there."

Once dug in on the Lübeck-Trieste line, the Russians could probably maintain power there "for some time" by sheer police methods. But this would not be easy. It would in fact become increasingly difficult for them with the passage of time. It was unlikely that they could permanently hold down one hundred million people.

As for Germany, the Russians would probably prefer perpetuation of the division of Germany to the establishment of a unified

Germany not under Communist control. We would therefore find ourselves obliged to make the best of a divided Germany. But this meant that we would have to find means, at some point, for bringing the western part of Germany into an acceptable relationship to other Western European countries.

So much for the first of these papers. I invite attention particularly to the passage about Czechoslovakia. The analysis proved correct. The crisis in that country came three and a half months later and culminated, as is well known, with the discarding of the last trappings of true democracy and the establishment of an unadulterated Communist dictatorship. Actually, as is readily apparent from the above, this development represented a defensive reaction — and one foreseen by ourselves — to the success of the Marshall Plan initiative. This, however, was understood neither by American opinion nor by people throughout our governmental bureaucracy. The result was that the Communist crackdown in Czechoslovakia, when it came, was received generally as a new Communist success — the evidence, in fact, of the inadequacy of the methods of containment employed up to that time. This had, as we shall see in another chapter, an effect on the origins of the NATO pact and on that militarization of thinking about the cold war generally that would overtake official Washington in the coming period.

The second of the two papers, completed and handed to the Secretary on the day before my departure for Japan, was a long analysis of the global problems of American policy. It is too voluminous to be summarized here. There are, however, certain features worth noting.

First, as to our relations with the Soviet Union: If it should prove possible, by means of the European recovery program and other measures, to put a halt to Communist expansionism in Europe, then, it was stated in this paper, the Soviet leaders would be prepared, for the first time since the German surrender, to do business with us seriously about Germany and about Europe in general. This would constitute a great test of American statesmanship. It would then be our task to demonstrate to them that it would be worth their while:

   (*a*) to reduce pressures in Europe and the Middle East to a point

where we could consent to a mutual withdrawal of forces in
Europe; and

(*b*) to acquiesce in a prolonged period of stability in Europe.

For all of this there would be need at some point for private, secret,
and informal discussions with the Soviet leaders.

(I mention especially this last, because in this rather cryptic formula there lay buried, though undetectable at that date, the germs
of the serious disagreements that would shortly emerge between
myself and others in the government, including General Marshall's
successor and the leaders of our military establishment in Germany,
concerning the manner in which the success of the European recovery program was to be followed up and exploited.)

A considerable part of this long paper was devoted to the danger,
which then seemed imminent, of further Soviet expansionism in the
eastern Mediterranean and the Middle East. The success of our
peaceful intervention in Greece was by no means as yet assured.
The establishment of the state of Israel (American military support
for which I resolutely opposed) seemed to heighten the danger of
Communist infiltration in the Arab countries. In this section of the
report I dealt at some length with the question (then hypothetical,
but destined to arise in acute practical form more than once in later
years) of what to do if there should be a serious prospect that Communists would be successful in seizing further areas through political penetration and subversion without the use of Soviet armed
forces. The answer I came up with was that in such an event it
would not be wise for us to react by employing our own armed
forces in combat with a view to correcting the situation at hand.
"The use of US regular armed force," it was stated,

. . . to oppose the efforts of indigenous Communist elements within
foreign countries must generally be considered as a risky and profitless
undertaking, apt to do more harm than good.

The best we could do in such a situation, I thought, would be to
advance wherever we could in the respective geographic region the
deployment of our regular peacetime military establishment. It

should be our purpose to make it evident to the Russians that extensions of their power by the methods of penetration and subversion would simply cause this country to expand and strengthen its military positions in adjacent areas, whereas reductions in the Communist threat might have the opposite effect in that they would create the conditions precedent for American military withdrawal. (It was my thought that if, for example, the Communists had been successful in consolidating their power in Greece, we should have responded by establishing bases, if our allies would agree, in other Mediterranean countries.)

Turning to the Far East, I expressed the view that we were greatly overextended. Things looked bad, and there was little we could do about it. We would have to show great restraint. Our means of influence were of necessity primarily military and economic. Japan and the Philippines would eventually constitute the cornerstones of a Pacific security system adequate for the protection of our interests. If we could retain effective control over these two archipelagoes in the sense of assuring that they would remain in friendly hands, there could be no serious threat to our security from the east within our time. Our objectives for the coming period, therefore, should be to:

(*1*) liquidate unsound commitments in China and try to recover our detachment and freedom of action with relation to that situation;

(*2*) devise policies toward Japan which would assure the security of that country from Communist penetration and domination as well as from military attack by the Soviet Union and would permit Japan's economic potential to become once again an important force in the affairs of the area, conducive to peace and stability; and

(*3*) permit Philippine independence, but in such a way as to assure that the archipelago remained a bulwark of American security in the Pacific region.

There was, as will be seen, no hint in this exposition of a view that we required for the assurance of our national security any special military position anywhere on the mainland of Asia.

* * *

On the day after the second of these papers was handed in —
February 26, I believe it was — I left for Japan. The mission was
one of the utmost delicacy. Relations between General Marshall
and General MacArthur were remote and, I sensed, not cordial.
They had been frayed, I supposed, by the enormous frictions of the
wartime competition between the Pacific and European theaters for
supplies and support — frictions of which General Marshall had
unavoidably found himself at the center. General Marshall seemed
reluctant to involve himself personally in any attempt to exchange
views with General MacArthur. The latter, on the other hand, as
we all knew from dozens of evidences, had a violent prejudice
against the State Department, resented any attempt by the State
Department to interfere in the conduct of the occupation in Japan,
and would be quick to sense in the arrival of any senior State Department official precisely this sort of an intention on the department's part. Liaison between the two institutions — the department
and SCAP — had been so distant and so full of distrust that my
mission was like nothing more than that of an envoy charged with
opening up communications and arranging the establishment of
diplomatic relations with a hostile and suspicious foreign government. And in the undertaking of this mission I was, in view of General Marshall's disinclination to become involved, and in view of the
unconcealed skepticism of the Far Eastern Division of the department as to the chances for success in such a venture, very much on
my own.

The War Department was, I suspect, both alarmed and intrigued
at the prospect of my undertaking. Some people there were also
aware of the need for a revision of the concepts and directives
under which we were operating in Japan; but even more than people in the State Department they were intimidated by MacArthur,
and I think they licked their lips as they watched a civilian David
prepare to call upon this military Goliath. Realizing that their own
interests were involved, they provided me with a military companion to keep them currently informed. This, fortunately, turned out

to be a highly competent, intelligent, and reasonable officer: General Cortlandt Van Rensselaer Schuyler (later Supreme Commander at SHAPE). I could not have wished for a more pleasant traveling companion; and I suspect that he, in his quiet, tactful way, was of considerable help behind the scenes in the accomplishment of my mission.

The State Department, too, provided me with a congenial companion and effective aide for this journey in the person of Mr. Marshall Green, a Foreign Service officer (destined many years later to be our ambassador in Indonesia) who had been private secretary to Ambassador Joseph Grew in Tokyo, and was then serving in the Division of Far Eastern Affairs. His excellent background knowledge of Japanese affairs and his tactful effectiveness in liaison with the intermediate levels of SCAP were invaluable to me in the performance of this mission.

General MacArthur was of course notified in advance of my impending visit. He did not refuse to receive me, but I was later told that his reaction to the news of my approach was a grim and cryptic: "I'll have him briefed until it comes out of his ears."

In these decidedly less than auspicious circumstances, General Schuyler and I took flight from Seattle on February 29, 1948. After a stop at Anchorage and another terrifying refueling stop in a nocturnal gale at the tabletop landing field of the tiny island of Shemya, fourteen hundred miles from nowhere in the northern Pacific, we reached Tokyo some thirty hours later — at four o'clock on a Sunday morning, to be exact — in a snowstorm. Once again, the heating had given out in the plane on the final two-thousand-mile lap from Shemya, and we were, by consequence, not only exhausted but thoroughly chilled on arrival.

After arriving at the Imperial Hotel, I tried to sleep; but correspondents and others kept calling me up at intervals through the morning, and it was no use. At one o'clock General Schuyler and I, having now been without sleep for nearly forty-eight hours, repaired to General MacArthur's residence for luncheon.

The general, in company with Mrs. MacArthur, received us courteously. We were joined at lunch, as I recall it, only by one of

his aides. Schuyler sat on one side of the general, I on the other. As
the meal neared its end — turning his back to me, addressing himself exclusively to Schuyler, and thumping the table for emphasis
with a single vertically held finger — the general embarked on a
monologue which lasted, by my recollection, approximately two
hours. Oppressed by weariness, I sat motionless in my humble corner. Unable of course to take anything in the nature of notes, I
could not make any detailed record of this discourse. I suspect that
it was much the sort of thing he was in the habit of saying to all
manner of visitors from Washington. Caesar's experience in the military occupation of Gaul was cited, I remember, as the only other
historical example of a productive military occupation. The Japanese were thirsty for guidance and inspiration; it was his aim to
bring to them both democracy and Christianity. They were now
tasting freedom; they would never return to slavery. The Communists were no menace in Japan. A year ago we might have had a
peace treaty. The Russians and the Chinese would then have gone
for it as a means of getting us out. Now, he felt it was more difficult.

This statement completed, we were politely dismissed, with the
assurance that suitable briefings would be arranged for us by members of headquarters.

The following day I listened to the first of these briefings. They
were helpful but not greatly illuminating. They embraced much
the same background information that would have been given, I
think, in off-the-record briefings to the press. Most of what they
contained was already known to Green and myself. They were, in
short, interesting enough, but far from meeting the basic purpose of
my mission.

Seeing that if I took no further initiative I would simply be put
off in this way, I sat down in my hotel room on that second evening
and wrote a note to General MacArthur expressing gratitude for
the briefings but pointing out to him that I had questions of some
moment which I was under instructions to discuss personally with
him and about which I would be expected to have inquired his opin-

ion by personal consultation before I left for home. I asked, accordingly, to be received by him at his earliest convenience.

The following evening after another day of briefing I was visited in my hotel room by General Charles A. Willoughby, who, as MacArthur's "G–2," was one of his senior aides and advisors. We passed a pleasant evening and found much to talk about. He was interested in the Soviet Union: in the progress of Soviet recovery, in the development of Soviet postwar foreign policy. He asked me if I would lecture, the following day, to a group of the senior officers of SCAP.

This last I gladly did. I had had much closer acquaintance than any of them had had in recent years with developments in the Soviet Union, and I think I was able to add to their knowledge and to clarify some of their impressions. General MacArthur did not appear to be present; but I later gained the impression that he was, in some way or other, excellently informed of what I had to say. Together with General Willoughby's account of our conversation, this lecture may have relieved some of the Supreme Commander's doubts as to the purpose of my mission and the nature of my interest in occupation policies.

In any case, a day or two later I was received, alone, by General MacArthur for a long evening's interview. We discussed — without exception, I think — all the leading problems of occupational policy as well as the problems of relations with our former allies in matters affecting the occupation and the peace treaty. He gave his views freely and encouraged me to do likewise. I could see that he was himself not unaware of some of the dangers that had suggested themselves to us, and that he felt, no less than we did, the need for changing and modifying a number of the occupational policies. What worried him particularly was the opposition that any such changes might be expected to encounter on the part of the Allies, as represented in the Far Eastern Commission. In just this respect I was able to make suggestions that were new to him and in which he saw, I think, possibilities for overcoming the impediments he had in mind. I pointed out that the advisory capacity of the Far

Eastern Commission related solely to the responsibility he bore for executing and enforcing the terms of the Japanese surrender. These in turn were based on the Potsdam Declaration. But the latter had envisaged only the demilitarization of Japan and the relinquishment by her of the administration of certain territories. These terms had now been carried out. He could thereby be said to have carried to completion that portion of his responsibility, flowing from the terms of surrender, with relation to which the Far Eastern Commission was qualified to advise him. The changes in occupation policy that were now required were ones relating to an objective — namely, the economic rehabilitation of Japan and the restoration of her ability to contribute constructively to the stability and prosperity of the Far Eastern region — the necessity of which did not flow from the terms of surrender but rather from the delay in negotiation of a peace treaty. There had been no international agreement on the policies and methods to be applied in this unforeseen situation. This being the case, the United States government and he as its commander in Japan had to exercise an independent judgment. I saw no need for him, in these circumstances, to consult the Far Eastern Commission or to feel himself bound by views it had expressed at earlier dates with a view to implementing the terms of surrender. So long as nothing was done that would undermine the measures envisaged in the Potsdam Declaration and the surrender document, the Allies could have no grounds for objection.

This thesis appeared to please the general mightily; he even slapped his thigh in approval; and we parted with a common feeling, I believe, of having reached a general meeting of the minds.

From that moment things went very well. In addition to completing the briefings at headquarters in Tokyo, Green and I made a tour of some of the main outlying centers of the occupation. For this we were kindly given the use of a private railway car, and every effort was made, so far as I could see, to provide us with whatever information we wanted.

The picture that emerged from this study of the situation in Japan confirmed in full the anxieties we in the staff had experienced when we first inquired into the matter the previous autumn. In no respect was Japan at that time in a position to shoulder and to bear successfully the responsibilities of independence that could be expected to flow at once from a treaty of peace.

It was true, in the first place, that no proper provision had been made for Japan's defense. SCAP had in Japan at that time a total of some 87,000 military personnel. Most of these were engaged in housekeeping duties. The most that could have been raised in the way of combat forces out of this number would have been one or two combat teams. The Japanese were themselves of course totally disarmed, and no one had any idea of rearming them.

Our occupational establishment was weighing heavily on Japanese life and preempting a good part of what was needed for economic recovery. In addition to the military personnel, we were maintaining there a staff of over 3500 civilians. The servicing personnel which the Japanese had to provide for these American occupiers, and for which they had to pay the entire costs, ran into the hundreds of thousands, including tens of thousands of personal servants. The Japanese government was engaged, at the time of our visit, in the construction at its own expense of some 17,000 new housing units for members of the American occupational establishment, and this at a time when it also faced the tremendous problem of providing new housing for millions of its own bombed-out city dwellers. The occupation costs were absorbing approximately one-third of the Japanese budget. The cumbersome occupational establishment was in many respects parasitical; and I am sorry to say that among the various purposes for which exactions were being made upon the Japanese, the personal enrichment of members of the occupation was not always absent.

Saddled with such a burden it would have been difficult for the Japanese to prepare themselves for independence even in the best of circumstances. But in addition to this, the effect of the reforms which SCAP had been conducting, and of the manner in which it had been conducting them, was such as to produce just at that time a high degree of instability in Japanese life generally.

The land reform, in itself constructive and desirable, had affected about one-third of the arable land of the country and had led to the purchase by the Japanese government of a very large part of this property with a view to its redistribution. Only about one-seventh of what had been purchased had, however, been resold up to that point. The result was a situation of great confusion and instability in the relationships of agricultural land ownership.

A similar situation existed on the industrial side. SCAP had embraced with an almost wild enthusiasm the trust-busting ideals that already commended themselves so powerfully to the antitrust division of the Department of Justice in Washington. Some two hundred and sixty Japanese companies, including some of the most tremendous industrial concerns, had been designated as "excessive concentrations of economic power." Their securities had in many instances been taken over by the Japanese government at SCAP's direction and were theoretically awaiting resale — to whom was not clear. The companies, meanwhile, existed in a state of uncertainty which could not help but interfere seriously with initiative and confidence of management. The ideological concepts on which these measures rested bore so close a resemblance to Soviet views about the evils of "capitalist monopolies" that the measures themselves could only have been eminently agreeable to anyone interested in the future communization of Japan. Their relation to the interests of Japanese recovery was less apparent.

Most serious of all, as I saw it, was the situation created by the wholesale "purging" of people in government, in education, and in business who were suspected of having had militaristic sympathies or of having abetted Japanese aggression in earlier days. Here SCAP had proceeded on a scale, and with a dogmatic, impersonal vindictiveness, for which there were few examples outside the totalitarian countries themselves. Seven hundred thousand people had already been involved, at the time of our visit, in the attendant screenings. Just in the educational establishment alone, some 120,-000 out of a half million teachers had been purged or had resigned to avoid purging. Nor was there any visible end to this process. SCAP had decreed that checks should henceforth be run under its supervision on all new governmental employees, so this sort of screening was apparently intended to go on indefinitely. The program, furthermore, had taken on a wholly unfathomable complexity. Orders, regulations, and institutions relating to this process had been piled on top of each other in appalling profusion. To the ordinary Japanese, as I later wrote in my report to the government,

. . . the operation of the purge must be thoroughly bewildering. I doubt, in fact, whether many persons in SCAP . . . could explain its history, scope, procedures and purpose.

All useful punitive psychological effect had been lost amid the confusion of ordinances, directives, and programs. The indiscriminate purging of whole categories of individuals, sickeningly similar to totalitarian practices, was in conflict with the civil rights provisions of the new constitution that we ourselves had imposed upon the Japanese. It had had the effect of barring from civil life many people who could not be regarded on any reasonable standards as exponents of militarism and whose only crime had been to serve their country faithfully in time of war. Important elements of Japanese society essential to its constructive development were being driven underground. Pressures were being engendered which, if not promptly relieved, were bound to come to the surface someday in extremely unhealthy ways. Particularly strange and unfortunate was the regularity with which the purge had seemed to hit persons known in the days before the war for their friendly attitude toward the United States. It was as though pro-Americanism, especially among upper-class Japanese, was particularly suspect. Here, again, the policies of SCAP had brought Japanese life to a point of great turmoil and confusion, and had produced, momentarily at least, a serious degree of instability.

Meanwhile, economic recovery was being further hampered by reparations deliveries, particularly of industrial equipment previously in use in Japan, to various allies — the Chinese, the Philippines, etc. Not only were these deliveries and the uncertainties connected with their possible continuation damaging the Japanese economy, but they were doing very little to strengthen anybody else's economy. Masses of this equipment lay rotting, we were told, on the docks at Shanghai and other Far Eastern ports.

Obviously, such conditions would constitute, in the event that the occupation should be suddenly removed, a high degree of vulnerability to Communist pressures. Yet nothing had been done to provide the Japanese with any adequate means of looking to their own internal security. The only police units under central control were some thirty thousand rural constabulary. The municipal police forces, amounting to some 77,000 men, were under only local control, with no provision for proper liaison among them or between them and the center in matters of political security; yet it was precisely here, in the cities, that the problem of Communist activity would be most acute. This whole establishment was armed, for the most part, only with pistols, and of these there was less than one weapon to every four men. There was no counterintelligence force. Although Japan was an island country, no maritime police force had been created. And there was, of course, no Japanese armed force to back up any of these units in case of emergency. It was difficult to imagine a setup more favorable and inviting from the standpoint of the prospects for a Communist takeover. The Japanese Communists at the same time were being given a free field for political activity and were increasing their strength rapidly.

One often heard it suggested at that time that this curious pattern of achievement on the part of SCAP was in part the result of Communist infiltration within the headquarters. General MacArthur was aware of these charges. They even entered into our discussions. He did not, if I understood him correctly, think it impossible that there might be party members among the thousands of persons attached to SCAP — on the contrary he rather assumed that there were. "We have probably got some of them. The War Department has some. So does the State Department. It doesn't mean very much," I seem to recall his saying. He did not think that such minor influence as they could exert was of any great importance.

I had no basis for judgment on the question of the extent to which SCAP policies reflected Communist influence in the lower levels. If governmental institutions were to be judged in this respect on the basis of the degree to which their operations appeared to favor or reflect Communist purposes (I myself can think of no

more improper a basis of judgment, but it was one sometimes applied in Washington), then SCAP headquarters would have been
many times more suspect than the State Department. Its members
could be happy in later years that their chief had been a high military officer and not a civilian; otherwise the hand of congressional
suspicion and denunciation would certainly have fallen upon them
in no uncertain way during the heyday of the late Senator Joseph
McCarthy. The very immunity that SCAP enjoyed to charges of
this nature gives rise, it seems to me, to interesting conclusions
about the motivation of the whole wave of governmental witch-
hunting that was at that time about to ensue.

On return to Washington I submitted to the Secretary of State a
report describing in much greater detail than has been done here
the situation I had encountered in Japan, and setting forth a comprehensive set of recommendations for American policy to meet
it.

The regime of control by SCAP over the Japanese government
should, I recommended, be relaxed. The Japanese should be encouraged to develop independent responsibility. No further reform
legislation should be pressed. The emphasis should shift from reform to economic recovery. The purges should be tempered, ta-
pered off, and terminated at an early date.

An effort should be made to reduce occupation costs. Reparations should be generally halted, the opposition of the other Far
Eastern Commission powers notwithstanding. The settlement of
property claims should be expedited.

Meanwhile, we should not press for a peace treaty. Precedence
should be given, for the time being, to the task of bringing the Japanese into a position where they would be better able to shoulder the
burdens of independence. When the time came for its negotiation
the treaty should be brief, general, and nonpunitive. (This last was
in contrast to the lengthy, legalistic, and largely punitive drafts that
had previously been circulating in the State Department.) Pending
conclusion of a treaty, we should retain tactical forces in Japan; but
their numbers, their cost to the Japanese, and their adverse impact

on Japanese life and economy should be reduced to a minimum. Whether we should plan to retain armed forces, bases, and other military facilities in Japan in the post-treaty period should be left for future decision. We should, however, make up our minds that we were in Okinawa for a long time to come, and should accordingly assume full responsibility for restoring economic stability and normal political conditions for the native population of the island. (We had heretofore refrained from doing this on the grounds that we did not know how long we were going to be there.) The Japanese police establishment, meanwhile, should be reinforced and re-equipped, and there should be added to it a strong, efficient coast guard and maritime police force.

These recommendations were passed on by the Secretary of State to the Far Eastern Division for its critical comment and clearance. The division accepted them with only one or two minor modifications. But because they involved so heavily our military interests and because their implementation had to proceed primarily through our military authorities, they had also to be submitted to the National Security Council, on which the armed services were powerfully represented, and thus to receive presidential sanction. This took time. Not all of the recommendations were agreeable to all echelons of the armed services whose responsibilities were engaged. Some of the recommendations would interfere, not only with existing armed service policies, but with cherished personal privileges, amenities, and advantages. Nevertheless, the recommendations met after some delay with practically complete acceptance in the National Security Council, and thus became, with presidential approval, the basis for orders issued — mostly at the end of 1948 or the beginning of 1949 — by the service departments to the occupational headquarters in Tokyo.

How, at what stages, and in what degree these decisions finally found realization in the actions and practices of SCAP, I cannot tell. I think it likely that General MacArthur, being largely in agreement with them and well informed of the deliberations in Washington that led to their final adoption, anticipated them at many points by the exercise of his own great executive powers.

Parts of them were no doubt well on the way to implementation before Washington had even finished its deliberations. If, on the other hand, there were certain features that did not meet with General MacArthur's full approval, he had ample means of delaying, if not frustrating, their execution. For these reasons the effect of the decisions in Japan was probably a gradual and to many an almost imperceptible one. Mr. Sebald says nothing in his memoirs* to indicate that he ever heard of these decisions, though he does refer to a number of the changes pursuant to them that took place in 1949. The memoirs of General Willoughby,† too, reveal no awareness on his part of any of the above. One has at times the feeling that Washington did not loom very large on the horizons of this highly self-centered occupational command.

Nevertheless, my own visit, the talk with General MacArthur, and the directives that finally emanated from Washington represented in their entirety a major contribution to the change in occupational policy that was carried out in late 1948 and in 1949; and I consider my part in bringing about this change to have been, after the Marshall Plan, the most significant constructive contribution I was ever able to make in government. On no other occasion, with that one exception, did I ever make recommendations of such scope and import; and on no other occasion did my recommendations meet with such wide, indeed almost complete, acceptance.

In recommending as I did in 1948 that no decision be made at that time regarding the possible stationing of American forces in Japan in the period following conclusion of a treaty of peace, it was my hope — shared at the moment, I believe, by General MacArthur — that we would eventually be able to arrive at some general understanding with the Russians, relating to the security of the northwestern Pacific area, which would make this unnecessary. Again, as in the case of Europe, I did not suspect the Russians of any intention to launch an outright military attack. The greatest

---

* William Sebald, *With MacArthur in Japan*. New York: Norton, 1965.
† Charles A. Willoughby, *MacArthur 1941-1951*. New York: McGraw-Hill, 1954.

danger to the security of Japan lay, as I saw it, in the possibilities for intrigue, subversion, and seizure of power by the Japanese Communists. Only in case such a process should be very far advanced — in its final stages, in fact — would there be any possibility that Russian forces might play some sort of a supplementary role. What Japan most needed, therefore, was not foreign military bases on her territory but the bolstering of her capabilities for assuring internal security. Once internal conditions in Japan had been stabilized and once the country was equipped with an adequate police establishment, and particularly with a smart, effective maritime police force that could prevent infiltration from the mainland, we would be able to afford, it seemed to me, to offer to the Russians in effect the withdrawal of our armed forces from the Japanese archipelago (about Okinawa I was not so sure) in return for some settlement that would give us assurance against the communization of all Korea. There was no need, of course, to face this problem in a final way until peace treaty negotiations were upon us; meanwhile, what was important was that the question be held open so that it could be used as a bargaining factor when the time came for serious international discussions.

Whether General Marshall would have gone along with this concept had he remained Secretary of State after the end of 1948, I do not know. Nor do I recall what did then finally cause our government — or Secretary of State Dean Acheson, at least — to decide by late summer of 1949 that the time had come to proceed with the effort to conclude a treaty of peace. I find in my diary for August 30, 1949, the following cryptic observation:

It is ironic that our principal reason for wanting a treaty of peace [with Japan] at this time is that it appears to be the only way of solving internal administrative difficulties within our own government.

This would strongly imply that the renewal of the quest for a peace treaty was forced upon us not by the needs of the objective situation we had before us but rather by the inability of our government to use the cumbersome occupational machinery, with its heavy involvement of the military side of the Washington bureaucracy, as an effective instrument of policy.

However that may be, Mr. Acheson and Mr. Bevin appear to have agreed, when they met in Washington in September 1949, that the time had come to proceed once more with efforts to conclude a treaty. The idea seems then to have met with resistance on the military side in Washington, where there was understandable reluctance to give up facilities and privileges then enjoyed by our armed forces in Japan. The conflict seems to have been resolved over the course of the ensuing winter by the emergence of a general understanding that, while the treaty would not itself provide for the retention of American bases in Japan, it would be accompanied by a separate agreement with the Japanese government sanctioning such an arrangement; and that if all this was not agreeable to the Russians, as it obviously would not be, we would not hesitate to conclude both treaty and agreement without them.

This, of course, departed basically from my own concept of the manner in which it was desirable for us to proceed. It foreclosed the question of the future of the American military presence in Japan before any effort had been made to see what use could be made of this as a bargaining factor in negotiations with the Russians. It is, as will be seen below, my own view that this probably had an important bearing on the Soviet decision to unleash the attack in Korea. But official Washington appeared, particularly at that time, impervious to any understanding of the possible effect of its own acts and policies on Soviet behavior beyond the rather primitive question as to whether what we did deterred or did not deter the Soviet government from its assumed desire to launch military attacks in every direction. I have seen no evidence that the possibility of a connection between our decision to proceed independently to the conclusion of a separate Japanese peace settlement, involving the indefinite retention of an American military presence in Japan in the post-treaty period, on the one hand, and the Soviet decision to unleash a civil war in Korea, on the other, ever entered the mind of anyone in Washington except myself.

The negotiation of the Japanese peace treaty was placed — in the spring of 1950, I believe it was — in the capable hands of Mr. John Foster Dulles. The decision to retain American forces indefinitely in Japan in the post-treaty period had of course by that time already been effectively taken. Whether Mr. Dulles influenced this decision I do not know. In any case, he went along with it. He consulted me briefly, as I recall, on one occasion at the outset of his preoccupation with this problem. I told him that I could not see, as yet, any need for American bases in Japan in the post-treaty period; I thought that if the Japanese were given adequate police forces and if they achieved sufficient domestic stability and economic security to enable them to cope successfully with the efforts of their own Communists, the islands could safely be left demilitarized and neutralized by international agreement. This view, obviously, commended itself no more to him than it did to Mr. Acheson.

Shortly thereafter the Korean War broke out. The shock thrown into SCAP by this development and the extent to which, in the course of the ensuing hostilities, we were obliged to draw on our military, naval, and air facilities in Japan as bases for the conduct of hostilities in Korea converted everyone who had not yet been converted to the view that the American military presence in Japan was wholly essential to any future security of the area. The Korean War demolished whatever slight possibility might ever have existed for a Russian-American understanding in relation to the problems of that region, based on the neutralization and demilitarization of Japan. What was later to occur in China made it doubly unfortunate that such an understanding never existed.

17

The North Atlantic Alliance

IN the last two chapters I have had occasion to describe efforts on my part, as a person connected now with the policy-making function in Washington, that were at least in the immediate sense successful. I must turn now to the first of the major undertakings of American policy in General Marshall's time with relation to which I failed to exert any effective influence, and which took, from the start, a course adverse in important respects to my own concept of what we ought to be attempting.

Over the winter of 1947-1948, prior to my departure for Japan, a number of things occurred with relation to the situation in Western Europe and in our relations with the Western European countries — things with regard to which I had no official responsibility and to which, foolishly and shortsightedly, I did not at the time attach much importance. The London Conference of the four foreign ministers (November 25 to December 15, 1947) ended in total failure. This was so much to be expected that it had made no impression whatsoever on my own thinking. Not so, however, in the case of the British and the French. No sooner were the Christmas holidays over than the British government turned to the question of what was to constitute the basis for British security, now that it was clear that the United Nations would not be able to act effectively to keep the peace in any question that involved cold war issues and differences. On January 13 the British foreign secretary, Ernest

Bevin, informed General Marshall that England proposed to approach France and the Benelux countries with a view to inaugurating discussions on common problems of defense; and he inquired what our attitude would be. Our reply, which must have gone out at some time between January 15 and 20, was encouraging. I cannot recall having had anything to do with it. Its tenor was influenced, I strongly suspect, by the views of Mr. John Foster Dulles. He had attended the London CFM meeting — in the interests, I suppose, of bipartisanship — as an advisor to Secretary Marshall. The French government, which had at that time just been heavily pressed by Communist-inspired strikes, was in a very anxious and almost panicky state of mind. Besides, the presence of senior American figures in London rather than in Paris was always upsetting in those days to French composure. For these reasons, presumably, Mr. Dulles, by agreement with Secretary Marshall, went to Paris on December 4. His purpose was to acquaint himself with the situation and to reassure the French. Although the peak of the French internal crisis had just been passed, Mr. Dulles returned shaken by the experience and convinced that the French were really in need of some sort of political reassurance. The Interim Aid Bill (the first installment on the Marshall Plan) had not yet been passed by our Congress. The main European recovery bill had yet to be presented for legislative approval. Not only were the French uncertain about their own internal situation but they were, as the British pointed out to us, reluctant to go along with the measures for the revival of the West German economy, as envisaged in the Marshall Plan, unless they had some sort of guaranty of support, and primarily American support, against a possible recrudescence of German military strength. All in all the French, as Mr. Dulles put it in his testimony to the Senate a year later, "felt naked." They required, as he saw it, our reassurance precisely in the military and political field, if they were to take a confident and constructive part in the European recovery program. This view commended itself to General Marshall and the President not only by reason of their respect for Mr. Dulles's experience and judgment but also by virtue of the impressions General Marshall had gathered independently from his experience at the London Conference.

The American reply, then, was encouraging; and on January 22 Bevin made a major speech in the House of Commons calling for the formation of a "Western Union" — a union, that is, among Britain, France, and the Benelux countries, to have political and military as well as economic connotations. The proposal found immediate support in Paris and in the Benelux capitals, and in February preparations were put in hand for a conference to give it further considerations. This meeting convened at Brussels in early March, and led to the signing on March 16 of the treaty establishing the so-called Brussels Union.

When I left for Japan on February 26, the Brussels talks had not yet begun. I was aware of the British initiative and of our response to it. I regarded the anxieties of the Europeans as a little silly; this was not, it seemed to me, the time to start talking about military defenses and preparations. I agreed that they needed some sort of reassurance; but I saw dangers in any form of such reassurance that would encourage them in their military preoccupations. In the long analysis of our problems of policy which I handed to Secretary Marshall on February 24 (see Chapter 16) I took the position that the British efforts toward the formation of a Western Union indeed deserved our support, but that further study was required before our position could be finally determined. I supposed, lightheartedly, that there was no urgency — that the whole matter could remain open until my return.

On the very day of my departure the Czech crisis reached its height. The realization of what had occurred burst with great violence upon the American press and public in the final days of February and the first days of March, while I was on the way to Japan. The shock was heightened, only too naturally, when on March 11 news was received of the mysterious death, either by murder or suicide, of Jan Masaryk, foreign minister of the Czechoslovak Republic and son of the former President of that country. Masaryk had been known as a friend of the West. His death dramatized, as few other things could have, the significance of what had just occurred in that country.

Of even greater importance, I believe, for its effect on American official opinion, was a telegram received from General Lucius Clay, in Berlin, on March 5. For many months, General Clay wired, logical analysis had persuaded him that war with the Soviet Union was unlikely "for at least ten years"; but

. . . within the last few weeks, I have felt a subtle change in Soviet attitude which I cannot define but which now gives me a feeling that it may come with dramatic suddenness.*

I strongly suspect that what General Clay's antennae had picked up in the highly charged atmosphere of Berlin was actually the first intimations of the Russian policy decisions leading to the establishment of the Berlin blockade. I cannot help but believe that a deeper background in Russian affairs would have saved him from the error of interpretation that this message reflected, and that the State Department, together with the rest of official Washington, would have done better in evaluating his message to rely on the judgment of some of us who knew something about Russia. The message was not shown to me until I arrived in the Philippines in mid-March. I immediately sent in my remonstrations but by this time it was too late. Washington, particularly the military establishment and the intelligence fraternity (where the military predominated), had already overreacted in the most deplorable way to the combination of Clay's telegram and the Czech coup. A real war scare ensued, the intensity of which may be judged from the fact that on March 16 the Central Intelligence Agency thought it necessary to hand to the President an estimate saying that war was "not probable within sixty days." A fortnight later, when the other services proposed to project this cautious estimate another two weeks into the future, the air force was even unwilling to associate itself with the extension.†

The effects of this misimpression were at once apparent in the

* *The Forrestal Diaries*, edited by Walter Millis, p. 387. New York: Viking Press, 1951.
† *Ibid.*, pp. 395 and 409.

reactions of the civilian echelons of the government in the matter of our relationship to the Brussels Union. On the very day the Brussels Treaty was signed — March 17 — the President addressed a joint session of Congress. He had originally planned to speak at a St. Patrick's Day observance in New York, but, as he has explained in his memoirs,

. . . the grave events in Europe were moving so swiftly . . . that I felt it necessary to report to the nation first through Congress.*

In this address he proceeded to welcome the Brussels agreement, to say that it had our support, and to express his confidence

. . . that the United States will, by appropriate means, extend to the free nations the support which the situation requires. I am sure that the determination of the free countries of Europe to protect themselves will be matched by an equal determination on our part to help them to protect themselves.

Even prior to the conclusion of the Brussels Treaty, the State Department had put in hand studies of the various ways in which this American support for the defense effort of the Brussels powers could be manifested.

In offering this brief summary of the March crisis of 1948, I must point out that both of the events that threw official Washington into such a dither — the consolidation of Communist power in Czechoslovakia and the inauguration of the attempt by the Russians to force the Western Allies out of Berlin — were defensive reactions on the Soviet side to the initial success of the Marshall Plan initiative and to the preparations now being undertaken on the Western side to set up a separate German government in Western Germany. They represented, like the Communist-inspired strike that France and Italy had just suffered in the autumn of 1947, Moscow's attempt to play, before it was too late, the various political cards it still possessed on the European continent. This reaction was

* Harry S Truman, *Memoirs*, Vol. II, p. 241. New York: Doubleday and Company, 1956.

something I had always expected and taken into account. I have mentioned above the basic paper that I wrote from Moscow at the time of the German surrender (see Chapter 9, pp. 247-251), entitled *Russia's International Position at the Close of the War with Germany.* The full text of this paper is enclosed in the Annex. Let me invite attention once more to certain of the language there used. Should the Western world, I then wrote,

. . . muster up the political manliness to deny to Russia either moral and material support for the consolidation of Russian power throughout Eastern and Central Europe, Russia would probably not be able to maintain its hold successfully for any length of time over *all* the territory over which it has today staked out a claim. In this case, the lines would have to be withdrawn *somewhat*.* But if this occurred, the nuisance value of Soviet power in the Western countries and in the world at large would be exploited to the full. The agents of Soviet power might have to abandon certain districts where they now hold sway; but they would, to use Trotsky's vivid phrase, "slam the door so that all Europe would shake." Every difficulty that could conceivably be created for the Western democracies by Communist parties and Communist claques would be used in this baring of the fangs; and the world would have cause to remember Molotov's warning at San Francisco that, if the conference did not give Russia peace and security on her own terms, she would seek it and find it elsewhere.

Should the Western world stand firm through such a show of ill temper and should democracies prove able to take in their stride the worst efforts of the disciplined and unscrupulous minorities pledged to the service of the political interests of the Soviet Union in foreign countries, Moscow would have played its last real card. It would have no further means with which to assail the Western world. Further military advances in the west would only increase responsibilities already beyond the Russian capacity to meet. Moscow has no naval or air forces capable of challenging the sea or air lanes of the world.

In 1948, nothing that had occurred in the three years since these words were written had shaken in any way my confidence in the

* It should be noted that both the Czech coup and the Berlin blockade occurred at a time when Moscow was already aware of the Yugoslav defiance of Soviet authority — when, in other words, the lines of Soviet authority in Eastern Europe had already been in effect "withdrawn somewhat."

accuracy of the analysis they embodied. I found, accordingly, nothing unexpected, nothing out of the ordinary, in any of the Communist behavior — the strikes in France and Italy, the Czech coup, and the Berlin blockade — that caused so much alarm in the Western capitals in late 1947 and early 1948. This was just the predictable "baring of the fangs." Nor did I see any reason why the development of military strength on our side, and particularly the development of new relationships of alliance between this country and European countries, was required to meet that behavior. In all of this I was, I think, justified. My mistake lay in my failure to realize that these views, despite all that had been said in the reporting from Moscow, in the X-Article, and in innumerable private conversations in the State Department, had made only a faint and wholly inadequate impression on official Washington. On the military establishment the impression had been practically nil. The same was true for all but one or two people in the State Department. General Marshall had been pleased, I know, with what I had done in the problem of European recovery; but he had, I fear, never fully understood the rationale behind it. If he ever read the warning I submitted to him in the autumn of 1947 to the effect that the Communists would inevitably crack down on Czechoslovakia in case the effort toward a European recovery program proceeded successfully, I am sure he had forgotten it by the end of February 1948 and that it was never brought to the attention of either the President or the Pentagon. The greatest mystery of my own role in Washington in those years, as I see it today, was why so much attention was paid in certain instances, as in the case of the telegram of February 1946 from Moscow and the X-Article, to what I had to say, and so little in others. The only answer could be that Washington's reactions were deeply subjective, influenced more by domestic-political moods and institutional interests than by any theoretical considerations of our international position. It was I who was naïve — naïve in the assumption that the mere statement on a single occasion of a sound analysis or appreciation, even if invited or noted or nominally accepted by one's immediate superiors, had any appreciable effect on the vast, turgid, self-centered, and highly emotional process by which the views and reactions of official Washington were finally evolved.

My journey to the Far East in February-March 1948 included not only Japan but also brief visits to the Philippines and Okinawa. It was the end of March before I returned to Washington. When I did return, I was ill with duodenal ulcers. I was taken to the Naval Hospital at Bethesda on the day after my arrival. On release from the hospital, a fortnight or so later, I went directly to my Pennsylvania farm for convalescence. It was not until April 19 that I finally got back to my desk in Washington; and it was only then that I became aware of all that had transpired in those recent weeks in the field of our relationship to the problem of European rearmament and defense.

The State Department had been continuing, over this entire period, its studies of the ways in which we might, conceivably, give support to the Brussels Union. The Planning Staff had even become occupied with this problem and had presented, on March 23, a preliminary paper dealing with it. Here it was recommended that while we should not now become a member of the Western Union, we should hold open the possibility of eventual association with it; that we should meanwhile give it assurance of our armed support; and finally, that we should try to bring into the Western Union a number of other European countries, including even Sweden and eventually Switzerland. A month later, on April 22, the department, drawing no doubt on this paper and on a number of other documents, presented its views to the President and the National Security Council. But meanwhile, it seems, discussions had also been in progress between Mr. Robert A. Lovett, Under Secretary of the department, and Senator Arthur H. Vandenberg, Republican foreign policy spokesman in the Senate.

Mr. Lovett, personally one of the most charming of men, a seasoned financier and a very smooth, capable operator, had been Under Secretary of the department since Mr. Acheson's departure from that position in the summer of 1947. He, like General Marshall, had a high sense of the importance of close liaison with the more influential members of the Senate on matters of foreign policy. This was wise and commendable; but I sometimes felt that it went so far as to assume on the part of the Senators a wisdom greater than was actually there, and took the form of a catering to senatorial opinion in instances where one might better have attempted to educate its protagonists to a more enlightened and effective view.

Senator Vandenberg I knew only slightly. I was aware of the important services he had just recently rendered in mobilizing support in Congress for the European recovery program. I found it hard to accept, however, the feeling prevalent in the department that for this reason we in the State Department were under great obligation to him. We were, after all, not the representatives of a foreign government but of one to whose interests his commitment was presumably no smaller than ours. He would, I thought, have been remiss had he not vigorously supported the Marshall Plan. He deserved credit no doubt for having supported it, but no more than we deserved for having proposed it. I could not accept the assumption that Senators were all such idiots that they deserved admiring applause every time they could be persuaded by the State Department to do something sensible.* For this reason, great as was my respect for Senator Vandenberg, I did not understand the rationale

---

* I find in my personal notes, under date of January 23, 1948, the following account of observations I had made that day to a Washington journalist who, in the course of a private conversation, had reproached me and the State Department for what he viewed as our failure to expose adequately to members of Congress the strategic realities underlying the Marshall Plan proposal:

I pointed out that personally I had entered a profession which I thought had to do with the representation of United States interests vis-à-vis foreign governments; that this was what I had been trained for and what I was prepared to do to the best of my ability; and that I had never understood that part of my profession was to represent the US government vis-à-vis Congress; that my specialty was the defense of US interests against others, not against our own representatives; that I resented the State Department being put in the position of lobbyists before Congress in favor of the US people; that I felt that Congress had a responsibility no less than that of ourselves toward the people; that we were not their keepers or their mentors; that it was up to them to inform themselves just as it is up to us to inform ourselves; that 98 percent of the information needed as background for judgments on questions of foreign policy can be found in the *New York Times* and that I had no sympathy with the allegations that Congress cannot act intelligently in these questions because "it has not been given the facts."

for the elaborate deference paid to him at that time in the State Department. And I did not assume that his views on the nature of our response to Europe's sudden attack of military jitters were necessarily the most profound and correct ones.

What came out of the Lovett-Vandenberg talks was the document that eventually emerged as Resolution 329, passed by the Senate on June 11, 1948, and commonly known as the Vandenberg Resolution. It was already taking shape when I returned to my desk on April 19. I saw it for the first time, as I recall it, in early May. It embodied two principles on which, I gather, Senator Vandenberg had insisted: first, that any undertaking on which we might enter should not imply any automatic commitment on the part of our government to go to war under any specific hypothetical circumstances — that the final decision, in other words, must always be left for congressional determination; and second, that it should not involve any unilateral benefits — that each of the countries participating in any arrangements for Atlantic security should be required to bestow benefits upon us in addition to receiving benefits from us. This last principle was borrowed from the Marshall Plan legislation. Both of these principles were considered necessary by the Senator, as I understood it, to assure approval of the resolution and of any arrangements made subsequently, under its authority, for American association with a North Atlantic defense grouping.

The Vandenberg Resolution and the State Department's part in producing it, made me very unhappy. I was willing to go along with the idea that it was desirable for us to encourage the Europeans in the Brussels Plan project. I could also understand it might be desirable for us, if this made them feel any better, to give them a unilateral political and military guarantee, and military aid as well, if they needed it — but this last only on the principle of the Marshall Plan: that they set up their own organization and that we appear as the great and good friends, but not participating members, of what they had set up. If we were to do these things at all, it seemed to me desirable that we should do them only in some sort of close partnership with the Canadians. For this reason, I favored what was sometimes referred to as the "dumbbell" concept: the combination, that is, of a unit at the European end based on the Brussels pact, and another unit at the North American end — Canadian-United States, this time — the two units being separate in identity and membership but linked by an acknowledgment on the North American side that the security of the European unit was vital to United States-Canadian security, and by a readiness on the United States-Canadian part to extend to the European participants whatever was necessary in the way of assistance in military supplies, forces, and joint strategic planning. This would have meant, in effect, a unilateral guarantee by the United States, in partnership with Canada if the Canadians were willing, of the security of those Western European nations that chose to associate themselves with the Brussels Union. Even for this, I saw no real necessity; but I was prepared to see us accept such an arrangement if this was the only way the Europeans could be given the reassurance necessary for them to proceed confidently with the task of economic and domestic-political recovery. But when I put forward in the department the suggestion of such a "dumbbell" arrangement, I was met with the objection that this would not do: it would conflict with Senator Vandenberg's principle of reciprocal aid. This last was interpreted to mean that each of the European parties would have to promise individually to defend *us* in addition to our undertaking to defend it. This, in turn, would inevitably involve something in the nature of a contract — a treaty, in other words — a treaty unprecedented in our history, and one requiring, of course, the most solemn and deliberate consideration and eventual approval by the Senate.

For this whole idea I had, I fear, little patience; and I shall attempt to explain why.

I saw, in the first place, no need for a full-fledged reciprocal military alliance at that stage of the game. It seemed to me regrettable that attention should even be drawn in a major way, in the circumstances of the moment, to the relationships of military strength as between Russia and the West. I was well aware that we had demobilized and the Russians had not. This I considered unfortunate but not fatal or even very important. The Russians had no idea of using regular military strength against us. Why then should we direct attention to an area where we were weak and they were strong? Time and again, in the ensuing weeks, I said to my colleagues: "All right, the Russians are well armed and we are poorly armed. So what? We are like a man who has let himself into a walled garden and finds himself alone there with a dog with very big teeth. The dog, for the moment, shows no signs of aggressiveness. The best thing for us to do is surely to try to establish, as between the two of us, the assumption that teeth have nothing whatsoever to do with our mutual relationship — that they are neither here nor there. If the dog shows no disposition to assume that it is otherwise, why should we raise the subject and invite attention to the disparity?"

Secondly, I had little confidence in the value of written treaties of alliance generally. I had seen too many instances in which they had been forgotten, or disregarded, or found to be irrelevant, or distorted for ulterior purposes when the chips were down. I had no confidence in the ability of men to define hypothetically in any useful way, by means of general and legal phraseology, future situations which no one could really imagine or envisage. What was needed, it seemed to me, was a realistic consciousness of where one's vital interests really lay. Given that, military policy would flow correctly of its own accord — it needed no legal obligations or prescriptions. The suggestion, constantly heard from the European side, that an alliance was needed to assure the participation of the United States in the cause of Western Europe's defense, in the event of an attack against it, only filled me with impatience. What in the world did they think we had been doing in Europe these last four or five years? Did they suppose we had labored to free Europe from the clutches of Hitler merely in order to abandon it to those of Stalin? What did they suppose the Marshall Plan was all about? Could they not see that we were well aware of the real dangers with which Western Europe was faced, and that we were acting, as generously and effectively as we could, to combat them? Why did they wish to divert attention from a thoroughly justified and promising program of economic recovery by emphasizing a danger which did not actually exist but which might indeed be brought into existence by too much discussion of the military balance and by the ostentatious stimulation of a military rivalry?

Finally, I had nothing but amused contempt for the legalisms and generalities of verbiage over which my colleagues, in their long and involved discussion with the Senators, were struggling. The Vandenberg Resolution struck me then, as did nine-tenths of the 1263 pages of testimony later taken by the Foreign Relations Committee of the Senate in connection with the NATO pact, as typical of that mixture of arid legalism and semantic pretentiousness that so often passes, in the halls of our domestic-political life, for statesmanship. I had no patience with that sort of thing then; I have none today. What we need, in order to make an effective foreign policy, is action — not promises to act; decisions — not legal undertakings or attempts to generalize future conduct.

These were the thoughts with which I took cognizance of, and followed, the course of the dealings between Secretary Marshall and Mr. Lovett and the Senators over the Vandenberg Resolution, and later — over the text of the treaty itself. But there was little I could do to affect the course of events. Unhappy over the paper the staff had submitted during my absence in Japan, but feeling partially committed by it, I wrote another in June, trying to put on the brakes. Here, I accepted (there was no alternative) the situation created by the Vandenberg Resolution but urged that military aid be granted only on the Marshall Plan principles (namely, that the Europeans must first draw up their own program and take responsibility for it) and that we should not discuss any further American political commitment along this line unless further conversations convinced us that this was necessary in order to bolster public confidence in Western Europe. But by this time, of course, the Senators had the bit in their teeth, and no words of this sort on my part could have had any effect.

More for the record, I suspect, than for any other reason, I set forth my views for General Marshall somewhat later in the year (November 23, 1948) in a paper entitled: *Considerations Affecting the Conclusion of a North Atlantic Treaty*. I realized that I could no longer affect the movement toward a treaty; but I was, after all, still the head of his planning staff, and I thought he should at least have available to him the view I took personally of the entire NATO project.

The danger that the European NATO partners faced in the political field — the danger, that is, of a spread of communism to new areas of the continent by political means — was still greater, I wrote, than any military danger that confronted them. The morale of the Western European peoples needed, of course, the stiffening that such a pact could give it; but hand in hand with any stiffening by this particular means went the danger

. . . of a general preoccupation with military affairs, to the detriment of economic recovery and of the necessity for seeking a peaceful solution to Europe's difficulties.

This preoccupation with military affairs was already widespread, I noted. It was regrettable. It addressed itself to what was not the main danger. We had to deal with it as a reality. To a certain extent we had to indulge it, for to neglect it would be to encourage panic and uncertainty among the Western European peoples and to play into the hands of the Communists. But it behooved us to bear in mind that the need for alliances and rearmament in Western Europe was primarily a subjective one, arising from the failure of the Western Europeans to understand correctly their own position. Their best bet was still the struggle for economic recovery and internal political stability. Intensive rearmament represented an uneconomical and regrettable diversion of their effort — a diversion that not only threatened to proceed at the cost of economic recovery but also encouraged the impression that war was inevitable and thus distracted attention from the most important tasks.

I urged, therefore, in conclusion, that while there was need over the long term for some formalization of defense relationships among the littoral countries of the North Atlantic, and while the pact now under consideration would have some value as a short-term reassurance to the Europeans, this pact should not be regarded as the main answer to the Russian effort to achieve domination over Western Europe, nor as a replacement for other needed steps. How pertinent this last formula was to decisions about to be taken will be seen presently, when we turn to the subject of Germany.

In addition to these reflections about the main purpose that such a pact might be expected to serve, I also recommended that it not be our policy to encourage the adherence to it of any country not properly a part of the North Atlantic area. This principle, if adhered to, would of course have excluded Greece and Turkey, and probably Italy as well. The thought behind it was the desirability of avoiding anything that could appear to the Soviet leaders as an aggressive encirclement of their country.

It was true that the regimes in Greece and Turkey were anti-Communist. But to make that, and that alone, a criterion for admission to the pact seemed to me a dangerous precedent. Nor could they — particularly the Turkish government — have qualified for membership on the standard of association with our ideas of democracy and individual liberty. Indeed, this could scarcely be cited as a criterion, in view of the inclusion of Portugal. The only sound standard for membership in the Atlantic pact was indeed the geographic one. This was the only one that was without ambiguity and could clearly be shown to have only defensive connotations. To this day I can see no reason for the admission of Greece and Turkey other than the desire on our part, or rather on the part of certain circles within our government, to have military bases there; and I find it regrettable that we yielded to these impulses. We could perfectly well have made a unilateral declaration of the importance to our security of the integrity of these countries; and within that framework we could have given them whatever military assistance we found it in our interests to give and they found it to their interest to accept. To require them, instead, to undertake an obligation to defend the United States in case of a war between the United States and Russia was not only to prejudice, unnecessarily and unfortunately, their own neighborly relations with the Soviet Union, but also to obscure the purely defensive nature of the pact, and to make a mockery of the term "North Atlantic" that appeared in its title.

In every attempt to define a circle of countries associating together for some political purpose, the greatest difficulty is never whom to include but always whom to exclude. So embarrassing, often, is the latter choice that this constitutes one very good argument against pacts of this nature in general — against any attempt, in other words, to define formally one's circle of friends. There was a tendency in the Department of State at that time, particularly among the gentlemen of the Office of European Affairs, to want to extend this alliance as far as possible — to jam it, so to speak, as close as possible to the Soviet borders. Some pressure was even brought to bear on the Swedes, if I remember correctly, to associate themselves with it. This seemed to me not only unnecessary but undesirable in the extreme. It would unquestionably have prejudiced such possibilities as the Finns possessed of continuing to pursue an independent political life in a neutralized status, and it could easily have led in this way to an actual expansion of the real limits of Soviet power.

Italy was another matter. Our continued military presence there was essential as a condition precedent to the clarification of the questions of Trieste and the Austrian peace treaty. Neither then nor at any later time did I question this necessity. But whether the best way to meet it was to take Italy into a military alliance with ourselves is another matter. Once the whole question of a military alliance between the United States and Western European countries had been raised, it became admittedly difficult to exclude Italy without this having misleading implications that could affect in unfortunate ways the delicate balance of the domestic-political struggle within that country. The best way to meet this problem would have been not to start talking about any North Atlantic alliance in the first place. Italy was, after all, not a member of the Brussels Union. Had we confined our action, in 1948-1949, to a guarantee of the Brussels Union and a military assistance program designed to give its members whatever was necessary to bolster their internal morale (which was, after all, the heart of the matter), the problem of Italy's membership in an Atlantic alliance would not have arisen in the first place.

Actual negotiation of the Atlantic pact was postponed, it will be recalled, until after the election in the autumn of 1948. (It seemed to me in those years that everything was always being postponed either because an election was in the offing or because an election recently held was expected to lead, at some point, to changes in appointments.) When the time finally came to negotiate the actual language of the pact, I found myself — somewhat ironically — appointed by Mr. Lovett to direct, in the capacity of chairman, the deliberations of the international "working group" in which the language of the pact was to be thrashed out. Formal responsibility for this work lay of course with Mr. Lovett; my instructions came from him; at the beginning and end of our labors there were meetings of the senior representatives — in some instances the same as those who functioned in the working group — which Lovett himself chaired; and it is he who deserves whatever credit is due for the successful accomplishment of this negotiating task.

I performed my share of the labor cheerfully and, I believe, satisfactorily. But I was never happy about it. I disliked, in particular, being placed in the position of spokesman for the views of unnamed figures in the legislative branch of our government — views which I could only relay in the most laconic form and the rationale of which I could neither explain nor, to tell the truth, myself accept. If senators were to constitute the final and unchallengeable arbiters of such proceedings, then, it seemed to me, they ought to conduct the negotiations themselves. I can recall an occasion, during one of the main plenary meetings, when some sort of suggestion made by one of the European representatives was crushed, properly and unavoidably, by Mr. Lovett, who said he could assure the gathering that anything in the nature of what had been suggested would be quite unacceptable to the Senate. The objection was final. It produced only a moment of glum silence. I could not help but wish, though, that one of our European friends had stood up at that point and said: "Mr. Lovett, if you and your colleagues in the State Department cannot speak responsibly for American policy in this matter, will you kindly introduce us to the people who can?" Our European friends had a right, it seemed to me, to deal with someone who had some latitude of decision, whose reflections and appreciations were relevant to the process of decision, and with whom it therefore paid to engage in rational discussion and argument.

Russia, winced under every evidence of superficiality and oversimplification in our public and official discussion of German matters,
and suffered from the realization of my own total isolation from
every form of decision-making that related to them.

I had, by this time, come to some rather basic views on the German problem. They revolved around the phenomenon of nationalism as a factor in Germany's experience and behavior. By and large,
it seemed to me, only those people had been able to cope successfully with the emotional power of national feeling who had known
national identity in the dynastic era — in the period before the Napoleonic wars — before the currency of the romantic linguistic nationalism of the nineteenth century. For those who acquired the
sense of national identity after that time, for the Germans in particular, national feeling was heady wine. Prior to the establishment of
the German Reich in 1870, the Germans had been no more and no
less of a problem to their neighbors than anyone else in Europe. It
was their attempt, beginning at that time, to think of themselves as a
single national community, unified on the primitive basis of a common tongue, and competing in this quality with the older established powers of Europe, that had caused the trouble. The great
mistake of the statesmen at Versailles in 1919 had been to reconsti-
tute Germany as a national entity, to give no wider horizon than
the national one to the aspirations of the German people, and at the
same time to set up nothing else in Europe that could rival Germany in physical strength. Now we were faced with this problem
once again. What were we to do this time? The idea of partition —
of breaking the country up once again into a multiplicity of small
sovereign entities, no longer seemed to me realistic. It had appealed
to me in 1942; but I had been obliged to recognize that the experiences of Hitlerism and the war, horrible and tragic as they were,
had probably deepened the sense of national community, and that
to attempt to keep the country partitioned in a Europe where
most other linguistic and ethnic bodies would be unified would
only be to re-create the aspirations and compulsions of the mid-
nineteenth century, and to place a premium on the emergence
of a new Bismarck and a new 1870. But if Germany could not be

broken up — if the problem of German nationalism could not be solved by thrusting Germany farther into the past — then the only thing to do was to thrust both Germany and Europe farther into the future: to create, that is, some sort of a united federal Europe into which the united Germany could be imbedded, and in this way to widen that horizon of aspiration and loyalty which, at its purely linguistic and national limits, had proved too narrow for the safety of Europe, too narrow for the safety of Germany herself. If Germany had to be united, then she must be a part of something larger than herself. A united Germany could be tolerable only as an integral part of a united Europe.

When stationed in Berlin during the war I had been struck with the fact that Hitler himself, albeit for the wrong reasons and in the wrong spirit, had actually accomplished much of the technical task of the unification of Europe. He had created central authorities in a whole series of areas: in transportation, in banking, in procurement and distribution of raw materials, in the control of various forms of nationalized property. Why, I asked myself, could this situation not be usefully exploited after an Allied victory? What was needed was an Allied decision not to smash this network of central controls when the war was ended but rather to take it over, to remove the Nazi officials who had made it work, to appoint others (and not necessarily all non-Germans) in their place, and then to supplement this physical unification with a new European federal authority. When I returned from Germany, in 1942, I tried to win understanding for this idea in the Department of State; but the effort was fruitless. The Russians, determined to exploit the economic potential of Western Germany and Western Europe and fearful of being excluded from having a voice in these regions, would not hear of anything along these lines. No one in Washington was prepared, at that moment, to consider schemes that would clearly be in conflict with Russian wishes. The members of the anti-Nazi resistance movements and exiled governments wanted only to get home and restore the *status quo ante*. And there was FDR's well-known aversion to anything that resembled a discussion of postwar political problems while the war was on. So no serious consideration was given at that time to the problems of postwar European unification as a means of solving the problem of Germany. Instead, one staggered into the post-hostilities period with a set of concepts which envisaged nothing more than an interim period of four-power collaboration in the occupation and military government of a defeated Germany, after which that country was to be restored once more, and launched again onto the sea of international life, as a sovereign entity among others, overshadowing once again all of its neighbors in potential physical strength, and with no higher focus for the collective ideals and aspirations of its people than the framework of German nationalism itself. Whatever elements of insecurity this might involve from the standpoint of the peace of the continent were apparently supposed to be contained and counteracted by the authority of the United Nations, supported by a continued collaboration among the great powers, including Russia and China.

To my own deep despair, this utterly unrealistic concept continued — despite the growing evidence of the unsubstantiality of its assumptions — to inspire American policy down to 1948. It was then modified to the extent that there was a new recognition, flowing from our preoccupation with the problems of European recovery, that Germany's prosperity was vital to the prosperity of Western Europe. But there was little understanding, as yet, of the need for European unification as the only conceivable solution for the problem of Germany's relation to the rest of Europe.

Up to the summer of 1948, policy with relation to Germany remained, after the pattern already noted in the case of Japan, largely the province of the War Department and the military-occupational establishment in Germany. There being no German government with which we could maintain diplomatic relations, the State Department — to my recollection — did not even have a German division at the political level — only an office of sorts for maintenance of liaison with the Pentagon on matters relating to "occupied areas." But the repeated meetings of the Council of Foreign Ministers compelled the Department of State to occupy itself increasingly with the German problem and to take under critical scrutiny the policies that had found their formal adoption at Potsdam. And with the breakdown of the CFM talks at the end of 1947, a new state of affairs was created, in which the responsibility of the Department of State could not fail to become prominently engaged. The demonstration that one could not hope to govern Germany successfully in collaboration with the Russians forced all three of the major Western countries to undertake a reexamination of their concepts and policies. It helped to remove the remaining French inhibitions against association with the British and Americans in the approach to the problem of economic recovery in Germany. And to the British and Americans it carried the connotation that one could no longer delay in proceeding to the establishment in Western Germany of some sort of a German political authority that could share the responsibility for economic recovery and provide a channel, if only initially a limited one, for the reenlistment of a sense of participation and responsibility on the part of the German population of that area. The first moves in this direction took place in the form of British-French-American exploratory discussions held at London in February and March, 1948.

There can be no doubt that, coming as it did on top of the European recovery program and the final elaboration and acceptance of the Atlantic alliance, the move toward establishment of a separate government in Western Germany aroused keen alarm among the Soviet leaders. It was no less than natural that they should do all in their power to frustrate this undertaking and to bring the three Western powers back to the negotiating table in order that Russia might continue to have a voice in all-German affairs. Their effort to do this took the form of the blockade of the Western sectors of Berlin. The first steps in this direction were instituted as early as March 1948, immediately after the first exploratory discussions among the Western powers. And when then, in June, a final round of further London discussions produced a publicly announced agreement — the so-called London Program — on the modalities of procedure looking to the establishment of a separate West German government, and when the Western powers proceeded, as a first step, to set up a separate currency for Western Germany, the Russian response was to make the blockade complete, except of course for the narrowly limited air channels which the Western powers by four-power agreement had the right to use.

The formal pretext for the blockade was the currency question; but actually it was conceived by its Russian authors as a species of squeeze play, designed to place the Western powers before an inescapable choice: either to abandon the great German capital to Communist political control, thus clearly weakening the competitive political attraction of the new regime they were about to set up in Western Germany, or to abandon the London Program in favor of a new round of talks in the CFM and the limitation of further action on Germany to whatever could command Russian agreement. Obviously, the Russians would hold out at any such CFM meeting for arrangements that would place them in a favorable position either to block German recovery or, if it could not be blocked, to assure that it operated to their benefit and not to the benefit of European recovery generally.

It was clear from the start that the Western powers might at some point find it necessary or expedient to agree to another meeting of the CFM in the interests of the removal of the blockade. (This was, indeed, what finally occurred in the spring of 1949.) It was impossible to know at the outset when such a development might occur; it could come at any time. There was thus urgent need for preparation of a new American negotiating position on the German problem, to be put forward if and when another CFM took place. The old one, plainly, would no longer do. At the end of 1947, at the last CFM meeting, the ministers had still been talking in terms of the conclusion of a treaty of peace with Germany and the establishment of an all-German government under Allied control, which would then sign the treaty and gradually take over responsibility for the conduct of German life. But now, by midsummer 1948, things had changed. The West Germans were already well launched on preparations for the election of the constituent assembly which, under the new London Program, was to devise the political framework for a purely West German government. Would we still wish, in these circumstances, to continue to talk with the Russians about an all-German solution? Would this not disorganize the procedures now in process of implementation under the London Program? But if not, what *would* we propose? And to what extent, in formulating new proposals, would we wish to take account of the precariousness of the situation of the Western sectors of Berlin, as illustrated by the blockade now in progress? Could we in fact, in the light of this situation, afford *not* to arrive at some broad general agreement with the Russians?

In the early days of July 1948, on the heels of the imposition by the Russians of the full blockade, the Planning Staff was charged with the study of these questions. Assisted by representatives from the State Department offices and from the War Department, we struggled with this task through the hot days of Washington's midsummer. The urgency of the exercise was emphasized by the preoccupation of everyone with the immediate problems imposed by the blockade. Night after night, several of us gathered in the communication center of the department to receive the latest news from Germany and to exchange views with General Clay and his advisors about our next move. No one was sure, as yet, how the Russian move could be countered or whether it could be successfully countered at all. The situation was dark, and full of danger. A tremendous premium appeared to rest on any new arrangements that would free Berlin from the virtual embrace of Russian military forces and make impossible the imposition of another blockade. To some of us on the Planning Staff, the possibilities for resolving the conflict in any satisfactory way by arrangements affecting only Berlin itself — by ones, that is, which would leave the Russians astride of Berlin's communication with the West — appeared to be small. The best prospects for solving the problem seemed to lie along the lines of a new arrangement for Germany as a whole that would involve retirement of the Russian forces from the entire area

around Berlin and make possible the establishment of normal communications between that city and the rest of Germany. Were
there, then, proposals along this line that might conceivably be put
forward by the United States government in the CFM — proposals
that would be sound in themselves, that we could live with if accepted by others, and that offered some possibility of at least eventual acceptance by the Russians? This was our problem. The results
of our preliminary inquiry suggested that there might well be such
proposals, although it would take time, and further study, to work
them out.

But did our government really wish to proceed along this line?
An important question of principle was involved. To make a new
attack on the problem of an all-German, four-power settlement
would imply a readiness to suspend the London Program during
negotiations, and to abandon it in the event negotiations should be
successful. If, on the other hand, we abandoned the effort to
achieve an all-German settlement, continued to pursue a solution to
the Berlin problem only within the framework of Berlin itself, and
contented ourselves otherwise with the elaboration and implementation of the London Program, the Russians would set up a rival
government in Eastern Germany; the fight would be on for fair;
the division of Germany, and with it the division of Europe itself,
would tend to congeal and to become more difficult of removal
with the passage of time. There would, furthermore, be no real and
permanent solution to the Berlin problem if this alternative was
adopted.

In a paper presented in mid-August, I brought this question to
the attention of my governmental superiors, and pointed out that
we really ought to have an indication of their preference before
proceeding with further planning for another CFM. No such indication was forthcoming. The query evoked, so far as its substance
was concerned, only a troubled and thoughtful silence. We were
encouraged, however — or permitted, at least — to continue our
exploration of what, hypothetically, another American proposal
for an all-German solution might look like, in the event we should

wish to press for a settlement of this nature. The study occupied us for some weeks. It included tapping the expertise and judgment of qualified experts within the government as well as a number of distinguished outsiders.

On November 15, we submitted the results of our work. We described the nature of the problem as we saw it. We presented a detailed "package" of proposals entitled "Plan A," to be put forward in the event we wished to push for a general German settlement. And we gave our own views as to which alternative might best be chosen.

The problem, we reiterated in this paper, was whether to come forward, at an eventual new CFM, with a positive program making clear the terms on which we would be prepared to consider the establishment of an all-German government and withdrawal of Allied forces from the major part of Germany, or whether we should rest on a purely negative position, advancing no positive proposals of our own and leaving it to the Russians to make proposals which we would then presumably decline on an ad hoc basis.

Plan A was conceived as a set of proposals to be put forward in the event we chose the first of these courses. It ran substantially as follows:

There would first have to be agreement on a new four-power control machinery to supervise the workings of the program. Here, we would have to insist that there be no individual veto power. The entrance into operation of the new control machinery would be followed by the early election and establishment of a provisional German government. These elections would take place under international supervision, exercised uniformly in all four zones. Simultaneously with the establishment of the provisional government, military government would cease and Allied forces would be withdrawn to garrison areas, within Germany but on its periphery. They would be so located that the lines of communication to and from them would not have to pass over German territory. It was suggested that the British area might be near Hamburg, the American near Bremen, and the Russian near Stettin, with access, in each case, to deep-water port facilities. The French area, on the other hand, would be adjacent to the French frontier and accessible directly from French territory. The territory thus liberated from Allied occupation (which would of course include most of Germany, and with it Berlin) would come under the administration of the new provisional German government. Elaborate safeguards were envisaged against any misuse of the German police by extremist elements of either right or left in the process of transition from military government to the establishment of a central German political authority. Timing and phasing of the individual elements of the program were so adjusted as to allow no opportunity at any point for control or undue influence of the transitional process from any side by undemocratic methods. Provision was made for the continued complete demilitarization of Germany.

Our recommendation was that in the event that a new CFM meeting should take place in the near future, our government should advance something along the lines of Plan A, provided we could get a sufficient measure of agreement to it on the part of the British and the French. We saw no satisfactory alternative. Merely to ask for the extension of the London Program to all of Germany, as others wished to do, did not seem to us to represent a satisfactory alternative. The London Program envisaged continuing supervision of German political life by an Allied high commission. This would scarcely be feasible on a four-power basis. The London Program also envisaged the retention of occupying forces in the various zones. But the authority of a non-Communist German government could never be effectively asserted, we thought, over an Eastern zone occupied by Soviet forces. The arrangements envisaged in the London Program were therefore simply not suitable as the basis for an all-German settlement. Something along the lines of Plan A, even if not immediately acceptable to the Russians (and we did not suppose that it would be), would at least serve to hold open the door for an eventual peaceful withdrawal of the Russians from the heart of Germany. Unless this door was held open by means of some sort of positive proposals on our part along these lines, the Russians might not feel able to withdraw even if a time should come when they would like to. Our position, we explained, was deeply affected by the impression we had gained that the Western position in Berlin could never be a comfortable one, and the people of the Western sectors as well as the Western garrisons there would be living constantly on the edge of an abyss, so long as the territory around the city remained under Russian occupation and Communist authority.

I must stress again — for this was in our view a vitally important feature of the recommendations — that we envisaged that these proposals would be put forward in the CFM only after careful and confidential exploration with the French and British and only in the event the latter were willing to go along with them. I was repeatedly asked, in the weeks that followed presentation of this paper, what we would do in case the French and British would not go along. My answer was that we would then not press the project but that we would place upon the French and British governments the onus of taking the lead in devising some other Western position; we would say to them, in effect: this is our best suggestion; if you don't like it, it is up to you to name the alternative, bearing in mind the urgent and pressing need for a solution to the Berlin problem; the main responsibility is now yours.

I was also asked, of course, what we would do if the French and British accepted the idea but the Russians — as was indeed to be expected — did not. My answer was that we would then proceed to implement the London Program (always assuming, of course, that we could find some other solution to the problem of the Berlin blockade), but that we would hold the offer open. In this way, we would place upon the Russians the onus of bringing about the final split of Germany, just as we had done in the case of the Marshall Plan with relation to all of Europe. We would then at least have named the terms on which we were prepared to agree to a removal of the division of Germany; we would have made it evident that we were not averse on principle to its removal. We would avoid the misunderstanding that could arise if we put forward proposals which appeared to offer no serious possibility for overcoming the division. By this means, the door would remain open for an eventual settlement; and we would guard against the propagandistic effect of any proposals for an all-German solution that the Russians might themselves put forward.

* * *

Around the turn of the year 1948-1949 General Marshall's place was taken by Mr. Dean Acheson. I had met him in earlier years, and had been associated with him briefly in 1947, before he retired (summer of 1947) from the position of Under Secretary of State. Now, on assuming the office of Secretary of State, he told me that he hoped I would remain, at least for the immediate future, in my position as director of the Planning Staff, and this I gladly agreed to do.

My relations with Mr. Acheson in the ensuing period were always agreeable. I respected and admired him, enjoyed his company, and profited constantly from exposure to the critical discipline of his fine mind. Realizing, as did all who knew him well, that he was a man of complete integrity — that the United States never had, in fact, a more honorable public servant — I resented the outrageous attacks directed against him at that time by certain congressional circles and portions of the press, and admired the dignity and fortitude with which he bore them. Our relations were then still untroubled by the difficulties over European policy that were to come out in the public discussions in later years.

Nevertheless, with Mr. Acheson's advent to the position of Secretary, there was a perceptible change in the position and the possibilities of the Planning Staff. He was a man who dealt, in his inner world, not with institutions but with personalities; and he was not always, I thought, a good judge of the latter. My Foreign Service experience was not only strange to him but was in his eyes, I suspect, of dubious value as a preparation for statesmanship or anything else. Although it was in the position of director of the Planning Staff that he asked me to remain, he saw me only as an individual — as one, in fact, of a group of individuals whom he had around him and with whom he liked to explore ideas — people of quite heterogeneous background and outlook, to whose disparate views he listened as might a judge to the arguments of opposing counsel. The thought of consulting the staff as an institution and conceding to it, as did General Marshall, a margin of confidence within which he was willing to respect its opinion even when that opinion did not fully coincide with his own — the thought, in particular, of conceding to the staff a certain function as the ideological inspirer and coordinator of policy, bringing into coherent interrelationship the judgments and efforts of the various geographic and functional divisions of the department — all this would have been strange to him. By such views as I had to voice in our oral discussions he was, I suspect, sometimes amused, sometimes appalled, usually interested; but there were times when I felt like a court jester, expected to enliven discussion, privileged to say the shocking things, valued as an intellectual gadfly on hides of slower colleagues, but not to be taken fully seriously when it came to the final, responsible decisions of policy.

* * *

Over the ensuing winter of 1948-1949 the operational levels of our government were fully occupied with the mounting and maintaining of the airlift as a means of frustrating the blockade, and with the implementation of the London Program. In this last, their efforts were of course merged with those of the French and British and the Germans themselves. The West German political leaders were busy, over the winter, with the drawing up of a constitution for the new West German state. The three Allied powers were busy working out a new occupation statute, to come into effect when the West German government was established. These procedures were elaborate; the attendant negotiations were difficult and full of anguish. As the process went forward, it gained steadily in momentum and in the aura of legitimacy. People's *amour propre* as well as their enthusiasms became engaged. There was growing personal commitment to what was being accomplished. Increasingly, as the months and weeks went by, the undertaking assumed in many minds an irrevocable character; and the idea of suspending or jeopardizing it for the sake of wider international agreement became for these people less and less acceptable. Once again, as is so often the case in American diplomacy, what was conceived as an instrument became, little by little, an end in itself. What was supposed to have been the servant of policy became its determinant instead.

In view of this preoccupation of our senior figures with the airlift and the London Program, and in the absence, as yet, of any agreement with the Russians on the convening of a new meeting of the CFM, the question raised by the Planning Staff concerning our position at an eventual meeting of this nature was placed, over the winter, on the "back burner." No formal decision was taken as to which course we would follow. Actually, of course, our position was being determined for us, from day to day, by the steady growth in the degree and solemnity of our commitment to the London Program.

I yielded to no one in my admiration for the achievement of the airlift. For the London Program, on the other hand, I could develop no interest or enthusiasm. This was partly because I recognized that it provided no basis at all for negotiation with the Russians, and meant in effect the abandonment of hope for any early removal of the division of Germany and the continent. But it was also because this program was, intellectually and in concept, the child of our occupational establishment in Germany. It was to be implemented under supervision of that establishment. It allowed for the establishment's continued existence and authority, even after the new West German government had been set up.

This was an establishment for which I had an almost neurotic distaste. I had been twice in Germany since the termination of hostilities. Each time I had come away with a sense of sheer horror at the spectacle of this horde of my compatriots and their dependents camping in luxury amid the ruins of a shattered national community, ignorant of the past, oblivious to the abundant evidences of present tragedy all around them, inhabiting the very same sequestered villas that the Gestapo and SS had just abandoned, and enjoying the same privileges, flaunting their silly supermarket luxuries in the face of a veritable ocean of deprivation, hunger, and wretchedness, setting an example of empty materialism and cultural poverty before a people desperately in need of spiritual and intellectual guidance, taking for granted — as though it were their natural due — a disparity in privilege and comfort between themselves and their German neighbors no smaller than those that had once divided lord and peasant in that feudal Germany which it had been our declared purpose in two world wars to destroy. That many Germans merited punishment was clear; but their delinquency was not the proof of our virtue. Nor was all that had gone down in the wreckage of Germany valueless or evil. Much — sickeningly much — that was innocent and precious had gone down with the rest. This was, however one viewed it, a tragedy of appalling dimensions. In the presence of this tragedy even the victors had, to my mind, a certain duty of self-effacement and humility. Perhaps it was necessary and unavoidable that so much should be destroyed that did not deserve to be destroyed; but if so, it was a profoundly tragic necessity; and we should ourselves have been sobered, saddened, and hushed by the realization that it was we who had been chosen by the Almighty to be the agents of it. To see so many of our people flaunting in the face of these reminders their smugness, their superficiality, their lack of imagination, and their preoccupation with the creature comforts was to me unendurable. I could not accustom myself to it. The tragedy of the decent Germany was in just sufficient degree my own tragedy that I could not close my eyes to it. That I overreacted is possible. That I could not react otherwise, and that this affected my political views, is clear.

In March 1949, anxious to refresh my impression of occupied Germany and to test my thought on the problems of policy, I paid a brief visit to Berlin, Frankfurt, and Hamburg. The diary notes of this visit are too voluminous to be reproduced here in full, but some of them may serve to illustrate the various factors and considerations that were at stake in the decisions of those crucial months.

I arrived in Berlin — on one of the airlift planes, of course — on the evening of March 12, and was driven

. . . through dark, deserted streets to the Harnack House — now an American club and guest house. The city seemed dead — a ghost of its former self.

Harnack House, brightly illuminated, stood out in the darkness like a garish honkey-tonkey that has stayed open too late in a sleepy provincial town. It was Saturday night. The thumping of dance music oozed out with the shafts of light from the windows of the building. Cars were lined up on the street and the little band of German chauffeurs, stamping up and down and muttering in the cold night air, seemed like an evil caricature of the bundled Russian coachmen of olden times, waiting for their masters outside the nightclubs of St. Petersburg and Moscow.

Inside, the lounge had that deserted and unappreciated air of most clubrooms in the evening; but the dining room had more life. It was equipped with candles in recognition of the festivity of the occasion (Saturday night). A German band was faithfully whacking out American dance tunes which they knew by heart. The faces of the musicians were drawn and worn, and so wearily deadpan that you could not tell whether they failed to see the colonels and the OMGUS civilians and their ladies who danced before them or whether they saw them and just didn't care. Plainly, they were interested in neither the occasion nor the music they were playing. Both were something inflicted upon them by others. Not theirs to reason why.

The patrons were generally decorous and well behaved. Only at one table, where they were having a birthday party, a major was raising his voice to command attention, and his monologue cut through the music and the murmur of conversation: "Look what's on de menu. Tuna fish. Tuna fish, for God's sake. We been feedin' it to our dog. He don't even like it any more. He jes' looks at me and says: 'Jeez, tuna fish again.'"

Late in the evening I took a long walk. The streets were silent and empty and utterly dark. This was the once fashionable suburb of Dahlem. The private villas — those which had escaped the bombing — stood out dimly in the shadows. What pretense, what eager hopes, what plans for personal happiness and prosperity lay behind the building of each of these houses? Whatever were these hopes and plans, they were now dashed. Today the villas stood mute and dark and cold. If Germans lived in them at all, they camped in them like barbarians in the palaces of Italy. There seemed little prospect of doing anything else. It was hard to tell whether this was in itself good or bad, deserved or undeserved. Whatever it was, every one of those dim architectural forms spelled a broken dream, spelled one more bit of frustration for people who had once felt the call of hope and initiative. However you looked at it, it seemed a pity.

Back in the club, I could not sleep. From my window, I watched the events of the night. In little groups, the guests emerged and departed in their cars. The last lingering lieutenant found his way into his jeep. Finally the musicians assembled, with great grumbling and scolding of their own latecomers, and rode off in an incredibly overloaded jalopy over which they appeared to dispose. And then the tall bare poplars, the same patient poplars which had waited and watched through the final years of the Weimar Republic and the Nazi era and the war and the bombings and the arrival of the Russian army, stood alone again through another night, until the battered cars of the first early subway train came clattering past through the open cut, a few yards away, and the sky lightened to the dawn of a gray, soggy March Sunday over airlift Berlin.

The following afternoon, a friend invited me to his home, to meet Ernest Reuter, then mayor of West Berlin. We picked him up at his home out near Wannsee and drove him to my friend's house in Dahlem. I had never met him before. He was, I noted,

a big man, clean-shaven and somewhat bejowled, with blue rings of fatigue under his eyes. He had just returned that afternoon from the Constituent Assembly at Bonn.

We sat in the window niche of the living room and drank tea. Beyond the windows, the Scotch pines, rising tall and erect from the melting snow, presided somberly over the conversation.

They were holding the line, he said, in Berlin. This was the hardest time of the year. Fresh food was at its lowest. The grippe season was upon them. But morale could be maintained as long as we Americans evidenced determination to remain.

The housing shortage was not really so bad in Berlin as in the Western zones. Berlin had lost 40 percent of its housing but also 25 percent of its population.

He saw no objections to dealings with the Russians about Berlin, provided we first created the requisite bargaining power. For this, we would have to install the Western Mark as the sole currency in the Western sectors and demonstrate that the airlift could hold an average of 8000 tons a day. Only then would the Russians believe that we had a real alternative to accepting eventually their terms, and only then would they do business with us seriously.

As for Western Germany, the youth was all right: it was the older people in whose minds and hearts Nazism still held sway. But youth was skeptical and suspicious about the old-line German politicians who headed the parties in Western Germany. He could not blame them. Those politicians were shortsighted and had learned little from experience. They were spoiled by having operated so long in the vacuum of irresponsibility. Only by having responsibility thrust upon them could they be brought down to earth; until then they would only sit around and dispute and criticize. Therefore, some form of German government was necessary, and the sooner the better.

But we should not, he begged us, rearm the Germans — not under any circumstances. I assured him that we had no intention of doing so, but he remained plainly unconvinced. There was too much talk about it among our own military people in Germany.

Darkness had now fallen. Reuter left. His place was taken by dinner guests, this time from the foreign colony. I had known them before, at another post. With their arrival, talk turned to the usual foreign colony gossip and chitchat. Forgotten were the ruin and desolation outside, forgotten — the two and a half million people who lived round about in hardship and uncertainty, forgotten — the great planes whose motors could be heard overhead at exact intervals of three minutes as they swept through the rain and the gloom. I marveled at the stubborn inertia of the social habits of us Anglo-Saxons, and asked myself the despairing question: How many more catastrophes would yet have to occur, how many more cities would have to be smashed, how much more horrible and insistent would have to become the visible evidences of cruelty and suffering in this world before we could be brought to stop handing each other drinks and discussing through the long evenings the price of antiques, the inadequacies of servants, and the availability of cosmetics in the PX.

After a couple of days in Berlin, I flew to Frankfurt, to attend various meetings of the High Commissioners among themselves and with senior German officials. To me, the spectacle of these latter meetings — the unlimited power of the one side and the abjectness of the other, was distasteful; but as among the various Allied officials involved, I felt a certain pride in our own. They struck me as the most serious, competent, and businesslike of the lot; and they made no effort to emphasize their position of power, or to preen themselves about it. They must, I thought, be the easiest ones for the Germans to deal with in the personal sense, though sometimes maddeningly naïve.

I took occasion, while in Frankfurt, to have a long talk with an old Berlin acquaintance, now an American citizen — a man of great experience and power of discrimination, who had been observing the sessions of the German Constituent Assembly. He, although himself a Berliner by birth, warned me against giving too much weight to the plight of Berlin and being thus pushed into the acceptance of a hasty unification of the country. The thought of trying abruptly to unite the two existing Germanies, already so different in social composition and habits, seemed to him full of danger. In the Soviet zone there had been, he said,

. . . something in the nature of a real social revolution. This was the only place in Germany where feudalism had been really done away with. This had been done brutally and destructively, and nothing positive had been put in its place; but it *had* been done. The ground had been broken. If an attempt were now made to reunite the Soviet zone with the rest of Germany, a civil war would ensue worse than that which had taken place in Spain. Neither the USSR nor the Western powers would be able to afford to see their friends defeated. They would therefore be forced to intervene. It would be the end of Germany and probably of Western European civilization. We should, therefore, make a virtue of necessity and cling to the split Germany as the only hope for the consolidation of Western Europe. A reunited Germany would probably be indigestible in Europe. The addition of Eastern-zone extremism to the ingredients already present in Western Germany would produce a political pattern too far from Western concepts to be acceptable. He said this with regret, as one who had been born a German.

Viewed unsentimentally, Berlin ought to be abandoned. It was not necessary as a German capital. Its retention had been illogical ever since the beginning of the cold war. Of course, it was true that this was perhaps psychologically impractical. There was no use underrating the bitterness of such a step. Not only the Western-sector politicians would be the victims. All the police of the Western sectors would likewise end up in Communist concentration camps.

Asked about Russian political capabilities for mischief with respect to Germany, he did not see much that they could do about frontiers unless they wanted again to profit from the ruins of the Polish state; but they had a very effective and powerful weapon in the question of the refugees. If they were to offer (or permit the German SED to offer in their name) a return of the refugees to their homelands, this would be popular with everyone in Germany: refugees and natives alike. Few could resist such a temptation. Furthermore, he thought the Communists still had interesting possibilities in the Ruhr. The feelings of the labor groups in that region were such that it would not take much to push them into a violent anti-Western attitude.

From Berlin, I went on to Hamburg. There I had a whole series of interviews, all interesting and revealing. Not all can be mentioned here. There was one man whom I described in my notes as "an editor, a half-Jew, who had been long in the emigration . . . a tall, thin man in whose sunken burning eyes there were the traces of long-suffering and thought."

He spoke about the youth. He felt, like others, that it was all right. It was the older people in whom the dangerous aspects of German chauvinism still resided. Youth saw no hopes. It had no prospects. In general, it wished to emigrate. For these young people, Germany was no longer a national home; it was a national prison. But even if emigration were permitted, those who left would turn out to be the enterprising and imaginative ones, and, above all, the young men. What good could this do for a country already staggering under a surplus of women and old people?

He spoke again with a sad sort of bitterness of Allied policy. To what avail this timidity, these halfway measures? Germans would remain unrealistic until they felt the bite of real responsibility.

In particular, he pleaded for the end of denazification: for some sort of amnesty which would finish the subject once and for all. He felt the issues involved in the determination of the guilt of persons with former Nazi associations too subtle, too subjective, too little susceptible of verbal classification to be a fit subject for legal procedure. The law, he said, must deal with clear and unambiguous situations of fact; it must not work with rubber concepts. The law must have validity without exception or not at all. Had we not had enough of this misconceived evil which had now been dragging along for years and the end of which was not yet in sight? Had we not already learned that it was not even possible to treat Nazism as a question of fact before the civil courts, to say nothing of committees of laymen, unfamiliar with the law? Every effort in this direction added new injustice to old injustice, new discord to old discord. We had to get used to the fact that it was impossible to scrape together before the courts a sufficient quantity of guilt and of culprits to compensate for the enormous crime that had been committed. The scales would come into balance only when a vast measure of human error and of human weakness had been added on the other side. But error and weakness should not be hailed before the courts of this world; for when one did this, one came nearer to revenge than to the law.

My next visitor was the mayor of Hamburg, Brauer. I described him as a "stocky, strongly built, blond man who looked as though he might have come from my native city of Milwaukee." This American aspect, I added,

was not misleading: he had indeed lived for years in the US and had at one time become an American citizen. He had come back after the war to assume this heavy and ungrateful office. He was, of course, an old Social Democrat. This alone made it possible for him to occupy this position in the socialistic city of Hamburg. The overtone of sadness and helplessness with which he spoke was ample proof to me that he was not remaining in this job for motives of personal ambition.

Fifty-two percent of Hamburg's housing, he said, had been destroyed. The population had at one time been reduced to one-half but had since increased again rapidly and was now nearing the prewar level of 1,600,000. An average of 6000 refugees were reaching the city per month, absorbing all the new housing that could be constructed, although building was proceeding at the peak prewar level. Every time he got something built, and a few people moved out of shacks and bunkers into houses, the shacks and bunkers were promptly filled with new arrivals from the Soviet zone. The port was working at 32 percent of normal capacity, although it had been restored to a potential handling capacity of 50 percent. There was not much hope of increasing this figure. The hinterland was gone. Ship-building was, of course, barred outside of minor exceptions. The great adjacent industrial district of Harburg had largely been laid waste by the bombings. In these circumstances the actual productive base of the city was far too slim for the enormous pyramid of population which rested upon it.

Employment was being kept up, but by what means? Captains with long experience on ocean-going vessels were working as streetcar conductors. Thirty-six thousand people were employed by the British, but at the cost of the municipality.

He was optimistic about the cold war. He thought we were winning it faster than was apparent. On the other hand, we were making a great mistake about the Western German government. Not only would we have to give to the central authority a workable portion of power vis-à-vis the *Länder*, but we would have to give the Germans real power in the economic field, if any good were to come of all this. And we ought also to drop the reeducation program, which was a farce and was influencing the Germans in exactly the wrong way. All in all, he had one great plea to make to the West: Let the Germans work.

The following day I was driven around Hamburg and given a tour, in particular, of the bombed-out areas. The spectacle was not a nice one to see, not a nice one to think about. "Here was sweeping devastation, down to the ground, mile after mile." It had all been done in three days and nights in 1943. Seventy thousand human beings had been killed in the process. More than three thousand bodies were estimated to be still in the rubble. I had experienced myself the first sixty of the British raids on Berlin, and had seen — since the end of the war — plenty of ruins; but these hit me particularly hard.

In the ruins of Berlin, there had seemed to be a certain tragic majesty. Berlin had been a great cold city, an imperial city, haughty and pretentious. Such cities invited the wrath of gods and men.

But poor old Hamburg: this comfortable, good-humored, seaport community, dedicated, like so many of our own cities, to the common sense humdrum of commerce and industry — for Hamburg, it seemed a great pity.

Here, for the first time, I felt an unshakable conviction that no momentary military advantage — even if such could have been calculated to exist — could have justified this stupendous, careless destruction of civilian life and of material values, built up laboriously by human hands over the course of centuries for purposes having nothing to do with war. Least of all could it have been justified by the screaming non sequitur: "They did it to us." And it suddenly appeared to me that in these ruins there was an unanswerable symbolism which we in the West could not afford to ignore. If the Western world was really going to make valid the pretense of a higher moral departure point — of greater sympathy and understanding for the human being as God made him, as expressed not only in himself but in the things he had wrought and cared about — then it had to learn to fight its wars morally as well as militarily, or not fight them at all; for moral principles were a part of its strength. Shorn of this strength, it was no longer itself; its victories were not real victories; and the best it would accomplish in the long run would be to pull down the temple over its own head. The military would stamp this as naïve; they would say that war is war, that when you're in it you fight with every means you have, or go down in defeat. But if that is the case, then there rests upon Western civilization, bitter as this may be, the obligation to be militarily stronger than its adversaries by a margin sufficient to enable it to dispense with those means which can stave off defeat only at the cost of undermining victory.

These were thoughts that were to pursue me into the trials and problems of future years: into arguments in Washington as to whether we should commit ourselves to the development of the hydrogen bomb, into the BBC Reith lectures of 1957 in which I inveighed against basing the defenses of the continental NATO members on nuclear missiles, into senatorial hearings of 1966 and 1967 where talk turned on the bombing of North Vietnam.

From Hamburg, I went on to Bremen. There I sat in the consul's home and talked with the president of the Bremen senate.

He was a strong, simple, quiet man, with old-fashioned, drooping moustaches: a farmer by origin, and a member of the pre-1914 generation. After his original imprisonment by the Nazis, at the outset of the Hitler era, he had gone back to the country and had worked the land, silently and patiently, for twelve years, paying no attention whatsover to politics. Called back to political life after the defeat, he had dropped his tools and returned, with equal simplicity and resolution, to take the top job in the Bremen enclave.

He spoke with a sad humor about the troubles of administering Bremen under our tutelage.

Military government told them they had to extend the basic grade school term from four to six years. They were not objecting. They would do it. But they wanted to do it gradually. The parents of the present fourth-year class weren't used to the idea. They had started their kids out on a different understanding. He had therefore asked military government whether they might not have a transition period. The answer had been no; they had to do it all right now.

Again: they had night school courses for ordinary workers — eight hours per week. Military government had come along and said this was not enough. They had to add eight hours of civics per week, thus doubling the scope of the course.

They did not have the buildings or the teachers to carry out these reforms. The city council was opposed to them. . . . It was embarrassing him with the council.

I asked the consul, who was sitting with us, just who it was in the military government who was handling these matters and giving these orders. He stated that it was the head of the educational section of the military government apparatus for the Bremen enclave. I asked what his background was. He was a high school teacher from Indiana. Was he a man of understanding and competence? The consul was taken aback by this question. He was, he replied, a good high school teacher in Indiana.

The president of the senate continued his story. The gas plant had been destroyed by the bombings. There was a shortage of fuel for homes; it was important to get the plant going again. It was owned by the city and had been operated before the war as a commercial enterprise. Its financial accounts were not part of the city budget. He now wanted to rebuild it, and the postal system was willing to lend him

10 million Marks for this purpose. Eventually the debt would be amortized from profits. But military government had now vetoed this. If the plant was to be reconstructed, it had, they said, to be done out of taxes. Now the Germans were stymied. They had enough financial troubles without adding another 10 million Marks to the tax burden.

"What," he said, "do you really want me to do? If you insist I can act like the Japanese. I can smile and bow and tell you that of course all this will be done just as you wish it. Then I can fuzz up actual performance in such a way that you will not know just what we really did do. In other words, I can pretend to comply, if that will make your people happier. But I do not want to deal with you in that way. I don't enjoy it myself. And in the long run no good will come of it."

I returned to Berlin more oppressed than ever with the realization of the enormity of the responsibility we had incurred and of our inadequacy to it.

It was a Sunday noon when I got back to the city. My official hosts were away for the weekend and I availed myself joyfully of the opportunity to walk around the place alone, incognito, and to feel myself once again a part of its ordinary life.

Despite occasional snow flurries, the weather was brighter than last week. It was suddenly the difference between winter and spring. The heavens were no longer all one tone. There were dark clouds and light clouds; and between them gleamed a new sky — the pale blue sky of spring, in the existence of which one had almost ceased to believe in the endless, dragging northern winter.

Even the children noticed it. On my way to the subway station, I passed three of them, walking an Airedale dog. "Oh look," the little boy was saying, "the dark cloud is the night fairy and the light cloud is the day fairy." The Airedale caught the hope and excitement in the boy's tone, looked eagerly at the others, and strained at the leash to show that he was one of the gang and ready for anything.

(You are right, my little fellow — I thought to myself — there is a day fairy and a night fairy, a light cloud and a dark cloud. And which of these clouds will hang over you and overshadow your life in the days of your maturity — which fairy will wield the wand over you — is the great question. The answer will depend partly on you, since none of us is without will and responsibility who is not completely a prisoner. But it will depend more on us Americans. For we have won great wars and assumed to ourselves great powers. And we have thus become the least free of all peoples. We have placed upon ourselves the obligation to have the answers; and anyone can come up and put a nickel in us and ask for an answer, and the rules of the game require us to give one. This, too, you will eventually discover; and, according to the answer we give, you may get mostly the day fairy or mostly the night fairy, hovering over yourself and your future. And I'd watch that one, if I were you, come to think of it; because we aren't too sure about all these things ourselves.)

It was the children, out in force, playing in the ruins, building dams out of bits of rubble in the flowing gutters, that monopolized my attention that afternoon, made me realize how profound had been the despair of recent days, and introduced a first faint note of hope. If only somehow, I thought to myself, "the inward influences of health and hope" could be brought to these children,

if it could be shown to them that somewhere, at the end of that faint rainbow that actually hovered over them on this afternoon whenever the March sun penetrated the snow flurries, there were such things as freedom and security and rewards for work accomplished and the chance to walk down the broad vistas of beauty and warmth in the human spirit: if these things could be done, then the ruins, like the charm of a wicked sorcerer, would lose their power over these children, and the day fairy would once again come into her own.

But whence was all this to come? From the parents? The parents were stoical and hardened, purged of many of their erstwhile illusions, but still bewildered, unenlightened, with a terribly restricted field of vision. From us Americans? We were doing our best. But we had no answers, yet, to the great political insecurity which hung over this area. And our own vision was clouded by our habits, our comforts, our false and corrupting position as conquerors and occupiers.

The following day was my last day in Germany. I flew to Frankfurt, had further interviews in the morning, and went out in the afternoon to the VIP guest house in the Taunus Mountains to rest. They were the same mountains where, fourteen years earlier, we internees had spent the dark hard winter of 1941-1942. Then, in the late afternoon, I drove down out of the hills to take the night train for Paris.

It had been a fine sunny day — the first day of good weather since I came to Germany. Now, although darkness had fallen, the sky was still bright in the west and the stars were out. In the villages, people were out strolling, enjoying the first evening of fine spring weather. There was brisk vehicular traffic all along the road, and most of it German. I thought of the whole bizonal area stretching off behind us in the dusk; and it seemed to me that you could hear the great low murmur of human life beginning to stir again, beginning to recapture the rhythm of work and life and change, after years of shock and prostration. Here were tens of millions of human beings, of all ages and walks of life, reacting, as human beings always have and must, to the myriad of stimuli of heredity and education and climate and economic necessity and emotion. Whatever we did, they would no longer stand still in thought or in outlook. Nothing could keep them from seeking again some outlet for the basic need of the human being to feel that he is doing something important and fruitful and necessary.

Would we be able to feel our way into this sea of human reaction and human will, heretofore so repugnant, so little interesting to us? Would we be able to realize that we are the doctor on whose understanding the recovery and health of this patient depend, without which recovery and health there may be no unity and no success for the Western world? Would we be able to steer its development into co-operative and constructive lines? Would we be able to give to it the sense of participation, the sense of being needed, which it so desperately required? Or would we turn our backs upon it in anger and revulsion, and leave it no choice but to grow again outside of us and against us, in the spirit of those bitter lines by Goethe with which the German Communist Party once used to close its meetings:

> *Du muss herrschen und gewinnen*
> *Oder dienen und verlieren,*

Leiden oder triumphieren,
Amboss oder Hammer sein? *

*   *   *

While I was paying this visit to Germany, the first signs became apparent of a readiness on the part of the Russians to desist from the blockade. On January 30, Stalin, in a statement made to a Western journalist, had mentioned as a precondition for abandonment of the blockade only the suspension (not even the permanent abandonment) of the plans for establishment of a West German government, and had omitted to mention the difficult currency problem which, up to that time, the Russians had allowed to appear as a principal formal impediment to agreement. Professor Philip Jessup, then serving as a sort of ambassador-at-large to the Secretary of State, had inquired on Mr. Acheson's behalf of Mr. Jacob Malik, Soviet representative at the United Nations, whether the omission had been accidental. Mr. Malik, after communicating with his government, had replied, on March 15, that it had not been. Further confidential exchanges, pursued by both men with skill and discretion, then ensued. They culminated at the end of April in an agreement which envisaged both the termination of the blockade and the early convening of a new meeting of the CFM. This last, it was finally arranged, should take place on May 23.

The imminence of a CFM meeting necessarily reactivated the question of what position we should adopt on the German problem as a whole. The matter was exhaustively treated in the press; and there were the usual intensive discussions within our governmental establishment. In these last, Plan A occasionally popped up and figured — as a curiosity of sorts — among the various alternatives. At no time did it have any serious chance of adoption. The London Program, now that the CFM meeting was upon us, was being rushed frantically to completion with the scarcely concealed intention that it should stand as a *fait accompli* before the Big Four for-

---

* *You must rule and win*
  Or serve and lose,
  Suffer or triumph,
  Be anvil or be hammer.

eign ministers. Its numerous authors clung to it like a mother to a child. Now that so much effort had gone into it, and now that its final realization was at hand, it seemed to them doubly unthinkable that anyone should contemplate jeopardizing it by pursuing other possible solutions in talks with the Russians, particularly since it was evident that the latter were now disposed to remove the Berlin blockade anyway. General Lucius Clay, just at that time retiring in a blaze of well-deserved glory from the position of commander in Germany which he had filled so long and with such distinction, prized the London Program particularly and regarded its final adoption, in the face of formidable difficulties, as a signal part of his achievement in Germany. I find nothing in his published memoirs* to suggest that he had ever, at any time, viewed it as expendable in favor of any sort of an agreement with the Russians. He believed, as he said in a press statement at the time of his retirement, that Allied occupational forces would be required in Western Germany for another five to twenty years to assure that the Germans abided by the new constitution. His veto alone, had it been necessary, would have sufficed to rule out any proposals by our government on the four-power level that envisaged the departure of Allied forces from most of Germany and the general abandonment of occupational controls.

Nor were opinions in the State Department any more favorable to the thought of proposing anything along the lines of Plan A. Mr. Acheson, if I read his mind correctly in retrospect, regarded it as no more than a curious, though not uncharacteristic, aberration on the part of one whose thoughts, while sometimes stimulating and amusing, lacked foundation in the daily grind of operational routine and were not generally to be taken seriously. So little, indeed, did the suggestion command interest in the department that no effort had been made, up to the eve of the new CFM meeting, to acquaint the French and British with it or to discuss with them the background of thinking out of which it arose. By mid-May of 1949 it was, therefore, far too late to gain serious consideration for it as a gen-

* Lucius D. Clay, *Decision in Germany*. New York: Doubleday and Company, 1950.

eral Western position, even had the will to do so been present.

Why, in these circumstances, someone within our government should have thought it necessary to give to Plan A a spectacular *coup de grace* on the eve of the Paris Conference was a mystery to me then, and remains one today. But this is what evidently occurred. With the meeting of the foreign ministers due to begin May 23, and with the Secretary of State preparing to depart for Paris about the 20th, it was decided that Messrs. Bohlen and Jessup should fly to Paris on the night of the 12-13th, with a view to inaugurating with the British and French the preliminary discussions necessary for the preparation of common Western negotiating positions. They were authorized, as I recall it, to mention Plan A to their British and French counterparts as one of the alternatives that had been given consideration in our government, but certainly not as one that had commended itself particularly to us. On the very day of their departure, however, there appeared on the front page of the *New York Times* a story from the pen of Mr. James Reston, then Washington correspondent of the *Times,* reporting in complete and faithful detail that portion of Plan A which dealt with a possible partial withdrawal of occupation forces and naming me as the author of the idea. It was explained, at the end of the story and on an inside page, that there was "not yet" agreement that this should be put forward in Paris as the American plan. It was further stated, inaccurately and somewhat inconsistently, that the plan was conditional on Russian readiness to accept the establishment of a central German government "along the lines of the London Program." (I say "inaccurately and somewhat inconsistently" because the London Program envisaged the indefinite continuation of occupational controls as well as the stationing of Allied forces throughout German territory, and thus embraced precisely those features we had been most concerned, in drawing up Plan A, to avoid.) No mention was made, furthermore, in the Reston story of the specific safeguards that had been built into Plan A. The impression conveyed to the French and British governments could only have been that the United States government was toying with the idea of withdrawing most of its forces from the heart of Germany, had previously concealed this from them, and was now about to spring it on them on the eve of the four-power meeting.

There could, obviously, have been no means of acquainting the French and British governments with the rationale of Plan A more calculated to frighten them and to dispose them against it, and none that was further from my own concept of how we should have proceeded. The reaction was calculable, and it did not fail to ensue. The French, in particular, shied and reared up like a frightened horse. So great was their alarm that Mr. Jessup was obliged to call on the French foreign minister, M. Robert Schuman, on the very morning of his arrival, to assure him that there was no substance in the story. The *New York Times* correspondent in Paris was told that same day by a high French official that "if there was one thing likely to frighten the French out of their newfound solidarity with the Western powers it was a proposal to liberate the bulk of Germany from Allied occupation before a peace treaty was signed." (Many Germans, this official added, somewhat absurdly, would be "in danger of death from nationalistic or Nazi organizations if the Western troops retired to the seacoast.") It became, unavoidably in the circumstances, the task of Mr. Jessup and Mr. Bohlen to assure both French and British that this idea had no real support in our government, and that the story was not to be taken seriously. Thus ignominiously was there interred — for better or for worse — my modest effort to prevent our government from locking itself into a position which would stand increasingly, with the passage of time, as a barrier to any overcoming of the division of Germany and Europe, and to persuade it to adopt, instead, a stance which would make clear the terms on which it was prepared to agree to the removal of that division, thus at least holding open the possibility of an eventual four-power agreement.

What was actually proposed at Paris from the Western side when the CFM met in May 1949 amounted merely to a grudging admission that if the various *Länder* of the Soviet zone showed a disposition to enter the West German Federation on the terms of the London Program and if the Soviet masters of that region were prepared to permit them to do it, we would graciously refrain from standing in the way. Aside from the fact that this envisaged acceptance *in toto* by the Soviet government of arrangements worked out exclusively on the Western side without their participation, and thus implied something like an unconditional capitulation of their position in Germany, it involved the very feature that had seemed to us in the staff, when we studied the question, most incongruous and unpromising: namely, the effort to operate a democratic political system on a territory occupied by Soviet troops and under the control of an inter-Allied body that included a Soviet commander.

Some years later, Mr. Acheson referred publicly to our disagreement of that time over policy toward Germany. It was a disagreement which was to be greatly increased in later years, first by the decision to rearm Western Germany and to bring it in, as a full-fledged partner, to the NATO alliance, and then by the further decision of the NATO powers, in 1957, to base the defenses of Germany and the continental NATO members on nuclear weapons. As of 1949, it was a disagreement serious in its long-term implications but scarcely more than one of procedure in its short-term significance. I was far then, and am far today, from being without sympathy for Mr. Acheson's position. The responsibility that rested on him was great. For him, too, the London Program, adopted and put in hand long before he became Secretary of State, represented a species of *fait accompli*. It could not be lightly placed in jeopardy. He had a solemn duty to preserve Western unity, to carry forward the improvement and consolidation of political and economic conditions in Western Germany, to avoid things that could unduly excite the ready suspicions and anxieties of our Western European Allies. No immediate Russian agreement could have been expected at that time to proposals along the lines of Plan A. The imprudent advancement of them, on the other hand, could easily alarm and disorient Western opinion. To ask him to toy with such proposals was, in the circumstances, asking a great deal.

Where we really differed was over such things as the need for the retention of greater negotiating flexibility in our relations with the Russians — the need for not permitting a new West German

government to become an end in itself and thus an enduring impediment to any agreement with Russia — the need for more searching
and less formal exploration with our French and British allies of the
problem of the future of the European continent — the weight to
be given to the views of a military occupational establishment
which I regarded as both politically illiterate and corrupted by the
misleading discipline of its own experience. These disagreements reflected the differences in our respective backgrounds. He, having
never lived in Eastern Europe or Russia (and perhaps sharing Sigmund Freud's view that the people east of the Elbe were "baptized
late and very badly") considered the possibility of agreement with
the Russians on the retirement of Russian forces from the Eastern
zone of Germany to be of relatively small importance and thus expendable, whereas our occupational establishment in Western Germany, and the Western unity it symbolized, were definitely not. I,
on the other hand, haunted by memories of long residence in both
Germany and Russia, considered our occupational establishment in
Western Germany decidedly expendable, but clung desperately to
the hope of getting the Russians to retire some day from the heart
of the continent, and fought to prevent our adopting a stance
which threatened to destroy every possibility of such a retirement
for an indefinite number of years to come.

Today, from the perspective of eighteen years, these problems
look somewhat different to me than they did at the time. I see my
own views as resting on some grievous miscalculations. I exaggerated the iniquities and inadequacies of our occupational establishment, took too tragically the painful aspects of its impact on the
Germans, suffered in fact more than most Germans probably did
from its lapses of tact and feeling. I was too pessimistic about the
prospects for recovery and prosperity in the Western zones under
the London arrangements. I overestimated the time it would take
for our occupational establishment to turn responsibility over to
the Germans and to bow, for the most part, out of the picture. I
overrated the immediate dangers that confronted the Western sectors of Berlin in the effort to continue to live in a Communist environment (although I am not sure that I overrated the long-term

ones). The political success of the London Program, and the economic "miracle" that was shortly to begin in Western Germany, stand now in the historical record as authoritative corrections to the extremisms of my outlook of 1949.

On the other hand, I was right in my fear that the path we were entering upon would stand for a long time to come as a decisive impediment to any removal of the division of Germany or Europe. It was a path to which we were shortly to become much more deeply committed by the decision to accept Western Germany, and to rearm it, as a member of the North Atlantic Treaty Organization — a decision which I must assume, especially from the record of the testimony of Mr. Acheson and others at the NATO hearings in 1949, to have been already in people's minds, at least as a possibility, at that time. These arrangements amounted to the acceptance, for an indefinite period to come, of the division of the continent; and in 1949 they represented certainly the safer — and in the immediate sense, the easier — way out. So long as the dominant Soviet influence over Eastern Europe remains firm, they are apparently adequate to the situation. But if some day there should be an insistent demand on the part of the Eastern European counties for some sort of reintegration into the European community generally, and if the nature of their relations with the Soviet Union is at that time such as to permit this to happen peacefully, then the limitations of the arrangements concluded in 1949 and 1954 will at once become apparent, and people will have to occupy themselves seriously once again with the logic, if not with the detailed provisions, of "Plan A."

19

The Future of Europe

THE breakdown of the attempts to reach agreement with the Russians on the future of Germany and the decision to set up a West German state had obvious implications from the standpoint of the future of international relationships across the European continent generally, and particularly from the standpoint of the various ideas and projects for European unification that agitated so many minds in the postwar period. A number of prominent Europeans, including Winston Churchill and Paul Henri Spaak, were pressing for a closer association among the European powers. The United States government, animated primarily by a belief that something should be done to "integrate" the economies of the European countries in the interests of economic recovery, had been adding words of encouragement, if not pressure. The fact that now, for the first time, one was in a position to ignore and defy any Rusian objections, so far as Western Europe was concerned, opened up at least a limited field for possible progress in this direction. Organizations, furthermore, had already been established, or were in process of establishment, to serve as vehicles for the realization of common interests of one sort or another among the European peoples. There was the Economic Commission for Europe (ECE), mentioned above, which embraced those European countries, including even some east of the iron curtain, that were members of the United Nations. There was the Organization for European Economic Cooperation (OEEC), which embraced those

European countries that were associated with the European recovery program, including five that were not members of the United Nations and did not, therefore, figure in the membership of the ECE. But the OEEC omitted, of course, the Eastern European UN members, since these were not associated with the Marshall Plan. Then there was the Atlantic pact grouping, just in process of establishment, which at that time included nine European countries but omitted a number of others that were members of the ECE and OEEC. There was likewise the Council of Europe, also in process of establishment in that winter and spring of 1949. The original membership of the council was similar to that of the European component of the Atlantic pact, but included Ireland and Sweden and omitted Portugal and Iceland. Finally, there was the Brussels Union, made up of Britain, France, and the Benelux countries: the only group of countries which belonged, without exception, to all these five organizations.

This proliferation of organizational forms, all differing in membership, naturally raised the question as to how, if we really wished to see European union become a reality, we envisaged it as proceeding: within what circle of countries, that is; through the development of which, if any, of these existing organizational forms; and to what degree of merging of sovereignty. These were problems in which there was need for a clarification of American opinion, not just because we were pressing the Europeans in the direction of unification and therefore had a duty to explain to them just what we had in mind when we used those words, but also because the questions at issue were ones bound to affect at many points our own determinations of policy: policy toward Germany, policy toward the Eastern European countries, policy toward Britain, policy in the face of the problems presented by Britain's position in world trade and finance and her relations with the Commonwealth. And since the question of European unification was one which, by common admission, related to Europe's long-term future rather than to the present, it presented a natural claim on the attentions of a State Department unit calling itself the Policy Planning Staff.

Of all the European countries, it was Britain for whom the various ideas and initiatives along this line presented the most perplexing difficulties. Caught between the pressures we were exerting and the enthusiasm for European union that existed in many places on the continent, on the one hand, and the restraints placed upon them by their overseas commitments, their unique position in world trade and finance, and the inhibitions of their own public opinion, on the other, British statesmen felt a particular necessity just at that time to clarify their own ideas and policies in this respect. At some time during the spring of 1949 I mentioned, in conversation with a friend from the British Foreign Office who was visiting Washington, that I would like to come to London and to talk these matters over with appropriate people in the British government, in order to get a clearer idea of what was involved from the British side. Shortly thereafter he wrote me from London, telling me that such a visit would be welcome in the Foreign Office, and listing a number of questions on which our reactions would be welcome. How far, for example, did we think that there was any actual possibility of progress toward European unification within the next five years? Was this, in other words, a real question at all? How did we envisage the future of Germany, and of Germany's relationship to a possible European union? What, in our opinion, would be the most desirable form of Britain's association with such a union? Did the idea imply a third force in Europe, comparable in strength to the US and the USSR? And what did the idea of an "Atlantic community" mean? Was it something that could be stretched beyond the confines of the Atlantic Ocean itself?

I was gratified by this response, and over much of the months of May and June the Planning Staff, assisted by a long series of distinguished outside consultants, wrestled with the task of drawing up a set of theses on this general subject that could serve as a basis for discussion within our own government and then with the British and, as I hoped, the French as well.

The question before us was, in essence, this: In what geographic area and in what framework of membership did we wish to see the movement toward European unification proceed, over the long term, and how far did we really wish it to go?

By early July, I was able to lay before the Secretary an outline of various views to which I, personally, had come with relation to these questions. I say "I, personally," because scarcely any of the outside authorities we had consulted, and indeed scarcely any of the members of my own staff, would have agreed fully with them. This, I think, was inevitable, given the complexity of the subject. In any case, I felt that I could do no other than I did. I could not go to England to put forward, as a basis of discussion, a set of ideas with which I did not agree and thus make of myself, in any discussions that might ensue, an advocate against my own cause. For this reason, the paper that I showed to the Secretary, and then took to Europe with me, represented no one's views but my own. This was made clear to everyone, both in Washington and in Europe, to whom I showed it.

Let me summarize the general tenor of the considerations set forth in this paper.

I first posed the question: Was European unification really necessary for economic reasons as a precondition for European recovery, as had been commonly supposed in Washington? The answer was generally "No"; at least, there was no adequate evidence that this was the case. But unification *was* needed to provide a framework in which the German problem could find a satisfactory solution. I reiterated, then, the views I have already described in the last chapter of this narrative: the idea of a renewed fragmentation of Germany was unrealistic; to leave Germany to continue to realize her national ideals and aspirations within the sovereign-national framework would almost inevitably lead to a repetition of the general sequence of development that had followed the Versailles settlement; only some sort of European federation could provide for Germany a place in the European community that would be comfortable and safe for everyone concerned.

I then analyzed the possibilities of the various conceivable organizational and geographic frameworks for European unity, and examined the attitudes of the various governments and the compulsions that were operating on them. I pointed out that there was least enthusiasm for the idea of unification in the countries of the Atlantic seaboard, with their strong traditional overseas involvements, and most enthusiasm among people in the heart of the continent, where the German problem presented itself most acutely. I examined in particular the problem of the British. I found both serious and compelling, in their totality, the reasons that caused the British to hesitate in associating themselves with any move toward a continental union — so serious and compelling that if any such movement had to include the British, then, I thought, it could not go very far. It could be taken as axiomatic, I wrote, that no framework of association which included the United Kingdom but excluded the United States and Canada would be permitted to advance to a stage resembling a real merging of sovereignty. British reservations and hesitations would thus inevitably constitute the ceiling beyond which unification would not be able to advance. This ceiling, I pointed out, would be far too low to allow for any real merging of sovereignties, and thus too low to be of value as a solution to the German problem. If we and the Canadians would participate, then some of these British inhibitions might be overcome — but not all. And that we and the Canadians could move in this direction seemed to me most implausible.

At the other end of the spectrum was the problem of the eventual relationship to any such European union of the Eastern European countries under Soviet influence. It was clear that at the moment there could be no question of their association with a union of this nature. But what of the distant future?

Most of the outside authorities whom we had consulted had tended to regard the division of Europe as a *fait accompli* so final and unalterable that they were disinclined to take the Eastern European countries into account at all as factors in the problem we had before us. They favored considering the problem only in terms of Western Europe and the Atlantic community. (Their position, I thought, was somewhat inconsistent, because when asked what they thought our policy should be toward the Eastern European countries, they would usually reply that we should be concerned to attract them away from their exclusive Soviet orientation and "get them to come over to our side"; yet they were unwilling to give

serious thought to the creation of an organizational framework in
which those countries could conceivably find a suitable place if and
when that objective might be realized.) I questioned the adequacy
of the assumption that the possibilities for a relaxation of the Soviet
hold over Eastern Europe were so far away that we could leave
these peoples entirely out of consideration in our thinking about the
future organization of the European community. Any concept
which did not offer a place for them meant leaving them, I pointed
out, no theoretical alternative other than a continued association
with Russia or some highly implausible neutralization and isolation.
Such a concept was really aimed in effect at the perpetuation of the
division of Europe.

On the other hand, I could not see these peoples fitting into any
sort of an Atlantic union that would go so far as to include the
Canadians and ourselves. The effects of their prolonged subjection
to Nazi and Communist influence and of the profound social
changes they were now experiencing made it most improbable that
they would ever come to share, within our time, Anglo-American
ideas on representative government or of state policy and behavior.
I could see a possibility of their finding a place, some day, in a union
of continental countries, or perhaps (though preferably not) even
one including the British, but certainly not in one that included the
United States and Canada. The idea of a federal union extending
from San Francisco to the eastern Carpathians and the Pripet
Marshes seemed to me wholly fantastic.

The conclusion I drew from these reflections was that what we
should aim for was a continental union, sufficiently detached from
Britain to have some chance of absorbing the Germans into something larger than themselves, sufficiently detached from ourselves
and the Canadians to be truly continental in character, quite separate from the Atlantic pact, and thus eligible, so to speak, to provide a framework into which the smaller Central and Eastern European countries could eventually be fitted, as and when suitable
possibilities might arise. There was no thought that anything of this
sort could be realized at an early date. What was important was to
guide the movement toward European unification along these lines,

so that when finally realized it could provide the institutional foundation for a stable Europe. Meanwhile, it was stressed in the paper, anything done within the Western European community should be held within the limits of the provisional; and the American military commitment should remain valid and adequately supported, right up to the line of Soviet power. This did not necessarily mean that we would keep American forces stationed indefinitely all the way up to this line; that would depend in part on what the Russians did. It simply meant that our military guarantee of the security of the Western European countries would remain fully operable until replaced by other security arrangements in Europe.

Not specifically expressed in the paper, but an integral part of the thinking that lay behind it and freely expressed to all with whom I discussed it, were two further assumptions. One was that the Germans, while perhaps contributing in certain suitable ways to arrangements for the defense of Western Europe, would themselves remain outside the NATO pact and without armed forces of their own. The other assumption was that the driving force behind any movement toward political unification on the continent, and the dominant influence within any federal union that came into being, would be, naturally and unquestionably, France.

The reader will note that this concept, if adopted, would have obviated a whole series of features of American policy that were actually to become prominent in the immediately succeeding years. There would have been, under this concept, no rearmament of Western Germany; that country would not have been taken into NATO; there would have been no such questions as that of the "multinational nuclear force." This being the case, we would have had incomparably greater flexibility in any negotiations with the Russians over the question of disengagement and German unification. There would also have been, in these circumstances, no reason for pressing the British to enter the European Economic Community; on the contrary, the EEC without Britain would have fitted excellently into the objectives of American policy. Finally, there would have been no appreciable conflict with General de Gaulle either over his misgivings about British membership in the Common

Market or over his desire to get on with the organization under French leadership of a continental Europe in which the United States would not be a participating entity. Nor would the United States have been able to view otherwise than with pleasure and satisfaction General de Gaulle's independent efforts to draw the Eastern European countries into a closer collaboration with France and with Western Europe generally. There would to be sure still have been differences with General de Gaulle over the extent to which European unification would go — how much, that is, of a merging of sovereignties it would involve — but not over the area to which it should extend.

A few days after preparing this paper, I took it to Paris and then to London for informal discussion with people in the Foreign Offices of those two capitals. I presented it very much as a personal paper, for it had not been possible, prior to my departure, to arrange any serious discussion of it by people within our government; and I had, as I recall it, no clear indication of the views of the Secretary of State.

The French reaction was predictable. The French at that time had only one preoccupation; and this was their anxiety lest there be some form of relationship between the British and ourselves from which they might be excluded. Even when, as was usually the case, our involvement in British affairs consisted primarily of struggling with the difficult problem of the British financial situation, from which one might have thought the French would be glad to be aloof, they were full of suspicion and resentment if any discussions were held to which they were not a party. To them at that time the idea of taking any sort of leadership among the continental powers, independently of ourselves and the British, was utterly foreign. It was impossible to make them understand that the idea of a continental union to which we Americans would not belong did not mean the withdrawal of our interest in the military security of the Western European peoples and the abandonment of France. In short, the French with whom I spoke were simply incapable of understanding what I was talking about. There was a certain irony in this fact, because before too many years those same French officials would be serving as instruments for the policies of a great Frenchman who understood these things very well, and their own tune would then change. But in 1949 they registered nothing but alarm at ideas of this nature.

The British were less edgy, calmer, and more thoughtful in their reaction, but cautious and not generally well disposed to the ideas I had to present to them. Like our American consultants, they saw no reason for taking into account the situation and possible future needs of the Eastern European countries. They, too, were content to talk in terms of the Atlantic community and Western Europe. They felt that in the development to date of their relationship with Western Europe they had something tangible to which they could cling and on which they could build. The rest was all theoretical and hypothetical. They felt committed, in particular, by the extent to which they had already involved themselves with the Council of Europe. Their approach was, as I noted in my diary, the usual "pragmatic tentative one, distrustful of logic and of hypothetical considerations, and directed primarily to the short term."

I returned therefore with empty hands; and the response in Washington itself, over the coming weeks, was not such as to give any greater comfort. My colleagues in the Western European Division, being responsible for the short-term rather than the long-term aspects of our relations with the Western European countries, having little interest in Eastern Europe, and being influenced to some degree by their contacts with people in the French and British governments, tended to take the European side of the argument. And while the Secretary of State, so far as I can recall, remained thoughtful and outwardly noncommittal, I was under no doubt that he viewed the concept I had presented, closely integrated as it was with my view of the German problem, skeptically and without enthusiasm.

If one intended, as I was suggesting, to promote the idea of European unification within a strictly continental framework, the concomitant of this concept was, of course, a closer relationship between the United States, Canada, and Britain. This had been my strong preference ever since I had assumed the directorship of the staff. A recommendation that studies be put in hand along this line was part of the original Marshall Plan recommendation. I had never ceased to believe in its desirability. I had visions of a world-trading, maritime bloc, to include not only the British, the Canadians, and ourselves but certain of the Commonwealth nations and possibly some entities of the Scandinavian and Iberian peninsulas as well, to be based on a single currency, to develop eventually into a federal unit with a common sovereignty, and to flank in this capacity a similar grouping on the continent. But in this respect, too, I was to suffer, in the course of that summer of 1949, a frustrating and discouraging experience.

Scarcely had I returned from the visit to Paris and London when we were faced with the ripening of one of those periodic crises over the solidity of the pound sterling that agitated the immediate postwar years. It was, this time, one of the worst. It was clear that the British ought to devalue and would have to do so. Before doing so, they wanted to send senior figures to Washington to confer with us and with the Canadians about the whole problem. The matter was not only a complex one, but was for us one of the utmost delicacy, for we could not accept the responsibility for their devaluation or place ourselves publicly in the position of having inspired it. Nor could we allow it to appear that any of the other measures of austerity which in our view they ought to take were being taken at our dictation or insistence.

For obscure reasons of domestic politics which to me remained unfathomable, it was decided that the talks should be conducted not by the Secretary of State but by the Secretary of the Treasury, Mr. John W. Snyder. Mr. Snyder had only recently toured Europe and had met in London with the Chancellor of the Exchequer, Sir Stafford Cripps, who was now to head the British delegation to Washington. For reasons which, again, escape me, Mr. Snyder now seemed full of hostility and suspicion toward the British, and determined, as the Washington talks neared, not only to keep the negotiations in his own hands but to assure that the British met with the coldest sort of a reception.

I was brought by the new Under Secretary of State, Mr. James Webb, only at a late date into the preliminary discussions within our government aimed at preparation of an American position for the forthcoming talks. I met with the two secretaries and Mr. Webb on the afternoon of August 23, and was shocked to discover that virtually no attention had been given to the political aspects of the whole problem; that the whole thing had been left, thus far, to the attentions of a few financial experts; and that we intended, from all appearances, to meet the British with nothing other than the maximum reserve and unhelpfulness. I therefore spoke up; and I still have the diary record of what I said:

At the present moment, with a great question mark hanging over the solidarity of Russian rule in the satellite area and with an extremely tense and unpleasant situation in the Far East, it would be catastrophic if anything happened to disrupt the spirit of confidence and solidarity and the reality of economic stability and progress in the Western world. This, however, was exactly what would happen if something drastic were not done about the British situation. If the British went home empty-handed and in despair, I had no doubt that the Labor government would fall soon thereafter to the accompaniment of a tremendous din of recriminations and bitter words against this country. It seemed to me that there was little we could do to help the British in the short term, for any help that required legislative action could not be expected in less than a year, and what we could do for them by administrative action was really very little. No matter what came out of these discussions, therefore, the British would have to return to take some bitter and difficult measures, on their own hook, in the weeks following the discussions. But it seemed to me that everything depended on the spirit in which they did that. If they went back feeling that the talks had yielded nothing and that we were going to give them no help at all, even over the long term, the worst results could be expected. If, on the other hand, we could give them the hope that even though we could not provide the short-term answers we would be willing to help them face the long-term aspects of their problem, I thought the entire picture might be a different one. I pointed out that their dollar drain arose from two factors: (a) their position as banker for the sterling area and (b) the adverse UK balance of trade with the dollar area. As to the first, I suggested that perhaps they ought to cease trying to be the bankers for at least a portion of the sterling area, and the respective countries ought to come direct to the US for their dollars. This would mean headaches for us — yes; but it would at least create clarity and public understanding where today there is confusion. As for the British adverse balance, that was a question of adjustment of the British economy to the economies of North America, and I thought that we ought at least to agree to join them in appointing a commission of inquiry to determine what institutional changes, if any, might be made in the relations between the three countries (US, UK, and Canada) which would ease this adjustment and prevent each single component of it from being made a particular issue and bone of contention in the relations between the respective countries.

Somewhat to my own surprise I was asked by Mr. Webb, despite this outburst, to set up and take the chairmanship of an interdepartmental committee which would work out a position paper to guide us in our handling of the talks; and the next days were taken up with this work. I can only conclude in retrospect that while the President and Mr. Webb wished, for domestic-political reasons, to see maximum political deference paid to Mr. Snyder and to allow it to appear that this was his show, they were also aware that matters of the utmost technical complexity and political delicacy were involved in the talks; and they wanted a real, if outwardly invisible, foundation of expert opinion.

Three days later, while my interdepartmental committee was still at work, the department received the draft of a speech the President proposed shortly to give which included a paragraph addressed to the forthcoming arrival of the British statesmen. It seemed to me cold and wholly devoid of sympathy or understanding for the British position. I therefore dictated a paragraph for inclusion in it; the Secretary read this over the phone to Clark Clifford in the White House; and to my own surprise it found its way into the speech. It was to the effect that the British statesmen would find the usual warm welcome in our country; that we would not forget our wartime associations with Britain or the strains and stresses to which the British people had been subject in the postwar years; that we would regard the matters under discussion as a common problem and would sit down to the discussions in a spirit of friendliness and helpfulness. When this speech appeared in the papers, on August 30, the general reception was highly favorable, but I later heard that it was the occasion of much anguish, and even phone calls of protest to the President, on the part of Secretary Snyder, to whom a friendly word of this sort appeared to harbor sinister dangers.

The position paper was completed on September 2; and there was a meeting with the two Secretaries and their principal advisors, late that day, ostensibly to consider it. To my amazement and indignation, Mr. Snyder began by remarking, very discontentedly, that while he had not had a chance to read the paper carefully, he did not think that any papers of this nature ought to be in circulation at all, and asked that all copies of it be immediately recalled and locked up. Much to my disgust this was done, with the sole proviso that the Secretary of State might keep one copy for discussion the following day with the President.

The talks began on September 7. Reluctant to participate in talks for which the Department of State did not have a clear responsibility, I asked Mr. Webb to excuse me from attendance. This request was granted. But what actually happened was, I thought, both amusing and indicative. Mr. Snyder, conducting the talks for the American side, began with an opening statement which had been prepared in the Treasury Department and which no one in the Department of State had seen. By this means, the Treasury's face, I suppose, was saved, and just enough of righteous vigilance and hostility was manifested vis-à-vis the British to satisfy the supicious anti-Anglicism of upstanding figures on Capitol Hill. But at the same time, just before the meeting, Mr. Webb quietly sent over to my office for six copies of the position paper I had drawn up; and the recommendations of the paper were then followed with greatest fidelity in all the practical aspects of the talks.

The domestic-political ramifications of these elaborate antics were not clear to me; but the episode depressed and disillusioned me, from two standpoints: first, as a revelation of the difficulty that would obviously be involved in trying to find understanding among Washington political circles for anything resembling a close and collaborative association with the British, much less anything approaching a union with them and the Canadians;* but secondly, as a revelation of the reaction of the French. The latter, for their part, lost no time in staging tantrums of anxiety and discontent over their own exclusion from these three-power discussions, despite the obvious fact that the discussions were ones forced upon us and ones in which the French could not conceivably have played any constructive role. In these two circumstances, there lay the demonstration of how far both Washington and Paris were from any view remotely resembling the one I had, in my effort of the earlier part of the summer, tried to put forward for discussion.

Enough has now been told, I think, to make clear the nature of the basic disagreement over European affairs that had by this time emerged as between myself and practically everyone else involved — either in our own government, in the Western European governments, or, for that matter, in the Benelux countries. Everyone else seemed content to accept the split of the continent as it then existed, to regard the possibility of its removal as too remote to constitute a factor in our calculations, and to conceive the future of Europe in terms of this existing situation. The Western Europeans were happy to have someone who would guarantee their security against both Russians and Germans and relieve them, in effect, of the necessity of having a policy of their own vis-à-vis either of those powers. It is characteristic that they were utterly unable to separate the political considerations from the military ones in their thinking, and could not (particularly the French and the Dutch) believe in the reality of an American military guarantee not backed

---

* This impression was greatly reinforced by what I had experienced in recent months in efforts I made, in my official capacity, to unravel and dissipate the tangle of misunderstanding between the British and ourselves inherited from our wartime collaboration in the development and production of the atomic weapon. These problems are still too highly classified, I assume, to permit of detailed discussion. I shall only say that I found our position in these matters, as determined in the light of existing legislation and pressures of one sort or another from the congressional side, harsh, boorish, shortsighted, and — for me — deeply discouraging.

up by some form of American political participation. The Americans, on the other hand, already committed to a militarized view of the cold war, their policy already largely dominated by the conviction that the overriding consideration was to set up the military strength necessary to "deter" the Russians from attacking Western Europe (an event for which, as I seem to recall, the year of 1952 at that time figured in Pentagon calculations as the most probable date), saw no reason to weaken this effort at military defense, just then finding its institutional form in NATO, by toying with plans which failed to include Britain, Canada, and the United States. The armed forces, furthermore, enjoyed their presence in Germany, as in Japan.

In the case of both German policy and policy toward Europe as a whole, as well as in the case of Japan, the question of principle underlying these differences was thus the same. My opponents, thinking in defensive terms, wished to see American military power held tightly at every point to the borders of the Soviet orbit — exactly the aberration of which Lippmann had accused me in 1947. I, in each case, wanted to hold the door open to permit the eventual emergence of large areas (a united, demilitarized Germany, a united Europe, a demilitarized Japan) that would be in the military sense uncommitted, as between the two worlds. In each case, I was prepared to see us withdraw our military forces if Soviet power would be equivalently withdrawn and if we could look forward to the rise, in the areas thus thrown open, of political authority independent of Soviet domination. The new, independent Communist Yugoslavia suited my book perfectly, as did Sweden and the neutralized Austria. I would have liked to see this uncommitted area increased until it came to constitute a large part of the European continent. I believed that a readiness on our side to withdraw would eventually stimulate a disposition on the Soviet side to do likewise. Only in this way, as I saw it, could one bring about the withdrawal of the lines of Soviet power to limits more compatible with the stability of Europe and thus make a beginning, at least, at the correction of the great geopolitical disbalance to which the outcome of World War II had led.

This was the first objective I had in mind. But the second was to get us as soon as possible out of the position of abnormal political-military responsibility in Western Europe which the war had forced upon us. I had no confidence that a *status quo* dependent on so wide an American commitment could be an enduring one. Such bipolarity, I thought, might do for a few years; it could not endure indefinitely. That we could not retire into a nineteenth-century isolation was clear; but it was also clear that we were not fitted, either institutionally or temperamentally, to be an imperial power in the grand manner, and particularly not one holding the great peoples of Western Europe indefinitely in some sort of paternal tutelage. Some day, it appeared to me, this divided Europe, dominated by the military presences of ourselves and the Russians, would have to yield to something more natural — something that did more justice to the true strength and interests of the intermediate European peoples themselves. What was important was that our plans for the future should be laid in such a way as to permit that "something" to come into being when the time for it was ripe — not in such a way as to constitute an impediment to it.

At the bottom of this difference lay, no doubt, two divergences of basic outlook. I was trying, as I think befitted one who directed a governmental unit concerned with "planning," to look ten to twenty years into the future. My friends in Washington, London, Paris, and The Hague were thinking of the problems we had immediately before us. But secondly, and even more important, I did not believe in the reality of a Soviet military threat to Western Europe. Not believing in it, I was concerned not so much to provide protection against the possibility of such an attack (although I recognized the need for some sort of military facade to quiet the anxieties of the jittery Western Europeans) as to facilitate the retirement of Soviet forces, and with them dominant Soviet political influence, to limits closer to the traditional boundaries of the Russian state. My friends, less concerned about the division of Europe, and indeed in many instances quite content with it, were thinking of how to deter — and if it could not be deterred, how to withstand — a Soviet attack envisaged by the military planners as likely to ensue in the early 1950s.

These were the real reasons for our differences. They serve to emphasize the importance, in the formulation of national policy, of two things: first, one's idea of one's own country, its capabilities, and its natural role in the world; the other, the interpretation given to the psychology, the political personality, the intentions, and the likely behavior of an adversary.

In mid-September 1949, difficulties arose over the handling of the papers of the Policy Planning Staff. Previously, these had always been submitted directly to the Secretary of State. The latter was of course at liberty to submit them for advice and criticism to whomsoever he cared to and then to accept or reject the conclusions as his own judgment might indicate. But at least he had before him, in doing so, a clear presentation of the views of the staff. Now, on September 16, a staff paper ready for presentation to the Secretary (on policy toward Yugoslavia, incidentally) was first laid, at Mr. Webb's expressed wish, before the body of senior officials — Assistant Secretaries and others — who attended the Under Secretary's regular morning meetings. Several of these gentlemen expressed disagreement with one or the other of its features, including some quite basic ones; whereupon the paper was returned to me with Mr. Webb's request that I reconcile these differences by discussion with the respective gentlemen and rewrite the paper before submitting it to the Secretary of State.

It was perfectly clear what was involved in this procedure: the staff was to be deprived of direct access to the Secretary of State in the presentation of its views; from now on, staff papers would be subject to the veto of any of the chiefs of the operational divisions of the department.

Three days later, I argued the matter out with members of the staff, some of whom favored acceptance of the new procedure. I remained unconvinced. I could not see my way to accepting it. It was, I said to them (as recorded in my diary, September 19):

a question of confidence. The whole *raison d'être* of this staff was its ability to render an independent judgment on problems coming before the Secretary or the Under Secretary. If the senior officials of the department do not wish such an independent judgment, or do not have confidence in us to prepare one which would be useful, then I question whether the staff should exist at all.

This lies in the nature of our work. When Secretary Byrnes called upon the Acheson-Lilienthal group to prepare for him a staff opinion on our policy with respect to the international control of atomic energy, he did not insist that it meet with the unanimous and detailed approval of the Assistant Secretaries before he was interested in reading it. Similarly, when Secretary Marshall first asked this staff to do work on the problem of European recovery, what he wanted was the staff's opinion and not a record of the extent to which the staff could find agreement with the various departmental chiefs on this subject.

On September 29 I told Mr. Webb that I desired to be relieved as soon as possible of the title and responsibilities of director of the Policy Planning Staff and would like to leave the government service the following June (when the school year was over). Subsequent discussion with him and with the Secretary culminated in an understanding that I would begin to turn over the staff work to my successor (Mr. Paul Nitze) at an early date; that I would leave the staff entirely by the end of December; and that when I left the department in June it would not be to retire completely from the governmental service, but to enter upon a long "leave of absence without pay" which would enable me to turn to academic pursuits and to approach in a more careful and leisurely fashion some of the great problems on which differences were clearly beginning to emerge between myself and senior officials of our government.

I may say that all these exchanges about my departure took place without acrimony or hard feeling. My relations with Mr. Webb were always personally pleasant; and those with Mr. Acheson, for whom I felt an affection and admiration so strong that they would even withstand the public controversy of ensuing years, were something more than that. The spirit in which I laid down my work in the staff and turned my face to a life outside the government is best shown, I think, by the following diary passages from that period:

Saturday, November 19, 1949

Pondering today the frustrations of the past week, it occurred to me that it is time I recognized that my Planning Staff, started nearly three years ago, has simply been a failure, like all previous attempts to bring order and foresight into the designing of foreign policy by special institutional arrangements within the department. Aside from personal shortcomings, the reason for this seems to lie largely in the impossibility of having the planning function performed outside of the line of command. The formulation of policy is the guts of the work of the department, and none of it can successfully be placed outside the hierarchy which governs operations. No one can regiment this institution in the field of ideas except the Secretary. He can take as much independent advice as he likes from outside the institution; he can take it orally from "special assistants" or "counselors" or other official advisors. But when it comes to any formalized staff effort, anything that has to be put down in writing and is designed to serve as a major guide for action, the operating units — the geographic and functional units — will not take interference from any unit outside the line of command. They insist on an effective voice in policy determination; if one of them cannot make its voice alone valid, it insists on the right to water down any recommendation going to the Secretary to a point where it may be meaningless but at least not counter to its own views. If an unwelcome recommendation does find the Secretary's approval, they will perhaps give it a perfunctory recognition, but they will pursue basically their own policies anyway, secure in the knowledge that no one can really survey their entire volume of work, that the issues which agitate the present will soon be outdated, and that the people who are trying to force their hand will soon be gone. This is only human, and much more justifiable than it sounds. It is my belief, in the light of this discouraging experience, that the only way the thing will work is if a Secretary of State will thresh out a basic theoretical background of his policy and then really set up some sort of an educational unit through whose efforts this system can be patiently and persistently pounded into the heads of the entire apparatus, high and low.

November 22, 1949

The heart of the difficulty lies in the fact that my concept of the manner in which our diplomatic effort should be conducted is not shared by any of the other senior officials of the department; and that the Secretary is actually dependent on these officials, for better or for worse, for the execution of any foreign policy at all. Even if he shared my views, he would not be able to find others who did; and lacking such others he would have to operate through people whose philosophy of foreign affairs would necessarily be a different one. The fact of the matter is that this operation cannot be unified and given real purpose or direction unless a firm theoretical groundwork has been laid to back up whatever policy is pursued and unless the persons most concerned, here, in our delegation in New York, in our occupied-area establishments, and in our field offices, have all been thoroughly and severely indoctrinated in this theoretical groundwork, so that they all have the same understanding of what it is that we are trying to do. Since our present governmental system lacks the disciplinary authority for such indoctrination, it can come really only through an intensive educational effort directed toward our public opinion in general and particularly toward the work of our universities. All this impels me to the thought that if I am ever to do any good in this work, having the courage of my convictions, it must be outside the walls of this institution [the Department of State] and not inside them.

I cannot recall exactly when, or in what circumstances, I finally abandoned the office in the premises of the Policy Planning Staff. It must have been around the end of the year. It was a change that gave me some sadness, for the relationship that had existed between myself and the various members of the staff, as they came and went over the course of the years, had been as close and meaningful as only intellectual intimacies can be. The staff had included a number of truly outstanding people: such people as Charles Burton Marshall, Louis Halle, Dorothy Fosdick and John Paton Davies, to mention only a few. Our relations had been those of affection and respect, if not invariably of intellectual agreement.

The departure from the staff, in Washington, thus escapes my memory. But I recall a morning out in the country, at my farm, when the change was very much on my mind.* I was driving that morning over to a nearby nursery to buy some trees. Driving along the highway, I fell to reflecting on the occasional successes and the frequent failures the staff had experienced, over those past two and a half years, in its efforts to enrich the intellectual and decision-taking processes of the United States government. The process put me in mind of the bee, planting his pollen here and there, then flying on and never seeing or knowing the fruits of his little labor. The result was that I stopped the car by the side of the road, found a piece of paper, and penned a parting missive in verse to my erstwhile associates on the Planning Staff. It may stand, in a way, as my last staff paper:

> *From: G. F. Kennan*
> *To: The Members of the Policy Planning Staff*
> *Subject: Their Peculiar Fate*
>
> *Friends, teachers, pupils; toilers at the wheels;*
> *Undaunted drones of the official hive,*
> *In deep frustration doomed to strive,*
> *To power and to action uncommitted,*
> *Condemned (disconsolate, in world of steel and glass confined)*
> *To course the foggy bottoms of the mind,*
> *Unaided, unencouraged, to pursue*
> *The rarer bloom, the deeper hue,*
> *The choicer fragrance — these to glean*
> *And, having gleaned, to synthesize*
> *And long in deepest reticence to hide . . .*
> *Until some distant day — perhaps — permitted,*
> *Anonymous and unidentified,*
> *The Great White Queen*
> > *at last*
> > > *to fertilize.*
>
> *Such is the life, the function,*
> > *such the fate*

---

* The time was actually some months later, when I was finally leaving the government.

Which I, the first to bear,
　　　　to you bequeathed.
Let not the foggy harshness of the air,
　　　　the season late,
The counsels of despair,
The prospect of the sword unsheathed,
Deter you from persistence in this task.
Do not, as I did, importune the skies . . .
The bureaucratic heavens do not ask . . .
To tell you where the reason lies
Why you . . . why no one else . . . should bear
　　　　this weight.

Who knows?
　　　　Perhaps in moment unforeseen
The Great White Queen,
Made fruitful by your seed,
　　　　may yet create
So dazzling and so beauteous a brood
That worlds will marvel, history admire.
And then the scorned, no-longer-wanted sire,
From bondage loosed, from travail freed,
Basking beside the rays these progeny exude,
May find the warmth to which all souls aspire
　　　　in autumn late.

asked me to conduct such a reexamination or whether I did so on my own initiative, I cannot recall. In any case, I and others worked on the problem over the final weeks of 1949; and on or about January 20 I submitted to the Secretary a long report of my findings and views. Since I was no longer director of the Planning Staff, the report had the character of a personal memorandum, and committed nobody except myself. I consider it to have been in its implications one of the most important, if not the most important, of all the documents I ever wrote in government. I regret that governmental policy precludes its publication at this time.

I began (this is by my recollection; I do not even have any notes on the document) with an examination of our existing position in the problem of international control. If, I concluded, it was really our desire to see atomic weapons excluded eventually from national arsenals, then our existing position did not do full justice to such a desire. There were ways — not vital ones, perhaps, but also not unimportant — in which our position could be safely moderated with a view to bringing us closer to the views of the Russians and other powers. But, I went on to ask, was it really our desire to see atomic weapons thus abolished? Did we really wish to move in a manner that would bring us and the world closer to that goal? The answer to these questions depended, as I saw it, on the attitude we took toward such weapons as a factor in our own defense policies. There were two ways they could be viewed. One could view them as an undesirable necessity, the very existence of which we regretted and deplored — a form of weapon we were obliged to hold because we had no assurance against its development and use by others against us, but the use of which we had no intention of initiating in any military encounter. In this case, we would of course not base plans for defense upon the presumption of its use. Or one could view this form of weapon as essential to our defense; as something we could not conceive ourselves as living without; and as something we would therefore expect to use deliberately, promptly, and spontaneously in any major encounter, regardless of whether it was first used against us. In this case, we would obviously base our defense structure on the assumption of its first use; and we would place ourselves in this way in a position where we would presumably not be able to afford *not* to use it, if war ever came.

Our statements to date, I pointed out, had been ambiguous and inconsistent on this point. We had done lip service, when we spoke in international forums, to a desire to see atomic weapons abolished. But it was perfectly clear from statements made by our political and military leaders as well as from the understanding that had been permitted to rest with our own Congress and with our NATO allies, that we were basing our defense posture on such weapons, and were intending to make first use of them, regardless of whether they had been or might be used against us, in any major military encounter.

If this was really our position, then, I said, there would be no point in readjusting our position in the international negotiations looking to the control or abolition of atomic weapons; for this was a direction in which we did not really wish to move.

The rest of the paper was devoted, then, to a plea — as earnest and eloquent as I was capable of making it — that before we decide to proceed with the development of the hydrogen bomb, thus committing ourselves and the world to an indefinite escalation of the destructiveness and expensiveness of atomic weapons, we reexamine once more, in the most serious and solemn way, the whole principle of the "first use" of atomic weapons or any other of the weapons of mass destruction; and I made it as clear as any language at my command could make it that if such a reexamination took place, my voice would be cast most decisively in favor of the abandonment of this principle altogether. It lay, I thought, at the heart of all our confusions. I did not question that we would have to retain weapons of this nature until we could arrive at some satisfactory understanding with others on their removal from national arsenals. But I described in words something along the lines of the following what I thought should be our public position:

We deplore the existence of all weapons of indiscriminate mass destruction. We regret that we were ever obliged to make use of one. We hope never to have to do so again. We do not propose ever to do so, unless we are forced to it by the use of such weapons against us. Meanwhile, we remain prepared to go very far, to show considerable confidence in others, and to accept a certain risk for ourselves, in order to achieve international agreement on their removal from international arsenals; for we can think of nothing more dangerous than a continued international competition in their development.

In arguing for this position, I made the point that the mere cultivation of such weapons would sooner or later present serious problems of public understanding (in view of their suicidal nature) and would raise questions as between ourselves and our allies that would be disruptive in their effect on the workings of existing alliances. But more importantly still, I argued — as I was destined to argue many times in the public discussions of future years — that there was no victory and no security to be won for our people by the sort of destruction these weapons were capable of working: the results they could produce would mean at best only a deterioration of the conditions of civilization for people everywhere, including ourselves; the victories that mattered would never be real victories unless they involved changes — beneficial changes, changes leading in the direction of greater tolerance and forebearance and hopefulness — in the minds of men; and such changes could never be brought about by destruction, and particularly the destruction of innocent life, on so vast and indiscriminate a scale.

I cannot remember that this paper was ever seriously considered or discussed. Nor can I recall what was the reaction to it of the Secretary of State. If I had to make a guess, I should think it was probably one of bewilderment and pity for my naïveté. The views put forward here conflicted with what was already established military policy. They conflicted with the ideas we had formed as to where the essentials of our own defense were to be found. They conflicted with the reactions of Congress, the military establishment, and the public to the news of the detonation by the Russians of an atomic weapon. They conflicted with the views we had communicated to our European allies, and with the manner in which we had taught these latter to see the needs and the guarantees of their own defense. (Some of them would have been the first to react with alarms and indignation at the very idea of attempting to live in a world where *our* atomic weapons did not stand as the guarantee of *their* security.) These views conflicted, furthermore, with the highly inflated estimates of Russian conventional military strength that had already become ingrained (we will not, at this point, ask why) in the official assessment of NATO defense needs, and with the resulting belief on our part that we could never meet the Russians successfully on non-nuclear ground. They conflicted, finally, with the growing tendency in Washington (a tendency doubly fateful now, in view of the demonstrated Russian capacity for producing atomic weapons) to base our own plans and calculations solely on the *capabilities* of a potential adversary, assuming him to be desirous of doing anything he could do to bring injury to us, and to exclude from consideration, as something unsusceptible to exact determination, the whole question of that adversary's real *intentions*. In the face of all these conflicts, one could well understand it if the Secretary of State saw no usefulness, nor even anything worth serious discussion, in the set of views I presented. In any case, on January 31, 1950, only some ten days after their presentation, the President announced our intention of proceeding with the development of the hydrogen bomb; and I knew that my labor had been, once again, in vain.

Years later, for reasons wholly independent of anything I then said, some of the thinking embodied in this paper would seep through into public discussion and into the official thinking of our government. After a lapse of twelve years President Kennedy and Mr. McNamara would recognize, for example, the basic unsoundness of a defense posture based primarily on weapons indiscriminately destructive and suicidal in their implications, and they would move, as far as they could in the existing circumstances, to correct this anomaly. The experience of two wars in which, as it turned out, the use of such weapons would prove impracticable, would tend to bring to the minds of many people, for the first time, the thought that they might not be the answer to every military problem. The complications presented by the question as to who, within the framework of the NATO alliance, should control the use of such weapons in case of war would come to constitute in the 1960s a knotty problem in the relations between ourselves and our allies, would play a part in changing the nature of the alliance itself, and would thus reveal some of the deficiencies of such weapons as a basis for a collective defense policy. But at the outset of 1950 even these mildly encouraging responses were still many years in the future; and it will be understood that I came away with nothing other than a heavy heart and the deepest sort of discouragement from this — my first and last responsible contact with the formulation of our official policy toward the cultivation and use of the weapons of mass destruction.

* * *

In February and March I made, with the permission of the Secretary of State, a journey to Latin America. I had never been there. I wanted to see something of it, before I left government. There was to be a meeting of our Latin American ambassadors in Rio de Janeiro, where there was need for the presence of someone from the senior echelons of the department. But beyond this, I realized that I had by this time come full circle in my effort to be of use to our government in the great problems of the relations between the major military powers of Europe and Asia. My possibilities were exhausted there. It was time, I felt, that I got away from all this and did something to gain an understanding of those parts of the world where things other than the cold war and the containment of communism were involved.

I set forth, accordingly, on February 18, 1950, by train to Mexico City and thence by air to Caracas and Rio. After the Rio meeting, I went on to São Paulo, Montevideo, Buenos Aires, and thence back, with stops at Lima and Panama City, to Miami.

I found the journey anything but pleasant. At Mexico City the altitude bothered me; the city made upon me a violent, explosive impression. I felt that it never slept at night (perhaps because I myself didn't). The sounds of its nocturnal activity struck me as disturbed, sultry, and menacing. Before continuing the journey, I spent one night, ostensibly for the purposes of rest, at the home of wealthy compatriots in Cuernavaca who kindly offered this hospitality to me sight unseen. They were themselves absent. Their home was a fantastic place: luxurious, intensely beautiful in the relation of building to landscape, and full of the most incredible antiques. But here, again, it was not my dish. I never felt at home in the halls of luxury. I lay sleepless, according to my diary records,

through the long night, under the huge crimson draperies which had once served a prince of the Church and still bore his insignia — while mosquitoes buzzed around my pillow, and outside a fountain tinkled softly in the patio and a fitful night breeze searched aimlessly back and forth among the cloisters, like a ghost, murmuring, as it seemed to me, "Lost, lost, lost." By this it referred, I was sure, to all of us: to myself, the guest, who had wandered where he did not belong; to the unhappy antiques, crowded together in such incongruous diversity like creatures in a zoo; finally, to itself, the wind, imprisoned in such beautiful walls and failing to find the concomitant of all this beauty.

And it finally occurred to me that this was the same wind which could always be found moving through the places of the lost people. It was the wind that blew through the Riviera and the Bahamas and the Sierra de Cintra: the wind of exiled royalty, of the hopelessly rich, of the tortured intellectuals; the wind of King Carol and the Windsors — the wind that gave its name to the Palace of the Seven Sighs. It was the wind of the last refuge, which turned out to be no refuge at all — the companion-wind of human pretense and despair, accompanying its charges, like an earnest, faithful animal, in the quest of that which was never there — troubling their dreams at night with its frantic naïve searching for that which would never be found.

Caracas, jammed in among its bilious-yellow mountains, appalled me with its screaming, honking traffic jams, its incredibly high prices, its feverish economy debauched by oil money, its "mushroom growth of gleaming, private villas creeping up the sides of the surrounding mountains." I commiserated, in the privacy of my diary, with those unfortunate American representatives who were obliged "to continue to carry on their work in this grotesque crevice of urbanization, fighting the claustrophobia imposed upon them by the isolation among the towering mountains and the life of the local millionaires, doing their part in this unhappy relationship in which each country was beholden to the other in a manner slightly disgraceful. . . ."

Rio, too, was repulsive to me with its noisy, wildly competitive traffic and its unbelievable contrasts between luxury and poverty; but my stay there was also rendered unpleasant for quite another reason. The Soviet propaganda machine had always followed the rule that when you enlist enthusiasm you may invoke ideas, but when it is a case of arousing hatred you always choose individuals as targets. It was considered necessary, therefore, to have at all times one or two individuals in each of the major non-Communist countries against whom hatred could suitably be directed. The identity of these individuals could vary with the situation. Sometimes natural targets presented themselves; but there were other times when one had to be content with whatever one could find. At this particular moment Jim Forrestal and I had been given the honor of selection in this capacity — as representatives, so to speak, of the United States; and our names consequently appeared (sometimes as those of the "hyenas" of American imperialism) in the products of Soviet propaganda outlets and Communist newspapers the world over. I had not realized this before departure from Washington; and it was therefore to my great astonishment and consternation that I found the walls of Rio — but hundreds and hundreds of them — decorated with large painted scrawls: *Fora Kennan* — Kennan Go Home! In addition to this, I was informed by my colleagues in the embassy that I had been buried in effigy four times, just in recent days, by processions of Communist students. I was even shown a photograph of one of these obsequies, and was moved to note that the students, while spelling the name wrongly, had done me the courtesy of providing me with a little child's coffin decently decorated with a large white cross — a Christian burial, in other words. The situation was not, however, entirely humorous — at least not in the view of the Brazilian government. Hawk-eyed Indian guards with sawed-off shotguns rode everywhere with me in my car with a few more in a car behind; and one of them sat all night, most uncomfortably, on a ballroom chair just outside the door of my hotel room. A normal acquaintance with the city was in these circumstances beyond the range of possibility.

In São Paulo it was still worse. Here a veritable army — half the city police force, I was told — was mobilized in my defense; and each of my comings and goings was the subject of wild confusion and controversy, what between police, photographers, other people's intelligence agents, and our own harassed officials. Montevideo, Buenos Aires, and the remaining places were more relaxed, but they all inflicted upon me a curious sense of mingled apprehension and melancholy. Particularly galling were the official interviews I was obliged to seek in each of the capitals. They were all similar, and all meaningless, as the diary records:

Visit at the President's residence: a dark drawing room; the President's son translating; and the President himself, sitting stiffly on the sofa, vibrating to my every word with a somber Latin sensitivity about himself and his country. ("You, Mr. Kennan, are an official of the government of a great country; and I am only the President of an obscure little country"; "Ah, Mr. President, that may be, but we are all aware that there is no connection between the size of a country and the amount of political wisdom its leaders can produce.")

And so it would go: sly provocation on their part, the indispensable flattery on mine — all painful and slightly disreputable.

In Lima, I was depressed by the reflection that it had not rained in the place for twenty-nine years, and by the thought that some of the dirt had presumably been there, untouched, for all that time. And the brief stops in Central America — again with the undercurrent of violence palpable even in the reception halls of the little airports — did nothing to cheer me up.

When I got back to Washington, I wrote a long report for the Secretary on the impressions of this trip. In it, I grappled with many aspects of the problem presented in the shaping of our relations with these countries, and found myself obliged, in doing so, to work out in my own mind and to enunciate in the report views on fundamental questions of political philosophy which I had never

before tried to formulate. These gropings belong, in reality, to another period of my own life and work, the academic one, that was
about to begin; and for this reason they will be more suitably saved
for another volume of these memoirs, if one ever comes to be written. But I think I should note here that the report came as a great
shock to people in the operational echelons of the department, so
much so that the Assistant Secretary for Latin America immediately persuaded the Secretary (I am not sure that he required much
persuading) to forbid its distribution within the department and to
have all copies of it locked away and hidden from innocent eyes,
which was promptly done. I was never told just what passages had
occasioned this drastic measure; but I have an idea they were ones
in which I dwelt on what seemed to me to be the tragic nature of
human civilization in all those countries to the south of us. Since the
report was never accepted and distributed, and must therefore be
assumed not to have entered into the official custody of the government files, I may feel at liberty to cite some of those passages which,
I suspect, caused the commotion.

There were, I wrote, certain appreciations concerning the Latin
American area as a whole which

strike the casual visitor with a heavy, melancholy force and claim the
right to a sort of precedence in all his thinking about it.

It seems to me unlikely that there could be any other region of the
earth in which nature and human behavior could have combined to
produce a more unhappy and hopeless background for the conduct of
human life than in Latin America.

As for nature, one is struck at once with the way in which South
America is the reverse of our own North American continent from the
standpoint of its merits as a human habitat.

North America is broad and ample in those temperate regions which
are most suitable to human life. As one moves southward into the
subtropical and tropical zones, it tapers off to the narrow and moun-
tainous isthmus, which is a part of Latin America.

South America, on the other hand, is wide and vast in those portions
of it which are close to the equator and least suited to human habitation, and it is the temperate zone into which the continent narrows at

its southern extremity, pinching off with a fateful abruptness the possibilities for a vigorous and hopeful development of human society.

In North America, the Mississippi drains and serves the huge basin of fertility which is the heart of the continent. The Amazon, on the other hand, reaches great fingers into a region singularly hostile to human activity.

In North America, the great country which stands in the center of the continent is highly developed, with a dense network of communications, and is well qualified to act as a bond for the continent as a whole. In South America, the pathless expanse of central Brazil, around the periphery of which the other countries are arranged, acts rather as a barrier to their mutual access and communication.

In North America, climate has permitted urban life to be led on the plains, in an organic intimacy with the natural hinterland. In South America, climate, together with Castilian tradition, has pressed a number of the more important urban communities up into poorly accessible mountain sites, at the price of a tragic and ineradicable artificiality.

I went on, then, to describe what I felt to be the tragic effects of the manner in which the Spaniards had introduced their civilization and their rule to the South American continent, and the further effects of the later importation of slaves and others from Africa. In these circumstances, I concluded,

the shadow of a tremendous helplessness and impotence falls today over most of the Latin American world. The handicaps to progress are written in human blood and in the tracings of geography; and in neither case are they readily susceptible of obliteration. They lie heavily across the path of all human progress; and the answers people have suggested to them thus far have been feeble and unpromising.

These bitter realities are ones which people cannot face fully and constantly. Human nature, with its insistence that life must go on, represses the consciousness of these things, turns away from them in healthy revulsion, and seeks to balance them out by overcompensation. Thus the inordinate splendor and pretense of the Latin American cities can be no other than an attempt to compensate for the wretchedness and squalor of the hinterlands from which they spring. And in the realm of individual personality this subconscious recognition of the

failure of group effort finds its expression in an exaggerated self-
centeredness and egotism — in a pathetic urge to create the illusion of
desperate courage, supreme cleverness, and a limitless virility where
the more constructive virtues are so conspicuously lacking.

For the foreign representative, this presents a terrible dilemma. In
an environment which ill supports the naked face of reality, he cannot
get very far with the sober and obvious concepts which are his stock
of trade in other parts of the world. He must take these neuroses as
the essence of the medium in which his activity must proceed; and he
must bear in mind that every impulse which he gives to his activity
must, if it is to be successful, find its translation into the terms of a
world where geography and history are alike tragic, but where no one
must ever admit it.

Thus the price of diplomatic popularity, and to some extent of diplomatic success, is constant connivance at the maintenance of a staggering and ubiquitous fiction: the fiction of extraordinary human achievement, personal and collective, subjective and objective, in a society
where the realities are almost precisely the opposite, and where the
reasons behind these realities are too grim to be widely or steadily entertained. Latin American society lives, by and large, by a species of
make-believe: not the systematized, purposeful make-believe of Russian
communism, but a highly personalized, anarchical make-believe, in
which each individual spins around him, like a cocoon, his own little
world of pretense, and demands its recognition by others as the condition of his participation in the social process.

Confronted with this phenomenon, many non-Latin diplomatists first
pause in dismay; for they see that only by accepting it can they achieve
many of their purposes. Yet to plunge deeply into it, as many finally
do, is to lose oneself in a sort of Alice's Wonderland, where normal
relations between cause and effect have lost their validity, where
nothing may be judged on its actual merits, where no idea has more
than a relative integrity, where real things receive recognition only by
their relation to the diseased and swollen human ego, where nothing is
ever wholly finished because things are never more than symbols and
there is no end to those things which are the objects of the symbols.

Here, for the sensitive foreigner, there are only three forms of escape: cynicism, participation, or acute unhappiness. Most foreign representatives find refuge in a combination of all three.

Such, I reiterate, were some of the passages of this report which I suspect to have rendered it intolerable to the embrace of the official files of the Department of State. On glancing over these passages today I understand better than I did at the time why even the vast slumbering archives of the department could find no comfortable place for them. But in the very fact that I, traveling around and reacting to stimuli, could not help but write such passages, whereas the Department of State, being what it was and facing the tasks it faced, could not help but reject them and refuse to take cognizance of them, there lay an excellent example of the logic that was now bringing to an end the usefulness of my career as a Washington official and forcing me out into a life where the deeper and more painful ranges of analysis and speculation could be more easily tolerated and more safely indulged.

I think I should add, lest a false impression be created, that despite the emphasis in the above passages on the tragic element in Latin American civilization, I have in another sense a high opinion of it and even look to it as perhaps humanity's best hope for the future. The human existence is everywhere tragic; that of Latin America is only tragic in its own manner; and this is a manner in some respects less menacing, certainly less apocalyptic, than that in which tragedy threatens to manifest itself elsewhere. Everywhere else, too, the human ego — demonic, anarchic, unbridleable — interferes in men's affairs and claims its own in their behavior. I am not sure that I do not prefer it in its Latin American manifestations: spontaneous, uninhibited, and full-throated, rather than in those carefully masked and poisonously perverted forms it assumes among the Europeans and the Anglo-Americans. Latin America is the only one of the world's great subdivisions where the human being is still entirely human, where no one has nuclear weapons or is even thinking of developing them, where the great fund of precept and experience and custom that has been created in the Christian West to reconcile man with God and with the requirements of a civilized condition is still wholly relevant. The South American continent may prove some day to be the last repository and custodian of humane Christian values that men in the European motherlands and in

North America — overfed, overorganized, and blinded by fear and ambition — have thrown away.

* * *

At no time in my governmental career, up to June 1950, had I ever been involved with any of the decisions relating to Korea. The significant ones had been taken at the military level; and if they had at any point engaged the responsibilities of the State Department, the resulting deliberations were not ones in which I had been asked to participate.

The withdrawal of American forces from Korea, in early 1949, had not alarmed me. It was my impression, for one thing, that those forces, encumbered as I understood them to be with the ponderous burden of dependents, PXs and other housekeeping paraphernalia which the Pentagon at that time seemed to find indispensable for any American forces stationed abroad, had very little combat capability anyway and would have been more of a nuisance than a help if a need had suddenly arisen for the conduct of military operations. But beyond this, I had been assured by a very high Air Force officer, on the occasion of my visit to Japan in 1948, that we had no need for any ground forces in Korea anyway, because the Air Force could control from Okinawa, through our strategic bombing capability, anything that went on in the way of military operations on the Korean peninsula — a boast, incidentally, which bears a most ironic relation to the situation in which we were to find ourselves three years later.

At some time in late May or early June, 1950, some of us who were particularly concerned with Russian affairs in the department were puzzled to note, among the vast "take" of information that flows daily into the ample maw of that institution, data suggesting that somewhere across the broad globe the armed forces of some Communist power were expecting soon to go into action. An intensive scrutiny of the Soviet situation satisfied us that it was not Soviet forces to which these indications related. This left us with the forces of the various satellite regimes, but which? Summoning the various experts to the table, we toured the horizons of the Soviet bloc. Korea came up in due turn. For information about military matters in that country, we were dependent on a long and indirect chain of communication, passing through two military establishments, as I recall it: the one in Japan and the Pentagon in Washington. The word that reached us through this indirect route was that an inauguration of military operations from the Communist side in that country was practically out of the question: the South Korean forces were so well armed and trained that they were clearly superior to those of the Communist north; our greatest task, we were told, was to restrain the South Koreans from resorting to arms to settle their differences with the north. Having no grounds to challenge this judgment, I accepted it (I have always reproached myself for doing so) and we passed on to other things. But nowhere else, understandably enough, could we see any possibility of an attack, and we came away from the exercise quite frustrated.

I was due to terminate my work in government and to leave Washington at the end of June. On the weekend of June 24-25 I drove up to the farm with Annelise on Saturday morning, and returned to Washington Sunday afternoon. We had no telephone at the farm, and received no Sunday papers. It was therefore only when I got back to Washington, late in the afternoon, and saw the headlines of the Sunday paper that I became aware of the attack that had occurred in Korea. Nobody had thought to notify me, and perhaps there was no reason anybody should have; but I could not help but reflect that General Marshall would have seen that this was done.

On arriving at the department, I found the Secretary of State in conference with Phil Jessup, Dean Rusk, and Doc Matthews. They had spent much of the day, so far as I could gather, pressing through the Security Council of the United Nations a resolution calling upon all its members not to assist the North Korean forces but rather to help the United Nations put a halt to the aggression. They were now considering what the American reaction should be.

It was clear to me from the start that we would have to react with all necessary force to repel this attack and to expel the North Korean forces from the southern half of the peninsula. I took this position unequivocally on that first day and in all the discussions that followed over the ensuing days and weeks. I also took occasion to emphasize, on that first occasion and on a number of others, that we would now have to take prompt steps to assure that Formosa, too, did not fall into Communist hands; for two such reverses coming one on the heels of the other, could easily prove disastrous to our prestige and to our entire position in the Far East.

At the time when I came to the department, that Sunday afternoon, the President was still airborne on his way back to Washington. The Secretary left at 6:15 P.M. for the airport to meet him. It had been arranged that the Secretary, accompanied by a few of the senior officials of the department, would later dine at Blair House with the President and with a similar group of military officials. The Secretary had left word, I was told, that he specifically wished me to be included in the group to meet with the President; but when the moment came for us to leave for Blair House, his secretary told me that somehow or other, by a process she did not understand, my name had been omitted from the list sent to the White House, and since the number of guests was limited there would be no place for me. This dinner had the effect of defining — by social invitation, so to speak — the group that would be responsibly engaged in the handling of the department's end of the decisions in the ensuing days. I found myself thus automatically relegated to the sidelines: attending the respective meetings in the Secretary's office, but not those that took place at the White House level. The Secretary asked, however, that I postpone my departure from government in order to be available in connection with the Korean crisis; and this I gladly agreed to do.

I remained, accordingly, over the summer, lending such help as I could. My principal function was to brief people at the daily morning meetings in the Secretary's office on the evidence relating to Soviet intentions. But I found myself involved in a dozen other ways as well, albeit always in the capacity which my friend Bohlen used to call that of the "floating kidney" (i.e., outside the chain of command and one step removed from the real decisions), in the hectic deliberations that the Korean crisis involved.

Three of the issues that agitated the discussions of those busy weeks were ones that had particular meaning for me.

The first of these related to the purpose of our military operations in Korea. In advocating from the outset a vigorous and determined military reaction on our part to the North Korean attack, I had in mind only the repelling of this attack and the expulsion of the North Korean forces from the area south of the 38th parallel. It never occurred to me, initially, that we would make it our purpose to go farther. So little did anything of this sort enter my thoughts that when, on Tuesday, June 27, two or three days after inauguration of the attack, I suddenly and unexpectedly found myself obliged to brief the assembled NATO ambassadors in Washington on what it was we were trying to do in Korea, I confidently and innocently assured them that we had no intention of doing more than to restore the *status quo ante*. I understood this, in fact, to be the view of our government as a whole; and it seemed to be implicit in the initial resolution of the UN Security Council on the subject.

Only one day later, however — June 28 — the Air Force was already pushing for authorization to operate beyond the parallel. This was discussed that same day in the Secretary of State's office; and I find in my own notes the following account of my part in the discussion:

I said I thought we might consider an alteration of our position about the 38th parallel, to the following effect: that while we would continue to state it as our purpose not to reoccupy any territory north of the parallel, we would not limit our forces to operation south of the parallel but would say that they would operate anywhere in Korea where their operations might promote the achievement of [their] missions. . . . This suggestion was generally welcomed; in fact it was clear that other people had been thinking along the same lines, and I can claim no originality for the thought. But I think it was instrumental in determining the establishment of a favorable State Department position on this point.

Just when and how the official Washington position changed is something which is still not clear to me. When, on July 9-10, the Chinese were reported to have accepted an Indian proposal that a solution be sought to the conflict along lines that involved, among other things, the restoration of the *status quo ante* in Korea, our government, as will be seen below, was quite unwilling to entertain this suggestion, considering that this would leave South Korea defenseless in the face of the possibility of a renewed North Korean attack. Then I find among my diary notes for July 21 the following significant entry:

First thing this morning two of the staff members came in to see me to voice their concern at the fact that we were not making clear our determination to stop at the 38th parallel in Korea. They were afraid that our reticence on this point might lead to misunderstandings on the Soviet side and cause the Kremlin to commit Soviet forces unnecessarily, in ways that might interfere with an eventual settlement.

I spoke of this at the [Secretary's] morning meeting, and said that I thought the question deserved careful attention. We must remember, I said, that what we were doing in Korea was, although for good political reason, nevertheless an unsound thing, and that the further we were to advance up the peninsula the more unsound it would become from the military standpoint. If we were actually to advance beyond the neck of the peninsula, we would be getting into an area where mass could be used against us and where we would be distinctly at a disadvantage. This, I thought, increased the importance of our being able to terminate our action at the proper point; and it was desirable that we should make sure we did not frighten the Russians into action which would interfere with this.

Similarly, under date of July 31, the following diary notation appears:

I was somewhat shocked to receive from the Bureau of United Nations Affairs a draft of a statement which it was proposed Senator

Austin should make if people should really get down to brass tacks in the Security Council about a settlement of the Korean matter by the United Nations. This draft put forward as a US position the proposition that the North Korean forces should be withdrawn to the 38th parallel, but added that they should surrender their arms to the United Nations commander and relinquish authority to him in order that he might create order throughout all of Korea. Elections throughout all of Korea were then to be held under UN auspices.

After some discussion of this draft with others, I phoned Matthews and said that while I did not consider it likely that we would get as far as any discussion of such matters in the Security Council tomorrow, I was very much disturbed about this draft, which carried us into entirely unclarified areas of policy, and recommended that there be high level discussions on these matters before any further consideration be given to it.

My reasons, which I stated to the others who discussed the matter with me, were the following: This could be interpreted by the Russians only to mean that we were pressing for the establishment of full military and police authority of General MacArthur right up to the northern borders of Korea, at the gates of Vladivostok. The Russians would never under any circumstances agree to this.

What influences were finally decisive in persuading us to go beyond the parallel and to enlist the support of the UN Assembly in this enterprise I do not know. They were, apparently, beginning to be strongly felt by mid-August; for on August 19 our representative in the Security Council, Senator Warren Austin, was already talking about the impossibility of leaving Korea "half slave and half free." Mr. John Foster Dulles, too, as we shall shortly see, appears to have favored an advance beyond the parallel as early as the end of July; and this could be, I should think, taken as evidence that such a view already represented the consensus of feeling in right-wing Republican circles on the Hill. But I also suspect that the change was partly the work of our wide-eyed enthusiasts for the UN, who, like so many other idealists, often promoted with the best of motives causes which ultimately only added to, instead of subtracting from, the total volume of violence taking place in the affairs of nations.

Our advance beyond the parallel was of course based, when it came, on a UN resolution. I never approved of the involvement of the United Nations in the Korean affair, or understood the rationale for it. This was, after all, an area in which we had taken the Japanese surrender and accepted the responsibilities of occupation. There was as yet no peace treaty with Japan to define its future status. We had accepted the responsibilities of military occupation in South Korea, and the fact that we had withdrawn our own combat forces did not mean, in the continued absence of a Japanese peace treaty, that these responsibilities were terminated. We had a perfect right to intervene, on the basis of our position as occupying power, to assure the preservation of order in this territory. We needed no international mandate to make this action proper. Nor did the Charter of the United Nations require us to involve the organization in such a conflict. Article 107, while somewhat ambiguous, conveyed the general impression that problems arising immediately from the recent war were not to be considered proper subjects for the attention of the UN. This was, finally, a civil conflict, not an international one; and the term "aggression" in the usual international sense was as misplaced here as it was to be later in the case of Vietnam. The involvement of the United Nations, hastily brought about by my colleagues in the State Department before I returned from my farm on that fateful Sunday, was thus in no way necessary or called for; and the later invocation of a UN resolution to justify military operations extending beyond the parallel seemed to me to represent an abuse, rather than a proper utilization, of the exceptional confidence accorded to us at that time by the international community.

The second of the issues that claimed my attention in those summer weeks following the attack on Korea was the question of the possible admission of Communist China to the United Nations. The way it came up was this. On July 10, we received word that the Indian government had approached both the Soviet and Chinese Communist governments with the suggestion for a settlement of the Korean question based on:

Last Months in Washington

> (*a*) admission of Communist China to the UN; and
>
> (*b*) restoration of the *status quo ante* in Korea by action of the expanded Security Council (i.e., after return of the Soviet representative, who had demonstrably absented himself in recent weeks).

According to the Indians, the Chinese Communists had shown themselves receptive to this suggestion, whereas the Soviet government had rejected the second point. Our initial reaction was, characteristically, to reject both points on grounds that have, today, a familiar ring: as already stated, we could not agree to the second one because this would leave the South Korean Republic defenseless and vulnerable to renewed aggression from the north; and as for the first — an admission of Communist China to the United Nations would be "a reward to the aggressor" and was therefore unthinkable.

This subject came up at the Secretary's morning meeting, the following day. "I made bold to say," the diary tells me,

that while I was not taking any exception to the proposed reply, I was a little worried lest it indicate an attitude too sweeping and too little deliberate in its high-minded rejection of the Indian ideas. I pointed out that if what the Indians had said was true . . . then here was indeed a serious difference of policy between the Soviet and Chinese Communist governments. Our action in Korea was after all only a negative action, occasioned by the manner in which we had been provoked . . . It did not represent any real strategic interests on our part, and it should be our concern to get ourselves out of the involvement as rapidly as this could be done on terms not detrimental to our prestige or the purpose of our action there. For this reason, we should not be negative about any efforts being made anywhere to solve the Korean affair, and especially when they appeared to reveal possibilities of splitting the Chinese Communists from the Russians on issues of real importance. I pointed out what an embarrassing position the Soviet government would be placed in if we were suddenly to favor and achieve the admission of the Chinese Communists to the UN and the Security Council under some understanding which involved Chinese Communist support for a settlement of the Korean affair along the lines the Indians had suggested. This might place the Soviet government before the dilemma of returning to the Security Council and publicly disagreeing with the Chinese Communists in the UN about Korea or remaining outside the Security Council while the Chinese Communists were in it, thus producing a very strange and embarrassing situation for themselves.

On July 17, the text of Stalin's reply to the Indian initiative lay before us. The circle of those who addressed themselves that morning to the discussion of it included now Mr. John Foster Dulles. His presence there was occasioned, as I recall it, primarily by the fact that he had been entrusted by the President with the conduct of the work and negotiations looking to conclusion of a Japanese peace treaty; but he participated in a number of the more general discussions among the Secretary of State's senior advisors.

Stalin's reply called, among other things, for action by the United Nations Security Council "with the obligatory participation of representatives of the five great powers, including the People's Government of China." In the discussion that ensued, I drew attention again to the advantages that might be gained, from the standpoint of the prospects for a favorable settlement of the Korean conflict, if we could accept admission of Communist China to the UN. Our position could be, I thought, that this question of China's admission was a separate one, and

if anyone thought that we had any ulterior motives about that, we would be prepared to abstain in any vote on the admission of the Chinese Communists and to leave the question entirely to the judgment of the international community. It was my thought that in this way we might get this question removed from the area of discussion, so that Stalin could no longer exploit it as an excuse for not facing up to the situation in Korea. As far as I can see, it makes not the slightest difference whether or not the Chinese Communists come into the UN; and the fact that they might come in would be no reason, in my opinion, why we should feel obliged to have diplomatic relations with them. I hate to see what seems to me a minor issue, on which we should never have allowed ourselves to get hooked in the first place, become something which the Russians can use to our disadvantage in the Korean affair.

I was shouted down on this. Mr. Dulles pointed out that if we were to do this it would look as though we were retreating on the Chinese Communist issue in the belief that we were thereby buying some Russian concessions about Korea; and that it would therefore look to our public as though we had been tricked into giving up something for nothing. I recognized the force of this and realize that nothing can be done; but I hope that some day history will record this as an instance of the damage done to the conduct of our foreign policy by the irresponsible and bigoted interference of the China lobby and its friends in Congress.*

Toward the end of July, the Soviet government made known its disposition to resume, as of the beginning of August, its seat on the Security Council. This confronted us once more with the question of how we should respond to possible renewed demands for seating of the Chinese Communists. Again: the diary (Friday, July 28):

In all the discussions of the morning I found myself for the most part in a lonely position of single opposition to the views of my associates. The main point at issue is the recognition of the Chinese Communists in the UN. I can see, myself, no fundamental objection from the standpoint of US interest to the seating of the Chinese Communists, provided we still wish to cling to the principle that the UN is a universal organization and can eventually be of some use in the adjusting of relationships between East and West by means other than a major war. The seating . . . would, in my opinion, constitute no new reality of any great significance. The significant reality was created when the Chinese Communists overran the mainland of China. Whether they should now be seated in the UN is only a question of the registration of an existing fact. It alters nothing in principle. We knew when we asked the Soviet Union to join us in setting up the organization, and when we admitted Soviet satellites to its membership in addition to conniving at the fiction of independent Ukrainian and Belorussian membership, that we would be dealing with an organization in which a certain number of the other members had political purposes antagonistic to ours. Admission of the Chinese Communists would add one hostile

* Diary, July 17, 1950.

vote in the General Assembly. This was insignificant. It would also give the Soviet Union one more friendly seat on the Security Council; but in doing so it would only restore, at best, the situation that had existed in this respect prior to the defection of Tito from the Kremlin leadership. An extra veto would be of no significance; two vetoes were not stronger than one. To insist, as my associates were doing, that the Chinese should not be admitted because they had taken an adverse attitude toward the UN action in Korea was to try to make form rather than substance the decisive factor in the handling of UN affairs.

The Chinese Communists were not as yet members of the UN and had not participated in its deliberations about Korea. There was nothing essentially illegitimate about their holding views with respect to Korea different from those of the majority of UN members. What we were dealing with here was a conflict of interest, founded in bitter strategic and political realities. It could not be considered a moral issue. Our insistence on the retention of the Security Council seat by the Chinese Nationalists was a source of confusion and unclarity in Asia. It was being alleged that we were governed by ulterior and imperialistic motives. I was not recommending that we vote for the seating of Communist China, nor that we say any kind words about the Peiping regime, toward which we have no reason to have any kindly feelings. On the contrary, my proposal was that we state frankly that in our opinion the Peiping regime had not shown a due sense of responsibility for its international obligations; that its international behavior had been offensive and childish and even such as to throw doubts on its independence of action in the international field; that we, for these reasons, had not recognized it and saw no reason to do so on the basis of its behavior to date; that since, however, our motives in this matter [of UN membership] had been widely questioned and since it had been alleged that we had ulterior purposes, we were prepared, as a pledge of the integrity of our position, to abstain completely from all further participation in the discussion or in the consideration of this problem in United Nations bodies, from any voting on the subject, and from any sort of pressure or intervention with any other power concerning the way that it should vote. It was our hope that each country would vote on this question as it thought best, in the light of a careful consideration of what was involved; we were prepared to abide entirely by the results of such a test of opinion.

My view was rejected by Dulles primarily on the ground that it would confuse American public opinion and weaken support for the President's program looking toward the strengthening of our defenses, and this position was eventually upheld by the Secretary. I said that I could very well understand this but that I shuddered over the implications of it; for it implied that we could not adopt an adequate defense position without working our people up into an emotional state, and this emotional state, rather than a cool and unemotional appraisal of national interest, would then have to be the determinant of our action. The position we were taking seemed to me to imply acceptance of the theory that in the last analysis the UN would not be universal but would be an Article 51 alliance against Russia. It seemed further to imply that the basis of our policy in the Far East from here on out would be an emotional anticommunism which would ignore the value to ourselves of a possible balance between the existing forces on the Asiatic continent, would force everyone to declare himself either for us (and incidentally for Chiang Kai-shek) or against us; that this would break the unity not only of the non-Communist countries in Asia but also of the non-Communist community in general, and would be beyond our military capacity to support. It rested, I said, on the encouragement in the minds of our people of a false belief that we were a strong power on the mainland of Asia, whereas we are in reality a weak one. Only the very strong can take high and mighty moral positions and ignore the possibilities of balance among the opposing forces. The weak must accept realities and exploit those realities to their advantage as best they can.

In the case of Dulles, as I say, the objectives were laid to public opinion. With Rusk and some of the others, I think there was a real sense of moral indignation about the Chinese Communists. These people, after all, are treading now the paths which we old Russian hands were treading over twenty years ago in our first experiences with the Soviet dictatorship. We were not unaware then, and we are not unaware now, of the fundamental ethical conflict between their ideals and ours. But we view the handling of our end, in this conflict, as a practical matter similar to many other matters with which diplomacy has had to deal through the course of the centuries. We have learned not to recoil from the struggle for power as something shocking or abnormal. It is the medium in which we work, as the doctor works in

the medium of the human flesh, and we will not improve our performance by failing to deal with its real nature or by trying to dress
it up as something else. In our own consciences — in our own concept,
that is, of our obligations to ourselves — we Americans may be profoundly convinced that we are "right." In our participation on the
international scene, we are only one of a number of contenders for the
privilege of leading a national existence on a portion of the territory of
this world. Other people are our enemies, and we must deal with them
accordingly. But let us recognize the legitimacy of differences of interest and philosophy between groups of men and not pretend that
they can be made to disappear behind some common philosophical concept.

This last discussion was, as indicated, on a Friday. On Monday
morning, just after the intervening weekend, one of the members of
the Planning Staff came in to tell me (again, the diary is the source)
that

he had learned from one journalist, who had learned it from another
journalist, that Mr. Dulles had said to journalist N. 2 that while he used
to think highly of George Kennan, he had now concluded that the
latter was a very dangerous man: that he was advocating the admission
of the Chinese Communists to the United Nations and a cessation of
US military action at the 38th parallel. This information had been
passed along to my friend under such solemn vows of discretion on
his part that I saw nothing I could do about it; but it seemed to me to
raise serious problems of the privacy of discussion among top officials
of the department in the presence of the policy advisor from the Republican Party.

There is little that need be added to these diary items. The reader
will recognize, of course, that had my view been accepted, there
would have been no advance by our forces to the Yalu, no Chinese
intervention, but distinctly better prospects for an early termination of the conflict. Against these consequences there will have to
be weighed whatever advantages can be construed to have flowed
from the bloody encounters of the remainder of the Korean War
and from the exclusion of the Chinese Communists, over a period of

at least seventeen years to come, from membership in the United Nations.

The third of the issues that preoccupied me in particular during that summer of 1950 was the question of Soviet intentions. As already stated, I was asked to brief the Secretary of State and his senior advisors daily on the evidence relating to this subject. This I was glad to do; and I have no doubt that what I had to say was listened to thoughtfully and with a certain amount of respect by most of those present. But it proved quite ineffective with relation to the development of governmental thinking generally.

Somehow or other, the North Korean attack came soon to appear to a great many people in Washington as merely the first move in some "grand design," as the phrase then went, on the part of the Soviet leaders to extend their power to other parts of the world by the use of force. The unexpectedness of this attack — the fact that we had had no forewarning of it — only stimulated the already existent preference of the military planners for drawing their conclusions only from the assessed *capabilities* of the adversary, dismissing his *intentions*, which could be safely assumed to be hostile. All this tended to heighten the militarization of thinking about the cold war generally, and to press us into attitudes where any discriminate estimate of Soviet intentions was unwelcome and unacceptable. In addition, it encouraged the military planners in another tendency against which I had fought long and bitterly but generally in vain: the tendency, namely, to view Soviet intentions as something existing quite independently of our own behavior. It was difficult to persuade these men that what people in Moscow decided to do might be a reaction to things we had done.

This last difficulty arose particularly in connection with the question of the background of the attack in Korea itself. Why had it been authorized by Moscow? True, we had not foreseen it. But once it had happened, it stood as a clue to what had been transpiring in recent weeks and months in the thinking of the Kremlin leaders; and much that was previously unintelligible then fell into place. The definitive historical study of the background in Soviet policy of the decision to authorize the Korean attack has yet to be made, and this is not the place to make it. But it is clear that among the various considerations which motivated Stalin in his decision to take this step, along with some that had no relation to our behavior (recent frustration in Europe, the Communist takeover in China, etc.), were several that represented direct reactions to moves of our own. This could be said with relation to our recent withdrawal of American forces from South Korea, the public statement that South Korea did not fall within the area of our vital strategic interest, and above all our recent decision to proceed at once with the negotiation of a separate peace treaty settlement with Japan, to which the Russians would not be a party, and to accompany that settlement with the indefinite retention of American garrisons and military facilities on Japanese soil. For some reason this connection — the idea that in doing things disagreeable to our interests the Russians might be reacting to features of our own behavior — was one to which the mind of official Washington would always be strangely resistant. Our adversaries, in the ingrained American way of looking at things, had always to be demonic, monstrous, incalculable, and inscrutable. It was unthinkable that we, by admitting that they sometimes reacted to what we did, should confess to a share in the responsibility for their behavior.

This state of affairs found a striking illustration in late August, during the final days of my service in the department, when we learned from the newspapers that American planes had been attacking certain ports on the northeast coast of North Korea in which there were reputed to be Soviet naval installations. Whether or not such installations existed there, the ports were uncomfortably close to Vladivostok and to waters that were, from a Soviet naval standpoint, ones of the utmost sensitivity; and the fact that the attacks were said to have been made through heavy cloud cover gave us no reassurance that our aviators really knew what they were hitting. Explanations given to the press by our military authorities on the spot to the effect that the raids were thought necessary in order to interdict the movement of supplies down the coast were, on investigation, found to have little verifiable substance.

Of all this, as I say, we learned only from the newspapers. At no point were we able to elicit through our own military channels any satisfactory information as to what they had done, were doing, or intended to do in this respect. For anyone kept thus in the dark — for anyone held officially ignorant of actions on our own part that obviously touched the Russians on the most sensitive sort of military nerves — it was obviously impossible to make any adequate assessment of Soviet intentions; for these would inevitably represent, in part, a reaction to our own behavior.

All through that summer, I had the feeling that the situation was slipping away not only from the control but from the influence of people like myself. I talked about this several times with Chip Bohlen, who I believe shared this impression; and on July 12 I noted the feelings I had on coming away from one of these discussions. "In general," I wrote:

the nervousness and consciousness of responsibility is so great around Washington that it is impossible to get people to set their signatures to anything as risky and as little founded in demonstrable fact as an analysis of Soviet intentions based on the subjective experience and instinct and judgment of persons like Chip and myself. Plainly, the government has moved into an area where there is a reluctance to recognize the finer distinctions of the psychology of our adversaries, for the reason that movement in this sphere of speculation is all too undependable, too relative, and too subtle to be comfortable or tolerable to people who feel themselves confronted with the grim responsibility of recommending decisions which may mean war or peace. In such times, it is safer and easier to cease the attempt to analyze the probabilities involved in your enemy's mental processes or to calculate his weaknesses. It seems safer to give him the benefit of every doubt in matters of strength and to credit him indiscriminately with *all* aggressive designs, even when some of them are mutually contradictory. In these circumstances, I was inclined to wonder whether the day had not passed when the government had use for the qualities of persons like ourselves — for the effort at cool and rational analysis in the unfirm substance of the imponderables — for an estimate of our Soviet adversaries based on their possible weaknesses as well as their possible strengths.

Altogether, I could find no comfort in what I could observe of the general conduct of foreign policy by our government in that hectic summer. The Korean attack had stirred us all up like a stone thrown into a beehive. People went buzzing and milling around, each with his own idea of what we were trying to do. Nothing seemed more futile than the attempt to infuse mutual understanding of concept, consistency of concept, and above all sophistication of concept into this turmoil of willful personalities and poorly schooled minds. "Never before," I wrote on August 14, 1950,

has there been such utter confusion in the public mind with respect to US foreign policy. The President doesn't understand it; Congress doesn't understand it; nor does the public, nor does the press. They all wander around in a labyrinth of ignorance and error and conjecture, in which truth is intermingled with fiction at a hundred points, in which unjustified assumptions have attained the validity of premises, and in which there is no recognized and authoritative theory to hold on to. Only the diplomatic historian, working from the leisure and detachment of a later day, will be able to unravel this incredible tangle and to reveal the true aspect of the various factors and issues involved. And that is why, as it seems to me, no one in my position can contribute very much more . . . unless he first turns historian, earns public confidence and respect through the study of an earlier day, and then gradually carries the public up to a clear and comprehensive view of the occurrences of these recent years.

These were the thoughts — this, the spirit — in which I finally left Washington, at the end of August 1950, and removed to Princeton, where Robert Oppenheimer had offered me hospitality at the Institute for Advanced Study. There, another environment, more kindly and receptive to whatever it was that I had to offer, and a new life, also not without its complications but with greater possibilities for creative expression than any I had ever known, awaited me.

Annexes

A. Russia — Seven Years Later
(*September 1944*)

IT is characteristic of the contradictory quality of all Russian reality that one can argue whether it is more presumptuous to write about Russia after a long presence or after a longer absence. Each doubtless has its values. Each also has its risks. It is the latter that I propose to undertake in this paper; and in justification of it I can cite only the subtlety of all change in a country where the relationship beweeen public feeling and official policy, between motive and action, between cause and effect, is a jealously guarded secret of state. This subtlety often makes invisible to the permanent resident of Moscow the movement of the society in which he lives. He himself moves with the stream; everything that he sees moves with him; and like the navigator at sea he has no subjective perception of the current upon which he is borne. This is why it is sometimes easier for someone who leaves and returns to estimate the speed and direction of movement, to seize and fix the subtleties of trend. And this, incidentally, is why no foreign observer should ever be asked to spend more than a year in Russia without going out into the outside world for the recovery of perspective.

In August 1937, the Soviet Union was not a happy place. In the material sense, conditions were indeed tolerable — better than they had been at any time since the late Twenties. But the purges, which had begun in earnest in 1935, were just then nearing their close; and the atmosphere which they left in their train was heavy and unpleasant. They had been enormously destructive in human values. The original generation of Communists was gone for good. Only Molotov, Voroshilov, Kalinin, and a handful of others had survived — to move like ghosts through the world of young new faces — their memories the only monuments to those fallen comrades hand in hand with whom they had once built the revolution and for whose fate they bore such heavy responsibility. And the great old names of communism had not died alone. With them had gone a full 75 percent of the governing class of the country, a similar proportion of the leading intelligentsia, and over half the higher officers' corps of the Red army.

The issue had been primarily this. Were the rank and file of the Communist Party, by virtue of the unique and limited type of democracy which originally existed among party members, to remain a living force in the political life of Russia? Or was the principle of unlimited autocracy — a principle rendered congenial to the Russian mind by centuries of Tsarist tradition and already reestablished in the state at large — to be established within the party as well? With the close of the purges, this issue had been decided. Stalin had settled firmly back into the throne of Ivan the Terrible and Peter the Great. He had become the "Batyushka Tsar" of the Russian fable. Those who longed instinctively for this sort of leadership could rejoice. But the cost had been undeniably great. The methods employed had been degrading. All but the most thick-skinned were a little ashamed. Life had now to be begun again with new and untried people. A new future had to be faced. The ship of state had been cut loose from the bonds of Communist dogma. Only the captain now plotted its course. And no one knew where it might be bound.

Today, seven years later, the Russian people stand again at the close of a great and destructive trial of their national worth. During the past three and a quarter years they have suffered invasion by the greatest military force in history; at least half of the developed portions of their country has been subjected to the devastations of war. Again there has been a tremendous toll of human life, far more costly than the purges on the population as a whole, although easier on the bureaucracy. To this has been added enormous material damage, and a heavy setback to national economy.

Yet how different this war from the purges, in its psychological effect. Here the national conscience is untroubled. And national self-confidence has been immeasurably increased. Aided by the mistakes of their adversaries, by the character of their country, by their recent industrialization, by the help of the Western powers, and by their own extraordinary capacity for heroism and endurance, the Russian people have repelled the invader and regained their territories in a series of military operations second in drama and grandeur to nothing else that the history of warfare can show.

In the life of a young and impressionable people this is the sort of experience that surpasses the receptivity of a single generation, that enters into the subconscious mind of a nation, to become legend, folk-lore, tradition — to determine the reactions of people yet unborn. And even in the present its effect is profound. It has pulled regime and people together, in a process for which the former, at any rate, can be highly thankful. It has clarified many of the riddles of the revolution. It has strengthened faith in the future. It has revived the hope, latent in every Russian soul, that the scope and daring of the Russian mind will some day overshadow the achievements of the haughty and conventional West. It has dispelled some of the suspicion, equally latent in every Russian soul, that the hand of failure lies heavily over all Russian undertaking, that the term "Russia" does not really signify a national society destined to know power and majesty, but only a vast unconquerable expanse of misery, poverty, inefficiency, and mud. In short, it has left behind it a Russian people once more impoverished (but hardened to poverty), once more decimated (but accustomed to decimation), brutalized by intimacy with brutality, united under firm and ruthless leadership, master of its own territory and its own philosophy, beholden to no one, thirsting for prosperity, power, and glory, looking into the future, as far as its weariness permits, with pride, confidence, and a new sense of national solidarity.

What are its chances?

It would be superfluous to trace out here the complicated channels through which estimates are arrived at for the effects of the period of the war on the Russian population. Such figures, in any case, must of course remain pure estimates for a considerable time to come. Nevertheless, competent experts have given careful study to this question, and their results are so close to one another that I think they may be accepted for the purposes of as rough a survey as this. If so, we may conclude that the war losses to the Soviet population have been in the neighborhood of 20,000,000, and that the present population of the Soviet Union proper, including all the new formal acquisitions in the west and allowing for all war losses, is approximately 185,000,000. To this — if we are to estimate the real power potential of Moscow — there should be added various population elements along the Russian borders not formally included in the Soviet Union but already amenable in one degree or another to Russian authority or influence, as well as the numbers which may shortly be added to this category in the Balkans, in Poland, in Finland, and elsewhere. While the scientist cannot deal with such loose conceptions, the statesman or the diplomat must take this factor into account. If this be done, and if due respect be paid to the indomitable fertility of the eastern Slav, we must reckon with the prospect that in a very short time despite all war losses, the power of the Kremlin will encompass something more than two hundred million souls.

The fact is that the losses brought about by the war have been substantially balanced off by the acquisitions of new territory and the further extensions of Soviet influence; so that we are dealing today with a Soviet population roughly equal in number to what we would probably have faced at this time had there never been any war in Eastern Europe in the last few years and had Hitler never given Stalin the opportunity to extend his authority to a further large zone of Eastern Europe.

Since these acquisitions of territory have been made at the expense of the total population of the remainder of Europe, the balance of population as between Russia and the remainder of the European peninsula (excluding the British Isles) has been somewhat altered. Europe, to be sure, can still count something like three hundred million people in the territories not yet subject to predominant Russian influence. These are, for the most part, highly developed and energetic people. They have just had intensive experience with foreign rule. They know the forms it takes. They know how to combat it. And their number is still sufficient to give grounds for second thought to those who regard Europe as "finished" and predict the early establishment of Russian domination throughout the continent. On the other hand, two hundred million people, united under the strong purposeful leadership of Moscow and inhabiting one of the major industrial countries of the world, constitute a single force far greater than any other that will be left on the European continent when this war is over; and it would be folly to underestimate their potential — for good or for evil.

The war and the German invasion have naturally had a profound effect on Russian economic life. Roughly 25 percent of the fixed capital of the country has probably been destroyed. The available labor fund has been reduced by at least three million people. If the war ends this fall, national income, according to best available estimates, will probably have been reduced by approximately 25 to 30 percent over the figure for 1940. And there are significant structural changes in the composition of national income. The income from agriculture will have been reduced by some 35 to 40 percent — that is, much more than the income from industry and other forms of economic life. In industry, due to transfer of enterprises to the east and to wartime construction, the decline is relatively small. Thus the relative importance of industry has undergone a great increase.

Yet for all these changes in the content of Russian economic life, its form remains just what it was seven years ago. With small and insignificant exceptions, the fruits of the labor of the entire population continue to pour, such as they are, into the hoppers of the government, which then sluices off this national income at will into the respective categories of consumption, capital investment, military expenditures, etc. Thus, while the total figure of national income must remain limited by the physical and nervous energies of the Russian people and by the amount of mechanical power at their disposal, and while there is also a limit of physical endurance beyond which their consumption for daily life cannot advantageously be reduced — for the rest, national economy is in the hands of the government. It is subject to no elemental laws of its own, such as the laws that govern economic life under conditions of free enterprise. And those who would understand its present state or define its future must look first of all to the minds and plans of the men who formulate economic policy.

This realization is the only reply to many of the questions one hears in Moscow about the future of Russian economic life: about the tempo of reconstruction, about the need for foreign assistance. All of these things will depend primarily on the policy of the Kremlin. If the war ends for Russia this fall, the Kremlin leaders will still presumably have an annual income slightly over twenty billion dollars to play with. (The figure is largely arbitrary, insofar as it depends on the exchange rate selected; but it will do for purposes of comparison.) They can allocate this as they like. At least ten billion, we may estimate, must go to consumption, if the energies of the people are to be sustained. (This would put the country back to the consumption expenditure of about 1934, but for a considerably larger population, and in the face of certain very special needs.) With the remainder, they can do what they please. They can use it in varying proportions for further consumption (i.e., for an improvement in living standards), for the increase of fixed capital (reconstruction, new industrial development, new tools for agriculture, etc.), or for military purposes. If they should choose to apply it all to the improvement of living standards, they could presumably restore the 1940 standard, even without outside assistance, in the course of a year or two. If they should choose to apply it all to fixed capital, they could likewise make good most of the war losses in a similar space of time. If they should choose to apply it all to the military machine, they could continue to maintain their present wartime force and improve considerably their equipment. Actually, of course, they will choose none of these extreme solutions, but will divide the expenditure between the three purposes in the way that they consider wisest.

It is idle for us to attempt to define the degree of altruism or of selfishness which will underlie this allocation. Gibbon teaches that "the rational wishes of an absolute monarch must tend to the happiness of his people." If we know anything of the minds of Stalin and his advisors we know enough to postulate that their decisions with regard to the future of Russian economic life will be predicated on the determination to increase the relative power and prestige of the Russian state in the world at large. And we may also guess that they will see the way to the achievement of this goal in the increase of fixed capital and in the maintenance of a large military establishment rather than in a rapid improvement of living standards. From this we may conclude that the Kremlin will promptly revert, after the war, to the basic program of military industrialization in which it was engaged from 1930 to 1941. A military establishment greater than any other in the world will be maintained. Reconstruction and new construction will be vigorously carried forward. We may expect that within three to four years, even barring outside credits, the overall industrial potential of the country will have been restored to its prewar figure. The standard of living will take considerably longer to recover — even to that 1940 level, the blessings of which our liberal commentators are so prone to exaggerate. In the two decades from 1920 to 1940 the individual security and comfort of one entire generation were sacrificed for the purposes of the Soviet program. With the present war, the sacrifice of a second generation began; and who should doubt that it will be carried to its completion in the ensuing period?

The average Russian of mature age today may some day have the moral satisfaction of seeing his government exercise a power unprecedented in history over the land masses of Asia and Europe. But it is not likely that he will ever know comforts, in the line of housing, clothing, and other conveniences of civilized living, comparable to those that have existed in the advanced countries of the West. That renunciation of comfort is his involuntary contribution to something: either to the future comfort of his own children or to the increased military power of Russia. He hopes — and we hope with him — that it will not be only the latter.

There remain, in the appraisal of Russian economic life, the questions of Russian foreign trade, of the need for foreign credits, of the dependence on the Western world. The answers to these questions are simpler than people are apt to think.

Despite all the prognostications of foreign editorial writers, the Soviet Union will not be economically dependent on the outside world when this war is over. If necessary, it will undertake to solve the problems of reconstruction, of national defense, and of the elevation of living standards alone, on its own resources. It would take longer to do it this way; and more years would have to elapse before any of these given objectives might be achieved. But it would not be out of the question.

Naturally, the Russian leaders will be pleased to have such help as they can obtain from the Western world in the completion of these tasks. In this respect, they will be interested in actual goods, not in money. Credits will interest them only insofar as they make possible the importation of those things which they wish to import at a given period. If they are able to satisfy the major portion of their import program — within the limitations of transport and absorption capacity — by means of foreign credits, they will not hesitate to do so. In doing so, they will not be worried by the extent to which this may influence their position one or two decades hence as a debtor or creditor nation. They learned from their experience with Germany in 1932 and 1933 when the Germans gave them interim credits to keep them above water that the more they owe to the Western world the greater the stake of Western capitalism in their financial prosperity and the less the Western world can afford to see them go bankrupt in their international business dealings.

If credits are not available they will probably still endeavor to maintain a high level of imports through the use of their present gold and foreign currency reserves, estimated at one and a half to two billion dollars. In their own thought, they have little respect for gold beyond what its utilitarian value would warrant, and I doubt that they have real faith in its ultimate endurance as a standard of value in international finance. I suspect that they wonder at our readiness to receive the commodity in exchange for things that have utilitarian value. This being the case, they will presumably not hesitate to exchange their gold in large measure, if necessary, for those things which they do consider to have intrinsic value proportionate to their cost.

To a certain extent, of course, their imports from the outside world will be paid for by exports. In case, for any reason, both gold and credits were to fail, exports of certain raw materials, particularly timber and oil, might be forced, as they were at the beginning of the 1930s, to make possible the execution of the import program. Regardless of the balance of exchange, they will certainly endeavor to export, for purposes predominantly political, to neighboring countries on both the Asiatic and European borders. These exports may assume sizable proportions. But beyond that, they will probably export only to the extent which they consider absolutely necessary in order to make possible the completion of their import program. And this in turn will depend on the availability of foreign credits and the negotiability, in terms of merchandise, of Soviet gold.

The points which Americans would do best to bear in mind with respect to Russian foreign trade after this war are the following:

1. Russia will not be dependent upon foreign trade.
2. Russia will not be inclined to give up anything for the sake of foreign trade which she deems vital or more important in terms of her own security and progress.
3. Russia will gladly accept any credits which will enable her to obtain needed imports for capital investment without immediate cost to herself.
4. Whatever credits are granted to her, Russia will assume that the foreign governments who made these credits possible will have acted in their own interests and with their eyes open. She will not permit this action to become the cause of widespread feelings of gratitude or sentimental enthusiasm among the Russian population which might weaken the relative respect of the latter for — and sense of dependence on — the Soviet government itself.

Through war, through peace, through drama, through suffering, unceasingly and irresistibly, there goes on that vast organic process which we can only describe as the spiritual life of the Russian people. It is at once the most important and the most mysterious of all the things that are happening in the Soviet state. It is important because it will some day determine the strength and character of Russia's national effort and of Russia's influence on the world. It is mysterious because it is governed by laws of its own, which not even the Kremlin understands.

Whether Moscow itself is aware of this, I cannot say. Moscow goes to the greatest possible lengths to control this phase of Russian life. No shepherd, real or spiritual, ever watched his flock with a more solicitous, a more jealous eye than that with which the Kremlin stands guard over the souls of its human charges. And the latter, in turn, respond with an agreeable acquiescence which could leave nothing to be desired. Bade to admire, they applaud generously and cheerfully. Bade to abhor, they strike a respectful attitude of hatred and indignation. But in the very readiness and regularity of this reaction, there lies the proof of its superficiality. The Russian people have dissembled for so many centuries that they have dignified the quality into a national virtue. In contrast to Western nations, they can dissemble graciously and good-naturedly — without resentment, without bad manners, without impatience. In this they have challenged, and challenged successfully, the power of the Kremlin.

By this, I do not mean to say that they are politically dissatisfied. But when the influence of the regime comes too close to those mysterious recesses that we may call — at the risk of banality — the Russian "soul," then the people quietly and politely disengage themselves behind an impeccable series of superficial responses, leaving their masters not quite sure just what they meant by the demure tone in which they murmured, "Why, yes. Of course."

Fifteen years of negation of the Russian classics on the part of the regime, all received with flawless acquiescence by the mass of the public, did not prevent Leo Tolstoy from becoming at the end of that period the most widely read of all authors in the Soviet Union. Fifteen years of Communist experimentation with the theater, all generously and unfailingly applauded by the spectators, have brought dramatic art in Russia back to a level of conservatism which makes the Moscow Art Theater once again, as forty years ago, the most daring venture in modernism on the Russian stage. Fifteen years of excursions by young people to antireligious museums have failed to yield a single word of indignation or criticism when, largely for reasons of foreign political expediency, superficial respite is now given to the Orthodox Church — when crowds of mothers surround the baptismal fonts on Sunday mornings and when a religious seminary — state controlled, to be sure, but nevertheless a seminary — opens its doors in the venerable walls of the New Virgin Monastery. In every way, on every hand, we see the people of Russia reverting quietly, triumphantly, to that point at which their spiritual and cultural development was interrupted by the violence and conceit of the revolution. We see them taking up the threads again where they once left off. And we see the Kremlin at long last following along in this development. Why? Because it does not know what else to do. Because it has seen the futility of any other course. The strength of the Kremlin lies largely in the fact that it knows how to wait. But the strength of the Russian people lies in the fact that they know how to wait longer.

In the demands of people for cultural and spiritual nourishment, there has been no change in the past few years. The Russians remain what they were seven years ago: the most unspoiled and the most curious of peoples. No other people has such a thirst for knowledge, such a zest for intellectual and artistic experience. They are as unspoiled in the immaterial things as they are in the comforts of life, and their tastes are as primitive in one sphere as in the other. They are grateful for anything. A Mack Sennett comedy would be as welcome as a performance of *The Fountain of Bakhchisarai*. If they have any preference, it is for nineteenth-century melodrama and romanticism. But in general, like children, they recognize no limit to their own ability to absorb and digest impressions. The world, as far as they are concerned, is their oyster. They want anything and everything that is in it.

What they get is another matter. The sum total of artistic and intellectual edification provided by the state has probably not changed much in recent years. But most of it has gone to the army rather than to the civilian population, since the war began. Throughout the countryside at large there has been a greater dearth than ever before of everything to do with culture and recreation: of books, of movies, of entertainment. Even before the war, the staggering figures of the publication and distribution of books in the Soviet Union were misleading. A large proportion of these publications were either strictly technical ones, not suitable for the public at large, or cheap pamphlets on various subjects, put out and distributed for political purposes. At the time Russia became engaged in the war, the Russian classics were only just beginning to become available to the Russian public in complete, cheap, and adequate editions. Of good contemporary Russian literature there was little. Translations from foreign languages of good fiction were few. Today, wartime restrictions — despite the earnest efforts of the authorities to combat this development — have further affected not only the distribution of literature, but movies, theater, and radio as well. For most of the women, the children, and the old people who today make up the civilian population of Russia, war has proved, as always, to be the most boring of human institutions; and the hunger for knowledge, for amusement, for artistic experience, is pitiful to behold.

What will be the effects of all this on Russia's future? If we may take again the psychology of children as a criterion, the effects will be all to the good for the future spiritual health of the race. Child psychologists know the benefits to children of quiet, of simplicity, of the avoidance of all that overtaxes the mind, the emotions, the imagination. Boredom, to a degree, spells relaxation; and relaxation spells spiritual health. The level of sophistication among the Russian people may, as a result of the limited intellectual stimuli, not be great. But the level of technical ability is growing. And the Russians, meanwhile, are spared at least that plethora of artificial stimuli and vicarious thrills which sap the emotional strength of big city people in the advanced countries of the West. They may have all this, at some future time. But they haven't got it yet. In contrast to our restless city dwellers, they can still take time to look at the earth and sky, to take note of the passage of the seasons, to sit quietly on a bench on a summer evening, to rest, to dream. And the chances are that in reward for this enforced abstinence they will emerge one or two decades hence with an emotional freshness and vigor which will make the Western peoples seem pale by contrast and which may play an important part in the national effort Russia is destined to make.

So much for the people at large. What about that relatively small nucleus of "intelligentsia" from which, in a state so organized as the Soviet Union, all cultural inspiration must flow? If the quantity of cultural output is limited by the war and the general standard of living, how about quality?

Here there has indeed been a marked change during the past decade. The revolution, in its early stages, destroyed much of the respect for past cultural achievements, and even some of their substance. But in their place it at least produced some noteworthy new manifestations of intellectual and artistic creation.

The value of these new manifestations — interestingly enough — seemed to be commensurate to the degree in which they had their roots in Russian culture of the past. The best writers, like Gorky and Bulgakov, were ones whose literary education had taken place before the revolution. The best poets, like Blok, were bred of the aestheticism of the turn of the century. The best theaters were rooted firmly in the impressionism of Chekhov. The same could be said of the composers, the actors, and the musicians.

But the upheavals and excitement of the revolution had a stimulating effect on all creative minds — the strong ones and the weak ones alike. A large portion of the cream of liberal and radical thinkers from other countries found its way to Moscow, either for permanent residence or for frequent visits. Strong threads bound the lecture rooms, the editorial offices, the ateliers and stages of Moscow with the feverish postwar intellectual life of Berlin and other Western European capitals. The Jewish intellectuals of Eastern Europe, now fully released from those bonds which Tsarism had once placed upon their education and their travel, were able to unleash in turn the full impact of their intellectual and artistic strength; and it was their restless genius which contributed most to the keen and analytical quality of Soviet thought and Soviet feeling in the years immediately following the revolution.

In all this, the past ten years have wrought a tremendous change. A great proportion of the original Soviet intelligentsia was carried off in the purges. Of the great intellectuals of the revolution, such men as Bukharin, Kamenev, and Radek, not one has remained. The Jewish intellectuals suffered particularly heavily, probably not by virtue of the fact that they were Jews, but because — as Jews — they had relatives scattered through a number of countries and had a tendency to maintain contact, both personal and intellectual, with persons outside the

Soviet Union. Finally, the stimulation of Russian nationalism and the embarrassing manifestations of anti-Semitic feeling that occurred during the early months of the war were probably the causes of the fact that after the evacuation of Moscow practically no Jews returned to the city, and this element, once so prominent and so prolific in the cultural life of the capital, has thus been largely, in fact almost entirely, eliminated.

The gradual disappearance of the radical intelligentsia has been accompanied by the steady reappearance of all that they had rebelled against. Along with revived Russian chauvinism there has been a veritable cult of the past in the field of culture. The great masters have been reintroduced — sometimes out of a considerable degree of obscurity — and held up for public admiration as testimonials to the greatness of Russian genius. Russian philosophy, Russian music, and Russian literature are now officially praised and commended with as little regard for their "social content" as for their general comparative value.

This cult of the past has found its culmination in the ballet, which — in its capacity as the formal representation of Russian artistic achievement — has probably now reached a state of technical perfection never known before. But in this flowering of the Russian genius and passion for display, there is a static quality — a congealment of artistic form — which shows how strong has been the influence of Byzantium on Russian culture. Not the quest for the new but the perfection of the old is the essence of this most respected and most characteristic of Russian cultural creations. Its genius, like that which underlay the construction of Santa Sophia or — at a later date — the classic school of Russian icon painting, leans to the elaboration and perfection of traditional detail rather than to the search for new forms. In this spirit, life and art go different ways. Life follows mysterious channels of its own. Art becomes a glorified form of ceremony.

In other forms of art, the scene is even less inspiring. It may be presumptuous for an American, in the year 1944, to deplore the lack of artistic originality in Russia. War is generally the enemy of art; and New York itself is hardly prolific of inspiration in these wartime years. But one may ask for more from a system which claims to have released the creative urge from the shackles of economic exploitation for the first time in history; and a political leadership which can go through a major war and two major reversals of foreign orientation without a single change in its personnel can be perhaps held to other standards than our own capricious and kaleidoscopic democracy. In any case, Soviet culture seems to have developed in inverse ratio to the military glory of the Soviet state. Painting and sculpture can hardly be said to have flourished in recent years. The last good novel was written — let me see — at least a decade ago. Dramaturgy and the theater are pleasing roughly in proportion to the age of the plays and age of the actors. The newer productions and the newer producers have gone back to a heroic style which can only be compared to our nineteenth-century melodrama at its loudest and broadest, with patriotic themes in the place of the romantic, with the traitorous villain in the place of the lecherous one, with the same screaming and groaning, the same flexing of muscles, and the same lack of humor which made the atmosphere of the Mississippi showboat. The Soviet screen, which never coped very well at any time with the problems of the talking film, now suffers from this same absence of lightness; and its subjects — in a world where a mistake in dogma can spell personal catastrophe — have a tendency to become more and more limited, more and more stereotyped. The works of Shostakovich and Prokofiev still stand out bravely in a musical world devoted principally to the cultivation of Glinka, Tchaikovsky, and Rimski-Korsakov. But at the mention of architecture, Moscow conversations have a tendency to drop; and even the warmest enthusiasts are apt to hang their heads and sigh significantly if asked to explain how Soviet creative feeling has expressed itself in architectural form.

I am afraid there can be no doubt of the trend of the life of the spirit in Russia. The exact sciences are flourishing, and may well produce great results in the service of the state. The social sciences have frozen into the rigid patterns of Byzantine scholasticism. In art, all that is decorative, all that partakes of ceremony and representation, will continue to be cultivated with Oriental fidelity and oriental devotion to detail. But the creation of new artistic form is too intimately connected with the freedom of the spirit, with the dignity of the individual, with the critical approach to human society, to take place in the heavy air of a vast and pompous despotism. When the star of Soviet power is on the wane, it may begin to give off again those effervescences of artistic genius with which Russia astounded the world in the latter decades of Tsardom. But while it is in the ascendant, its light will be cold, collected, inscrutable; and Western eyes, always peering from a distance, may wonder whether it is menace or promise that they discern in its austere and formal gleam.

In wartime Russia, domestic politics do not exist. In the army, their place is taken by discipline. And the squabbles and complaints of camp followers (for what else are the civilians, in a military totalitarian state in wartime?) do not deserve the name of politics. The civilian population is only a labor fund of women and children and old people. Beyond forcing them to endure hardship and to work long hours, the regime treats them with exceptional consideration. It is undesirable, from the standpoint of the war, that they should be any unhappier than necessary. But their feelings cannot be said to cause political concern or to have political significance.

With the higher army officers, it is another matter. This is the only group in the Soviet state whose disaffection, at the present moment, might cause critical difficulties for the regime. Stalin appears to have solved this problem satisfactorily by placing himself and his leading political assistants into high military positions. While the institution of political commissars has been abolished in the rank and file of the army, it cannot be said that this has occurred at the top. The position of such men as Zhdanov, Khrushchev, and Bulganin can hardly be other than that of political counterchecks to the operational generals on the sections of the front in which they serve. The Red army is still outstandingly apolitical; and due respect must be paid to the adroitness with which Stalin has reconciled professional military prowess with the most intimate civilian control of the military machine.

In these circumstances domestic politics are quiescent, and apparently will remain so for the duration of the war. What will come after that is another story. It would be premature and dangerous to make predictions. That there will be discontent and restlessness among demobilized officers and men seems scarcely open to doubt. But no one knows better than Stalin the technique of authoritarian rule.

If political conditions are quiet internally, the same cannot be said for foreign policy. Ever since the conclusion of the purges and the establishment of Stalin's power beyond question in the internal political life of the country, the political effort of the Kremlin has concentrated in increasing measure on relations of Russia to the outside world.

It is depressing to reflect how many volumes could be filled with the speculation that has appeared in the foreign press during the past two years on Russia's foreign political aims. The questions involved have been repeated with a monotony that almost discourages the attempt to answer. Has Russian policy changed? Does Russia want to "communize" other countries? Does Russia propose to "cooperate," etc.?

These questions are ones which, in the Soviet view, are very elementary. The reader must, therefore, not take it amiss if the answers are the same.

The Soviet leaders have never forgotten the weak and vulnerable position in which the Soviet regime found itself in the early days of its power. The treaty of Brest-Litovsk, the intervention of Allied forces in various parts of Russia, the repulse of the Red army from the Baltic states, the invasion of the western provinces in the Polish-Russian war of 1920: all these left in Soviet minds an indelible and undoubtedly exaggerated impression of the dangers which threatened Soviet power from without. Fed by the traditional Russian mistrust of the stranger, and reinforced by the continual reverses suffered in the early attempts to increase Russian power through communization, this feeling of fear and insecurity lived and flourished and came to underlie almost all Soviet thought about the outside world.

In the early days of communism it was still officially held, and widely believed, that Russia could and would be saved from what was felt to be its perilous predicament by the growing conflicts between the imperialist powers and by the world revolution which was bound to ensue. Orders given to foreign Communist parties to direct their efforts to the earliest possible achievement of social and political revolution were therefore considered to serve the cause of Soviet military security as well as the broader purposes of Communist ideology. To Stalin's own sense of realism must go the credit for the gradual appreciation that not only were there no real chances for the success of this world revolutionary undertaking, but that the Communist parties operating under such instructions were actually of less practical advantage to the Soviet Union than the groups of bourgeois-liberal enthusiasts for whom — somewhat to Moscow's own surprise — the Soviet Union soon came to have so powerful an attraction. Soviet policy thus began with time to lay less stress on the immediate bringing about of revolution in other countries and to concentrate on using all foreign sympathizers, Communist and otherwise, as vehicles for a purely nationalistic Soviet foreign policy. This was indeed a change, and an important change. But it did not alter the basic conception of Soviet policy, which was to increase in every way and with all possible speed the relative strength of the Soviet Union in world affairs, and to exploit to the utmost for this purpose the rivalries and differences among other powers.

During the years just preceding Hitler's rise to power in Germany the Kremlin, enamoured of its role as the innocent object of evil designs, began — like Shakespeare's lady — to protest too much. It fussed and fumed about the dangers of capitalistic encirclement and about the plans for "intervention" on the part of the "Anglo-French imperialists." It held propaganda trials to impress the population with the proximity of these dangers. All realists knew that the substance behind these fears was not great, and that the value of this constant beating of the alarm lay rather in the stimulus it might bring to the domestic efforts of the Russian population than in the meeting of any real need for national defense. But it served its purpose in large measure, and the Soviet leaders succeeded in convincing many people, themselves included, that mortal danger was at hand.

With Hitler's rise to power, the Kremlin — having cried "wolf" largely out of ulterior motives for a number of years — suddenly found a real wolf at the door. What had once been declamation now became grim reality. During the years from 1933 to 1938, it was well understood in Moscow that the Soviet Union did not have the strength to sustain alone, without aid from outside, a German attack. It seemed to Russian minds, therefore, that the best chance of safety lay in inducing somebody else to fight Hitler before his plans for aggression in the east could develop. Had not Lenin himself said that the "contradictions between the imperialist powers" should always be ruthlessly exploited in the interests of communism? Perhaps this was not only Russia's mortal danger but also Russia's golden opportunity, depending on how it was played.

The result was a sudden enthusiasm for collective security. The Soviet press developed marked solicitude for the precarious position of the Western Democracies in the face of the Nazi menace. The Soviet Union joined the League of Nations. Litvinov went to Geneva, spoke eloquently of the dangers of aggression, of the indivisibility of peace and of the hopelessness of supposing that war, once begun, would not become universal. The Western powers, he argued, should agree to fight at the first sign of German aggression anywhere. He advanced one legalistic formula after another designed to assure that there could be no German aggression which would not involve the Western powers. He was generous in his offers to join anyone and everyone in pacts of mutual assistance.

In all of this, there was no real evidence that Moscow had any serious intention of undertaking major military activities on anyone else's behalf. Traditional Russian preoccupation with the *interpretation* rather than the *letter* of an agreement quickly suggested to the Russian mind that there could be little danger in incurring obligations which Russia herself would be able to interpret unilaterally when the time came to deliver. The main thing was to assure that Germany could not fight in the east without fighting in the west. Once military complications in the western theater were assured, Russia could take care of herself.

This, incidentally, is the answer to the Russian attitude at the time of Munich. Russia, on the precedent of the Spanish war, would have been glad to give token military assistance to Czechoslovakia — particularly in the air. There was no will — and, as the Germans well knew, no possibility — for the dispatch of any sizable ground force to Czechoslovakia at that time.

Litvinov's efforts tided over a difficult period, during which both German and Russian armaments were built up. But they did not succeed in drawing the Western powers into obligations which would compel them to fight Hitler if the latter embarked on a policy of expansion; and the chances of accomplishing this looked progressively dimmer as Nazi power increased and Western appeasement continued.

If Russia could not rely on the Western nations to save her, it then seemed to Russian minds that the alternative lay not only in the utmost development of Russian military power within the 1938 borders, but also in new territorial acquisitions designed to strengthen Russia's strategic and political position, and in the creation of a sphere of influence even beyond these limits. In drawing up this expansionist program, Soviet planners leaned heavily on the latter-day traditions of Tsarist diplomacy.

The experience of Munich, at which moment the nightmare of an isolated German-Russian war seemed close to becoming reality, finally dispelled all serious hopes in the prospects of inducing the Western world to fight Hitler except in direct self-defense, and the stage reached at that moment in the military industrialization of Russia lent justification to the final junking of Litvinov's tenuous program. The road was now open for a policy of open territorial expansion, designed if possible to forestall attack on Russia, but at any rate to soften the shock of the attack when it came. In this way it came about that the Kremlin, in the summer of 1939, rejected the advances of the Western powers, who had neither the will nor the strength to hand over whole sections of Eastern Europe to the Soviet Union, and accepted the advances of the Germans, in whom neither this will nor this strength were lacking.

It would be useful to the Western world to realize that despite all the vicissitudes by which Russia has been afflicted since August 1939, the men in the Kremlin have never abandoned their faith in that program of territorial and political expansion which had once commended itself so strongly to Tsarist diplomatists, and which underlay the German-Russian Nonaggression Pact of 1939. The program meant the reestablishment of Russian power in Finland and the Baltic states, in eastern Poland, in northern Bukovina, and in Bessarabia. It meant a protectorate over western Poland, and an access to the sea for the Russian Empire somewhere in East Prussia. It meant the establishment of dominant Russian influence over all the Slavs of Central Europe and the Balkans, and, if possible, the creation of a corridor from the western to the southern Slavs somewhere along the border between Austria and Hungary. Finally, it meant Russian control of the Dardanelles through the establishment of Russian bases at that point. This program was intended not only to increase the physical military strength of Russia. It was intended to prevent the formation in Central and Eastern Europe of any power or coalition of powers capable of challenging Russian security.

It was considered in Moscow in 1939 that if a portion of this program could be realized by an agreement with the Germans such as was actually concluded, an agreement which would at the same time turn the point of German weapons toward the west, this would be a handsome achievement. While it was recognized that it would hardly prevent the growth of a power in Central Europe dangerous to Russia it did seem to assure that that power would first exhaust itself against the Western nations, and would in any event not be turned against Russia alone.

The course of the war provided a bitter disappointment to this line of Russian thought. The West collapsed rapidly, without having brought any serious exhaustion to German military power. Hitler turned out to be in a position to turn a large portion of German strength against Russia in a period of quiescence of military activity in the west. And the territorial gains of the Nonaggression Pact proved to have little real military value. The Russians lost their eastern half of Poland more rapidly, when the time came, than the Poles had lost their western half in 1939. What minor strategic advantages the newly acquired territories might have brought were at least partially balanced off by the ruin of the national armies they had once supported. If still in existence, these armies might have taken up at least some of the shock of the German attack. Their disappearance, to which Russia herself had so largely contributed, left the Red army face to face with the Reichswehr.

But all these reversals failed to shake Russian confidence in the ultimate efficacy of this policy of expansion. The Russian conclusion was not that the policy had been unsound. It was rather that it had not been carried far enough. When, after the first war winter, the prospects of victory began to grow on the horizon, Russian minds saw the possibility of completing successfully in 1945 what had been unsuccessfully begun in 1939. This time there would be no powerful Germany to be reckoned with. An exhausted and war-torn Eastern Europe would provide a plastic and yielding mass from which the objectives of Russian statesmanship could easily be molded.

Until June 1944, all such Russian aims had to await the exertion of a real military effort by the Western powers. Without that effort, not even Russian victory was assured. The second front was a paramount requirement of all Russian policy. The suspicious Russian mind naturally exaggerated the danger of Russia being left in the lurch by her Western allies. To offset this danger the Kremlin was prepared to go a long way to meet the requirements and the prejudices of the Western world.

Western conceptions of future collective security and international collaboration seemed naïve and unreal to the Moscow eye. But if talking in unreal terms was the price of victory, why not? If the Western world needed Russian assurances of future collaboration as a condition of military support, why not? Once satisfied of the establishment of her power in Eastern and Central Europe (and who, after all, would be able to prevent the establishment of that power when the day of German collapse arrived?), Russia would presumably not find too much difficulty in going through whatever motions were required for conformity with these strange Western schemes for collaboration in the preservation of peace. What dangers could collaboration bring to a country which already held in its hand the tangible guarantees of its own security? On the contrary, if it were properly exploited, participation in arrangements for world security might even be made into a form of reinsurance for the protection of Russia's interests. Considerations of prestige, furthermore, would demand that Russia not be missing from any of the councils of the world powers.

In this way, thoughts of international collaboration settled down only too easily beside dreams of empire in minds schooled from infancy to think and deal in even sharper contradictions than these. As long as no second front existed, expediency suggested that the idea of collaboration be kept rather to the fore, the idea of spheres of interest rather in the background. But when the second front became reality, there was no longer any need for excessive delicacy. The resultant bluntness of Soviet policy has caused some surprise and questioning in the West.

People at home would find Soviet words and actions easier to understand if they would bear in mind the character of Russian aims in Eastern and Central Europe. Russian efforts in this area are directed to only one goal: power. The form this power takes, the methods by which it is achieved: these are secondary questions. It is a matter of indifference to Moscow whether a given area is "communistic" or not. All things being equal, Moscow might prefer to see it communized, although even that is debatable. But the main thing is that it should be amenable to Moscow influence, and if possible to Moscow authority. If this can be achieved inconspicuously, with the acquiescence of most of the inhabitants and through a concealed form, so much the better. If not, it will be achieved by other means. For the smaller countries of Eastern and Central Europe, the issue is not one of communism or capitalism. It is one of the independence of national life or of domination by a big power which has never shown itself adept at making any permanent compromises with rival power groups. Neither the behavior of Red army occupying forces nor the degree of "communization" of the country is any criterion of the eventual outcome of this issue. It is not a question of boundaries or of constitutions or of formal independence. It is a question of real power relationships, more often than not carefully masked or concealed. As such — and in no other way — should it be judged.

Today, in the autumn of 1944, the Kremlin finds itself committed by its own inclination to the concrete task of becoming the dominant power of Eastern and Central Europe. At the same time, it also finds itself committed by past promises and by world opinion to a vague program which Western statesmen — always so fond of quaint terms agreeable to their electorates — call collaboration.

The first of these programs implies taking. The second implies giving. No one can stop Russia from doing the taking, if she is determined to go through with it. No one can force Russia to do the giving, if she is determined not to go through with it. In these circumstances, others may worry. The Kremlin chimes, never silent since those turbulent days when Lenin had them repaired and set in motion, now peal out the hours of night with a ring of self-assurance and of confidence in the future. And the sleep of those who lie within the Kremlin walls is sound and undisturbed.

Who are these men who sleep so well?

Joseph Vissarionovich Stalin, now in the sixty-fifth year of his life and the twentieth year of his power in Russia, is the most powerful and the least known of the world's rulers. Only a handful of foreigners have ever seen him. None have ever had any intimate contact with him. No one knows exactly where, or with whom, he lives. His personal life remains a mystery which not even the curiosity of the American press has been able to penetrate. Only his political figure is apparent; and that figure is revealed at best in a series of brief and enigmatic glimpses.

From the standpoint of one who would understand Russia today, there are certain points about Stalin which it is important to remember.

First — that he is a Georgian. That strange law of psychology which has more than once caused great peoples to accept the rule of obscure and untypical persons from their own peripheries has brought Stalin from the barren hills of Georgia to the seclusion of the Kremlin. He does not now consider himself much of a Georgian; and history will have to admit that he has become one of the greatest of *Russian* national figures. But he has not lost the characteristics of his native environment. Courageous but wary; quick to anger and suspicion but patient and persistent in the execution of his purposes; capable of acting with great decision or of waiting and dissembling, as circumstances may require; outwardly modest and simple, but jealous of the prestige and dignity of the state which he heads; not learned, yet shrewd and pitilessly realistic; exacting in his demands for loyalty, respect, and obedience; a keen and unsentimental student of men — he can be, like a true Georgian hero, a great and good friend or an implacable, dangerous enemy. It is difficult for him to be anything in between.

Second — his ignorance of the Western world. Stalin's youth is shrouded in the mists of underworld revolutionary activity — largely in his native Caucasus. From that he graduated into the Dostoyevskian atmosphere of revolutionary conspiracy in European Russia. His life has known only what Lenin called "the incredibly swift transition from wild violence to the most delicate deceit." A brief glimpse of Stockholm, in his younger days, left little or no impression on his fevered imagination. Of Western life in general, he could not possibly understand very much. The placid give and take of Anglo-Saxon life, in particular; the tempering of all enmity and all intimacy, the balancing function of personal self-respect, the free play of opposing interests — these things would remain incomprehensible, implausible to him.

Third — his seclusion. Foreign representatives, fretting over their isolation in Moscow's diplomatic ghetto, should bear in mind that of all the people in Moscow, Stalin himself is probably the most isolated. It is doubtful if in the course of the past fifteen years he has ever had the sensation of being alone or of mingling unobserved with other people. During all this time, he has probably never known what it is to walk down a street by the light of day, like anybody else, and to see life as others see it. If not even the humble diplomatic secretary can visit a Russian provincial town quietly and normally, on his own, without swarms of guides and escorts, without elaborate preparations for his reception, without vodka and caviar and speeches, think what it must be for Stalin to try to catch his countrymen off guard. His beat from his Kremlin office to his dacha is no more revealing than the well-worn cowpaths of the Moscow diplomatic corps; and the precautions taken for his safety must make it nearly as hard for him to survey Moscow as it is for Moscow to survey him. The Moscow police, they say, are instructed to view with suspicion diplomats found to be anywhere except in an automobile, in a museum, or at the *Swan Lake* ballet. Stalin's life is even poorer. His visits to the ballet are few. And the whole Kremlin, when closely observed, bears a depressing resemblance to a chilly museum.

Why do I single out for attention these three aspects of Stalin's life and character? I single them out because they all point to the same thing: namely, to his extreme dependence on his own friends and advisors. In every authoritarian state, political life too readily becomes a struggle for access to the ruler and for the control of his sources of information. In Russia, with its passion for secrecy and conspiracy, this has been particularly pronounced. In the case of Stalin's relations to the Western world the role of his political intimates must — in view of his own ignorance, his extreme seclusion, and his suspicious Georgian nature — be little short of decisive. In the conviction of the writer it is here, in the relations between Stalin and his advisors, that we must seek the explanations for the puzzling, often contradictory, manifestations of Soviet attitude toward Western nations.

The most indisputable, and perhaps the most important, point about Stalin's advisors is that for the past six years there has been practically no change among them. After a period of turnover in high government positions unprecedented except in the most wildly revolutionary eras, Russian political life suddenly froze, about 1938, into an equally unprecedented immobility. There were not even any noteworthy deaths. The Kremlin, having successfully defied so many other rules of human behavior, seemed now to have defied even the laws of human frailty. The deductions of those cynical wits among the foreign observers who insisted that no one could survive the purges who was not endowed with the gift of immortality now seem to be finding confirmation. For years there have been, as far as the outside world is aware, no changes of note in the composition of the Politbureau, the Central Committee of the party, or even the leading provincial party positions. This is extraordinary enough for a country that has been through two major reorientations of foreign policy and a military ordeal which rocked the state to its foundations. It is even more extraordinary for a political system which has never before failed to produce a few sacrificial political victims for every major reverse in the fortunes of the country. At best, it is an unhealthy situation, and one which will take on added importance when the war is over. The danger, in Russian circumstances, is that if changes are not made gradually and in good time, they may come all at once and start another landslide of panic, intrigue, and denunciation similar to that which took place at the time of the purges.

What strikes the Western observer most strongly about this state of affairs is that it means there is not a single person in prominent position in Russia who is in any way personally identified with the present policy of collaboration with the Western democracies. There is not a person who was not doing business pretty much at the same old stand back in the days when policies — and let us hope convictions — were entirely different.

To those who have come to Russia recently for the first time there is nothing unusual in the association of such men as Molotov, Vyshinski, Lozovski, and Manuilski with the policies of Moscow and Tehran. But in the minds of those whose memories of Russia are longer these names arouse strange images.

One can see the figure of Molotov at the ceremonial meeting of the Moscow Soviet in the Great Theater, on November 6, 1939, denouncing England and France ("who are constantly dragging into war not only their own population but also the populations of the dominions and colonies") for opposing Hitler in this "criminal" war. They recall that only a few days earlier, at the session of the Supreme Soviet, he had called England and France "the instigators of the second imperialist war" and had accused them of portraying themselves deceitfully "as fighters for the democratic rights of the peoples."

One sees before him once again the figure of Vyshinski in the prosecutor's box in the Hall of Columns. It is the trial of Bukharin; and Vyshinski is sounding the cry of suspicious, secretive Russia against the fancied hostility of the outside world. It is not only Germany he talks about. "Here in this dock," he thunders, pointing an accusing finger at the last of the great names of the revolution, "is not just one anti-Soviet group, not the agents of just one foreign intelligence service. Here in the dock are a number of anti-Soviet groups, the agents of the intelligence services of a number of foreign powers hostile to the USSR . . . Implicated in the case are . . . at least . . . four foreign intelligence services, the Japanese, German, Polish, and British — and, it goes without saying, all the other foreign intelligence services which maintain friendly, so-called operative contact with the above-mentioned intelligence services." "This trial," one can hear him conclude, "has reminded us again that two worlds face each other as irreconcilable and deadly enemies — the world of capitalism and the world of socialism."

Memories shift to Lozovski, the old operative head of the Red International of Labor Unions, now — like Vyshinski — Assistant People's Commissar for Foreign Affairs. For years on end he harangued despairing foreign workers of the Profintern, gathered together in Moscow for the improvement of their morale. He pleaded with them above all things to understand that apparent Soviet departures from the quest of world revolution did not mean that the goal had been lost sight of. "The situation has changed," he would cry, "and the tactics change. If any particular slogan has outlived its usefulness or any particular formula needs to be changed for a new one, that doesn't mean that everything that there was in the past was wrong." Would he say that today, one wonders? And would he still maintain, as he was maintaining in 1935, that "no force in the world will prevent the collapse of capitalism and the victory of the working class over the bourgeoisie?"

And Manuilski, the old workhorse of the Comintern, now People's Commissar for Foreign Affairs of the Ukraine. At the recent armistice negotiations with the Rumanians, which he attended as the Foreign Minister of a neighboring state to Rumania, he was friendly, agreeable, concerned for the condition of his liberated Ukraine, anxious that the British and American ambassadors should come to Kiev and view the destruction wrought by the Germans there. Did he really want their sympathy? Had he forgotten that in 1939 he was saying: "The years will pass. Not a stone will remain unturned of the cursed capitalistic structure, of its wars, its reaction, its vileness, its bestiality, and its progressive savagery. People will think back on the days of capitalism as on a bad dream." Poor Manuilski. The years *have* passed. The upturned stones are to be found everywhere: in socialism and in capitalism alike — in Kiev as well as in London. The bad dreams of this age are of war and occupation, not of capitalism. Does he know that his analysis was unsound? Does he regret the words of 1939?

The men I have mentioned are all men prominently connected with Russia's formal diplomatic relations with the Western world. They are men who have contact with foreigners in their work and presumably access to the foreign press and foreign literature. Possibly this has indeed widened their horizons to some extent. But what about those other leading figures of the regime whose voice in the inner councils of state is obviously greater than the voice of any of these four, except possibly Molotov? What about such men as Beria, Zhdanov, Shcherbakov, Andreyev, Kaganovich, etc.? What advice do these men give to Stalin about foreign policy?

These prominent Soviet leaders know little of the outside world. They have no personal knowledge of foreign statesmen. To them, the vast pattern of international life, political and economic, can provide no associations, can hold no significance, except in what they conceive to be its bearing on the problems of Russian security and Russian internal life. It is possible that the conceptions of these men might occasionally achieve a rough approximation to reality, and their judgments a similar approximation to fairness; but it is not likely. Independence of judgment has never been a strong quality of leading Communist figures. There is evidence that they are as often as not the victims of their own slogans, the slaves of their own propaganda. To keep a level head in the welter of propaganda and autosuggestion with which Russia has faced the world for the past twenty years would tax the best efforts of a cosmopolitan scholar and philosopher. These men are anything but that. God knows what strange images and impressions are created in their minds by what they hear of life beyond Russia's borders. God knows what conclusions they draw from all this, and what recommendations they make on the basis of those conclusions.

There is serious evidence for the hypothesis that there are influences in the Kremlin which place the preservation of a rigid police regime in Russia far ahead of the happy development of Russia's foreign relations, and which are therefore strongly opposed to any association to Russia with foreign powers except on Russia's own terms. These terms would include the rigid preservation of the conspiratorial nature of the Communist Party, of the secrecy of the working of the Soviet state, of the isolation of the population from external influences, of feelings among the population of mistrust of the outside world and dependence on the Soviet regime, of the extreme restriction of all activities of foreigners in the Soviet Union, and the use of every means to conceal Soviet reality from world opinion.

There is reason to believe that these influences have a certain measure of control over the information and advice that reach Stalin. Certainly there has been no appreciable relaxation, as compared with seven years ago, in the restrictions on association between foreigners and Russians; and representatives of Russia's allies continue to be treated today with no less suspicion than was shown to German representatives in the days of the most violent anti-Fascist press polemics, prior to the conclusion of the Nonaggression Pact. Fortunately, however, there is as yet no reason to conclude that this issue is finally decided and that the isolationists have entirely won the day. The overwhelming sentiment of the country is against them, so much so that this may become a serious internal issue in the aftermath of the war. So is the pressure of events in international life. They are undoubtedly balanced off by many men who have a healthier, a saner, a more worthy conception of Russia's mission in the world. But that this xenophobian group exists and that it speaks with a powerful voice in the secret councils of the Kremlin is evident. And that it is in no way accessible to the pleas or arguments of responsible people in the outside world is no less clear.

As long as the situation endures, the great nations of the West will unavoidably be in a precarious position in their relations with Russia.

They will never be able to be sure when, unbeknownst to them, people of whom they have no knowledge, acting on motives utterly obscure, will go to Stalin with misleading information and with arguments to be used to their disadvantage — information which they cannot correct and arguments which they have no opportunity to rebut. As long as this possibility exists, as long as it is not corrected by a freer atmosphere for the forming of acquaintances and the exchange of views, it is questionable whether even the friendliest of relations could be considered sound and dependable.

Those men of good will, among the foreign representatives in Moscow, for whom the relations of Russia with the world at large have become one of the great experiences and hopes of contemporary life, may go on with their patient work of unraveling the never-ending tangle of misunderstandings and difficulties which lies across the path of Russia's foreign relations. They will continue to be borne up in this trial of patience by their unanimous faith in the greatness of the Russian people and by their knowledge of the need of the world for Russia's talents. But at heart they all know that until the Chinese Wall of the spirit has been broken down, as the actual Chinese Wall of Moscow's business district was recently broken — until new avenues of contact and of vision are opened up between the Kremlin and the world around it — they can have no guarantee that their efforts will meet with success and that the vast creative abilities of Russia will not lead to the tragedy, rather than to the rescue, of Western civilization.

Russia remains today, more than ever, an enigma for the Western world. Simple American minds imagine that this is because "we don't know the truth about it." They are wrong. It is not our lack of knowledge which causes us to be puzzled by Russia. It is that we are incapable of understanding the truth about Russia when we see it.

We are incapable, in the first place, of understanding the role of contradiction in Russian life. The Anglo-Saxon instinct is to attempt to smooth away contradictions, to reconcile opposing elements, to achieve something in the nature of an acceptable middle ground as a basis for life. The Russian tends to deal only in extremes, and he is not particularly concerned to reconcile them. To him, contradiction is a familiar thing. It is the essence of Russia. West and East, Pacific and Atlantic, Arctic and tropics, extreme cold and extreme heat, prolonged sloth and sudden feats of energy, exaggerated cruelty and exaggerated kindness, ostentatious wealth and dismal squalor, violent xenophobia and uncontrollable yearning for contact with the foreign world, vast power and the most abject slavery, simultaneous love and hate for the same objects: these are only some of the contradictions which dominate the life of the Russian people. The Russian does not reject these contradictions. He has learned to live with them, and in them. To him, they are the spice of life. He likes to dangle them before him, to play with them philosophically. He feels competent to handle them, to profit from them. Perhaps he even expects, at some time in the dim future, to lead them out into a synthesis more tremendous than anything the world has yet seen. But for the moment, he is content to move in them with that same sense of adventure and experience which supports a young person in the first contradictions of love.

The American mind will not apprehend Russia until it is prepared philosophically to accept the validity of contradiction. It must accept the possibility that just because a proposition is true, the opposite of that proposition is not false. It must agree never to entertain a proposition about the Russian world without seeking, and placing in apposition to it, its inevitable and indispensable opposite. Then it must agree to regard both as legitimate, valid conceptions. It must learn to understand that Russian life at any given moment is not the common expression of harmonious, integrated elements, but a precarious and ever-shifting equilibrium between numbers of conflicting forces.

But there is a second, and even more daring, *tour de force* which the American mind must make if it is to try to find Russian life comprehensible. It will have to understand that for Russia, at any rate, there are no objective criteria of right and wrong. There are not even any objective criteria of reality and unreality.

What do we mean by this? We mean that right and wrong, reality and unreality, are determined in Russia not by any God, not by any innate nature of things, but simply by men themselves. Here men determine what is true and what is false.

The reader should not smile. This is a serious fact. It is the gateway to the comprehension of much that is mysterious in Russia. Bolshevism has proved some strange and disturbing things about human nature. It has proved that what is important for people is not what is there but what they conceive to be there. It has shown that with unlimited control over people's minds — and that implies not only the ability to feed them your own propaganda but also to see that no other fellow feeds them any of his — it is possible to make them feel and believe practically anything. And it makes no difference whether that "anything" is true, in our conception of the word. For the people who believe it, it becomes true. It attains the validity, and all the powers, of truth. Men can enthuse over it, fight for it, die for it — if they are led to believe that it is something worthy. They can abhor it, oppose it, combat it with unspeakable cruelty — if they are led to believe that it is something reprehensible. Moreover, it becomes true (and this is one of the most vital apprehensions) not only for those to whom it is addressed, but for those who invent it as well. The power of autosuggestion plays a tremendous part in Soviet life.

Let not the brash American think that he personally stands above these disturbing phenomena of the Russian world. Unless he is a man of great mental obtuseness or of great mental strength, he too, upon the first contact with Russian life, will begin to react strongly to these man-made currents, the reality of which he would have contemptuously rejected from a distance. He will soon take them as real forces, as real threats or as real promises. In that, he will be right. But he will not know what he is doing. He will remain the tool, rather than the master, of the material he is seeking to understand.

Soberly viewed, there is little possibility that enough Americans will ever accomplish these philosophical evolutions to permit of any general understanding of Russia on the part of our government or our people. It would imply a measure of intellectual humility and a readiness to reserve judgment about ourselves and our institutions of which few of us would be capable. For the foreseeable future the American, individually and collectively, will continue to wander about in the maze of contradiction and the confusion which is Russia with feelings not dissimilar to those of Alice in Wonderland, and with scarcely greater effectiveness. He will be alternately repelled or attracted by one astonishing phenomenon after another, until he finally succumbs completely to one or the other of the forces involved or until, dimly apprehending the depth of his confusion, he flees the field in horror.

Distance, necessity, self-interest, and common sense may enable us, thank God, to continue that precarious and troubled but peaceful coexistence which we have managed to lead with the Russians up to this time. But if so, it will not be due to any understanding on our part of the elements involved. Forces beyond our vision will be guiding our footsteps and shaping our relations with Russia. There will be much talk about the necessity for "understanding Russia"; but there will be no place for the American who is really willing to undertake this disturbing task. The apprehension of what is valid in the Russian world is unsettling and displeasing to the American mind. He who would undertake this apprehension will not find his satisfaction in the achievement of anything practical for his people, still less in any official or public appreciation for his efforts. The best he can look forward to is the lonely pleasure of one who stands at long last on a chilly and inhospitable mountaintop where few have been before, where few can follow, and where few will consent to believe that he has been.

B. Russia's International Position at the Close of the War with Germany

(*May 1945*)

PEACE, like spring, has finally come to Russia; and the foreign resident, weary of both Russia's wars and Russia's winters, finds himself wanly wishing that the approaching political season might not be like the Russian summer: faint and fleeting, tinged with reminders of rigors that recently were and rigors that are soon to come.

Of the two occurrences, the advent of peace and the advent of spring, the latter is by far the more noticeable on the Moscow scene. A mere cessation of hostilities brings little outward change to a people which has lived under martial law and war conditions without respite, in peace as in war, for thirty-one years. So long as strong Allied forces remain in Europe, Stalin has no intention of beginning a demobilization of his legions. Even when the Allied armies have departed, considerations of general policy and the consolidation of power in newly conquered areas will make it necessary that a great armed force be maintained and that the national energies continue to be directed toward the building-up of military power. Finally, mobilization is an indispensable feature of the police state. Thus for an indefinite period to come, we may expect the lives of the Russian people to continue to be dominated by the requirements of the making and bearing of arms. And the outward aspects of Russian life, which have now been conditioned largely by this factor for over three decades, must not be expected to show any early change.

But regardless of externals, the cessation of hostilities must bring great modifications to the environment in which Russia must live. For this reason, the formal advent of peace in the West provides a suitable occasion for an estimation of the position of Russia in the world at large; the position at which it has arrived out of the ordeal of war and invasion and from which it must take its departure into a future as obscure and uncertain as any that the Russian people has ever faced.

The greatest change which the war has brought to Russia's world position has come not from any development of Russia herself but from the disintegration of the power of neighboring peoples. Russia's own overall potential has probably undergone little alteration since 1940. Losses in manpower and in physical property have been substantially balanced off by new compulsory labor forces available from German prisoners and the civil population of conquered areas, by the stricter regimentation of Russian society, by the greater exploitation of woman's labor, and by the development of new industrial districts.

But there has been an extensive decline in the rival power which confronts Russia across her land frontiers. By the time the war in the Far East is over Russia will find herself, for the first time in her history, without a single great power rival on the Eurasian landmass. She will also find herself in physical control of vast new areas of this landmass: some of them areas to which Russian power had never before been extended. These new areas (although their exact frontiers are deliberately kept vague) will probably contain well over one hundred million souls — most of them in the European sector. Those are developments of enormous import in the development of the Russian state.

Plainly, such a relative increase in Russia's power will bring with it a similar increase in her responsibilities. It is now Russia which must be at least morally responsible to the world for the happiness and prosperity of the newly acquired peoples, for the development of their resources, the ordering of their industrial and social relationships, the securing of their military defense. But this is not the greatest of the new responsibilities. Russian government now has a heavy responsibility to itself: namely, to hold the conquered provinces in submission. For there can be little doubt that many of the peoples concerned will be impatient and resentful of Russian rule. And successful revolts on their part against Moscow authority might shake the entire structure of Soviet power.

The great question of Russia's new world position, as seen from Moscow, is whether the Soviet state will be able to carry successfully these new responsibilities, to consolidate its hold over the new peoples, to reconcile this with the traditional political structure of the Russian people, to make of its conquests a source of strength rather than weakness. This is the real question of Russia's future, as seen from the Kremlin.

Behind Russia's stubborn expansion lies only the age-old sense of insecurity of a sedentary people reared on an exposed plain in the neighborhood of fierce nomadic peoples. Will this urge, now become a permanent feature of Russian psychology, provide the basis for a successful expansion of Russia into new areas of east and west. And if initially successful, will it know where to stop? Will it not be inexorably carried forward, by its very nature, in a struggle to reach the whole — to attain complete mastery of the shores of the Atlantic and the Pacific?

It should not be forgotten that the absorption of areas in the west beyond the Great Russian, White Russian, and Ukrainian ethnological boundaries is something at which Russia has already once tried and failed. Students of Russian history have given too little attention to the connection between the Russian Revolution and Tsardom's policies of western expansion in the eighteenth and nineteenth centuries. The acquisition of the Baltic provinces by Peter the Great led to no difficulties for a century and a half, due to Peter's wise forebearance in confining the patents of the local gentry and not interfering with the language, the laws, or the social structure of the provinces. As long as the eighteenth-century principles of tolerance and good form were observed, even Poland did not seem to cause much trouble. But the nineteenth century, with its abolition of serfdom, its industrialism, and its attempts at Russification, made of the western provinces a hotbed out of which there grew the greater part of the Russian Social Democratic Party which bore Lenin to power. What would Russian Social Democracy have been without the powerful support of the Jewish "Bund," of the Polish Socialists, the Lettish proletarian leaders? They, together with the other minority groups from the Caucasus, made up the bulk of the party. Without them, there would have been no revolution. And without a revolution, without a breakup of Tsardom, these provinces would not have gained their independence.

These western districts, in other words, proved indigestible to Tsardom. The responsibility of retaining power over them proved in 1917 to be too much for the backward political institutions of Russia, already shaken by social change and the strain of modern war. In a convulsion of violence and confusion, they were disgorged.

But by this very token, Soviet Russia came to enjoy a robust political health. Back among the Russians, the most tractable of peoples — back in the traditional capital of Muscovy, untouched by even the memories of western conquests — back within the comfortable western borders of the good Tsar Alexis — Bolshevism could revert without danger to the Russian political traditions of the seventeenth century: to the unlimited centralization of autocratic power, the Byzantine scholasticism of political thought, the exclusive self-segregation from the Western world, and even the mystic dreams of becoming the world's "Third Rome."

The loss of the western provinces, in other words, was a relief to the Russian state, and one of the factors which made it possible for the Kremlin to indulge successfully in what was really an antiquated system of government and a dogma replete with wishful and unrealistic thinking.

The Soviet state has now repeated in the brief space of two decades much of the history of Tsardom in its last two centuries. Stalin in the first ten years of his rule relived the era of Peter the Great. The outbreak of the war in Europe found him already enjoying Russian power in the grand manner of Catherine II. The end of the war finds him in a position strikingly similar to that of Alexander I at the close of the Napoleonic era. And the shades of Nicholas I are already present in the growing ponderousness and inelasticity of Russian police power, in many of the aims and methods of Russian policy. . . . If this comparison is apt, then we may expect that the seeds of a new convulsion are already being sown, as the seeds of Russian revolution were planted by the condemned Decembrists nearly one hundred years before that revolution took place. And if this same telescoping of time continues, another five or ten years should find Russia overshadowed again by those clouds of civil disintegration which darkened the Russian sky at the outset of this century.

Will this process again be hastened and brought to maturity by the germs of social and political ferment from the restless conquered provinces of the west? Or is the Soviet state better equipped than Tsardom was to hold in submission peoples who, unlike the Russians, have felt at one time or another in their history the ordering and yet vitalizing touch of law-abiding Rome?

Soviet Russia, as an imperialist power, has great sources of strength. It has that readiness of access to the territories it has subjugated which was named by Gibbon as one of the prerequisites for success in the unnatural task of holding in submission distant peoples. It has those advantages which the development of modern technical weapons has given to the exercise of police power by dictatorial authority — advantages which made it impossible for the subject peoples to revolt against German power during this past war. Finally, it has, as the greatest and most important of these sources of strength, the general bankruptcy of rival political tendencies and the widespread confusion and disorientation in the popular mind. Since the collapse of German power, the movement directed by Moscow has been unrivaled throughout this part of Europe in energy, initiative, unity, discipline, and ruthlessness. Any political movement which leads the field in all these qualities is hard to stop.

Yet for all this, the Russian machine in Eastern and Central Europe is not without its weaknesses.

In the first place, it bears the inevitable drawbacks of foreign rule. The peoples of this area are familiar with the devices of puppet government. After their experiences with the Germans it is not easy to fool them in this respect. Moscow would wish that those who accept its authority and convey its will to the peoples in question might pose as independent patriotic leaders of the peoples to which they belong. This is a fond hope. Europe has not spent five years smelling out quislings and collaborationists for nothing; and it is a hard thing today for any man in these areas to conceal or disguise his efforts in the service of a foreign state.

To the non-Russian peoples, the erstwhile native agents of the Comintern may have been traitors; but they were traitors openly and courageously, in the name of a faith no less universal in application than that of Christianity itself, a faith which could profess with good justification to have at heart the interests of all peoples great and small. Those who now enlist to do the Kremlin's bidding must be suspected of having at heart first and foremost the interests of the Russian people; and if they are nationals of nations which have fallen under Soviet power, it is not easy for them to pose at home as the saviors of their peoples. He who holds that national salvation can come only through bondage to a greater nation may be, in some cases, a farseeing man. It is not easy for him to be a popular figure.

The implications of this fundamental fact are aggravated by the wave of chauvinism and arrogance which has swept over the Soviet army and bureaucracy in connection with this war and with Russian victories. This has given to Russian imperialism a naked bluntness little calculated to inspire confidence and sympathy in foreign hearts. Russia was better served, in a sense, by the unabashed fanatics of the Comintern who carried the torch of revolutionary socialism to other peoples in the early days of Soviet power than by these heavy-handed generals and commissars who now command the capitals of Central Europe and whose girth is no less and subtlety no greater than those of the Tsarist satraps of a hundred years ago.

To all this must be added the sad fact that Soviet policy in the conquered territories is not much richer than its rivals in constructive content. It may be superior in discipline and drive. But it has behind it no great idea which could inspire the various peoples of the area and bind them together into a single political entity with a single purpose. Pure Marxism is dated; and if its flame still animates to any appreciable degree the power of the Kremlin (which is questionable), the Russians do not dare put it to the test as a straight political program for Eastern Europe. Lacking this, they have themselves no overall constructive thought to put forward, and their appeals, thus far, have not been impressive.

The call for drastic action against those accused of former collaboration with the Germans is at best a short-lived expedient and by no means one that always arouses confidence or enthusiasm. Too often people feel that it is misused by the Russians to effect the removal from the scene of elements which might conceivably stand in the way of their own political purposes.

The promulgation of land reform is not the first but the last trump of the demagogue in an agricultural country. It can be played only once; and human nature is such that the enthusiasm it evokes yields rapidly to the consciousness of the new problems it creates. It is not likely to lead to that increase of agricultural production of which all the countries of Eastern and Central Europe have such urgent need just at this juncture. And it brings with it in its train a series of new problems — problems of new tools, of housing, of transportation, and of organization of labor — which cry out for solutions and which, in the wake of a long and destructive war, are particularly difficult to solve. So this idea, too, can be used at best, as it was used after the Russian Revolution, to reconcile a sullen peasantry to a revolutionary shift of power in the cities. The slogan "Peace, Bread, and Land," as the history of the Soviet regime has taught, is by no means the final answer to the problems of the agricultural peoples of Eastern Europe.

Finally, it may well be questioned whether the Soviet Union is capable, without assistance from the advanced Western nations, of reconstructing and ordering the economic life of these countries in what could be called a successful manner. By the word "successful" I mean in this instance a manner which would serve to reconcile the peoples concerned to the continuation of Soviet domination.

Soviet power is by nature so jealous that it has already operated to segregate from world economy almost all of the areas in which it has been established. In the nature of things, this can hardly be otherwise. The power of Moscow is a secret police power founded on the elimination of all rival influences and contacts. The conduct of trade between private circles in these countries and countries outside the sphere of

Russian influence would be bound to arouse the liveliest suspicions in Russian police circles and would surely lead to trouble in the end. International trade with the non-Russian sphere conducted through individual government trade monopolies in individual puppet states is not unthinkable, and will probably eventually come about. But the irrepressible instinct of Moscow to retain control of economic processes as a political weapon means that such trade monopolies will function only as branches of the parent monopoly in Moscow and that to all intents and purposes the country in question will remain entirely a part of the Russian economic sphere.

Now the competence of Soviet officials in economic administration is a debatable point. It must certainly be said that in the Soviet Union the regime has succeeded at long last in bringing about a sufficient concentration of human energy to build and maintain a vigorous war industry without sacrificing the principles of government ownership and operation. But the cost at which this has been accomplished has been enormous. To achieve this end, manpower was burned up or sacrificed to the figure of some millions; living standards were kept appallingly depressed for two decades; the cottage handicraft industry, which once played so great a role in the production of consumer goods, was almost entirely lost to the economy of the country; the housing fund was permitted to deteriorate to a point where there is probably not 5 percent of the housing of this whole great people which would not deserve immediate condemnation on any normal Western standards; the country's livestock took a beating from which it has never recovered; and there has been a vast dislocation of human life, which has seriously affected the general institutions of marriage and the home and undermined the sense of security and emotional balance of an entire generation. It still remains to be demonstrated that had there never been a Socialist revolution and had Russian industrialism continued to develop along the lines of private initiative at the prerevolution rate, Russian industry would not by 1940 have attained a level at least equal to that actually reached by the Soviet state, and at an incomparably smaller cost.

There is every reason to believe that in the newly acquired areas the Russians will continue to put politics before economics, cost what it may. They will not hesitate to ruin the productivity of entire branches of economic life, if by doing so they can reduce to helplessness and dependence elements which might otherwise oppose their power. The resulting decline in living standards will appear to them, in many cases, a well-deserved corrective to the smug philistinism of the peoples involved; and they will be astonished and disgusted at the unwillingness of these peoples to accept a standard of living as low as that of the Soviet peoples.

But, on the other hand, they will also strive —from motives of prestige and military security — to develop to the maximum certain branches of production particularly useful to the state; and they will seek various outward economic effects which can be exploited for propaganda purposes at home and abroad to prove that Soviet rule has been an economic blessing. The development of all industry that relates to the defense of the state will be forced. This will be done with more energy than discrimination, and with a crude concentration of effort which may well lead to depreciation of subsidiary facilities and to a decline in real working conditions. The latter phenomena, on the other hand, will be combatted with pretentious workers' clubs, with lottery awards, with prizes to individual workers, and with similar showy benefits which can be easily publicized. Similarly, in the countryside, such devices as the conversion of erstwhile manor houses into rest homes and museums, the building up of individual model collective farms, the creation of individual machine tractor stations, and spectacular mass deliveries of grain during the harvest season will all be used to build up the impression of thriving country life to mask over what will probably be a real decline in agricultural production and in rural living standards. In all of this, outside of branches of production vital to the internal and external security of the state, emphasis will be placed not on the real economic content but on the external political effect. The Russians are a nation of stage managers; and the deepest of their convictions is that things are not what they are, but only what they seem.

As applied to Russians, these methods work, to a point. Confronted with bread and circuses, the Russian accepts with gratitude the circuses, and is fatalistic about the amount and quality of the bread. He does not regard himself as entitled to anything at all at the hands of the state. If he gets an unexpected handout of some sort, he pockets it with pleased, if skeptical, satisfaction; and is neither surprised nor indignant when it is taken away from him again. And he is naturally careful to do lip service at all times to whatever impression it was that the state wished to create with this show of generosity. Life is safer, that way — and more tranquil.

But whether these methods will be successful among non-Russian peoples further to the west is another matter. Certainly they will not work as well; and this will be one of the serious problems the Russians will have to face.

In no circumstances will the Russians compromise in the use of eco-

nomic weapons for political purposes, however costly this may prove
to be. But having been successful on more than one occasion in eating
their cake and having it too in matters of government policy, they will
search for means of accomplishing this with respect to the economic
life of dependent areas. Here, their eyes will light — indeed, have lit —
on the economic resources of the West; and it will be their hope that
the economic losses caused by their own political and social manipulations will be made good by the Western nations in the form of deliveries and services on credit.

There remains to mention perhaps the greatest difficulty which the
Russians will have to face in controlling the newly won areas, a difficulty inextricably entwined with all those that have been mentioned
above. This is the question of personnel and manpower. In the West, the
countries of Finland, Estonia, Latvia, Lithuania, Poland, Germany up
to the Oder and Neisse, Ruthenia and Slovakia, Hungary, Rumania,
Bulgaria, and Yugoslavia have a total population of roughly ninety-five
million people. This does not take into account Bohemia and Moravia
or Austria, where the Russians also obviously intend to exercise considerable influence. None of these peoples are Russian-speaking and only
about 60 percent of them use Slavic languages. To administer them and
to hold them in submission as reluctant members of a Russian security
sphere will take probably a greater administrative and police force than
was necessary even in normal times; and this last must have numbered
in the millions.

Here the Russians are faced with a dilemma. If they rely extensively
on local officials they run the risk of eventual disaffection, intrigue, and
loss of control as soon as they remove their military forces. If they try
to use Russians in their places a number of difficulties arise. In the first
place they have not got enough of them who know the languages and
customs of the other peoples. If they try to maintain large numbers of
them for long periods abroad, to learn these customs and languages and
to obtain really valuable experience, they run a strong risk of their
becoming corrupted by the amenities and temptations of a more comfortable existence and more tolerant atmosphere. They can attempt to
combat this, as they do at present in the case of their diplomats abroad,
by concentrating them in closely controlled Soviet communities and
forbidding them to have unsupervised close personal contact with the
local population. Or they can send them abroad for brief periods only.
But in neither case is it easy for the individuals concerned to obtain
the thorough experience of a foreign tongue and a foreign system of

thought which they require if they are to be useful as administrators. Here the Soviet government is faced with the problem which confronts all good students of linguistics: namely, the fact that it is impossible to acquire an intimate knowledge of a foreign language and culture without becoming to a degree a part of it and accepting something of the validity of its outlook. For the Soviet government this fact is particularly distressing. The average Soviet citizen, nursed along from infancy by the unbending and infallible propaganda machine of the state, has little independence of thought or individual sense of intellectual responsibility. Left to himself in the turbulent crosscurrents of foreign thought and feeling, he cannot be depended upon to find and maintain his balance by virtue of individual self-respect and common sense. The outlook on life with which he proceeds abroad is not a part of himself but is an artificial structure which has been produced by the devices of modern propaganda and is easily susceptible to destruction and replacement by the same devices.

Here we come close to one of the most vital and little known facts of the current stage of development in Soviet Russia. This is the extent to which the government has lost moral dominion over the masses of the Russian population. I mention this with some trepidation, because it is so susceptible to serious misinterpretation. It does not mean that there is any serious disaffection in Russia. It does not mean that people are unwilling to do what they are asked by the Kremlin to do. It does not mean that they are no longer prepared to do lip service to whatever slogans are suggested by the state. Finally, it does not mean that large numbers of them do not experience a genuine sensation of pride and enthusiasm in the nationalist traditions and aspirations of which the Kremlin has now made itself the sponsor. But it does mean that there are no longer many illusions among the Russian people as to the moral or spiritual quality of all that the state represents. The fire of revolutionary Marxism has definitely died out. What remains is capable of inspiring patriotism and nationalist sentiment, both for defense and for imperialist aggrandizement. But it is incapable of commanding that ultimate fund of human idealism on which the revolution, like the churches of all ages, was once able to draw. The deepest confidence, the most intimate hopes, the finest ideals: these are no longer the Kremlin's to command. It has before its gates a submissive but no longer an inspired mass of followers.

This subtle but vital change, which bears some of the greatest implications for the future, could have found no more startling illustration than in the demonstrations of religious feeling to which the past months have been witness. For twenty-five years every means of influencing, organizing, and channeling public sentiment has been monopolized by the Communist Party. Press, radio, the privilege of public meetings, facilities for public announcement, facilities of transportation of the public, innumerable other technical aids, even the control of the education of the youth: all these have been the complete monopoly of the party and the state. The Church has never been able to work outside the confines of the few run-down church edifices which were left to it when the antireligious crusade was over. And even here it has labored under staggering disadvantages. It has not been able to announce its services publicly. It has not been able to transport its congregations to its services. It has been unable to influence directly the youth of the country. It has never been allowed to reply to the unnumbered attacks and attempts of the state to disrupt its moral authority. It has had to suffer in silence the conversion of many churches into antireligious museums. Never, at any time, has it been permitted to say a word in its own defense.

Nevertheless, when it becomes known today by word of mouth throughout the population that an important religious event is scheduled, people crowd the churches and even the whole city districts surrounding them in an atmosphere of intense excitement and emotion. The party can call out its members and even other Soviet citizens for demonstrations at any time, in any number and in any form. They will appear without question, will carry whatever banners are put in their hands, and will comply with any orders that are given to them. But the party cannot produce among them even a shadow of the atmosphere of real emotional excitement and experience which was stamped on the faces of tens of thousands of people on the recent Easter night in Moscow. The party has been successful in retaining that which is Caesar's; but its initial bid to retain that also which was God's has been quietly and decisively rejected.

For the moment, and even for decades to come, this may have little visible practical significance. But it constitutes a possibility with which the state must reckon. The sources of fanaticism have been lost to state control. As long as the Church is kept in harmless channels, and as long as no other force is permitted to touch these particular springs of human nature and human action, there is no danger. But if they are ever to be grasped and activated by outside influence, the danger to the regime would be incalculable. This increases still further the necessity for isolation of the Soviet public from foreign contacts. And it makes more delicate than ever the problems of control of the non-Russian peoples.

All in all, therefore, it can be seen that Russia will not have an easy time in maintaining the power which it has seized over other people in Eastern and Central Europe unless it receives both moral and material assistance from the West. It must therefore be Russian policy in the coming period to persuade the Western nations, and particularly the United States (1) to give its blessing to Russian domination of these areas by recognizing Russian puppet states as independent countries and dealing with them as such, thus collaborating with the Soviet government in maintaining the fiction by which these countries are ruled; and (2) to grant to Russia the extensive material support which would enable the Soviet government to make good the economic damages caused by its costly and uncompromising political program and to claim credit for bringing economic as well as political progress to the peoples in question.

If it seems at first sight remarkable that the Kremlin should hope to win the support of democratic peoples for purposes so contrary to Western democratic ideals, it should be remembered that the Russian views all currents of public sentiment as the sailor views the winds. He is convinced that even if he cannot sail directly against them he can at least use their power to tack in general directions contrary to that in which they blow. It would not appear to him impossible to exploit Western enthusiasm for democracy and national independence in order to further the interests of authoritarianism and international oppression. He knows, to use a classical expression, that "mankind is governed by names"; and he has no compunction in adopting to his own use any slogan which he finds appealing to those whom he wishes to influence.

Furthermore, in the particular case of the United States, the Kremlin is counting on certain psychological factors which it knows will work strongly in Russia's favor. It knows that the American public has been taught to believe:

(a) That collaboration with Russia, as we envisage it, is entirely possible;
(b) That it depends only on the establishment of the proper personal relationships of cordiality and confidence with Russian leaders; and
(c) That if the United States does not find means to assure this collaboration (again, as we envisage it), then the past war has been fought in vain, another war is inevitable, and civilization is faced with complete catastrophe.

The Kremlin knows that none of these propositions is sound. It knows that the Soviet government, due to the peculiar structure of its authority, is technically incapable of collaborating with other governments in the manner which Americans have in mind when they speak of collaboration. It knows that the Soviet secret police have no intention of permitting anything like the number of personal contacts between the two peoples that would be required to lead to a broad basis of personal confidence and collaboration. It knows that throughout eleven years of diplomatic relations between the two countries it has been the United States government in at least ninety-nine cases out of a hundred which has taken the initiative to try to establish relationships of confidence and cordiality; that these efforts have met almost invariably with suspicion, discourtesy, and rebuff; and that this will not, and cannot, be otherwise in the future. Finally, it knows that the type of intimate collaboration for which Americans yearn is by no means necessary for the future of world peace. It knows, as a body thoroughly versed in the realities of power, that all that is really required to assure stability among the present great powers for decades to come is the preservation of a reasonable balance of strength between them and a realistic understanding as to the mutual zones of vital interest.

But it is no concern of the Soviet government to disabuse the American public of prejudices highly favorable to Soviet interests. It is entirely agreeable to Moscow that Americans should be indulged in a series of illusions which lead them to put pressure on their government to accomplish the impossible and to go always one step further in pursuit of the illusive favor of the Soviet government. They observe with gratification that in this way a great people can be led, like an ever-hopeful suitor, to perform one act of ingratiation after the other without ever reaching the goal which would satisfy its ardor and allay its generosity. As long as these prejudices can be kept alive among large sections of the American public, the Kremlin will not give up the hope that the Western democracies may, for the time being, be used as the greatest and most powerful auxiliary instrument in the establishment of Russian power in Eastern and Central Europe.

It is this hope which lies behind all Russian action in the question of international security. Russia expects from an international security organization that it will effectively protect Russian dominion in this belt of puppet states. It expects the organization to enlist automatically the support of the Western democracies against any forces which might undertake the liberation of the peoples in question. In addition to this, it expects to be repaid immediately in the form of credits and economic assistance for its generosity in consenting to join an organization of this nature at all.

There are undoubtedly thoughtful people in the higher councils of the Soviet government who see the preposterousness of this program and the possibilities for its failure. But they apparently still represent the weaker voice in the councils of state. And why should it be otherwise? Others can always talk them down by pointing to the extraordinary record of patience and meekness which the Western Allies have thus far exhibited. They can point out that there has been no act of Russian power, however arbitrary, which has not evoked an approving echo and at least some attempt at defense on the part of a considerable portion of the American and British press. They can point to the unshakable confidence of Anglo-Saxons in meetings between individuals, and can argue that Russia has nothing to lose by trying out these policies, since if things at any time get hot all they have to do is allow another personal meeting with Western leaders and thus make a fresh start, with all forgotten. Finally, they can point again to the fact that "getting along with the Russians" is political capital of prime importance in both of the Anglo-Saxon countries and that no English or American politician can pass up any halfway adequate opportunity for claiming that he has been successful in gaining Russian confidence and committing the Russians to a more moderate course of action. In other words, they consider that Anglo-Saxon opinion can always be easily appeased in a pinch by a single generous gesture, or even in all probability by a few promising words, and that Western statesmen can always be depended upon to collaborate enthusiastically in this appeasement.

As long as a number of Stalin's leading advisors are able to use these arguments and to point to an unbroken record of success in reliance upon this line of thought the Soviet government will continue to proceed on the theory that with the Western countries anything is possible, and that there is no reason to fear that serious difficulty will be encountered either in reconciling the Western world to Russia's program of political expansion in Europe or even in obtaining Western assistance for the completion of that program.

Before its own people the Soviet government is committed to nothing with respect to the Western Allies. In its own unceasing press campaign against reactionary elements and "vestiges of fascism" abroad, it has carefully kept a door open through which it can retire at any moment into a position of defiant isolation. Through the puppet government system which it has employed for the domination of Eastern and Central Europe, it can always withdraw the battle lines of its political power without damage to its own prestige.

Should the Western world, contrary to all normal expectations, muster up the political manliness to deny to Russia either moral and mate-

C. *Excerpts from* Telegraphic Message from Moscow of February 22, 1946

IN view of recent events, the following remarks will be of interest to the department.

I. *Basic features of postwar Soviet outlook, as put forward by official propaganda machine.*

A. The USSR still lives in antagonistic "capitalist encirclement" with which in the long run there can be no permanent peaceful coexistence. As stated by Stalin in 1927 to a delegation of American workers: "In course of further development of international revolution, there will emerge two centers of world significance: a socialist center, drawing to itself the countries which tend toward socialism, and a capitalist center, drawing to itself the countries that incline toward capitalism. Battle between these two centers for command of world economy will decide fate of capitalism and of communism in entire world."

B. Capitalist world is beset with internal conflicts inherent in nature of capitalist society. These conflicts are insoluble by means of peaceful compromise. Greatest of them is that between England and US.

C. Internal conflicts of capitalism inevitably generate wars. Wars thus generated may be of two kinds: intracapitalist wars between two capitalist states, and wars of intervention against socialist world. Smart capitalists, vainly seeking escape from inner conflicts of capitalism, incline toward latter.

D. Intervention against USSR, while it would be disastrous to those who undertook it, would cause renewed delay in progress of Soviet socialism and must therefore be forestalled at all costs.

E. Conflicts between capitalist states, though likewise fraught with danger for USSR, nevertheless hold out great possibilities for advancement of socialist cause, particularly if USSR remains militarily powerful, ideologically monolithic, and faithful to its present brilliant leadership.

F. It must be borne in mind that capitalist world is not all bad. In addition to hopelessly reactionary and bourgeois elements, it includes (1) certain wholly enlightened and positive elements united in acceptable communistic parties, and (2) certain other elements (now described for tactical reasons as progressive or democratic) whose reactions, aspirations and activities happen to be "objectively" favorable to interests of the USSR. These last must be encouraged and utilized for Soviet purposes.

G. Among negative elements of bourgeois-capitalist society, most dangerous of all are those whom Lenin called false friends of the people, namely moderate Socialist or Social Democratic leaders (in other words, non-Communist left-wing). These are more dangerous than out-and-out reactionaries, for latter at least march under their true colors, whereas moderate left-wing leaders confuse people by employing devices of socialism to serve interests of reactionary capital.

So much for premises. To what deductions do they lead from standpoint of Soviet policy? To the following:

A. Everything must be done to advance relative strength of USSR as factor in international society. Conversely, no opportunity must be missed to reduce strength and influence, collectively as well as individually, of capitalist powers.

B. Soviet efforts, and those of Russia's friends abroad, must be directed toward deepening and exploiting of differences and conflicts between capitalist powers. If these eventually deepen into an "imperialist" war, this war must be turned into revolutionary upheavals within the various capitalist countries.

C. "Democratic-progressive" elements abroad are to be utilized to bring pressure to bear on capitalist governments along lines agreeable to Soviet interests.

D. Relentless battle must be waged against Socialist and Social Democratic leaders abroad.

II. *Background of outlook.*

Before examining ramifications of this party line in practice, there are certain aspects of it to which your attention should be drawn.

First, it does not represent natural outlook of Russian people. Latter are, by and large, friendly to outside world, eager for experience of it, eager to measure against it talents they are conscious of possessing, eager above all to live peace and enjoy fruits of their own labor. Party line only represents thesis which official propaganda machines puts forward with great skill and persistence to a public often remarkably resistant in the stronghold of its innermost thoughts. But party line is binding for outlook and conduct of people, and government — and it is exclusively with these that we have to deal.

Second, please note that premises on which this party line is based are for most part simply not true. Experience has shown that peaceful and mutually profitable coexistence of capitalist and socialist states is entirely possible. Basic internal conflicts in advanced countries are no longer primarily those arising out of capitalist ownership of means of production, but are ones arising from advanced urbanism and industrialism as such, which Russia has thus far been spared not by socialism but only by her own backwardness. Internal rivalries of capitalism do not always generate wars; and not all wars are attributable to this cause. To speak of possibilities of intervention against USSR today, after elimination of Germany and Japan and after example of recent war, is sheerest nonsense. If not provoked by forces of intolerance and subversion "capitalist" world of today is quite capable of living at peace with itself and with Russia. Finally, no sane person has reason to doubt sincerity of moderate Socialist leaders in Western countries. Nor is it fair to deny success of their efforts to improve conditions for working population whenever, as in Scandinavia, they have been given chance to show what they can do.

Falseness of these premises, every one of which predates recent war, was amply demonstrated by that conflict itself. Anglo-American differences did not turn out to be major differences of Western world. Capitalist countries, other than those of Axis, showed no disposition to solve their differences by joining in crusade against USSR. Instead of imperialist war turning into civil wars and revolutions, USSR found itself obliged to fight side by side with capitalist powers for an avowed community of aims.

Nevertheless, all these theses, however baseless and disproven, are being boldly put forward again today. What does this indicate? It indicates that the Soviet party line is not based on any objective analysis of the situation beyond Russia's borders; that it has, indeed, little to do with conditions outside of Russia; that it arises mainly from basic inner-Russian necessities which existed before recent war and exist today.

At the bottom of the Kremlin's neurotic view of world affairs is traditional and instinctive Russian sense of insecurity. Originally, this was insecurity of a peaceful agricultural people trying to live on vast exposed plain in neighborhood of fierce nomadic peoples. To this was added, as Russia came into contact with economically advanced West, fear of more competent, more powerful, more highly organized societies in that area. But this latter type of insecurity was one which afflicted rather Russian rulers than Russian people; for Russian rulers have invariably sensed that their rule was relatively archaic in form, fragile and artificial in its psychological foundation, unable to stand comparison for contact with political systems of Western countries. For this reason they have always feared foreign penetration, feared direct contact between Western world and their own, feared what would happen if Russians learned truth about world without or if foreigners learned truth about world within. And they have learned to seek security only in patient but deadly struggle for total destruction rival power, never in compacts and compromises with it.

It was no coincidence that Marxism, which had smoldered ineffectively for half a century in Western Europe, caught hold and blazed for first time in Russia. Only in this land which had never known a friendly neighbor or indeed any tolerant equilibrium of separate powers, either internal or international, could a doctrine thrive which viewed economic conflicts of society as insoluble by peaceful means. After establishment of Bolshevist regime, Marxist dogma, rendered even more truculent and intolerant by Lenin's interpretation, became a perfect vehicle for sense of insecurity with which Bolsheviks, even more than previous Russian rulers, were afflicted. In this dogma, with its basic altruism of purpose, they found justification for their instinctive fear of outside world, for the dictatorship without which they did not know how to rule, for cruelties they did not dare not to inflict, for sacrifices they felt bound to demand. In the name of Marxism they sacrificed every single ethical value in their methods and tactics. Today they cannot dispense with it. It is fig leaf of their moral and intellectual respectability. Without it they would stand before history, as best, as only the last of that long succession of cruel and wasteful Russian rulers who have relentlessly forced their country on to ever new heights of military power in order to guarantee external security for their internally weak regimes. This is why Soviet purposes must always be solemnly clothed in trappings of Marxism, and why no one should underrate the importance of dogma in Soviet affairs. Thus Soviet leaders are driven by necessities of their own past and present position to put forward a dogma which pictures the outside world as evil, hostile, and menacing, but as bearing within itself germs of creeping disease and destined to be wracked with growing internal convulsions until it is given final coup de grace by rising power of socialism and yields to new and better world. This thesis provides justification for that increase of military and police power in Russia state, for that isolation of Russian population from the outside world, and for that fluid and constant pressure to extend limits of Russian police power which are together the natural and instinctive urges of Russian rulers. Basically this is only the steady advance of uneasy Russian nationalism, a centuries-old movement in which conceptions of offense and defense are inextricably confused. But in new guise of international Marxism, with its honeyed promises to a desperate and wartorn outside world, it is more dangerous and insidious than even before.

It should not be thought from above that Soviet party line is necessarily disingenuous and insincere on part of all those who put it forward. Many of them are too ignorant of outside world and mentally too dependent to question self-hypnotism, and have no difficulty making themselves believe what they find it comforting and convenient to believe. Finally we have the unsolved mystery as to who, if anyone, in this great land actually receives accurate and unbiased information about outside world. In an atmosphere of Oriental secretiveness and conspiracy which pervades this government, possibilities for distorting or poisoning sources and currents of information are infinite. The very disrespect of Russians for objective truth — indeed, their disbelief in its existence — leads them to view all stated facts as instruments for furtherance of one ulterior purpose or another. There is good reason to suspect that this government is actually a conspiracy within a conspiracy, and it is hard to believe that Stalin himself receives anything like an objective picture of outside world. Here there is ample scope for the type of subtle intrigue at which Russians are past masters. Inability of foreign governments to place their case squarely before Russian policy makers — extent to which they are delivered up in their relations with Russia to good graces of obscure and unknown advisors whom they never see and cannot influence — this is a most disquieting feature of diplomacy in Moscow, and one which Western statesmen would do well to keep in mind if they would understand nature of difficulties encountered here.

III. *Projection of Soviet outlook in practical policy on official level.*

We have now seen nature and background of the Soviet program. What may we expect of its practical implementations?

Soviet policy is conducted on two planes: (1) official plane represented by actions undertaken officially in the name of the Soviet government; and (2) subterranean plane of actions undertaken by agencies for which the Soviet government does not admit responsibility.

Policy promulgated on both planes will be calculated to serve basic policies A to D outlined in "I." Actions taken on different planes will differ considerably, but will dovetail into each other in purposes, timing, and effect.

On official plane, we must look for following:

A. Internal policy devoted to increasing in every way strength and prestige of Soviet state; intensive military-industrialization; maximum development of armed forces; great displays to impress outsiders; continued secretiveness about internal matters, designed to conceal weaknesses and to keep opponents in dark.

B. Wherever it is considered timely and promising, efforts will be made to advance official limits of Soviet power. For the moment, these efforts are restricted to certain neighboring points conceived of here as being of immediate strategic necessity, such as northern Iran, Turkey, possibly Bornholm. However, other points may at any time come into question, if and as concealed Soviet political power is extended to new areas. Thus a "friendly" Persian government might be asked to grant Russia a port on Persian Gulf. Should Spain fall under Communist control, question of Soviet base at Gilbraltar Strait might be activated. But such claims will appear on official level only when unofficial preparation is complete.

C. Russians will participate officially in international organizations where they see opportunity of extending Soviet power or of inhibiting or diluting power of others. Moscow sees in UNO not the mechanism for a permanent and stable world society founded on mutual interest and aims of all nations, but an arena in which aims just mentioned can be favorably pursued. As long as UNO is considered here to serve this purpose, Soviets will remain with it. But if at any time they come to the conclusion that it is serving to embarrass or frustrate their aims for power expansion and if they see better prospects for pursuit of these aims along other lines, they will not hesitate to abandon UNO. This would imply, however, that they felt themselves strong enough to split unity of other nations by their withdrawal, to render UNO ineffective as a threat to their aims or security, and to replace it with an international weapon more effective from their viewpoint. Thus Soviet attitude toward UNO will depend largely on loyalty of other nations to it, and on degree of vigor, decisiveness, and cohesion with which these nations defend in UNO the peaceful and hopeful concept of international life which that organization represents to our way of thinking. I reiterate, Moscow has no abstract devotion to UNO ideals. Its attitude to that organization will remain essentially pragmatic and tactical.

D. Toward colonial areas and backward or dependent peoples, Soviet policy, even on official plane, will be directed toward weakening of power and influence and contacts of advanced Western nations, on theory that insofar as this policy is successful, there will be created a vacuum which will favor Communist-Soviet penetration. Soviet pressure for participation in trusteeship arrangements thus represents a desire to be in a position to complicate and inhibit exertion of Western influence at such points rather than to provide major channel for exerting of Soviet power. Latter motive is not lacking, but for this Soviets prefer to rely on other channels than official trusteeship arrangements. Thus we may expect to find Soviets asking for admission everywhere to trusteeship or similar arrangements and using levers thus acquired to weaken Western influence among such peoples.

E. Russians will strive energetically to develop Soviet representation in, and official ties with, countries in which they sense strong possibilities of opposition to Western centers of power. This applies to such widely separated points as Germany, Argentina, Middle Eastern countries, etc.

F. In international economic matters, Soviet policy will really be dominated by pursuit of autarchy for Soviet Union and Soviet-dominated adjacent areas taken together. That, however, will be underlying policy. As far as official line is concerned, position is not yet clear. Soviet government has shown strange reticence since termination hostilities on subject foreign trade. If large-scale long-term credits should be forthcoming, the Soviet government may eventually again do lip service, as it did in 1930s, to desirability of building up international economic exchanges in general. Otherwise it is possible that Soviet foreign trade may be restricted largely to Soviet's own security sphere, including occupied areas in Germany, and that a cold official shoulder may be turned to principle of general economic collaboration among nations

G. With respect to cultural collaboration, lip service will likewise be rendered to desirability of deepening cultural contacts between peoples, but this will not in practice be interpreted in any way which could weaken security position of Soviet peoples. Actual manifestations of Soviet policy in this respect will be restricted to arid channels of closely shepherded official visits and functions, with superabundance of vodka and speeches and dearth of permanent effects.

H. Beyond this, Soviet official relations will take what might be called "correct" course with individual foreign governments, with great stress being laid on prestige of Soviet Union and its representatives and with punctilious attention to protocol, as distinct from good manners.

IV. *Following may be said as to what we may expect by way of implementation of basic Soviet policies on unofficial, or subterranean, plane; i.e., on plane for which Soviet government accepts no responsibility.*

Agencies utilized for promulgation of policies on this plane are the following:

A. Inner central core of Communist parties in other countries. While many of the persons who compose this category may also appear and act in unrelated public capacities, they are in reality working closely together as an underground operating directorate of world communism, a concealed Comintern tightly coordinated and directed by Moscow. It is important to remember that this inner core is actually working on underground lines, despite legality of parties with which it is associated.

B. Rank and file of Communist parties. Note distinction is drawn between these and persons defined in paragraph A. This distinction has become much sharper in recent years. Whereas formerly foreign Communist parties represented a curious (and from Moscow's standpoint often inconvenient) mixture of conspiracy and legitimate activity, now the conspiratorial element has been neatly concentrated in inner circle and ordered underground, while rank and file — no longer even taken into confidence about realities of movement — are thrust forward as bona fide internal partisans of certain political tendencies within their respective countries, genuinely innocent of conspiratorial connection with foreign states. Only in certain countries where Communists are numerically strong do they now regularly appear and act as a body. As a rule they are used to penetrate, and to influence or dominate, as the case may be, other organizations less likely to be suspected of being tools of Soviet government, with a view to accomplishing their purposes through front organizations, rather than by direct action as a separate political party.

C. A wide variety of national associations or bodies which can be dominated or influenced by such penetration. These include: labor unions, youth leagues, women's organizations, racial societies, religious societies, social organizations, cultural groups, liberal magazines, publishing houses, etc.

D. International organizations which can be similarly penetrated through influence over various national components. Labor, youth, and women's organizations are prominent among them. Particular, almost vital, importance is attached in this connection to international labor movement. In this, Moscow sees possibility of sidetracking Western governments in world affairs and building up international lobby capable of compelling governments to take actions favorable to Soviet interests in various countries and of paralyzing actions disagreeable to the USSR.

E. Russian Orthodox Church with its foreign branches, and through it the Eastern Orthodox Church in general.

F. Pan-Slav movement and other movements (Azerbaijan, Armenian, Turcoman, etc.) based on racial groups within the Soviet Union.

G. Governments or governing groups willing to lend themselves to Soviet purposes in one degree or another, such as present Bulgarian and Yugoslav governments, North Persian regime, Chinese Communists, etc. Not only the propaganda machines but the actual policies of these regimes can be placed extensively at the disposal of the USSR.

It may be expected that the component parts of this far-flung apparatus will be utilized, in accordance with their individual suitability, as follows:

1. To undermine general political and strategic potential of major Western powers. Efforts will be made in such countries to disrupt national self-confidence, to hamstring measures of national defense, to increase social and industrial unrest, to stimulate all forms of disunity. All persons with grievances, whether economic or racial, will be urged to seek redress not in mediation and compromise, but in defiant violent struggle for destruction of other elements of society. Here poor will be set against rich, black against white, young against old, newcomers against established residents, etc.

2. On unofficial plane particularly violent efforts will be made to weaken power and influence of Western powers over colonial, backward, or dependent peoples. On this level, no holds will be barred. Mistakes and weaknesses of Western colonial administration will be mercilessly exposed and exploited. Liberal opinion in Western countries will

be mobilized to weaken colonial policies. Resentment among dependent peoples will be stimulated. And while latter are being encouraged to seek independence of Western powers, Soviet-dominated puppet political machines will be undergoing preparation to take over domestic power in respective colonial areas when independence is achieved.

3. Where individual governments stand in path of Soviet purposes pressure will be brought for their removal from office. This can happen where governments directly oppose Soviet foreign policy aims (Turkey, Iran), where they seal their territories off against Communist penetration (Switzerland, Portugal), or where they compete too strongly, like Labor government in England, for moral domination among elements which it is important for Communists to dominate. (Sometimes, two of these elements are present in a single case. Then Communist opposition becomes particularly shrill and savage.)

4. In foreign countries Communists will, as a rule, work toward destruction of all forms of personal independence, economic, political, or moral. Their system can handle only individuals who have been brought into complete dependence on higher power. Thus persons who are financially independent — such as individual businessmen, estate owners, successful farmers, artisans, and all those who exercise local leadership or have local prestige, such as popular local clergymen or political figures, are anathema. It is not by chance that the USSR local officials are kept constantly on move from one job to another.

5. Everything possible will be done to set major Western powers against each other. Anti-British talk will be plugged among Americans, anti-American talk among British. Continentals, including Germans, will be taught to abhor both Anglo-Saxon powers. Where suspicions exist, they will be fanned; where not, ignited. No effort will be spared to discredit and combat all efforts which threaten to lead to any sort of unity or cohesion among others from which Russia might be excluded. Thus, all forms of international organization not amenable to Communist penetration and control, whether it be the Catholic Church, international economic concerns, or the international fraternity of royalty and aristocracy, must expect to find themselves under fire.

6. In general, all Soviet efforts on unofficial international plane will be negative and destructive in character, designed to tear down sources of strength beyond reach of Soviet control. This is only in line with basic Soviet instinct that there can be no compromise with rival power and that constructive work can start only when Communist power is dominant. But behind all this will be applied insistent, unceasing pressure for penetration and command of key positions in administration and especially in police apparatus of foreign countries. The Soviet re-

gime is a police regime par excellence, reared in the dim half-world of Tsarist police intrigue, accustomed to think primarily in terms of police power. This should never be lost sight of in gauging Soviet motives.

V. *Practical deductions from standpoint of US policy.*

In summary, we have here a political force committed fanatically to the belief that with US there can be no permanent modus vivendi, that it is desirable and necessary that the internal harmony of our society be disrupted, our traditional way of life be destroyed, the international authority of our state be broken, if Soviet power is to be secure. This political force has complete power of disposition over energies of one of the world's greatest peoples and resources of the world's richest national territory, and is borne along by deep and powerful currents of Russian nationalism. In addition, it has an elaborate and far-flung apparatus for exertion of its influence in other countries, an apparatus of amazing flexibility and versatility, managed by people whose experience and skill in underground methods are presumable without parallel in history. Finally, it is seemingly inaccessible to considerations of reality in its basic reactions. For it, the vast fund of objective fact about human society is not, as with us, the measure against which outlook is constantly being tested and reformed, but a grab bag from which individual items are selected arbitrarily and tendentiously to bolster an outlook already preconceived. This is admittedly not a pleasant picture. Problem of how to cope with this force is undoubtedly greatest task our diplomacy has ever faced and probably the greatest it will ever have to face. It should be the point of departure from which our political general staff work at the present juncture should proceed. It should be approached with same thoroughness and care as solution of major strategic problem in war, and if necessary, with no smaller outlay in planning effort. I cannot attempt to suggest all the answers here. But I would like to record my conviction that the problem is within our power to solve — and that without recourse to any general military conflict. And in support of this conviction there are certain observations of a more encouraging nature I should like to make:

(One) Soviet power, unlike that of Hitlerite Germany, is neither schematic nor adventuristic. It does not work by fixed plans. It does not take unnecessary risks. Impervious to logic of reason, and it is highly sensitive to logic of force. For this reason it can easily withdraw — and usually does — when strong resistance is encountered at any point. Thus, if the adversary has sufficient force and makes clear his readiness to use it, he rarely has to do so. If situations are properly handled there need be no prestige-engaging showdowns.

(Two) Gauged against Western world as a whole, Soviets are still by far the weaker force. Thus, their success will really depend on degree of cohesion, firmness, and vigor which Western world can muster. And this is factor which it is within our power to influence.

(Three) Success of Soviet system, as form of internal power, is not yet finally proven. It has yet to be demonstrated that it can survive supreme test of successive transfer of power from one individual or group to another. Lenin's death was first such transfer, and its effects wracked Soviet state for fifteen years after. Stalin's death or retirement will be second. But even this will not be final test. Soviet internal system will now be subjected, by virtue of recent territorial expansions, to a series of additional strains which once proved severe tax on Tsardom. We here are convinced that never since termination of the civil war have the mass of Russian people been emotionally farther removed from doctrines of Communist Party than they are today. In Russia, party has now become a great and — for the moment — highly successful apparatus of dictatorial administration, but it has ceased to be a source of emotional inspiration. Thus, internal soundness and permanence of movement need not yet be regarded as assured.

(Four) All Soviet propaganda beyond Soviet security sphere is basically negative and destructive. It should therefore be relatively easy to combat it by any intelligent and really constructive program.

For these reasons I think we may approach calmly and with good heart the problem of how to deal with Russia. As to how this approach should be made, I only wish to advance, by way of conclusion, the following comments:

1. Our first step must be to apprehend, and recognize for what it is, the nature of the movement with which we are dealing. We must study it with the same courage, detachment, objectivity, and the same determination not to be emotionally provoked or unseated by it, with which a doctor studies unruly and unreasonable individuals.

2. We must see that our public is educated to realities of Russian situation. I cannot overemphasize the importance of this. Press cannot do this alone. It must be done mainly by government, which is necessarily more experienced and better informed on practical problems involved. In this we need not be deterred by ugliness of the picture. I am convinced that there would be far less hysterical anti-Sovietism in our

country today if the realities of this situation were better understood by our people. There is nothing as dangerous or as terrifying as the unknown. It may also be argued that to reveal more information on our difficulties with Russia would reflect unfavorably on Russian-American relations. I feel that if there is any real risk here involved, it is one which we should have the courage to face, and the sooner the better. But I cannot see what we would be risking. Our stake in this country, even coming on the heels of tremendous demonstrations of our friendship for Russian people, is remarkably small. We have here no investments to guard, no actual trade to lose, virtually no citizens to protect, few cultural contacts to preserve. Our only stake lies in what we hope rather than what we have; and I am convinced we have a better chance of realizing those hopes if our public is enlightened and if our dealings with Russians are placed entirely on realistic and matter of fact basis.

3. Much depends on health and vigor of our own society. World communism is like malignant parasite which feeds only on diseased tissue. This is the point at which domestic and foreign policies meet. Every courageous and incisive measure to solve internal problems of our own society, to improve self-confidence, discipline, morale, and community spirit of our own people, is a diplomatic victory over Moscow worth a thousand diplomatic notes and joint communiqués. If we cannot abandon fatalism and indifference in face of deficiencies of our own society, Moscow will profit — Moscow cannot help profiting by them in its foreign policies.

4. We must formulate and put forward for other nations a much more positive and constructive picture of the sort of world we would like to see than we have put forward in the past. It is not enough to urge the people to develop political processes similar to our own. Many foreign peoples, in Europe at least, are tired and frightened by experiences of the past, and are less interested in abstract freedom than in security. They are seeking guidance rather than responsibilities. We should be better able than the Russians to give them this. And unless we do, the Russians certainly will.

5. Finally, we must have courage and self-confidence to cling to our own methods and conceptions of human society. After all, the greatest danger that can befall us in coping with this problem of Soviet communism is that we shall allow ourselves to become like those with whom we are coping.

D. *Excerpt from* The United States and Russia
(*Winter 1946*)

HISTORICALLY, the foreign affairs of Russia have developed along lines entirely different from those of the United States. Our most important foreign relations, historically speaking, have been along the lines of peaceable overseas trade. These have set the pattern of our thinking on foreign affairs. The Russians, throughout their history, have dealt principally with fierce hostile neighbors. Lacking natural geographical barriers, they have had to develop, in order to deal with these neighbors, a peculiar technique (now become traditional and almost automatic) of elastic advance and retreat, of defense in depth, of secretiveness, of wariness, of deceit. Their history has known many armistices between hostile forces; but it has never known an example of the permanent peaceful coexistence of two neighboring states with established borders accepted without question by both peoples. The Russians therefore have no conception of permanent friendly relations between states. For them, all foreigners are potential enemies. The technique of Russian diplomacy, like that of the Orient in general, is concentrated on impressing an adversary with the terrifying strength of Russian power, while keeping him uncertain and confused as to the exact channels and means of its application and thus inducing him to treat all Russian wishes and views with particular respect and consideration. It has nothing to do with the cultivation of friendly relations as we conceive them.

We would find it much easier to deal with Russia if we would recognize frankly in our own minds the fact that its leaders are, by their own choice, the enemies of all that part of the world they do not control, and that this is a recognized principle of thought and action for the entire Soviet machine. Let us also remember that in the Soviet Union decisions are rarely taken by individuals. They are taken by collective bodies. These collective bodies are required to proceed on the theory that the outside world is hostile to Russia and would be incapable of a generous or unselfish act toward the Russian state or people. It follows from this that no act of a foreign government could be officially recognized as an act of good will. Any Soviet official who would dispute this principle and try to demonstrate in a Soviet body that a foreign state had gone out of its way to be nice to the Soviet Union and deserved credit for it would risk — at the least — his job. Everyone in the Soviet government must assume that foreign governments act only in their own interests, and that gratitude and appreciation are unknown qualities in foreign affairs.

In this way, the machinery by which Soviet foreign affairs are conducted is capable of recognizing, and reacting to, only considerations of concrete Soviet interest. No one can argue any proposition in the councils of the Soviet government unless he can show concretely how the interests of the Soviet Union stand to gain if it is accepted or to suffer if it is rejected. This principle is applied with the most serene objectivity. In examining a position taken by a foreign state, the Russians make no effort to look at it from the standpoint of the foreign state in question or from any fancied community of aims on the part of themselves and the state involved. They assume it is dictated by purposes which are not theirs, and they examine it only from the standpoint of its effect on them. If the effect is favorable, they accept it without gratitude; if it is unfavorable, they reject it without resentment. We could make it much easier for them and for ourselves if we would face these facts.

In the light of the above, I would like to suggest the following rules to govern our dealings with the Russians:

A. *Don't act chummy with them.*

This only embarrasses them individually, and deepens their suspicions. Russian officials abhor the thought of appearing before their own people as one who has become buddies with a foreigner. This is not their idea of good relations.

B. *Don't assume a community of aims with them which does not really exist.*

There is no use trying to swing Russians into line by referring to common purposes to which we may both have done lip service at one time or another, such as the strengthening of world peace, or democracy, or what you will. They had their own purposes when they did lip service to these purposes. They think we had ours. For them it's all a game. And when we try to come at them with arguments based on such common professions, they become doubly wary.

C. *Don't make fatuous gestures of good will.*

Few of us have any idea how much perplexity and suspicion has been caused in the Soviet mind by gestures and concessions granted by well-meaning Americans with a view to convincing the Russians of their friendly sentiments. Such acts upset all their calculations and throw them way off balance. They immediately begin to expect that they have overestimated our strength, that they have been remiss in their obligations to the Soviet state, that they should have been demanding more from us all along. Frequently, this has exactly the opposite effect from that which we are seeking.

D. *Make no requests of the Russians unless we are prepared to make them feel our displeasure in a practical way in case the request is not granted.*

We should be prepared as a matter of principle to accompany every expression of our wishes by some action on our part proving that Russian interests suffer if our wishes are not observed. This requires imagination, firmness, and coordination of policy. If we cannot find these qualities in our foreign affairs, then we should begin to prepare for serious trouble.

E. *Take up matters on a normal level and insist that Russians take full responsibility for their actions on that level.*

Requests should not, as a rule, be taken to higher levels just because we have failed to get satisfaction on a lower level. This merely encourages the Russian bureaucracy to be uncooperative and causes our relations with high-level Soviet authorities to be encumbered with matters of second-rate importance. Instead of this, we should take our retaliatory or corrective action promptly and unhesitatingly when we do not obtain satisfaction on the lower level. It is only in this way that we can teach the Russians to respect the whole range of our officials who must deal with them. By failing to back up our subordinate officials in their dealings with the Russians, we make it difficult for ourselves to accomplish anything in the intervals between high-level meetings. This works in the interests of the Russians and prejudices our interests. This is a very important point and goes to the heart of many of our failures of the last two or three years. The top level is physically incapable of encompassing the whole range of our dealings with the Soviet government and of assuring the collaboration which we are seeking. Agreements reached there can be — and frequently are — sabotaged successfully and with inpunity on the lower levels. We must train the Russians to make their whole machine, not just Stalin, respond sensibly to our approaches.

F. *Do not encourage high-level exchanges of views with the Russians unless the initiative comes at least 50 percent from their side.*

Russians can be dealt with satisfactorily only when they themselves want something and feel themselves in a dependent position. It should be a matter of technique with us to see that they are not dealt with on a high level except when these conditions prevail.

G. *Do not be afraid to use heavy weapons for what seem to us to be minor matters.*

This is likewise a very important point, and one which many Americans will receive with skepticism. In general, it may be bad practice to take a sledgehammer to swat a fly. With the Russians it is sometimes necessary. Russians will pursue a flexible policy of piecemeal presumption and encroachment on other people's interests, hoping that no single action will appear important enough to produce a strong reaction on the part of their opponents, and that in this way they may gradually bring about a major improvement in their position before the other fellow knows what's up. In this way, they have a stubborn tendency to push every question right up to what they believe to be the breaking point of the patience of those with whom they deal. If they know that their opponent means business, that the line of his patience is firmly established and that he will not hesitate to take serious measures if this line is violated even in small ways and at isolated points, they will be careful and considerate. They do not like a showdown unless they have a great preponderance of strength. But they are quick to sense and take advantage of indecision or good-natured tolerance. Whoever deals with them must therefore be sure to maintain at all times an attitude of decisiveness and alertness in the defense of his own interests.

H. *Do not be afraid of unpleasantness and public airing of differences.*

The Russians don't mind scenes and scandals. If they discover that someone else does mind them and will go out of his way to avoid them, they will use this as a form of blackmail in the belief that they can profit from the other fellow's squeamishness. If we are to reestablish our prestige with the Soviet government and gain respect in Russia we must be prepared to undertake a "taming of the shrew" which is bound to involve a good deal of unpleasantness. On the other hand, we need not fear that occasional hard words will have permanent bad effect on our relations. The Russian is never more agreeable than after his knuckles have been sharply rapped. He takes well to rough play and rarely holds grudges over it. Let us not forget Stalin's first reaction when he met Ribbentrop. It was to joke good-naturedly and cynically about the bitter propaganda war which had been waged for so many years between the two countries. The Russian governing class respects only the strong. To them, shyness in dispute is a form of weakness.

I. *Coordinate, in accordance with our established policies, all activities of our government relating to Russia and all private American activities of this sort which the government can influence.*

The Russians are quick to take advantage of conflicts, inconsistencies, and the seeking of private aims on the part of our nationals or agencies of our government. Their own system is designed to produce the maximum concentration of national energies. We cannot face them effectively unless we do all in our power to concentrate our own effort.

J. *Strengthen and support our representation in Russia.*

The American embassy in Moscow is the symbol of our country to the Russians. It is watched intently by many people. It must be not only the representation of our society but also a guiding brain center of our policy toward Russia. In the face of frequent neglect and discouragement, always the object of attacks by jealous self-seekers and discontented liberals, never enjoying the full backing or understanding of people in Washington, never properly staffed or properly housed, it has nevertheless managed to become a pioneering establishment in the American Foreign Service and the most respected diplomatic mission in Moscow. It could do far more and play a far greater role in the Soviet Union if it received proper support. This means that failure of the Soviet government to grant quarters and other facilities for the performance of diplomatic work in Moscow must sooner or later be made an open issue between the governments and pressure must be brought to bear to improve these conditions. It means that the mission must be adequately staffed with American personnel. Finally it means that the mission must at all times be led by someone capable of and prepared for hard and tedious work over a long period of time, someone who has in high degree the qualities of modesty and patience, who is animated solely by devotion to the interests of our country, and is generally fitted by personality and background to earn the respect of a nation unexcelled in the psychological analysis of the human individual. In the case of Ambassador Harriman, I can sincerely say that I consider these prerequisites fulfilled. But I make this observation with an eye to the future. The post of ambassador to Moscow is not a sinecure which can be lightly disposed of; and the department must be prepared to use its influence to see that it is effectively filled. The Moscow mission works, and has always worked, under strain, in the face of multitudinous obstacles. A vain, fussy, and ignorant ambassador is capable of breaking its back, and of doing lasting (if not readily apparent) damage to the fabric of Russian-American relations.

Index

About the Author

George F. Kennan, a Pulitzer Prize and National Book Award winner, is the author of some eighteen books on Russia and the Soviet Union, the nuclear issue, and diplomatic history. He is one of the founders of the Kennan Institute for Advanced Russian Studies, and is an honorary chairman of the American Committee on U.S.-Soviet Relations. He is a member, and past president, of the American Academy and Institute of Arts and Letters. He is Professor Emeritus at the Institute for Advanced Study in Princeton, New Jersey.